Lecture Notes in Computer Science   10292

Commenced Publication in 1973
Founding and Former Series Editors:
Gerhard Goos, Juris Hartmanis, and Jan van Leeuwen

More information about this series at http://www.springer.com/series/7409

Theo Tryfonas (Ed.)

Human Aspects of Information Security, Privacy and Trust

5th International Conference, HAS 2017
Held as Part of HCI International 2017
Vancouver, BC, Canada, July 9–14, 2017
Proceedings

Springer

Editor
Theo Tryfonas
University of Bristol
Bristol
UK

ISSN 0302-9743   ISSN 1611-3349   (electronic)
Lecture Notes in Computer Science
ISBN 978-3-319-58459-1   ISBN 978-3-319-58460-7   (eBook)
DOI doi.org/10.1007/978-3-319-58460-7

Library of Congress Control Number: 2017939727

LNCS Sublibrary: SL3 – Information Systems and Applications, incl. Internet/Web, and HCI

This Springer imprint is published by the registered company Springer Nature Switzerland AG
The registered company address is: Gewerbestrasse 11, 6330 Cham, Switzerland

Foreword

The 19th International Conference on Human–Computer Interaction, HCI International 2017, was held in Vancouver, Canada, during July 9–14, 2017. The event incorporated the 15 conferences/thematic areas listed on the following page.

A total of 4,340 individuals from academia, research institutes, industry, and governmental agencies from 70 countries submitted contributions, and 1,228 papers have been included in the proceedings. These papers address the latest research and development efforts and highlight the human aspects of design and use of computing systems. The papers thoroughly cover the entire field of human–computer interaction, addressing major advances in knowledge and effective use of computers in a variety of application areas. The volumes constituting the full set of the conference proceedings are listed on the following pages.

I would like to thank the program board chairs and the members of the program boards of all thematic areas and affiliated conferences for their contribution to the highest scientific quality and the overall success of the HCI International 2017 conference.

This conference would not have been possible without the continuous and unwavering support and advice of the founder, Conference General Chair Emeritus and Conference Scientific Advisor Prof. Gavriel Salvendy. For his outstanding efforts, I would like to express my appreciation to the communications chair and editor of *HCI International News*, Dr. Abbas Moallem.

April 2017   Constantine Stephanidis

HCI International 2017 Thematic Areas
and Affiliated Conferences

Thematic areas:

- Human–Computer Interaction (HCI 2017)
- Human Interface and the Management of Information (HIMI 2017)

Affiliated conferences:

- 17th International Conference on Engineering Psychology and Cognitive Ergonomics (EPCE 2017)
- 11th International Conference on Universal Access in Human–Computer Interaction (UAHCI 2017)
- 9th International Conference on Virtual, Augmented and Mixed Reality (VAMR 2017)
- 9th International Conference on Cross-Cultural Design (CCD 2017)
- 9th International Conference on Social Computing and Social Media (SCSM 2017)
- 11th International Conference on Augmented Cognition (AC 2017)
- 8th International Conference on Digital Human Modeling and Applications in Health, Safety, Ergonomics and Risk Management (DHM 2017)
- 6th International Conference on Design, User Experience and Usability (DUXU 2017)
- 5th International Conference on Distributed, Ambient and Pervasive Interactions (DAPI 2017)
- 5th International Conference on Human Aspects of Information Security, Privacy and Trust (HAS 2017)
- 4th International Conference on HCI in Business, Government and Organizations (HCIBGO 2017)
- 4th International Conference on Learning and Collaboration Technologies (LCT 2017)
- Third International Conference on Human Aspects of IT for the Aged Population (ITAP 2017)

Conference Proceedings Volumes Full List

1. LNCS 10271, Human–Computer Interaction: User Interface Design, Development and Multimodality (Part I), edited by Masaaki Kurosu
2. LNCS 10272 Human–Computer Interaction: Interaction Contexts (Part II), edited by Masaaki Kurosu
3. LNCS 10273, Human Interface and the Management of Information: Information, Knowledge and Interaction Design (Part I), edited by Sakae Yamamoto
4. LNCS 10274, Human Interface and the Management of Information: Supporting Learning, Decision-Making and Collaboration (Part II), edited by Sakae Yamamoto
5. LNAI 10275, Engineering Psychology and Cognitive Ergonomics: Performance, Emotion and Situation Awareness (Part I), edited by Don Harris
6. LNAI 10276, Engineering Psychology and Cognitive Ergonomics: Cognition and Design (Part II), edited by Don Harris
7. LNCS 10277, Universal Access in Human–Computer Interaction: Design and Development Approaches and Methods (Part I), edited by Margherita Antona and Constantine Stephanidis
8. LNCS 10278, Universal Access in Human–Computer Interaction: Designing Novel Interactions (Part II), edited by Margherita Antona and Constantine Stephanidis
9. LNCS 10279, Universal Access in Human–Computer Interaction: Human and Technological Environments (Part III), edited by Margherita Antona and Constantine Stephanidis
10. LNCS 10280, Virtual, Augmented and Mixed Reality, edited by Stephanie Lackey and Jessie Y.C. Chen
11. LNCS 10281, Cross-Cultural Design, edited by Pei-Luen Patrick Rau
12. LNCS 10282, Social Computing and Social Media: Human Behavior (Part I), edited by Gabriele Meiselwitz
13. LNCS 10283, Social Computing and Social Media: Applications and Analytics (Part II), edited by Gabriele Meiselwitz
14. LNAI 10284, Augmented Cognition: Neurocognition and Machine Learning (Part I), edited by Dylan D. Schmorrow and Cali M. Fidopiastis
15. LNAI 10285, Augmented Cognition: Enhancing Cognition and Behavior in Complex Human Environments (Part II), edited by Dylan D. Schmorrow and Cali M. Fidopiastis
16. LNCS 10286, Digital Human Modeling and Applications in Health, Safety, Ergonomics and Risk Management: Ergonomics and Design (Part I), edited by Vincent G. Duffy
17. LNCS 10287, Digital Human Modeling and Applications in Health, Safety, Ergonomics and Risk Management: Health and Safety (Part II), edited by Vincent G. Duffy
18. LNCS 10288, Design, User Experience, and Usability: Theory, Methodology and Management (Part I), edited by Aaron Marcus and Wentao Wang

Human Aspects of Information Security, Privacy and Trust

Program Board Chair(s):Theo Tryfonas, UK

The full list with the Program Board Chairs and the members of the Program Boards of all thematic areas and affiliated conferences is available online at:

http://www.hci.international/board-members-2017.php

HCI International 2018

The 20th International Conference on Human–Computer Interaction, HCI International 2018, will be held jointly with the affiliated conferences in Las Vegas, NV, USA, at Caesars Palace, July 15–20, 2018. It will cover a broad spectrum of themes related to human–computer interaction, including theoretical issues, methods, tools, processes, and case studies in HCI design, as well as novel interaction techniques, interfaces, and applications. The proceedings will be published by Springer. More information is available on the conference website:http://2018.hci.international/.

General Chair
Prof. Constantine Stephanidis
University of Crete and ICS-FORTH
Heraklion, Crete, Greece
E-mail: general_chair@hcii2018.org

http://2018.hci.international/

Contents

Cyber Security Policies

Human Factors in Security

The Design of Messages to Improve Cybersecurity Incident Reporting

Pam Briggs[1], Debora Jeske[2], and Lynne Coventry[1(✉)]

[1] Northumbria University, Newcastle upon Tyne, UK
{P.briggs,lynne.coventry}@northumbria.ac.uk
[2] University College Cork, Cork, Ireland

Abstract. Cybersecurity suffers from the problem of poor incident reporting. We explored message influences on incident reporting rate. Participants were presented with messages that differed in terms of (i) whether the problem was framed as a technical or a security issue and (ii) the perceived beneficiaries of making a report (benefit to the user, to others vs. no benefit message). Participants were more likely to report a problem if so doing implied some benefit to self, where making the problem more personally relevant might act to reduce social loafing in group settings. They were also more likely to report a technical rather than a security problem and qualitative data suggested that users were sometimes suspicious of messages reporting a security incident – believing that the message itself might be a cybersecurity attack. The findings provide starting points for future research aimed at improving incident reporting.

Keywords: Security · User behavior · Incident reporting · Behavior change · Protection-motivation theory · Social loafing

1 Introduction

Users are generally poor at incident reporting. Research evidence for this comes primarily from studies of technical error reporting, where failure to report is generally seen as problematic both from an organizational, situational awareness perspective [1] but also from an engineering perspective, as such error reports can help in the design of interventions and software improvements [2, 3]. However, failure to report an incident is even more problematic in relation to cybersecurity, where intrusion detection is an important component in cybersecurity defense. The little research that exists reveals that users pay scant attention to warning messages [4] but also shows that passive warnings, i.e. those requiring no user action, are almost universally ignored [5]. There is comparatively little research that shows how incident reporting behavior relates to an organization's security vulnerability – but we do know that the ability to detect and respond to a cybersecurity attack is paramount, just as we recognize that the volume and diversity of attacks are growing exponentially [6].

Security warnings can include notifications about lapsed security certificates or software updates as well as alerts about mobile applications or websites. It is difficult for users to interpret them properly in order to differentiate between real threats, potential threats and false alarms [7]. Well-designed messages can be effective, for

© Springer International Publishing AG 2017
T. Tryfonas (Ed.): HAS 2017, LNCS 10292, pp. 3–13, 2017.
DOI: 10.1007/978-3-319-58460-7_1

example, Egelman et al. [5] found that active warnings helped deter 79% of participants from visiting a potentially harmful website, but overly complex messages are much less effective [8, 9] and can also be misleading [10]. This is particularly problematic for the novice user, who is unclear about the proper meanings of system settings and messages [11]. Given that users are typically under time-pressure to complete other, high-priority tasks, both the intelligibility and the resource demands of messages are important considerations [12] as is over-exposure to a particular message, which can lead to habituation [13].

It is possible to manipulate the design and content of warning messages so as to nudge users into action. Security messages are more effective when the authority of message sender is emphasized [14]; the severity of threat is highlighted [15]; personal risks rather than technical risks are communicated [16, 17] and when the risk to users' private information is highlighted [16]. Messages are also more effective when they are 'active warnings' that require action from the user before progressing, such as swiping over the text to be read [5, 7]. Contextualized, concrete warnings are superior, i.e. those that take the user's current intention into account in order to evoke realistic consequences of action or inaction [14, 18]. We should, however, note that some studies have found no effect of message design. For example, [19] found no difference in the effect of a generic warning compared to one that highlighted specific consequences and [20] showed that altering text and color improved user attention but this was not sufficient to change behavior.

Given these inconsistent findings, it is important to understand more about why people ignore warnings or requests for specific behaviors. Several useful approaches have been adopted here. Firstly, as we have seen, there is the *productive security* approach (e.g. [21]) that sees the decision to ignore messages as a rational choice. Typically, warning messages and requests for action are often unanticipated, potentially disruptive and unquantified in terms of effort required, and while they may be genuine indicators of security threat, they may also be false alarms. Thus, many users prefer to ignore information when they feel the costs of action outweigh the benefits [22] or when they feel that engaging with the new information would disrupt their primary task performance [23]. There will also be individual differences at play here. For example, those with less capacity to respond (e.g. those with low working memory capacity [24] or those experiencing higher task demands [25]) may possess a reduced cybersecurity 'compliance budget' and as a consequence will struggle to make a proactive response.

A second relevant approach is Protection Motivation Theory (PMT) [26], which supposes that users make two important appraisals, a threat appraisal and a coping appraisal. For the first, they assess both the severity of the threat and their own vulnerability to it and for the second, they assess their own understanding and ability to respond as well as the efficacy of making a response. In relation to the first issue of threat appraisal, the average user has a poor understanding of security threats [27] and security incident reporting has been linked to misperceptions of threat and poor cybersecurity beliefs [29, 30]. In relation to the second point, users may be unsure of the appropriate action to take but can also be unconvinced about the efficacy of taking any action. Some evidence for this comes from Workman et al. [30] who observed that perceived response efficacy was one predictor of inaction. This situation is compounded by the fact that many system errors are encountered repeatedly, reducing the sense that a report will be useful or lead to some personal or organizational benefit (see also [31]).

A third approach draws upon the concept of social loafing [32]. That is, in the presence of many other users, an individual user may not react to a request, perhaps assuming that others will make the required response. Certainly, any individual user would not wish to duplicate the input generated by others - a trend particularly prominent in collective work settings [33]. Also, we should note that while users can be persuaded that their own, possibly unique contribution is important [34], social loafing becomes more likely if they believe their own failure to respond goes unnoticed or if they know they cannot be personally identified [35]. Users may be uncomfortable when personally identifiable information is included in problem reports that are sent back to the corporation and shared with others. This, paradoxically, means that inaction can result from either anxiety about being held accountable for the outcome [36–38] or lead to a lack of accountability [33]. Perceived task characteristics may also contribute to social loafing and the underreporting of errors. For example, unattractive tasks often require the use of incentives to encourage employees to report [39]. Also, complex tasks are less likely to lead to personal engagement [37, 40]. If there is no specific information provided regarding the complexity of the reporting task, then users may assume potential complications or excessive work demands [41] which may or may not exist. Thirdly, the efficacy of reporting may be unclear – lack of change or lack of response to user action may reduce motivation to act, thus returning to the earlier point: the perceived redundancy of effort – it will not make a difference.

To a certain extent, reporting can be improved by making users more aware of the personal relevance of an issue or threat [42]. For example, it may be possible to reduce habitual ignoring of system-generated messages by making those messages more personally relevant [7, 11]. The implication is that providing a better rationale for the request may reduce perceptions of response redundancy, i.e. leave people less exposed to social loafing effects. This could be achieved by either personalizing the message or outlining the repercussions of leaving a potential issue unaddressed over time.

This study is a direct response to calls for more research to help us understand how and why individuals may be persuaded to respond to information requests area [1]. The aims were to investigate how the wording of an incident message might influence the reporting of that message and also to explore individual differences in this area. These aims are expressed as three research questions: 1. Are users more likely to report a problem when it is framed as a security or as a technical issue (framing effect)? 2. Can the inclusion of a 'benefits' statement (explaining the benefits to either self or others) improve rates of problem reporting? 3. What individual differences might affect users' problem reporting behaviors?

2 Method

2.1 Study Design

The main focus of this study was an incident reporting task that had been embedded in a distractor task requiring the participants to rate four travel websites.

Distractor Task. The distractor task (and the focus in the participant recruitment message) asked participants to rate four accommodation booking websites:

(1) Booking.com (2) Tripadvisor.com, (3) Bookingbuddy.com and (4) Airbnb.com. Participants were presented with screenshots of the home page for each site.

Incident Reporting Task. After the third booking site screenshot, all participants were presented with a dialogue box that opened with the statement: *"We noted a problem on this page"*. This statement was followed by either a security or technical message frame: *"This problem may indicate a security/technical issue"*. The second part of the message presented one of three possible benefit conditions. In the benefit-to-self condition, the message stated *"Problem reporting will help us identify the source of the problem and protect you."* In the benefit-to-others condition, the message reported *"Problem reporting will help us identify the source of the problem and protect others in your organization"*. In the third (control) condition, no benefit message was presented. Each message ended with the same question: *"Do you want to report the problem?"* The user was required to click on either the "Report" or "Don't report" button to continue. This was thus a 2 (technical vs security framing) * 3 (benefit to self, benefit to others, no benefit statement) factorial design (see Fig. 1 for an example message). Full ethical approval was received from the departmental Ethics Committee.

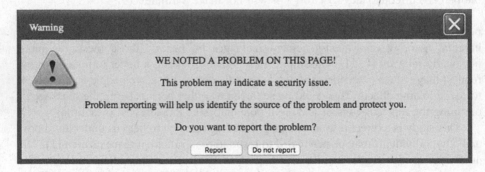

Fig. 1. Example of incident report request message.

2.2 Participants

Participants were university students situated in different departments (social and natural sciences). Information about the study was circulated via email and a dedicated university online recruitment portal. Students are a relevant sample in this case as they tend to use many different online services and had experienced recent server failures. All participants could earn research credits for their respective programs. All participants were recruited between December 2014 and March 2015. In total, the study was accessed by 147 participants. All participants completed the study with a computer and at a location of their choice. Hits that had not led to full completion of the survey were excluded ($n = 19$). This reduced the final dataset to $N = 126$. Participants were 18 to 36 years old ($M = 20.15, SD = 2.79, n = 125$). Eighty-four percent of the participants were female ($n = 105$, two missing values), only 16% were male ($n = 20$; one missing value).

2.3   Procedure

Participants were randomly allocated to the six experimental conditions. Once participants had given their consent to participate, they were presented with instructions about how to rate the four online travel sites and each of the four screen shots was then presented separately. Before the fourth screenshot, they encountered a message stating that a problem was found and gave them the choice to report the problem. This was followed by questions about their online use of travel sites, familiarity and review activity of such sites, in turn followed by demographic and short personality questionnaires (no details are included here as no personality effects were found). The questionnaire ended with demographics and the debrief statement about the study.

3   Results

In terms of the message framing, 65 participants received the technical framing, 61 the security framing. In terms of the implied benefit conditions, 41 participants were in the benefit-to-self condition, 37 were in the benefit-to-others condition and 48 participants were in the control condition.

3.1   Incident Reporting Across All Conditions

Overall, 42% of participants ($n = 73$) reported the incident. Table 1 gives a more detailed breakdown and shows, for each condition the number of people who reported the incident with the number who failed to report given in parentheses. The χ^2 statistic revealed a significant overall effect across the six conditions in a 2×3 contingency table ($\chi^2(2) = 8.16$, $p < .05$) but separate analyses for the two experimental manipulations are given below.

Table 1. Number of participants who reported (failed to report) the incident across the six experimental conditions.

	Benefit to self ($n = 41$)	Benefit to other ($n = 37$)	No benefit statement ($n = 48$)
Technical framing ($n = 65$)	24 (0)	6 (11)	5 (19)
Security framing ($n = 61$)	7 (10)	9 (11)	2 (22)

3.2   Effects of Security vs. Technical Framing

There was a significant reporting difference when security vs. technical framing conditions were compared ($\chi^2(1) = 7.65$, $p = .006$). Reporting was higher when the problem was framed as a technical (obs/exp. 35/27.3) rather than a security issue (obs/exp. 18/25.7). The Phi statistic (Phi $= -.25$) also indicates that there is a moderately strong relationship between framing and reporting. Incident reporting was lower when the problem message suggested a security issue.

3.3   Effects of the Benefit Statement

The χ^2 statistic revealed a significant effect of including a benefit statement $(\chi^2(2) = 33.84, p < .001)$. Incident reporting was higher when a benefit was implied, particularly a benefit to self (obs/exp. 31/17.2). In the absence of such a statement, reporting was much lower (obs/exp. 7/20.2). The Cramer's V statistic (Cramer's V = .52) also indicates a strong relationship between message contents and reporting responses.

3.4   Qualitative Analysis of General Problem Reporting

Comments were available from 121 of 126 participants. An exploratory analysis was conducted using thematic analysis in order to understand the factors that drove a decision whether or not to report an incident. The quotes provided in this section illustrate the themes that were identified. These themes illustrate the tension between threat perception, the cost of responding and the efficacy of reporting. Non-reporting appeared to be influenced by the extent to which participants sensed a potential threat (fear appraisal), or lack thereof. Some participants actually felt that the message itself represented a threat (as an indicator of a virus or spam). For example, some do not report the problem because: "*I always feel like the message is a virus rather than an actual warning;*" "*[it] could be a virus;*" and "*in case it's a scam or a virus*". Others did not perceive a threat and said they felt the message was unimportant or that they had sufficient protection in place and were safe because, for, example "*I have anti-virus software.*"

Another factor was the perceived efficacy of responding to the threat with participants reporting that it "*was not worth the effort*" and would make no difference on the grounds of past experience: "*when reporting incidents in the past nothing has happened*". Failure to report may also be linked to uncertainty and lack of information. For example, two participants said that they were "*not sure how it works*" and "*don't know what it means or what it is*". That is, they were unsure of what was required of them or where the information would end up.

A third factor concerned the potential costs associated with incident reporting (e.g., in terms of productivity costs incurred by the process of reporting). Individuals who did not report problems were particularly attentive to the potential time and effort costs associated with making the report. For example, one participant stated that it "*makes it go away quicker if I say no*". In addition, participants reported that "*I just want to continue doing what I was previously and did not want to report an error because of the potential for disruption that may result in terms of "time and redirection."* Lastly there was a suggestion that the request was inappropriate as they had previously been "*taught not to*", suggesting lessons learnt from another part of the security policy (i.e. not clicking on links) was being misapplied in this context.

The participants who accept the error message as legitimate were more likely to go on and report the error. This group recognized the importance of error reporting both for themselves and others, seeking: "*To hopefully draw attention to the problem and ensure it is more likely to be fixed;*" "*to bring the problem to the attention of the website administrator so they can sort it out quicker;" "to try and stop it from happening from again;" "because it may improve future services;"* and *"improve site."*

4 Discussion

We found that the framing of a message could directly influence incident reporting. Reporting was significantly higher when participants were presented with a technical as opposed to a security framed message, which may relate to concerns participants expressed about security-related messages as a possible social engineering attack. This is a troubling finding when we consider how important security notifications could be in helping us deal effectively with a threat. An additional interpretation (derived from PMT) relates to the user's judgment about whether incident reporting will be effective. Again, users may be more likely to feel that their own organization could respond more swiftly and more effectively in response to a technical problem than to a cybersecurity threat. To a certain extent, people are beginning to habituate to such threats – believing that they must simply accept cybersecurity incidents as part of the working environment. Finally, users may know how to report a technical problem, but be unsure of what action to take in regard to a cybersecurity problem [11].

We also found a significant effect of the benefit message. Reporting frequencies were higher when the message implied a benefit to self, followed by a benefit to others. Reporting was lowest when no benefit information was provided. This was a simple, but effective manipulation and it is interesting to speculate what further information might be used to move users away from social loafing and nudge them into action. Again, in theoretical terms we can see a link to PMT in that a benefit statement explicitly tells users that making a report will produce a positive impact, either to self or other.

4.1 Practical Implications

We deal firstly with the implications that are specific to cybersecurity contexts and here we should note that attempts to nudge action within a security context can backfire. Our manipulations were less effective in the security context and we are particularly concerned about the way that participants felt the message itself could constitute a security threat. We note work by [20] who found that users chose to ignore warnings, believing them to be irrelevant, see [18] who showed that the contextualisation of a message could create distrust and [44] showed that users are often reluctant to use an electronic system to report an incident.

More generally, incident reporting typically represents a situation with unknown "return on investment." Investment here can be understood as the time a user spends on making a report. We would suggest that feedback is important here to boost feelings of efficacy. There should be some acknowledgement that a report has been made and if possibly, some signal of that report's usefulness would be helpful. This point relates to work by [31], who argued that incident reporting will only be perceived as useful when the data is also used in system improvement and when reporters are made aware that it was their feedback that led to these improvements.

While this study provides interesting evidence about the role of framing in requesting action from a user, we acknowledge that this study was with a group of students using work machines. As such it serves as a proof of concept, and the robustness and transferability of the findings needs to be established as we move forward. An important implication for researchers is to ensure that more work is carried out in this area and that we establish a reliable evidence base about the effectiveness of design interventions within cybersecurity.

4.2 Limitations and Future Steps

Our study provides some important insight into cybersecurity behavior, however, we do acknowledge certain aspects of the study that may be perceived as limitations. In terms of the use of a student sample, it is not unusual for researchers to pilot test interventions with student samples (see examples such as [45–47] or cross-sectional samples that include students (e.g., [7, 48]).

Given the design of the study, it was necessary to carefully monitor of the number of individuals being allocated into each condition. As students are incentivized to complete studies, the drop-out rate was speculated to be lower than with an organizational sample. Choosing students allowed us to anticipate data collection issues (including mid-terms and similar).

However, the use of student samples in the development of potential organizational interventions provide an interesting sample. Students are exposed to cybersecurity messages from their university. They are also unlikely to have had extensive IT training or specific awareness training when joining the university. This provided us with a homogeneous sample than we might get in a more age-diverse organizational setting where individuals may have more expertise (and our effects may be diluted due to less controllable factors). Students will take the behaviors they learn at university into their working life.

This study was a pilot study to test experimental effects for which we lacked a solid foundation, as cybersecurity research has not tackled this issue before. This provides some evidence that these nudges can have a positive effect. However, replication of this study is needed to validate this evidence. The next step would be to implement this approach in organizational settings. This would allow us to ascertain if an effect is still present in a real world setting.

Acknowledgements. We gratefully acknowledge the technical and data collection support of James Turland from the School of Computing at Newcastle University. The work presented in this paper was part of a project (2013–2016) that was funded through the Choice Architecture for Information Security (ChAIse) project (EP/K006568/1) from Engineering and Physical Sciences Research Council (EPSRC), UK, and Government Communications Headquarters (GCHQ), UK, as a part of the Research Institute in Science of Cyber Security.

References

1. Zhao, B., Olivera, F.: Error reporting in organizations. Acad. Manag. Rev. **31**(4), 1012–1030 (2006). http://www.jstor.org/stable/20159263
2. August, T., Niculescu, M.F.: The influence of software process maturity and customer error reporting on software release and pricing. Manag. Sci. **59**, 2702–2726 (2013). doi:10.1287/mnsc.2013.1728
3. Singh, R., Pace, W., Singh, A., Fox, C., Singh, G.: A visual computer interface concept for making error reporting useful at the point of care. In: Henriksen, K., Battles, J.B., Keyes, M. A., et al. (eds.) Advances in Patient Safety: New Directions and Alternative Approaches, Assessment, vol. 1. Agency for Healthcare Research and Quality, Rockville (2008)
4. Felt, A.P., Ha, E., Egelman, S., Haney, A., Chin, E., Wagner, D.: Android permissions: user attention, comprehension, and behavior. In: Proceedings of the Eighth Symposium on Usable Privacy and Security (SOUPS). ACM, New York (2012). Article No. 3. doi:10.1145/2335356.2335360
5. Egelman, S., Cranor, L.F., Hong, J.: You've been warned: an empirical study of the effectiveness of web browser phishing warnings. In: Proceedings of the SIGCHI Conference on Human Factors in Computing Systems, pp. 1065–1074. ACM, New York (2008). doi:10.1145/1357054.1357219
6. ICS CERT. (2015). https://ics-cert.us-cert.gov/sites/default/files/Annual_Reports/Year_in_Review_FY2015_Final_S508C.pdf
7. Bravo-Lillo, C., Komanduri, S., Cranor, L.F., Reeder, R.W., Sleeper, M., Downs, J., Schechter, S.: Your attention please. Designing security-decision UIs to make genuine risks harder to ignore. In: Proceedings of Symposium on Usable Privacy and Security (SOUPS). ACM, New York (2013). Article 6. doi:10.1145/2501604.2501610
8. Bauer, L., Bravo-Lillo, C.L., Cranor, F., Fragkaki, E.: Warning Design Guidelines. Carnegie Mellon University, Pittsburgh (2013)
9. Harbach, M., Fahl, S., Yakovleva, P., Smith, M.: Sorry, I don't get it: an analysis of warning message texts. In: Adams, A.A., Brenner, M., Smith, M. (eds.) FC 2013. LNCS, vol. 7862, pp. 94–111. Springer, Heidelberg (2013). doi:10.1007/978-3-642-41320-9_7
10. Motiee, S., Hawkey, K., Beznosov, K.: Investigating user account control practices. In: Proceedings of the 28th of the International Conference Extended Abstracts on Human Factors in Computing Systems, pp. 4129–4134. ACM (2010)
11. Maxion, R.A., Reeder, R.W.: Improving user-interface dependability through mitigation of human error. Int. J. Hum.-Comput. Stud. **63**, 25–50 (2005). doi:10.1016/j.ijhcs.2005.04.009
12. Böhme, R., Grossklags, J.: The security cost of cheap user interaction. In: Proceedings of the New Security Paradigms Workshop (NSPW 2011). pp. 67–82. ACM, New York (2011). doi:10.1145/2073276.2073284
13. Akhawe, D., Porter Felt, A.: Alice in warning land: a large-scale field study of browser security warning effectiveness. In: Proceedings of the 22nd USENIX Security Symposium, pp. 257–272 (2013). https://www.usenix.org/system/files/conference/usenixsecurity13/sec13-paper_akhawe.pdf
14. Modic, D., Anderson, R.: Reading this may harm your computer: the psychology of malware warnings. Comp. Hum. Behav. **41**, 71–79 (2014). doi:10.1016/j.chb.2014.09.014
15. Sunshine, J., Egelman, S., Almuhimedi, H., Atri, N., Cranor, L.F.: Crying wolf: an empirical study of SSL warning effectiveness. In: Proceedings of the USENIX Security Symposium, pp. 399–416. ACM, New York (2009). http://static.usenix.org/legacy/events/sec09/tech/full_papers/sec09_browser.pdf

16. Harbach, M., Hettig, M., Weber, S., Smith, M.: Using personal examples to improve risk communication for security and privacy decisions. In: Proceedings of the SIGCHI Conference on Human Factors in Computing Systems, pp. 2647–2656. ACM, New York (2014). doi:10.1145/2556288.2556978

17. Kauer, M., Pfeiffer, T., Vokamer, M., Theuerling, H., Bruder, R.: It is not about the design - it is about the content! Making warnings more efficient by communicating risks appropriately. In: Proceedings of Conference: Sicherheit– Sicherheit, Schutz und Zuverlässigkeit   (2012).   http://tuprints.ulb.tu-darmstadt.de/3092/4/ ItIsNotAboutTheDesignItIsAboutTheContent.pdf

18. Bartsch, S., Volkamer, M., Theuerling, H., Karayumak, F.: Contextualized web warnings, and how they cause distrust. In: Huth, M., Asokan, N., Čapkun, S., Flechais, I., Coles-Kemp, L. (eds.) Trust 2013. LNCS, vol. 7904, pp. 205–222. Springer, Heidelberg (2013). doi:10. 1007/978-3-642-38908-5_16

19. Krol, K., Moroz, M., Sasse, M.A.: Don't work. Can't work? Why it's time to rethink security warnings. In: Proceedings of 7th International Conference on Risks and Security of Internet and Systems (CRiSIS), pp. 1–10. IEEE (2012). doi:10.1109/CRISIS.2012.6378951

20. Egelman, S., Schechter, S.: The importance of being earnest [in security warnings]. In: Sadeghi, A.-R. (ed.) FC 2013. LNCS, vol. 7859, pp. 52–59. Springer, Heidelberg (2013). doi:10.1007/978-3-642-39884-1_5

21. Beautement, A., Sasse, M.A., Wonham, M.: The compliance budget: managing security behaviour in organisations. In: Proceedings of the New Security Paradigms Workshop (NSWP 2008), pp. 47–58. ACM, New York (2008). doi:10.1145/1595676.1595684

22. Herley, C.: So long, and no thanks for the externalities: the rational rejection of security advice by users. In: Proceedings of the New Security Paradigms Workshop (NSPW), pp. 133–144. ACM, New York (2009). doi:10.1145/1719030.1719050

23. Duggan, G.B., Johnson, H., Sørli, P.: Interleaving tasks to improve performance: users maximise the marginal rate of return. Int. J. Hum.-Comput. Stud. **71**, 533–550 (2013). doi:10.1016/j.ijhcs.2013.01.001

24. Drews, F.A., Musters, A.: Individual differences in interrupted task performance: one size does not fit all. Int. J. Hum.-Comput. Stud. **79**, 97–105 (2015). doi:10.1016/j.ijhcs.2015.01. 003

25. Nurse, J.R.C., Creese, S., Goldsmith, M., Lamberts, K.: Guidelines for usable cybersecurity: past and present. In: Proceedings of the 5th International Conference on Network and System Security (NSS), pp. 21–26 (2011). doi:10.1109/CSS.2011.6058566

26. Rogers, R.W.: A protection motivation theory of fear appeals and attitude change. J. Psychol. **91**, 93–114 (1975). doi:10.1080/00223980.1975.9915803

27. Furnell, S., Shams, R., Phippen, A.: Who guides the little guy? Exploring security advice and guidance from retailers and ISPs. Comput. Fraud Secur. **12**, 6–10 (2008). doi:10.1016/ S1361-3723(08)70175-1

28. Herath, T., Raghav Rao, H.: Protection motivation and deterrence: a framework for security policy compliance in organisations. Eur. J. Inf. Syst. **18**, 106–125 (2009). doi:10.1057/ejis. 2009.6

29. Howe, A.E., Ray, I., Roberts, M., Urbanska, M., Byrne, Z.: The psychology of security for the home computer user. In: Proceedings of IEEE Symposium on Security and Privacy. IEEE, pp. 209–223 (2012). doi:10.1109/SP.2012.23

30. Workman, M., Bommer, W.H., Straub, D.: Security lapses and the omission of information security measures: a threat model and empirical test. Comput. Hum. Behav. **24**, 2799–2816 (2008). doi:10.1016/j.chb.2008.04.005

31. Holden, R.J., Karsh, B.-T.: A review of medical error reporting system design considerations and a proposed cross-level systems research framework. Hum. Factors **49**, 257–276 (2007). doi:10.1518/001872007X312487
32. Karau, S.J., Williams, K.D.: Social loafing: a meta-analytic review and theoretical integration. J. Pers. Soc. Psychol. **65**, 681–706 (1993). doi:10.1037/0022-3514.65.4.681
33. Karau, S.J., Williams, K.D.: Social loafing: research findings, implications, and future directions. Curr. Dir. Psychol. Sci. **4**, 134–140 (1995). doi:10.1111/1467-8721.ep10772570
34. Kerr, N.L., Bruun, S.E.: Dispensability of member effort and group motivation losses: free-rider effects. J. Pers. Soc. Psychol. **44**, 78–94 (1983). doi:10.1037/0022-3514.44.1.78
35. Harkins, S.G.: Social loafing and social facilitation. J. Exp. Soc. Psychol. **23**, 1–18 (1987). doi:10.1016/0022-1031(87)90022-9
36. Hembree, R.: Correlates, causes, effects, and treatment of test anxiety. Rev. Educ. Res. **58**, 47–77 (1988). doi:10.2307/1170348
37. Jackson, J.M., Williams, K.D.: Social loafing on difficult tasks: working collectively can improve performance. J. Pers. Soc. Psychol. **49**, 937–942 (1985). doi:10.1037/0022-3514.49.4.937
38. Tobias, S.: Test anxiety: interference, defective skills, and cognitive capacity. Educ. Psychol. **20**, 135–142 (1985). doi:10.1207/s15326985ep2003_3
39. Zaccaro, S.J.: Social loafing: the role of task attractiveness. Pers. Soc. Psychol. Bull. **10**, 99–106 (1984). doi:10.1177/0146167284101011
40. Harkins, S.G., Petty, R.E.: Effects of task difficulty and task uniqueness on social loafing. J. Pers. Soc. Psychol. **43**, 1214–1229 (1982). doi:10.1037/0022-3514.43.6.1214
41. Robbins, T.L.: Social loafing on cognitive tasks: an examination of the "sucker effect". J. Bus. Psychol. **9**, 337–342 (1995). doi:10.1007/BF02230973
42. Petty, R.E., Cacioppo, J.T., Goldman, R.: Personal involvement as a determinant of argument-based persuasion. J. Pers. Soc. Psychol. **41**, 847–855 (1981). doi:10.1037/0022-3514.41.5.847
43. Vance, A., Siponen, M., Pahnila, S.: Motivating IS security compliance: insights from habit and protection motivation theory. Inf. Manag. **49**, 190–198 (2012). doi:10.1016/j.im.2012.04.002
44. Kingston, M.J., Evans, S.M., Smith, B.J., Berry, J.G.: Attitudes of doctors and nurses towards incident reporting: a qualitative analysis. Med. J. Aust. **181**, 36–39 (2004)
45. Brustoloni, J.C., Villamarin-Salomon, R.: Improving security decisions with polymorphic and audited dialogs. In: Symposium on Usable Privacy and Security (SOUPS) 2007, 18–20 July 2007, Pittsburgh, PA, USA (2007)
46. Gross, R., Acquisti, A.: Information revelation and privacy in online social networks (the Facebook case). In: ACM Workshop on Privacy in the Electronic Society (WPES), 7 November 2005, Alexandria, Virginia, USA (2005)
47. Sun, J., Ahluwalia, P., Koong, K.S.: The more secure the better? A study of information security readiness. Ind. Manag. Data Syst. **111**, 570–588 (2011)
48. Wang, Y., Leon, P.G., Acquisti, A., Faith Cranor, L., Forget, A., Sadeh, N.: A field trial of privacy nudges for Facebook. In: CHI 2014, 26 April–01 May 2014, Toronto, ON, Canada (2014)

Overcoming Fear of the Threat Model

Scott Cadzow[✉]

Cadzow Communications Consulting Ltd., Sawbridgeworth, UK
scott@cadzow.com

Abstract. In recognising that it is the human factor that generally identifies risk and maps out the functionality of a system - its goal in other words - it is clear that this strength can be undermined by fallibility. The question we need to ask is how do we optimise the strengths of the human element and minimise the risk they present to the system? How do we do the security job effectively without leading to a climate of fear? Unfortunately undertaking a critical security analysis of a design will almost inevitably point out critical errors, or required design adjustments. When applied late in the design process the impact is high - often working against the analyst when presenting the results. This time around the fear starts with the analyst. The purpose of this paper is to mark those elements of the connected world and the publicised attacks on it, and to identify steps that security engineers should be taking to minimise the concerns raised. Addressing the fear of the threat model, promoting why good design works, relegating the "movie plot" threats to the fiction they belong in.

Keywords: Human factors · Standards · Risk modelling

1 Extended Introduction

The purpose of this short paper, and its accompanying presentation material, is to open a debate that marks out those elements of the connected world and the publicized attacks on it that give rise to fear. From a view of that world of risk and uncertainty we need to ask what should security engineers be doing that will minimize the concerns raised without escalating the level of fear. The worry is that in looking at all the issues of what could possibly go wrong and working out means to ensure they don't ever happen is that they find those things that could go wrong and end up in some endless loop of despair. So the paper is going to assert that we need to know what can go wrong, how we can be exploited, and use that knowledge to learn to recognize wrongness and the exploits, and then defend against them. This is something I'm terming "overcoming the fear of the threat model" by taking steps to address the fear of the threat model, promoting why good design works, and relegating the "movie plot" threats to the fiction they belong in.

The role of standards in this endeavor should not be understated. As engineers and scientists we need to respect issues such as scientific method, repeatability, ethical behavior and presentation of results, and we need to be as objective as possible - presenting facts and evidence that support any claim. This paper will assert that

© Springer International Publishing AG 2017
T. Tryfonas (Ed.): HAS 2017, LNCS 10292, pp. 14–24, 2017.
DOI: 10.1007/978-3-319-58460-7_2

standards, when used correctly, underpin scientific method and can be used to give greater assurance to users that a product will not be a liability with regards to security.

2 Human Fallibility

We start with a simple assertion: Humans design, operate and are the net beneficiaries of most systems. We can also assert as a consequence that humans are the net losers when systems go wrong. If that failure is in the security systems trust in the system can disappear.

Humans are fallible and make mistakes. One of the roles of security engineers is to recognize this fallibility and to be up front about what can and cannot be done with respect to countering threats that limits the damage of such fallibility. In doing this it is essential to also recognize that humans are adaptable and resourceful in both designing systems and correcting them when they go wrong. These characteristics mean that humans can be both the strongest and the weakest link in system security. It also means that there is an incentive to manage the human element in systems such that those systems work well (functionality matches the requirement), efficiently (don't overuse resources), safely and securely. Thus human centric design, even for mostly machine based systems, is essential.

The need to understand risk, attack vectors, mitigation strategies, attacker motivation, resilience, cryptography, protocols, data value and many other application specific topics in order to be effective in designing security into systems from day zero marks the rounded security engineer out as a maverick entity.

In recognizing that it is the human factor that generally identifies risk and maps out the functionality of a system - its goal in other words - it is clear that this strength can be undermined by fallibility. The question we need to ask is how do we optimize the strengths of the human element and minimize the risk they present to the system? How do we do the security job effectively without leading to a climate of fear?

Unfortunately undertaking a critical security analysis of a design will almost inevitably point out critical errors, or required design adjustments. When applied late in the design process the impact is high - often working against the analyst when presenting the results. This time around the fear starts with the analyst.

The purpose of this paper is to mark those elements of the connected world and the publicized attacks on it, and to identify steps that security engineers should be taking to minimize the concerns raised. Addressing the fear of the threat model, promoting why good design works, relegating the "movie plot" threats to the fiction they belong in.

3 Security Controls? Security Awareness?

The set of Critical Security Controls (CSC) published by the SANS [SANS] Institute (see list below) are proposed as key to understanding the provision of security to systems, however selling the benefits of such controls, and the threat modelling that underpins many security programmes, including Common Criteria [CC] and ETSI's Threat Vulnerability Risk Analysis (TVRA) [E-TVRA] method to the end user is difficult and more often appears to induce fear rather than contentment that the experts understand their work.

Misapplication of the Critical Security Controls by human error, malicious or accidental, will lead to system vulnerabilities. The importance of such controls has been widely recognized and they can be found, either duplicated or adopted and adapted for sector specific spaces, in ETSI, ISO and in a number of industry best practice guides.

1. Inventory of Authorized and Unauthorized Devices
   (a) On the face of it this is relatively simple - identify the devices you want to authorize and, those you don't. However this introduces the Rumsfeld[1] conundrum "... there are known knowns ... there are known unknowns ... there are also unknown unknowns ...", it is not possible to identify everything.
2. Inventory of Authorized and Unauthorized Software
   (a) As for devices the Rumsfeld conundrum applies.
3. Secure Configurations for Hardware and Software on Mobile Device Laptops, Workstations, and Servers
4. Continuous Vulnerability Assessment and Remediation
5. Controlled Use of Administrative Privileges
6. Maintenance, Monitoring, and Analysis of Audit Logs
7. Email and Web Browser Protections
8. Malware Defenses
9. Limitation and Control of Network Ports, Protocols, and Services
10. Data Recovery Capability
11. Secure Configurations for Network Devices such as Firewall Routers, and Switches
12. Boundary Defense
13. Data Protection
14. Controlled Access Based on the Need to Know
15. Wireless Access Control
16. Account Monitoring and Control
17. Security Skills Assessment and Appropriate Training to Fill Gaps
18. Application Software Security
19. Incident Response and Management
20. Penetration Tests and Red Team Exercises

The more flexible a device is the more likely it is to be attacked by exploiting its flexibility. We can also assert that the less flexible a device is it is less able to react to a threat by allowing itself to be modified.

The use of the Johari Window [JOHARI] to identify issues is of interest here (using the phrasing of Rumsfeld).

---

[1] "Reports that say that something hasn't happened are always interesting to me, because as we know, there are known knowns; there are things we know we know. We also know there are known unknowns; that is to say we know there are some things we do not know. But there are also unknown unknowns – the ones we don't know we don't know. And if one looks throughout the history of our country and other free countries, it is the latter category that tend to be the difficult ones." Attributed to Donald Rumsfeld on 12-February-2002.

	Known to self	Not known to self
Known to others	Known knowns - BOX 1	Unknown knowns - BOX 2
Not known to others	Known unknowns - BOX 3	Unknown unknowns - BOX 4

The human problem is that the final window, the unknown unknowns, is the one that gives rise to most fear but it is the one that is not reasonable (see movie plot threats below). The target of security designers is to maximize the size of box 1 and to minimize the relative size of each of box 2 and box 3. In so doing the scope for box 4 to be of unrestrained size is hopefully minimized (it can never be of zero size).

We can consider the effect of each "box" on the spread of fear:

BOX 1: Knowledge of an attack is public knowledge and resources can be brought to bear to counter the fear by determining an effective countermeasure

BOX 2: The outside world is aware of a vulnerability in your system and will distrust any claim you make if you do not address this blind spot

BOX 3: The outside world is unaware of your knowledge and cannot make a reasonable assessment of the impact of any attack in this domain and the countermeasures applied to counter it

BOX 4: The stuff you can do nothing about as as far as you know nothing exists here.

The obvious challenge is thus to bring tools such as the 20 controls listed above to bear to maximize box 1 at the same time as using education and dissemination to minimize the size of boxes 2 and 3. Box 3 is characteristic of the old, mostly discredited, approach of security by secrecy, whereas Box 1 is characteristic of the open dissemination and collaborative approach of the world of open standards and open source development. Box 1 approaches are not guarantees of never having a security problem ever, problems migrate from box 4 to boxes 2 and 3 before reaching box 1 and, hopefully, mitigation.

In the security domain we can achieve our goals both technically and procedurally. This also has to be backed up by a series of non-system deterrents that may include the criminalisation under law of the attack and a sufficient judiciary penalty (e.g. interment, financial penalty) with adequate law enforcement resources to capture and prosecute the perpetrator. This also requires proper identification of the perpetrator as traditionally security is considered as attached by *threat agents,* entities that adversely act on the system. However in many cases there is a need distinguish between the threat source and the threat actor even if the end result in terms of technical countermeasures will be much the same, although some aspects of policy and access to non-system deterrents will differ. A *threat source* is a person or organisation that desires to breach security and ultimately will benefit from a compromise in some way (e.g. nation state, criminal organisation, activist) and who is in a position to recruit, influence or coerce a threat actor to mount an attack on their behalf. A *Threat Actor* is a person, or group of persons, who actually performs the attack (e.g. hackers, script kiddy, insider (e.g. employee), physical intruders). In using botnets of course the coerced actor is a machine and its recruiter may itself be machine. This requires a great deal of work to eliminate the innocent threat actor and to determine the threat source.

The technical domain of security is often described in terms of the CIA paradigm (Confidentiality Integrity Availability) wherein security capabilities are selected from the CIA paradigm to counter risk to the system from a number of forms of cyber attack. The common model is to consider security in broad terms as determination of the triplet {threat, security-dimension, countermeasure} leading to a triple such as {interception, confidentiality, encryption} being formed. The threat in this example being interception which risks the confidentiality of communication, and to which the recommended countermeasure (protection measure) is encryption.

The very broad view is thus that security functions are there to protect user content from eavesdropping (using encryption) and networks from fraud (authentication and key management services to prevent masquerade and manipulation attacks). What security standards cannot do is give a guarantee of safety, or give assurance of the more ephemeral definitions of security that dwell on human emotional responses to being free from harm. Technical security measures give hard and fast assurance that, for example, the contents of an encrypted file cannot, ever, be seen by somebody without the key to decrypt it. So just as you don't lock your house then hang the key next to the door in open view you have to take precautions to prevent the key getting into the wrong hands. The French mathematician Kerchoff has stated "A cryptosystem should be secure even if everything about the system, except the key, is public knowledge". In very crude terms the mathematics of security, cryptography, provides us with a complicated set of locks and just as in choosing where to lock up a building or a car we need to apply locks to a technical system with the same degree of care. Quite simply we don't need to bother installing a lock on door if we have an open window next to it - the attacker will ignore the locked door and enter the house through the open window. Similarly for a cyber system if crypto locks are put in the wrong place the attacker will bypass them.

It may be argued that common sense has to apply in security planning but the problem is that often common sense is inhibited by unrealistic threats such as the movie plot scenarios discussed below.

4 Movie Plot Threats

Bruce Schneier has defined movie plot threats as "... *a scary-threat story that would make a great movie, but is much too specific to build security policies around*"[2] and rather unfortunately a lot of the real world security has been in response to exactly these kind of threats. Why? The un-researched and unproven answer is that movie plots are easy to grasp and they tend to be wrapped up for the good at the end.

The practical concerns regarding security and the threats they involve is that they are somewhat insidious, like dripping water they build up over time to radically change the landscape of our environment.

Taking Schneier's premise that our imaginations run wild with detailed and specific threats it is clear that if a story exists that anthrax is being spread from crop dusters over

---

[2] https://www.schneier.com/blog/archives/2014/04/seventh_movie-p.html.

a city, or that terrorists are contaminating the milk supply or any other part of the food chain, that action has to be taken to ground all crop dusters, or to destroy all the milk. As we can make psychological sense of such stories and extend them by a little application of imagination it is possible to see shoes as threats, or liquids as threats. So whilst Richard Reid[3] was not successful and there is no evidence to suggest that a group of terrorists were planning to mix a liquid explosive from "innocent" bottles of liquid, the impact is that due to the advertised concerns the policy response is to address the public fears. Thus we have shoe inspections and restrictions on carrying liquids onto planes. This form of movie theatre scenario and the response ultimately diverts funds and expertise from identifying the root of many of the issues.

Again taking Schneier's premise the problem with movie plot scenarios is that fashions change over time and if security policy is movie plot driven then it becomes a fashion item. The vast bulk of security protection requires a great deal of intelligence gathering, detail analysis of the data and the proposal of targeted counter measures. Very simply by reacting to movie plots the real societal threats are at risk of being ignored through misdirection.

Movie plot derived security policy only works when the movie plot becomes real. If we built out bus network on the assumptions behind Speed we'd need to build bus stops for ingress and egress that are essentially moving pavements that don't allow for the bus to ever slow down, and we'd need to be able to refuel and change drives also without slowing the bus. It'd be a massive waste of money and effort if the attackers did a Speed scenario on the tram or train network or didn't attack at all.

A real problem is that for those making security policy, and for those implementing the countermeasures, they will always be judged in hindsight. If the next attack targets the connected vehicle through the V2I network, we'll demand to know why more wasn't done to protect the connected vehicle. If it targets schoolchildren by attacking the exam results data, we'll demand to know why that threat was ignored. The answer "we didn't know ... " or "we hadn't considered this ..." is not acceptable.

The attractiveness of movie plot scenarios is probably hard to ignore - they give a focus to both the threat and the countermeasures. In addition we need to consider the role of Chinese Whispers[4] in extending a simple story over time.

We can imagine dangers of believing the end point of a Chinese Whispers game:

* Novocomstat has missile launch capability
* Novocomstat has launched a missile
* Novocomstat has launched a bio weapon
* Novocomstat has launched a bio weapon at Neighbourstat
* Neighbourstat is under attack
* Neighbourstat is an ally and we need to defend them
* We're at war with Novocomstat because they've attacked with the nuclear option

---

[3] https://en.wikipedia.org/wiki/Richard_Reid => The "shoe bomber".

[4] https://en.wikipedia.org/wiki/Chinese_whispers => A parlour game that passes a message round introducing subtle changes in meaning with each re-telling.

As security engineers the guideline is to never react without proof. Quite simply acting on the first of these Chinese Whispers is unwarranted, and acting on the 6th is unwarranted unless all the prior statements have been rigorously verified, quantified and assessed. The various risk management and analysis approaches that exist (there are many) all come together by quantifying the impact of an attack and its likelihood. In recent work in this field in ETSI the role of motivation as well as capability in assessing risk has been re-assessed and now added to the method [E-TVRA]. The aim in understanding where to apply countermeasures to perceived risk requires analysis. That analysis requires expertise and knowledge to perform. In the approach defined by ETSI in TS 102 165-1 this means being able to quantify many aspects of carrying out a technical threat including the time required, the knowledge of the system required, the access to the system, the nature of the attack tools and so forth.

5 The Role of Standards

Standards are peer reviewed and have a primary role in giving assurance of interoperability. Opening up the threat model and the threats you anticipate, moving everything you can into box 1, in a format that is readily exchangeable and understandable is key.

Standards are at the root of sharing a common syntactical and semantic understanding of our world. This is as true for security as it is for any other domain and has to be embraced.

The corollary of the above is that if we do not embrace a standards view we cannot share knowledge effectively and that means we grow our box 2, 3, 4 visions of the world and with lack of knowledge of what is going on the ability of fear to grow and unfounded movie plot threats to appear real gets ever larger.

Let us take health as a use case for the role of standards in achieving interoperability. When a patient presents with a problem the diagnostic tools and methods, the means to describe the outcome of the diagnosis, the resulting treatment and so on, have to be sharable with the wider health system. This core requirement arises from acceptance that more than one health professional will be involved. If this is true they need to discuss the patient, they need to do that in confidence, and they need to be accountable for their actions which need to be recorded. Some diseases are "notifiable" and, again, to meet the requirement records have to be kept and shared. When travelling a person may enter a country with an endemic health issue (malaria say) and require immunisation or medication before, during and following the visit. Sharing knowledge of the local environment and any endemic health issues requires that the reporting and receiving entities share understanding.

Shared understanding and the sharing of data necessary to achieve it is the essence of interoperability. A unified set of interoperability requirements addresses syntax, semantics, base language, and the fairly obvious areas of mechanical, electrical and radio interoperability.

Syntax derives from the Greek word meaning ordering and arrangement. The sentence structure of subject-verb-object is a simple example of syntax, and generally in formal language syntax is the set of rules that allows a well formed expression to be formed from a fundamental set of symbols. In computing science syntax refers to the normative structure of data. In order to achieve syntactic interoperability there has to be a shared understanding of the symbol set and of the ordering of symbols. In any language the dictionary of symbols is restricted, thus in general a verb should not be misconstrued as a noun for example (although there are particularly glaring examples of misuse that have become normal use, e.g. the use of "medal" as a verb wherein the conventional text "He won a medal" has now been abused as "He medalled"). In the context of eHealth standardisation a formally defined message transfer syntax should be considered as the baseline for interoperability.

ASSERTION: All systems that need to share information require a formally defined message syntax.

Syntax cannot convey meaning and this is where semantics is introduced. Semantics derives meaning from syntactically correct statements. Semantic understanding itself is dependent on both pragmatics and context. Thus a statement such as "Patient-X has a heart-rate of 150 bpm" may be syntactically correct but has no practical role without understanding the context. Thus a heart-rate of 150 bpm for a 50-year old male riding a bike at 15 km/h up a 10% hill is probably not a health concern, but the same value when the same 50 year old male is at rest (and has been at rest for 60 min) is very likely a serious health concern. There are a number of ways of exchanging semantic information although the success is dependent on structuring data to optimise the availability of semantic content and the transfer of contextual knowledge (although the transfer of pragmatics is less clear).

ASSERTION: Semantic interoperability is essential to allow any machine based processing to be commonly understood across nodes in a network.

Underpinning the requirements for both syntactic and semantic interoperability is the further requirement of a common language. From the eHealth world it has become clear that in spite of a number of European agreements on implementation of a digital plan for Europe in which the early creation of 'e-health' was eagerly expected the uneven development of the digital infrastructure has in practice made for differing levels of initiative and success across the member states. These led to a confusing vocabulary of terms and definitions used by e-health actors and politicians alike. The meaning of the term e-health has been confused with 'tele-health' which in turn is confused with 'm-health;' 'Telemedicine,' a term widely used in the USA has been rejected in Europe in favour of 'tele-health.' There is general agreement that for these terms to be effective we need to redefine them in their practical context. Without an agreed glossary of terms, it will be hard to improve semantic interoperability - a corner stone for the effective building of e-health systems. The vocabulary is not extensive but at present it fails to address the need for clarity in exchange of information in the provision of medical services.

Finally we have to consider basic mechanical, electrical and radio interoperability. Quite simply a device with a power connector using, for example, a Type- IEC 60906-2 connection cannot accept power from anything other than a IEC 60906-2 connector. Similarly, for example, a serial port complying to USB-Type-A will not be able to directly interconnect with a USB-Type-C lead.

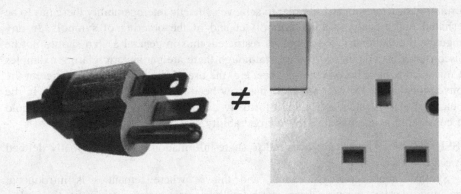

In addition to simple mechanical compatibility there is a requirement to ensure electrical interoperability covering amongst others the voltage level, amperage level, DC or AC, frequency if AC, variation levels and so forth. In the eHealth environment devices have to be able to interconnect and if wireless communication is deployed then it is obvious that the communicating end-points use the same means to communicate. In the radio sense this means sharing knowledge of frequency band, modulation technique, symbol rate, power, and so forth. The current Industrial Scientific Medical (ISM) band allocations are in this respect not strongly protected and many non-ISM devices use the ISM bands ("A" bands are allocated to ISM applications, "B" bands may be used by ISM and non-ISM applications). A consequence of the current management of the ISM bands is that knowledge of the frequency does not determine modulation waveform and vice versa.

Standards therefore enable and assert interoperability on the understanding that:

$$\text{Interoperability} = \textit{Semantics} \cup \textit{Syntax} \cup \textit{Language} \cup \textit{Mechanics}$$

Quite simply if any of the elements is missing then interoperability cannot be guaranteed. However we do tend to layer standards on top of one another, and alongside each other, and wind them through each other. The end result unfortunately can confuse almost as much as enlighten and unfortunately the solution of developing another standard to declutter the mess often ends up with just another standard in the mess.

However we can reasonably state that interoperability is the key to a solution where more than one stakeholder is involved and moreover that achieving interoperability requires standards. The nature of the standard is unimportant - it simply has to be accepted by the stakeholders. If the stakeholders are global and largely unknown then an internationally accepted standard is most likely to be the way forward. If, however, the stakeholders are members of a small local team the standard could be as simple as a set of guidance notes maintained on a shared file.

In the security domain understanding that we need interoperability is considered the default but simply achieving interoperability is a necessary but insufficient metric for making any claim for security. As has been noted above the technical domain of security is often described in terms of the CIA paradigm (Confidentiality Integrity Availability) wherein security capabilities are selected from the CIA paradigm to counter risk to the system from a number of forms of cyber attack. The common model is to consider security in broad terms as determination of the triplet {threat, security-dimension, countermeasure} leading to a triple such as {interception, confidentiality, encryption} being formed. The threat in this example being interception which risks the confidentiality of communication, and to which the recommended countermeasure (protection measure) is encryption.

The very broad view is thus that security functions are there to protect user content from eavesdropping (using encryption) and networks from fraud (authentication and key management services to prevent masquerade and manipulation attacks). Technical security, particularly cryptographic security has on occasion climbed the ivory tower away from its core business of making everyday things simply secure.

6 Where to Go?

How do you get rid of fear and get acceptance of the threat model? Shared knowledge, shared understanding and willingness to educate each other about what we know and what we may not know. This is the only real way forward. This result is close to zero in boxes 2 and 3 and a bounteous box 1.

7 Conclusions

As stated in Sect. 6 of this paper the approach to getting rid of fear and get acceptance of the threat model is in the wider acceptance of shared knowledge, shared understanding and willingness to educate each other about what we know and what we may not know. The role of standards in giving assurance of interoperability as the key to a solution where more than one stakeholder is involved is difficult to argue against. The nature of the standard is unimportant - it simply has to be accepted by the stakeholders. If the stakeholders are global and largely unknown then an internationally accepted standard is most likely to be the way forward. If, however, the stakeholders are members of a small local team the standard could be as simple as a set of guidance notes maintained on a shared file.

Spreading of fear through a combination of movie plot threats and Chinese Whispers is an inevitable consequence of human curiosity and imagination.

Standards are at the root of sharing a common syntactical and semantic understanding of our world. This is as true for security as it is for any other domain and has to be embraced.

Acknowledgements. Contributions made by the author in development of this paper have in part been supported by EU projects i-locate (grant number 621040), SUNSHINE (grant number 325161) and UNCAP (grant number 643555).

24   S. Cadzow

References

[SANS]   CIS Critical Security Controls, version 6.1. http://www.cisecurity.org/critical-controls/
[E-TVRA]   ETSI TS 102 165-1. https://portal.etsi.org/webapp/WorkProgram/SimpleSearch/QueryForm.asp by searching
[CC]   The Common Criteria. www.commoncriteriaportal.org
[JOHARI]   Luft, J., Ingham, H.: The Johari window, a graphic model of interpersonal aware-ness. In: Proceedings of the Western Training Laboratory in Group Development, Los Angeles (1955)

"No Good Reason to Remove Features"
Expert Users Value Useful Apps over Secure Ones

Steve Dodier-Lazaro, Ingolf Becker, Jens Krinke$^{(\boxtimes)}$, and M. Angela Sasse

University College London, London WC1E 6BT, UK
s.dodier-lazaro@cs.ucl.ac.uk, j.krinke@ucl.ac.uk
http://www0.cs.ucl.ac.uk/

Abstract. Application sandboxes are an essential security mechanism to contain malware, but are seldom used on desktops. To understand why this is the case, we interviewed 13 expert users about app appropriation decisions they made on their desktop computers. We collected 201 statements about app appropriation decisions. Our value-sensitive empirical analysis of the interviews revealed that *(a)* security played a very minor role in app appropriation; *(b)* users valued plugins that support their productivity; *(c)* users may abandon apps that remove a feature – especially when a feature was blocked for security reasons. Our expert desktop users valued a stable user experience and flexibility, and are unwilling to sacrifice those for better security. We conclude that sandboxing – as currently implemented – is unlikely to be voluntarily adopted, especially by expert users. For sandboxing to become a desirable security mechanism, they must first accommodate plugins and features widely found in popular desktop apps.

Keywords: Value-Sensitive Design · Security · Productive security · Sandboxing · Apps · Appropriation

1 Introduction

Sandboxes are security mechanisms that execute processes in a fully controlled and isolated environment. They are typically used to isolate apps from one another on operating systems (OSs). They protect users both against malicious apps and against exploits targeting legitimate apps. Sandboxes have become an essential building block of modern OSs [2,3,12,19]. However, sandboxes impact how app features can be implemented, and sometimes prevent the implementation of features found in apps, because the methods used to implement those features are also useful for malware writing. Therefore, sandboxed and unsandboxed versions of the same app can differ slightly in behaviour or affordances.

The security benefits of sandboxes are tangible. On Mobile OSs, all apps are sandboxed, which prevents malware-ridden and malicious apps from affecting other apps on the system. On desktop OSs, however, sandboxes are only partially deployed. Desktop developers struggle to make their apps compatible with

© Springer International Publishing AG 2017
T. Tryfonas (Ed.): HAS 2017, LNCS 10292, pp. 25–44, 2017.
DOI: 10.1007/978-3-319-58460-7_3

sandboxing without sacrificing important features and plugins. Many ultimately opt out from supporting this security feature [8, 13, 15, 20, 26]. Plugin infrastructures (which allow third-party developers to augment an app with additional features or user experience improvements) and features such as emulating keyboard input, screen sharing, audio recording, inter-process communication and bulk file processing are forbidden in sandboxes to prevent malicious behaviours, but they are sometimes too critical for apps to abandon [22, 31]. These incompatibilities are not, *per se*, technological constraints that cannot be overcome. They are design decisions made by sandbox designers. Instead, designers could have chosen to complicate sandboxed apps' security policies to support those potentially dangerous features.

On Windows, many popular apps like Dropbox, Steam, iTunes, Google Drive, VLC, Office, Photoshop, etc. are not sandboxed, or only in rudimentary versions with missing features [14]. Tech reporters argued that sandboxed apps are rarely downloaded and used on Windows, as they lack critical features and degrade productivity [6]. After five years, the adoption of sandboxing stagnates on Windows, and even dwindles on OS X where developers have publicly announced abandoning the Mac App Store [20, 26, 31]. On Linux desktops, sandboxed app stores exist [7, 9, 10], but none have a substantial user base. Consequently, desktop users are not currently taking advantage of the security benefits of sandboxes, despite being exposed to phishing attacks, malware, ransomware, etc. Still, many productive activities such as software development, complex information work, data science, etc. require the use of desktop OSs.

Moreover, assuming sandboxing meets usability requirements, users still need to either abandon their current apps in favour of new, sandboxed apps. How users will arbitrate such decisions about app adoption or retainment has not been addressed in past research.

We hypothesise that developers refuse to support sandboxing because it would degrade what makes their apps valuable to their users. Our analysis of developer discussions on sandboxing revealed two main issues: some types of features cannot be implemented in sandboxed apps, and sandboxed apps cannot have plugins. If the consequences of sandboxing upset users or make apps useless, it would explain why developers are reluctant to support it.

To answer these questions, we interviewed 13 expert users to explore the values they seek to fulfil when they make choices about apps. We aim to unveil the *de facto* requirements that sandboxed apps must meet in order to entice user adoption, support app adaptation needs, and prevent app abandonment.

We show that our users struggle with explaining and accepting feature loss, and may choose to abandon apps that remove features – especially for security reasons. We show that plugins are useful and valuable to expert users, and are a crucial way to improve their productivity. We also show our participants do not consider security as a prime factor in their decisions related to app appropriation.

We also make the following contributions: we perform a value-sensitive analysis of app adoption, adaptation via plugins and abandonment. We find that different values underpin each of these processes, and that the values recruited to think about content consumption and production apps differ. We identify short-comings in past usable security research: temporal aspects of appropriation (e.g. use of plugins, which address issues that were experienced in use and reflected upon by users) can only be studied in-the-wild; and participants' appreciation of security must not be distorted by priming.

We first present relevant research. Next, we explain our study design and research questions. Then, we present our value analysis of three aspects of app appropriation. We continue with a detailed analysis of participants' reactions to feature loss. We finish with a list of limitations, and conclude with a summary of our findings and open problems.

2 Background and Related Work

Usability evaluations of security mechanisms are mostly restrained to their user interfaces. We argue there is more to technology adoption than usable interfaces. If a tool does not perform a function that is useful to users, or if this function conflicts with other valued artefacts, the tool may be ignored. This is why Smetters and Grinter [27] have called for usable security to ensure that designed systems are useful. Likewise, Mathiasen and Bødker [17] examine usable security from the lens of experience-driven design [18]. They "concern [themselves] with how, on the one hand, the use experience is determining the security technology, while on the other hand, the security technology resists, constrains and directs the use experience". By framing sandboxing as an appropriation problem rather than a usability one, we can focus on the compositional and spatio-temporal aspects of user experience, which are usually ignored in usable security.

2.1 The Usability of Sandboxes

Only two usability studies of sandboxes exist [23,25]. Both had participants perform scripted scenarios in a lab, emulating basic app interactions. These studies do not model the impact of introducing sandboxes on the complex app ecosystems of the real-world. Expert users may rely on features that are more demanding on security policies, or sometimes not possible to formulate safely with current app sandbox models. These differences in technological needs are masked by seemingly successful usability studies, but it remains unclear if users would be able to appropriate a fully sandboxed OS.

2.2 Value-Sensitive Design

We did not want to just document participants' preferences, but understand why they held such preferences. Value-Sensitive Design (VSD) [11] is a methodology that reveals values involved in user behaviours and the frictions between them. It combines three forms of analysis. Conceptual analysis is used to identify stake-holders, their goals and potential value tensions between them. Empirical analysis reveals tensions in studied environments where technologies are deployed.

Technical analysis probes how artefact designs position themselves with regards to values and value conflicts. We used a VSD conceptual analysis to design the interview we report on, and an empirical study to model the values involved in app appropriation and relate them to security, which we report on here.

3 Study Design

We aim to identify how sandboxes clash with the needs of expert users. We performed semi-structured interviews with 13 users about the apps they use.

3.1 Research Questions

Feature loss and plugin loss are externalities of sandboxing that developers expect and dislike, and thus focus most of our investigation on these aspects. However, other tensions might yet have to be uncovered. We hence explore the relationship between users and their apps more thoroughly, including situations like app adoption and abandonment which are have been ignored in past studies. We treat plugin usage as acts of app adaptation, and thus include their use in our value analysis. If the presence of features emerges as an important value for users, and if plugins play a distinct and important rules in users' practices, it would corroborate developers' worries about these two aspects of apps that conflict with sandboxing.

We first investigate what users *value* and prefer in their apps, and the relation between these values and security. Our research questions are:

RQ1: Which values drive app appropriation? Is security one such value?
RQ2: How much do expert users rely on plugins? What value do plugins provide to expert users?

After that, we turn to how users relate to and *react to* feature removal in their apps. We discuss their own experiences and beliefs, and then explore how they make sense of feature removals motivated by security reasons.

RQ3: Is feature loss acceptable? How does it impact users' choices of apps?
RQ4: How does security-motivated feature loss differ from other types of loss with regard to acceptance and reaction?

3.2 Data Collection and Coding

We performed semi-structured interviews centred around participants' usage of apps, how they manage and value their apps, and about their information management and security strategies. The interviews lasted 40 min to 1:50 h (median 1:14 h), and we collected 81 to 227 statements per participant (median 140).

We coded our data separately for the value analysis and questions about feature loss. In the next section on value analysis, we allocated all participant's statements for each topic to characteristics of the apps that they relate to (we call those *app traits*), e.g.: apps being slow or costly, or the fact that an app offers new features. We re-coded previous answers and refined app traits as we went along, until all participants answered could be unambiguously classified. We then mapped these app traits to the value they support, to enable a value-sensitive empirical analysis of participants' behaviours. In the section on feature loss, we used Grounded Theory's open coding [30] to identify themes in participants' answers, e.g. how they made sense of feature loss statements or the expected compensations for feature loss.

Self-reported data suffer from accuracy issues. To eliminate potential demand traits biases [21], we only retained strong statements – which participants justified or supported with prior experiences. We eliminated 18 hypothetical, vague or contradictory statements, and used 201 in our findings.

3.3 Recruitment and Demographics

We advertised our study on a Reddit community dedicated to Linux. We used Linux users because participants were recruited as part of a larger field study, parts of which include deploying software components that cannot be written for closed-source OSs. Linux is for this reason the *de facto* standard OS in systems research. We paid participants £20 for participating to the interview this paper is based on, out of a total of £100 for participating to the whole project.

We recruited 13 Xubuntu users from 7 EU countries and from the USA, aged between 18 and 54, representative of desktop Linux users for age, occupation, gender and degree of Linux proficiency. Most were expert Linux users, except P6 and P12 (beginners), and P3 and P10 (IT professionals). P10 and P13 are security experts, and P12 attends security classes. Our participants include a Web developer, two (adult) high school students, two tech support representatives, a musician, a consumer retail employee, a student teacher, a sales engineer and four computer science students. 8 of them write code, 7 perform information work, and 7 produce media content (e.g. graphics, audio, video, photos).

3.4 Use of Deception

We told participants the study focused on their multitasking habits, to avoid non-respondent bias from participants with limited motivation to engage with security, and social desirability biases and demand trait biases during the study. We chose multitasking to attract participants who have a need for productivity, as opposed to leisure users of computers. We revealed the deception to participants near the end of the interview. Unless when mentioned otherwise, all the data we use was obtained before we revealed the deception. This study was approved by the UCL Research Ethics Committee under identifier 6079/001.

4   Value-Sensitive Analysis of App Appropriation

Sandboxes can make an impact in terms of everyday security only if they are *used*, rather than merely *usable*. To this end, we aim to determine how sandboxing interplays with three aspects of app appropriation: adoption, adaptation and retainment. Sandboxes may conflict with users' ability to obtain features and may incur a performance penalty. If users' adoption and abandonment behaviours are driven by the presence or absence of features and by performance considerations, then sandboxing will conflict with users' main decision factors. This could lead to sandboxed apps being adopted less often, or apps being abandoned after they become sandbox-compatible.

Besides, sandboxes prevent apps from providing plugins. Plugins are part of how apps can be adapted to better suit workflows. Users of plugins must compare the benefits afforded by plugins with the sandbox's benefits and decide whether to adopt or circumvent the sandbox based on such a cost/benefit analysis. We aim to find out where plugins are used, and what value they provide.

4.1 Method

We classified participants' statements on how they appropriate apps and on the plugins they use, based on the app traits they relate to (e.g. "Ad-blocking" or "Access to content" for plugins; "Unresponsive UI" or "Privacy Issues" for app abandonment). For plugins, we paid attention to their *reported purpose*, e.g. P11 uses a VPN service to access foreign media rather than for security. When participants added or replaced components of their desktop Environment (DE), we recorded those events as DE plugins.

Next, we categorised traits into values: *usefulness, security & privacy, usability, productivity, credibility, affordability, mobility, stability* and *flexibility*. We chose values to highlight known tensions in the usable security literature (*security* vs. *usability* [1], *usefulness* [27] and *productivity* [4]) and to capture concerns identified in our conceptual analysis (*usefulness* and developers' *credibility*).

We classified apps into categories: browsers, communication apps (email and messaging), file sharing apps (cloud storage and torrent), media consumption apps (e.g. music and video players, news aggregators, etc.), media and document editors (e.g. Office, audio, video, image editors), code editors, DEs and security apps. When a statement refers to an app's feature or to a past experience with an app, we assign it to the category that fits the app.

4.2 App Adoption and Abandonment

We look at the values governing app adoption and app abandonment, in order to discover potential challenges during the transition to sandboxed apps. When developers port their apps to a sandbox, externalities can include features being incompatible, loss of plugins or performance degradation. They must decide if those changes will put users off from adopting or continuing to use their app. Hence, we asked participants what would convince them not to try a new app, and what would convince them to abandon an app they are using.

Losing Interest in Potential Apps. We recorded 20 statements of interest loss. P4 gave no answer, and P2's answers were too weak to be included.

As Fig. 1 shows, half of our 12 respondents stopped considering an app because it lacked a feature. Feature loss is a possibility when porting an app to a sandbox, either because the feature relied on privileged operations (e.g. bulk file processing, access to hardware, IPC) or on libraries that are themselves not compatible with the sandbox. Thus, if an app developer removes a key feature because of sandboxing, fewer users will adopt their app in the future.

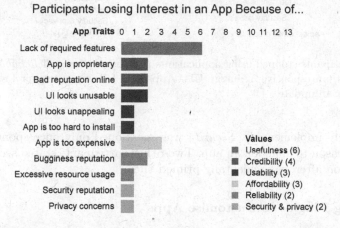

Fig. 1. Participants decided not to install potential new apps primarily because they lacked a required feature. Other reasons revolve around *Credibility* and alleged *Usability* and *Reliability*.

P10 mentioned avoiding apps that have a reputation for "breaking other programs somehow" or "security stuff". He also avoids apps that are hard to install. Apps with such a reputation might benefit from being sandboxed owing to the benefits of app stores. Ultimately however, sandboxes appear more detrimental than beneficial to adoption for our cohort.

Abandoning a Current App. We also analysed what reasons participants have to stop using their current applications, to identify the impact of sandbox introduction for the current users of an app. 11 participants provided 21 statements on app abandonment. P2's data was again removed.

Figure 2 shows that *Reliability* is the primary factor for app abandonment: participants stopped using apps because they became too slow, buggy, or used too much RAM. *Usefulness* follows in users' reasons for app abandonment. It is by changes in apps or in user needs. Two participants no longer needed an app, and two had a better replacement available. Five abandoned an app because it was missing a feature (in four cases, it was lost to an update; in one case, it was

Fig. 2. Participants stopped using applications primarily because of *Reliability* issues: bloated apps, unresponsive or buggy UIs. Apps also fell out of use, or lost required features after an update.

only partially implemented). *Security* was mentioned only once spontaneously as a good reason to abandon an app. Two other participants stated security was a good reason after we accidentally primed them.

4.3   Using Plugins to Customise Apps

Expert users commonly install plugins on their apps to improve them. Plugins are routinely found on browsers, but also code editors, media editors, information work apps, communication apps, media players, etc. They are written by third-party developers, and are banned from the Windows App Store, the OS X App Store (partially) and on Mobile platforms. Browsers run unsandboxed in order to retain the ability to provide plugins.

Our participants reported using 73 plugins (2 to 9, average 5), for all app categories except media consumption apps (46 for browsers; 14 for code editors; 2 to 4 for communication apps, document editors, DEs and security apps). When asked, seven participants mentioned 11 additional plugins they would like to have. Participants plausibly had more plugins installed than they recalled, as many Linux productivity apps and media players are distributed with some plugins enabled by default. If all Linux apps were sandboxed, participants would resultingly miss out on a significant part of their user experience. In this section, we document the role of plugins to understand how users would be affected if they chose to adopt sandboxed apps. This informs us on the values that security mechanisms compete against when they compromise the ability to have plugins.

Desired Plugins and Features. We asked participants to imagine an additional feature or plugin they would like to have, to check if specific types of features are in demand, or if plugins are wanted for specific app categories. Plugins were desired for browsers, communication apps, code editors and DEs.

We found that the 73 installed plugins and 11 desired plugins and features were similar in terms of the values they support and concerned similar app categories. Consequently and for space reasons, we discuss 'installed plugins' and 'desired plugins' together in this paper.

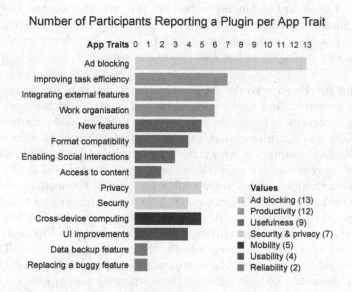

Number of Participants Reporting a Plugin per App Trait

Fig. 3. The plugins installed and wanted by our participants primarily support *Ad-blocking*, *Productivity* (task efficiency, external features, work organisation) and *Usefulness* (new features, format compatibility, access to content, social interactions).

The Role of Plugins. Plugins were predominantly used for browsers, but also for content production apps such as code or image editors and for communication apps. The features provided by plugins supported a variety of app traits, e.g. making an app compatible with a new format. Our classification aims to show what exactly participants would lose if plugins were removed. Some types of users or some apps' userbases may be more affected than others. We highlight the app traits for which sandboxes may be able to replace plugins with other techniques. We counted how many participants mentioned each trait and assigned traits to values, as shows Fig. 3. The Ad-blocking trait was mentioned by all participants and not classified into a value due to its unique nature.

Plugins mostly support the *productivity* value, with three traits relating to it. Firstly, plugins help participants perform small tasks faster, e.g. code snippets or tools to accelerate browsing through Web pages. Secondly, they integrate features normally found in other apps to make them faster to access, e.g. image processing features in browsers or source version control in code editors. Thirdly, plugins help participants organise their work sessions in browsers, DEs and code editors, e.g. tools to manage tabs or improve window placement.

Plugins also support *Usefulness*, with traits such as the compatibility with new document formats, enabling new social interactions, granting access to copyrighted content, and with the introduction of new features. *Security* plugins consisted of script and Flash blockers, HTTPS Everywhere, and a password manager. *Privacy* plugins comprised end-to-end encryption for instant messaging and email apps and of plugins to prevent user tracking on the Web and on Facebook. Sandboxes can partially emulate some features of network security plugins, albeit without proper integration into apps' UIs. They cannot compensate for the loss of plugins in the *Usefulness* category.

Accounting for Productivity Apps. Our participants used plugins for code editors and document and media editors, as well as DEs and browsers. We call both editor categories 'production apps' – apps used in productivity contexts. Browsers, DEs and communication apps are hybrid, relevant to all sorts of use contexts. Media consumption apps (music and media players, online social networks, news aggregators, etc.) are, themselves, rarely ever useful in productivity contexts. Even though plugins are available for most of the media consumption apps mentioned by our participants, none of them used plugins for this category. Thus, plugins are particularly in demand for production apps. This is especially true for code editors where 6/8 participants used plugins. The *Productivity* value also accounted for 7/15 plugin mentions for the code editor category. Therefore, users of code editors are particularly dependent on plugins to boost their productivity. They would be more affected than others by plugin loss.

4.4   Values Driving Appropriation over Time

We recorded other value statements that are not specific to adoption, abandonment or plugins. Two values were frequently mentioned: stability and flexibility.

6 participants expressed, in 8 statements, discontent when their user experience is disrupted by changes in apps, therefore preferring *stable* experiences. P7 and P5 expressed disbelief about feature removal. P5 said: "If there is a need and there something covering this need, if you remove it it's really hard to explain to your users that it's just not there any more". Three participants were attached particularly to a specific feature (e.g. the ability to browse books or albums by their cover for P5, or the reopening of documents at the page they were last closed for P10) while we discussed their work habits. Finally, P13 expressed not wanting to change the apps he was habituated to, and disliking when those apps' UI changed after an update.

4 participants also praised, in 6 statements, software that is *flexible* and can be adjusted to their needs. P4 and P12 told us how they take advantage of settings and plugins to speed up keyboard-driven workflows. P4, P5, P12 and P13 mentioned customising applications like their document editors or DE. P5, for instance, says "I have been able to basically make my own toolbars with everything that I use. That's really flexible. [...] And it's pretty much the same idea in all applications".

4.5 Summary of Findings

RQ1: Which values drive app appropriation behaviours? Is security one such value? We found apps are:

adopted if they are *useful*, appear *usable* and *affordable*, and have a reputation of *reliability*, *security* and *credibility*

adapted with plugins to boost *productivity* and *usefulness* and sometimes to provide *security* and *ad blocking* capabilities

abandoned when they lose their *usefulness* or *reliability*

Users also valued a *stable* user experience, and *flexible* apps that can be adjusted to their needs.

RQ2: How much do expert users rely on plugins? What value do plugins provide to expert users? All our participants used plugins – for browsers, DEs and all types of editors, but not for media consumption apps. Plugins mainly provide usefulness and productivity. They also provide ad-blocking in browsers, and security for Internet-facing apps. Few of the benefits provided by plugins could be replaced by other mechanisms, if plugins were to become unavailable.

Productivity plugins were more prevalent for productivity apps and DEs, and our participants were in demand for more productivity plugins than they already had. Thus, people who use computers for productive work, and specifically users of some types of apps, would see their productivity decrease if they no longer had access to plugins.

4.6 Implications for Sandboxing

Sandboxing threatens *usefulness* by preventing the implementation of some features, *reliability* by degrading performance and resource usage, and *stability* by causing developers to transform or drop some features. Sandboxes thus conflict with the values recruited by participants when they decide to adopt and abandon apps. Owing to their effects on plugins, sandboxes further threaten *productivity* and *usefulness*, the main values supported by the use of plugins. Developers who chose to drop features and plugins to support sandboxing will be confronted to loss of users and potential new users, according to our value-sensitive analysis.

Our participants' liking of *stability* suggests sandbox designers shouldn't expect user experience sacrifices as a prerequisite to sandbox adoption. Mobile OSs never had plugin infrastructures, and so their users have adopted what was available. Android and iOS are dominated by media consumption apps [28,29], and since there is no plugin demand for consumption apps, plugins are not as crucial for Mobile OSs as they are for desktops. Users might refuse to switch to sandboxed versions of desktop apps if this means losing plugins they have already integrated into their work practices.

Plugin loss will particularly affect users with productivity goals, and some demographics e.g. users who write code (and expectedly, over demographics that were not represented in our cohort). When productivity is put in competition with security, users respond by implementing "shadow security" practices, which involve disengagement from sanctioned, verified security mechanisms, even if they do value security [16]. It is advisable that plugins be supported by sandboxes, especially since there is no technical barrier to distributing plugins on the Windows and Mac App Stores, just like standalone apps.

5   Feature Loss

We learnt that usefulness is a major driver of appropriation decisions, and we know that sandboxes conflict with usefulness by forbidding some features. We now explore the value arbitrations made by participants when they are confronted with feature loss. We query how they explain feature loss in an app they use, and how they react to it, especially if "security reasons" motivate it.

5.1   Method

We asked participants, if a feature was removed from an application, what they would do and how it would affect them. We also asked them what good and bad reasons a developer could give to justify this change. When possible, we asked participants about features they mentioned during the interview. Otherwise, we would ask about "a feature" or "the ability to have plugins" for an app they mentioned using. Most participants responded with hypothetical scenarios based on apps they used.

We formulated the security question as such: we asked participants what they would think if a developer were to remove a feature or plugin "for security reasons". P12 spontaneously mentioned security as a valid reason for removing a feature, obviating the security question. P5 and P9 were mistakenly asked about justifications to feature removal after we had revealed the security deception.

We refer to answers based on participants' features as "own experiences", and answers to the security question as "security reasons". As the interviews were semi-structured, some participants did not answer, especially P3 and P11.

5.2   Justifying Feature Removal

We wanted to know what determined whether users would accept the disappearance of a feature. If a specific reason makes sense to users, they will be less incredulous and suspicious when a feature is removed for that reason. Inversely, if users are told a feature is removed for a reason they do not understand, they might deplore the developer's decision and be more prone to switch apps.

We collected 18 reasons which participants thought were acceptable (see Fig. 4) and 8 unacceptable (Fig. 5) to justify feature removals. 5 participants recalled actual experiences of feature loss, showing it is a commonplace experience, though overall participants did not find it easy to answer those questions.

Maintainability was seen as the most valid reason to remove features, by 3 participants, with 2 mentions from P4. This included removing code that was too difficult to maintain or not stable enough, or making plugins temporarily unavailable after an update. However, one of the "feature loss" app abandonment reasons we discussed in the previous section was justified with maintainability: P4 abandoned the GNOME DE because its plugins would often stop working after an update. So the reason is not unanimously accepted.

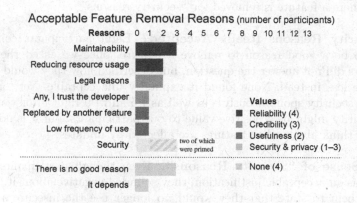

Fig. 4. Number of participants citing a reason as acceptable to justify feature removal.

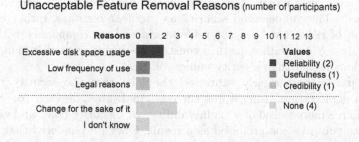

Fig. 5. Number of participants citing a reason as *not* acceptable.

Security was mentioned thrice, albeit two times by participants whom we accidentally primed to think about security beforehand, as we forgot to ask the question about feature removal until right after revealing the security topic of the study and before discussing security practices. Legal reasons were mentioned both as a good and as a bad justification. So was reliability, with participants claiming that excessive CPU or RAM usage were valid reasons, but excessive disk usage wasn't. Likewise for usefulness: P6 mentioned not caring about a feature he did not use, whereas P12 strongly opined that developers should not remove a feature used only by a minority of users.

Participants could conceptualise why feature are removed (maintainability, legal issues, reliability, and security), but none of the enumerated reasons seem to be *always* justified. Besides, three participants thought feature removal to be inexcusable, no matter the reason. Therefore, there is no *blanket rationale* that developers can invoke to explain away a decision to remove a feature.

5.3 Security Reasons

We asked eleven participants (except P3 and P11) what they would think of a scenario where a feature is removed for "security reasons".

Are Security Reasons Really Accepted? Eight participants considered security to be a good reason to remove a feature, once we asked them. The three others did not answer the question, but described how they would analyse the feature loss instead. None found it explicitly unacceptable. Yet, only P12 mentioned security spontaneously – as well as P5 and P9 right after we primed them. Security might be a positive value to our participants, but it is not something they think about when features are affected by updates.

Making Sense of "Security Reasons". Even though participants agreed security was an acceptable justification, they sounded negative about it. We had expected them to state that they would no longer use the insecure software. Instead, they showed us they would attempt to understand the announcement and to decide for themselves if they should be concerned and adjust their practice.

Participants were mostly defiant because of how they made sense of "security reasons". They understood security as *incident response*, rather than the *anticipation* of risks that have not yet materialised, or *compliance* with external constrains. Yet, sandbox feature constraints derive from risk management considerations rather than security vulnerabilities.

Three participants clearly expressed the idea that the security risk had resulted in exploitation, using words such as "malware", "breach" or "security exploit". Three more talked of a "vulnerability" or "security hole" and wondered if their data could be compromised as a result. Only P8 pondered that the feature itself might have represented a danger, without mentioning the existence of a fault attributable to the developer.

5.4 Deciding What to Do About Feature Removals

How many users would abandon an app if its developers decided to remove an important feature from it? The answer to this question is relevant to developers who must decide whether to adopt feature-degrading sandboxes or not. We thus asked our participants how they would react to the loss of a feature they had previously mentioned to us, or to the loss of plugins. We sometimes asked participants about more than one feature. Figure 6 presents the 20 reactions we collected from 11 participants for feature loss in general (some participants answered for several features, P9 gave weak answers, P11 was not asked). It also shows the 11 reactions collected for security-induced feature loss from 9 participants (P1 gave two answers, and P3, P9, P11 and P13 gave none).

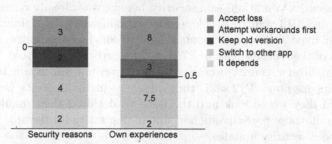

Fig. 6. Participants are more likely to accept an update that induces feature loss for reasons other than security. Some will deploy workarounds to emulate or replace the lost feature, before seeking a replacement app. Over a third of participants would abandon an app that lost a feature and seek another one with an equivalent feature either way.

For updates motivated by security reasons, participants decided to stay on the old, insecure version of the app in 2/10 cases. In 4/10 cases, they preferred switching to another app. 2/10 said their reaction would depend on the feature or the developer's attitude. This leaves only 3/10 cases where participants would accept the update. This reaction contradicts our finding that nearly all participants agreed security is a valid reason to remove features. We hypothesise this discrepancy is due to usefulness taking precedence over security in driving participants' choices. Another possible conjecture is that our expert users have become *prejudiced* against security announcements, owing to dissonance between alleged and perceived security benefits in past security experiences.

The cost of feature loss was viewed as higher than the security benefits in our security question. In contrast, when we asked about feature removal in a generic update, participants rooted for the imagined benefits of the update more often: they would use the new version in 11/21(52%) cases – including 3/21(11%) cases where they would attempt to emulate the lost feature with the new version, but would switch back to the old one or to a new app if their coping mechanism fails to satisfy them. Security is, after all, a secondary goal [24,32], so it comes after features which support a primary goal. Our value analysis corroborates this: factors like usefulness, productivity or reliability trump security in participants' decisions. P10 would either switch to another app or stay on the old version. In 7.5/21(36%) cases in total, participants would switch to another app. In 2/21(10%) cases, participants said it depends on the feature.

5.5   Getting Something Out of the Loss

In both conditions, three participants expected lost features to be re-introduced after some time. When a disruption is temporary, participants might tolerate it as a necessary evil. P1, P10 and P13 also expected the app to be improved in some way (e.g. reducing RAM usage, speeding up the UI, or integrating popular plugins into the app) in the general case. This desire for *compensation* was not seen in the security condition, as a security benefit was already communicated.

P5, P10 and P13 wanted developers to explain what the vulnerability was that had been fixed. Other participants sought to convince themselves of the well-foundedness of the security reason. P7 stated he expected to be told "how much time has there been a security breach, why have they not warned me beforehand, and what happens now". P12 said "they'd have to justify it pretty well". P2, P8 and P10 said they would look into the issue to decide if they should feel concerned. Overall, those participants had untrusting attitudes towards developers who announced security updates.

5.6 Summary of Findings

RQ3: Is feature loss acceptable? How does it impact users' choices of apps and practices? Feature removal has a substantial impact on users: over a third may abandon an app when a feature they used disappears. Half won't consider updating an app with a missing feature, and they may also abandon an app that loses a feature. A forth of participants expected feature loss to be temporary, and a forth also expected it to be compensated with improvements.

There is no consensus among participants over what constitutes good reasons to remove a feature. Maintainability, reliability and legal issues were mentioned, although as bad reasons too. Security was mentioned spontaneously by one participant, and after security priming by two more participants. Given the prevalence of *stability* in user values, we find feature loss hard to justify overall.

RQ4: How does security-motivated feature loss differ from other types of loss with regard to acceptance and reaction? When asked, our participants claim security is a valid reason to remove features. Yet, they are four times more likely to ignore a security update than a non-security update that removes features. This illustrates how security is a secondary goal to users.

Participants view security-motivated feature removals as incident response rather than a preventative measure. They expect developers to explain why a security risk existed and the consequences if it. Thus, developers' credibility may paradoxically suffer when they announce security improvements.

5.7 Implications for Sandboxing

Sandboxes restrain the ability to implement some features as a form of *risk management*, rather than because these features cause systematic vulnerabilities. As our participants understand security as *incident response*, they are likely to attribute a sandbox-related feature loss to a fault on behalf of app developers. Besides, we've seen that there is no *blanket rationale* that developers can invoke to explain away a decision to remove a feature, which all participants would believe is legitimate. Therefore, the task of explaining a sandbox-motivated feature loss to users seems particularly strenuous and hazardous for developers.

Feature removal can lead to user base attrition. As we've seen, this is more so the case when feature loss is justified by security. In competitive app ecosystems where many apps provide similar features, having to remove features from one's app may act as a deterrent for developers to consider sandboxing. We argue that the current restrictions on features and plugins place an unfair burden on app developers, and that sandbox designers must review those decisions rather than wait out for developers to finally 'get it' and adopt sandboxing. Presently, there are valid incentives in place for app developers to stay away from sandboxing.

6   Limitations

6.1   Cohort Size

The field study we are running involves sustained interactions with participants, forcing us to keep a small cohort. We thus have too few participants to provide statistical significance for our results. We provide quantitative data as much as possible to allow for our results to be aggregated to future studies on this topic. Besides, we view the presentation of our method as a contribution in itself, relevant to security designers who need to study barriers to the adoption of security technologies in their app ecosystems.

6.2   Deception

We ensured the validity of our data by using deception. This means less data was available as we could not incite our participants to detail their mental models of security without drawing their attention to our actual topic of interest.

6.3   Method of Report

App appropriation events are rare, and participants sometimes struggled to recall details of their past experiences. We helped them recall past events by using diary data to discuss the apps which we knew they used, and we eliminated statements where participants sounded hesitant or were inaccurate.

6.4   Linux Users

We recruited Linux users. They are reflective about technology and often have experience with multiple OSs. This is not a threat to validity, but reduces the scope of our findings to experienced and reflective practitioners. Many Windows and OS X users are experts, too – including developers, digital artists, researchers, etc. Linux users prefer software that is open-source. Thus, our data likely overstates the importance of the app traits related to proprietary licenses.

7   Implications for Usable Security Research

Some of our findings would not have been possible to make if we had stuck to the methods used in previous sandbox usability research [23, 25]. We derive methodological implications for future usability evaluations of security mediators.

7.1 Productive Security Is Achieved over Time, Not in the Lab

Beautement et al. [5] argue that the cost of security might be accepted during initial interactions, but rejected over time as users wear out their "compliance budget" – their ability to comply with security when the cost of it exceeds its benefits. When newly introduced security artefacts disrupt stability (e.g. with feature loss) or flexibility (e.g. by removing plugins), these artefacts cannot be declared usable solely on the basis of one-off interactions in a lab setting. Those values are fulfilled over time, and so the impact that changes in users' practices have on them must be studied over time too.

Previous usability studies of sandboxing [23,25] failed to study how participants ultimately react to the cumulative frustrations caused by a degraded user experience, or how they can improve their productivity once sandboxes hinder apps' flexibility. Ergo, sandboxes must be introduced in-the-wild and their impact on practice monitored until they are completely appropriated or rejected by participants. Otherwise, researchers may falsely conclude that sandboxes are usable, when participants' compliance budget is exhausted in superficial interactions settings and their interaction would not have been sustained in-the-wild.

7.2 Deception Is Necessary to Discover Actual Behaviour Drivers

Participants overwhelmingly agreed that security is an acceptable reason to remove a feature, when we asked them. Yet, they would be less likely to continue using an app that lost a feature for security, rather than for other types of improvements. We conclude from that that querying participants directly about their attitude to security can mislead researchers into thinking that security is sufficiently valued to influence user behaviour. We've shown that explicit attitudes towards one value are not the proper measure for drivers of behaviour. Instead, researchers should focus on building value hierarchies and identifying the main values that users recruit in making decisions that impact security. This means that study designs must include deception to avoid non-respondant and social desirability biases, and to produce valid value hierarchies.

8   Conclusion

Sandboxes do not provide support for several types of features, and for plugins, resulting in second-class apps. Sandboxes also decrease app performance slightly. Sandbox adoption is low on desktop OSs, and some developers even forsake sandboxed versions of their apps. We investigated how expert desktop users arbitrate different values in apps, and how they cope with feature loss, to understand how they arbitrate between usefulness, productivity and security, and how likely they are to adopt or retain apps that sacrifice features for security improvements. If users are likely to abandon newly sandboxed apps, it would explain developers' reluctance to support sandboxing.

We built a model of values involved in three desktop app appropriation processes: adoption, adaptation, and abandonment. We found that lack of features was the primary reason for users to reject a potential app, and one of two reasons (along with reliability) for users to abandon an app they're using. We also found that users like to adapt and customise their apps, primarily to meet productivity goals, especially for browsers and productivity apps like code editors. Besides, feature loss is a seldom understood phenomena that is poorly accepted by users. A non-negligible portion of our participants would abandon an app that removes a feature they use, especially if justified by security improvements.

Sandbox designers must identify the features threatened by the changes sandboxing brings about, and they must improve support for the relevant APIs so that these features survive sandboxing. They could support plugins by distributing them on app stores and subjecting them to the same security checks as apps. These corrections are essential to avoid putting security in competition with usefulness and security. Indeed, our value analysis clearly shows that security will not be privileged by expert users, and thus, that sandboxed apps are less likely to be adopted than their insecure counterparts.

In future work, we will continue to investigate how app sandboxing and our participants' digital lives fit together. We will assess the fitness of app sandboxing for the information management strategies of our participants using qualitative and quantitative data we collected, and we will investigate how many of the apps they used contain features typically threatened by sandboxing.

References

1. Adams, A., Sasse, M.A.: Users are not the enemy. Commun. ACM **42**(12), 40–46 (1999)
2. Apple Inc.: App Sandboxing, September 2016. https://developer.apple.com/app-sandboxing/
3. Apple Inc.: iOS Security iOS 9.3 or later, May 2016. https://www.apple.com/business/docs/iOS_Security_Guide.pdf
4. Beautement, A., Becker, I., Parkin, S., Krol, K., Sasse, A.: Productive security: a scalable methodology for analysing employee security behaviours. In: SOUPS 2016. USENIX Association (2016)
5. Beautement, A., Sasse, M.A., Wonham, M.: The compliance budget: managing security behaviour in organisations. In: NSPW 2008. ACM (2008)
6. Chacos, B.: And the study says: Windows 8 users rarely touch Metro apps, May 2013. http://www.pcworld.com/article/2039445/
7. Canonical: Ubuntu Core Documentation - Security and Sandboxing (2016). http://docs.ubuntu.com/core/en/guides/intro/security
8. Counsell, D.: Not on the Mac App Store, November 2015. https://www.dancounsell.com/not-on-the-mac-app-store/
9. Docker Inc.: Overview of Docker Hub (2016). https://docs.docker.com/docker-hub/
10. Flatpak: Flatpak - the future of application distribution (2016). http://flatpak.org/
11. Friedman, B.: Value-sensitive design. Interactions **3**(6), 16–23 (1996)

12. Google: Android: application security, September 2016. https://source.android.com/security/overview/app-security.html
13. Hoffman, C.: Why the Mac App Store Doesn't Have the Applications You Want, March 2015. http://www.howtogeek.com/210605/
14. Hoffman, C.: Why Desktop Apps Arent Available in the Windows Store (Yet), March 2016. http://www.howtogeek.com/243559/
15. Paul, I.: The 10 most glaring Windows Store no-shows, April 2013. http://www.pcworld.com/article/2033876/
16. Kirlappos, I., Parkin, S., Sasse, M.: Learning from shadow security: why understanding non-compliance provides the basis for effective security. In: Workshop on Usable Security, USEC 2014, February 2014
17. Mathiasen, N.R., Bødker, S.: Threats or threads: from usable security to secure experience? In: NordiCHI 2008. ACM (2008)
18. McCarthy, J.C., Wright, P.: Technology as Experience. MIT Press, Cambridge (2004)
19. Microsoft: Windows 8 Security Overview, June 2013. https://technet.microsFFoft.com/en-us/library/dn283963(v=ws.11).aspx
20. Dzhumerov, M.: Mac App Store: The Subtle Exodus, October 2014. http://blog.helftone.com/mac-app-store-the-subtle-exodus/
21. Nichols, A.L., Maner, J.K.: The good-subject effect: investigating participant demand characteristics. J. Gen. Psychol. **135**(2), 151–165 (2008)
22. Cohen, P.: The Mac App Store and the trouble with sandboxing, April 2014. http://www.imore.com/mac-app-store-and-trouble-sandboxing
23. Potter, S., Nieh, J.: Apiary: easy-to-use desktop application fault containment on commodity operating systems. In: USENIX ATC 2010 (2010)
24. Sasse, M.A., Brostoff, S., Weirich, D.: Transforming the 'weakest link' a human/computer interaction approach to usable and effective security. BT Technol. J. **19**(3), 122–131 (2001)
25. Schreuders, Z.C., McGill, T., Payne, C.: Empowering end users to confine their own applications: the results of a usability study comparing SELinux, AppArmor, and FBAC-LSM. ACM Trans. Inf. Syst. Secur. 14(2): (2011)
26. Sketch: Leaving the Mac App Store, December 2015. http://bohemiancoding.tumblr.com/post/134322691555/leaving-the-mac-app-store
27. Smetters, D.K., Grinter, R.E.: Moving from the design of usable security technologies to the design of useful secure applications. In: NSPW 2002. ACM (2002)
28. Statista: Most popular Google Play app categories in February 2014, by device installs, February 2014. http://www.statista.com/statistics/279286/
29. Statista: Most popular Apple App Store categories in June 2016, by share of available apps, June 2016. http://www.statista.com/statistics/270291/
30. Strauss, A., Corbin, J.: Basics of Qualitative Research: Techniques and Procedures for Developing Grounded Theory. Sage Publications Inc., Thousand Oaks (1998)
31. Streeting, S.: Between a rock and a hard place our decision to abandon the Mac App Store, February 2012. http://blogs.atlassian.com/2012/02/between-a-rock-and-a-hard-place-our-decision-to-abandon-the-mac-app-store/
32. Yee, K.P.: Aligning security and usability. IEEE Secur. Priv. **2**(5), 48–55 (2004)

Mobile Online Proficiency and Mobile Internet Use - Findings from Finland

Titiana Ertiö[✉] and Pekka Räsänen

Economic Sociology, Department of Social Research,
University of Turku, Turku, Finland
{titiana.ertio, pekka.rasanen}@utu.fi

Abstract. This paper investigates Finnish mobile Internet use and mobile payments, playing on the dual roles of citizens as users of a technology and consumers of services. The empirical section of the paper consists of an analysis of a nationally representative survey (n = 5,405) collected in 2012 and 2014. The data represent individuals aged 15 to 79. Our results indicate that Finns have become more active users of the mobile Internet and services such as mobile payment. The observed differences in user categories continue to be associated with age, education level and other socio-demographic factors. This also applies to expressing worries regarding information security, which continue to associate not only with use purposes, but also with age and other individual characteristics.

Keywords: Mobile Internet · Mobile payments · Mobile security proficiency

1 Introduction

Mobile phones have radically changed our patterns of communication, time use, consumption, and everyday life. There is no doubt that phones are very powerful and cost-effective communication tools for most people at the moment. Not so long ago, phones were widely thought of as offering the freedom to make and receive calls anywhere. Mobile phones established themselves as real timesavers for those who needed to be in touch with others at all times. Today, phones are 'standard accessories' for many consumers and their popularity rose dramatically. Indeed, phones are capable of so much more as their functionalities diversify. Due to technological convergence, smartphones equipped with calendars, cameras, GPS, voice recognition sensors and even health tracking sensors are just another step in the "mobile revolution". Access to new technical gadgets is likely to significantly influence people's social practices both directly and indirectly [1, 2].

Mobile phones break down the 'chains of time and space' [3, 4], offering users increased opportunities for information, entertainment or social interaction via applications (apps). On the other hand, the mobile phone also constitutes a private communication tool in that it is intended for one user only. The owner of the phone is expected to answer calls personally, use their own identity online and agree to the terms of use of third-party services personally. Naturally, the patterns of mobile phone use differ considerably from one person to another. The basic criterion for adopting any

T. Tryfonas (Ed.): HAS 2017, LNCS 10292, pp. 45–56, 2017.
DOI: 10.1007/978-3-319-58460-7_4

new product is that consumers use the product and its features, inevitably affected by personal preference. Broadly speaking, some products are cheaper, easier to use or provide other advantages over competing alternatives. Consumers feel that the basic functions of mobile phones are comfortable and easy to use. This helps to explain why mobile phones have diffused so quickly on a global scale.

As a response to the mass adoption of smartphones, firms of all types are integrating a mobile presence, or "mobile first", into their services. "Always online" consumers' demands for cross-platform services are met through mobile offerings. According to Eurostat [5], mobile Internet use has increased rapidly over recent years. In 2012, for instance, less than 40% of Europeans used a mobile device to connect to the Internet. By 2015, this share had already risen to 57% in Europe. Across the EU, only 25% of Internet users faced security concerns [5]. Notably, recent studies of the mobile Internet are country and area-specific, e.g. Indonesia [6], Thailand [7], Europe [8], India [9], Germany [10], African countries [11], Chile [12] or Denmark [13].

These studies focus on the plethora of tailored offerings for local customers in a hyper-connected, modern digital society. In Finland and other Nordic countries, mobile Internet use rose to 70% and beyond [5]. After only 8 months in the making, Denmark's "Mobile Pay" application has been adopted by 40% of Danes [13]. The striking availability of mobile Internet and mobile commerce opportunities, however, comes with a variety of security loopholes. There are common misconceptions tied to mobile usage, such as the fact that young people are less concerned about security and privacy and therefore more prone to adopt new services like mobile payments.

Recent studies found that socio-economic background variables do not influence mobile payments intentions or use [14, 15]. Such findings are puzzling in the light of technology adoption studies, which have consistently provided evidence of the importance of socio-economic variables. In this paper, we investigate Finnish mobile Internet use and mobile payments, playing on the dual roles of citizens as users of a technology and consumers of services. Mobile payments enable consumers to wave their phones over a terminal and secure a fast and seemingly secure transaction. But the adoption of such novel payment methods takes place at different speeds for consumers. We use demographic, social and economic data of repeated random-sampling, nationally representative surveys collected since 2006 by Statistics Finland. The 'ICT use by individuals and households' dataset represents individuals aged 15 to 74.

Our paper is structured as follows: first, we review literature on accessing the Internet from a mobile phone, a necessary but not sufficient condition of mobile payment usage. We single out mobile purchases as actions which mobile users can make. We then describe the data and methods used in the study. After the empirical analyses, we conclude with a short discussion on future developments of the mobile Internet revolution.

2   Mobile Internet and Mobile Purchases: Citizens as Users and Consumers?

Access to technology more broadly has been associated with a series of cumulative types of access [16, 17]. Much of the research has been focused on material access, namely devices, subscriptions and costs associated with accessing information. This is both the case with owning a mobile device, and with having the resources to access the Internet – namely to pay the mobile operator's fees.

The industry standard for mobile Internet fees is based on data volume. In Finland, on the other hand, mobile operators offer flat-rate, unlimited access to the mobile Internet. Furthermore, subscriptions are also affordable which allows users to go about their daily business without worrying about costs. Such a bold move results in Finland having the highest data mobile usage in the world [18]. Particularly for mobile phone users, the Internet allows them to stay connected at all times [19]. An "activation effect" occurs when using a specific service (mobile Internet) by triggering the usage of other related services (mobile commerce applications and services [19]). Wei claims that mobile phone users spend "empty time periods" surfing the Internet. Being "always online" also comes with a high diversification of services used, which are highly context dependent. For instance, the mobile Internet is associated with free time and leisure activities, which are situated outside of the home and office in "other meaningful places" [20].

Figure 1 shows the rapid adoption of mobile Internet use in Finland. After a steady growth period between 2006 and 2008, the mobile Internet grew dramatically until 2014. In just eight years, adoption has grown from zero to 80% of the population. Outside wireless networks, Internet is accessed through 3G/4G connections. For instance, in 2015, 69% of Finns owned a smartphone and used it primarily to read emails and news, 61% [21].

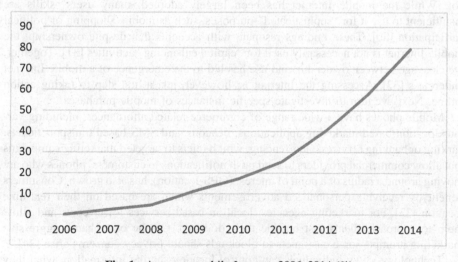

Fig. 1. Access to mobile Internet, 2006–2014 (%)

In general terms, one way of explaining the process of global technological diffusion and adaptation of the mobile Internet and mobile payments derives from the perspectives of diffusion theory. Rogers [22], for example, proposed that the characteristics of new products as perceived by consumers, determine their rate of adaptation. According to him, there are a total of five important attributes of an innovation.

These are: (1) relative advantage, (2) compatibility, (3) ease of use, (4) reliability, and (5) observability. Rogers also argued that any technological innovation (such as mobile Internet) is distributed along an S-curve over time [23]. Groups of early and late adopters of the technology perceive the benefits of the new products differently. Early adopters are immediately able to exploit or make use of the new offering, while late adopters are likely to use new products only after the general attitude toward adopting them has become positive. Mobile phones, in particular, present a variety of relative advantages, which explain their rapid diffusion; these include mobility, social status and opportunities to save time and money. Relative advantage is the degree to which an innovation is perceived as better than the idea it supersedes [23: 229]. Adopting technological innovations is also a function of people's willingness to try new products [24: 704]. The five attributes, however, are not the ultimate factors driving the adoption of mobile phones but rather the extent to which they fit seamlessly into daily life [14, 25: 12–13, 26].

Personal, social, economic and demographic factors such as age, gender, education and income influence mobile Internet usage [27]. Massoud and Gupta [28] found that beyond ease of use, security and privacy are the most important factors in adopting mobile services. Age is also negatively correlated with phone ownership, mobile Internet access and mobile Internet usage [6]. In addition, the differences in skills and usage become a type of social inequality [29]. Puspitasari and Ishii [6] found that mobile Internet on smartphones correlates with information acquisition levels (search and handling capacity) while mobile Internet on earlier models of mobile phones was not. While the mobile Internet has been largely adopted, many users' skills are insufficient to use it for "sophisticated" purposes, such as mobile shopping or political participation [30]. These findings resonate with accounts that despite ownership, the mobile Internet is not necessarily used for "capital enhancing" activities [31]. Together, the cleavage between ownership and use has led to the emergence of a mobile Internet underclass [32]. Accessing the Internet is, however, just a first step to taking action online. Next, we turn to investigate specific instances of mobile purchases.

Mobile phones have a wide range of commerce-related affordances, including various location-based marketing applications, beacons, and SMS-based transport tickets, parking or banking services. Geo-fencing, which refers to targeted marketing campaigns that allow commercial providers to send push notifications to customers' phones who are moving around a radius of a point of interest (GPS-location), has also grown. Consumers benefit by receiving personalized advertisements which are based on their real-time location [33]. For marketing agencies, location-based services lower costs and allow them to approach clients just outside their doorstep. On the other hand, aggressive marketing prompts some customers to block ads should privacy concerns arise [34].

Technology-savvy individuals can control location-sharing information, what they share and with whom. Trust in mobile advertisers and a positive attitude towards m-commerce predicts mobile payment activity [33]. Chung's study [14] found that mobile users found advertising information to be up-to-date and relevant. Moreover, when permission is granted, personalized marketing messages to a phone are considered trustworthy as well [14, 35]. Yet, many users notoriously only accept the "Terms of service" without reviewing its content. In doing so, the information collected by the services they subscribe to is no longer private because the user cannot control it. Simultaneously, information may be secure if accessed by authorized personnel only (for a distinction between security and privacy, see [36]). Privacy concerns of data collection, awareness of collection methods and location sharing with marketers do not predict mobile payments. On the other hand, perceived control over one's data and unauthorized access to personal information have significant negative influence on mobile payments [33].

Prior studies of the factors mitigating mobile purchases offer quite conflicting findings. Some studies find no influence of demographic or socio-economic variables [15, 33]. There seems to be some agreement that gender has no influence in mobile purchase behaviour [14, 37]. Yet, the effects of other variables are more diversified. The presence of children in the household and the time-constraints derived lead young parents to shop from their mobile phones [38]. Chong [37] found that age, education and income correlate with mobile purchases. Age has significant, negative effects on mobile purchases; education and income have significant, positive effects [37–39]. Younger users need fewer external impetuses to adopt mobile payments; moreover, trust and ease of use are also age dependent [39]. Younger users and users with higher levels of educational were also more likely to use mobile payments, location-based services, and entertainment than older users [37]. Older and younger adults have also been found to make mobile purchases at similar levels. More generally, many prefer to use their phones more for entertainment purposes than shopping [38].

Literature suggests that certain socio-demographic groups are characterized by high skills in mobile purchases as well as high purchasing power. However, on the other hand, they also face constraints of time, which makes the ubiquity of mobile payments particularly lucrative [38]. Next, we examine disparities that can be found when examining the use patterns of the mobile Internet in Finland during the past few years.

3 Research Questions, Data and Methods

In the empirical part of the paper, we examine mobile Internet access and online purchases in Finland in 2012 and 2014. Our main interest relates to the interconnections between these activities and online security proficiency, along with the basic sociodemographic background of different population segments. We refer to (1) mobile Internet access as whether the respondent has access to the Internet on his/her mobile phone, and (2) mobile purchase activities users perform to buy a product or service online with their mobile phone. We summarize the following two research questions:

RQ1: How do mobile Internet access and mobile purchases associate with online security proficiency in Finland in 2012 and 2014?
RQ2: Were there any associations after controlling for basic socio-demographic factors?

The data utilized covers the years 2012 and 2014, and were derived from the official Finnish statistics dataset 'ICT use by individuals and households' collected by Statistics Finland (n = 5,405). The data represents Finns aged 15 to 79 years. The data were primarily collected by phone interviews. However, data also include information derived from population statistics, such as information on respondents' age, gender, education, residence and income [40].

As dependent measures, we use two variables: overall access to mobile Internet (3G or 4G connection) and mobile purchases during the past 12 months or earlier. Both of these variables were measured using the dichotomous options 'yes' and 'no'. Thus, these items only offer us a rough overview of information on mobile Internet uses. For instance, they do not reveal anything about the frequency of the given use purposes. At the same time, however, this measurement is the most straightforward way to make a distinction between mobile Internet users and non-users.

The primary explanatory factor for mobile Internet access and mobile purchases is online security proficiency. In our data, online security proficiency was measured using a question on whether respondents verified or modified an app or service other than the Internet browser. The response options were 'yes' and 'no'. In addition, our independent variables include age, education, and gender. Age was measured as age in years and is coded as a continuous variable. Education reflects the three educational levels of Statistics Finland's official education categorization, which are 'Bachelor/higher', 'secondary' and 'primary'. Finally, the variable 'gender' reports the sex of the respondents. Descriptive statistics for all independent and dependent variables are given in Table 1.

Table 1. Measurement, coding and descriptive statistics for dependent variable and independent variables by year

Variables	Coding	2012	2014
Dependent variables			
Do you have an Internet connection on your mobile phone (either 3G or 4G)	1 = Yes 0 = No	40.1%; 1,042 59.9%; 1,559	74.2%; 1,940 19.3%; 505
Have you made online purchases using a mobile phone during the past 12 months?	1 = Yes 0 = No	5.3%; 137 94.0%; 2,166	10.0%; 243 90.0%; 2,184
Independent variables			
Gender	1 = Female 0 = Male	51.2%; 1,332 48.8%; 1,269	49.7%; 1,299 50.3%; 1,313
Age (numerical variable)	Years of age (15–79)	47.23; 2,601 (16.60)	45.15; 2,613 (16.49)
Education	1 = Primary level 2 = Secondary 3 = BA or higher	24.9%; 648 42.7%; 1,111 58.3%, 1,414	21.6%; 564 41.5%; 1,085 36.9%; 964
Have you verified or modified an application or service other than the Internet browser?	1 = Yes 0 = No	58.3%; 1,414 41.7%; 1,009	60.3%; 1,500 39.7%; 986

Note: Percentages represented for categorical variables, means represented for numerical variables. Frequencies represented for both categorical and numerical variables (standard deviation in parenthesis).

Our starting point is that mobile Internet activities have become more common between 2012 and 2014. As already shown in Fig. 1, mobile Internet access increased from 40% to 80% during this two-year period. However, we may also assume that those citizens who are proficient in online security issues are more likely to access the mobile Internet and make mobile purchases (Hypothesis 1). We also assume that the use of the mobile Internet as well as making purchases is likely to decline according to age (Hypothesis 2). Similarly, less educated citizens are probably less likely to use the mobile Internet and make online purchases (Hypothesis 3). Gender, on the other hand, does not necessarily associate strongly with mobile Internet access or making purchases (Hypothesis 4). In order to examine the hypotheses listed above, we will use descriptive and explanatory techniques. First, the aim of the analysis is to describe the interconnections between mobile Internet use purposes and online security proficiency over time. Afterwards, logistic regression models will be applied in the explanatory analysis.

4 Results

The overall aim of the analysis is to examine whether online security proficiency connects with general mobile Internet access and mobile purchases. In addition, we were interested in how the possible associations with online security proficiency are affected by the general increase in mobile Internet access. We first examined these assumptions using simple cross tabulations. Tables 2 and 3 show findings from this descriptive analysis for 2012 and 2014.

Table 2. Mobile Internet by online security proficiency. Percentages

Year	Access to mobile Internet	Verified settings	
		Yes	No
2012	Yes	53.6	27.3
2014	Yes	87.4	67.5

Table 3. Mobile purchases by online security proficiency. Percentages

Year	Mobile purchases during the last 12 months	Verified settings	
		Yes	No
2012	Yes	8.3	2.2
2014	Yes	14.0	3.6

Tables 2 and 3 indicate that out of those who have accessed the mobile Internet, approximately 54% had verified online security settings on some other device or application than a web browser. In 2014 the share was already 87%. The shares were significantly lower for those who have not verified security settings (27% and 68%). Similarly, when we look at the consumption-related item, we can see that those who have made purchases have checked online security settings more often than those who have not. The shares were 8% and 14% in 2012 and 2014, respectively. Despite the fact that very few had made online purchases through their mobile phone, it appears that this activity is clearly more common for those who have verified security settings in their devices. In this sense, it seems that mobile security proficiency is connected with the increased likelihood of both of the activities examined.

Tables 2 and 3 also capture the significance of online security proficiency's stability over time. In other words, this does not mean that the associations between online security proficiency, mobile Internet access and online purchases are going to disappear; the mobile environment is in a continual state of transformation as new technologies or innovations emerge. Next, we examine whether the associations with online security proficiency remain significant after controlling for basic socio-demographic factors.

Tables 4 and 5 show the results of logistic regression main-effect tests for mobile Internet access and mobile purchases in 2012 and 2014. In the tables, the effects of the independent variables in the models are presented with odds ratios (OR) and overall significance of the predictors with a chi square test (namely, Wald's χ^2). The pseudo-coefficients of the determination (Nagelkerke Pseudo R^2) of the models are also reported. The odds ratio is the increase or decrease if the ratio is less than one, in the odds of being in one outcome category when the value of the independent variable increases by one unit. Odds ratios are thus used to compare the relative strength of the independent variables.

Table 4. Access to mobile Internet by independent variables in 2012 and 2014. Logistic regression models

	2012			2014		
	OR	SE	CI 95%	OR	SE	CI 95%
Independent variables						
Age	0.965***	0.003	(0.959–0.971)	0.934***	0.004	(0.926–0.942)
Did not verify settings	1			1		
Verified settings	1.782***	0.100	(1.464–2.169)	1.555***	0.122	(1.225–1.975)
Female	1			1		
Male	1.312**	0.091	(1.098–1.567)	1.245 (ns)	0.116	(0.991–1.563)
BA or higher education	1			1		
Secondary education	0.556***	0.101	(0.456–0.678)	0.554*	0.130	(0.422–0.702)
Primary education	0.285***	0.134	(0.219–0.371)	0.406***	0.162	(0.296–0.558)
Pseudo R-Square (Nagelkerke) 0.185				Pseudo R-Square (Nagelkerke) 0.271		

Note: ***$p < 0.001$; **$p < 0.01$; *$p < 0.05$; (ns) = $p > 0.05$; OR = odds ratios; SE = standard errors; CI = confidence intervals.

Table 4 focuses on mobile Internet access. In both years, those who have verified online security settings are more likely than others to access the Internet with their mobile phones. The odds ratio is nearly 1.8 against 1 in 2012, and nearly 1.6 against 1 in 2014. In addition, it can be seen that age and education levels seem to have strong

Table 5. Mobile purchases by independent variables in 2012 and 2014. Logistic regression models

	2012			2014		
	OR	SE	95% CI	OR	SE	95% CI
Independent variables						
Age	0.968^{***}	0.007	(0.954–0.982)	0.964^{***}	0.006	(0.953–0.975)
Did not verify settings	1			1		
Verified settings	2.218^{***}	0.262	(1.327–3.706)	2.779^{***}	0.203	(1.867–4.136)
Female	1			1		
Male	2.451^{**}	0.199	(1.660–3.620)	1.186 (ns)	0.143	(0.897–1.569)
BA or higher education	1			1		
Secondary education	0.807	0.208	(0.537–1.212)	0.569^{*}	0.160	(0.416–0.779)
Primary education	0.515^{***}	0.291	(0.291–0.912)	0.365^{***}	0.233	(0.231–0.577)
Pseudo R-Square (Nagelkerke) 0.097				Pseudo R-Square (Nagelkerke) 0.109		

Note: $^{***}p < 0.001$; $^{**}p < 0.01$; $^{*}p < 0.05$; (ns) = $p > 0.05$; OR = odds ratios; SE = standard errors; CI = confidence intervals.

effects in both years, while gender is no longer significant in 2014. Highly educated and younger Finns are more likely than other demographic segments to access the mobile Internet. Overall, the pseudo-coefficients of the determinations indicate that mobile Internet access can be predicted rather efficiently by the selected independent variables in both years.

Table 5 shows the results for mobile purchases. Again, those who have verified online security settings are more active in making purchases than those who have not done so. In fact, the models indicate that the effects are relatively strong. The odds ratios indicate likelihoods of 2.2 and 2.8 against 1. This means that users proficient in online security are more than twice as likely to make mobile purchases as others. In addition, age and education are also significant in both years. Again, gender is significant only in 2012. The variances accounted for were smaller here compared to mobile Internet access. However, they indicate at least modest shares for both 2012 and 2014.

Together, the tables reveal that all background variables are statistically associated with Internet use activities, except for gender in the 2014 sample. As assumed, even in 2012, the effect of gender is weaker when compared to the effect of other independent variables. These findings by age are hardly surprising, since younger people are usually more interested in new ICTs than older segments of the population. However, it is notable that none of the observed differences by mobile phone proficiency have significantly diminished over time.

5 Discussion and Conclusion

This paper examined associations between online security proficiency and mobile Internet use in Finland. The Finnish case is particularly interesting because Finland has one of the highest adoption rates of the mobile Internet, which suggests that consumers make use of this ubiquitous tool for many aspects of social life. We contribute to the growing literature on the mobile revolution in a consumer society by investigating not only the factors determining mobile commerce but also how it changes over time.

The mobile Internet plays a major role in terms of social participation by providing relatively easy access to information on various activities and events. In the near future, we expect to witness a remarkable extension of the software and application market aimed at private consumption and the use of public services. This extension is significant because the Finnish population is ageing rapidly. It may well be that older adults are less interested in mobile shopping due to lower levels of consumption after retirement [38]. Yet, a variety of future mobile well-being services might increase interest, which should be investigated in future research.

Our research shows that mobile Internet access is not associated with online purchases. While access to the Internet is as high as 80%, mobile purchases barely make the 10% cut. In light of the diffusion theory, our results suggest that even for a high-tech country like Finland, mobile purchases are only reaching a tipping point. By 2014, only innovators and early adopters used mobile purchases. There is a clear cleavage between the rate of adoption of the mobile Internet and task-based activities like mobile shopping.

We have posited and demonstrated that mobile online security proficiency is associated with mobile purchases (H1). As for age (H2) and education (H3), they also correlate significantly with mobile purchases. Interestingly, gender (H4) is significant for 2012 but not 2014. These findings expand our understanding of recent studies on mobile purchases [13–15, 26, 33, 35, 37–39]. We also posited that there would be a significant change in mobile purchase activities between the two years. Even though the numbers doubled, there is no evidence for mobile purchases becoming common for the general population.

Regarding our first research question, both mobile Internet access and mobile purchases correlate strongly with online security proficiency. Regarding our second research question, both mobile access and purchases correlate with the socio-demographic variables tested in 2014, excluding gender. Our results can be discussed in the light of consumer empowerment: when mobile users feel they can set security criteria themselves, they are more likely to use the mobile Internet and engage in mobile commerce. When access and shopping take place on terms that they can modify, consumers are more likely to engage in them.

Our study has its limitations as well. First of all, comparative research is required both from an international and a domestic perspective. Given the Finnish context, the results cannot be generalized beyond one Nordic country. At the general level, however, the results are strikingly similar to findings from different countries regarding mobile purchases. Secondly, we only assess the change over two years, which may not be sufficient to capture the overall phenomena.

Acknowledgements. This research was funded by the Strategic Research Council of the Academy of Finland (Digital Disruption of Industry research consortium, DDI).

References

1. Lievrouw, L.A.: Determination and contingency in new media development: diffusion of innovations and social shaping of technology perspectives. In: Lievrouw, L.A., Livingstone, S. (eds.) Handbook of New Media: Social Shaping and Consequences of ICTs, pp. 183–199. Sage, London (2001)
2. Wellman, B., Salaff, J., Dimitrova, D., Garton, L., Gulia, M., Haythornthwaite, C.: Computer networks as social networks: collaborative work, tele-work, and virtual community. Ann. Rev. Sociol. **22**, 213–238 (1996)
3. Kopomaa, T.: The City in Your Pocket: Birth of the Mobile Information Society. Gaudeamus, Helsinki (2000)
4. Mäenpää, P.: Mobile communication as a way of urban life. In: Gronow, J., Warde, A. (eds.) Ordinary Consumption, pp. 107–123. Routledge, London (2001)
5. Eurostat. http://ec.europa.eu/eurostat/statistics-explained/index.php/Digital_economy_and_society_statistics_-_households_and_individuals
6. Puspitasari, L., Ishii, K.: Digital divides and mobile internet in Indonesia: impact of smartphones. Telematics Inform. **33**(2), 472–483 (2016). http://dx.doi.org/10.1016/j.tele.2015.11.001
7. Srinuan, C., Srinuan, P., Bohlin, E.: An analysis of mobile Internet access in Thailand: implications for bridging the digital divide. Telematics Inform. **29**(3), 254–262 (2012)
8. Mascheroni, G., Olafsson, K.: The mobile internet: access, use, opportunities and divides among European children. New Media Soc. **15**, 1–23 (2015)
9. Rangaswamy, N., Arora, P.: The mobile internet in the wild and every day: digital leisure in the slums of urban India. Int. J. Cult. Stud. **19**(6), 611–626 (2015)
10. Gerpott, T.J.: SMS use intensity changes in the age of ubiquitous mobile internet access - a two-level investigation of residential mobile communications customers in Germany. Telematics Inform. **32**(4), 809–822 (2015)
11. Stork, C., Calandro, E., Gillwald, A.: Internet going mobile: internet access and use in 11 african countries. Info **15**(5), 34–51 (2013)
12. Ramirez-Correa, P.E., Rondan-Cataluña, F.J., Arenas-Gaitán, J.: Predicting behavioral intention of mobile internet usage. Telematics Inform. **32**(4), 834–841 (2015). http://dx.doi.org/10.1016/j.tele.2015.04.006
13. Hedman, J., Henningsson, S.: The new normal: market cooperation in the mobile payments ecosystem. Electron. Commer. Res. Appl. **14**(5), 305–318 (2015). http://dx.doi.org/10.1016/j.elerap.2015.03.005
14. Chung, K.: Gender, culture and determinants of behavioural intents to adopt mobile commerce among the Y Generation in transition economies: evidence from Kazakhstan. Behav. Inform. Technol. **33**(7), 743–756 (2014). doi:10.1080/0144929X.2013.805243
15. Cocosila, M., Trabelsi, H.: An integrated value-risk investigation of contactless mobile payments adoption. Electron. Commer. Res. Appl. **20**, 159–170 (2016). http://dx.doi.org/10.1016/j.elerap.2016.10.006
16. van Dijk, J.A.: The Deepening Divide: Inequality in the Information Society. SAGE Publications, Thousand Oaks (2005)
17. Räsänen, P.: The consumption disparities in information society: comparing the traditional and digital divides in Finland. Int. J. Sociol. Soc. Policy **25**(1–2), 48–62 (2006)
18. Tefficient. http://media.tefficient.com/2016/01/tefficient-industry-analysis-1-2016-mobile-data-usage-and-pricing-1H-2015.pdf
19. Wei, R.: Motivations for using the mobile phone for mass communications and entertainment. Telematics Inform. **25**, 36–46 (2008)

20. Karikoski, J., Soikkeli, T.: Contextual usage patterns in smartphone communication services. Pers. Ubiquit. Comput. **17**(3), 491–502 (2013). doi:10.1007/s00779-011-0503-0
21. Statistics Finland. Väestön tieto- ja viestintätekniikan käyttö, Internetin käyttö mobiililait-teilla (The population's use of ICT, use of Internet on mobile devices). http://www.stat.fi/til/sutivi/2015/sutivi_2015_2015-11-26_kat_002_fi.html
22. Rogers, E.M.: Communication Technology: The New Media in Society, 1st edn. The Free Press, New York (1986)
23. Rogers, E.M.: Diffusion of Innovation. The Free Press, New York (2003)
24. Hargittai, E.: Weaving the western web: explaining difference in internet connectivity among OECD countries. Telecommun. Policy **23**, 701–718 (1999)
25. Fidler, R.: Mediamorphosis: Understanding New Media. SAGE Publications Ltd., Thousand Oaks (1997). doi:10.4135/9781452233413
26. Bouwman, H., Carlsson, C., Molina-Castillo, F.J., Walden, P.: Barriers and drivers in the adoption of current and future mobile services in Finland. Telematics Inform. **24**(2), 145–160 (2007). http://dx.doi.org/10.1016/j.tele.2006.08.001
27. Potongsangarun, R., Worasesthaphong, T., Taveechat, O., Somkane, S.: Factors influencing decision to subscribe mobile phone services. Procedia-Soc. Behav. Sci. **40**, 473–477 (2012)
28. Massoud, S., Gupta, O.K.: Consumer perception and attitude toward mobile communication. Int. J. Mobile Commun. **1**(4), 390–408 (2003)
29. Zillien, N., Hargittai, E.: Digital distinctions: status-specific types of internet usage. Soc. Sci. Q. **90**(2), 274–291 (2009)
30. Lin, W.Y., Zhang, X., Jung, J.Y., Kim, Y.C.: From the wired to wireless generation? Investigating teens' internet use through the mobile phone. Telecommun. Policy **37**(8), 651–661 (2013). http://dx.doi.org/10.1016/j.telpol.2012.09.008
31. Pearce, K.E., Rice, R.E.: Digital divides from access to activities: comparing mobile and personal computer internet users. J. Commun. **63**(4), 721–744 (2013)
32. Napoli, P.M., Obar, J.A.: The emerging mobile internet underclass: a critique of mobile internet access. Inform. Soc. **30**(5), 323–334 (2014)
33. Eastin, M.S., Brinson, N.H., Doorey, A., Wilcox, G.: Living in a big data world: predicting mobile commerce activity through privacy concerns. Comput. Hum. Behav. **58**, 214–220 (2016). http://dx.doi.org/10.1016/j.chb.2015.12.050
34. PageFair The 2015 Ad blocking report. https://blog.pagefair.com/2015/ad-blocking-report/
35. Martín-Consuegra, D., Gómez, M., Molina, A.: Consumer sensitivity analysis in mobile commerce advertising. Soc. Behav. Pers.: Int. J. **43**(6), 883–897 (2015). doi:10.2224/sbp.2015.43.6.883
36. Chen, J.Q., Zhang, R., Lee, J.: A cross-culture empirical study of M-commerce privacy concerns. J. Int. Commer. **12**(4), 348–364 (2013). doi:10.1080/15332861.2013.865388
37. Chong, A.Y.L.: Mobile commerce usage activities: the roles of demographic and motivation variables. Technol. Forecast. Soc. Change **80**(7), 1350–1359 (2013). http://dx.doi.org/10.1016/j.techfore.2012.12.011
38. Kuoppamäki, S.M., Taipale, S., Wilska, T.A.: The use of mobile technology for online shopping and entertainment among older adults in Finland. Telematics Inform. **34**(4), 110–117 (2017). http://dx.doi.org/10.1016/j.tele.2017.01.005
39. Liébana-Cabanillas, F., Sánchez-Fernández, J., Muñoz-Leiva, F.: Antecedents of the adoption of the new mobile payment systems: the moderating effect of age. Comput. Hum. Behav. **35**, 464–478 (2014). http://dx.doi.org/10.1016/j.chb.2014.03.022
40. Statistics Finland. Väestön tieto- ja viestintätekniikan käyttö, Internetin käytön muutoksia 2015 (The population's use of ICTs, changes in the use of the Internet 2015). http://www.stat.fi/til/sutivi/2015/sutivi_2015_2015-11-26_kat_001_fi.html

Usability in Solutions of Secure Email – A Tools Review

Lucas Ferreira$^{(\boxtimes)}$ and Junia Anacleto

Advanced Interaction Laboratory (LIA), Computer Science Departament,
Federal University of São Carlos, São Carlos, Brazil
{lucas.ferreira, junia}@dc.ufscar.br

Abstract. The adoption of Information and Communication Technologies in personal, social and corporative environments is increasingly evident, bringing complexity, interdisciplinarity and diversity to the study on information security in an era marked by decentralization and ubiquity. As this phenomenon becomes increasingly common, concerns intensify regarding security, secrecy, privacy, and information governance. Consequently, secure tools have gained more evidence and new solutions are emerging. However, literature shows the difficulty of adopting these secure solutions, even though they are efficient for information security, reinforcing the need for more effective security and privacy models on the Web to increase their adoption by users in general. Thus, it is necessary that the approaches to the development of security and privacy solutions be understood by the users, facilitating their adoption, without disregarding their contexts of use. Therefore, a review of such solutions seems necessary. In this article, we instantiate the usable security field for secure email and presented a review of the main tools, seeking to understand the implemented task model of each tool. With an analytical evaluation, we verified the compliance of these solutions with the usable security guidelines existing in the literature. Finally, we contribute to the usable security field by indicating in which directions secure email tools might be developed to accommodate the usable security guidelines.

Keywords: Security and usability · Secure email · Secure email tools

1 Introduction

We live in an era guided by the third paradigm of Human-Computer Interaction (HCI) regarding the contextualization of technologies to the user's culture, emphasizing the adoption of these technologies in a natural way [1]. In this paradigm, the relationship between users and their technology artifacts gain different proportions from those identified until then, ruled by the human factors and delimited by the work environment with emphasis to the execution of tasks.

Aligned to this technological paradigm, there are major changes that are changing the relationship of people with the computers. The hyperconnectivity and technological dependence are increasingly evident, making people more connected and dependent on

T. Tryfonas (Ed.): HAS 2017, LNCS 10292, pp. 57–73, 2017.
DOI: 10.1007/978-3-319-58460-7_5

technology in the personal, social and corporate contexts. In addition, the growth of the cloud services and data storage capacity are contributing to the end of the ephemeral. Now, all interactions and people's activities can be recorded and they will hardly be forgotten with time [2].

If on one hand the widespread adoption of Information and Communication Technologies (ICTs) and the major changes are inevitable phenomenons, on the other hand, there is an increasing concern over security, confidentiality, privacy, information governance and communication in this era marked by decentralization and ubiquity. Consequently, the need for better security and privacy support on the internet is evident, as showed in the cases of Ashley Madison [3], Hilary Clinton [4] and Greenwald and Macaskill [7]. Such cases had a huge impact on the lives of the people involved.

However, as experienced by Greenwald and Macaskill [7] and presented by Routi et al. [6] and Whitten and Tygar [5] designing secure and usable tools is not a trivial task, going beyond the general techniques of encryption, architecture and engineering, as well as security software design. Therefore, it is necessary to use specific usability and security approaches to develop these solutions, in order to make them ease to be understood by users, considering their contexts, facilitating their use and, consequently, their adoption by users in general.

In this paper, we instantiated the usable security study for secure email tools and presented a review of the main tools in literature, aiming at understanding the implemented task model of the tools and evaluating their compliance with the usable security guidelines.

2 Related Work

Whitten and Tygar [5] conducted the first user test using a secure email tool (PGP 5.0), exploring the usability of the tool through usability evaluation methods. This paper presents very convincing results that explain the inconsistency between the conceptual model implemented by the PGP 5.0 tool and the mental model of the users and serious usability problems with key management. In addition, they found that most users were not able to successfully send secure emails. Finally, they concluded that the PGP 5.0 tool is not usable enough to provide effective security for the vast majority of ordinary users.

Replications of the Whitten and Tygar [5] study were made by Sheng et al. [8] and Garfinkel and Miller [9]. Sheng et al. [8] performed an evaluation in a version of the PGP tool (PGP 9.0) seven years after the Whitten and Tygar study. They concluded that despite the improvements in usability, the conceptual model implemented by the tool is still not consistent with the user's mental model and, consequently, the problems persisted in this new version. In addition, they demonstrate that transparency in the PGP 9.0 email security process made the tool less secure in users' perceptions. Garfinkel and Miller [9] showed that automatic key management is closer to the user model. However, the study also revealed that the tool was excessively transparent in its integration with Outlook Express.

More recently, Routi et al. [10] continued the study of the PGP tool, now with the PGP tool (Mailvelpe). They concluded that the tool is not yet usable enough for most users. The results of the paper show that despite advances in Mailvelope, it still has very low usability and very complex operation for users without knowledge of public key cryptography, in other words, the manual management of encryption keys does not correspond to the mental model of the users.

Routi et al. [11] discussed security transparency in sending encrypted messages using the secure Private WebMail email tool. Authors noticed that excessive transparency of the tool confused users about the level of security. They conclude that the in a secure email tool, showing the encrypted message before actually sending it had a significant effect on usability and contributes to the users' perception of security.

Two papers seek to understand the adoption of users in use of secure email tool. In the first one, Renaud et al. [13] explored the user's understanding of how email works and at the end they reported some possible reasons to explain why secure email tools' adoption is low. The second one is Gaw et al. [12], which interviewed users in an organization using secure email. They stated that the adoption was conducted by the organization deciding that cryptography was necessary (due to secrecy concerns). However, there were users who did not want to use the software regularly because of usability concerns and social factors.

Ruoti et al. [6] evaluated the usability of three secure email tools (Private Webmail, Virtru and Tutanota) using a user-peer evaluation. The paper shows very convincing results that explain that tools that are integrated with some conventional webmail (e.g. Gmail, Outlook etc.) are more propitious to be used and adopted by ordinary users.

3 Task Model and Analysis – ConcurTaskTrees (CTT)

For Diaper and Stanton [19], task analysis (TA) is "the expression used to represent all methods of collection, classification and interpretation of data on the performance of a system that has at least one person as a component." In other words, task analysis is a set of methods for describing users' tasks in order to understand how they perform them and why. In this type of analysis, the basic approach is to describe the task having a specific goal and a set of steps to your execution. However, it is not just a list of actions, but of understanding how the system affects the application domain.

Analyzing tasks in a specific domain produces an explicit description of tasks, called the task model (TM). Such models represent the results of the task analysis, in which each model emphasizes a perspective. The task models allow a detailed understanding of the steps and relationships between them and contribute to the simplicity, effectiveness and usability of the computational system [20].

ConcurTaskTrees (CTT) is a task model focused on the design and evaluation of interactive systems in Human-Computer Interaction. CTT provides a rich set of temporal operators to describe the relationships between tasks, allowing concurrency. In addition, CTT provides more information on tasks such as their type, category, objects, and attributes [21]. CTT also has an editing and support tool, named CTT Environment (CTTE), which facilitates the creation and editing of the task model and is also capable of simulating tasks [22].

3.1 Task Allocation

CTT has four types of tasks to allocation, Theses types are showed in the Fig. 1.

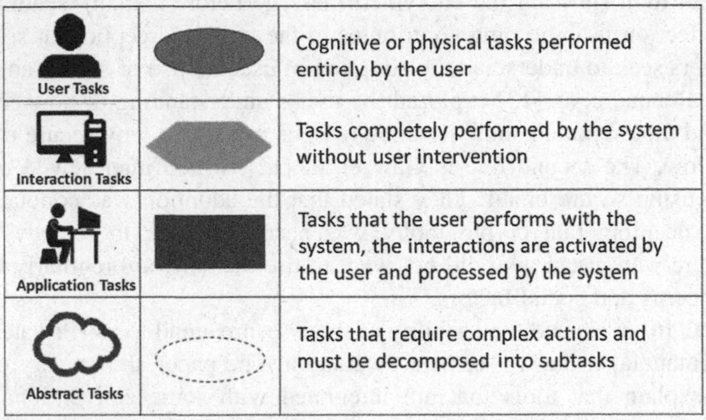

User Tasks		Cognitive or physical tasks performed entirely by the user
Interaction Tasks		Tasks completely performed by the system without user intervention
Application Tasks		Tasks that the user performs with the system, the interactions are activated by the user and processed by the system
Abstract Tasks		Tasks that require complex actions and must be decomposed into subtasks

Fig. 1. Types of tasks of the CTT (figure adapted from [21])

3.2 Temporary Relationships

Temporal operators are used to indicate the temporal relationship between the tasks of the same hierarchical level, so that they can model the behavior of the systems. The list of temporal operators available in CTT is presented in Table 2.

In addition to the operators mentioned above, CTT includes a set of three unary operators (applicable to one task individually). The complete list of unary operators available in CTT is presented in Table 1.

Table 1. Unary operators [21]

Operator	Symbol	Form	Description
Iteration	*	T*	Task is iterative, only terminates if interrupted by another task
Optional tasks	[]	[T]	Task is indicated as optional
Connection between models	↔	T↔	Task can be used in a cooperative model where several users participate

Table 2. Temporal relationships available in CTT [21]

Operator	Symbol	Form	Description
Choice	[]	T1 [] T2	It is possible to choose one task among others, but when started the others become unavailable until the chosen task finishes
Independence of order	|=|	T1 |=| T2	Both tasks must be performed in any order, but must be performed individually
Independent Concurrency	|||	T1 ||| T2	It specifies that tasks can be performed in any order or at the same time
Concurrency with information exchange	|[]|	T1 |[]| T2	Tasks can be performed concurrently, but they must be synchronized for information exchange
Deactivation	[>	T1 [>T2	(T1) is completely interrupted by (T2)
Suspend-resume	|>	T1 |>T2	(T1) can be interrupted by (T2) and is resumed from the point where it stopped as soon as (T2) ends
Enabling	≫	T1 ≫ T2	(T2) only starts when (T1) ends
Enabling with information passing	[] ≫	T1 [] ≫ T2	When the (T1) ends it sends the information produced to the start of (T2)

4 Usable Security

Saltzer and Schroeder [14] were the first to note that security systems should be usable to users to be truly secure. In their paper, they identified "acceptability psychology" as one of the eight principles for building secure tools. Zurko and Simon [15] defined three categories of research to explore the concept of security and usability: (1) application of usability testing and systems protection techniques; (2) development of safety models and mechanisms for user-friendly systems; (3) users' need as a primary goal of developing secure tools. They brought a radical idea to the security community, so the community saw the need to perform usability testing on security tools to establish not only usability but also security.

Despite these definitions, the concept of usable security gained notoriety in the paper of Whitten and Tygar [5]. In this paper, they defined that software is secure and usable if users: (1) are aware of the security tasks need to perform; (2) are able to find out how to perform their tasks successfully; (3) do not make compromising mistakes; (4) are comfortable enough with the interface. In summary, usable security or human-computer interaction and security (HCI-Sec) is a field of research that aims to unite usability and security concepts in order to provide secure solutions that can be usable by users.

4.1 The Demotivation of Users and Challenges

The demotivation of users in learning to use complex tools and applications is well known and such problem is already widely considered by several HCI guidelines.

However, in the case of information security, this demotivation becomes even greater, since the vast majorities of users treat security and privacy as a secondary issue and are hardly willing to waste time with training and manuals [5].

Even in the corporate environment, where you have firewalls and security policies the information can be compromised because of the user's extra effort. For example, to share a file between with a friend on a workstation next door, a user with enough experience in email exchanges prefers to send him an email with the attached file going through the frustration of setting up folders shared in the corporate network [16].

Due to this demotivation of the vast majority of users learning new security and privacy mechanisms, it is clear that developing solutions to such a scenario is a complex task and goes beyond common design patterns. Thus, Whitten and Tygar [5] proposed the five challenges of usable security systems:

- **The unmotivated user:** Security is usually a secondary goal, the users are not disposed to waste time managing their security.
- **Abstraction:** Users do not share the same level of abstraction as system developers, if this is not taken into account, there is a maximized risk of the interface is not intuitive.
- **Lack of feedback:** The need to avoid dangerous errors makes feedbacks an essential task for users, but the misuse of the feedbacks can confuse them.
- **Barn door:** If the secret has been accidentally left unprotected, regardless of the length of time, there is no way to be sure if it is still intact.
- **Weakest link:** In the case of security a single error can be fatal and compromise the entire security system.

4.2   Usable Security Guidelines

Yee [17] proposed a set of ten guidelines created through a continuous experience of observations, which aims to guide the design of security and usable systems, which are:

1. **Path of Least Resistance.** The most natural way to do any task should also be the most secure way.
2. **Appropriate Boundaries.** The interface must be consistent and distinguish actions and objects that are important to the user.
3. **Explicit Authorization.** The user's authorities must only be provided to other actors as a result of an explicit user action that is understood to imply grating.
4. **Visibility.** The interface should always show users the status of the system.
5. **Revocability.** The interface should allow the user to revoke designed actions whenever possible such revocation.
6. **Expected Ability.** The interface should not give the user the impression that it is possible to do something that is not really possible.
7. **Trusted Path.** The system must provide "trusted paths" for users to perform their actions on the interface, so that these paths can't be corrupted.

8. **Identifiability.** The interface must be able to identify essential objects and actions, ensuring consistency in this identification.
9. **Expressiveness.** The interface should provide enough expressive power (a) to describe a safe security policy without undue difficulty; and (b) to allow users to express security policies in terms that fit their goals.
10. **Clarity.** Indicate with clarity the consequences of possible decisions of users in use of the system.

4.3   Secure Email

As already mentioned, security is a secondary goal for most users and security tools that require a lot of cognitive effort and extra work may not be understood and unused [5]. In email services, most users already have a mental model more definite for email exchange, because they already use conventional services (e.g., Gmail and Outlook). Thus, change the model implemented by such services may affect directly the users' understanding in the email exchange.

Routi et al. [6] verified this difficulty of users in understanding tools that alter the model already implemented by conventional services. They evaluated three secure email tools: Private Webmail, Virtru and Tutanota. These tools had different integration models with conventional services, thus they concluded that users preferred the tools integrated to such services. The integration models identified were:

- **Integrated.** Tools that integrate with the conventional email service interface and do not need new domains.
- **Depot-Based.** Tools that do not integrate with conventional email services, are other email services fully unbound and often require the creation of new domains.
- **Hybrid.** Tools that are integrated, however, perform specific functions outside the interface of conventional email services.

5   Tools Review

In this section, we present the tools review, which aims to identify, categorize and evaluate the implemented task model and the compliance of the tools with usable security guidelines. For this, we will use the interaction models [6], the guidelines [17], the challenges [5] and all the knowledge acquired through the related works.

This review is divided in four parts: (i) identification of the main tools; (ii) categorization of the main characteristics; (iii) refinement and (iv) evaluation.

5.1   Identification of the Main Tools of Secure Email

At the identification stage, we research for scientific papers that refer to secure email tools and solutions, based on keywords that describe such tools. The search string used to search for such tools in several search engines was:

(("email encryption" OR "encrypted email" OR "safe email" OR "secure email" OR "email security" OR "email safety") AND (usability OR usable) AND (tool OR system OR solution OR implementation OR prototype) NOT (phishing))

After some refinements, we defined our inclusion (I) and exclusion (E) criterias to refine the set of returned articles:

I1. Published articles that present, evaluate, or implement secure email tools/ solutions;
I2. Articles published only in English;
E1. Published articles dealing only the new cryptographic methods and their efficiency.

Beyond the search the digital libraries (ACM, IEEE and Springer) using the academic engines, we also did a research for the security community on the Quora[1] site and a general search on the internet and in the application and extension stores, seeking to identify more consolidated tools (products). Finally, we found 10 secure email tools. However, it is worth mentioning that this review does not make an exhaustive search of the available tools, but only the solutions recommended by the community. The Table 3 shows the list of identified tools.

Table 3. Email secure tool identified in the tools review

	Email secure tools identified	
1	Jumble Mail	https://www.jumble.io/
2	Mailvelope	https://www.mailvelope.com/
3	Private WebMail (PWM)	https://pwm.byu.edu/home/
4	ProntonMail	https://protonmail.com
5	SCRYPTmail	https://scryptmail.com/
6	SecureGmail	https://www.streak.com/securegmail
7	Startmail	https://www.startmail.com
8	Tutanota	https://tutanota.com
9	Virtru	https://www.virtru.com
10	Xmail	https://xmail.shwyz.ca/

5.2 Categorization of the Main Characteristics

For a better understanding of the tools, we will categorize the main characteristics of the identified tools, following some criteria (Table 4) that we believe are the main ones for the usable safety study. The final result of this categorization is shown in Table 5.

---

[1] https://www.quora.com/.

Table 4. Criteria used to categorize identified tools

Criteria to categorization	
Criteria	Description
Solution type	**Plug-in (P-in):** The tool is a plugin of an existing provider **Private service (Ps):** The tool is a service fully separated
Maturity	**Beta (β):** The tool is in development, but a version is already available and can be evaluated **Product (P):** The tool is already marketed
License	**Free (F)** **Partially free (Pf):** Free, but only with the premium it is possible to use all the functions **Premium (P)**
Open code	**Available (A)** **Unavailable (U)**
Key management	**Automatic (A):** The user does not manage the keys **Manual (M):** The user manages the keys of the senders
Private key empowerment	**Tool (T):** The private key is generated automatically and managed by the tool **User and tool (Ut):** The user creates a "password" and from it the tool generates the keys
Integration models [6]	**Integrated (It):** The tool interface integrates directly with the conventional webmail service **Depot-Based (Db):** The tool does not integrate with conventional webmail services **Hybrid (Hy):** The tools integrate with webmail, but perform specific functions outside the webmail interface

Table 5. Categorization of the main characteristics of the identified tools

Tools	Main characteristics						
	Solution type	Maturity	License	Open code	Key management	Private key empowerment	Integration model
Jumble Mail	P-in/Ps	P	Pf	U	A	Ut	Hy/Db
Mailvelope	P-in	P	F	A	M	Ut	Hy
Private WebMail	P-in	β	F	U	A	T	It
ProntonMail	Ps	P	Pf	A	A	Ut	Db
SCRYPTmail	Ps	P	Pf	U	A	Ut	Db
SecureGmail	P-in	P	F	A	–	–	It
Startmail	Ps	P	Pf	U	A	Ut	Db
Tutanota	Ps	P	Pf	A	A	Ut	Db
Virtru	P-in	P	Pf	U	A	T	Hy
Xmail	P-in	β	F	U	A	Ut	It

5.3   Tools Refinement

In order to identify the tools that are closest to usable security guidelines, this section aims to refine the set of tools selected, seeking to filter solutions that do not conform to the interaction model and the management of the keys found in the literature. Below we show the filtered tools and wounds directives

- **Mailvelope: Key management**
  - As previously shown [5, 8–10], tools with manual key management require a lot of cognitive effort from most users and will hardly be used.
- **ProntonMail, SCRYPTmail, Startmail, Tutanota: Integration model**
  - When it comes to secure email tools, users prefer to use solutions that have the design close to conventional services [6]. Thus, in this study we decided to filter the tools that offer disintegrated services to conventional ones.

5.4   Tools Evaluation

After the refinement, this section aims to evaluate the filtered tools (Table 6). For this, we present the task model of each tool, together with an evaluation of the tools.

Table 6. Tools after refinement

Email secure tools			
1	Jumble Mail	4	Virtru
2	Private WebMail (PWM)	5	Xmail
3	SecureGmail		

In the task models, we simulate the use of tools in the task "write and send email". For a better understanding of these models, we compare with the Gmail[2] task model (Figs. 2 and 3), highlighting the main differences. It is worth mentioning that the models simulate the perception of the users in use of the tools. In addition, the model

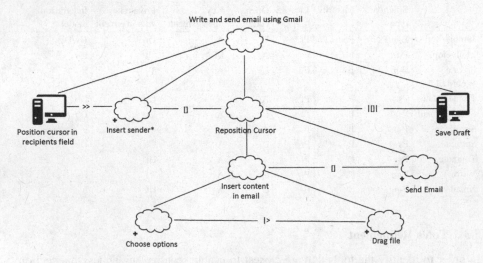

Fig. 2. Task model implemented by Gmail on task "write and send email"

---

[2] https://www.gmail.com.

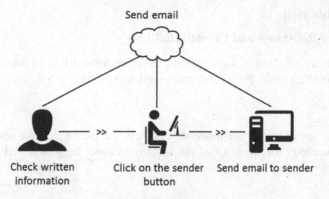

Fig. 3. Subtask "send email" in Gmail

focuses mainly on the most critical information of each tool, that is, details such as small adjustments may not be represented.

In the evaluate the tools, we analyze the conformity of each guideline and challenge in the tools. We also note that some of the challenges and guidelines complement each other. Thus, we combine such challenges and guidelines into just one evaluation topic. The results of this evaluation are presented in Table 7.

Table 7. Compliance of selected tools with usable security challenges and guidelines

<table>
<tr><td colspan="3"></td><td colspan="5" align="center">Tools Selected</td></tr>
<tr><td colspan="3"></td><td>Jumble Mail</td><td>Private WebMail</td><td>Secure Gmail</td><td>Virtru</td><td>Xmail</td></tr>
<tr><td rowspan="20">Guidelines (Yee [17])</td><td rowspan="18">Challenges (Whitten and Tygar [5])</td><td>Path of Least Resistance</td><td rowspan="2">-</td><td rowspan="2">-</td><td rowspan="2">-</td><td rowspan="2">-</td><td rowspan="2">-</td></tr>
<tr><td>Unmotivated user</td></tr>
<tr><td>Appropriate Boundaries</td><td>X</td><td>X</td><td>X</td><td>X</td><td>X</td></tr>
<tr><td>Explicit Authorization.</td><td>X</td><td>-</td><td>X</td><td>-</td><td>X</td></tr>
<tr><td>Visibility</td><td>X</td><td>X</td><td>X</td><td>X</td><td>-</td></tr>
<tr><td>Revocability</td><td>X</td><td>X</td><td>-</td><td>X</td><td>X</td></tr>
<tr><td>Expected Ability</td><td>X</td><td>X</td><td>X</td><td>X</td><td>X</td></tr>
<tr><td>Trusted Path</td><td>X</td><td>X</td><td>X</td><td>X</td><td>X</td></tr>
<tr><td>Barn door</td><td>-</td><td>-</td><td>X</td><td>-</td><td>X</td></tr>
<tr><td>Identifiability</td><td rowspan="2">X</td><td rowspan="2">X</td><td rowspan="2">X</td><td rowspan="2">X</td><td rowspan="2">X</td></tr>
<tr><td>Weakest link</td></tr>
<tr><td>Expressiveness</td><td rowspan="2">X</td><td rowspan="2">-</td><td rowspan="2">-</td><td rowspan="2">-</td><td rowspan="2">X</td></tr>
<tr><td>Abstraction</td></tr>
<tr><td>Clarity</td><td rowspan="2">-</td><td rowspan="2">X</td><td rowspan="2">X</td><td rowspan="2">X</td><td rowspan="2">X</td></tr>
<tr><td>Lack of feedback</td></tr>
</table>

5.4.1   Jumble Mail

Path of Least Resistance and Unmotivated User

- Tool treats the sending of secure emails as an additional task in the interface and requires an extra effort for each secure email to be sent.

Barn Door

- As we can see in Fig. 4, the tool only encrypts the message in the sending of the e-mail, therefore, the integrity of the message cannot be guaranteed only to the sender and receiver.

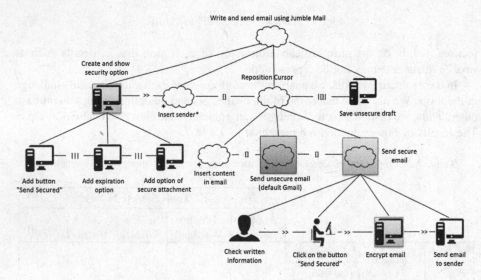

Fig. 4. Task model implemented by Jumble Mail on task "write and send email"

Clarity and Lack of Feedback

- Tool does not explicitly tell users the potential risk of sending an unsecured email.

5.4.2   Private WebMail e Virtru

Path of Least Resistance and Unmotivated User

- The tools approach the security in a disruptive way and change the standard interface of the Gmail emphasize security status. Although it contributes to the perception of users, it can demotivate them in daily use.

Explicit Authorization

- As shown in Table 5, these tools do not explain to users how security is achieved, since users do not share passwords or keys.

Barn Door

- Tool task model (Figs. 5 and 6) show that tools only guarantee integrity between sender and receiver if the user activates the security option before writing the message.

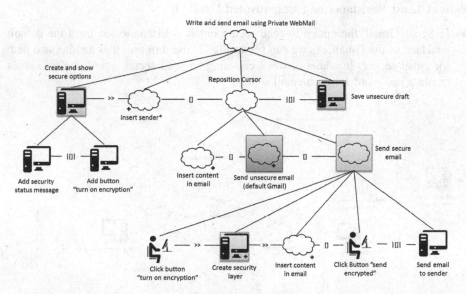

Fig. 5. Task model implemented by Private WebMail on task "write and send email"

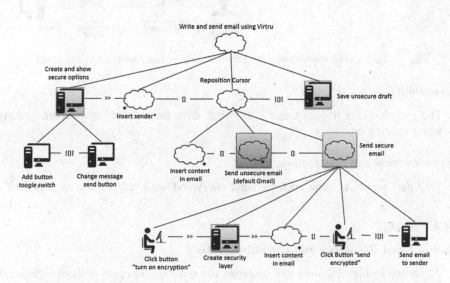

Fig. 6. Task model implemented by Virtru on task "write and send email"

Expressiveness and Abstraction

- Tool use technical terms such as "send encrypted" and "cryptographic password".

5.4.3   SecureGmail

Path of Least Resistance and Unmotivated User

- In SecureGmail, the option to send secure email is disconnected from the default interface of the Gmail. As we can see in Fig. 7, the tool provides an alternate path for email secure. In addition, when choosing to send secure email, the user must create a password for each email sent.

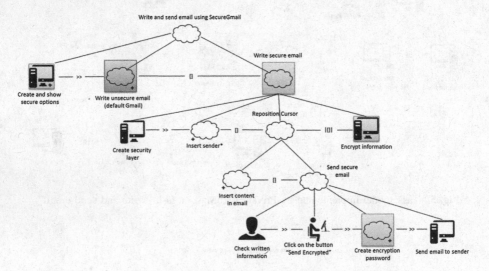

Fig. 7. Task model implemented by SecureGmail on task "write and send email"

Revocability

- The user does not have autonomy to switch over the safe and non-secure options when sending emails.

Expressiveness and Abstraction

- Tool uses technical terms such as "send encrypted" and "cryptographic password".

5.4.4   Xmail

Path of Least Resistance and Unmotivated User

- As shown in Fig. 8, Xmail tool proposes the send secure email without significant changes to the standard Gmail interface. However, it requires extra effort from the user to send unsecured emails.

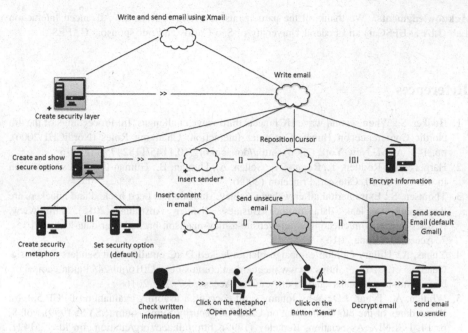

Fig. 8. Task model implemented by Xmail on task "write and send email"

Visibility

- Xmail proposes a non-disruptive interface to the Gmail interface, however, this may disrupt the user's perception of security.

6   Conclusion

Events demonstrate the need for better security and privacy in the Web. However, as presented in this paper, designing secure and usable tools for most users is not a trivial task, going beyond the general techniques of encryption, architecture and engineering, as well as security software design. For this, it is necessary to use specific usability and security approaches to develop these solutions, so that they are understood, facilitating their use.

In this paper, we present a review of main secure email tools, together with an understanding of the task model implemented by the tools that meet the key usable security criteria. In addition, we evaluate the compliance of these tools with usability and security policies.

With this review of the tools, we bring significant contributions to the usable security arena and an overview of the main secure email tools. We have also shown that the efforts of the security and usability community have had an effect on the development of the tools, since the tools have gained in usability. In the future work, we will involve evaluations with the users with the objective to further investigate the usability and mental model of security of the users in use of these tools.

Acknowledgments. We thank all the participants, the fellows from the Advanced Interaction Lab (LIA at UFSCar) and Federal University of São Carlos and our sponsors CAPES.

References

1. Bødker, S.: When second wave HCI meets third wave challenges. In: Proceedings of the 4th Nordic Conference on Human-Computer Interaction: Changing Roles (NordiCHI 2006), pp. 1–8. ACM, New York (2006). http://doi.acm.org/10.1145/1182475.1182476
2. Harper, E.R., Rodden, T., Rogers, Y., Sellen, A., Human, B.: Human-Computer Interaction in the Year 2020. Citeseer, Princeton (2008)
3. Thomsen, S.: Extramarital affair website Ashley Madison has been hacked and attackers are threatening to leak data online. Business Insider Australia (2015). http://www.businessinsider.com/cheating-affair-website-ashley-madison-hacked-user-data-leaked-2015-7. Accessed 5 June 2016
4. Yuhas, A.: Hillary Clinton campaign blames leaked DNC emails about Sanders on Russia. Guard. (2016). https://www.theguardian.com/us-news/2016/jul/24/clinton-campaign-blames-russia-wikileaks-sanders-dnc-emails. Accessed 7 Aug 2016
5. Whitten, A., Tygar, J.D.: Why Johnny can't encrypt: a usability evaluation of PGP 5.0. In: Proceedings of the 8th Conference on USENIX Security Symposium (SSYM 1999), vol. 8, p. 14. USENIX Association, Berkeley (1999). http://dl.acm.org/citation.cfm?id=1251421.1251435
6. Ruoti, S., et al.: We're on the same page: a usability study of secure email using pairs of novice users. In: Proceedings of the 2016 CHI Conference on Human Factors in Computing Systems (CHI 2016), pp. 4298–4308. ACM, New York (2016). http://doi.acm.org/10.1145/2858036.2858400
7. Greenwald, G., Macaskill, E.: NSA Prism program taps in to user data of Apple, Google and others. Guard. (2013). https://www.theguardian.com/world/2013/jun/06/us-tech-giants-nsa-data. Accessed 7 June 2016
8. Sheng, S., et al.: Why Johnny still can't encrypt: evaluating the usability of email encryption software. In: Symposium on Usable Privacy and Security, pp. 3–4 (2006)
9. Garfinkel, S.L., Miller, R.C.: Johnny 2: a user test of key continuity management with S/MIME and outlook express. In: Proceedings of the 2005 Symposium on Usable Privacy and Security (SOUPS 2005), pp. 13–24. ACM, New York (2005). http://dx.doi.org/10.1145/1073001.1073003
10. Ruoti, S., et al.: Why Johnny still, still can't encrypt: evaluating the usability of a modern PGP client. arXiv preprint arXiv:1510.08555 (2015)
11. Ruoti, S., et al.: Confused Johnny: when automatic encryption leads to confusion and mistakes. In: Proceedings of the Ninth Symposium on Usable Privacy and Security (SOUPS 2013), pp. 5:1–5:12. ACM, New York (2013). http://doi.acm.org/10.1145/2501604.2501609
12. Gaw, S., et al.: Secrecy, flagging, and paranoia: adoption criteria in encrypted email. In: Proceedings of the SIGCHI Conference on Human Factors in Computing Systems, pp. 591–600. ACM (2006)
13. Renaud, K., Volkamer, M., Renkema-Padmos, A.: Why doesn't jane protect her privacy? In: Cristofaro, E., Murdoch, S.J. (eds.) PETS 2014. LNCS, vol. 8555, pp. 244–262. Springer, Cham (2014). doi:10.1007/978-3-319-08506-7_13
14. Saltzer, J.H., Schroeder, M.D.: The protection of information in computer systems. Proc. IEEE **63**(9), 1278–1308 (1975). IEEE

15. Zurko, M.E., Simon, R.T.: User-centered security. In: Proceedings of the 1996 Workshop on New Security Paradigms, pp. 27–33. ACM (1996)
16. Dix, A.: Designing for appropriation. In: Proceedings of the 21st British HCI Group Annual Conference on People and Computers: HCI...But Not As We Know It (BCS-HCI 2007), vol. 2, pp. 27–30. British Computer Society, Swinton (2007). http://dl.acm.org/citation.cfm?id=1531407.1531415
17. Yee, K.-P.: User interaction design for secure systems. In: Deng, R., Bao, F., Zhou, J., Qing, S. (eds.) ICICS 2002. LNCS, vol. 2513, pp. 278–290. Springer, Heidelberg (2002). doi:10.1007/3-540-36159-6_24
18. Norman, D.A.: The Design of Everyday Things: Revised and Expanded Edition. Basic Books, New York (2013)
19. Diaper, D., Stanton, N.: The Handbook of Task Analysis for Human-Computer Interaction. CRC Press, Boca Raton (2003)
20. Winckler, M.A., Pimenta, M.S.: Análise e modelagem de tarefas. In: Congresso Brasileiro de Fatores Humanos em Sistemas Computacionais, p. 3 (2004)
21. Paterno, F.: Model-Based Design and Evaluation of Interactive Applications, 1st edn. Springer, London (1999)
22. Mori, G., Paterno, F., Santoro, C.: CTTE: support for developing and analyzing task models for interactive system design. IEEE Trans. Softw. Eng. **28**(8), 797–813 (2002). ISSN 0098-5589

A User-Centered Model for Usable Security and Privacy

Denis Feth[✉], Andreas Maier, and Svenja Polst

Fraunhofer Institute for Experimental Software Engineering,
Kaiserslautern, Germany
{denis.feth,andreas.maier,
svenja.polst}@iese.fraunhofer.de
http://www.iese.fraunhofer.de

Abstract. Security, privacy and usability are vital quality attributes of IT systems and services. Users and legal authorities demand that systems are secure and preserve privacy. At the same time, security and privacy mechanisms should not complicate workflows and must be transparent for the user. In order to master this challenge, a close involvement of the users is necessary—both at development and at run-time. In this paper, we present a user-centered model for usable security and privacy that is aligned with user-centered design guidelines [34] and the Human-Centered Design process [28]. Based on this model, we present an initial method for the design of usable security systems. Through active involvement of the user, the model and the method are meant to help developers to identify and solve shortcomings of their security and privacy mechanisms. We motivate our work and present our results based on an Internet of Things/smart home scenario. Due to the amount of private data and strong data protection laws, both usability and privacy are of major importance in this domain. However, our model and method are not limited to the smart home domain, but can be applied whenever usable security and privacy are of particular interest for a system under development.

Keywords: Usability · Security · Privacy · Security modelling · User-centered design · Continuous improvement

1 Introduction

1.1 Context and Motivation

Security, privacy, and usability are important and inherent quality attributes of IT systems. However, it is often hard to optimize all attributes at the same time [8]. From the users' perspective, systems must be adequately secure and respect their privacy in order to be trustworthy. At the same time, the systems, especially the security mechanisms they provide, must be usable. However, security measures and privacy enhancing technologies are complex by nature and typically complicate workflows. Thus, they frequently have a negative impact on usability [45, 46], e.g. with respect to efficiency.

© Springer International Publishing AG 2017
T. Tryfonas (Ed.): HAS 2017, LNCS 10292, pp. 74–89, 2017.
DOI: 10.1007/978-3-319-58460-7_6

1.2 Ideas and Contributions

We introduce a model that focuses on the user´s privacy as the bridging element of security and usability and which is aligned with the Human-Centered Design process. The U.S. Department of Health and Humans Services [40] defines privacy as "the control over the extent, timing, and circumstances of sharing oneself (physically, behaviorally, or intellectually) with others". As the perception of privacy is highly individual to each user, it will be a major challenge for IT corporations to get their users to understand and trust privacy measures. At the same time, the European Union´s "General Data Protection Regulation" [12] provides for fines up to 4% of the annual worldwide company turnover if the company lacks comprehensive privacy mechanisms. Gartzke and Roebel [22] state that "getting their approach to privacy right while remaining consumer friendly will be absolutely critical to their [both startups and established corporations] future." In that respect, we consider three relevant goals:

1. Adequate privacy enhancing technologies and control mechanisms for the protection of personal data must exist.
2. Control mechanisms must be made transparent for the users and be understood by them.
3. Users have to be capable of building an individual perception of the control mechanism and the preservation of their privacy. This mental model decides whether a user trusts or mistrusts a system.

Through active user involvement, our approach is able to identify and quantify problems with respect to the understanding, application and acceptance of privacy measures following the stated requirements. Our method covers a variety of interdependent aspects to be considered and questions to be answered in terms of usable privacy mechanisms. Besides the requirements stated by Fischer-Hübner et al. [16] (representation of legal requirements, transparency, and trust), we primarily consider the user's mental model and the overall effect on the acceptance of the system. Our model is aligned with the User-Centered Design (UCD) guidelines [34] and the Human-Centered Design (HCD) process [28], and it is a key part of an iterative improvement process. This allows for the evaluation and optimization of privacy with respect to usability at development-time and at run-time [15]. The application of our model and method is meant to help security developers to gain a better understanding of the user's objectives and needs with respect to privacy (e.g., security-relevant information about missing encryption [4]). Thereby, developers will be empowered to optimize privacy enhancing technologies in this respect and improve their acceptance.

To motivate our work in more detail and to provide a base line for subsequent discussions, we use an example from the Internet of Things (IoT) domain. However, both the model and the method are not limited to this domain, but can be applied to each system development process that draws particular attention to usable security and privacy.

At the time being, the work presented here is research in progress and lacks a comprehensive evaluation. We will present our evaluation plan as part of our future work.

1.3   Structure

The paper is structured as follows: We continue with an example scenario in Sect. 2. In Sect. 3, we present our model and its integration into UCD and our iterative improvement process. Related work is presented in Sect. 4 and we conclude the paper in Sect. 5.

2   Usable Security and Privacy in the Internet of Things

The Internet of Things (IoT) offers a plethora of possibilities to customers and service providers. The basic idea is that all kinds of things—including physical objects, sensors, vehicles, buildings—are interconnected with each other and to the Internet. By 2020, there will be approx. 28 billion [10] to 50 billion [13] things. Based on the things and on the data collected by them, services can be offered, optimized and tailored to the user. Famous IoT applications are Smart Home devices (e.g., intelligent heating, smart metering, door locks), wearables (e.g., Smart Watch, intelligent clothing), and connected vehicles (e.g., autonomous vehicles). In summary, the IoT can be described as an "inextricable mixture of hardware, software, data and service" [33].

2.1   Privacy in the Internet of Things

Especially the sheer amount of data that is collected by things is a huge burden for users. In Smart Homes, fewer than 10,000 households can generate 150 million discrete data points every day [14]. This amount of data leads to massive privacy concerns. According to [25], 71% of consumers share the fear that their personal information may get stolen and 64% of customers fear that their data may be collected and sold. Besides the amount of data, this fear is also caused by the sensitivity of the data. The combination of data from different sources allows—at least in theory—the creation of a complete profile of the user. The problem is that users do not have, or at least do not feel like they have, control about their data. Privacy statements are hard to read and understand, and control mechanisms are hardly known or understandable. According to [11], only 15% of EU citizens feel that they have complete control over the data they provide online. 31% even feel they have no control at all. However, the perception of privacy highly differs between countries. While Germans are most concerned about lacking control (only 4% think that they have complete control, 45% think that they have no control at all), Greeks are the least concerned (31% think that they have complete control, only 22% think that they have no control at all).

All of this leads to two conclusions: First, existing control mechanisms are perceived as non-sufficient by users. This might be the case because convincing control mechanisms are missing completely, or because existing mechanisms are not known, understood, or trusted by users. Second, the perception of the quality of privacy and control mechanisms highly differs between different users. A one-for-all solution might thus not be possible and mechanisms need to be tailored to different user groups or even individuals to provide a comprehensive and convincing privacy experience. Companies are starting to realize this problem and are looking for solutions to handle data transparently and legally. This includes processing data only with explicit user consent and only for permitted purposes. However, it is still unclear how processes, technologies, and user interactions must be designed. Relating to our stated conclusions, we believe that the solutions must be approached iteratively and with close contact to the users whose needs have to be in the focus of the development.

2.2   Application Scenario: Privacy in the Smart Home

For further discussions, consider the following scenario: Uma recently bought a new house that is equipped with several smart home services:

- *Locks and shutters* that open and close automatically or remotely using an app.
- A *heating system* that regulates the room temperature according to Uma's needs and helps to save energy costs. For example, if Uma locks her front door, the heating automatically turns off until she approaches her home again.
- *Lights* that can be controlled remotely and that turn on and off automatically when Uma enters or leaves a room.

Additionally, she already owns some smart devices, which can be perfectly integrated:

- Modern *entertainment* systems (e.g., Smart TV) that are connected to Internet services and can be controlled via voice commands and modern apps—a welcome and efficient way of interacting with her TV in Uma's point of view.
- A *baby monitor* that Uma can access remotely to check on her child's safety.

All of these functions are of high value to Uma. However, Uma also has a variety of privacy concerns. The baby monitor and the smart TV continuously record audio and/or video data in sensitive areas. While this is good for the dedicated purposes, all private conversations could also be recorded. Uma wonders how she can be sure that vendors do not store these records and how they are used exactly. Additionally, Uma is concerned that data from smart locks, lights and heating are used to create a detailed profile of her movements.

In order to resolve these concerns, she has to understand how her privacy is protected in order to trust the vendor. However, it is in the nature of IoT systems that they being continuously changed (e.g., via updates) and extended (e.g., new remote control app). With every change, privacy would need to be reassessed.

For IoT developers, this is a challenge, as he does not know which information Uma needs in order to trust/accept his service. In turn, if Uma lacks information, there are seldom suitable ways to get it.

3   A Usable Security and Privacy Model

Especially in the IoT, continuous user involvement and system optimization are very important, as systems, users and contexts continuously change. We divided our model into several (intersecting) sub-models and aligned with to user-centered design [34] and the Human-Centered Design (HCD) process [28]. HCD is an iterative process aimed at making systems usable and increasing their user experience by taking into account users' needs and requirements.

The process we are following consists of four steps (cf. Fig. 1), namely Context of Use, System Awareness, System Design and Design Evaluation. Each of these will be described in the subsequent sections.

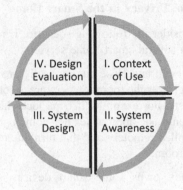

Fig. 1. Design process

3.1   Context of Use

The goal of this step is to understand and to specify the context of use regarding a usable security and privacy system. The context of use is defined by the users and tasks (cf. Fig. 2) and by the environment (cf. Sect. 3.4) [16]. Through the interplay of these aspects, security goals emerge, which can be refined into concrete security requirements. Considering the security requirements in the process of (re-)building a system will contribute to the trustworthiness of the system.

Definition of the System Context. The first step in defining the context of use is to create a description of the information system context. Information systems are defined as the total of all components, interacting to fulfill a certain functionality [32], including applications, services, information technology assets, or other information handling components [29]. The information system has to fulfill privacy goals to protect a user's privacy. Privacy goals can stem from legal regulations or from the user. To comply with legal regulations, system developers have to identify the assets that have to be protected according to legal regulations. Assets are resources that are of real or ideal value for at least one stakeholder [32].

For users, personally identifiable information and their privacy are assets. These assets are exposed to threats—potential causes of an unwanted incident, which may result in harm to a system or organization [29]. With the rising number and increasing severity of threats, the risk for these assets to get harmed increases. To keep the risk low, security mechanisms including privacy-enhancing technology have to be built into the system. These mechanisms fulfills security goals, including the privacy goals. A security goal describes a property of a component or system that has to be fulfilled to protect a

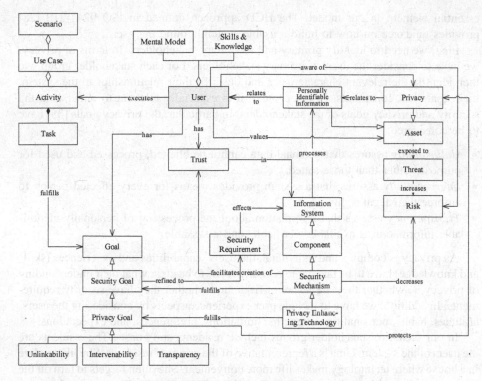

Fig. 2. Model Pt. 1: system context & awareness

user's concrete assets [32] from concrete threats. In the ISO 27000 standard [29] Confidentiality, Integrity, Availability, Authenticity, Non-Repudiation, and Authorization are the main security goals that must be investigated to derive corresponding security requirements. Additionally, the overall system goals are based on the system's security goals in terms of a usable security and privacy system.

Regarding the scenario, Uma is interested in using the information system "Smart Home". Uma has to understand how her privacy is protected. She knows that the information system processes data that concern her privacy, e.g., audio data recorded by the baby monitor. However, she knows that there are legal regulations that force the company to use mechanisms to protect Uma's privacy. For instance, the company must not save or share recorded data. However, in order to trust the system, Uma needs to know how the system adapts certain security mechanisms. In addition, she must be able to control specific smart products, including their security features, if necessary. For this reason, the system needs to provide appropriate usability, which has to be implemented according to Uma's individual needs, preferences, skills, and knowledge.

Creation of Personas. In the next step, we have to create personas of all user groups in order to better understand the users and their privacy goals. If a system is not designed for and with the users, it will offer a poor user experience due to missing trust in the system and will counteract efficient and effective work. Therefore, the user is an essential element in our model. The HCD approach defined in ISO 9241-210 [28] provides guidance on how to build a usable system around the user.

First, we need to identify primary and secondary stakeholders. In terms of privacy, we have to consider the users as primary stakeholders. For each stakeholder group, we then identify the relevant characteristics and describe their relationships to the system, their goals and constraints. In our context, it is especially relevant to understand the security and privacy goals of the stakeholders. In particular, the privacy goals [35] have to be considered:

- *Unlinkability* assures that personal data cannot be elicited, processed and used for purposes other than those stated.
- *Intervenability* assures that a system provides means for every affected person to enforce their legal rights.
- *Transparency* assures that information about the processing of personally identifiable information is available, verifiable, and assessable.

As privacy is complex and individual, the users' capabilities and experiences (skills and knowledge) have to be taken into account. It has to be clear what their understanding of privacy is, whether they are aware of risks, and whether they have security requirements. In addition, we have to include user experience aspects by considering the users' attitudes, habits, personalities, strengths, limitations, preferences, and expectations.

In our scenario, stakeholder groups include residents and guests. The residents are the users of the system. Uma is a representative of the group of residents. She likes to live in a house where technology makes life more convenient. She often forgets to turn off the light when she suddenly has to care for her child. Therefore, she expects her house to take care of switching the lights off when she leaves the house. Turning lights on and off could be an indication of being at home. She needs to be sure that nobody with bad intention (e.g. a potential burglar) can access the data. As she knows something about information security, all three privacy goals are highly important to her.

Creation of Use Cases. Once we know the system context and the goals of its users, we can start to define use cases. Use case specifications describe all activities that have to be performed with the help of the system under development. They describe ideal standard procedures embedded into a realistic sequence of interactions from the personas' points of view. Every task in a use case needs to be characterized with respect to its impact on usability, accessibility, as well as security and privacy. Furthermore, it needs to be refined into activities the user needs to execute. Several use cases are integrated into a scenario, which again can be used to identify missing use cases. The results of this step can be recorded in activity descriptions, use case specifications, use case diagrams, and scenario descriptions.

Regarding the scenario, Uma wants to set up a movie mode for her smart home in order to watch movies in a suitable atmosphere. Therefore, she defines a set of system reactions that are executed when she starts a movie. For example, the shutters close, the lights dim and the baby monitor is set on maximum volume. However, Uma likes to keep her choice of movies secret. Therefore, a requirement to the smart TV is that it does not forward the selection of movies to 3rd party vendors (e.g., the vendor of the baby monitor).

3.2   System Awareness

The goal of this step is to create concepts to make the user aware of important things in the system. Especially for the security and privacy, this is an important aspect with respect to transparency and user involvement. Usable security guidelines, like the ones collected by the USecureD project [41], Yee [45] and the usable security principles by Whitten [42], Garfinkel [20], by Furnell [19], and by Herzog and Shahmehri [24] can help to accomplish this step.

Conceptual System Model. The first step is to develop a conceptual model of the system that cap-tures the important parts of the operation of the device and that is appropriate and understandable for the user [16]. This means that the conceptual model of the system has to be mapped to the user's mental model of the system. At this point, it is important to pay particular attention to the security goals that have to be fulfilled by the system and the privacy goals of the user. This step helps to cover the basic security and privacy mechanisms (cf. Fig. 2, and Sect. 1.2, Goal 1).

Regarding the scenario, Uma is concerned that data from smart locks, lights, and heating can be used to create a detailed movement profile of herself. Therefore, the system must ensure that data cannot be used by unauthorized persons in any way. It must provide security mechanisms that prevent unauthorized access while keeping the use of the smart home functionality comfortable at the same time. Additionally, the smart home functionality must be controllable with respect to Uma's skills and knowledge. Since Uma is skillful in using mobile apps on her smartphone, the system should provide a mobile app to control the smart home. Data conveyed from the mobile app to the system must be encrypted to prevent the system from being controlled by unauthorized persons. However, Uma must not be annoyed when using the mobile app by being forced to enter a password whenever she uses the mobile app. In her mental model of the system, the system behaves like another person. Therefore, she wants to talk to her smart home. Thus, the mobile app should be designed in a way that allows for natural interaction. Among other things, this requires a speech recognition component.

Obviously, there are many interdependencies to consider. The user's mental model has to be consistent with the behavior of the system. Thus, every internal and external component of the system has to match to the user's skills and knowledge. This includes all security mechanisms and privacy-enhancing technologies. The user needs to understand how the security mechanisms achieve the security goal(s) and the privacy goal(s).

Continuous Visibility of System States and User Actions. For each dialog step, the system must ensure that the user's currently possible actions, alternative actions, and results of actions are visible [34]. In this step, the focus is particularly on security-relevant information and user actions that mitigate risks in this step. This step contributes to the fulfillment of transparency (cf. Sect. 1.2, Goals 2 & 3). To that end, it has to be analyzed which security-relevant information is important for being conveyed to the user at which time and at which level of detail. However, individual perception and trust in privacy and control mechanisms can highly vary between, but also within user groups. If security and privacy measures require user interactions, the user needs to be made aware of possible actions and the results of actions.

Regarding the scenario, Uma is informed about every change in the smart home elements. Whenever a light is switched on or off, a heater is adjusted, or a door is opened, closed, locked or unlocked, Uma gets informed both on her smartphone and via an LED and an acoustic signal located directly on the corresponding element. The mobile smart home control app is designed like her apartment. Therefore, Uma has a very good overview of each room and the smart elements in the rooms. The status of each smart element is continuously presented and only functions that make sense can be performed. For example, when a light is switched on, Uma can only switch it off instead of being able to switch it on a second time. The app only allows controlling those smart elements that can be controlled without any security risk. For example, the mobile app allows unlocking the front door only when Uma is located within a radius of 200 m.

Transparency and Guidance. In this step, we have to ensure that the user knows the current state of the system and that the interaction follows natural mappings between intentions and required actions and between actions and resulting effects. Simply speaking, the user shall always know what is currently happening on the system's side. This step contributes to Goals 2 and 3 (cf. Sect. 1.2).

Security-relevant, meaningful information needs to be conveyed in the user's language [16] at an appropriate abstraction level. For each action on security-relevant information, it needs to be decided whether this action should be made transparent for the user. A variety of aspects contribute to this decision. For example, the presented information might differ according to the user group. Some information is not understandable to certain user groups and leads to an opposite effect. In addition, making internal information public might lead to security risks. Finally, we have to decide whether information is presented to the user only upon demand or also actively to make the user aware of certain risks.

In addition to transparency, there needs to be guidance on the mitigation of risks and the use of security mechanisms that require user actions. The user needs to know immediately what to do and not suffer from confusion or information gaps.

Regarding the scenario, Uma is concerned about third parties hacking into her system. Due to the system's transparency concerning the current system state and the implemented security mechanisms, Uma gains trust in the system's security regarding unauthorized access. Whenever the system identifies an unauthorized access, Uma is immediately informed and guided through a security mechanism that asks her to authorize the access and to identify herself as an authorized user.

3.3   System Design

This section corresponds to the step 'Producing design solutions' of the HCD process provided by ISO 9241-210 [28], but we draw particular attention to the security mechanisms of the system under development. This section deals with the identification and implementation of appropriate user interface patterns, the creation of an appropriate interaction design, and the creation of prototypes (cf. Fig. 3), which are important for evaluating the proper operation of the security mechanisms as well as their usable operability in the next step.

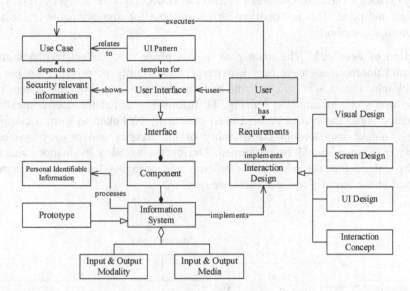

Fig. 3. Model Pt. 2: system design

Selection of User Interface Patterns. To support the performance of tasks, it is useful to draw on fast and proven solutions for particular human-system interactions given in use case specifications. We have to pay particular attention to usable security patterns from pattern libraries (e.g., [41]) to identify fast and proven solutions for particular human-system interactions. This is especially true for the usable security and privacy issues described in the use cases and scenarios created in step 1.

Creation of Interaction Design. Based on the personas, use cases, scenarios, and user interface patterns, we have to illustrate interaction ideas as interaction concepts, user interface design, and screen design. A Usability Walkthrough is an adequate instrument for the early evaluation of the usable security and privacy of the interaction ideas, user interface design, and the screen design. This can be performed before the actual evaluation of the system takes place.

Creation of Prototypes. Finally, we have to create interactive and realistic prototypes of interaction designs to facilitate discussing ideas with stakeholders, especially the end-users of the system. Compliance with conceptual usability criteria can and should be checked at this stage. We have to design user tasks, user-system interactions and the user interface to meet user requirements, especially those user requirements that concern usable security and privacy. We then create the essential design concept and the essential outcomes as well as appropriate input and output modalities and appropriate media for conveying information.

3.4   Design Evaluation

The evaluation of the design corresponds to the HCD phase "Evaluating the design" [28] and closes the iterative cycle of the method for the design of a usable security and privacy system. Through systematic feedback collection and analysis, issues are identified and rated. This information serves as input for improvements in the next iteration of the method.

Collection of Feedback. The main goal of this phase is to collect feedback about issues and uncertainties users face with respect to security or privacy. To put the feedback into context, it is enriched with additional information about the system state and the user's current situation (cf. Fig. 4). Information about the user context and information about the system context must eventually be linked to form a complete picture. To take into account the usability of the security and privacy system, a usability evaluation should be performed. During the usability evaluation, check if usability criteria that are relevant for smooth and engaging use of the system as described in the scenario and use cases are met.

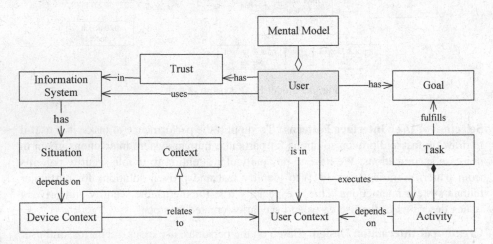

Fig. 4. Model Pt. 3: user context at runtime

For the purpose of a usability evaluation, an evaluation should be performed according to usability heuristics. This evaluation is performed by experts who check if usability criteria are violated. The experts should perform a walkthrough and check the suitability of the design decisions for daily use. Ultimately, the system is evaluated by real end-users. Here, particular hypotheses are proposed. The end-users follow the scenarios created in step 3.1. In laboratory environments, the test can be documented with video and audio records.

In the field, users execute (or want to execute) certain activities to fulfill one or more goals in a certain context. For example, if Uma is at home, she can perform several activities that belong to that context: relaxing, cooking, watching TV, and so on. The status of the devices (i.e., things) she is using includes information about their internal states and their environment. Similar to the relationship between activity and user context, device context and situation would always match in an ideal world. However, due to technical limitations, several distinct device situations lead to the same device context. Further details about this kind of context modeling and its application can be found in [30]. The main goals is to collect feedback about issues and uncertainties users face with respect to security or privacy. To put the feedback into context, it is enriched with additional information about the system state and the user's current situation. Information about the user context and information about the system context finally have to be linked to form a complete picture.

If usability issues are found, these issues should be prioritized according to their severity, especially regarding on their impact on system usage, security, and privacy. The most severe usability issues should be solved first. Appropriate solutions can be found in the descriptions of the patterns and corresponding design solutions identified and created in the previous steps.

Analysis. At this point, we combine static information from the system design with feedback we collected from users of the system or prototype. As user feedback is typically vague and informal, a *root cause* has to be identified, i.e., we have to map feedback to one or more security or privacy measures. The effect of the issue on the user has to be *rated* in order to assess the severity of the issue and its influence on system acceptance. To that end, we have to combine information about the currently performed activity, the context of use, the user's mental model, and the system state.

The continuous collection and analysis of these mappings allows for iterative improvement and tailoring of the solution. This phase is especially challenging, as usability issues are typically the result of a combination of different aspects. In order to utilize and automate the rating, our model has to be extended by corresponding metrics, which is part of our future work (cf. Sect. 5).

4   Related Work

Since the mid-1990s, huge efforts have been made to develop approaches for aligning usability and security. Unfortunately, the number of security incidents caused by unusable security measures or usable, but insecure systems is still high [18]. In [21] Garfinkel and Lipfort summarize the history and challenges of the "usable security" domain.

Whereas some guidelines and checklists exist for the design and evaluation of a usable security system, only few general requirements on a usable security system can be found in the scientific literature. For the harmonization of security and usability, Fischer-Hübner et al. [16] formulate three major requirements:

- Legal data protection requirements must be represented in a user-friendly manner in order to increase the user's comprehension, consciousness, and controllability.
- *Through a system's transparency, t*he user must understand security and privacy mechanisms and concepts in order to create a mental model that supports him in achieving his goals.

- A user has to be able to create trust in security mechanisms and be aware of the risks that might be caused by missing security mechanisms. The user must be able to perceive these risks. Important criteria are the conveyance and the comprehension of the plausibility of the security mechanisms.

Existing literature on usable security shows that the user is an important and active part of modern security chains. The research field of usable security and privacy has been approached both in a theoretical fashion and in the form of case studies. Famous case studies analyze the usability of email encryption with PGP [42, 44], of file sharing with Kazaa [23], and of authentication mechanisms and password policies [6, 9, 26, 30]. However, case studies are specific to one system, system class, or application domain and can hardly be generalized. On the other hand, theoretical work [1, 7] is typically more abstract and hard to apply in practice.

This gap is closed by design principles for usable, yet secure systems [20, 24, 39, 44, 45]. These principles focus on the development of usable security systems by supporting developers and emphasizing the importance of considering the user. However, they do not adopt the user's viewpoint or active involvement of users in the development process. However, it is crucial to both consideronsidering both the user's viewpoint and to involve users in the development process, as the user is an important, but often weak, link in the usable security HCI chain [3, 5, 37, 44, 46]. We consider design principles to be complementary to our work. By quantifying the effect and acceptance of design principles in different contexts, a knowledge base can be built that supports developers.

Looking specifically at the IoT, a survey on security and privacy issues and corresponding mitigation techniques is provided by Tank et al. [38]. Related work is provided by Ismail et al. [27], who propose a framework for evaluating transparency in cloud applications. This framework is comparable to parts of our model, but not integrated into design and optimization processes.

5 Summary and Conclusion

The preservation of privacy is becoming more and more important. Demands in terms of privacy are coming both from legal regulations and from users themselves. However, the implementation of a secure and privacy-preserving, yet usable system is a challenge for software and service providers. This challenge can be solved only by actively involving the users. Especially in the IoT, where systems are changing frequently, it is important to continue this involvement also at run-time. Unfortunately, corresponding user-centered design approaches do not explicitly include security and privacy. In this paper, we presented a usable security and privacy model and a corresponding method, both of which focus on the user as the central element. Not only does this focus separate our approach from other existing approaches, but we believe that it is also the only way to help elaborate and quantify the users' privacy needs and their perception of privacy- enhancing technologies. Based on the model and the method, developers are supported in optimizing appropriate usable security and privacy mechanisms.

In its current state, the model is quite abstract and cannot be applied directly to full extent. Thus, the next important step is to derive attributes and metrics for each model element. Based on that, measures have to be researched to provide the required data at development time and at run-time. In addition, a technical implementation, for example by using the Eclipse Modeling Framework (EMF), is necessary to support the use of the model. Finally, the evaluation with respect to applicability and generalizability remains to be done. We are planning to evaluate the model's applicability together with a large German IT company by collecting and analyzing feedback from their users. Additionally, we are planning expert reviews from different domains to generalize our model.

The work presented here is a first step towards the consideration and integration of privacy into UCD and HCD. In the future, this will become a vital aspect, which will not be limited to the IoT. The provision of comprehensive and understandable security and privacy mechanisms will be a major prerequisite to achieving compliance and high user acceptance by enhancing user experience through increased trustworthiness of the system.

Acknowledgements. The research presented in this paper is supported by the German Ministry of Education and Research (BMBF) project Software Campus (grant number 01IS12053). The sole responsibility for the content of this document lies with the authors.

References

1. Adams, A., Sasse, A.: Users are not the enemy. Commun. ACM **42**(12), 40–46 (1999)
2. Al-Saleh, M.: Fine-grained reasoning about the security and usability trade-off in modern security tools. Dissertation, The University of New Mexico (2011)
3. Blythe, J., Koppel, R., Smith, S.W.: Circumvention of security: good users do bad things. IEEE Secur. Priv. **11**(5), 80–83 (2013)
4. Botha, R.A., Furnell, S.M., Clarke, N.L.: From desktop to mobile: examining the security experience. Comput. Secur. **28**, 130–137 (2009)
5. Caputo, D.D., Pfleeger, S.L., Sasse, A., Ammann, P., Offutt, J., Deng, L.: Barriers to usable security? Three organizational case studies. IEEE Secur. Priv. **14**(5), 22–32 (2016)
6. Choong, Y.-Y., Theofanos, M.: What 4,500+ people can tell you – employees' attitudes toward organizational password policy do matter. In: Human Aspects of Information Security, Privacy, and Trust, pp. 299–310 (2015)
7. Cranor, L., Garfinkel, S.: Security and Usability. O'Reilly Media, Inc., Sebastopol (2005)
8. Cranor, L., Garfinkel, S.: Secure or usable? IEEE Secur. Priv. **2**(5), 16–18 (2004)
9. Eljetlawi, A.M., Ithnin, N.: Graphical password: comprehensive study of the usability features of the recognition base graphical password methods. In: Proceedings of the 3rd International Convergence and Hybrid Information Technology ICCIT 2008, vol. 2, pp. 1137–1143 (2008)
10. Ericsson: Ericsson Mobility Report – on the pulse of the networked society (2015)
11. European Commission: Special Eurobarometer 431 - Data Protection (2015)
12. European Union: Regulation (EU) 2016/679 of the European parliament and of the Council on the protection of natural persons with regard to the processing of personal data and on the free movement of such data, and repealing Directive 95/46/EC (General Data Protection Regulation) (2016)

13. Evans, D.: The internet of things - how the next evolution of the internet is changing everything (2011)
14. Federal State Commission: IoT Privacy & Security in a Connected World (2015)
15. Feth, D.: User-centric security: optimization of the security-usability trade-off. In: Proceedings of the 2015 10th Joint Meeting on Foundations of Software Engineering - ESEC/FSE 2015, pp. 1034–1037 (2015)
16. Fischer-Hübner, S., Iacono, L., Möller, S.: Usable security und privacy. Datenschutz und Datensicherheit - DuD **34**, 773–782 (2010)
17. Fogg, B.: A behavior model for persuasive design. In: Proceedings of the 4th International Conference on Persuasive Technology 2009, pp. 40:1–40:7 (2009)
18. Furnell, S.: Making security usable: are things improving? Comput. Secur. **26**(6), 434–443 (2007)
19. Furnell, S., Jusoh, A., Katsabas, D.: The challenges of understanding and using security: a survey of end-users. Comput. Secur. **25**(1), 27–35 (2006)
20. Garfinkel, S.: Design principles and patterns for computer systems that are simultaneously secure and usable. Gene **31**, 234–239 (2005)
21. Garfinkel, S., Lipford, H.R.: Usable security: history, themes, and challenges. Synth. Lect. Inf. Secur. Priv. Trust **5**(2), 1–124 (2014)
22. Gartzke, U., Roebel, M.: Balancing privacy and user experience: the challenge of the digital age (2016). http://techonomy.com/2016/01/balancing-privacy-and-user-experience-the-challenge-of-the-digital-age/
23. Good, N., Krekelberg, A.: Usability and privacy: a study of KaZaA P2P file-sharing. In: Proceedings of the Conference on Human Factors in Computing Systems CHI, no. 5, p. 137 (2003)
24. Herzog, A., Shahmehri, N.: Usable set-up of runtime security policies. In: Proceedings of the International Symposium on Human Aspects of Information Security and Assurance (HAISA 2007), Plymouth, UK, 10 July 2007, pp. 99–113 (2007)
25. IControl Networks: 2015 State of the Smart Home Report (2015)
26. Inglesant, P., Sasse, M.A.: The true cost of unusable password policies: password use in the wild, pp. 383–392 (2010)
27. Ismail, U., Islam, S., Ouedraogo, M., Weippl, E.: A framework for security transparency in cloud computing. Futur. Internet **8**(1), 5 (2016)
28. ISO 9241-210: Ergonomics of human-system interaction—Part 210: Human-centred design for interactive systems (2010)
29. ISO 27000 Series: Information security management systems
30. Jermyn, I., Mayer, A., Monrose, F., Reiter, M.K., Rubin, A.D.: The design and analysis of graphical passwords. In: Proceedings of the 8th USENIX Security Symposium, 23–36 August 1999
31. Jung, C., Eitel, A., Feth, D., Rudolph, M.: Dealing with uncertainty in context-aware mobile applications. In: Mobility 2015, p. 9 (2015)
32. Kompetenzzentrum für angewandte Sicherheitstechnologie: "Begriffsdefinitionen in KASTEL". https://www.kastel.kit.edu/651.php
33. Noto, G., Diega, L., Walden, I.: Contracting for the 'Internet of Things': looking into the Nest. Queen Mary School of Law, Legal Studies Research Paper No. 219/2016 (2016)
34. Norman, D.: The design of everyday things. Doubled Currency (1988)
35. Rost, M., Pfitzmann, A.: Datenschutz-Schutzziele – revisited. Datenschutz und Datensicherheit (DuD) **33**(6), 353–358 (2009)
36. Rudolph, M.: User-friendly and tailored policy administration points. In: 1st International Conference on Information Systems Security and Privacy (2015)

37. Sasse, A., Brostoff, S., Weirich, D.: Transforming the 'Weakest Link': a human/computer interaction approach to usable and effective security. BT Technol. J. **19**(3), 122–131 (2001)
38. Tank, B., Upadhyay, H., Patel, H.: A survey on IoT privacy issues and mitigation techniques. In: Proceedings of the Second International Conference on Information and Communication Technology for Competitive Strategies - ICTCS 2016, pp. 1–4 (2016)
39. Quay-de la Vallee, H., Walsh, J.M., Zimrin, W., Fisler, K., Krishnamurthi, S.: Usable security as a static-analysis problem. In: Proceedings of the 2013 ACM International Symposium on New Ideas, New Paradigms, and Reflections on Programming & Software - Onward! 2013, pp. 1–16 (2013)
40. U.S. Department of Health and Human Services: "Institutional Review Board Guidebook". https://archive.hhs.gov/ohrp/irb/irb_guidebook.htm
41. USecureD Project. https://www.usecured.de
42. Whitten, A.: Making security usable. Comput. Secur. **26**, 434–443 (2004)
43. Whitten, A., Tygar, J.D.: Usability of security: a case study. Comput. Sci. 1–41 (1998)
44. Whitten, A., Tygar, J.: Why Johnny can't encrypt: a usability evaluation of PGP 5.0. In: Proceedings of the 8th Conference on USENIX Security Symposium - Volume 8, p. 14. USENIX Association, August 1999
45. Yee, K.-P.: Aligning security and usability. IEEE Secur. Priv. Mag. **2**(5), 48–55 (2004)
46. Zurko, M.E., Simon, R.T.: User-centered security. In: Proceedings of the 1996 Workshop on New Security Paradigms - NSPW 1996, pp. 27–33 (1996)

Information Security, Privacy, and Trust in Social Robotic Assistants for Older Adults

Thomas Given-Wilson, Axel Legay$^{(\boxtimes)}$, and Sean Sedwards

Inria, Rocquencourt, France
axel.legay@inria.fr

Abstract. People with impaired physical and mental ability often find it challenging to negotiate crowded or unfamiliar environments, leading to a vicious cycle of deteriorating mobility and sociability. To address this issue the ACANTO project is developing a robotic assistant that allows its users to engage in therapeutic group social activities, building on work done in the DALi project. Key components of the ACANTO technology are social networking and group motion planning, both of which entail the sharing and broadcasting of information. Given that the system may also make use of medical records, it is clear that the issues of security, privacy, and trust are of supreme importance to ACANTO.

1 Introduction

People with impaired physical and mental ability often find it challenging to negotiate crowded or unfamiliar environments, leading to a vicious cycle of deteriorating mobility. This also severely impacts sociability, and increases isolation, that in turn provides an additional cycle of deteriorating health and well-being. To address these issues the ACANTO project[1] is developing a robotic assistant (called a *FriWalk*) that supports its users by encouraging and supporting them to engage in therapeutic group social activities.

The key components of the ACANTO project that act to counteract these vicious cycles are social networking and group motion planning. Both of these entail the sharing and communicating of information about the users. In the social networking setting, to encourage communication between users and organise groups who share common interests and locations. In the group motion planning setting, to coordinate groups of users participating in shared activities while maintaining both group and individual safety and comfort of users (even in different groups) in a shared environment. The goal of the social networking aspect of ACANTO is to support and encourage group activities, while the group activity and related motion planning are the key challenges of the project. Thus, the rest of this work focuses on this setting.

A significant aspect of the ACANTO project is the inclusion of medical professionals and medical information. Users may be prescribed therapeutic activities by a medical professional for maintaining health and well-being or to recover

---

[1] www.ict-acanto.eu.

© Springer International Publishing AG 2017
T. Tryfonas (Ed.): HAS 2017, LNCS 10292, pp. 90–109, 2017.
DOI: 10.1007/978-3-319-58460-7_7

from mobility affecting injury. Thus, the information used in ACANTO about users may derive from medical records. This yields a particular challenge to information sharing aspects of ACANTO, since such user information must be handled with great care, to respect user security, privacy, and trust.

More generally, the ACANTO project by definition exploits user information to assist in developing social networks for group activities, and to aid in group motion planning. Both of these require the sharing of user information to function effectively. Since the target users of the ACANTO project are likely to be particularly vulnerable (physically or mentally impaired, recovering from injury, etc.), issues of information security, privacy, and trust are major challenges for the ACANTO project.

This paper considers challenges for the implementation of group activities and group motion planning in the ACANTO project. These can be divided into four broad challenges.

The first challenge is that the requirement to plan group activities must account for all the users in the group, thus leaking user information to other members of the group. Since the group activity must not violate the constraints of any user (such as not straying too far from a bathroom), this may be observable to other members of the group, and so members could conceivably infer sensitive private information about other group members.

The second challenge is that the sharing of information during navigation yields information about user location; to other group members and to other ACANTO users (even from different groups). The navigation and reactive planning assistance of the FriWalk exploit information from other ACANTO users and environmental sensors. This can lead to information about the location of other users being inferred, even across different groups.

The third challenge is that using medical information as part of group planning and social networking place a very high burden on the security and privacy of this information. Further, using medical information often has legal requirements that must be met. Thus, information derived from medical records must be handled with particular care.

The fourth is a different kind of challenge; trust in the ACANTO project by users. The users must feel that the ACANTO social network and FriWalk are trustworthy and that they will look after users. Since, without this, users will not use ACANTO and gain the benefits.

With this overview of the kinds of challenges the ACANTO project must address, in the sequel we give more information about the ACANTO project, the technologies exploited, the challenges, and possible solutions in the context of security, privacy, and trust.

The rest of the paper is structured as follows. Section 2 presents a more detailed view of the ACANTO project itself and sets the scope of the project. Section 3 discusses the technological choices made in ACANTO so far. Section 4 considers the challenges of the ACANTO project in more detail, including the limitations and requirements placed upon them by the project and technological choices. Section 5 sketches possible solutions to the challenges that can address the challenge within the bounds of the choices already made. Section 6 concludes.

2   Project Scope

The ACANTO project builds on work done in the DALi project[2]. DALi created
a robotic motion planning assistant, based on a standard wheeled walker, to
aid those with reduced physical and mildly reduced mental ability to negotiate
complex and potentially crowded environments, such as shopping malls or muse-
ums. The ACANTO project extends upon this in three directions. (1) the single
user scenario of DALi is now generalised to include many users, including users
who perform activities and navigate in groups. (2) a social network is created
that helps ACANTO users find others to undertake group activities with and
to maintain social support. (3) clinical versions of the walker can assist medical
professionals with diagnostics and therapeutic activities for users.

These three extensions in ACANTO require various extensions to the work
of DALi, and add new aspects that yield new challenges. The rest of this section
overviews the ACANTO project and its requirements as they pertain to challenges for human aspects of information security, privacy, and trust.

2.1   FriWalk

The walker in the ACANTO project is called a *FriWalk* and extends upon the
DALi walker. Despite these extensions to support group activities and medical
assistance, many aspects of the FriWalk are carried over from the DALi walker.

The FriWalk assists in motion planning at two levels; a *long term planner* [4]
and a *reactive (short term) planner* [3]. The architecture of the ACANTO motion
planner is similar, but we wish to provide robotic guidance to a number of people
with reduced ability who are taking part in a group activity within the same
type of environments. The typical goal of such an activity is to facilitate social
interaction and provide therapeutic exercise in an enjoyable way. Thus both
the long term and reactive planners need to consider the notion of a group.
To facilitate this group notion and maintain group cohesion, communication
between FriWalks is considered a vital part of ACANTO.

An activity will be defined in advance, considering many user preferences.
This in turn has requirements about how information about users is shared and
handled outside the FriWalk and planning. For further detail see below.

During the activity, the ACANTO system comprises a fixed server and mobile
client applications on the FriWalks, which interact via radio communication.
The server collects, processes and distributes information gathered by sensors
attached to the client devices. This information comprises the pose and location
of the user and any other agents visible to his sensors. (These agents are any
other humans in the environment, and are not assumed to be recognised by the
sensors as being other FriWalk users or not.)

We assume that the high level goals of an activity are (eventually) translated
into a *global plan* (a path for the group to follow through an environment),
based on pre-existing knowledge of the layout of the environment. Hence we do

² www.ict-dali.eu.

not consider the activity explicitly and simply assume the existence of a global plan. Each FriWalk attempts to follow the global plan, using a *reactive planner* that makes planning decisions according to the dynamic local conditions (e.g., the position of other agents) and the constraints and requirements imposed by the individuals and the activity. Dynamic conditions may require that the global plan is modified (e.g., an encountered obstruction not present in the plan of the environment), but in this work we focus on the challenges related to information security, privacy, and trust when performing distributed group planning and communication. Note that changes to the activity plan may also result from feedback during the activity, and so some care has to be taken with information leakage through (re)planning as well.

We want to guide the users to follow the global plan as a group, while allowing them to move around within the group. We want to achieve this by efficiently distributing the problem among the FriWalks and server, while ensuring that the loss of an individual will not cause the activity to fail. We must accommodate the possibilities that people have different physical abilities and that some members of the group will not be cooperative and may decide to temporarily or permanently quit the group.

2.2 Social Network

The creation of activities is largely driven by the social network of the ACANTO project. Users of the social network can propose activities, join groups to find or be recommended activities, or add their preferences and be recommended activities by the social network. Once an activity has been created, an activity plan is generated taking into account the goals of the activity, the preferences of the users participating, and the safety requirements assured by the ACANTO system. This requires gathering significant information about the users, and balancing potentially conflicting or competing requirements.

For example, an activity may include visiting various locations in a shopping mall. Taking into account user preferences, the activity global plan may need to ensure the following. The global plan does not travel too far from any bathroom. The distance traveled is within a lower and upper bound. The projected time taken is within lower and upper bounds. The global plan does not include any flights of stairs. There is at least one trained medical professional included among the users. Observe that these requirements will likely by synthesised from information gathered regarding the users subscribed to the activity. (Note that in theory it may be impossible to meet all requirements, or the solution may be unlikely to be achieved in practice, these concerns are not considered here.)

Observe that to generate such activity plans, it is necessary for user information and preferences to be considered. It would be impossible to create such an activity plan without user information, and unsafe to proceed with some plans if user information is withheld. For example, when a user requires a medical professional to be nearby at all times, and the activity plan may not include a medical professional in the list of users, and this would be unsafe.

2.3   Therapeutic Rôle

The ACANTO project also includes a therapeutic aspect where FriWalks are used in diagnosis and treatment. In particular, FriWalks may be used to gather, compare, and exploit medical information in collaboration with medical professionals. This allows for therapeutic care and support for those recovering from mobility impairments. Some FriWalks are planned to be certified as medical devices equipped with more sensors and capable of (assisting in) diagnosing or monitoring patient health. Since FriWalks may thus yield medical information that will be considered and exploited in therapeutic activities, the handling of medical information requires some care. However, these diagnostic rôles of FriWalks shall not be considered directly here, as this paper focuses on aspects related to the group activities and group motion planning.

As part of therapeutic care and other support, medical professionals may recommend a regime of activities to patients. Thus, medical information (both direct and inferred) may be used by the ACANTO system. This is most obvious in the creation of activity plans; since these must consider the users and their preferences, which in turn may be information directly by medical records, diagnoses, and treatment plans.

3   Technology

This section overviews the technology choices made in the ACANTO project. The focus here is on the technological choices made from the group motion planning—the generation of a global plan is straightforward, and the aspects of social networks and medical records are already well known from other contexts. Thus, the rest of this section presents key points of the technology used in ACANTO for group motion planning.

Activity planning generates an a priori global plan of therapeutic and social activities defined by the activity generator. Reactive planning refers to local motion planning that copes with the actual conditions encountered by the users, given the activity plan. In addition to accounting for unforeseen changes to the environment and other pedestrians who are not part of the activity, the reactive planner also accounts for the random, potentially uncooperative behaviour of users of the system. Activity monitoring is performed in real time and ensures that the concrete suggestions offered to the users will achieve the goals of the activity with high probability.

Although the ACANTO system will have powerful centralised infrastructure, communication latency and potential interruption require that reactive motion planning is both autonomous and cooperative. The algorithms must therefore be efficient because the motion planning problem is complex and the algorithms will be executed on low powered embedded hardware. In general, we require the system to be robust and able to take advantage of increased computational power and additional information as these become available.

This section presents key details about the chosen hierarchical framework to analyses the local environment and classify the behaviour of moving agents or groups of agents. The framework takes as input a series of instantaneous snapshots of behaviour observed by the sensors. From these it constructs traces that evolve over time. In future, following developments of the ACANTO sensor technology, the framework will take traces or partial traces as input.

The more complex behaviour evident in the traces is clustered to infer grouping and other metrics that also evolve over time. The interpretation of these dynamic metrics allows ever more complex patterns of behaviour to be classified. To improve efficiency, we propose a group-based model abstraction that takes advantage of the fact that the motion of people walking together is strongly correlated. We thus motion plan at the level of groups, while incorporating a sliding level of abstraction that allows groups to consist of a single pedestrian.

3.1 Reactive Planning

Figure 1 gives a diagrammatic overview of the ACANTO reactive planner, the key elements of which are summarised below.

The global objectives, comprising the specification of the chosen activity and the preferences of the users, is provided as input a priori. During the course of the ensuing activity, sensors locate the users and other pedestrians with respect to the fixed objects in the environment. This information is used to parametrise a predictive stochastic model of human motion based on the social force model (SFM [2,9]). The SFM is overviewed in Sect. 3.4. This model is used to simulate multiple future trajectories with respect to alternative immediate behaviour of the users. The sets of simulated trajectories corresponding to each alternative immediate behaviour are validated against the global objectives using statistical model checking (SMC). The basic notions of SMC are described in Sect. 3.3. The immediate behaviour that maximises the probability of achieving the global objectives is recommended to the users.

The measurements of the sensors contain an element of noise, but for the purposes of the SFM are treated as deterministic best approximations. To account for their potential inaccuracy and the fact that the model is necessarily an incomplete representation of reality, we include a random "noise" term that allows the SFM to explore non-smooth behaviour and behaviour that is not explicitly modelled by forces (see also Sect. 3.4). Simulations of the model are

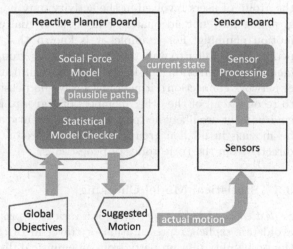

Fig. 1. Overview of reactive planning.

therefore samples of a random variable and it is for this reason that we then use SMC to estimate the probability of "successful" trajectories.

Our reactive planner is in fact a combination of reactive and predictive planning. A purely reactive approach might be adequate if we could guarantee perfect sensing with no latency. On the other hand, with a perfect predictive model we would have minimal need to sense the environment. Since neither of these are feasible, we adopt a "predictor-corrector" approach. We make a recommendation to the user based on a prediction with an efficient human motion model (i.e., the SFM), then correct our recommendation with updated predictions as the user progresses. Using this approach we significantly improve on the performance of the SFM [2] and can accommodate unpredictable eventualities that would be difficult to include in any reasonable model.

3.2 Group Motion Planning

The notion of groups of pedestrians and their interaction is key to ACANTO. While the reactive planning approach described in Sect. 3.1 has been shown to be efficient on embedded hardware for the case of a single user [2], using the same ideas with a group of users leads to a potential exponential explosion of hypothesised initial behaviour. Given that each user may go left, right or straight with respect to their current direction, there are a minimum of $3^{\#users}$ alternatives to try. In practice there are also different degrees of left and right choices, so the number of alternatives is much higher. Our approach is to construct the group behaviour compositionally and to first hypothesise alternative initial behaviour of groups as a whole. Suggestions to individuals within the group will aim to respect the group motion and maintain the group cohesion. Similar ideas for crowd simulation have been explored in [12].

One of our principal concerns is therefore the detection of groups. Although the group of users involved in the activity may be known a priori, this notional grouping may not adequately reflect the actual grouping for the purposes of motion planning. For example, it is known that when part of a large group people often prefer to walk together in smaller groups of between two and four to facilitate conversation [10]. In addition, for technical reasons (e.g., temporary loss of network connection), it may not always be possible for an individual FriWalk to recognise all of the other members of a group. Moreover, most people in the environment are likely not part of the therapeutic activity, but may nevertheless be moving in ad hoc groups [10]. It is therefore necessary to infer grouping directly from the trajectories of pedestrians.

3.3 Statistical Model Checking

Statistical model checking (SMC) is a variety of probabilistic model checking that avoids an explicit representation or traversal of the state space and estimates the probability of a property from an empirical distribution built by verifying a property ϕ against multiple independent executions (simulations) of the system.

Given N independent simulation traces ω_i and a function $z(\omega_i) \in \{0, 1\}$ that indicates whether $\omega_i \models \phi$ (read "ω_i *satisfies* ϕ"), the probability γ that, in general, $\omega \models \phi$ can be estimated using the unbiased estimator $\tilde{\gamma} = 1/N \sum_{i=1}^{N} z(\omega_i)$. The confidence of the estimate can be guaranteed by standard statistical bounds, allowing SMC to trade certainty for reduced confidence plus tractability. For example, the sequential probability ratio test [13,14] efficiently evaluates the truth of an hypothesis without needing to calculate the actual probability, while the Okamoto bound [11] asserts a level of confidence for a given number of simulations N, expressed as $\Pr[|\gamma - \tilde{\gamma}| > \epsilon] < 1 - \delta$. In words, this formula reads that the probability that the absolute error of the estimate is greater than ϵ is less than $1 - \delta$, where δ is a function of N and ϵ. In comparison to the 'certain' varieties of model checking, SMC does not require a finite or even tractable state space. This makes SMC particularly suitable for the present application that considers continuous time and space.

3.4   The Social Force Model

The social force model (SFM) [6–9] combines real and psychological "forces" to predict the behaviour of pedestrians in crowds under normal and panic situations. The model recognises that pedestrians are constrained by the physical laws of motion and also by social rules that can be modelled as physical forces. The model considers an environment comprising fixed objects (walls) and moving agents (pedestrians) that respond to attractive and repulsive forces that arise from social and physical interactions.

The SFM here considers (groups of) agents that have a mass a their centre, a velocity, and an ellipsoid shape. Additionally, fixed objects in the environment are modelled with solid forms according to their footprint. The SFM then determines the forces that act upon the (groups of) agents due to their desired path, current velocity, and the forces of other elements of the system. Thus the influence of all these forces can be used to predict the (group of) agents' future path. In addition to these forces, random "noise" is added, that serves to represent fluctuations not accounted for by the model, and to avoid deadlocks.

In general the forces in the SFM can be defined and exploited in many different ways. For example, these may include: repulsive forces away from unknown agents, repulsive forces from fixed objects, attractive forces towards friends or other users, attractive forces towards activity goals, attractive forces to maintain proximity to a perimeter, etc. Thus, many different effects upon the agents can easily be represented and balanced by manipulating these forces in the SFM.

3.5   Our Approach

In ACANTO the reactive planner will be collaborative and cooperative. Sensor information obtained by each user will be shared between other users of the ACANTO platform, effectively giving the planner a much wider view. The planner will explicitly consider group motion and identify pedestrians who are part of the same social activity as the user. Due to potential communication latency or interruption, planning will nevertheless be local to the user. The significantly increased complexity of the planning task thus necessitates an approach that is efficient. Figure 2 shows a diagrammatic representation of our behaviour classifier.

The classifier takes as input sensor information provided by the sensor board, as shown in Fig. 1. This information will at least contain the estimated positions and velocities at a given time point of moving agents in the vicinity of the sensors of a number of users of the ACANTO platform. The current sensor technology (based on Microsoft Kinect) does not recognise the identity of

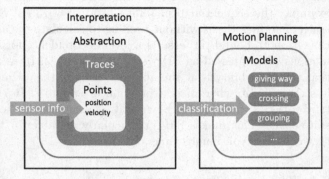

Fig. 2. Hierarchical structure of behaviour classifier.

individuals between consecutive readings by the same sensor. Future developments may allow the sensor technology to directly infer traces or partial traces and to identify users of the FriWalk, reducing the computation from sensor input to traces and clusters.

Combining the output of multiple sensors incurs the additional challenge of identifying pedestrians who leave the view of one sensor and appear in another. Pedestrians may also appear and disappear as a result of sensors being obscured, because of communication unreliability or because users just leave. Our trace inference algorithm therefore makes minimal a priori assumptions about the data, but will take advantage of whatever information is available. If no additional input is available from other users, an individual reactive planner can still function using the information provided by its local sensors, along the lines of the DALi short term planner [3].

Having inferred a set of active traces, the classifier then clusters them into groups of traces with characteristics that imply the pedestrians are or will be moving as a group. Mere proximity is not a sufficient indicator, since two close pedestrians may be trying to get away from each other. The classifier therefore also considers velocity and acceleration (inferred from successive observations of velocity or predicted by the SFM). It is possible for the framework to include higher level information (e.g., we may know that two pedestrians are part of the same activity group), but if pedestrians are close and moving in a similar direction at a similar speed, for the purposes of motion planning they are already moving as a group, regardless of whether they are involved in the same activity. Finally, note that groups are not necessarily disjoint and may overlap.

Identifying de facto gròups allows us to plan motion at a more efficient level of abstraction. When hypothesising the alternative directions for a number of users of the platform, we believe that it is a reasonable compromise to only hypothesise the overall motion of the groups to which they belong. We feel it is not necessary to consider all the possible combinations of suggestions to those within the same group given that, by virtue of how we define a group, their motion is strongly correlated. Note that suggestions are nevertheless tailored to the actual position of an individual within the group, in order to maintain its "social" structure. A further advantage of this approach is that we may also identify behavioural templates at the level of groups, rather than at the computationally prohibitive level of individuals. We may also quantify temporal properties over traces of group-related metrics.

Finally, it is important to note that a group may comprise a single pedestrian, so our framework allows us to choose a level of abstraction that is appropriate for the available computational power. In general, our approach is to plan the motion of an individual against an abstraction of the environment that may be as detailed or complex as the available computational capacity allows.

4   Challenges

This section considers information security, privacy, and trust challenges raised within the ACANTO project. Some of these are very strong: requiring careful handling of medical information in a social and collaborative setting. While others are more general, relating to handling of private location information, and indirect information leakage. The goal of this section is to provide an overview of four main areas of challenge, particularly as they relate to the group activities and group motion planning required for the ACANTO project.

4.1   Group Planning Leakage

One main area of challenge is in the leakage of information through the group activity planning. The planning of an activity must take into account all the constraints of all the group members, and so the end result must account for all of these constraints. This in turn implies that *some* potentially secure or private information must be shared and thus could be inferred by other group members based on the chosen group activity and global plan. The rest of this section considers the scope and risks of such information leakage in ACANTO.

To illustrate this leakage, consider the scenario where one group member has a particular medical issue that requires them to always be within five minutes of a bathroom. To satisfy this user, the activity and global plan must keep the group within five minutes of a bathroom at all times. In general this can lead to global plans that will not appear optimal or natural to a user who does not have this constraint.

For example, consider the paths presented in Fig. 3. The shortest path is represented in gray, while the path that remains within five minutes travel time of a bathroom is in red.

Of course, inferring the cause for a particular global plan may not be a trivial exercise, particularly when several competing or complementary constraints are in play. After all, if bathrooms and access ramps are co-located in an environment, the inference may be that a group member is unable to use stairs, rather than a member of the group having issues that require a bathroom.

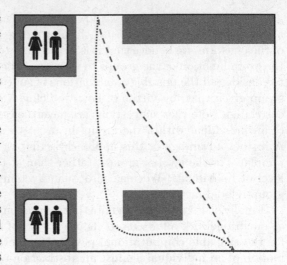

Fig. 3. Paths with and without bathroom constraints. (Color figure online)

Such issues are not always as simple and obvious as the global plan chosen. Groups may have members that have upper or lower bounds on exercise, on time spent, on rest taken, and many other factors. Thus, the activity plan may approximate all of these initially, but require the plan to be recalculated and changed based upon these constrains, that may appear arbitrarily to another user.

For example, if the group has been moving too slowly, a re-plan to ensure sufficient calorie burn may lead to longer (non-intuitive) paths between the next activity locations. Similarly, if too much time has been spent resting, the global plan may alter or even drop activities, which would indirectly yield information both about the status and requirements of the users, but also about the importance of the activities themselves.

4.2   Shared Server Leakage

Another path for information leakage to occur is through the shared server infrastructure. Since information is shared between FriWalks through the server, it is possible for information about one FriWalk user to be leaked to others, even FriWalk users not in the same group. Similarly to the above, the goal of collaborative and group activities in ACANTO requires some communication and thus information leakage between users. Although this could be largely ignored for planning as discussed here, this would lead to significantly less user safety, which is considered a top priority in the ACANTO project.

The underlying goal of the shared server infrastructure is to allow for shared sensor data to be used, improving planning for both the long term planner, and the reactive planner. However, this also allows information to be inferred about where other agents are.

Consider the example illustrated in Fig. 4. A user (here in blue with sensor range shown as the blue triangle) approaches a corner that obstructs vision. Another user (green here) around the corner may have shared (via the server) that an agent (in red) is about to turn around the corner from the obscured side. The reactive planner will advise the blue user whose vision is obstructed (both sensor vision, and natural vision) to turn away or stop in order to avoid a collision.

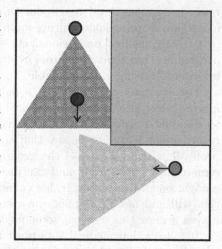

In such a scenario it is easy to see how leakage of user location can occur, since the FriWalk reactive planner will react to things that can only be sensed from another source. Thus, the approximate location of the other source could be inferred.

Fig. 4. Inferring user location around corners. (Color figure online)

On the larger scale, the server will also be aware of obstructions and traffic behaviours from different locations due to information from other agents. Thus, a change in global plan could yield information about the prior locations of other users.

For example, the global plan may have originally been to cross a food court in a mall, however a previous user or group attempted to cross the food court (or is in the process of doing so) and reports significant traffic and issues with avoiding collisions. Thus, a user may have their plan updated due to server information that the path ahead will be densely trafficked and may not be suitable for them.

Thus, information about the location of other agents will be implicitly shared with users of the system. Although this is considered an overall benefit to the design of the system, and should improve overall safety and comfort for users, it cannot be ignored that some location information could be inferred about users by other users.

4.3 Medical Information

One particular challenge in the ACANTO project is the use of medical information. The ACANTO project includes medical personnel as part of the social aspects, and in assisting impaired adults with designing and completing preventative and recovery activities. However, this implies the use of medical data and potentially medical records in various aspects of the project. Further, some FriWalks are also equipped with more advanced sensors that can both aid in, and perform, medical diagnostics.

The use of medical records and medical information is more obvious in the planning for (group) activities. As part of rehabilitation and preventative care, activity plans should account for specified actions. These can include: minimum and maximum calories spent in activities; minimum and maximum distances walked; minimum and maximum time spent in a single walk; minimum and maximum sustained pace during walking; requirement to always be accompanied by a trained medical professional, etc. Thus an activity plan must adhere to these constraints that are derived from medical information without the source medical information being made available.

For example, consider when a patient's medical records indicate that they must always have a trained medical professional in the vicinity, perhaps due to some heart condition that may require intervention. Clearly the global and reactive planners must ensure that this user is not separated from any medical professional who is part of the group. However, in general the group need not remain in a single group and can instead split into sub-groups for parts of the navigation and activities. If this vulnerable user is to be appropriately cared for, this will add new constraints on the planning, and may yield behaviour that makes it clear this user has some medical issue.

It follows that medical data must be used as part of the planning and activities, but this should be handled with great care since even indirect information may yield significant breaches of patient information security and privacy.

Legal Limitations. To further complicate medical records use, in most jurisdictions there are many specific laws with respect to the use of medical records and in the general handling of privileged medical information. Although the ACANTO project is being developed in partnership with medical professions and with these in mind, larger outcomes and a general application of the ACANTO system will need to consider these issues with great delicacy.

4.4   FriWalk Trust

A different challenge is for adoption of ACANTO by users, there will also need to be user trust in the FriWalk and ACANTO social network. In addition to ensuring security to a sufficient level for users to feel comfortable with the FriWalks and social network, there must also be trust in the FriWalk itself behaving in a good, reliable, and user-centric manner. That is, FriWalks should rarely conflict with user perceptions and about planning (or only do so in a comprehensible manner), and must establish trust with the user that the FriWalk has their interests foremost.

The behaviour and advice of the FriWalk needs to be reliable and comprehensible to the extent that the user trusts that the directions and suggestions made are sensible. This is particularly pertinent when the directions given by the FriWalk may be in conflict with the expectations of the user.

For example, the user may be familiar with the environment and already know the "best" way to the next location in the activity plan. However, the FriWalk may suggest an alternative path. This could reduce user trust if the user does not see any reason or benefit to the suggested alternative plan.

Another example would be when the reactive planner suggests a direction that seems at odds with the immediate observations by the user. This could occur when the server has provided information about obscured agents moving in the environment, and the user may not (yet) be aware of their existence (as discussed above in Sect. 4.2).

These general scenarios bring into consideration how to best support the user while providing good information, even in conflict with the user's knowledge or observations.

Another dimension of trust is that the behaviour of the FriWalk must act in the best interest of the user. It is possible that a user may feel that the FriWalk is acting to force them into some conformity with the group, rather than taking into account the individual's needs. This is most likely to appear when activities are designed to meet the requirements of many, and so may be suboptimal for many (or even all) users if considering the activity individually. This can include planning poor paths through the environment, choosing unnatural movement patterns to maintain group cohesion, guiding members to continue when they feel they need a break, or alternatively suggesting breaks or delays when users are keen to continue.

All of these provide a complex interplay of balancing the individual desires of a user, and the group plans and actions. To some degree the FriWalk should incentivise the user towards maintaining group cohesion and following the group activity plan. At the same time, it must be flexible and reactive to the needs of an individual; perhaps splitting the group easily when one user indicates a need to visit the bathroom and adding others to this sub-group to ensure no user is left alone.

5   Proposed Solutions

This section considers possible solutions to the challenges of Sect. 4. The focus here is upon how to solve the challenges within the framework of the ACANTO project, the technologies chosen, limitations, and in a manner that does not introduce new overhead or concerns. The goal of this section is to consider such possible solutions and their effectiveness. The details of their implementation (and related experiments) are left to future work.

5.1   Group Planning Leakage

In a general sense the issue of some information being leaked in such scenarios is unsolvable; it is not possible to create a global plan that both achieves the constraints required, and does not yield any information about those constraints. That said, it is feasible to mitigate the leakage of information, and address the manner in which it is leaked.

The most obvious "solution" to this issue is in the complexity and conjunction of the constraints themselves. While a constraint such as "must always be close to a bathroom" may appear strict, many other constraints could also lead to the kinds of paths features in Fig. 3. As hinted in Sect. 4.1, it may not be obvious that this is the constraint imposed, since avoiding stairs could coincide.

More generally, this kind of leakage can be mitigated by the conjunction of other constraints. Consider that the global plan may be due to wishing to increase caloric burn, duration, or to avoid traffic and other issues the users are not aware of. All of these other plausible explanations make inferring a particular constraint much more complex, particularly given limited information.

To complicate such inferences further, the global plan is not made evident to the users initially. Thus, the users may not even be aware of the global plan having this initial constraint. Since replanning may occur due to a variety of factors, it is quite conceivable that the path followed by the users was emergent rather than designed.

Indeed, such emergent paths through the environment may dominate any global plan that was initially created. Considering that any local traffic factor or updated information could change the global plan, it is likely that perturbations of the global plan would be normal rather than an exception.

Even further, the above all assume that the users follow the directions and plans without agency. However, one key consideration in ACANTO is that the FriWalk provides guidance, but the user may ignore or alter their behaviour. Thus, even if there was the potential to reasonably infer some secure or private information from observing the plan followed, it would not be clear that this was planned, or simply emergent from the actions of users, reactive planning, and general constraints to maintain group cohesion.

For example, the global plan may have indicated a direct path that did not remain close to bathrooms. However, one user could have opted to ignore the suggested direction (or varied their actions due to reactive planning) and ended up shifting the whole group down an alternate path that was always close to bathrooms. (The reverse is also possible, with users opting to ignore the guidance to remain close to a bathroom. In such a scenario the FriWalk would strongly suggest directions to the users to maintain the constraint of staying close to a bathroom, but this cannot be forced by the FriWalk.) Thus, an observed path cannot be reliably assumed to have been the global plan chosen to satisfy user constraints, and thus inferring information from the global plan is non-trivial, and likely to be highly erroneous in practice.

In instances where it is obvious that a replan has occurred due to violation of constraints (such as when key activities are dropped, or the activity prematurely ended), it is still unclear which possible constraint this could be related to. Consider that a premature end could signal an overrun of: calorie burn, distance, time, scheduling, etc., or even that some emergency has occurred or some updated traffic information made the plan impossible.

Thus, although information leakage is impossible to avoid, the details are suitably obscured to make this a minor issue in the implementation of ACANTO.

5.2   Shared Server Leakage

Like the previous challenge, the leakage of information between users or other sensors in the environment cannot be completely prevented (and indeed would contradict the choice in ACANTO to exploit this data to improve reactive planning). Again the solution here is to limit the amount of data that is directly evident to a user.

In a general sense the challenge is to prevent the location of another FriWalk user from being easily inferred by exploiting the location of agents that is provided by the server. This can be mitigated in four different ways.

In many environments the infrastructure also includes several fixed sensors, such as fixed cameras. This allows for the environment to be augmented with agent information that does not come from any user or FriWalk. That is, the fixed sensors of the environment can also provide the location (and trajectory information) of agents. Thus, when reactive planning exploits information about agents outside the sensor range of the FriWalk (doing the reactive planning), it is not certain that the agents being considered were observed by another user/FriWalk. Thus, while there *may* be another user in the vicinity, it is not necessary for another user to be in the vicinity to have information about the location of agents outside sensor range. That said, if the location of fixed sensors is known, the shared information through the server can still leak approximate location information about other users/FriWalks.

Even in this case, it is not clear that the information from the server can be used to infer the location of another agent with high precision. The information sent from the server is an n-dimensional cube (three dimensions: x, y, and maybe z for Euclidean space, and t for time) and so does not contain all the information observed by other users/FriWalks. Thus, it is not in general possible to infer precise location information about the sensor(s) that observed the other agents. Consider the diagram in Fig. 5. The blue user may be able to infer that there is another user/FriWalk in the area to be informed about the red agent, but any of the green locations (as well as many others) are potential locations for the other user/FriWalk.

To further complicate the problem of inferring information from agent locations provided by the server, the server and reactive planner may both project the future locations of recently observed agents, even if no longer "visible" to any sensor. This arises because observations are recorded and sent asynchronously by FriWalks, while it may be necessary for both the server and individual FriWalks to predict the current state of the environment from stored data (for the purpose of disambiguating different observations of the same agent and if communication breaks down). Thus, even though an agent's location was observed in the past and sent to a FriWalk, this does not imply that the agent is still observable.

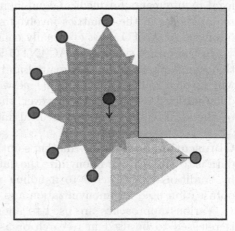

Fig. 5. Possible information about other user/FriWalk from server information. (Color figure online)

Their location may be projected forward by the reactive planner, thus giving the location of an agent that is not actually observed to be there by any sensor. This makes inferring possible sensor information (and from this other user/FriWalk location information) much more difficult.

Lastly, location information is not perfect and the reactive planning itself is not deterministic. The location information is refined by further observations, so it is possible that locations will be made more accurate or altered when the server aggregates information form multiple devices. This can lead to location information changing (slightly). Further, the reactive planner itself is not deterministic: adding noise to the SFM and using SMC to derive the best outcome. This ensures a non-deterministic outcome, and so means that even with the same input, it is possible for different suggestions to be made to the user. Since the user only observes the direction suggestions of the reactive planner, this can obscure information that might lead to leakage of other user/FriWalk locations.

5.3 Medical Information

The handling of medical data in the ACANTO project raises several complications, particularly related to the shared information aspects of the project. The proposed solutions to prevent issues here fall into three general categories: legal solutions, data obfuscation solutions, and user trust solutions.

Legal Solutions. In a sense the legal complications and challenges raised when handling medical data are the easiest to resolve. While the various jurisdictions and variations in legal requirements are on their own a challenge, the solution can be easily applied on the scale of the project implementation. At this stage the ACANTO project is approaching clinical trials overseen by medical professionals and in a research environment. Thus, for now the solution is to abide by the legal requirements for medical equipment trials, and thus comply with all legal requirements in the countries involved so far (UK, Spain). As an EU project, however, ACANTO must eventually comply with all subscribing nations.

In the future the goal of ACANTO is to build a larger scale social network that can support mobility impaired and older adults in various locations. This will involve rolling out the social network to different jurisdictions and with different legal requirements. However, the solution is clear in all cases – to abide by the legal requirements for medical data used in all jurisdictions.

Obfuscation Solutions. Another solution to the challenge of handling medical data is to obfuscate or anonymize the data being used. This approach is inspired by traditional approaches to handling medical data in research, and in data obfuscation used for anonymization and as discussed in Sects. 5.1 and 5.2.

Various approaches are used to anonymize medical (and other) data that is released to be used in research or as part of the results of a study. These techniques can be used within the ACANTO project to reduce leakage of medical information being tied to any particular user. Although this is non-trivial to resolve and relies upon the data set and other information, techniques such as differential privacy [5] could be used at the activity and group planning stages to ensure that the data does not leak medical information about any individual.

Further efforts to reduce the medical information leakage can also be taken, such as adding noise to the various results that derive from medical data. This could be considered by extending the bounds of differential privacy to ensure greater distances, or by adding some randomness to the outcomes of derived results that depend upon medical information.

User Trust. A further solution to the challenge is to provide the users with the choice of what medical information can be used in social and planning aspects of ACANTO. This could be approached in a similar manner to various current social networks that let the user choose what information applications and other users have access to. Thus, a user of the ACANTO network could choose to share their preferences (derived from medical information) or keep these secret.

For example, a user may be happy to allow the ACANTO social network and activity planning to know that they require rests regularly or have a very low top speed. The user may not be recognised as the source of this information due to other proposed solutions (above), or may be happy to share this and merely note it as part of their recovery. On the other hand, a user may choose to keep such requirements to themselves and merely trust that the activity monitoring and planning aspects of the activity planner and FriWalk will adjust for the slow speed and frequent rests during the activity.

This approach allows users to have greater control over how their medical information may be used by the ACANTO system. This should provide transparency and control to users, allowing them to better understand how the ACANTO systems works, and to gain trust in the ACANTO system accounting for their needs.

5.4 FriWalk Trust

This section considers general approaches and concerns with gaining user trust of the ACANTO system and FriWalk. This area is difficult to approach within the technology and scope of the implementation of the ACANTO project, yet on the other hand is also relatively straight forward to gain useful information from other domains and from user feedback during clinical trials.

The challenge of reliable and comprehensible behaviour for the FriWalk significantly falls back to the FriWalk respecting the requirements and constraints of the user. Thus, the global and reactive planners should clearly behave in the best interest of the user. This is simple to implement for an individual, though slightly more complex when multiple users may have competing constraints.

Competing constraints and scenarios where there is no "good" solution is a hot topic in the related domain of autonomous vehicles [1]. The proposed resolutions of ethical dilemmas in that field can potentially provide a basis for solutions within the ACANTO project.

To further support such choices, ACANTO also has clinical trials that can be used to gather more information, and also implement different solutions to gain user feedback. This is discussed further below in Sect. 5.4.

The other aspect of when the user and the FriWalk/FriTab believe separate paths are "better" can be resolved by the FriWalk not being rigid in the choices. By having the global and reactive planners both willing and able to replan as the situation changes, ensures that the user can override what they think is a "poor" choice and have the FriWalk smoothly adjust to this change. This is similar to GPS/navigation in vehicles, whether the user not taking the nominated path causes a replan, rather than the device attempting to override the user or force them back to the original plan.

Another challenge is when the individual and the group may be in competing positions. For example, when an individual needs to use the bathroom or in some other manner wishes to diverge from the group/activity. In such scenarios, the proposed solution is to provide the user of a FriWalk an option to notify their device of this scenario. Thus, the device can react to the requirements of the individual user, and also relay this to the server and other devices. This will allow for the user's FriWalk to immediately support their needs, overriding any constraints imposed by the group. Further, this can allow other users to react accordingly, such as ensuring a companion or medical professional is aware of the situation and can support the user, or perhaps the group will be split to ensure the user is not left behind.

Clinical Trials. Various proposed solutions have been suggested above or in related works and projects. In addition to considering and learning from other projects and results, the ACANTO project will be conducting clinical trials of groups of users and will be able to experiment with different approaches. This can be used to determine which solutions work best, and also which behaviours of the FriWalk and the ACANTO project as a whole are most accepted, and also which cause tension or distrust in users. It is expected that feedback from clinical trials will be used to refine proposed solutions, and be able to test different solutions to see which are most effective and more trusted by users in practice.

6   Conclusions

The ACANTO project's aim to assist physically and mentally impaired users with therapeutic and social support via social networking and group activities clearly raises several challenges in the context of security, privacy, and trust. Further, the choices of technology to implement the ACANTO project also influences and implies other challenges.

These challenges range across several areas. Information sharing where users of ACANTO join or participate in group activities that must account for the safety and support of all users. Information leakage during motion planning where other users of ACANTO even outside the group may have location information leaked. The handling of medical information of users, both in the legal and privacy dimensions. Gaining user trust and providing a trustworthy platform for users so they can feel safe in interacting with ACANTO.

Several ways to address these challenges have been presented, and their feasibility to implement within the design and technological choices of ACANTO. In general these provide effective solutions that balance the need to, for example, share information with the need to maintain user security, privacy, and trust.

References

1. Bonnefon, J.-F., Shariff, A., Rahwan, I.: The social dilemma of autonomous vehicles. Science **352**(6293), 1573–1576 (2016)
2. Colombo, A., Fontanelli, D., Gandhi, D., De Angeli, A., Palopoli, L., Sedwards, S., Legay, A.: Behavioural templates improve robot motion planning with social force model in human environments. In: 2013 IEEE 18th Conference on Emerging Technologies Factory Automation (ETFA), pp. 1–6, September 2013
3. Colombo, A., Fontanelli, D., Legay, A., Palopoli, L., Sedwards, S.: Motion planning in crowds using statistical model checking to enhance the social force model. In: 2013 IEEE 52nd Annual Conference on Decision and Control (CDC), pp. 3602–3608, December 2013
4. Colombo, A., Fontanelli, D., Legay, A., Palopoli, L., Sedwards, S.: Efficient customisable dynamic motion planning for assistive robots in complex human environments. J. Ambient Intell. Smart Environ. **7**, 617–633 (2015)
5. Dwork, C.: Differential privacy. In: Bugliesi, M., Preneel, B., Sassone, V., Wegener, I. (eds.) ICALP 2006. LNCS, vol. 4052, pp. 1–12. Springer, Heidelberg (2006). doi:10.1007/11787006_1
6. Helbing, D., Farkas, I., Molnár, P., Vicsek, T.: Simulation of pedestrian crowds in normal and evacuation situations. In: Schreckenberg, M., Sharma, S.D. (eds.) Pedestrian and Evacuation Dynamics. Springer, Heidelberg (2002)
7. Helbing, D., Farkas, I., Vicsek, T.: Simulating dynamical features of escape panic. Nature **407**, 487–490 (2000)
8. Helbing, D., Farkas, I.J., Vicsek, T.: Freezing by heating in a driven mesoscopic system. Phys. Rev. Lett. **84**, 1240–1243 (2000)
9. Helbing, D., Molnár, P.: Social force model for pedestrian dynamics. Phys. Rev. E **51**, 4282–4286 (1995)
10. Moussaïd, M., Perozo, N., Garnier, S., Helbing, D., Theraulaz, G.: The walking behaviour of pedestrian social groups and its impact on crowd dynamics. PLoS ONE **5**(4), e10047 (2010)
11. Okamoto, M.: Some inequalities relating to the partial sum of binomial probabilities. Ann. Inst. Stat. Math. **10**, 29–35 (1959)
12. Raupp-Musse, S., Thalmann, D.: Hierarchical model for real time simulation of virtual human crowds. IEEE Trans. Vis. Comput. Graph. **7**(2), 152–164 (2001)
13. Wald, A.: Sequential tests of statistical hypotheses. Ann. Math. Stat. **16**(2), 117–186 (1945)
14. Younes, H.L.S., Simmons, R.G.: Probabilistic verification of discrete event systems using acceptance sampling. In: Brinksma, E., Larsen, K.G. (eds.) CAV 2002. LNCS, vol. 2404, pp. 223–235. Springer, Heidelberg (2002). doi:10.1007/3-540-45657-0_17

Android App Permission and Users' Adoption: A Case Study of Mental Health Application

Hsiao-Ying Huang[1,2(✉)] and Masooda Bashir[1,2]

[1] Illinois Informatics Institute, University of Illinois at Urbana-Champaign,
Champaign, USA
{hhuang65,mnb}@illinois.edu
[2] School of Information Sciences, University of Illinois at Urbana-Champaign,
Champaign, USA

Abstract. The prevalent use of mobile devices makes mobile applications (apps) a promising approach to enhance mental healthcare. However, at the same time, users' information privacy and security becomes a serious concern due to the ubiquitous data collection of mobile device, especially when it comes to mental health information. With the exponential development of the current Android app market, hundreds of mental health apps are available to users. We are interested in how app permission, as the only information available about app privacy, is related to users' adoption of mental health apps. Considering that mental health is a broad field, this study focuses on one mental health condition: anxiety. A systematic search of anxiety apps was conducted on the Android app store. A total of 274 apps were collected and analyzed. In this study, we revealed the relationship between app permission and users' anxiety app adoption. We found that anxiety apps with more app permissions have higher installs. Also, certain app permissions are significantly related to the installation and rating of apps, such as the permission of in-app purchases, cameras, and location. This study provides a big picture of how app permission is connected with mental health app adoption. We believe this is an important step before we can identify which apps may pose higher risks for compromising users' information privacy and security.

Keywords: Information privacy · Security · Mobile device · Smartphone

1 Introduction

Recently, mobile technologies have advanced to the point that today's mobile devices function like handheld computers and are highly integrated into our daily lives. The prevalent use of mobile devices makes mobile applications (apps) a promising approach to engage users in beneficial activities or therapeutic sessions in the context of mental health [1]. While the majority of these mental health apps provide some level of confidentiality for their users' personal information, the information privacy and security of these mobile apps is still a vital concern, especially when it comes to the sensitivity of mental health information.

When using mobile apps for mental healthcare, users may be exposed more to information privacy risks and security breaches due to the "always-on" feature of

© Springer International Publishing AG 2017
T. Tryfonas (Ed.): HAS 2017, LNCS 10292, pp. 110–122, 2017.
DOI: 10.1007/978-3-319-58460-7_8

ubiquitous data collection [2]. For instance, users' information privacy can be compromised when third parties collect, store, and analyze their information without their consent and knowledge. Previous studies have indicated that patients are concerned about their information privacy while using mobile devices [3, 4]. Also, users' selection of apps can be affected by how they perceive the apps' risk to privacy and security [5, 6]. Users seem to prefer apps that collect less personal information [7].

From the user's perspective, information privacy represents a state of limited access to personal information [8]. However, when it comes to mobile privacy, users are often given no choice. For example, before app installation in the Android system, users can only see a dialogue of permission groups informing them what system function and data the app can access. In the iOS system, there is no privacy notice about apps although users can turn the app's access to personal information on or off after installation. The effect of these two mechanisms on users' information privacy protection is unclear. Prior research suggests that most Android users do not pay attention to the app permission dialogue [9–11]. Also, app permissions seem to have less of an effect on user adoption compared to other types of information (e.g., price, review, rating) [7]. Although the existing literature has indicated some important factors involved in users' decision-making processes for app adoption, the literature about mental health app adoption is scarce. To the best of our knowledge, no previous study has investigated how app permission, as displayed information of app privacy and security, is related to users' adoption of mental health apps.

To investigate the relationship between app permission and the adoption of mental health apps, we selected Google Play as our research site for two reasons. First, it is currently one of the leading app markets [13], and second, it exhibits the dialogue of information about app permission, which notifies users about app privacy and security. In addition, considering that mental health is a broad field, we focus this study on one mental health condition: anxiety, which is also one of the most common mental health issues among U.S. adults [12]. The aim of this study is to examine the relationship between different types of app permission and users' adoption of anxiety apps. As far as we know, this study is the first work focusing on examining the relationship between app permission and mental health app adoption.

2 Background

2.1 Mobile Privacy and Android App Permission

Information privacy has become one of the most concerning issues in mobile technologies due to the exponential use of mobile apps. According to Google Play [27], approximately 65 billion apps have been downloaded to users' mobile devices. The enormous number of apps downloads by users make the misuse of user data and the security breach of users almost inevitable. For instance, Felt et al. [11] found that around 93% of free Android apps had at least one potentially malicious data usage, such as accessing the camera to take pictures, and sending messages on the users' behalf.

Mobile apps often attempt to collect a wide range of user data stored on mobile devices for functionality purposes and to personalize advertising [14]. Android apps can request access to mobile system functionality via the Android app permission system. To inform users which type of data may be accessed by apps, Google Play displays the permissions to the user at the time of installation. Nevertheless, it does not provide an explanation about how and why these permissions are requested. From the users' perspective, previous studies [9–11] found that only 3% of users had a full understanding of what access the permissions were requesting. In addition, most users do not pay attention to the permissions screen. That is, the majority of users do not have a comprehensive understanding about an apps' capacity to access personal data. The lack of adequate knowledge and attentiveness to app permissions could lead users to make inappropriate decisions, which may put users' information privacy at risk.

2.2   Mobile App Adoption

A substantial amount of studies have identified a variety of factors that can influence users' app adoption, including prices, ratings, reviews, rankings, installs, titles, descriptions, functions, and privacy issues of apps [6, 7, 15–22]. Furthermore, the search ranking of results is a significant factor of users' adoption [25], which can influence app adoption. Although app adoption is a complicated decision-making process, users often apply the simple "take the first" heuristic approach. This approach is mainly dominated by the most accessible information, such as price, ratings and rankings of apps [7, 22]. Even though prior research has pointed out that users would prefer the app to collect less personal data [7, 26], how app permissions affect users' app adoption remains unclear, especially when it comes to mental health apps. Since mental health apps can collect sensitive personal information (e.g., mental health state, health conditions, daily routine), we are interested in whether app permission is related to users' adoption of mental health apps.

3   Method

3.1   Anxiety Apps Search and Selection

To imitate the users' app search process, we used keyword search strategies to identify apps that most likely would be adopted by users seeking anxiety-related apps. This is similar to the approach employed by Ramo et al. [23]. Based on DSM-5 [24], we first identified three main keywords related to anxiety disorders including: anxiety, fear, and avoidance. Each term reported 250 results on Google Play. We dropped the term "avoidance" because its search results did not yield the result of anxiety-related apps. To identify other potential keywords, we performed a search for the word "anxiety" on the website UrbanDictionary.com. Twenty-seven commonly used terms were listed. We selected two of the words most compatible with anxiety and fear, which are "anxious" and "worry." We used four keywords as our final search terms on Google Play, including: anxiety, anxious, fear, and worry. The term "anxiety" was our primary search term and the other three keywords were used for supplementary searches.

A two-phase app search was conducted. Our first app search was conducted on Google Play between July and September 2016. Researchers collected the information for all of the apps and selected the anxiety-related apps based on the apps' descriptions. A second round of app searches by keyword was conducted on October 7, 2016. Twenty-four new apps were identified and 14 apps no longer existed. A total of 274 apps were chosen for analysis.

3.2   App Permission

According to the list provided by Google Play [28], there are 138 types of system permissions that Android apps can request. App developers can also create their own app permission request if there is a need. Although many app permission requests are available to developers, only certain types of app permissions are commonly requested by most apps, such as in-app purchase, location, and Wi-Fi connection. Users can review these app permission requests before they download the app. Google Play categorizes their system permission and only displays 16 common groups of app permission. Additional app permission requests fall under the 'Other' category. To identify app permissions, we included these 16 types of app permission requests and added other app permissions by manually reviewing the 'Other' section of apps, which resulted in 11 additional app permission requests. Table 1 provides the full list of app permissions identified in this study.

Table 1. List of app permission request

App permission group	Other app permission
1. In-app purchases	17. Storage
2. Device & app history	18. Receive data from Internet
3. Cellular data settings	19. Control vibration
4. Identity	20. Prevent device sleeping
5. Contacts	21. View network connections
6. Calendar	22. Change your audio settings
7. Location	23. Full network access
8. SMS	24. Modify system settings
9. Phone	25. Run at startup
10. Photos/Media/Files	26. Google play license
11. Camera	27. Manage access to documents
12. Microphone	
13. Wi-Fi connection information	
14. Bluetooth connection information	
15. Wearable sensors/activity data	
16. Device ID & call information	

3.3   Indicators of App Adoption: App Installs and Ratings

We collected two types of observational data as indicators of app adoption from the app store, which are: app installs and ratings. We reassigned a number to the installs because we could only access the approximate range of installs on Google Play, instead of the exact number. Based on the range of categories, the number of installs ranges from level 1 (<10) to level 12 (>1000000). The mean of anxiety app installs is 6.42 and the average rating is 3.43 (SD = 1.61).

3.4   App Price, Review, and Ranking

We also collected the price and number of anxiety app reviews. App ranking on the search results page is defined by an algorithm and may be customized based on individuals' preferences. To collect the average mean ranking for each app, three researchers manually searched web browser apps by keyword and recorded their rankings between October 7 and October 11, 2016.

4   Results

4.1   Overview of Anxiety App Permission

The average of app permission requests is 5.84 (SD = 4.01). As exhibited in Fig. 1, approximately 80% of anxiety apps request full network access permissions, which is followed by 'view network connection,' 'storage,' and 'photos/media/files.' Forty percent of apps request permissions to prevent the phone from going into sleep mode. These results suggest that many anxiety apps provide functions that require Internet access, data storage, or constant operation. Around 30% of apps request 'phone' and 'device and app information,' which indicates that these apps may access users' phone numbers and that the phone number is connected by calls, web bookmarks, and browsing history. Seventeen percent of apps request permission to access users' contact information, location, and identify users' accounts on the device. Approximately 10% of apps request permission to access the camera and microphone. Also, very few apps request permission to access the log history of the device and app, SMS messages, and calendar schedule. No apps request permission for 'cellular data settings,' 'Bluetooth connection,' and 'wearable sensors/activity data.' Thus, we exclude these three types of permission in our analysis.

4.2   Anxiety App Permission and App Adoption

We investigated the relationship between anxiety app permission requests and their adoption by correlational analysis. As shown in Table 2, the permission requests of 'in-app purchase,' 'control vibration,' 'prevent device from sleeping,' 'view network access,' and 'run at startup' have a significant positive correlation with app install and rating. These indicate that anxiety apps with the aforementioned permission requests have higher installs and ratings. In addition, the apps with permission requests for 'photo/media/files,' 'change audio settings,' 'full network access,' and 'modify system settings' have more installs. On the other hand, anxiety apps with camera permission requests have both lower installs and lower ratings. Apps with location and microphone permission requests show lower ratings. In general, the more permissions the apps request, the higher rate of installation the apps have (r = .200, p = .001).

App Permission and App Installs. The first hierarchical multiple regression with 24 predictors revealed that app permissions contributed significantly to the regression model F(24, 270) = 3.73, p < .001 and accounted for 26.8% of the variance in app

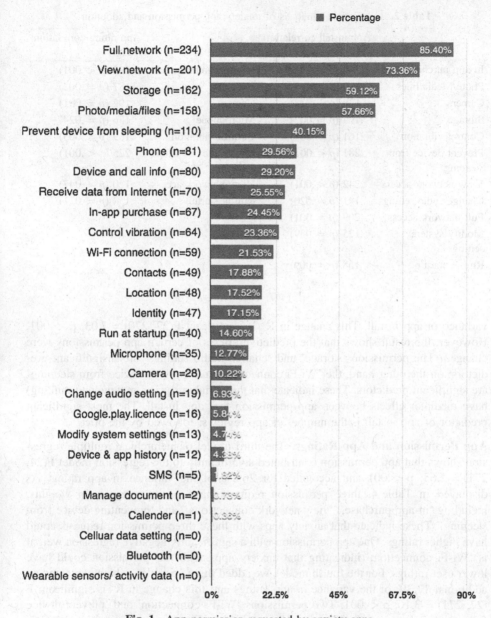

Fig. 1. App permission requested by anxiety apps

install. As displayed in Table 3, four permission requests have positive regression weights, including 'in-app purchase,' 'storage,' 'view network connections,' and 'change audio settings.' These results suggest that anxiety apps with these four permission requests will demonstrate higher installs. In the second model, we added three variables: price, review, and ranking, which explained an additional 37.6% of the

Table 2. Correlational analysis of anxiety app permission and adoption

	App install correlation r (sig.)		App rating correlation r (sig.)
In-app purchase	.341 ($p < .001$)	In-app purchase	.242 ($p < .001$)
Photo/Media/Files	.120 ($p = .048$)	Location	−.187 ($p = .002$)
Camera	−.138 ($p = .023$)	Camera	−.192 ($p = .001$)
Storage	.164 ($p = .007$)	Microphone	−.136 ($p = .024$)
Control vibration	.161 ($p = .008$)	Control vibration	.169 ($p = .005$)
Prevent device from sleeping	.281 ($p < .001$)	Prevent device from sleeping	.225 ($p < .001$)
View network access	.242 ($p < .001$)	View network access	.120 ($p = .047$)
Change audio settings	.141 ($p = .020$)	Run at startup	.154 ($p = .011$)
Full network access	.209 ($p = .001$)		
Modify system settings	.125 ($p = .039$)		
Run at startup	.158 ($p = .009$)		

variance in app install. This change in R^2 is significant $F(27, 270) = 7.03$, $p < .001$. However, the result shows that the predictive effects of certain app permissions were changed. The permission 'storage' and 'change audio settings' are insignificant predictors; on the other hand, the 'Wi-Fi connection' and 'prevent device from sleeping' are significant predictors. These indicate that the variables (price, review, and ranking) have mediator effects between app permission and app install. The most significant predictor of app install is the number of app reviews, followed by the price.

App Permission and App Ratings. The third model of hierarchical multiple regression shows that app permission contributed significantly to the regression model $F(24, 271) = 2.65$, $p < .001$ and accounted for 26.8% of the variance in app rating. As displayed in Table 4, three permission requests have positive regression weights, including 'in-app purchase,' 'view network connections,' and 'preventing device from sleeping.' These indicate that anxiety apps with these three permission requests could have higher ratings. One app permission with a significantly negative regression weight is 'Wi-Fi connection,' indicating that anxiety apps with this permission could have lower user ratings. For the fourth model, we added three variables, which explained an additional 17.3% of the variance in app ratings and this change in R^2 is significant $F(27, 271) = 3.10$, $p < .001$. Two permissions 'Wi-Fi connection' and 'prevent device from sleeping' remain significant positive predictors. However, the permission 'in-app purchase' and 'view network connection' are no longer significant predictors. Instead, location permission request becomes a significant negative predictor of ratings. This means that anxiety apps with location permission requests will have lower ratings. Furthermore, app price is the most significant predictor of ratings, followed by ranking.

Table 3. Hierarchical regression model of app permission and app install

Independent variables: app permission	Model 1: install		Model 2: install	
	Standardized beta	t-value (sig.)	Standardized beta	t-value (sig.)
In-app purchase	.231	3.78 ($p < .001$)	.111	1.99 ($p = .048$)
Device & app history	−.098	−1.56 ($p = .121$)	−.054	−.96 ($p = .339$)
Identity	−.109	−.70 ($p = .483$)	−.070	−.51 ($p = .608$)
Contacts	.047	.30 ($p = .763$)	.054	.39 ($p = .697$)
Calendar	−.044	−.78 ($p = .437$)	−.027	−.55 ($p = .583$)
Location	−.094	−1.22 ($p = .223$)	−.129	−1.89 ($p = .060$)
SMS	.085	1.46 ($p = .147$)	.077	1.48 ($p = .139$)
Phone	−.056	−.32 ($p = .753$)	−.099	−.63 ($p = .527$)
Photo/Media/Files	−.369	−1.96 ($p = .052$)	−.267	−1.60 ($p = .111$)
Camera	−.081	−.96 ($p = .339$)	−.067	−.89 ($p = .372$)
Microphone	−.107	−1.38 ($p = .169$)	−.040	−.58 ($p = .566$)
Wi-Fi connection	−.104	−1.62 ($p = .107$)	−.139	−2.39 ($p = .018$)
Device ID & call information	.125	.71 ($p = .481$)	.193	1.23 ($p = .219$)
Storage	.435	2.29 ($p = .023$)	.287	1.70 ($p = .090$)
Receive data from Internet	−.018	−.21 ($p = .831$)	−.040	−.54 ($p = .589$)
Control vibration	.043	.59 ($p = .558$)	.039	.60 ($p = .552$)
Prevent device sleeping	.142	1.90 ($p = .058$)	.145	2.19 ($p = .030$)
View network connections	.167	2.12 ($p = .035$)	.144	2.07 ($p = .039$)
Change audio settings	.143	2.31 ($p = .022$)	.073	1.31 ($p = .192$)
Full network access	.032	.43 ($p = .666$)	−.029	−.44 ($p = .662$)
Modify system settings	.062	.99 ($p = .322$)	.007	.12 ($p = .903$)
Run at startup	.030	.47 ($p = .643$)	.026	.45 ($p = .651$)
Google play license	−.010	−.17 ($p = .869$)	.094	1.64 ($p = .103$)
Manage access to documents	.030	.53 ($p = .595$)	.030	.59 ($p = .557$)
Price			−.264	−5.01 ($p < .001$)
Review			.285	5.43 ($p < .001$)
Ranking			−.157	−3.03 ($p = .003$)
(Constant)		10.64 ($p < .001$)		12.81 ($p < .001$)
R^2	.268		.439	

5   Discussion

This study investigated the relationship between app permission and the adoption of anxiety apps by analyzing observational data collected from the Google Play store. We found that the most requested permissions by anxiety apps are mainly for Internet access, data storage, or device operation. Interestingly, our results show that anxiety

Table 4. Hierarchical regression model of app permission and app rating

Independent variables: app permission	Model 3: rating		Model 4: rating	
	Standardized beta	t-value (sig.)	Standardized beta	t-value (sig.)
In-app purchase	.162	2.53 (p = .012)	.101	1.57 (p = .118)
Device & app history	−.030	−.45 (p = .653)	−.016	−.25 (p = .801)
Identity	−.136	−.84 (p = .400)	−.114	−.72 (p = .470)
Contacts	.051	.31 (p = .758)	.046	.29 (p = .775)
Calendar	−.030	−.51 (p = .613)	−.016	−.29 (p = .775)
Location	−.155	−1.92 (p = .056)	−.163	−2.07 (p = .040)
SMS	.058	.94 (p = .346)	.054	.91 (p = .366)
Phone	.112	.66 (p = .513)	.065	.39 (p = .699)
Photo/Media/Files	−.096	−.49 (p = .627)	−.037	−.19 (p = .846)
Camera	−.108	−1.22 (p = .223)	−.098	−1.13 (p = .261)
Microphone	−.065	−.80 (p = .424)	−.034	−.42 (p = .673)
Wi-Fi connection	−.196	−2.90 (p = .004)	−.186	−2.78 (p = .006)
Device ID & call information	−.068	−.40 (p = .690)	−.013	−.08 (p = .936)
Storage	.134	.68 (p = .500)	.055	.28 (p = .779)
Receive data from Internet	−.036	−.42 (p = .677)	−.059	−.70 (p = .486)
Control vibration	.124	1.61 (p = .108)	.112	1.49 (p = .138)
Prevent device sleeping	.164	2.10 (p = .037)	.177	2.33 (p = .021)
View network connections	.164	1.99 (p = .047)	.154	1.92 (p = .056)
Change audio settings	.092	1.41 (p = .159)	.071	1.09 (p = .275)
Full network access	−.055	−.71 (p = .479)	−.093	−1.21 (p = .228)
Modify system settings	−.014	−.22 (p = .825)	−.024	−.37 (p = .714)
Run at startup	.013	.20 (p = .840)	.010	.15 (p = .883)
Google play license	.006	.08 (p = .933)	.043	.65 (p = .517)
Manage access to documents	.031	.51 (p = .610)	.020	.35 (p = .729)
Price			−.173	−2.87 (p = .005)
Review			.051	.84 (p = .402)
Ranking			−.139	−2.33 (p = .021)
(Constant)		12.25 (p < .001)		12.00 (p < .001)
R^2	.205		.256	

apps with higher installs request more permissions. A possible explanation is that the apps with higher installs may provide users with more functionality, and these request more permissions. Furthermore, we found that certain app permission requests correlated significantly with app adoption (see Table 5). For instance, apps with permission requests for 'in-app purchase' have higher installs and ratings. We infer that apps requesting permission for an in-app purchase would have lower prices, which could

Table 5. Overview of app permission and app adoption

	Install	Rating
In-app purchase	Higher	Higher
Control vibration	Higher	Higher
Prevent device from sleeping	Higher	Higher
View network access	Higher	Higher
Run at startup	Higher	Higher
Photo/Media/Files	Higher	X
Storage	Higher	X
Change audio settings	Higher	X
Full network access	Higher	X
Modify system settings	Higher	X
Camera	Lower	Lower
Location	X	Lower
Microphone	X	Lower

lead more users to install them. Also, apps with an in-app purchase request may provide users more autonomy to decide if they want to purchase certain functions in the app, rather than automatically including them at the time of installation. This may result in higher ratings. Our findings also indicate that anxiety apps with permission of 'control vibration,' 'prevent device from sleeping,' 'view network connections,' and 'run at startup' have higher installs and ratings. These four permissions are involved with the operating functions of mobile devices, suggesting that these anxiety apps may either provide functions that users need or they have better functionality. On the other hand, apps with permission requests for the device's camera have significantly fewer installs and lower ratings than apps without camera permission. Also, anxiety apps with location and microphone permissions have lower ratings. Although it is difficult to infer whether these apps have lower installs or ratings because they evoke users' privacy concerns, these findings may suggest that these three permission types could reduce users' adoption of anxiety apps. We encourage future studies to investigate whether or not the camera, location, and microphone permission requests elicit more concern in users about their privacy and if this further affects their adoptions.

We conducted hierarchical multiple regression analysis to examine the predictive effect of app permission and other influential factors (price, review, and ranking) on app adoption. Our findings show that the price, review, and ranking of anxiety apps remain the dominant predictors of app installation and rating. In another words, app permission does not appear to be an impactful factor on anxiety app adoption, but certain app permissions still have impacts. For instance, two types of permissions: 'in-app purchase' and 'prevent device from sleeping' are positive predictors for both app installs and ratings. Interestingly, our results reveal the mediator effects of price, review, ranking on app permission and app adoption. A salient example is the Wi-Fi connection permission that only showed effects on the installation and rating of apps after adding price, review, and ranking. The location exhibited a similar effect on app rating. Since users' app adoption is an intricate process involving various factors, how informational factors such as price, review, and ranking, mediate the effect of app permissions on app adoption needs further investigation.

6 Limitations

We want to note several limitations in this study. First, we acknowledge that the correlational coefficient between app permission and app adoption is rather weak, although we have enough of a sample size to show the significance. Second, we only examined anxiety apps on Google Play, which may limit our findings to a specific mental health context and app market. Since we did not compare the results of anxiety apps to other kinds of apps (e.g., game, health and fitness), we have no conclusion about whether anxiety apps request more or different app permissions than other kinds of apps request. We recommend that future studies adopt a similar approach and compare the permission requests among mental health apps and other kinds of apps. Furthermore, due to the observational nature of our data, we cannot identify the cause and effect of app permission on users' app adoption. We suggest that future studies conduct empirical work for further investigation on the effect of app permission on mental health app adoption.

7 Conclusion

In this study, we revealed the relationship between app permission and users' anxiety app adoption by analyzing the observational data of apps collected from Google Play. Interestingly, our findings show that anxiety apps with more app permissions have higher installs. Also, app permissions associated with the operating functionality are significantly related to the install and rating of apps, such as the permission to access users' 'in-app purchase', 'camera', and 'location'. We found the mediator effect of app price, review, and ranking on app permission and adoption that still needs further investigation. Overall, this study contributes a general picture of how app permission is connected with mental health app adoption, which is an important step before we can identify which apps may have higher risks of compromising users' information privacy and security.

References

1. Matthews, M., Doherty, G., Coyle, D., Sharry, J.: Designing mobile applications to support mental health interventions. In: Handbook of Research on User Interface Design and Evaluation for Mobile Technology, pp. 635–656. IGI Global (2008)
2. Martínez-Pérez, B., De La Torre-Díez, I., López-Coronado, M.: Privacy and security in mobile health apps: a review and recommendations. J. Med. Syst. 39(1), 181 (2015)

3. George, S.M., Hamilton, A., Baker, R.: Pre-experience perceptions about telemedicine among African Americans and Latinos in South Central Los Angeles. Telemed. e-Health **15** (6), 525–530 (2009)
4. Price, M., Williamson, D., McCandless, R., Mueller, M., Gregoski, M., Brunner-Jackson, B., Treiber, F.: Hispanic migrant farm workers' attitudes toward mobile phone-based telehealth for management of chronic health conditions. J. Med. Internet Res. **15**(4), e76 (2013)
5. Racherla, P., Babb, J.S., Keith, M.J.: Pay-what-you-want pricing for mobile applications: the effect of privacy assurances and social information. In: Conference for Information Systems Applied Research Proceedings, vol. 4, no. 1833, pp. 1–13 (2011)
6. Krasnova, H., Eling, N., Abramova, O., Buxmann, P.: Dangers of 'Facebook Login' for Mobile Apps: Is There a Price Tag for Social Information? (2014)
7. Kelley, P.G., Cranor, L.F., Sadeh, N.: Privacy as part of the app decision-making process. In: Proceedings of the SIGCHI Conference on Human Factors in Computing Systems, pp. 3393–3402. ACM, April 2013
8. Smith, H.J., Milberg, S.J., Burke, S.J.: Information privacy: measuring individuals' concerns about organizational practices. MIS Q. 167–196 (1996)
9. Felt, A.P., Egelman, S., Finifter, M., Akhawe, D., Wagner, D.: How to ask for permission. In USENIX Workshop on Hot Topics in Security (HotSec) (2012)
10. Felt, A.P., Egelman, S., Wagner, D.: I've got 99 problems, but vibration ain't one: a survey of smartphone users' concerns. In: 2nd Annual ACM CCS Workshop on Security and Privacy in Smartphones and Mobile Devices (SPSM) (2012)
11. Felt, A.P., Ha, E., Egelman, S., Haney, A., Chin, E., Wagner, D.: Android permissions: user attention, comprehension, and behavior. In: Symposium on Usable Privacy and Security (SOUPS) (2012)
12. NIMH: Any Anxiety Disorder Among Adults (2016). https://www.nimh.nih.gov/health/statistics/prevalence/any-anxiety-disorder-among-adults.shtml. Archived at: http://www.webcitation.org/6lHXIjlha. Accessed 6 Feb 2017
13. Statista: Number of apps available in leading app stores as of June 2016 (2016). https://www.statista.com/statistics/276623/number-of-apps-available-in-leading-app-stores/. Archived at: http://www.webcitation.org/6lHWw0RUk. Accessed 6 Feb 2017
14. Zhang, B., Xu, H: Privacy nudges for mobile applications: effects on the creepiness emotion and privacy attitudes. In: Proceedings of the 19th ACM Conference on Computer-Supported Cooperative Work & Social Computing, pp. 1676–1690. ACM, February 2016
15. Nikou, S., Mezei, J.: Evaluation of mobile services and substantial adoption factors with Analytic Hierarchy Process (AHP). Telecommun. Policy **37**(10), 915–929 (2013)
16. Kim, G.S., Park, S.B., Oh, J.: An examination of factors influencing consumer adoption of short message service (SMS). Psychol. Mark. **25**(8), 769–786 (2008)
17. Wang, T., Oh, L.B., Wang, K., Yuan, Y.: User adoption and purchasing intention after free trial: an empirical study of mobile newspapers. Inf. Syst. e-Bus. Manag. **11**(2), 189–210 (2013)
18. Luxton, D.D., McCann, R.A., Bush, N.E., Mishkind, M.C., Reger, G.M.: mHealth for mental health: integrating smartphone technology in behavioral healthcare. Prof. Psychol.: Res. Pract. **42**(6), 505 (2011)
19. Xu, H., Teo, H.H., Tan, B.C., Agarwal, R.: The role of push-pull technology in privacy calculus: the case of location-based services. J. Manag. Inf. Syst. **26**(3), 135–174 (2009)
20. Xu, H., Teo, H.H., Tan, B.: Predicting the adoption of location-based services: the role of trust and perceived privacy risk. In: ICIS 2005 Proceedings, p. 71 (2005)
21. Dehling, T., Gao, F., Schneider, S., Sunyaev, A.: Exploring the far side of mobile health: information security and privacy of mobile health apps on iOS and Android. JMIR mHealth uHealth **3**(1), e8 (2015)

22. Dogruel, L., Joeckel, S., Bowman, N.D.: Choosing the right app: an exploratory perspective on heuristic decision processes for smartphone app selection. Mob. Media Commun. **3**(1), 125–144 (2015)
23. Ramo, D.E., Popova, L., Grana, R., Zhao, S., Chavez, K.: Cannabis mobile apps: a content analysis. JMIR mHealth uHealth **3**(3), e81 (2015)
24. American Psychiatric Association: Diagnostic and statistical manual of mental disorders (DSM-5®). American Psychiatric Pub. (2013)
25. Granka, L.A., Joachims, T., Gay, G.: Eye-tracking analysis of user behavior in WWW search. In: Proceedings of the 27th Annual International ACM SIGIR Conference on Research and Development in Information Retrieval, pp. 478–479. ACM, July 2004
26. Sadeh, J.L.B.L.N., Hong, J.I.: Modeling users' mobile app privacy preferences: restoring usability in a sea of permission settings. In: Symposium on Usable Privacy and Security (SOUPS), vol. 40, July 2014
27. Statista: Cumulative number of apps downloaded from the Google Play as of May 2016 (in billions). https://www.statista.com/statistics/281106/number-of-android-app-downloads-from-google-play/. Accessed 6 Feb 2017
28. Google Play: Manifest.Permission. https://developer.android.com/reference/android/Manifest.permission.html. Accessed 6 Feb 2017

"If It's Urgent or It Is Stopping Me from Doing Something, Then I Might Just Go Straight at It": A Study into Home Data Security Decisions

Norbert Nthala[✉] and Ivan Flechais

Department of Computer Science, University of Oxford, Oxford OX1 3QD, UK
{norbert.nthala,ivan.flechais}@cs.ox.ac.uk

Abstract. Data security incidents have led to a wave of security awareness campaigns by public institutions targeted towards the so-called
home user. Despite this rise, studies have shown poor adoption rates
of security measures by the target. In this paper, we conduct a qualitative investigation of 15 home users, analyse the data using Grounded
Theory and present a model of factors of data security decisions made in
the home. We further consolidate the literature on this topic and analyse
our findings against it using meta-synthesis. From this we identify the
critical issues that surround data security in the home environment. We
finally present a consolidated theoretical model for investigating factors
that influence security practices in the home, and suggest future work
based on our findings.

Keywords: Home user · Data security · Decision making · Security-
related behaviours · Grounded theory · Meta-synthesis

1 Introduction

Incidents affecting personal information services and assets regularly hit the
news headlines, and raising security awareness is the most commonly proffered
solution to the widely perceived problem of inadequate security in the home
[5]. Set against a backdrop of government-backed efforts to improve security,
increases in spending on organisational IT security and a greater emphasis on
compliance and data protection, securing the "home user" has received far too
little attention. Despite a real, and growing, series of existing and foreseeable
threats targeting the home user, research thus far has only scratched the surface
of the breadth and depth of the problem domain – not least of which by tacitly
proposing that home users are broadly defined as "not professionals in computing". Furthermore, given that homes are also targeted to enable attacks on third
parties (e.g. DDoS through compromised home devices, attacks on company
data through compromised home computers tunneling into protected company
networks, or attacks aiming to compromise key employees at home), the security
benefits of improving home data security are clear, and yet more needs to be
done to understand how we can better achieve home data security.

© Springer International Publishing AG 2017
T. Tryfonas (Ed.): HAS 2017, LNCS 10292, pp. 123–142, 2017.
DOI: 10.1007/978-3-319-58460-7_9

The use of information technology in households is increasing, and the number of networked devices available to household users is also increasing and likely to continue to do so with the advent of smart cities, wearable computing, and other Internet of Things devices. Networked devices in the home include laptops/PCs, mobile phones, tablets, games consoles, routers, networked cars, smart meters, medical equipment and many more. Home networks can be wired, wireless, or both, and connect one or more household devices to the Internet through local Internet Service Providers (ISP) or through mobile data connections. In 2015, the International Telecommunications Union (ITU) reported that households with a computer in developed countries had increased from 55.5% in 2005 to 80.8% in 2015, while that of developing countries jumped from 14.6% in 2005 to 32.9% in 2015 [10]. ITU further reported that households with Internet access at home increased from 44.7% in 2005 to 81.3% in 2015 for developed countries, and from 8.1% in 2005 to 34.1% in 2015 for developing countries [10].

While organisations manage the security of their data and systems strategically through security policies, the protection of home users is left to the initiative of the users [11]. Home users utilise different online services, each requiring different security behaviour from users (e.g. passwords, tokens, privacy settings, and others). The complexity of these security requirements has led users to devise their own mechanisms and workarounds for managing the security for the online services. And while the number of services and devices that need security is growing, the time, knowledge, and budget that typical home users allocate to securing their data is small, and likely to remain so. Consequently, a large number of exploited vulnerabilities in computing systems involve users of the systems making bad choices [6,16]. Despite efforts by governments and commercial entities to improve the security of cyberspace by raising security awareness to home users, various studies [1–3,9] show that home users still do not adequately apply security controls for their home systems and often ignore or do not act in ways that would keep them secure. Work has been undertaken on how to analyse and improve security awareness, including [4,8], but a larger question remains as to whether awareness is the correct solution to the problem.

Many studies, including [2,11–15], have referred to the concept of 'the home (computer) user' without satisfactorily defining this. Most do not define the concept [2,11–13], and those that do tend to settle on broad generalities, e.g. "the distinguishing characteristic is that the users are not professionals in computing" [15], or "a citizen with varying age and technical knowledge who uses Information Communication Technologies (ICTs) for personal use anywhere outside their work environments" [14]. We argue that home user security is a growing concern that has not received sufficient attention, and that improving home data security needs to start from a more grounded understanding of home users, the context of use in which they operate, and how they make data security decisions.

This study focusses on understanding data security decisions made by home users: factors that influence outcomes of these decisions, common scenarios in which security decisions are made in the home, sources of information to enable decision-making, and sources of support and assistance for decision-making.

This helps to provide clear evidence for future work to improve education, technology, and practices for home data security. This is all the more important in light of the October 2016 attack on Dyn which took down a number of major websites in the USA and is thought to have been enabled by insecure IoT devices in homes.

2   Literature Review

2.1   Understanding the Home

Home users consist of individuals from any demographic, ranging from children, teenagers, parents, working and non-working professionals, retired, elderly, infirm, and disabled individuals, each with different resources, education, skills, capabilities, and interests. To further clarify and define home users, and drawing from the work of Venkatesh [17] and Meshkova et al. [18], we present a model of home computer users that spans three distinct spaces: social, activity, and technological.

Social Space. The social space of home users is complex and has been explored according to Household (people living in one building) and Family (exploring different types of family unit) [19]. To this we add a third category of Neighbourhood and Friends (which encompasses geographical proximity such as housing estates, but also social proximity such as common interest groups, friendships, and other social groupings). This is supported by the study from Ng and Rahim [11] that found that home users are influenced by different factors to practice security, among them family and peer influence. While the importance of individual stakeholders in home security decisions has not been explored, research exploring the role of individuals in the context of security design activities has clearly highlighted the importance of individual involvement, motivation, responsibility and communication in the decision-making process [20].

Activity Space. The activity space aims to represent the type of computer centric pursuits that occur in a home. Different priorities exist in different homes, much determined by the home social space. The activities comprise, but are not limited to, family communications, correspondence, home shopping, remote (online) education, school work, word processing, and entertainment. The services and event of the ontology of the home environment presented in [18] belong to this space.

Technology Space. According to Venkatesh [17], the technological structure of the home is complex and determines the operation of the system of its activities, and the patterns of home interactions relative to its goals. The level of technology is distinct from one home to the next, however this is a crucial space to understand in exploring the issues of data security, as it intimately informs the threat and vulnerability space, and also strongly influences the type and complexity of technical controls.

2.2 Security Behavioural Theories

Several studies have utilised a number of predictive theories to study specific security behaviours of home users. These models are most often extensions of existing social cognitive theories of factors that produce risky behaviour in other decision situations [15]. Prominent among these models are the Theory of Planned Behaviour (TPB) [21], and the Protection Motivation Theory (PMT) [22]. Researchers have sought to explore antecedents from such theories as factors that influence a home user's security behaviour.

When applied to security behaviour, these two predictive theories operate on a general assumption that there are assets which are facing security threats, and that there are security controls available to counter the threats. We call this the security space. TBP considers the intention of a person to be an immediate determinant of an action or a behaviour. The behaviour in this case being applying appropriate security controls. TPB states that intentions are determined by three factors: attitude towards the behaviour, subjective norm (social influence), and perceived behavioural control. Ng and Rahim [11] used decomposed TPB (an extended version of TPB) to investigate the factors that influence a user's intention to practice home computer security. Their study found that both attitude and subjective norms had a significant positive relationship with the intention to practice computer security. However, the study could not clearly identify the relationship between perceived behavioural controls and the intention to practice home computer security due to a number of unexplained differences in the results. In a different study, Lee and Kozar [29] extended TPB with concepts from diffusion of innovations model, and IT ethics and morality to investigate factors affecting an individual's decision to adopt anti-spyware software. Their study found that attitude, subjective norms, perceived behavioural control, and denial of responsibility significantly affected an individual's intention to adopt.

PMT posits two closely related pathways whose balance determines the likelihood of a risky behaviour to occur. The *threat appraisal pathway* compares perceived rewards (intrinsic and extrinsic) with perceived threats (severity and vulnerability) that the behaviour poses. The *coping appraisal pathway* compares coping efficacy (self-efficacy and response efficacy) with perceived response costs of the behaviour. Milne et al. [23] draw upon PMT and social cognitive theory to investigate the extent to which the level of perceived threat and likelihood of threat along with online self-efficacy affect online behaviours. Thus what factors lead consumers to make adaptive and maladaptive responses in the face of privacy and security threats. A national online survey was designed based on these theories and administered to 449 non-students. The researchers found out that self-efficacy plays a key role in a consumer's choice to perform risky online behaviours, and perceived threat and likelihood of threat influence the decision to choose an adaptive or maladaptive behaviour.

Other researchers have however used other approaches, such as qualitative interviews to study security behaviours of home users. Redmiles et al. [7] interviewed 25 participants in investigating where users learn security behaviours, and why users accept or reject different advice. The study reported that users get security advice from sources they trust which include workplace, service providers, IT professionals, family members and friends [7]. The study found that users reject advice due to too much marketing information, and threatening users' privacy. The researchers also indicated users disregard some security roles because they assume somebody is responsible for that. In a similar study, Herley [5] found three reasons that lead to users' rejection of security advice: they are overwhelmed; the benefit is moot in some cases or is perceived to be moot; and claimed benefits are not based on evidence.

3 Methodology

3.1 Grounded Theory

The aim of this study is to elicit data regarding data security decisions made by home users. For this purpose, we conducted semi-structured interviews to get the benefits of using a rigid script of well-defined, ordered questions to control the flow and consistency of the interview, while keeping the interview opened up for both depth and breadth topic exploration [24]. All respondents were asked identical questions in the same sequence, but the interviewer probed inductively on key responses. The questions took into consideration all the three home environment spaces discussed in Sect. 2.1 to ensure the home context was fully explored. We asked questions about participant demographics; devices and services they use; their concerns about data security, and if they have ever experienced a data security breach; what they did/do to secure their data, and who did it; what informs their choice of security measures; their attitude toward data security, largely elicited through specific scenarios; the kind of support they need(ed), and where they seek/sought it; and their expectations about the security of their data.

As the interview data was being collected, it was qualitatively analysed using Grounded Theory [25] to identify significant themes emerging from the data and to inform the next data collection. Due to its theory-building qualitative nature, grounded theory is well-suited to problems where little is already known. This makes it the ideal choice for studying factors and issues that affect the home user data security decision making.

Participants. Fifteen participants from Oxford took part in the study: 9 Male (4 married, 5 single), and 6 Female (2 married, 4 single). Of these, 4 were Asian, 5 White, 4 African, and 2 Black American. Their ages ranged from 18 to 34. The participants were recruited through snowball sampling, with the first set purposefully selected.

Our study was ethically reviewed and approved by the Social Sciences and Humanities Inter-divisional Research Ethics Committee at the University of Oxford.

3.2   Meta-Synthesis

As explained in Sect. 2.2, several studies on the security behaviour of home users have reported varying reasons and factors that influence such behaviour. In this view, we sought to consolidate the literature on this topic, and later compare it with results from our study to identify common elements and attempt to bridge the gaps that exist in the different findings. We used meta-synthesis [26] to achieve this. This is a non-statistical technique used to integrate, evaluate, and interpret the findings of multiple qualitative research studies. The studies may be combined to identify their common core elements and themes. Meta-synthesis involves analysing and synthesising key elements in each study, with the aim of transforming individual findings into new conceptualisations and interpretations.

A conventional literature search was done using different terms such as 'home user', 'home computer user', 'security behaviour', and many more. The databases searched included ACM Digital Library, IEEE Xplore, Compendex, Science Direct, ProQuest, and others. All papers published in English on the subject were included. Papers with a quantitative research focus, such as those using the behavioural theories to conduct surveys, were excluded. However, these excluded papers gave us a lead to the original qualitative papers of the theory employed, which we included in our study. Other relevant literature was identified through an iterative process based on the research papers.

4   Interview Results

Our analysis of security decision-making in the home highlighted four main themes that surround the process (see Fig. 1): **Stimuli** (cues to action), **Support**, **Stakeholders**, and **Context**. We explore these in more detail below:

4.1   Stimuli

The participants outlined the following five different cues that drive their security decisions. All the cues however share one thing in common, security concern.

Security Concern. Home user data security concerns fall into three groups: *Uncertainty*, where the user is not sure about particular security aspects; *Loss*, where the user is concerned about losing either data or some material thing; and *Nuisance*, where the user is concerned about something causing inconvenience or annoyance.

Uncertainty includes issues like not being sure about how secure a user's credentials are with a service provider, who has access to them on the back-end? Should one accept access permission requests from applications? If accepted, what kind of data are the applications accessing in the background? One male participant said:

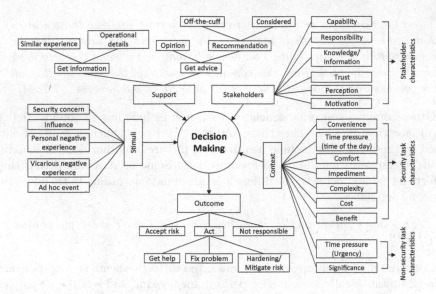

Fig. 1. Home data security decision-making factors model

Like for my android, I am not sure about the permissions. Of course when you install an app, you give it permissions to read your mic, to use your camera, and use your storage. So I don't know to what extent those apps are doing the right thing. Is there a possibility that may be they are viewing my messages without me knowing, so I don't know. That's about all. For android, it's the permissions on the apps. I don't know what they are doing because I know that facebook, for example, has access to my photos. So I don't know how often it accesses my photos. Does it access the photos when am not using the app? And what does it do with my photos? [P3,M]

Loss was noted to be multifaceted with participants referring to both material and non-material loss. Loss of money (which is linked to loss of banking details) from a bank account through unknown transactions, for instance, was a common concern for all participants, with some having experienced this before *(personal negative experience)*. One participant talking about his online banking experience said:

Something happened. That was the time I just stopped. I have been following up with the bank to find out who was removing the money, but because of my job I don't have time. So they have been sending me letters. I just went there and told them I don't need it any more, so cancel it. Mostly I have cash in hand, so I don't bother much. [P2,M]

Some reported having heard about someone's *(vicarious) negative experience* from which they were motivated to act on their security behaviours:

... on the newspaper or whatever, from time to time you read those stories that some people lost their money in the bank and the bank denied the responsibility of controlling... So basically may be someone else withdrew money from the bank, from this person's account, but the bank say that all the process was authorised, 'there is no problem in our process'. [P7, M]

Other common concerns associated with loss include loss of confidentiality, loss of integrity, data loss, data theft, and loss of privacy. Different kinds of data linked to these concerns include health data, pictures, contact details, banking details, communication data, and location data. Some users reported that they perform a trade-off between the different kinds of data according to their specific needs, for instance:

... So I don't quite mind to share location, but I don't share my photos. [P14, F]

Concerns under nuisance include unwanted advertisements sent to personal address, nuisance calls, poor device performance, spam, and scam. One participant said:

I thought they were just gonna try and steal my data so they could call me all the time with nuisance calls, or they might just send a virus across, or you know use the data to find out about me and send me specific advertising things I don't like. [P10, F]

As can be seen here, security decisions, influenced by a concern, arise in a number of ways, including personal or vicarious negative experience, an ad hoc encounter such as a pop-up, or based on social influence, as can be seen below:

Normally, if I get a pop-up saying that isn't secure, I usually stop. [P15, M]

I'm only concerned because people think I should be concerned. I do understand the risks, but so far, like my bank account has never been hacked... Colleagues that I work with, the media say we should all be concerned about our privacy, and that's it really. [P4, F]

However, our analysis revealed that home users respond differently to different cues. Those who have had a negative experience put in much more effort to avoid similar or other breaches compared to those who are socially influenced. One respondent who had not experienced a security breach before said:

I mean it's like being concerned about not being chased by a dog that you have never seen. [P12, F]

4.2 Stakeholders

The analysis brought to light the importance of understanding the stakeholders who are crucial in ensuring data security in the home environment. These include all who play a role in home data security and/or in security decision-making. Security responsibility in the home lies with two distinct groups of stakeholders (see Fig. 2): **informal stakeholders**, composed of the social space in the home environment; and **business stakeholders**, composed of service providers, vendors, governments, and others.

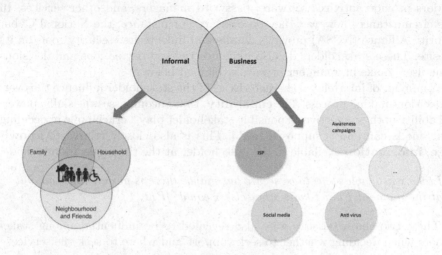

Fig. 2. Home data security stakeholders

As depicted in Fig. 2, the social spaces in the informal sector can overlap (i.e. family can exist within one household or many, within one neighbourhood or multiple; households may contain families but do not have to, etc.). These differences influence the extent to which individuals become involved, motivated, and responsible for data security activities and decisions. For instance, just to quote some participants:

We always try to consult each other about security issues. As I'm an expert, I can differentiate between security and privacy, but my wife doesn't. So we look at those security issues in general... what I try to do is to try to explain the potential risks, and leave my partner to make a decision herself. [P5, M]

My mum will sometimes ring me and say I have got a text message that says I have won a mountain bike, and I will be like you should just delete that because it's just spam. Or she had once where it said she had entered a competition to win a car and she needed to follow the following link to verify her details. And she rang me up and say I haven't been to the airport, why am I getting these messages. I explained to her that people just got your data from somewhere, just delete it. [P4, F]

My supervisor is my security lecturer, is the one who recommended it. So I followed her advice... We had a short chat, and she explained how it works, and why it's important. Then I bought the idea.[P3, M]

The stakeholders in the business sector however frequently operate independently of each other. For instance, governments provide awareness campaigns; vendors provide antivirus software, password managers, and other services. In rare circumstances however, they do overlap. For instance, the National Cyber Security Alliance (NCSA) provides details and links to free security tools on its website. These stakeholders do also influence the security actions and decisions home users make in a number of ways explained below.

A number of interrelated characteristics of the stakeholder influence the overall decision-making process. The **capability**, that encompasses the skills, power, and ability of the respective responsible stakeholder play a crucial role in deciding what one is can and is supposed to do. This is also closely related to **knowledge/information** available to the stakeholder at the time a decision is made.

I take reasonable steps to be secure but maybe there is more I could do, but at the moment I don't know what else I could. [P11, F]

These two characteristics were also revealed to be influential among stakeholders when deciding whether to seek support and where to seek the service.

... usually I come and check with ... in IT. I tell him that I was trying to install this application, this popped up. I have tried Googling what it was or check if it is fine, but couldn't find anything. Do you think it will be ok? [P1, M]

I would probably have to read a bit more, or may be call someone who has a bit more experience than me, and see what they suggest. Because am not an expert so I would call someone who is much more familiar with IT related things. [P8, M]

I told you my friend, ... , because he is a Computer Engineer, mostly he has to put some security. [P2, M]

Another important characteristic in security decision-making is **responsibility**. The participants reported having considered whether they are responsible for doing a particular action or not. For some actions, stakeholders in the home believe someone, either among their social space or in the business sector, is responsible for keeping their data secure. Asked about who they think is responsible for implementing what they expect to be a good level of security, some participants said:

If it's a corporation [the service provider], a big company, then the government should be responsible. [P6, M]

would say it could be apple, it could be google I guess. When they allow those developers to upload their product to apple store or google store, I think they should be responsible for the security. [P7, M]

I guess [service providers should] limit the number of people that have access to the data. And for example on Facebook, I don't want any of my own personal information shared with advertisers. Yeah, just to not share personal information with advertisers or second hand parties or things like that. [P9, F]

So both parties. Both the providers of services and also the users of the services. The providers should ensure that the data of the users is secure enough that it is not likely to end in random people, but also important that the user inputs like good passwords, is able to make sure that whatever setting that they are in is also secure enough for them to use the service. [P12, F]

Another important influential characteristic about stakeholders is their perception. Users reported to make security decisions based on brand recognition. Well-known service providers or tools are considered to be more secure (**trustworthy**), and therefore require little to no attention. One participant said:

But what I believe is that I only install apps from the big companies. I don't install apps from private developers. So that would mean that I somehow trust those big companies, and usually if anything goes wrong, it doesn't affect only me. It affects a lot of people. [P7,M]

Apart from trusting service provider and/or tools/services, **trust** also extends to a source of security information. This includes colleagues, IT professionals, family members, peers, and websites providing the information. This comprises a combination of both informal and business stakeholders. Some participants said on this:

I'm slightly more confident with those that haven't got hacked yet, so I'm more trusting of them. [P1, M]

The most trusted data for me is from the service provider, rather than others. [P5, M]

Usually I look at the developers in case of software. Well are they credible, or at least big developers or they are open source developers well regarded in the community, then I will trust. [P6, M]

The last characteristic of stakeholders that plays a role in security decision-making in the home is **motivation**. Our analysis revealed a number of ways that motivate users to make security decisions or to carry out security actions. Among these are influence from the peers and the media, perceived capability, perceived responsibility, and availability of security information through well known channels among others.

4.3 Support

The results showed that home users seek different kinds of support, from different sources based on the purpose. Three different types of support have been identified: **Provision of labour**, which involves provision of actual security work; **information provision**, which involves sharing experiences and/or operational details of some security tool for example; and **Advice**, which involves the provision of an opinion, an off-the-cuff recommendation, or a considered recommendation. Based on the context, users need either information or advice to help them make a decision or to act. The information can pertain to operational details, such as instructions to remove a virus from a device. A participant said:

Yeah, just to be able to use it and how it works, and what I should do and not just have this installed on my computer... [P14, F]

At other times, users seek to learn from someone who has had a similar experience and how they tackled it. This normally applies to experiences of those one is close to and trusts. One participant said:

I have a few friends who do IT and know more, kind of comfortable with more complex things of computers. Sometimes I ask them, but most of the times it's about whether they have experienced the same or if they have done the same thing. So it's not always the specialists. Sometimes am even [more] competent [than the friends I ask] though. It's just if they have ever downloaded an app or something some other time, if they have seen any issues. [P1, M]

In addition to information, home users also seek advice from trusted stakeholders (colleagues, IT Professionals, relations and peers, and websites). Advice comes in two forms; first as an opinion, where the advice helps the user make their own decision. For instance:

It's more of an opinion. I want to ask someone because sometimes there is a tendency to overlook certain things. [P1, M]

Second as a recommendation, which can be further divided into two. An off-the-cuff recommendation does not involve much effort from the provider of the recommendation. The provider simply gives advice from s/he knows. For instance:

Usually which antivirus is good? Is it ok if someone installed this kind of software? [P15, M]

Asked what kind of support she sought online, one participant said:

I just wanted a recommendation of what would be the most effective thing to do. [P9, F]

A considered recommendation requires the provider to put in extra effort to have a clear understanding of the problem in question before giving the recommendation. Asked what they would do in a scenario where someone they gave advice to suffered a breach, one participant said:

> I would just go back to what I said before and see what the problem is, and then investigate ways to try and solve the problem. I would probably have to read a bit more, or maybe call someone who has a bit more experience than me, and see what they suggest. [P8, M]

The third and final type of support commonly sought in the home is labour. Users who perceive themselves as not capable of acting on security issues turn to trusted and skilled stakeholders for technical help. This is usually sought from colleagues, IT professionals, relations, and peers. Some participants said:

> There is a friend who usually comes here. Mostly he is the one. If the laptop has a virus, I give it to him. He just wipes it and upgrades it again. [P2, M]

> Yes, for my grandmother... She is not very competent when it comes to technological applications, or computers or anything of that nature... So I just had to install something to scan her emails to make sure there are no malicious things in there. [P8, M]

> I usually check my mum's computer every now and again. Check if it's looking alright, especially if she says she has had some pop-ups and things, to see if there is anything I can do to help her out. And sometimes my partner will have a look at it as well to see if there is a bit more we are able to do. [P4, F]

4.4   Context

The context in which a security decision is made has two characterising categories; **security task characteristics**, which defines issues related to the required security task that stakeholders take into consideration when making security decisions, and **non-security task characteristics**, which relates to issues about the primary task that a user is required to do.

One influential theme on security task characteristics is **convenience**. Users weigh the convenience of available security countermeasures against the importance of their activities. If functionality is preferred to security, users are willing to bypass or ignore recommended secure behaviours. Talking about two-factor authentication, one participant said:

> ... the time that I'm working where there is no network, I can't login to gmail. So it's a big disadvantage. [P11, M]

Next, **time pressure (time of the day)** has been noted to influence the outcome of security decisions made in the home. This has been shown to influence what a user would do when faced with a security decision at a particular time. One such scenario is:

> There was something that was preventing me from going on a website and I was pretty sure it was fine. It wanted me to install something. I wasn't convinced I actually needed to install it. It was actually crashing the site when I wasn't installing it, but this was in the evening and I really wanted to get this done. [P1, M]

Comfort is another issue taken into consideration on the subject at hand. Home users care about the security of their data, and take actions to keep it secure. However, they would like to do what they want comfortably and not let security overheads get in their way. As one way of ensuring this, they tend to differentiate between important services and those that are less secure. In doing so, much effort is put on securing the most important services. One of the participants echoed their experience:

> It is much more comfortable if you can save your password in the browser. Well, I have been tempted to do that you know – just save it in the browser – I just don't need to retype it over and over again. I occasionally do that for something not so important: accounts like twitter; but for something much more important like bank account or email, I will never save it there. [P13, M]

Impediment: If a security-related task stands in the way of users in achieving their primary task, we found that users weigh the two and do a trade-off.

> If it's urgent or it is stopping me from doing something, then I might just go straight at it. [P1, M]

The **complexity** of a security task in relation to the stakeholder's capability influences what s/he can do or decide. In most cases, there is an interplay of the different factors that influence the outcome of a security decision. For instance, complexity would be weighed against capability, and availability of required support in cases where the stakeholder is not capable of undertaking a decision or action.

> I read online that we should delete cookies to keep our data secure, but I don't know how to do it and there is no one to do it for me at home. So I just accept the risk, and maybe some hackers have already stolen my data. [P14, F]

Cost and **Benefit:** The cost of performing a security task includes time, effort, financial resources. These are usually weighed against the expected reward after performing the required action. Asked about seeking information to inform security decision in a particular scenario, one participant said:

I think it's only a 3 seconds decision, I don't spend any more time on this. So just to look at what they wrote and then make a decision. [P7, M]

All but four of the participants shared the idea that they installed a free antivirus to keep viruses in check. They did not care much about having a virus at some point because they could always have someone clean their devices, which they state is to different from losing money in the bank.

The non-security characteristics that come to users' attention in light of security include **time pressure (Urgency)**, which revolves around the time constraints for completing the primary task, for instance

... I urgently wanted an Internet connection to do some work. I connected to a network which had the same name as our usual library network and required the same login details, but a warning showed up saying it was not a secure connection. Since I wanted the Internet badly, I just ignored the warning and connected. When I finished working, I realised someone had been reading my unread emails. [P11, F]

Another consideration is the *significance* of the primary task. Users consider the importance of what they are doing or the importance of what they are looking for. They are ready to trade security for something else in order to achieve what they want if the situation calls for it.

It depends on how much I want to use the thing. If it's just a curiosity thing, and something flashes, I just close it down. If it's something am actively looking for, I might go back out and look on other stuff to find out if this is the only place I can find it. Then I go ahead and do it. [P1, M]

... it did this with one website, but I knew that it was OK. So I kept browsing. It was always like 'this website is not secure, are you sure you want to continue?'. I did so because I think it was something for the University. Usually if they say this, if it's not important then I leave it. [P10, F]

5   Analysis of Interview Results Against Literature

As discussed in Sect. 2.2, the two main theories that have been used in studying the security behaviour of home users are TPB and PMT.

One clear area that is not in covered by either theory is the situation where users state that they do not feel responsible for performing a particular behaviour. This has been reported by two independent field studies: our study and Redmiles et al. [7]. To make sense of this phenomenon, we turn to the widely used Triangle Model of Responsibility (TMR) [27]. In security studies, though not explicitly stated, TMR comes into play in the study by Blyth [28]. In this study, the researcher developed a socio-technical model of trust that utilises the concepts of responsibilities and roles so as to link the technical and social aspects of trust into a single inductive logical framework.

TMR states that in order to make evaluative reckonings concerning responsibility, one must have information related to prescriptions (rules and norms that guide an agent's conduct), an event (the action in question), and identity (the agent's role and abilities). TMR also seeks to understand if there is connectedness between the agent and the event due to the agent's role and perception of control. Interdisciplinary studies have also shown that perceived control is directly and significantly related to responsibility. Those who perceive the capability to perform an action are more likely to feel internally obligated, and hence motivated, to produce positive outcomes [30]. We argue that understanding the three antecedents from TMR, together with the factors from TPB and PMT, can give us a more complete understanding of the home data security context.

Security decisions and behaviours are executed in a world of risk and uncertainty. We noted during our analysis of the interviews and as can be seen in Fig. 1, that participants frequently referred to the concept of understanding the risk, and in some cases going further to accept the risk. Studies and theories such as risk homeostasis claim that individuals adjust their behaviours in response to changing variables to keep what they perceive as a constant accepted level of risk. Pearman [31] explored home-user computer security behaviour and concluded that risk compensation occurs. Adams [32,33] explains the notion of risk compensation by presenting a risk thermostat. He claims that individuals execute a balancing behaviour between their propensity to take risks (risk appetite) and perceived danger (risk perception), where risk propensity is determined by perceived rewards, whereas accidents (negative experiences) influence perceived danger.

We consolidate all these concepts from the different theories and models from literature and our model in Fig. 1, and present a breakdown of the different factors that affect home data security decisions. Three general categories of Motivation, Capability, and Context are complemented by perception factors (see Fig. 3). In turn, capability and contextual factors influence a home user's motivation to practice security behaviours.

It is important to note that there are two dimensions of responsibility: *perceived responsibility*, which is presented by TMR referring to individual responsibility; and *actual responsibility*, where users fully understand their role. For instance, our study identified stakeholders in the home environment who make decisions and/or carry out security tasks on behalf of others (who are not capable), which presents an understanding of the actual responsibility that one has towards the others. This included parents/guardians making data security decisions on behalf of their children, and competent children/nephews/nieces deciding on behalf of their parents or grand parents.

From this understanding of the home data security environment, we develop a consolidated theoretical model that can be used to investigate factors that influence home data security decisions and behaviours (see Fig. 4).

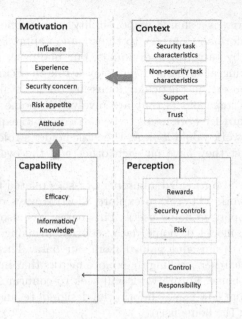

Fig. 3. Home data security environment

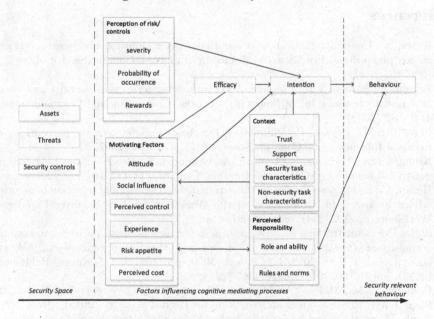

Fig. 4. Consolidated model of home data security behaviour

6   Conclusion and Future Work

Home users are concerned about the security of their data, and do not deliberately ignore security advice or choose to behave insecurely. Our study reveals

that home data security is a shared responsibility among different stakeholders, both business and informal. Contrary to the common approach of investigating home data security by targeting individuals, our findings suggest adopting a broad approach looking at all issues that play a role in security decisions and behaviours of home users, in particular focussing on the stakeholders and the context. A model of stakeholders that are involved in home data security has been presented, but further work needs to be carried out to explore this model in greater detail. Such work would look at the stakeholder's role, level of involvement, and the impact they have on each other and the overall data security practice in the home.

Our findings have also revealed a number of issues related to support. Building on this, future work will seek to explore effective ways of delivering more tailored kinds of support to home users. This paper has also presented a consolidated theoretical model of home data security, bringing together existing models informed by the insights gained from our data. This presents a good starting point for researchers seeking to explore factors that influence data security decisions in the home. Future work will seek to confirm and/or expand on this model, and explore how it may inform the design of technology and security approaches targeting the home user.

References

1. Aytes, K., Connolly, T.: Computer security, risky computing practices: a rational choice perspective. In: Advanced Topics in End User Computing, vol. 4, p. 257 (2005)
2. Bryant, P., Furnell, S.M., Phippen, A.D.: Improving protection, security awareness amongst home users. In: Advances in Networks, Computing and Communications 4, p. 182 (2008)
3. Furnell, S.M., Bryant, P., Phippen, A.D.: Assessing the security perceptions of personal Internet users. Comput. Secur. 26(5), 410–417 (2007)
4. Kumaraguru, P., Sheng, S., Acquisti, A., Cranor, L.F., Hong, J.: Teaching Johnny not to fall for phish. ACM Trans. Internet Technol. (TOIT) 10(2), 7 (2010)
5. Herley, C.: So long, no thanks for the externalities: the rational rejection of security advice by users. In: Proceedings of the Workshop on New Security Paradigms Workshop, pp. 133–144. ACM (2009)
6. Styles, M.: Constructing positive influences for user security decisions to counter corporate or state sponsored computer espionage threats. In: Marinos, L., Askoxylakis, I. (eds.) HAS 2013. LNCS, vol. 8030, pp. 197–206. Springer, Heidelberg (2013). doi:10.1007/978-3-642-39345-7_21
7. Redmiles, E.M., Malone, A., Mazurek, M.L.: I Think They're Trying To Tell Me Something: Advice Sources and Selection for Digital Security (2015)
8. Nouh, M., et al.: Social information leakage: effects of awareness and peer pressure on user behavior. In: Tryfonas, T., Askoxylakis, I. (eds.) HAS 2014. LNCS, vol. 8533, pp. 352–360. Springer, Cham (2014). doi:10.1007/978-3-319-07620-1_31
9. Mendes, M.S., Furtado, E., Militao, G., Castro, M.F.: Hey, I have a problem in the system: who can help me? An investigation of facebook users interaction when facing privacy problems. In: Tryfonas, T., Askoxylakis, I. (eds.) HAS 2015. LNCS, vol. 9190, pp. 391–403. Springer, Cham (2015). doi:10.1007/978-3-319-20376-8_35

10. ITU. Itu world telecommunication/ict indicators database (2016). http://www.itu. int/en/ITU-D/Statistics/Pages/stat/default.aspx. Accessed 16 Apr 2016
11. Ng, B.-Y., Rahim, M.: A socio-behavioral study of home computer users' intention to practice security. In: PACIS Proceedings, p. 20 (2005)
12. Rao, U.H., Pati, B.P.: Study of internet security threats among home users. In: Fourth International Conference on Computational Aspects of Social Networks (CASoN), pp. 217–221. IEEE (2012)
13. Anderson, C.L., Agarwal, R.: Practicing safe computing: a multimedia empirical examination of home computer user security behavioral intentions. MIS Q. **34**(3), 613–643 (2010)
14. Kritzinger, E., von Solms, S.H.: Cyber security for home users: a new way of protection through awareness enforcement. Comput. Secur. **29**(8), 840–847 (2010)
15. Howe, A.E., Ray, I., Roberts, M., Urbanska, M., Byrne, Z.: The psychology of security for the home computer user. In: IEEE Symposium on Security and Privacy (SP), pp. 209–223. IEEE (2012)
16. Rader, E., Wash, R.: Identifying patterns in informal sources of security information. J. Cybersecur. **1**(1), 121–144 (2015)
17. Venkatesh, A.: A Conceptualization of the household/technology interaction. In: NA - Advances in Consumer Research, vol. 12, pp. 189–194. Association for Consumer Research, Provo (1985)
18. Meshkova, E., Riihijarvi, J., Mahonen, P., Kavadias, C.: Modeling the home environment using ontology with applications in software configuration management. In: International Conference on Telecommunications, ICT 2008, pp. 1–6. IEEE, June 2008
19. Hammel, E.A., Laslett, P.: Comparing household structure over time and between cultures. Comp. Stud. Soc. Hist. **16**, 73–109 (1974). Cambridge University Press
20. Flechais, I., Sasse, M.A.: Stakeholder involvement, motivation, responsibility, communication: how to design usable security in e-science. Int. J. Hum.-Comput. Stud. **67**, 281–296 (2009). Elsevier
21. Ajzen, I.: From intentions to actions: a theory of planned behavior. In: Kuhl, J., Beckmann, J. (eds.) Action Control. SSSP, pp. 11–39. Springer, Heidelberg (1985)
22. Rogers, R.W.: A protection motivation theory of fear appeals and attitude change1. J. Psychol. **91**(1), 93–114 (1975)
23. Milne, G.R., Labrecque, L.I., Cromer, C.: Toward an understanding of the online consumer's risky behavior and protection practices. J. Consum. Aff. **43**(3), 449–473 (2009)
24. Lazar, J., Feng, J.H., Hochheiser, H.: Research Methods in Human-Computer Interaction. Wiley, Hoboken (2010)
25. Glaser, B.G., Strauss, A.L.: Strategies for Qualitative Research. Transaction Publishers, Piscataway (2009)
26. Walsh, D., Downe, S.: Meta-synthesis method for qualitative research: a literature review. J. Adv. Nurs. **50**(2), 204–211 (2005)
27. Schlenker, B.R., Britt, T.W., Pennington, J., Murphy, R., Doherty, K.: The triangle model of responsibility. Psychol. Rev. **101**(4), 632 (1994)
28. Blyth, A.: Responsibility modelling and its application trust management. In: Tryfonas, T. (ed.) HAS 2016. LNCS, vol. 9750, pp. 114–127. Springer, Cham (2016). doi:10.1007/978-3-319-39381-0_11
29. Lee, Y., Kozar, K.A.: An empirical investigation of anti-spyware software adoption: a multitheoretical perspective. Inf. Manag. **45**(2), 109–119 (2008)

30. Fishman, E.J.: With great control comes great responsibility: The relationship between perceived academic control, student responsibility, and self-regulation. Br. J. Educ. Psychol. **84**(4), 685–702 (2014)
31. Pearman, S.: Risk compensation in home-user computer security behavior: a mixed-methods exploratory study. Poster presented at SOUPS, Colorado, USA, June 2016
32. Adams, J.: Risk compensation in cities at risk. In: Joffe, H., Rossetto, T., Adams, J. (eds.) Cities at Risk. ANTHR, pp. 25–44. Springer, Netherlands (2013). doi:10.1007/978-94-007-6184-1_3
33. Adams, J.: Risk. University College Press, London (1995). ISBN 1-85728-067-9 (HB), ISBN 1-85728-068-7 (PB)

Assessing the Impact of Affective Feedback on End-User Security Awareness

Lynsay A. Shepherd$^{(\boxtimes)}$, Jacqueline Archibald,
and Robert Ian Ferguson

School of Arts, Media and Computer Games,
Abertay University, Dundee DD1 1HG, UK
{lynsay.shepherd,j.archibald,i.ferguson}@abertay.ac.uk

Abstract. A lack of awareness regarding online security behaviour can leave users and their devices vulnerable to compromise. This paper highlights potential areas where users may fall victim to online attacks, and reviews existing tools developed to raise users' awareness of security behaviour. An ongoing research project is described, which provides a combined monitoring solution and affective feedback system, designed to provide affective feedback on automatic detection of risky security behaviour within a web browser. Results gained from the research conclude an affective feedback mechanism in a browser-based environment, can promote general awareness of online security.

Keywords: End-user security behaviours · Usable security · Affective feedback · User · Monitoring techniques · User feedback · Security awareness

1 Introduction

Risky behaviour exhibited by the end-user may place devices at risk, despite the widespread availability of security tools [1]. This has become a growing concern owing to the reliance on the internet for online banking, e-commerce transactions, consumption of media, and the maintenance of social ties. This paper describes an approach whereby the concept of affective feedback is applied to the domain of a browser-based environment via the use of an extension. The extension has been developed in an attempt to educate users regarding online security, with the end-goal of raising security awareness.

2 Background

Security measures on devices are often seen as restrictive and obtrusive by end-users, potentially limiting users' ability to perform tasks. To circumvent these measures, users may engage in behaviours which are deemed to be risky, placing their devices at risk of compromise.

This section explores previous research, highlighting risky security behaviours users may inadvertently engage in, and perception of risk. Previous attempts at

T. Tryfonas (Ed.): HAS 2017, LNCS 10292, pp. 143–159, 2017
DOI: 10.1007/978-3-319-58460-7_10

educating the end-user are discussed, before proposing the concept of affective feedback as a possible method to educate the end-user.

2.1 Risky Security Behaviour

What constitutes risky behaviour is not necessarily obvious to all end-users and can be difficult to recognise. In the context of a browser-based environment there are multiple examples of behaviour which could be perceived as risky, e.g., creating weak passwords/sharing passwords with colleagues [2, 3], downloading data from unsafe websites [4] or interacting with a website containing coding vulnerabilities [5].

Attempts have been made to categorise behaviours displayed by users which could be classified as risky, including a 2005 paper by Stanton et al. [2]. Following interviews with both security experts and IT experts, and a study involving end-users in the US, across a range of professions, a taxonomy of 6 behaviours was defined: intentional destruction, detrimental misuse, dangerous tinkering, naïve mistakes, aware assurance and basic hygiene.

Padayachee [6] discussed compliant security behaviours whilst investigating if some users had a predisposition to adhering to security behaviour. A taxonomy developed highlighted elements which have the potential to influence security behaviours in users i.e. extrinsic motivation, identification, awareness and organisational commitment. The paper acknowledges the taxonomy does not present a complete overview of all possible motivational factors regarding compliance with security policies. Despite this, it may provide a basis as to how companies could start to improve security education of employees.

Weak passwords are associated with poor security behaviour and a trade-off exists between the usability of passwords and the level of security they provide [3]. Whilst exploring the issue of security hygiene, Stanton et al. [2] touched on the subject of passwords noting that 27.9% of participants wrote their passwords down and 23% revealed their passwords to colleagues Others have explored the usability of passwords and have acknowledged the difficulties end-users can experience in choosing a password whereby it was determined "*length requirements alone are not sufficient for usable and secure passwords*" [7].

Another risky behaviour category relates to how users perceive technology flaws, e.g. vulnerability to XSS attacks or session hijacking. Social engineering can also be considered to fall into this category: e.g. an attacker could potentially clone a profile on a social networking site and utilise the information to engineer an attack against a target (e.g. via a malicious link) [5]. Such attacks can be facilitated by revealing too much personal information on social networking sites [8].

A paper by Milne et al. [9] also investigated risky behaviours and compared this with self-efficacy. The paper concludes that depending on the demographic and the self-efficacy of the end-user, different types of behaviour are exhibited online. 449 people participated in the web-based study. During the survey, participants were asked if they had engaged in specific risky behaviours online. These suggestions were drawn from previous research into risky behaviours [10, 11].

Specific behaviours users were asked about in the survey included the use of private email addresses to register for contests on websites, selecting passwords consisting of dictionary words, and accepting unknown friends on social networking sites. The most common risky behaviour which participants admitted to was allowing the computer to save passwords: 56% of participants admitted to this.

Whilst there has been a number of attempts to categorise risky security behaviours, users may also exhibit a lack of perception regarding risk.

2.2 Perception of Risk

A number of research papers have explored techniques to gauge the perception of risk. Farahmand et al. [12] explored the possibility of using a psychometric model originally developed by Fischoff et al. in 1978 [13] in conjunction with questionnaires, allowing a user to reflect on their actions and gauge their perception, providing a qualitative overview.

Takemura [14] also used questionnaires when investigating factors determining the likelihood of workers complying with information security policies defined within a company, in an attempt to measure perception of risk. Participants were asked a hypothetical question regarding whether or not they would implement an anti-virus solution on their computer if there was a risk of being infected by a virus. Results revealed that 52.7% of users would implement an antivirus solution if the risk was only 1% however, 3% of respondents still refused to implement antivirus, even when the risk was at 99%. This displays a wide range of attitudes towards risk perception.

San-José and Rodriguez [15] used a multimodal approach to measure perception of risk. In a study of over 3000 households with PCs connected to the internet, users were given an antivirus program to install which scanned the machines on a monthly basis. The software was supplemented by quarterly questionnaires, allowing levels of perception to be measured and compared with virus scan results. Users were successfully monitored and results showed that the antivirus software created a false sense of security and they were unaware of how serious certain risks could be.

In a different study, Hill and Donaldson [16] proposed a methodology to integrate models of behaviour and perception. The research attempted to assess the perception of security the system administrator possessed. It also created a trust model, reducing the threat from malicious software. The methodology engaged system administrators whilst developing the threat modelling process, and quantified risk of threats, essentially creating a triage system to deal with issues.

Understanding the level of risk perception a user possesses can help identify the best methods to educate users regarding security behaviour.

2.3 Tools to Educate End-Users

Since there is the potential for end-users to inadvertently engage in behaviours deemed risky, many tools have been developed to help users.

Furnell et al. [17] conducted a study in 2006, to gain an insight into how end-users deal with passwords. The survey found that 22% of participants said they lacked security awareness, with 13% of people admitting they required security training. Participants also found browser security dialogs confusing and in some cases, misunderstood the warnings they were provided with. The majority of participants considered themselves as above average in terms of their understanding of technology, yet many struggled with basic security.

Much of the research conducted into keeping users safe online, educating them about risky security behaviour revolves around phishing attacks. Various solutions have been developed to gauge how to educate users about the dangers of phishing attacks, with the view that education will reduce engagement in risky security behaviours.

Dhamija and Tygar [18] proposed a method to enable users to distinguish between spoofed websites and genuine sites. A Firefox extension was developed providing users with a trusted window in which to enter login details. A remote server generated a unique image used to customise the web page the user is visiting, whilst the browser detects the image and displays it in the trusted window e.g. as a background image on the page. Content from the server is authenticated via the use of the secure Remote Password Protocol. If the images match, the website is genuine and provides a simple way for a user to verify the authenticity of the website.

Sheng et al. [19] tried a different approach to reducing risky behaviour, gamifying the subject of phishing with a tool named Anti-Phishing Phil. The game involves a fish named Phil who has to catch worms, avoiding the worms, on the end of fisher- men's hooks (these are the phishing attempts). The study compared 3 approaches to teaching users about phishing: playing the Anti-Phishing Phil game, reading a tutorial developed or reading existing online information. After playing the game, 41% of participants viewed the URL of the web page, checking if it was genuine. The game produced some unwanted results in that participants became overly cautious, producing a number of false-positives during the experimental phase.

PhishGuru is another training tool designed by Kumaraguru et al. [20] to discourage people from revealing information in phishing attacks. When a user clicks on a link in a suspicious email, they are presented with a cartoon message, warning them of the dangers of phishing, and how they can avoid becoming a victim. The cartoon proved to be effective: participants retained the information after 28 days didn't cause participants to become overly cautious.

Similarly, an Android app called NoPhish has been developed to educate users about phishing on mobile devices [21]. The game features multiple levels where users are presented with a URL and are asked if is a legitimate link or a phishing attempt. In a study conducted after playing the game, participants gave significantly more correct answers when asked about phishing. A further long-term study was conducted 5 months later. The long-term outcomes showed participants still performed well however, their overall performance decreased.

Besmer et al. [22] acknowledged that various applications may place users at risk by revealing personal information. A tool was developed and tested on Facebook to present a simpler way of informing the user about who could view their information. A prototype user interface highlighted the information the site required, optional in- formation, the profile data the user had provided and the percentage of the users' friends who could see the information entered. The study showed that those who were already interested in protecting their information found the interface useful in viewing how applications handled the data.

In addition to security tools which have been developed to target privacy issues on social networking sites, studies have also focused on more general warning tools for the web. A Firefox extension developed by Maurer [23] attempts to provide alert dialogs when users are entering sensitive data such as credit card information. The extension seeks to raise security awareness, providing large JavaScript dialogs to warn users, noting that the use of certain colours made the user feel more secure.

More recently, Volkamer et al. [24] developed a Firefox Add-On, called PassSec in attempt to help users detect websites which provided insecure environments for entering a password. The extension successfully raised security awareness and significantly reduced the number of insecure logins.

Despite the number of tools created to help protect users online, users continue to engage in risky security behaviour. The tools developed span a number of years, indicating users still require security education. Therefore, this suggests that a different approach is needed when conveying information to end-users. Ongoing research is described and explores the use of affective feedback as a suitable method of educating the end-user, raising security awareness.

2.4   Affective Feedback

In terms of computing, this is defined as *"computing that relates to, arises from, or deliberately influences emotions"* [25]. Types of affective feedback include, specific text or phrases, and avatars with subtle facial cues. Such feedback has previously been beneficial in educational environments [26–28].

Several methods can be employed to inform the user that they are exhibiting risky behaviour. Ur et al. [29] investigated ways in which feedback could be given to users, in the context of aiding a user in choosing a more secure password. Research conducted found that users could be influenced to increase their password security if terms such as "weak" were used to describe their current attempt. In the research, colour was also used as a factor to provide feedback to users. When test subjects were entering passwords into the system, a bar meter was shown next to the input field. Depending upon the complexity of the password, the meter displayed a scale ranging from green/blue for a good/strong password, to red, for a simplistic, easy to crack password. Affective properties of colour were highlighted by Osgood and Adams in 1973 [30], and colours such as red signify danger in Western culture. Data gathered from the experiments showed that the meters also had an effect on users, prompting them to increase system security by implementing stronger passwords.

Multimedia content such as the use of colour and sound can also be used to provide feedback to the user. In a game named "Brainchild" developed by McDarby et al. [26], users must gain control over their bio-signals by relaxing. In an attempt to help users relax, an affective feedback mechanism has been implemented whereby the sounds, colours and dialogues used provides a calming mechanism.

Textual information provided via the GUI can be used to communicate feedback to the user. Dehn and Van Mulken [31] conducted an empirical review of ways in which animated agents could interact with users. They provided a comparison between the role of avatars and textual information in human-computer interaction. It was hypothesised that textual information provided more direct feedback to users however, avatars could be used to provide more subtle pieces of information via gestures or eye contact. Ultimately it was noted multimodal interaction could provide users with a greater level of communication with the computer system.

Previous research has indicated that affective feedback could be utilised when aiding users in considering their security behaviour online, since it can detect and help users alter their internal states [26]. Work conducted by Robison et al. [27] used avatars in an intelligent tutoring system to provide support to users, noting that such agents have to decide whether to intervene when a user is working, to provide affective feedback.

Hall et al. [28] concurs with the notion of using avatars to provide affective feedback to users, indicating that they influence the emotional state of the end-user. Avatars were deployed in a personal social and health education environment, to educate children about the subject of bullying. Studies showed that the avatars produced an empathetic effect in children, indicating that the same type of feedback could potentially be used to achieve the same result in adults.

2.5 The Relationship Between Security Behavior, Education, and Affective Feedback

Although there's a number of security tools available which have been designed to help the end-user, people are still falling victim to online attacks. This suggests that perhaps a different approach is required. The ongoing research discussed in the following sections offers the application of affective feedback in the context of a browser-based environment, in attempt to raise the security awareness of end-users.

3 Methodology

The work developed as part of the research project proposes the use of a browser extension to automatically detect risky security behaviour. Previous research has indicated affective feedback has the potential to serve as a suitable method to educate users regarding risky security behaviours [26–28]. Within the scope of the browser environment, on detection of risky security behaviour, the browser is used as a delivery mechanism for affective feedback, warning users about their actions.

3.1 Testing Harness Overview

The research project proposed the creation of a testing harness, in the form of a XUL (XML User Interface Language) browser extension for Mozilla Firefox, including the ability to monitor user behaviour and provide suitable affective feedback (Fig. 1).

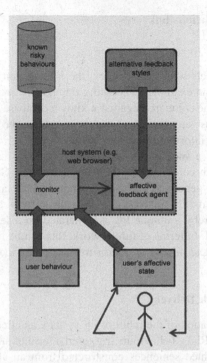

Fig. 1. Overview of the Spengler-Zuul extension

The extension developed was named Spengler-Zuul, and utilises several feedback agents. Should the monitoring system detect a user engaging in a known, potentially risky security behaviour whilst browsing the internet e.g. entering a commonly used password into a website, an affective feedback mechanism triggers, warning users regarding the dangers of their actions.

3.2   Monitoring Solution

To detect potentially risky security behaviours, and trigger affective feedback at opportune moments, a monitoring system had to be created within the confines of a browser- based environment.

Research conducted by Bubaš, Orehova and Konecki [32] and, Milne, Labrecque and Cromer [9] define specific risky security behaviours. A smaller subset of these behaviours were chosen for implementation, owing to their suitability for monitoring in the context of a web browser. Checks for these behaviours were built into a monitoring solution:

- Commonly used words in a password
- Password contains personal information
- Password length
- Malicious links found on page

- Current page is a malicious link
- Site is served via HTTP
- Current page is a top 20 social media site

When the user interacts with the browser, the information is encrypted, and processed on the server. As an example, processing the information on a server allows the URL of a current site to be compared against a known database of malicious sites [33]. Detection of a malicious site can then trigger the affective feedback mechanism, delivering some form of information to the end-user.

The development of a monitoring solution required a method of logging user actions. Previous research conducted by Fenstermacher and Ginsburg [34] noted the use of an XML log file generated by users' actions within a particular application. Drawing inspiration from this approach, a logging system was developed for the monitoring solution whereby a unique log is generated on a server for each user, and their actions are recorded. In terms of future work, this can be used to build-up a local profile of the end-user, determining common mistakes they may engage in.

3.3   Affective Feedback Delivery

Following the implementation of the monitoring system, an affective feedback delivery system was put in place. Risky behaviours triggered a form of affective feedback within the browser, using weighted sentences constructed from an affective word list [35], colour, and avatars to alert users to possible risks.

Previous research has indicated there are a number of types of affective feedback which could be utilised within the web browser window, to help guide users into making more appropriate security decisions. Depending on the actions of the user, they may be offered positive reinforcement because of their behaviour, negative reinforcement, or a mixture of both positive and negative. The 3 affective methods chosen were colours, avatars and text. The following section will discuss each type of feedback in more detail.

3.3.1   Text-Based Feedback

Research highlighted text-based feedback as an appropriate form of affective feedback for disseminating information to the end-user. When Ur et al. [29] investigated password strength meters, text-based feedback was also applied to describe users' passwords e.g. "*weak*". Other research, such as the work conducted by Dehn and Van Mulken [31] concluded that textual information provided more direct feedback to end-users.

The Spengler-Zuul extension developed required a word list in order for affective sentences to be constructed, with an indication as to the whether they were positively or negatively weighted.

The AFINN database developed by Finn °Arup Nielsen at DTU Informatics, Technical University of Denmark [35] was chosen for this purpose. A 2011 paper describes the construction of the wordlist, scoring of the words, and the overall impact. Specifically, it was the AFINN-111.txt wordlist which was used during the experimental design process. The wordlist was specifically developed for microblogs e.g. services such as Twitter where users post short messages. This concept fits in with this research project as the affective feedback solution aims to regularly updates end-users with short messages depending upon their actions.

Text-based feedback has been split into 3 sections, or bars: password information, general information, and malicious site information.

The final pieces of affective text integrated into the Spengler-Zuul extension had to be designed in such a way that when weighted words were placed into the phrases, the phrases themselves still made sense. In addition to this, positive and negative versions of phrases were required for triggers e.g. if a user visited a safe site or a malicious site.

In the case of unencrypted sites (HTTP) and social media sites, users were provided only with a general warning. It is possible to visit a social media site and stay safe, provided you are mindful regarding the information you are sharing with others. Similarly, you can visit an unencrypted website and behave in a completely safe way e.g. not entering sensitive information.

When writing affective phrases, care was taken to provide balanced text. As an example, the malicious links message telling users they are safe has a positive rating of 2. Conversely, the negative message for the opposing trigger has a rating of −2, meaning the warnings carry the same severity. In some cases, multiple weighted words were added to affective phrases to provide the same level of weighting. Within the positive malicious links message, the weighted words "validated" and "safe" have been included. These each carry a weighting of 1, giving an overall score of 2. In terms of the opposing, negative message, the only weighted word which has been used is "harmful", which has a negative weighing of −2.

The final affective phrases for the malicious links are as follows-

- Positive text: *"Links found on the page have been validated and deemed safe."*
- Negative text: *"Harmful links have been found on the page."*

3.3.2 Colour-Based Feedback

Another method of providing affective feedback to the end-user involves the use of certain colours in a bid to influence users. To provide an example, in Western culture, the colour red has long been associated with danger. Research carried out by Kralik et al. [36] has even proposed that the link between the colour red and dangerous situations may be rooted in evolutionary psychology.

In terms of cyber security, a number of studies have been conducted, into the use of colour-based feedback including Ur's 2012 paper [29] on password meters.

Colour-based feedback, in combination with sound, was also one method of affective feedback successfully implemented in a game called "Brainchild" developed by McDarby et al. [26] which attempts to help users relax.

During the development of the extension, the following colours were chosen for inclusion to denote affect: a shade of red (#CF4250), yellow (#EBA560), and green (#78BF60), producing a traffic-light system.

3.3.3   Avatar-Based Feedback

Avatar-based feedback may be an appropriate form of affective feedback when attempting to educate users. Again the Brainchild tool by McDarby et al. [26] indicated affective feedback can help users alter their internal states. Avatars have been used to good effect in intelligent tutoring systems [27], with Hall et al. [28] agreeing that the use of avatars may prove effective in influencing the emotional state of the end-user, thus forming part of this research.

To allow for delivery of avatar-based affective feedback within the browser-based environment, 2 avatars displaying subtle facial cues were selected from the paper by Sacharin et al. [37]. The paper makes reference to the previously identified 6 basic emotions [38]: happiness, anger, sadness, fear, disgust, and surprise, and also includes a neutral avatar, devoid of any such emotion. The 2 avatars selected for inclusion in this research project were happiness and sadness, to denote positive and negative feedback accordingly.

Research has shown that people are uncertain about emotions displayed in expression sequences in comparison to simple static images [37]. Due to this finding, static images of avatars were implemented into the Spengler-Zuul extension.

3.3.4   Combining Feedback

Within the affective feedback solution, there is also a system of flags in place, which is designed to provide an overall level of feedback, depending on users' actions.

One example of this would involve the password feedback. There are multiple areas of password feedback which can be shown to the user involving length and commonality. A password may be short (bad) however, it may be a non-dictionary word (good). To prevent the system from providing users with positive feedback when they have failed any of the password security checks, the password flags are checked and provide an override. So whilst users may have an uncommon, yet short password, they are still shown negative affective text, colours and avatars. They will only be shown positive feedback when they meet all levels of the password security criteria. Each bar has its own set of flags which determine the overall colours of the password, general info and malicious links bar.

3.3.5   Spengler-Zuul Extension Developed

A number of versions of the final tool, named the Spengler-Zuul extension were developed, allowing the impact of different combinations of affective feedback to be tested against a control environment. 5 versions of the tool were created:

- Spengler-Zuul (none)- monitors users but showed no on-screen feedback.
- Spengler-Zuul (text)- monitors users and displays text-based affective feedback.
- Spengler-Zuul (text and avatar)- monitors users and displays text-based affective feedback, alongside an avatar situated in the bottom right of the screen.
- Spengler-Zuul (text and colour)- monitors users and displays text-based affective feedback, with a colour coded traffic light system background.
- Spengler-Zuul (text and colour and avatar)- monitors users and displays text- based affective feedback, with a colour coded traffic light system background. Additionally, an avatar is situated in the bottom right of the screen (see Fig. 2).

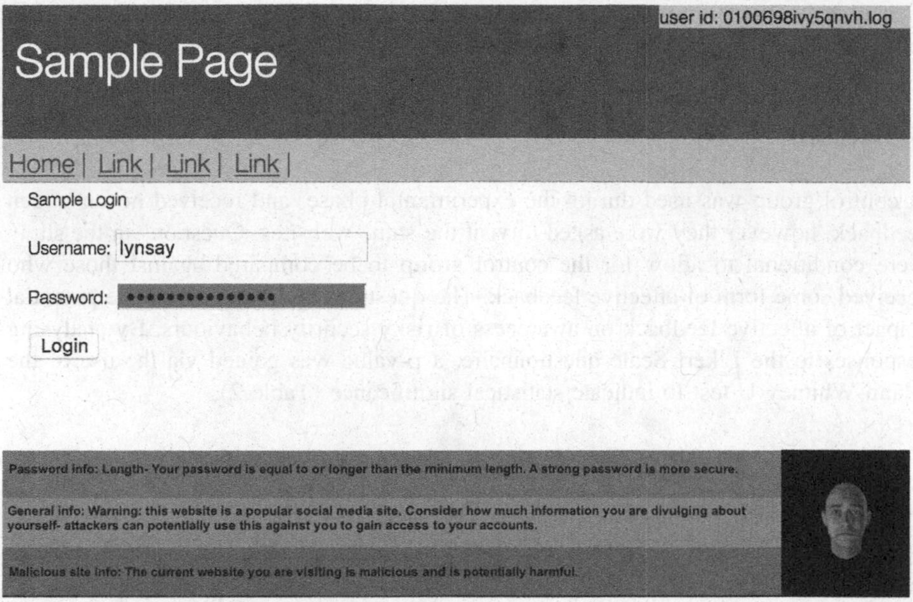

user id: 0100698ivy5qnvh.log

Sample Page

Home | Link | Link | Link |

Sample Login

Username: lynsay

Password: ●●●●●●●●●●●●●●●

Login

Password info: Length- Your password is equal to or longer than the minimum length. A strong password is more secure.

General info: Warning: this website is a popular social media site. Consider how much information you are divulging about yourself- attackers can potentially use this against you to gain access to your accounts.

Malicious site info: The current website you are visiting is malicious and is potentially harmful.

Fig. 2. Affective feedback displayed in the browser via the Spengler-Zuul extension

3.4   Experiments

Participants were initially given a briefing handout, outlining the experimental process. Participants were drawn from Abertay University, and many had a computing background. No reference was made to the type of feedback which would be provided. The fact that risky security behaviours and awareness were also being measured was omitted from the information for participants, in order to avoid bias.

Participants were then given a USB stick labelled with a number from 1–5. Each USB stick contained a portable version of the Firefox browser, and a version of the Spengler-Zuul extension. The types of feedback delivered corresponded to the numbers 1–5, and are outlined in Table 1. Participants were asked to visit a number of pre-defined websites, following on-screen instructions. Some of the websites were chosen to purposely trigger feedback e.g. a HTTP warning. On completion of the computer-based part of the experiment, participants were asked to complete a paper-based questionnaire utilising Likert Scales. This allowed participants to assess

Table 1. Experiment groups and feedback types

Group	Feedback type	Participants (n)
1	Control	12
2	Text	13
3	Text, avatar	16
4	Text, colour	14
5	Text, colour, avatar	17

their response to the on-screen feedback received. Participants were only allowed to take part in the experiments once only, regardless of the experiment group they were in.

4 Results

A control group was used during the experimental phase, and received no on-screen feedback, however they were asked to visit the same websites. Questions in the study were conditional to allow for the control group to be compared against those who received some form of affective feedback. The questions sought to assess the potential impact of affective feedback on awareness of risky security behaviours. By analysing responses to the Likert Scale questionnaire, a p-value was gained via the use of the Mann-Whitney U test to indicate statistical significance (Table 2).

Table 2. Control group vs. affective feedback results

Statistical significance- question vs. experiment				
Question	Group 1 vs. 2	Group 1 vs. 3	Group 1 vs. 4	Group 1 vs. 5
If you received negative password-related feedback, did it make you consider changing your Facebook password?	No	No	No	No
If you received social media-related feedback, did it make you consider the information you share online?	No	No	No	No
If you received feedback about malicious links on a page, did it make you consider which links you were clicking on?	No	Yes	No	No
Did the feedback make you hesitate to provide information online?	No	Yes	No	Yes
Did the feedback clearly highlight any issues with the page?	No	No	No	No
Do you think the feedback provided helped to increase your security awareness?	Yes	Yes	Yes	Yes
Did you find the feedback useful?	Yes	No	Yes	Yes
Did the feedback encourage you to learn more about online security?	Yes	Yes	Yes	Yes

In comparing data from the control experiment when participants were asked "*Do you think the feedback provided helped to increase your security awareness?*", all affective experiments produced a positive, statistically significant result. This indicates participants feel the affective feedback has had an impact on security awareness.

Similarly, when asked "*Did the feedback encourage you to learn more about online security?*", again, all affective experiments produced a statistically significant result in comparison to the control responses. This indicates that in the opinion of the participants, the affective feedback has had some form of impact on them, encouraging them to improve their behavior in the future.

In terms of finding the feedback useful, the only group which failed to produce a statistically significant result in this instance was experiment 3 (text and avatar-based feedback) in comparison to the control group. Other results were mixed, with text and avatar-based feedback proving successful in eliciting a hesitant response in participants when they were clicking on links, and when they were asked to provide information online.

5 Discussion

Participants were asked to answer 8 questions during the study relating to on-screen feedback, in an effort to determine the potential impact of affective feedback on security awareness. The results of the two questions "*Do you think the feedback provided helped to increase your security awareness?*" and "*Did the feedback encourage you to learn more about online security?*" produced positive, statistically significant results for all affective experiments. This indicates that no form of affective feedback delivered out-performed the other. In this study any form of affective feedback (text, colour, avatars) had an impact on overall awareness.

When comparing the questionnaire results regarding the impact of the affective feedback, there were statistically significant differences when experiment 1 (control) participants were compared to those who engaged with the affective feedback-based experiments.

When participants were asked "*Do you think the feedback provided helped to increase your security awareness?*", all affective experiment questionnaire results produced a positive, statistically significant result when compared to the control group questionnaire data. This indicates that in this study, the affective feedback was successful in creating a positive impact on the security awareness of the end-user.

A similar statistically significant result was generated when participants were asked "*Did the feedback encourage you to learn more about online security?*". All affective experiment questionnaire results produced a positive, statistically significant result when compared to the control group questionnaires. This result highlights again that the affective feedback appears to have influenced the participants into thinking about their security behaviours online, with the possibility of prompting them to engage in better security choices in future web-browsing. The result also links to the need for education: in this instance it appears the participants were eager to learn.

Again, results of the two questions "*Do you think the feedback provided helped to increase your security awareness?*" and "*Did the feedback encourage you to learn more about online security?*" were interesting as no form affective feedback delivered surpassed the other in terms of the impact on the end-user. This is an interesting result as a separate part of the questionnaire asked participants which type of affective feedback they felt had the largest impact. Raw results gained from this question indicated participants felt colour had the largest impact, though it was only used in 2 of the experiment groups.

When asked if the feedback provided was useful, only one comparison group failed to produce a statistically significant result. The group in question was experiment 3 (text and avatar-based feedback). This result correlates with the raw results in another part of the questionnaire, where participants indicated that colour had the largest impact during the experimental process, though it should be noted that experiment 2 (text-based feedback) produced a statistically significant result, despite the lack of colour-based feedback.

The other results gained from the experiments were mixed. When asked if the feedback made them hesitate to provide information online, both experiment 3 (text and avatar-based feedback) and experiment 5 (text, colour and avatar-based feedback) were successful, again highlighting a potential impact on end-user security behaviour. Experiment 3 also appeared to have an impact on the way they browsed online, making them consider the links they were clicking on, guiding them to avoid engagement in risky security behaviours.

In terms of the affective feedback delivered, some participants left free-form comments on the questionnaire, stating some participants thought the affective solution is a useful application, with comments such as *"I find the extension useful for people who do not know much about online security"*, *"Very helpful, especially for strong passwords"*, and *"I think this is a good idea to raise awareness on online security especially people that are new to technology"*.

As of August 2015, Mozilla announced XUL-based extensions would be depre- cated, and they would move to a new API named WebExtensions [39]. In addition to this, at the start of 2017, Mozilla started to integrate warnings (text-based) in Firefox regarding password entry on a non-HTTPS website [40]. This is a feature which was integrated into the Spengler-Zuul extension in 2015, and highlights the importance of security awareness in the context of a browser-based environment.

6 Conclusion/Future Work

To conclude, this research study found that the delivery of affective feedback within the confines of a browser-based environment enhanced users' general awareness of security risks online, though it didn't have an impact on specific behaviours such as the information they shared on social media websites. When compared to the control group, statistically significant results were recorded by those who received some form of affective feedback. Those who received affective feedback felt it helped to increase their security awareness, and that the feedback encouraged them to learn more about online security, a factor which could potentially improve their security awareness in the future, and modify their behaviour. Overall this suggests that affective feedback allows users to consider whether their online behaviours could be perceived as risky.

This piece of research was a preliminary study to investigate if it was plausible to apply affective feedback in the context of a browser-based environment. If affective feedback was delivered over a longer period of time, on a regular basis, this has the potential to reflect positive behavioural changes as end-users become more knowl- edgeable regarding the subject matter. Future work seeks to investigate the impact of a long-term study in this area, utilising varying affective agents e.g. differing wordlists and avatars.

Further research could be explored, in a way to modify the delivery and application of the affective feedback to make it appeal to specific groups. The Office of National

Statistics in the UK has noted the rise of Internet users who are aged 75 and over [41]. Regardless of the users' age, they still need to be educated about the dangers of risky security behaviour. Modifying the extension to deliver more appropriate feedback e.g. have less of a focus on colour as the lens of older people become yellow, distorting colours [42] could provide another avenue for investigation. Similarly, the affective feedback delivered could be modified to appeal to children, helping to educate them about staying safe online from a young age, enhancing their security awareness.

References

1. Li, Y., Siponen, M.: A call for research on home users information security behaviour. In: PACIS 2011, Proceedings, p. 112 (2011)
2. Stanton, J.M., et al.: Analysis of end user security behaviors. Comput. Secur. **24**, 124–133 (2005). Elsevier
3. Payne, B., Edwards, W.: A brief introduction to usable security. IEEE Internet Comput. **12** (3), 13–21 (2008)
4. Fetscherin, M.: Importance of cultural and risk aspects in music piracy: a cross-national comparison among university students. J. Electron. Commer. Res. **10**, 45–55 (2009). http://www.csulb.edu/journals/jecr/issues/20091/Paper4.pdf
5. Hadnagy, C.: Social Engineering: The Art of Human Hacking. Wiley Publishing, Indianapolis (2011). pp. 23–24
6. Padayachee, K.: Taxonomy of compliant information security behavior. Comput. Secur. **31** (5), 673–680 (2012). http://dx.doi.org/10.1016/j.cose.2012.04.004
7. Shay, R., et al.: Designing password policies for strength and usability. ACM Trans. Inf. Syst. Secur. **18**(4) (2016). http://doi.org/10.1145/2891411
8. Balduzzi, M.: Attacking the privacy of social network users. HITBSECCONF2011, Malaysia (2011). http://conference.hitb.org/hitbsecconf2011kul/materials/D1T1%20% 20Marco%20Balduzzi%20-%20Attacking%20the%20Privacy%20of%20Social% 20Network%20Users.pdf. Accessed 21 Sept 2012
9. Milne, G.R., Labrecque, L.I., Cromer, C.: Toward an understanding of the online consumer's risky behavior and protection practices. J. Consum. Aff. **43**(3), 449–473 (2009). http://doi.org/10.1111/j.1745-6606.2009.01148.x
10. Larose, R., Rifon, N.J.: Promoting i-safety: effects of privacy warnings and privacy seals on risk assessment and online privacy behavior. J. Consum. Aff. **41**(1), 127–149 (2007). doi:10.1111/j.1745-6606.2006.00071.x
11. Milne, G.R., Rohm, A.J., Bahl, S.: Consumers' protection of online privacy and identity. J. Consum. Aff. **38**, 217–232 (2004). doi:10.1111/j.1745-6606.2004.tb00865.x
12. Farahmand, F., et al.: Risk perceptions of information security: a measurement study. In: Proceedings of the 2009 International Conference on Computational Science and Engineering, CSE 2009, vol. 3, pp. 462–469 (2009). http://dx.doi.org/10.1109/CSE.2009.449
13. Fischoff, B., et al.: How safe is safe enough? A psychometric study of attitudes towards technological risks and benefits. Policy Sci. **9**(2), 127–152 (1978)
14. Takemura, T.: Empirical analysis of behavior on information security. In: Proceedings of the 2011 International Conference on Internet of Things and 4th International Conference on Cyber, Physical and Social Computing, ITHINGSCPSCOM, pp. 358–363 (2011). http://dx.doi.org/10.1109/iThings/CPSCom.2011.8

15. San-Jose, P., Rodriguez, S.: Study on information security and e-Trust in Spanish households. In: Proceedings of the First Workshop on Building Analysis Datasets and Gathering Experience Returns for Security, BADGERS 2011, pp. 1–6 (2011). http://doi.acm.org/10.1145/1978672.1978673

16. Hill, R., Donaldson, D.R.: Bridging the trust gap: integrating models of behavior and perception. In: NSPW 2015 Proceedings of the 2015 New Security Paradigms Workshop, pp. 148–155 (2015). doi:10.1145/2841113.2841125

17. Furnell, S., et al.: The challenges of understanding and using security: a survey of end-users. Comput. Secur. 25(1), 27–35 (2006). doi:10.1016/j.cose.2005.12.004

18. Dhamija, R., Tygar, J.: The battle against phishing: dynamic security skins. In: Symposium on Usable Privacy and Security (SOUPS 2005), pp. 1–12 (2005). http://cups.cs.cmu.edu/soups/2005/2005proceedings/p77-dhamija.pdf

19. Sheng, S.: Anti-phishing phil: the design and evaluation of a game that teaches people not to fall for phish. In: Symposium on Usable Privacy and Security (SOUPS 2007), pp. 1–12 (2007). http://cups.cs.cmu.edu/soups/2007/proceedings/p88_sheng.pdf

20. Kumaraguru, P., et. al.: School of phish: a real-world evaluation of anti-phishing training. In: Symposium on Usable Privacy and Security (SOUPS 2009), pp. 1–12 (2009). http://cups.cs.cmu.edu/soups/2009/proceedings/a3-kumaraguru.pdf

21. Canova, G., Volkamer, M., Bergmann, C., Reinheimer, B.: Nophish app evaluation: lab and retention study. In: NDSS Workshop on Usable Security (2015)

22. Besmer, A.: Social applications: exploring a more secure framework. In: Symposium on Usable Privacy and Security (SOUPS 2009), pp. 1–10 (2009). http://cups.cs.cmu.edu/soups/2009/proceedings/a2-besmer.pdf

23. Maurer, M., De Luca, A., Kempe, S.: Using data type based security alert dialogs to raise online security awareness. In: Symposium on Usable Privacy and Security (SOUPS 2011), pp. 1–13 (2011). http://cups.cs.cmu.edu/soups/2011/proceedings/a2_Maurer.pdf

24. Volkamer, M., Renaud, K., Canova, G., Reinheimer, B., Braun, K.: Design and field evaluation of PassSec: raising and sustaining web surfer risk awareness. In: Conti, M., Schunter, M., Askoxylakis, I. (eds.) Trust 2015. LNCS, vol. 9229, pp. 104–122. Springer, Cham (2015). doi:10.1007/978-3-319-22846-4_7

25. Picard, R.W.: Affective Computing. MIT Press, Cambridge (1997). p. 15

26. McDarby, G., Condron, J., Hughes, D., Augenblick, N.: Affective feedback. Media Lab Europe (2004). http://medialabeurope.org/mindgames/publications/publicationAffectiveFeedbackEnablingTechnologies.pdf. Accessed 22 May 2012

27. Robison, J., McQuiggan, S., Lester, J.: Evaluating the consequences of affective feedback in intelligent tutoring systems. In: Proceedings of International Conference on Affective Computing and Intelligent Interaction (ACII 2009), Amsterdam, Netherlands, 10–12 September 2009, pp. 37–42 (2009)

28. Hall, L., Woods, S., Aylett, R., Newall, L., Paiva, A.: Achieving empathic engagement through affective interaction with synthetic characters. In: Tao, J., Tan, T., Picard, Rosalind W. (eds.) ACII 2005. LNCS, vol. 3784, pp. 731–738. Springer, Heidelberg (2005). doi:10.1007/11573548_94

29. Ur, B., et al.: How does your password measure up? The effect of strength meters on password creation. In: Security 2012 Proceedings of the 21st USENIX Conference on Security Symposium (2012)

30. Adams, F.M., Osgood, C.E.: A cross-cultural study of the affective meanings of color. J. Cross-Cultural Psychol. 4(2), 135–156 (1973)

31. Dehn, D., Van Mulken, S.: The impact of animated interface agents: a review of empirical research. Int. J. Hum.-Comput. Stud. 52(1), 1–22 (2012). http://dx.doi.org/10.1006/ijhc.1999.0325

32. Bubaš, G., Orehova, T., Konecki, M.: Factors and predictors of online security and privacy behavior. J. Inf. Organ. Sci. **32**(2), 79–98 (2008)
33. HpHosts (2016). http://www.hosts-file.net/
34. Fenstermacher, K.D., Ginsburg, M.A.: Lightweight framework for cross-application user monitoring. IEEE Comput. **35**, 51–58 (2002)
35. Nielsen, F.: A new ANEW: evaluation of a word list for sentiment analysis in microblogs. In: Proceedings of the ESWC2011 Workshop on 'Making Sense of Microposts': Big Things Come in Small Packages. CEUR Workshop Proceedings, vol. 718, pp. 93–98 (2011)
36. Association For Psychological Science: Stop On Red! The Effects of Color May Lie Deep in Evolution (2011). http://www.psychologicalscience.org/index.php/news/releases/stop-on-red-a-monkey-study-suggests-that-the-effects-of-color-lie-deep-in-evolution.html
37. Sacharin, V., Sander, D., Scherer, K.R.: The perception of changing emotion expressions. Cogn. Emot. **26**, 1273–1300 (2012). http://doi.org/10.1080/02699931.2012.656583
38. Ekman, P.: Basic emotions. Cognition (1999). http://doi.org/10.1002/0470013494.ch3
39. Mozilla: The Future of Developing Firefox Add-ons (2015). https://blog.mozilla.org/addons/2015/08/21/the-future-of-developing-firefox-add-ons/
40. Mozilla: Designed to protect your privacy (2017). https://www.mozilla.org/en-GB/firefox/desktop/trust/
41. Office for National Statistics: Internet users in the UK (2016). http://www.ons.gov.uk/businessindustryandtrade/itandinternetindustry/bulletins/internetusers/2016#recent-internet-use-is-on-the-increase-for-those-aged-65-and-over
42. Salvi, S.M., Akhtar, S., Currie, Z.: Ageing changes in the eye. Postgrad. Med. J. **971**, 581–587 (2006). http://doi.org/10.1136/pgmj.2005.040857

A Generic Cognitive Dimensions Questionnaire to Evaluate the Usability of Security APIs

Chamila Wijayarathna$^{(\boxtimes)}$, Nalin A.G. Arachchilage, and Jill Slay

Australian Centre for Cyber Security,
University of New South Wales (UNSW Canberra),
Australian Defence Force Academy, Canberra, Australia
c.diwelwattagamage@student.unsw.edu.au, {nalin.asanka,j.slay}@adfa.edu.au

Abstract. Programmers use security APIs to embed security into the applications they develop. Security vulnerabilities get introduced into those applications, due to the usability issues that exist in the security APIs. Improving usability of security APIs would contribute to improve the security of applications that programmers develop. However, currently there is no methodology to evaluate the usability of security APIs. In this study, we attempt to improve the Cognitive Dimensions framework based API usability evaluation methodology, to evaluate the usability of security APIs.

1 Introduction

In January 2014, hackers posted user-names and telephone numbers of 4.6 million US Snapchat account holders on-line due to an insecure Application Programming Interface (API) used in Snapchat app [12]. Snapchat is one of the most popular mobile apps among teens that allows its users to send and receive "self-destructing" pictures and videos. However, hackers claimed that their intention was to raise public awareness around the insecure API issue and also to put public pressure on Snapchat to get this security flow fixed. As reported in May 2015, Starbucks suffered from a similar fate that hackers drained money from its customers' bank and PayPal accounts through an insecure API [26]. Nevertheless, programmers in the software development industry have been heavily dependent on the use of APIs [33,34].

An API is a salient part of a reusable software component which acts as the interface where programmers can call the features of the component. Using features of a reusable software component through an API helps the programmer to use them effectively for developing applications, even without a knowledge of implementation details of the component. Therefore, the use of APIs has become an inseparable part of a programmer's life.

One of the functionalities that APIs provide is security. Due to high complexity of security concepts, security related components are designed and implemented by designers specialized in security [16,33]. Programmers use those components through APIs exposed, which we call as security APIs. Programmers use

T. Tryfonas (Ed.): HAS 2017, LNCS 10292, pp. 160–173, 2017.
DOI: 10.1007/978-3-319-58460-7_11

security APIs to achieve various security functionalities such as authentication and authorization, input validation, encryption, decryption, hashing, etc.

Even though APIs are important in software development process, often they are not very easy to learn and use in software development environment [3, 30, 31, 34]. Less usability of APIs causes to reduce efficiency of programmers where they have to spend significant time to learn the APIs [23]. Also less usable APIs lead programmers to incorrectly use them, which causes unintended behaviors in resulting systems.

The situation is worse with less usable security APIs. When the programmer uses a security API incorrectly, that causes security vulnerabilities in the system s/he develops. In a study Fahl et al. carried out using 13500 popular free Android apps, they found that 8% of the apps are vulnerable to attacks like man in the middle attack, due to improperly using the Secure Socket Layer (SSL)/Transport Layer Security (TLS) APIs [13]. The authors have identified that the cause for this is not only the carelessness of the programmers, but also the usability issues of the SSL/TLS APIs used by programmers for developing those apps.

If the usability of security APIs can be improved, they will be less prone to erroneous usages and therefore, will be less subject to introduce security vulnerabilities to the applications [16, 22]. As per the knowledge of the authors, currently there is no existing methodology to evaluate the usability of security APIs. Thus, in this study our contribution focuses on developing a methodology to evaluate the usability of security APIs.

The rest of the paper is organized as follows. Section 2 presents the related work from existing literature. Section 3 describes the new dimensions and questionnaire we propose in this study. In the final section, we summarize the work presented and conclude with an outlook on future work.

2 Related Work

2.1 Usability of Security APIs

APIs provide a mechanism for code reuse, where programmers can build their software applications on top of other software components which already exist rather than writing the code from scratch [20, 23, 27, 28, 33, 34]. Hence, effective APIs are important to ensure the better use of the underlying components, and the usability of APIs demands increasing interest [11, 34]. Due to the impact that API usability seems to have, Myers and Stylos [23] suggest that "Following its design, a new API should be evaluated to measure and improve its usability". There has been a number of studies that introduce and use various methods to evaluate the usability of APIs [3, 8, 14, 19, 27, 28, 31]. Some of the most popular methods for evaluating usability of APIs are empirical evaluation [8, 9, 27], heuristic evaluation [19], conducting user studies [3, 29–31], API peer reviews method [14] and API concepts framework based automated methodology [28].

Even though, number of methods for evaluating API usability have been suggested as mentioned above, evaluating usability of security APIs is still a less attended topic [16, 22, 23]. Security APIs are a subset of APIs which are used to secure the boundary between trusted and untrusted code [1]. Bond [5] defined a security API as "an application programming interface that uses cryptography to enforce a security policy on the interaction between two entities". However, this definition by Bond exclude some APIs which provide security functionalities without using cryptography (e.g.: input validation APIs such as Open Web Application Security Project (OWASP) esapi). Hence in this study, we consider security APIs as "application programming interfaces that provides developers with security functionalities that enforce one or more security policies on the interaction between atleast two entities", as defined by Gorski and Iacono [16].

Several previous studies have discussed the importance of the usability of security APIs and the effects of the security APIs which are not usable [5,13,15, 22,23,32,33]. Fahl et al. [13] and Georgiev et al. [15] list and discuss number of software, which were vulnerable to cyber attacks because of the usability issues in SSL/TLS API that has been used to develop the software. Myers and Stylos [23] also discussed the importance of the usability of security APIs, pointing to the results obtained by Fahl et al. [13]. Weber [32] describes the importance of the usability of APIs such as authentication API provided by Facebook. He suggests that APIs like those should be usable, otherwise cyber-security failures will result on the software which makes use of them.

Wurster and van Oorschot [33] highlight that most of the times programmers are not the experts of security, and also most programmers believe that their code is not security critical. Authors suggest that educating all the programmers about security concepts is not feasible and the most feasible solution is making the APIs that they use more secure and usable.

Mindermann [22] discusses the importance of the usability of security APIs for developing more secure software. He claims that the security of developed applications will be far better if the security libraries are more usable. He also highlights the importance of applying usability research for security APIs to deliver more usable security APIs.

Even though the importance of the usability of security APIs has been discussed, only a limited work has been done to achieve this [16,17]. By referring and analysing the outcomes of existing security studies, Gorski and Iacono [16] list 11 security API specific usability characteristics. According to the authors, this set is not complete, so there can be more characteristics that describe usability of security APIs. Green and Smith [17] also point out 10 rules to create a good crypto API. Furthermore, they urge the need for qualitative and quantitative empirical studies in this area.

From looking at the existing literature, even though different methods have been identified to evaluate the usability of APIs, none of them has been used to evaluate the usability aspects of security APIs. In this study, we try to address this problem and propose a methodology to evaluate the usability of security APIs.

We are proposing an empirical evaluation methodology similar to the one used by Microsoft Visual Studio Usability group in their API usability evaluations [8,9]. We choose this methodology over other usability evaluation techniques (i.e. heuristic evaluation, API peer review method, API concepts framework and conducting unstructured user studies) due to several reasons. First of all, empirical evaluation requires involvement of programmers who are the actual end users of the API. In our point of view, this is essential for evaluating the usability of security APIs, because security vulnerabilities caused by the usability issues that exist in security APIs, occur when programmers incorrectly use security APIs. Getting them involve in the evaluation process will help evaluators to identify what usability issues persuade programmers to use the API incorrectly. Furthermore, getting end users of the product involved in the usability evaluation process is considered as the gold standard among Human Computer Interaction (HCI) specialists [23,24]. In addition to that, this methodology requires less expert intervening and also sensitive to wide range of usability aspects compared to API peer review method and API concepts framework. Therefore, we believe that conducting empirical evaluations using Cognitive Dimensions framework will be more effective than using other mentioned methodologies, for evaluating the usability of security APIs.

2.2 Cognitive Dimensions Framework Based Usability Evaluation

Cognitive Dimensions of Notation framework was first introduced by Green [18] as a broad-brush discussion tool to discuss usability issues of programming tools. In 1999, Kadoda et al. [21] used this framework to empirically evaluate usability of educational theorem provers. They changed the evaluation procedure by getting end user involved in the evaluation process through a questionnaire. Blackwell and Green [4] acknowledge the importance of this method saying that users do all the work here, so less expert involvement is required. However, this approach used by Kadoda et al. [21] have few drawbacks. Blackwell and Green [4] point out that, since system designer is the person who designs the questionnaire to evaluate the system and selects the dimensions to use, some usability aspects that may important in users perspective will be ignored. Furthermore, Blackwell and Green [4] mention that it adds extra burden since a different questionnaire has to be developed for each system to be evaluated.

As a solution to these problems, Blackwell and Green [4] describe an enhancement for this method which uses a generic questionnaire. They presented a complete questionnaire which covers all 16 cognitive dimensions of the Cognitive Dimensions Notation Framework of Green [18]. There are many advantages of using a generic questionnaire over using a questionnaire specific to a system. When using a generic questionnaire, user do all the work related to the usability evaluation and data retrieved through evaluation will only demonstrate user's judgement. Furthermore, same questionnaire can be used to evaluate any system. Therefore, burden of creating questionnaire per each system has removed here.

In 2004, Clarke [8] presented a methodology used by Microsoft Visual Studio Usability Group to evaluate the usability of APIs. He used the same methodology described by Blackwell and Green [4] with a modified set of cognitive dimensions and a different questionnaire [10]. The framework Clarke used consisted of 12 dimensions which are,

- Abstraction level
- Learning style
- Working framework
- Work-step unit
- Progressive evaluation
- Premature commitment
- Penetrability
- API elaboration
- API viscosity
- Consistency
- Role expressiveness
- Domain correspondence

Clarke alleges that Microsoft Visual Studio Usability Group has proved the relevance and the utility of the cognitive dimensions framework for evaluating API usability, however the usage of the above mentioned questionnaire has not been backed by any empirical evidence. Clarke mentions that he developed this questionnaire based on his experience and the feedbacks of participants who involved in usability tests at Microsoft [10]. Following is the methodology they used for evaluating usability of APIs.

Firstly, experimenters recruit participants and ask them to write code that accomplishes various tasks using the API that need to be evaluated. While participants are doing this, evaluators recorded data such as video records of participants' behaviour and participants' verbal accounts for their actions (Participants were employed in a think-aloud study [2,6]). After the tasks are completed, the evaluators ask participants to answer the questionnaire [8]. Based on the participants' feedback, evaluators identify the usability issues that exist in the API.

Other researchers have also used this methodology for evaluating the usability of APIs. For an example, Piccioni et al. [27] used the same approach with slight modifications to evaluate the usability of a data persistence library API written in Eiffel. Without using the 12 dimension cognitive dimensions framework introduced by Clarke, they have only considered 4 dimensions which are *understandability, abstraction, reusability* and *learnability*. They have used their own questionnaire developed based on these dimensions.

As discussed in the previous subsection, we propose the same methodology to evaluate the usability of security APIs. Even though we can use the same methodology described by Clarke [8] to evaluate usability of security APIs, the dimensions and questionnaire he used are not sufficient to do this. This is supported by the fact that Gorski and Iacono [16], and Green and Smith [17] recommend more different characteristics to consider when discussing usability of security APIs. Also, improving usability with respect to some aspects can cause to reduce the security [23]. Thus, when evaluating usability of security APIs, we may have to omit some of the dimensions listed by Clarke and add some new dimensions. Therefore, in this study, we are proposing an enhanced and fine tuned version of Cognitive Dimensions framework and the questionnaire, that can be used to conduct empirical usability evaluations for security APIs.

3   Questionnaire Design

We considered Microsoft's version of Cognitive Dimensions framework [8] as the starting point to develop the new questionnaire. Then we improved it by referring to the past studies conducted in this area [16,17] and by taking usability guidelines those studies have mentioned into consideration.

First, we took 10 rules mentioned by Green and Smith into account. Their first rule is **Easy to learn - even without crypto background**. This is related to the **Learning Style** dimension in the Microsoft's version of Cognitive Dimensions framework. **Learning Style** describes the knowledge about the API that the programmer needs to have before start using the API, and how user would gain the knowledge he requires about the API [7,8]. However, Green and Smith talk about the cryptographic knowledge requirements that the programmer needs to have. In previous sections, we discussed that most programmers who use security APIs are not security experts. Therefore, **Easy to learn without crypto or security background** is an important aspect to consider when evaluating usability. Since this is related to **Learning Style** dimension, without introducing as a new dimension, we added new questions to Learning Style dimension to cover this aspect.

- Do you think your previous computer security related knowledge made it easy to use the API? What previous knowledge helped in using the API?
- Do you think, if you had previous knowledge of any specific area related to computer security, it would have been easier to use the API? What are those areas you think would have been useful?

We did not consider the **Easy to use - even without documentation**, **Sufficiently powerful to satisfy non-security requirements**, **Hard to circumvent errors - except during testing/development** and **Assist with/ handle end-user interaction** rules. We could not get a proper idea about what the authors tried to convey from these properties by referring to the resources available. Also, since our objective is to improve the Cognitive Dimensions framework to support security APIs, we assume that not using these rules which are not related to security will not reduce the effectiveness of the framework.

Hard to misuse is an important rule to consider when evaluating usability of security APIs, because most security related issues occur when programmers misuse security APIs intentionally and unintentionally. This aspect is not covered in the Clarke's version of Cognitive Dimensions framework. Thus, we included this rule with the following questions.

- Have you come up with incidents where you incorrectly used the API and then identified the correct way of doing that? Did the API give any help to identify that you used the API incorrectly? If there were any similar incidents, please explain.
- Did the API give proper error messages in case of exceptions and errors, or did you have to handle them at your programme level? If you had to handle them at your level, please mention the scenario/s.

We decided to omit remaining rules, because Cognitive Dimensions framework already covered those rules by its existing dimensions. **Easy to read and maintain code that uses it** rule says the same as the **Role Expressiveness** dimension. Similarly **Hard to override/change core functionality** rule is covered by **API Eloboration** dimension and **Appropriate to audience** rule is covered by **Learning Style** dimension.

Then we took 11 characteristics of the usability of security APIs suggested by Gorski and Iacono [16] into consideration. The first characteristic they have mentioned is **End-user protection**. This characteristic says that security of an application which uses a security API should not depend on the programmer who develops the application. It could be argued that this is something that needs to be considered when evaluating usability of a security API. Since this aspect is not covered in our questionnaire, we added a new dimension with questions to cover that.

- Do you think the security of the end user of the application you developed, depends on how you completed the task? Or does it depend only on the security API you used?
- If you think security of the end user depends on how you completed the task, in which ways does it depend?

The next characteristic Gorski and Iacono have listed is **Case distinction management**, which refers to the handling of exceptional events and errors that occur related to the API. When these errors and events need to be handled by the programmer, most of the time they do it incorrectly, which leads to vulnerabilities in resulting applications [13,15,16]. This is the same issue which we discussed at **Hard to misuse** rule by Green and Smith [17]. Since we added new questions to **Hard to misuse** rule, we didn't add new questions to **Case distinction management** rule again.

We did not include the third characteristic mentioned by Gorski and Iacono, which is **Adherence to security principals**. It says that a security API must follow security guidelines such as "OWASP coding practises" [25]. This is not a property that can be evaluated by observing programmers who use API to implement their applications. So we did not add this characteristic in to the questionnaire.

Fourth characteristic mentioned by Gorski and Iacono is **Testability**, which means API must support reliable test routines written by security experts. This closely relates to **Learning Style** and **Progressive Evaluation** dimensions of the Microsoft's version of Cognitive Dimensions framework. However, those dimensions do not address whether the API provide means to test the security of the application developed using the security API or not. Therefore, we added a new dimension **Testability** with following questions.

- Did you test the security of your application after completing the task using security API? If not, can you explain why?
- If yes, can you explain how did you do that?
- Did the API provide any guidance on how to test the security of the application you developed?

Next characteristic is **Constrainability**, which means letting programmers do configurations related to security causes security vulnerabilities. This is the same we discussed with **API Elaboration** and **Hard to misuse**, so we did not add new questions for **Constrainability**.

Information obligation characteristic describes the extent which the API informs the programmer about the security relevant aspects of the security API. Even though the **Penetrability** dimension talks about the API related information exposed by the API to the programmer [7,8], it does not address whether the API's security related specifics are properly communicated to the programmer. Therefore, without adding a new dimension, we added a new question to the **Penetrability** dimension to cover this characteristic.

- Did the API (including its documentation) provide enough information about the security relevant specifics related to the task you completed? What information was missing or you had to find by referring to external sources?

Next characteristic by Gorski and Iacono, which is **Degree of reliability**, does not talk directly about a property of the API. It talks about the reliability of web resources that the programmer refers while using the API to achieve a task. However, the programmer refers to external unreliable resources (e.g.: stackoverflow), because API does not expose enough information to the programmer who is using it. We have considered whether the API is providing enough information to the programmer or not, at **Penetrability** dimension. Therefore, we did not add a new dimension to the questionnaire to cover the **Degree of reliability** characteristic.

Security prerequisites characteristic says that there are mandatory prerequisites that need to be fulfilled by programmers when using security APIs, which are often unknown and unclear. These prerequisites are also a type of security related information that an API needs to communicate to the programmer, which we described under **Information obligation**. Therefore, we did not add new questions to cover this characteristic, since this is already covered in our questionnaire. Similarly, we did not add new questions to **Execution platform** characteristic. It discusses the target execution platform that API is developed for and whether or not the information has been properly communicated to the programmer. We believe this characteristic is also covered by questions under **Penetrability** dimension.

Next characteristic, which is **Delegation** says that, the security APIs delegating implementation of security functionalities to the application programmer, can cause vulnerabilities in applications that the programmer develops. In **End user protection**, we discussed that security of the developed application should not depend on the application programmer, and we already included questions to cover this. Therefore, we did not included new questions into **Delegation**.

The last characteristic, **Implementation error susceptibility**, says that security API usability research should aim to minimize the error susceptibility. According to the authors, error susceptibility is caused by ignoring the first 10 characteristics that Gorski and Iacono mentioned. Hence, we assumed that this aspect is also covered by previous questions added.

Based on our arguments in this section, we have formed a generic questionnaire by improving Clarke's cognitive dimensions questionnaire to conduct empirical evaluations for security API usability, which contains questions of 15 dimensions (refer Appendix A for the complete questionnaire).

4   Conclusion and Future Work

In this work, we improved the version of Cognitive Dimensions framework introduced by Clarke [8] and introduced a generic questionnaire, to evaluate the usability of security APIs. We added new questions into Learning Style and Penetrability dimensions to cover the security related aspects. Furthermore, we introduced 3 new dimensions (i.e. **Hard to misuse**, **End-user protection** and **Testability**) with questions which we argued referring to existing literature, to be important for evaluating the usability of security APIs.

As a continuation of this work, we would be conducting empirical studies to prove the validity of the model and the questionnaire proposed.

Acknowledgements. We would like to thank Steven Clark from Microsoft Visual Studio usability group for providing details about API usability studies at Microsoft. We would also like to thank anonymous reviewers for their feedback.

A   Appendix

Appendix A - Complete Questionnaire

Abstraction Level

- Do you find the API abstraction level appropriate to the tasks?
- Did you need to adapt the API to meet your needs?
- Do you feel that you had to understand the underlying implementation to be able to use the API?

Learning Style

- Did you had to learn about different components exposed by API before starting to do anything useful related to your task? What are the components that you had to learn?
- Did you had previous experience working with any of the components of the API? If you had, do you think, that knowledge was essential to do anything useful related to your task?
- Did you had to learn about dependencies between different components exposed by API before starting to do anything useful related to your task? What are the dependencies that you had to learn?
- Did you had to learn about the underlying architecture of the API and other conceptual information before starting to do anything useful related to your task?

- Does the API support learning (the stuff required to complete the task), while you progressing with the task?
- Do you think your previous computer security related knowledge made it easy to use the API? Specifically what previous knowledge helped in using the API?
- Do you think, if you had previous knowledge of any specific area, it would have been easier to use the API? What are they?

Working Framework

- What are the information you had to maintain while completing the tasks?
- Which of them were represented in the API you had to use?
- Which of them were not directly represented in API, but was represented in the way that your code is structured?
- Which of them were not represented at all in the API or the code that you were writing?

Work Step Unit

- Does the amount of code required for this scenario seem just about right, too much, or too little? Why?
- Does the amount of code required for each subtask in this scenario seem just about right, too much, or too little? Why?

Progressive Evaluation

- How easy is it to stop in the middle of the scenario and check the progress of work so far?
- Is it possible to find out how much progress has been made? If not, why not?

Premature Commitment

- When you are working with the API, can you work on your programming task in any order you like, or does the system force you to think ahead and make certain decisions first?
- If so, what decisions do you need to make in advance? What sort of problems can this cause in your work

Penetrability

- What are the places where you had to distinguish between different methods and classes while you work on your programming task?
- Were you able to find enough information to distinguish between different methods and classes while you work on your programming task? If not, what are the information you think is missing?
- What are the places where you had to understand the context or scope of the particular parts of the API you worked with?
- Were you able to find enough information to understand the context or scope of the particular parts of the API you worked with? If not, what are the information you think is missing?

- What are the places where you had to understand the intricate working details of the API while you work on your programming task?
- Were you able to find enough information to understand the intricate working details of the API while you work on your programming task? If not, what are the information you think is missing?
- Did the API (including its documentation) provide enough information about the security relevant specifics related to the task you completed? What are the information that was missing or you had to find by referring to external sources?

API Elaboration

- Did you had to extend types exposed by the API by providing their own implementation of custom behavior to accomplish task? What are the types you had to extend? Explain why you needed to extend the original type provided by the API in each case.
- Did you had to replace existing types or introduce new types to accomplish task? What are the types you had to replace/introduce? Explain why you needed to replace existing types or introduce new types in each case.

API Viscosity

- When you need to make changes to previous work, how easy is it to make the change? Why?
- Are there particular changes that are more difficult to make? Which ones?

Consistency

- Were there different parts of the API that mean similar things, is the similarity clear from the way they appear? Please give examples.
- Are there places where some things ought to be similar, but the API makes them different? What are they?

Role Expressiveness

- When reading code that uses the API, is it easy to tell what each section of code does? Why?
- Are there some parts that are particularly difficult to interpret? Which ones?
- When using the API, is it easy to know what classes and methods of the API to use when writing code?

Domain Correspondence

- Did the types exposed by the API map directly onto the types and concepts you expected? If not, please mention the the types you expected and how it was supported in the API?
- Were there any types exposed by the API do not map directly onto the types and concepts you expected? What are they?

Hard to Misuse

- Have you came up with incidents where you incorrectly used the API and then identified the correct way of doing that? Did API give any help to identify that you used the API incorrectly? If there any similar incidents, please explain?
- Did the API give proper error messages in a case of exceptions and error, or did you had to handle them at your programme level? If you had to handle them at your level, please mention the scenarios.

End-user Protection

- Do you think the security of the end user of the application you developed, depends on how you completed the task? Or does it depend only on the security API you used?
- If you think security of the end user depends on how you completed the task, in which ways does it depend?

Testability

- Did you tested the security of your application after completing the task using security API? If not, why?
- If yes, how did you do that?
- Did the API provided any guidance on how to test your application?

References

1. Anderson, R.: Security Engineering. Wiley, New York (2008)
2. Arachchilage, N.A.G., Love, S., Beznosov, K.: Phishing threat avoidance behaviour: an empirical investigation. Comput. Hum. Behav. **60**, 185–197 (2016)
3. Beaton, J., Jeong, S.Y., Xie, Y., Stylos, J., Myers, B.A.: Usability challenges for enterprise service-oriented architecture APIs. In: IEEE Symposium on Visual Languages and Human-Centric Computing, pp. 193–196. IEEE (2008)
4. Blackwell, A.F., Green, T.R.: A cognitive dimensions questionnaire optimised for users. In: Proceedings of the Twelth Annual Meeting of the Psychology of Programming Interest Group, pp. 137–152 (2000)
5. Bond, M.K.: Understanding security APIs. Ph.D. thesis, University of Cambridge (2004)
6. Boren, T., Ramey, J.: Thinking aloud: reconciling theory and practice. IEEE Trans. Prof. Commun. **43**(3), 261–278 (2000)
7. Clarke, S.: Evaluating a new programming language. In: 13th Workshop of the Psychology of Programming Interest Group, pp. 275–289 (2001)
8. Clarke, S.: Measuring API usability. Dr. Dobbs J. **29**(5), S1–S5 (2004)
9. Clarke, S.: Describing and measuring API usability with the cognitive dimensions. In: Cognitive Dimensions of Notations 10th Anniversary Workshop, p. 131. Citeseer (2005)
10. Clarke, S.: Re: [ppigdiscuss] cognitive dimensions questionnaire for evaluating API usability, October 2016. Email by: Steven.Clarke@microsoft.com
11. Daughtry, J.M., Farooq, U., Stylos, J., Myers, B.A.: API usability: CHI 2009 special interest group meeting. In: CHI 2009 Extended Abstracts on Human Factors in Computing Systems, pp. 2771–2774. ACM (2009)

12. Eng, J.: Snapchat hacked, info on 4.6 million users reportedly leaked, 1 January 2014. http://www.nbcnews.com/business/snapchat-hacked-info-4-6-million-users-reportedly-leaked-2D11833474. Accessed 08 Sept 2016
13. Fahl, S., Harbach, M., Perl, H., Koetter, M., Smith, M.: Rethinking SSL development in an appified world. In: Proceedings of the ACM SIGSAC Conference on Computer and Communications Security, pp. 49–60. ACM (2013)
14. Farooq, U., Zirkler, D.: API peer reviews: a method for evaluating usability of application programming interfaces. In: Proceedings of the ACM Conference on Computer Supported Cooperative Work, pp. 207–210. ACM (2010)
15. Georgiev, M., Iyengar, S., Jana, S., Anubhai, R., Boneh, D., Shmatikov, V.: The most dangerous code in the world: validating SSL certificates in non-browser software. In: Proceedings of the ACM Conference on Computer and Communications Security, pp. 38–49. ACM (2012)
16. Gorski, P.L., Iacono, L.L.: Towards the usability evaluation of security APIs. In: Proceedings of the Tenth International Symposium on Human Aspects of Information Security and Assurance, pp. 252–265 (2016)
17. Green, M., Smith, M.: Developers are users too: designing crypto and security APIs that busy engineers and sysadmins can use securely. In: Talk at the USENIX Summit on Hot Topics in Security (HotSec 2015) (2015)
18. Green, T.R.: Cognitive dimensions of notations. In: People and computers V, pp. 443–460 (1989)
19. Grill, T., Polacek, O., Tscheligi, M.: Methods towards API usability: a structural analysis of usability problem categories. In: Winckler, M., Forbrig, P., Bernhaupt, R. (eds.) HCSE 2012. LNCS, vol. 7623, pp. 164–180. Springer, Heidelberg (2012). doi:10.1007/978-3-642-34347-6_10
20. Henning, M.: API design matters. Queue 5(4), 24–36 (2007)
21. Kadoda, G., Stone, R., Diaper, D.: Desirable features of educational theorem provers? A cognitive dimensions viewpoint. In: Proceedings of Psychology of Programming Interest Group conference (1999)
22. Mindermann, K.: Are easily usable security libraries possible and how should experts work together to create them? In: Proceedings of the 9th International Workshop on Cooperative and Human Aspects of Software Engineering, pp. 62–63. ACM (2016)
23. Myers, B.A., Stylos, J.: Improving API usability. Commun. ACM 59(6), 62–69 (2016)
24. Nielsen, J.: Usability Engineering. Academic Press, Boston (1994)
25. OWASP: OWASP secure coding practices - quick reference guide (2010). https://www.owasp.org/index.php/OWASP_Secure_Coding_Practices_-_Quick_Reference_Guide. Accessed 26 Sept 2016
26. Pagliery, J.: Hackers are draining bank accounts via the Starbucks app, 14 May 2015. http://money.cnn.com/2015/05/13/technology/hackers-starbucks-app/. Accessed 8 Sept 2016
27. Piccioni, M., Furia, C.A., Meyer, B.: An empirical study of API usability. In: ACM/IEEE International Symposium on Empirical Software Engineering and Measurement, pp. 5–14. IEEE (2013)
28. Scheller, T., Kühn, E.: Automated measurement of API usability: the API concepts framework. Inf. Softw. Technol. 61, 145–162 (2015)
29. Stylos, J., Clarke, S.: Usability implications of requiring parameters in objects' constructors. In: Proceedings of the 29th International Conference on Software Engineering, pp. 529–539. IEEE Computer Society (2007)

30. Stylos, J., Graf, B., Busse, D.K., Ziegler, C., Ehret, R., Karstens, J.: A case study of API redesign for improved usability. In: IEEE Symposium on Visual Languages and Human-Centric Computing, pp. 189–192. IEEE (2008)
31. Stylos, J., Myers, B.A.: The implications of method placement on API learnability. In: Proceedings of the 16th ACM SIGSOFT International Symposium on Foundations of software engineering, pp. 105–112. ACM (2008)
32. Weber, S.: Empirical evaluation of API usability and security (2016). https:// insights.sei.cmu.edu/sei_blog/2016/01/empirical-evaluation-of-api-usability-and-security.html. Accessed 08 Sept 2016
33. Wurster, G., van Oorschot, P.C.: The developer is the enemy. In: Proceedings of the 2008 Workshop on New Security Paradigms, pp. 89–97. ACM (2009)
34. Zibran, M.F., Eishita, F.Z., Roy, C.K.: Useful, but usable? Factors affecting the usability of APIs. In: 18th Working Conference on Reverse Engineering, pp. 151–155. IEEE (2011)

Managing User Experience: Usability and Security in a New Era of Software Supremacy

Panagiotis Zagouras[1], Christos Kalloniatis[1(✉)],
and Stefanos Gritzalis[2]

[1] Privacy Engineering and Social Informatics Laboratory,
Department of Cultural Technology and Communication,
University of the Aegean, University Hill, 81100 Mytilene, Greece
{ctdl6015, chkallon}@aegean.gr
[2] Information and Communication Systems Security Laboratory,
Department of Information and Communications Systems Engineering,
University of the Aegean, 83200 Samos, Greece
sgritz@aegean.gr

Abstract. Software is now the driving force behind our daily lives. At work, everyone is affected to a greater or lesser extent by software, which exerts a significant influence in every activity of our daily lives. It is clear that software and the way it interacts with humans has a significant impact on the life and future of everyone who uses it. There is thus a self-evident need to balance usability and security, with usability now defined as an outcome of a product's interaction rather than a property inherent to that product, and assessed by means of usability evaluations rather than by measurements. Still, the problems of achieving a balance between usability and security remain. Recent research would indicate that the concept of 'user experience' needs to be broken down into the complementary factors of usability and security to create new methodologies for producing modern, reliable, user-friendly software. The current paper moves into this direction by presenting scientific definitions for the concepts of 'user experience', 'usability' and 'security', their extensions and implications, and the research which has explored ways of harmonizing usability and security in contemporary software. It highlights how hard this is to achieve and how important it is for the software industry to incorporate the concept of 'user experience' into usability-security so as to develop products capable of automatically adapting to any given environment or user.

Keywords: User experience · Usability · Security · Interaction

1 Introduction

The need for user-friendly, high-quality software is now axiomatic. However, a large number of information systems [1] are rejected, despite the large sums invested in their development, due to their failure to interact with the system or fulfill their task. Usability thus has a significant impacts on the success of a given software package.

© Springer International Publishing AG 2017
T. Tryfonas (Ed.): HAS 2017, LNCS 10292, pp. 174–188, 2017.
DOI: 10.1007/978-3-319-58460-7_12

And while it remains a highly complex concept with fuzzy characteristics, it is crucial that we manage usability correctly in every function of a given piece of software. User involvement plays an important role in defining the usability of software and the level of security it can provide when it is operated by a given user.

We live in a world in which privacy and security have assumed greater importance than ever before. In this post-Snowden era [2], companies assign greater significance to data security and as software users, we are increasingly aware of threats to our privacy. And yet we still demand software that is personalizable, user-friendly, intuitive and flawless. As users, we demand 24/7 access to out information without constantly having to log back in to the system.

This is the contradiction between security and user experience (UX). We do not want our data falling into the wrong hands, but we do not want our added security to impact on our user experience, either. In fact, we want ever-easier access to our data.

Everyone has a double-edged relationship [3] with the products and services they make use of: they simplify but complicate our lives; they divide us and bring us together. But all this software is made by people who will take the credit if it works well and the blame if it fails to do so. This means that, in order to design software that provides a better user experience, we need to foresee every action a user may conceivably take and understand their intentions at every stage in every process they execute, all of which must take place in a secure and private environment. Correctly applying UX principles and guidelines will boost security.

This is encapsulated in the following formula:

$$Security + UX = Security^2$$

There is a need to create user-centric information systems. The concept of 'user experience' is crucial to such developments and its implications for usability—security has still to be fully explored by researchers.

This paper illustrates the need to research the concept of user experience in tandem with usability and security, given the lack of scientific methodologies, which consider all three concepts in parallel in order to produce easy to use and secure software meeting contemporary requirements.

Specifically, Sect. 2 provides a thorough analysis of the qualities of user experience-usability-security and their lines of scientific demarcation. Section 3 reviews scientific methodologies, which have been developed to complement usability-security as well as respective tools that have been developed in this direction and provides useful findings. Finally Sect. 4 argues the case for more specific, categorized solutions in the design of secure and usable information systems and concludes the paper and provides guidelines for future research.

2   Core Concepts

The Internet of Things (IoT) is a system of interrelated computing devices, mechanical and digital machines, objects, animals or people that are provided with unique identifiers and the ability to transfer data over a network without requiring human-to-human or human-to-computer interaction [4]. Yet along with the many societal, environmental and economic benefits of the IoT, the rapidly-expanding connected world represents a growing surface which adversaries of all stripes can attack, and IoT vulnerabilities are being exploited with malicious intent every day.

The IoT (Internet of Things) has changed the way consumers behave in the marketplace. A large number of different devices now interact using a range of technologies. Major corporations are investing heavily in connectable devices. In this context, it is self-evident that the way in which businesses and individuals interact with the IoT will impact significantly on user experience-usability-security.

2.1 User Experience

Recent years have seen vast changes [5] in the systems architecture sector. The data organization and search landscape has changed utterly over the last decade or so, and the nineteen nineties are now most definitely a bygone era. Complex information systems with different technologies, users and goals now interact and exchange personal data and financial figures under regulatory systems of varying strictness, creating obstacles, issues and delays for users. Figure 1 below illustrates why we must strike a unique balance on each project between business goals and context, user needs, behavior and content.

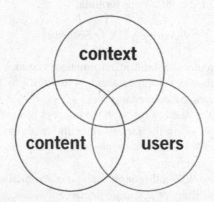

Fig. 1. Three circles of information architecture [5]

The above figure represents the concept of Information Architecture, but it is also useful for understanding user experience as well. If the content has structure and all the information a user needs, it will help create a good user experience [6]. The context refers to the physical, digital, and social structures that surround the point of use.

Users have several characteristics including their age, professional responsibilities, software, hardware, environment (home, shared office, private office, shared public terminal), computer experience and Web experience. User characteristics can also include types of disability, adaptive strategies used, and experience with specific assistive technologies.

User experience has multiple significant extensions, which make it clear that we have to expand into a large number of parameters beyond usability. The following diagram presents this in detail (Fig. 2):

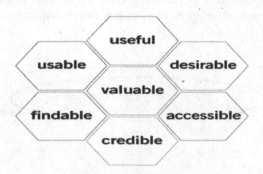

Fig. 2. User experience honeycomb [5]

This is how the facets or qualities of the user experience can be explained [5]:

Useful. Practitioners cannot simply paint within the lines drawn up by managers. They must be brave and creative enough to question the degree to which products and systems are useful and use their expertise in both the craft and the medium to come up with innovative improvements.

Usable. Usability remains crucial, but there are aspects of web design, which go beyond methods of, and perspectives on, human-computer interaction which center on the interface. We can thus say that ease of use, while necessary, is not sufficient in itself.

Desirable. Efficiency is not the be-all-and-end-all of design. It is important not to underestimate the power of emotional design and the value of image, identity, brand etc.

Findable. Users must be able to find what they are looking for on a web site easily, so objects need to be locatable and navigable.

Accessible. Given that people with disabilities account for upwards of 10% of the population, web sites need to ensure they are accessible to this group. It is not only the ethical thing to do, it is good for business, too. E-accessibility is sure to be required by law at some point, in the same way that physical accessibility is now.

Credible. The Web Credibility Project is helping us understand how design elements can impact on the degree to which users believe web content.

Valuable. Site sponsors need to receive value for their money. In the case of not-for-profit organizations, the experience of site users must contribute to the fulfill-ment of the organization's mission. In the case of for-profit businesses, the on-line experience must enhance customer satisfaction and profits.

UX specialists, designers and developers [7] no longer work in a one-way workflow (or waterfall). Rather, two-way communication is the norm between UX specialists and designers, UX specialists and developers, and developers and designers, given that the definition, design and development processes can be concurrent. This does, however, create the need for an integrator to coordinate this interaction. The coordinator will thus work closely at different times with UX specialists in realizing the UI architecture (e.g. screen layout), with designers in providing technical support to generate XAML or MXML code, and with developers in ensuring that functionality is integral to the design (Fig. 3).

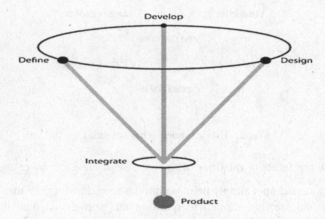

Fig. 3. An illustration of the new UX design and development workflow [7]

Petrie and Bevan [8] found that users of new technologies are less intent on completing a task than on amusing and entertaining themselves. Table 1 illustrates that, rather than being distinct concepts, UX and usability have interrelated aspects that contribute equally to a system's overall UX and usability.

Table 1. Factors contributing to UX [8].

Quality characteristic	UX	Functionality	User interface usability	Learnability	Accessibility	Safety
Product attributes	Aesthetic attributes	Appropriate functions	Good UI design (easy to use)	Learnability attributes	Technical accessibility	Safe and secure design
UX pragmatic do goals	To be effective and efficient					
UX hedonic be goals	Stimulation, identification and evocation					
UX: actual experience	Visceral	Experience of interaction				
Usability (=performance in use measures)	Effectiveness and productivity in use: effective task completion and efficient use of time			Learnability in use: effective and efficient to learn	Accessibility in use: effective and efficient with disabilities	Safety in use: occurrence of unintended consequences
Measures of UX consequences	Satisfaction in use: satisfaction with achieving pragmatic and hedonic goals					
	Pleasure	Likability and comfort				Trust

2.2 Usability

More recently, usability experts [9] have worked with the ISO/IEC JTC1 SC7 Software Engineering subcommittee to integrate usability into software engineering and software quality standards.

Standards relating to usability are primarily concerned with:

- The product in use (the effectiveness, efficiency and satisfaction derived from a particular use).
- The user interface and interaction.
- The process used to develop the product.

The capability of an organization to apply user- centered design.

The above are inter-related: the product's purpose is to be effective, efficient and satisfying when it is used to achieve the desired result. That it has a suitable interface and interaction is a prerequisite for all of these. This requires a user-centered design process, which, if it is to be consistent, requires an organizational capability to support user-centered design.

The most challenging aspect of software development is not simply providing the required functionality; it is fulfilling specific properties such as performance, security and maintainability, which contribute to software quality [10].

Usability engineering has several benefits. Specifically:

- It improves software
- It saves customers money
- It minimizes engineering costs

Proper usability engineering leads to software that is usable, which translates itself into productive, satisfied customers, a better reputation for the product, and hence increased sales. Proper usability engineering can reduce the cost overruns in software projects.

A framework is presented which visualizes how and to what extent usability can be integrated at the architectural level using specific methods of design, and how and to what extent we can assess architectures in terms of the degree to which they support usability. Usability should drive design at all stages, but current usability engineering practices fail to fully achieve this goal. Our survey shows that there are no design techniques or assessment tools that allow for usability to be integrated at the architectural level.

Figure 4 below illustrates an integrated approach to the extensions/implications of usability.

2.3 Information and Computer Security

Information security [11] is described as a set of properties that must be upheld.

The ISO/IEC 27000:2016 [12] provides an overview of information security management systems and describes terms and definitions.

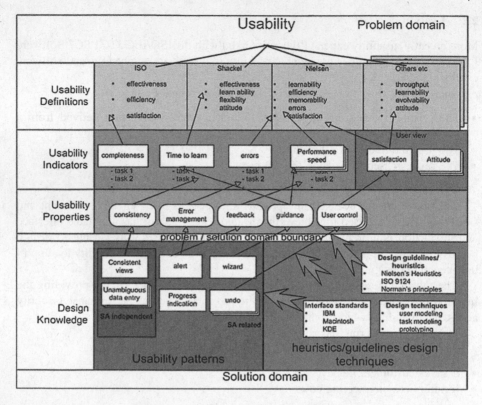

Fig. 4. A usability framework approach [10]

Computer Security can be defined [13] as the technological and managerial procedures applied to computer systems to ensure the availability, integrity and confidentiality of the information managed by the computer system.

Confidentiality, integrity and availability—or CIA–are the fundamental elements of any IT security system. However, their inclusion often detracts from the usability of IT systems. Other researchers have offered more complex variations on the classic CIA triad; Don Parker [14], for instance, has written about the Parkerian Hexad of Confidentiality, Integrity, Availability, Possession, Authenticity and Utility. Other scientists have proposed other desirable properties.

Gollman [15] proposed accountability and dependability. He defined security as the protection of assets and introduced the concepts of prevention, detection and reaction. Two equally important concepts relevant to security are avoidance and deterrence.

A threat is something that has the potential to cause us harm. Vulnerabilities are weaknesses that can be exploited in order to harm us. Risk is the likelihood that something bad will happen.

The table below lists the potential consequences of various types of threats to an information system's security attributes [16]. An interception means that some unauthorized party has gained access to an asset. In an interruption, an asset of the system becomes lost, unavailable, or unusable. If an unauthorized party not only accesses but tampers with an asset, the threat is a modification. Finally, an unauthorized party might fabricate counterfeit objects on a computing system (Table 2).

Table 2. Various types of threats

Security attribute	Threats
Confidentiality	Interception
Integrity	Interruption
	Modification
	Fabrication
Availability	Interruption
	Modification
	Fabrication

There are various ways of building increased security into information systems. These break down into:

- Descriptive and *ad hoc* methods.
- Checklists.
- Guidelines.
- Risk management.

Providing security for, but also against, the different people around our information is one of the most difficult aspects of information security. These can include service providers, employees, partners, contractors, customers and many others. We can expect all these groups to behave in different unforeseen and unexpected ways, doing so innocently, ignorantly or maliciously. In all cases, it can be a challenge to provide security in this area. Given that humans are the weakest link, they must be taught to be more aware of security.

Applying design patterns can have multiple benefits in the security sphere. The seven security patterns as shown in Fig. 5 and proposed by Yoder and Barcalow [17] can be applied when developing security for an application.

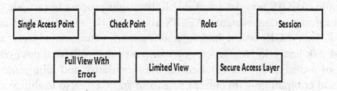

Fig. 5. Yoder and Barcalow's seven security patterns [17].

This is an excellent approach to take into consideration in this research, given that it considers an application to be only as secure as its component parts and its interactions with them. It is a user-focused approach.

3 Academic Approaches

It is extremely difficult to harmonize security with usability. The fundamental goal of security is to protect assets. But protecting infrastructure from risks requires security systems to access these risks. Moreover, it should be noted that security is a process not a product.

3.1 Usable—Security

HCISec is a scientific field which has advanced enormously in recent years. A number of research projects have focused on the usability of password policies and security controls. The HCISec community has approached the design of usable-security from two different directions:

- Design principles and idioms.

Examples include Yee's [18] guidelines and strategies for secure interaction as well as Garfinkel's [19] patterns for usable-security.

- User-centered security

Sasse et al's [20] work on applying HCI design approaches to the design of security mechanisms and Zurko and Simon's [21] work on user-centered security contain significant material.

Very little research has been conducted into the design of usable and secure systems with a view to the designer's, rather than the end user's, needs. Composing HCI with security technics is a development that has inspired a good many researchers.

Gerd tom Markotten's research [22] seeks to connect the security engineering process to usability engineering. It begins with functional analysis, threat and risk analysis, a security strategy and model, and the design and implementation of testing. This corresponds to Analysis, Design, Testing in usability engineering.

AEGIS [23] (Appropriate and Effective Guidance for Information Security) is another example. AEGIS was designed as a lightweight process to provide guidance to developers designing secure systems. AEGIS assets and their relationships are modeled using UML [24]. AEGIS asset models make useful boundary objects, while asset modeling and risk analysis are carried out with respect to different environments.

The lack of a design approach based on the singularity and requirements of individual users and compatible with current scientific approaches to usability and security is obvious. Procedures need to be created which allow software to be designed in line with these singular needs, while sticking to the rules of usability-security.

3.2   Usability—Design

The ISO 9241 on usability definitions is detailed in Table 3 below.

Table 3. Usability Definitions based on ISO 9241

Concept	Description
Product	The part of the equipment (hardware, software, materials) for which usability is to be specified or evaluated
User	Person who interacts with the product
Goal	Intended outcome
Effectiveness	Accuracy and completeness with which users achieve specified goals
Efficiency	Resources expended in relation to the accuracy and completeness with which users achieve goals
Satisfaction	Freedom from discomfort, and positive attitudes towards to the use of the product
Context of use	Users, tasks, equipment (hardware, software and materials) and the physical and social environments in which a product is used

A number of usability professionals have taken the philosophy of user-centered design on board and have created various usability design processes informed by this philosophy, such as: Goal-Directed-Design [25], Contextual Design [26] and Usage Centered Design [27]. The above processes share the following features:

- Tasks and scenarios
- Goals
- Personas and Assumption personas

We have still to produce modern, user-friendly software, and there is a pressing need to adopt a contemporary approach informed by the new balance of priorities in Information Technology.

3.3   Requirements Engineering

Requirements engineering [23] is a research nexus between HCI and information security. It encompasses many approaches, but the best fits for this area are Problem Frames, Goal-Oriented Approaches, and Use Cases. These approaches are valuable in this area, because they have published security extensions and relate to the elicitation and specification of requirements.

Problem Frames: A tool [28] for structuring software problems and analyzing them.

Problem analysis or the problem frames approach is a set of concepts which can be employed when collating requirements and deciding on specifications for software. Its underlying philosophy differs markedly from other methods of collecting software requirements in so far as it:

- Takes a parallel rather than a hierarchical approach to breaking down user requirements.
- Views user requirements as real-world relationships–which is to say in the application domain, rather than within the software system itself or its interface.

Goal-oriented approaches: Goal-Oriented Requirements Engineering (GORE) [29] is about the use of goals for requirements evaluation, elicitation, documentation, quality assurance and evolution. Two goal-oriented RE Frameworks emerged independently for GORE, KAOS [30] and NFR/i* (Non-Functional Requirements/Intention Strategic Actor Relations) [31]. Both frameworks address common targets such as goal refinement and conflicts, but while there are complementarities there are also differences between them. KAOS was more focused on semi-formal and formal reasoning about behavioral goals for deriving goal refinements, goal operationalization, goal-based risk analysis and conflict management. In NFR/i*, too, the focus was more on qualitative reasoning and soft goals for analyzing goal contributions, evaluating alternative goal refinements, and reasoning about goal dependencies among organizational agents.

Use Cases: Scenario-based approaches to specifying, validating and eliciting are popular in Requirements Engineering. The best-known approaches are Use Cases [32]. Sindre and Opdahl [33] proposed Misuse Cases, a sequence of actions including variants that a system or entity can perform, interacting and causing harm to stakeholders.

Castro et al. propose yet another approach, which combines Usability with Requirements Engineering [34]. In order to take usability into account at early stages of software development, he adds various new activities: relating behavior patterns to usability mechanisms, building use cases with usability mechanisms, and building mock-ups with usability mechanisms. The activities that gained the most were the elicitation and analysis of requirements relating to user knowledge and user modeling respectively.

The above approaches relate to the users' goals and knowledge, but do not return the expected results, primarily because neither the individual user nor their behavioral characteristics have as yet been properly and fully researched.

3.4   Methodologies—Frameworks

The community adopts social science research methodologies to examine the difficult issue of secure information system research. The two basic methodologies are (i) Action Research [35, 36] and (ii) Grounded Theory [37, 38].

The Action Research approach has a five-phase process:

- Diagnosing
- Action Planning
- Action Taking
- Evaluating
- Specifying learning

Grounded Theory has three basic stages:

- Open Coding
- Axial Coding
- Selective Coding

Hausawi [39] proposed the Usable-Security Engineering Framework (USEF), which consists of three components (Assessment Framework for Usable Security—AFUS, Usable-Security Guidelines, and a Usable Security Measuring Matrix). Each component focuses on one of the three phases (Requirements Engineering, Design, and Evaluation/Testing) of the Software Engineering Development Life-Cycle (SDLC) in order to enhance the alignment of security and usability for better usable-security (Fig. 6).

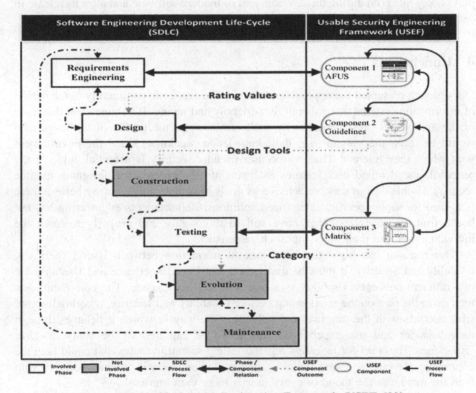

Fig. 6. The Usable-Security Engineering Framework (USEF) [39]

Faily [23] proposed the IRIS (Integrating Requirements and Information Security) framework as a paradigm for integrating existing techniques and tools with the design of usable and secure systems. The IRIS medal model is sub-divided into six views—environment, asset, task, goal, risk and responsibility—which correspond with the different perspectives associated with a secure system's use contexts. Each view is modelled using a UML class diagram.

The meta-model facilitates the specification of requirements for usable and secure systems by stipulating the concepts that need to be elicited. However, the meta-model is agnostic about how this is to be done, which makes it necessary to provide guidance on how the concepts should be elicited and specified. To this end, we have broken the meta-model up into three intersecting groups (which Faily calls perspectives): Usability, Requirements and Security.

The same researcher has also developed CAIRIS (Computer Aided Integration of Requirements and Information Security), a software tool which embodies the characteristics required to support the IRIS framework. The design principles of CAIRIS are: Familiarity, Extensibility, Process, Centricity, Security and Usability centricity.

These two approaches deliver excellent results in the management of usability and security, but there would still appear to be considerable scope for further research into how user experience relates to the characteristics in question, given that the user now plays a key role both during the development of modern software and after its release in determining its success or otherwise.

4   Conclusions

Our research presented the approaches taken by the academic community to the design of information systems that are both user-friendly and secure. It became clear that none of the approaches presented actually took into account the profile of the users who would be using the system—i.e. their knowledge, weaknesses and the environment with which they interact. Thus, while user-friendly security is essential, none of the proposals use detailed user features as input into the process for designing useable security. Usable design seeks to achieve its goals in various ways, but we believe there is a need for more specific, categorized solutions. Requirements engineering has not borne fruit, because researcher have still to thoroughly and properly research the individual user and their behavioural characteristics.

Our research has highlighted the lack of interaction between User Experience, Usability and Security. It must be understood that User Experience and Usability are two different concepts. Usability is a subset of user experience. The community has focused in the past on the relationship between usability and security, ignoring the user who interacts with the program and influences the way in which it behaves through their behavior and use experience. This could be captured in the study on User Experience. The need for investigating and testing scientific routes that could help the community develop software building methodologies that will interact securely with both the mind and the mood of every user is more than immense.

We believe that the future of software engineering lies in the creation of software whose nature adapts to every context and user it finds itself in. The need for establishing rules and procedures that will enable everyone involved in software development to work together and create safe and user-friendly software which will draw its character from the environment in which it is operating, respect every user, and interact in a different way with different users depending on their needs and requirements is a goal that the new technological trends along with users' expertise demand to be implemented as soon as possible.

References

1. Ankita M., et al.: Usability evaluation methods: a literature review. Int. J. Eng. Sci. Technol. **4**(2) (2012)
2. Jasper, O.: Security + Usability = Security^2 (2015). http://www.thenextview.nl/blog/security-user-experience. Accessed 11 Jan 2017
3. Garret, J.J.: The Elements of User Experience: User-Centered Design for the Web and Beyond. New Riders, Berkeley (2011)
4. http://internetofthingsagenda.techtarget.com/definition/Internet-of-Things-IoT
5. Morville, P.: User Experience Design (2004). http://semanticstudios.com/user_experience_design/. Accessed 11 Jan 2017
6. Techved: (2016). https://uxmag.com/articles/the-user-experience-of-good-content. Accessed 15 Jan 2017
7. Zheng, X.S., Wang, M., Matos, G., Zhang, S.: Streamlining user experience design and development: roles, tasks and workflow of applying rich application technologies. In: Jacko, J.A. (ed.) Human-Computer Interaction, Part I, HCII 2011. LNCS, vol. 6761, pp. 142–151. Springer, Heidelberg (2011). doi:10.1007/978-3-642-21602-2_17
8. Petrie, H., Bevan, N.: The evaluation of accessibility, usability and user experience. In: Stephanidis, C. (ed.) The Universal Access Handbook, pp. 20.1–20.14. CRC Press, Boca Raton (2009)
9. Bevan, N.: International Standards for HCI. Idea Group Publishing, Hershey (2006)
10. Folmer, E., Bosch, J.: Architecting for usability: a survey. J. Syst. Softw. Issue **70**(1) (2002)
11. Fléchais, I.: Designing secure and usable systems. Ph.D. thesis, University College London (2005)
12. ISO: ISO/IEC 27000:2016 Information technology – Security techniques - Information security management systems - Overview and vocabulary. ISO/IEC (2016)
13. http://www.digitalguards.com/glossary.php
14. Parker, D.B.: Fighting Computer Crime. Wiley, Hoboken (1998)
15. Gollman, D.: Computer Security. Wiley, Hoboken (1999)
16. Andress, J.: The basics of Information Security: Understanding the Fundamentals of InfoSec in Theory and Practice. Elsevier, Amsterdam (2014)
17. Yoder, J., Barcalow, J.: Architectural patterns for enabling application security. Urbana **51**, 61801 (1998)
18. Yee, K.-P.: Guidelines and strategies for secure interaction design. In: Cranor, L.F., Garfinkel, S. (eds.) Security and Usability: Designing Secure Systems that People Can Use. O'Reilly Media, Newton (2005)
19. Garfinkel, S.L.: Design principles and patterns for computer systems that are simultaneously secure and usable. Ph.D. thesis, Cambridge (2005). (Adviser-David D. Clark and Adviser-Robert C. Miller)
20. Sasse, M.A., et al.: Transforming the 'weakest link'—a human/computer interaction approach to usable and effective security. BT Technol. J. **19**(3), 122–131 (2001)
21. Zurko, M.E., Simon, R.T.: User-centered security. In: Proceedings of the 1996 New Security Paradigms Workshop, pp. 27–33 (1996)
22. tom Markotten, D.G.: User-centered security engineering. In: Proceedings of the 4th EurOpen/USENIX Conference (2002). Unpublished workshop proceedings
23. Faily, S.: A framework for usable and secure system design. Ph.D. thesis, University of Oxford (2011)
24. Rumbaugh, J., et al.: The Unified Modeling Language Reference Manual, 2nd edn. Addison-Wesley, Boston (2005)

25. Cooper, A., et al.: About Face 3: The Essentials of Interaction Design. Wiley, Hoboken (2007)
26. Beyer, H., Holtzblatt, K.: Contextual Design: Defining Customer-Centered Systems. Morgan Kaufmann, Burlington (1998)
27. Constantine, L.L., Lockwood, L.A.D.: Software for Use: A Practical Guide to the Models and Methods of Usage-Centered Design. Addison-Wesley, Boston (1999)
28. Jackson, M.: Problem Frames: Analyzing and Structuring Software Development Problems. Addison-Weslay, Boston (2001)
29. van Lamsweerde, A.: Requirements Engineering: From System Goals to UML Models to Software Specifications. Wiley, Hoboken (2009)
30. Dardenne, A., et al.: Goal-directed requirements acquisition. Sci. Comput. Program. **20**(1–2), 3–50 (1993)
31. Chung, L., et al.: Non-functional Requirements in Software Engineering. Kluwer Academic, Dordrecht (2000)
32. Jacobson, I.: Object-Oriented Software Engineering: A Use Case Driven Approach. Addison-Wesley, Boston (1992)
33. Sindre, G., Opdahl, A.L.: Eliciting security requirements with misuse cases. Requir. Eng. **10** (1), 34–44 (2005)
34. Castro, J.W., et al.: Integrating the personas technique into the requirements analysis activity. In: Proceedings of the 2008 Mexican International Conference on Computer Science, pp. 104–112. IEEE Computer Society (2008)
35. Baskerville, R.: Investigating informations systems with action research. Commun. AIS **2** (1999)
36. Stringer, E.T.: Action Research. SAGE Publications, Thousand Oaks (2007)
37. Martin, P.Y., Turner, B.A.: Grounded theory and organizational research. J. Appl. Behav. Sci. **22**(2), 141–157 (1986)
38. Goulding, C.: Grounded Theory: A Practical Guide for Management, Business and Market Researchers. SAGE Publications, Thousand Oaks (2002)
39. Hausawi, Y.: Towards a Usable-Security Engineering Framework for Enhancing Software Development. Florida Institute of Technology (2015)

Usable Authentication

PSV (Password Security Visualizer): From Password Checking to User Education

Nouf Aljaffan[1,2], Haiyue Yuan[1], and Shujun Li[1(✉)]

[1] University of Surrey, Guildford, UK
shujun.li@surrey.ac.uk, hooklee@gmail.com
[2] King Saud University, Riyadh, Kingdom of Saudi Arabia

Abstract. This paper presents the Password Security Visualizer (PSV), an interactive visualization system specifically designed for password security education. PSV can be seen as a reconfigurable "box" containing different proactive password checkers (PPCs) and visualizers of password security information, allowing it to be used like a "many in one" or "hybrid" PPC. PSV can provide many new features that do not exist in traditional PPCs, thus having a greater potential to achieve its goals of educating users. Using purely client-side Web-based technologies, we implemented a prototype of PSV as an open-source software tool on a 2-D animated canvas. To evaluate the actual performance of our implemented PSV prototype against traditional PPCs, we conducted a semi-structured interview involving 20 human participants. Our qualitative analysis of the results showed that PSV was considered the most informative and recommended by most participants as a good educational tool. To the best of our knowledge, PSV is the first system combining different PPCs together for user education, and the user study is the first of this kind on comparing educational effectiveness of different PPCs (and PPC-like password security tools such as PSV).

Keywords: Password · Security · Visualization · Password strength · Password checker · Password strength meter · Password cracking

1 Introduction

Despite being older than half a century, passwords remain the mostly-used form for user authentication, which can be attributed to their simplicity (ease to use) and cost effectiveness. Because the pervasive use of passwords, they are frequently targeted in cyber attacks and many large-scale password leakage incidents have been reported especially in recent years [9,22]. Password strengthening technologies such as password hashing and salting have been developed to provide more protection on passwords stored on the server side, but human users remain a weak link because they often choose weak passwords to compromise security for usability, thus making password cracking much more effective [11,17,31,32].

© Springer International Publishing AG 2017
T. Tryfonas (Ed.): HAS 2017, LNCS 10292, pp. 191–211, 2017.
DOI: 10.1007/978-3-319-58460-7_13

In order to avoid the use of weak passwords by human users, many technologies have been developed to assist users and network administrators. Password checkers are among the most widely-used technologies for this purpose. Password checkers are software tools used to check the strength of given passwords in order to detect and/or prevent use of weak passwords. There are two types of password checkers: proactive password checkers (PPCs) and reactive password checkers (RPCs). PPCs are client-side tools interacting with end users when they are creating passwords and giving immediate feedback on the user interface to inform users about the password strength. They are often combined with password policies so that known weak passwords are banned. RPCs are server-side tools performing regular scans of the password database by launching simulated password cracking attempts. Detected weak passwords by RPCs will be sent to network administrators and/or affected users for actions. In this paper, we focus on PPCs because they can offer more opportunities to educate end users directly.

A PPC needs to work with one or more password strength metering (PSM) algorithms, each of which normally returns a numerical or categorical value indicating the overall strength of a given password[1]. Many researchers use the term "PSM" (password strength meters) or simply "password meters" for PPCs, which can lead to confusion. In this paper, we used the term PSM for the underlying ("invisible") algorithms calculating password strength and PPC for the ("visible") software system with a clear user interface, empowered by one or more PSMs, to inform users about the strength of a given password.

PPCs are normally not designed for educational purposes, but can achieve such goals as a natural byproduct (e.g., by repeatedly using PPCs a user can naturally gain knowledge about password security). Insights learned from research work on PPCs and PSMs [4, 5, 25–27] have suggested that educating users about password security and attacks is an important aspect to make PPCs more effective, but very few tools have been developed and evaluated for this purpose.

This paper tries to fill the gap between password checking and user education by presenting Password Security Visualizer (PSV), an *interactive* visualization system specifically designed for password security education. PSV extends the main concepts behind all PPCs to a *reconfigurable* "box" containing different proactive password checkers and other non-PPC tools for visualizing useful information around the security of a given password, where "reconfigurable" refers to the capability of adding new PPCs into and removing existing ones from the PSV "box". Although being designed as an educational tool, PSV can still be used like a normal PPC, with much richer information about the security of the given password. To some extent, in addition to being a password security education tool, PSV can also be seen a "many in one" or "hybrid" PPC.[2] At the user interface (UI) level, PSV can be designed in many different ways, two of which will be explained in this paper. Using purely client-side Web-based technologies,

---

[1] In principle, a PSM algorithm can return more than one value each representing a different aspect of the password strength. Such algorithms are however very rare.

[2] We originally developed PSV as Visual Password Checker (VPC) [10], which was later extended/renamed to be more education-oriented rather than yet another PPC.

we implemented one possible PSV design as an open-source software tool on a 2-D animated canvas. We followed some educational principles to design and implement PSV, so we hoped it can a greater potential to achieve its goals of educating users. To evaluate the actual performance of the PSV prototype, we conducted a semi-structured interview with 20 human participants. Since there are not many other password security education tools and PPCs do have a side feature of educating users about password security, we decided to compare our PSV prototype's performance with three different designs of existing PPCs. Our results suggested that our PSV prototype was considered the most informative tool for educating users about password security.

The rest of this paper is arranged as follows. In the next section we present related work on PPCs. Section 3 discuss design considerations of PSV, and Sect. 4 gives details on the web-based PSV prototype system. In Sect. 5 we explain how we conducted the semi-structured interview and analyzed the results. The final section concludes the paper with further discussions and future work.

2 Related Work

PPCs can be traced back to research work conducted in the early 1990s [11,15]. Nowadays PPCs have become ubiquitous on computer systems and websites, as a standard component of the password creation and update processes. The basic functionality of a PPC is to give *immediate* feedback on the strength of the password the user is entering so that the user can make a more informed decision on if the current password is strong enough to be used.

It has been observed that PPCs could influence users to choose stronger passwords [4,5,26], but users can also be confused by inappropriate/inconsistent strength ratings given by different PPCs [3]. Much research [13,16,23,30,33] has therefore been done to develop more robust PSMs so that the estimated password strength matches the actual risk against password crackers better.

At the UI level, some studies [5,28] have showed that the PPC UI design matters in terms of influencing users to create stronger passwords, and some designs could be more effective. The most common UI design is a (horizontal or vertical) 1-D bar (or segmented box) showing the estimated password strength score as a progress bar, a colored bar/box, and sometimes a very short textual description such as "weak" and "very strong" as well. Some PPCs also show a more detailed textual description (maybe visible only after a link/button being clicked), which can cover recommendations on how to improve the current password and password policies. Some PPCs choose to use different PSMs e.g. those based on peer pressure [23] and fear appeal [28], which also require the UI to be designed differently. Among all PPCs we are aware of, one PPC [24] is quite unique in displaying multiple 1-D bars, which show details about how the overall password strength score is calculated based on multiple sub-ratings. Although the multi-bar PPC is much more informative, Ciampa found out it is the hardest to understand compared with other simpler PPCs [5]. The general absence of *clear* feedback and *sufficient* information about the returned password strength scores in PPCs can leave users confused about why a password is given a specific rating by a PPC thus let them choose to neglect PPCs and depend on their own subject judgments on passwords [4,25].

Ciampa studied the effectiveness of four different UI designs on password feedback mechanisms in PPCs [5]. Besides a common 1-D bar PPC, he also examined (1) a dial reading based PPC [19], (2) a fear appeal based PPC [29], (3) the multi-bar PPC "The Password Meter" [24]. His results showed that the fear appeal based PPC is the most effective among all the four tested feedback mechanisms on influencing users towards stronger passwords. However, the majority of participants were observed preferring the multi-bar PPC, even though it was the hardest to understand. Ciampa also reported the need of supporting users with the required security level based on the used context.

Ur et al. conducted a comparative study on PPCs used by 14 popular websites in 2012 [26]. They found out that most PPCs studied have a simple 1-D bar based UI design. They also found out that different PPCs' appearances did not have major effect on either users' attitudes or password arrangement. Although using PPCs did motivate users to creating longer passwords, which were not observed to be less memorable, users often did not have a clue about the reason behind ratings given by PPCs, which might cause confusion and mislead them when improper PSMs are used. They also found out that participants had tended to select weaker passwords when they became frustrated, and lost trust in the PPC. Similar observations around the psychological phenomenon "frustration" and "discomfort" were also reported by Haque et al. in a 2014 study [8].

Two more recent studies [25,27] suggested that many users do have prior knowledge on how to strengthen their passwords, but they do not always follow the knowledge to create strong passwords in real world. One study [25] further suggested that this knowledge-behavior gap may be the result of neglecting to educate users about different attacks to passwords.

Furnell's study [6] revealed great inconsistencies among PPCs on 10 popular websites, and the password composition recommendations given by those websites were largely unclear and insufficient to guide users. The same observations were reported by de Carné de Carnavalet and Mannan in their work [3], in which they examined 13 PPCs deployed at 11 widely-used web services.

Komanduri et al. proposed a system called Telepathwords [12], which predicts most likely weak passwords based on the current password as the prefix and show them to alert users about such choices (since guessable passwords are weak). Telepathwords is not a PPC per the standard definition, but it show the security of the current password in a different way to guide users. They reported that the quality of passwords created using Telepathwords were higher than a number of PPCs they used for comparison. However, although users found that the feedback given by Telepathwords was helpful, many of them also reported it being difficult and annoying to use. This again highlighted the difficulty of designing good password security tools.

Some recently-reported personalized attacks on passwords [13,31] imply that PSMs and PPCs need to be personalized and contextualized. This is also echoed by Loge et al.'s work on a PPC for Android unlock patterns [14], in which they observed that the password strength could be influenced by individual features such as age and gender.

3 Password Security Visualizer (PSV): Design Considerations

Our overall aim for PSV is to help enhance users' overall understanding of password security, based on what we have learned from existing PPCs and other password security tools with an educational effect. This lets us to reflect about what users truly need if we want to educate them about password security, eventually leading us to design PSV as a system going beyond password checking. Our main design goals for PSV include: (1) to help users gain more knowledge and have less confusions on *all* aspects of password security, including but not limited to password strength, (2) to highlight the *complexity* of password security by *externalizing* inconsistencies between different PPCs and more advanced attacks on passwords; (3) to *engage* users actively so that the process of learning is enjoyable, (4) to produce an *open* system that can be easily executed and customized by users on different platforms.

To achieve those design goals, we decided to follow some well-established design principles to design and implement PSV. In the following, we will discuss those design principles, which will be followed by two example designs and a discussion on some key supporting algorithms running in the background.

3.1 Design Principles

For designing PSV, we followed a number of widely-recognized principles across different application domains [1,21], including cyber security [34]. Here, we explain all these principles and discuss how we considered them for PSV.

Informative Feedback: This principle aims to provide users with essential and sufficient information to make more informed decisions [21]. This has been observed for many simple PPCs where users only see a single rating of the given password without any further information on why the password is rated as such and what to do to improve. Therefore, supporting users with more informative feedback could help raise their awareness on password security and correct any misconceptions, which in turn will help them to make better security-related decisions such as choosing a stronger password.

The informative feedback PSV can provide include different aspects of password security such as the following (but not limited to these) categories: (1) basic password attributes such as length, types of characters used, and structural information e.g. repeated patterns or character transformation rules, (2) risks against simple and advanced dictionary-based attacks, and (3) an overall password strength like what is given by a typical PPCs or PSM. For the third category, it will be beneficial to show estimates from multiple PPCs and PSMs to inform users about the complexity and limitations around the overall password strength estimation, thus educating them that they should not blindly follow an arbitrary PPC or PSM. Being able to understand the complexity and limitations will also help them become less confused when they enter such inconsistent ratings of different PPCs/PSMs. PSV will thus include a number of Password Information Units (PIUs), each showing one aspect of password security.

While offering more information is in general helpful, we must not lose sight of implications for overloading users with too much information, which can harm their learning performance. After a certain point, information overload will occur, which consequently may prevent users from processing the provided information. This requires controlling the amount of information shown to users by adapting some strategies (e.g., filtering and zooming). Some other principles discussed below can help in this regard as well.

Visualization: Information visualization can facilitate exploring and understanding rich information at a glance to attract users' interest and motivate them to learn, so it has been advocated by researcher over textual contents for superior learning outcome [34]. Most PPCs already support some level of visualization, however, this needs further strengthening in PSV as there will be more PIUs and more interactions with users. One focus will be to minimize possible distractions caused by too many PIUs and visualization itself.

Segmentation and Contiguity: Both principles can help to manage information being presented by reducing its complexity, thus helping users to understand the information better. Segmentation is about breaking information into small chunks [34]. This may involve grouping related information into different units. Contiguity is about keeping related information near to each other to maintain a smoother information flow, which can help users to achieve a better comprehension of the information presented [34]. For PSV, the segmentation principle is naturally done by grouping information into PIUs. We will need to consider how to map each PIU to visual features such as shape, size, orientation, etc. Figure 1 shows two examples of how the combination of shapes and orientations can be used to map various PIUs. The contiguity principle can be applied by providing more detailed information about each PIU (e.g., using a pop-up tooltip) while the user is interacting with the PIU. The additional information should be placed close to the PIU of interest so the information contiguity is maintained.

Signaling: This principle is about drawing users' attention to significant information only if it is necessary, which can help enhance users' learning performance [34]. For PSV, different visual features can be used to signal important information in each PIU. Information can be signaled by many distinct visual features (e.g., more prominent color, unique shape, larger size, animation, change of styles, etc.). For example, different icons or shapes can be used to indicate different information categories of a PIU, and a PIU's location relative to a reference can signal a specific level of risk. Such signaling can help users to recognize important information more quickly. Another example is about using animation: a PIU can move smoothly from an old location to a new one once its risk level changes. This interactive visualization could help raise users' awareness on such risk changes w.r.t. any changes to the password being evaluated, thus achieving a better understanding of how password security risks are estimated and why.

Interactive and Immediate Feedback: It is known that providing interactive and immediate feedback to users can foster their learning performance [21,34]. Immediate feedback can help to engage users via giving them a quick chance to reflect on what they just learned [34], and interactivity would allow users to absorb complex concepts and enjoy the learning process more. All PPCs have this principle built-in since the password strength estimate is always updated immediately when any change to the current password is made. For PSV, we can provide users with more interactive and immediate feedback by drawing users' attention to important security issues beyond the password strength estimate. For example, the interactive fear appeal idea proposed in [28] can be used to warn users about potential risk of password attacks immediately after a weak password is detected against some specific attacks. The risk level can be visualized by a number of "negative" icons such as skulls to achieve the fear appeal effect.

Reconfigurability and Personalization: Further information enrichments are also obtainable from allowing the system to be easily reconfigured. Such reconfiguration can allow users to create a personalized space to enhance their learning experience and gain more relevant knowledge [1]. As far as we know, all existing PPCs are designed to offer the same information to all users, which cannot adapt to different users' needs. To support reconfigurability and personalization, special UI elements and lower-level programming interfaces should be introduced in PSV to allow easy addition and removal of PIUs and other supporting components (e.g. PPCs, PSMs, password dictionaries and personal information), and also easy modification of the behavior and look of each PIU and any supporting algorithm. Different levels of reconfigurability and personalization can be supported, ranging from simple information filtering to customization of how an individual PIU or component looks/works and to even completely change of the look or working mechanism of the whole system.

Portability: This principle is about the need to make a system more available when users are moving across devices and platforms. An installation-free system that can run cross different platforms will be ideal. For PSV, a natural choice is to implement it as a web-based system based on pure client-side technologies (HTML, CSS and JavaScript) so that any computing device and OS with a standard-compliant web browser can allow the user to use PSV.

3.2   Two Example Designs

Following all the design principles discussed above, we can have many different designs of PSV. To accommodate more information and enrich interactions with users, it is necessary to move from the simple 1-D bar based design of most PPCs to a large space for visualization. In other words, we need to use a 2-D or a 3-D space to show a number of visualized PIUs. The space should have a layout easy for reconfiguration and personalization. To balance informativeness and information overload, the information shown in PSV can be put into several layers and visual metaphors can be used to invite users to interact with each PIU to get more detailed information related to the PIU. Since working with a 2-D space is easier and requires less computation, we decided to adhere to 2-D designs but will consider extensions to 3-D spaces in future.

Two example designs of PSV on a 2-D canvas are shown in Fig. 1. In both designs, the following groups of PIUs are included: (1) a number of PPCs showing the overall strength of the current password; (2) a number of PIUs showing basic password attributes (PA); (3) a number of weak passwords closer to the current password. Each weak password is visualized as an icon with a negative meaning following the fear appeal concept (e.g. a skull) and located at a position proportional to the edit distance (ED) [18] between the weak password and the current password. The number of weak passwords around the current password can be used as a proxy of the level of risk against dictionary-based attacks: the closer a dictionary entry to the current password and the more such entries are around, the more risky the current password is. The edit distance between a weak password and the current password can be related to a hybrid password attack which combines a dictionary-based attack with a simple brute force up to a number of character changes. The whole canvas can be extended to accommodate more PIUs easily, and removing or relocating existing PIUs is easy as well.

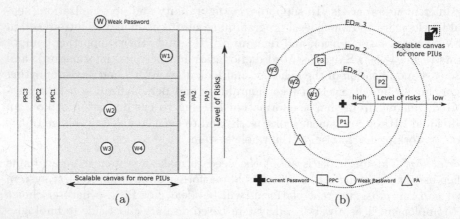

Fig. 1. Two example designs of PSV on a 2-D canvas, which is divided into (a) horizontal bars and (b) concentric circles representing different levels of security risk.

3.3 Supporting Algorithms

Different PIUs in PSV require a range of supporting algorithms which include at least the following groups.

PSMs: PSV can include a number of PPCs as PIUs and as mentioned before each PPC needs to work with one or more PSMs.

Password Dictionary Handling Algorithms: PSV will support dictionary-based attacks so some algorithms will be needed to read and search in one or more dictionaries. A trie-based data structure can be used to efficiently store dictionaries and to accelerate the search process. A major subset of algorithms in this group are for detecting weak passwords with a specific edit distance. Another subset of algorithms are for calculating the edit distance between two given strings.

Algorithms Linking PSMs with PIUs: For some designs of PSV, the location of a PPC (as a PIU) is used to signal the password strength estimated (e.g., in the second design shown in Fig. 1). In this case, some algorithm will be needed to translate the password strength estimated to a location in the visualized space.

Algorithms for Selecting and Positioning of PIUs: Since multiple PIUs are displayed in a limited space, some algorithms are needed to decide what PIUs to show (how many) and where. Dynamic adjustment to some PIUs (e.g., reducing the size of a PIU or rotating it) may also be considered. These algorithms need to consider prioritization and randomization when not all PIUs can be shown due to limited space.

Parallelization and Pre-computation Algorithms: To ensure immediate feedback to users, the visualization of all PIUs needs to be fast enough to catch up with the typing speed of the user, even on relatively less powerful computing devices (e.g., smart phones). This requires most time-consuming computation to be done in an asynchronous manner (e.g., using HTML5 workers and AJAX), and be parallelized as much as possible. Pre-computation should be included, e.g., when a new character is added into the current password, each dictionary trie does not need to be searched from scratch, but from the last visited node.

4 Our PSV Prototype

We implemented a prototype of the second example design of PSV shown in Fig. 1(b). This prototype is developed using pure client-side web technologies including HTML5, CSS and JavaScript, which makes the prototype highly portable. We also made a simple interface for the PSV prototype to be incorporated into password creation/update pages of any HTML5-ready websites. The prototype can be found online at http://passwords.sccs.surrey.ac.uk/PSV/. In this section, we describe how we implemented the front-end and back-end parts of the prototype.

4.1 Front-End UI

The PSV prototype includes three groups of visual elements: a 2-D canvas, a configuration panel and a number of PIUs.

2-D Canvas and Overall Look. A 2-D canvas is used as the container of PIUs. Figure 2 shows a screenshot of the PSV prototype's canvas whose background is rendered as an active radar with a rotating beam "scanning" for security concerns constantly (indicating the working status of PSV). The radar canvas as a visual metaphor matches the cyber security context well, which was the main reason why we decided to go for the second example design of PSV. The center of the radar canvas represents the current password and a number of (three as a default value, which is reconfigured) concentric circles are drawn to accommodate all PIUs. The three concentric circles allow us to locate weak passwords with a particular distance with the current password (following the segmentation principle). Other PIUs (mainly PPCs) are mapped to any point from the radar center to the largest circle linearly so that the distance to the center represents the level of risk. A PIU will disappear if the risk is considered lower than a threshold (the value corresponding to the largest circle) so that it is unnecessary to show it any longer. From a user's perspective, while he/she is entering a password the radar canvas is dynamically updated with immediate feedback (via relevant PIUs), and the task of defining a strong password is to remove as many (ideally all) PIUs out of the radar so that no risks are visible (i.e., high). When the task is not to define a password, the user can play with the system by entering different passwords to learn more about password security. The design allows easy reconfiguration and personalization as a PIU can be easily added to or removed from the 2-D canvas. Each PIU's look and settings can also be configured separately or as a group (e.g., one can refine how a PPC is located by introducing a new linear or nonlinear mapping between the password strength estimate and the distance to the radar center). For three example passwords, Fig. 3 shows how the whole PSV's UI looks like.

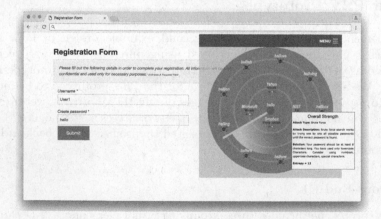

Fig. 2. The screenshot of an example user registration page of our PSV prototype.

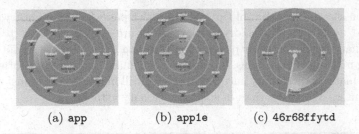

(a) app   (b) apple   (c) 46r68ffytd

Fig. 3. Screenshots when three passwords were being entered into our PSV prototype. (Color figure online)

PIUs. There are four different types of PIUs we include in our PSV prototype. Password attributes are not currently included because we found them least useful for user education purposes. We may add some in future versions.

The first type is the center of the 2-D canvas. As mentioned above, the center represents the current password. We use a small circle filled with a specific color to visualize three different states: light blue (normal), red (the password itself is a weak password), yellow (the password contains at least one weak password segment). On top of the small circle the current password is shown in clear. We do not hide the password since PSV is designed as an educational tool. If the PSV is used as a PPC, the password can be simply removed or asterisks are shown as usual.

The second type covers PPCs. The current version incorporates four PPCs based on the common 1-D bar design: a PPC we developed based on the NIST password entropy [2] as the underlying PSM, the open-source password checker zxcvbn (which has been deployed by Dropbox) [33][3], the PPCs used by Microsoft and Yahoo! (for which we implemented our own versions). Note that the four are just used as examples and more PPCs can be added easily.

The third type covers weak passwords signaling the risks against dictionary-based attacks. We use a skull icon by following the fear appeal concept used by some PPCs such as those in [28]. Our prototype considers three different types of dictionary attacks to detect weak passwords related to the current password: (1) *naive* dictionary attack where each entry is checked as is, (2) *smart* dictionary attack where some common character transformation rules are considered, and (3) *targeted* dictionary attack where the user's personal information is used to build a small personalized dictionary. As a demonstrator, the targeted dictionary attack currently gets the user's first and last names by asking them to log into his/her Facebook account via the Facebook API. This can be extended to cover more personal information such as what was used in [13,31].

The last type covers tool-tips that are shown when the user moves mouse over any PPC or weak password. Such tool-tips provide more detailed explanation to the corresponding PIU in order to provide more information about the risks of concern and guidance on how to reduce such risks. A unique part of the

---

[3] We incorporated an older version of the PPC zxcvbn downloaded from https://github.com/dropbox/zxcvbn.

information shown on each tool-tip is about weak password segments, which are highlighted using different colors so that users are encouraged not to include any dictionary entries in their passwords. This can educate users about attacks combining multiple dictionaries. In addition, when a character transformation is applied to match a dictionary entry, the tool-tip will highlight the transformation to inform users about the risks of smart dictionary attacks.

Fig. 4. The menu bar of our PSV prototype.

Configuration Panel. To support reconfigurability and personalization, we also created a configuration panel as part of our PSV prototype on the top of the 2-D canvas. The configuration panel has two versions, one is shown in Fig. 4 for a typical layout on a PC, and a more mobile-friendly version as shown in Fig. 2 which breaks down the menu items into smaller items. The configuration panel empowers the user to make the following changes to the behavior and look of the PSV prototype.

Information Filtering: The panel provides two ways to filter information shown on the 2-D canvas: a slider enabling dynamic control of the number (i.e., density) of weak passwords shown on the canvas, and a number of menu items to switch some types of PIUs on or off which includes indirect control via enabling or disabling existing password dictionaries and password attacks.

Adding New Dictionaries: The PSV prototype allows users to add their own dictionaries into the system. This include personalized and normal dictionaries through "Facebook" and "New Dic" menu items, respectively. Normal dictionaries added will be stored in the system and can be enabled/disabled as built-in dictionaries, while the personalized dictionary is only accessible in the memory after the user logs into his/her Facebook account and will be released once he/she logs out.

4.2 Supporting Algorithms

Our PSV prototype is supported by some underlying algorithms for different purposes, which can be categorized based on five steps of the whole information processing chain: data storage, creation of candidate PIUs, positioning of PIUs, selection of PIUs, and visual presentation of selected PIUs. These steps are explained briefly below.

Data Storage. Since multiple dictionaries are used in PSV, we need an efficient data structure and corresponding algorithms for creating and modifying dictionaries in the selected data structure. For our PSV prototype, we decided to use the succinct trie data structure implemented by Hanov [7]. A segment of such a trie can be seen in Fig. 5(a), where red nodes represent dictionary entries (concatenating all letters from the root node sequentially).

For personalized dictionaries, our PSV prototype currently extracts the user's first and last names from his/her Facebook account (after login), which are stored in the volatile memory and deleted permanently once the user logs out.

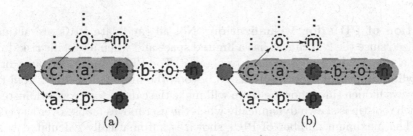

(a)   (b)

Fig. 5. The process of searching for weak passwords in a dictionary, where the password given is "car" and two detected weak passwords are "car" and "carbon". (Color figure online)

Creation of Candidate PIUs. To create candidate PIUs that can be further selected for visualization, some algorithms are needed to produce information needed by all candidate PIUs. Information needed for the current password PIU is straightforward, so we ignore it here and focus on other three types of PIUs.

Detection of Weak Passwords: An algorithm was developed to search through all enabled dictionaries to detect weak passwords whose edit distance from the current password is not greater than 3. In our prototype, we used Levenshtein distance as the edit distance since it is the most common metric used [18]. An example of the searching process is shown in Fig. 5. The results are stored as an array in which each element represent a weak password. We implemented multi-threading capability using HTML5 Web workers to improve performance of the searching process and to avoid blocking the main user interface.

Password Strength Metering (PSM): To visualize any PPC, the underlying PSM has to be executed on the current password. For our PSV prototype, there are four PSMs each serving one PPC. A PSM produces either a numeric value such as an entropy value or an ordinal value (among three or four different levels) to represent the strength of a given password.

Tool-Tip Generation: For each weak password and PPC PIU, a tool-tip object is also created to contain more detailed information and guidance to users.

Positioning of PIUs. One algorithm is needed to map each PIU type to a specific position on the 2-D canvas. For weak passwords, they can be naturally mapped to one of the three circles based on their edit distance from the current password. For PPCs, this will depend on the format of the password strength value: (1) if the underlying PSM returns an ordinal value then the PPC can be naturally mapped to one of the three circles as well (outer circles correspond to stronger passwords); (2) if the underlying PSM returns a numeric value like an entropy then the PPC is linearly mapped to a position on a radial line starting from the center of the 2-D canvas, where the most outer circle will be set to correspond to a specific value considered as "very strong".

Selection of PIUs for Visualization. Not all candidate PIUs are actually visualized since the 2-D canvas has a limited space and when a specific risk drops below a threshold we do not need to show it. For PPCs and weak passwords, they will disappear if their positions go beyond the most outer circle. Tool-tips are always hidden since showing them will make the canvas too crowded, instead, one such tool-tip is shown dynamically when the user moves mouse over a specific PIU. The maximum number of PIUs shown is automatically calculated based on the size of the canvas. The configuration panel also allows the user to tailor the number of weak passwords which will also influence what PIUs are selected.

Visual Presentation of Selected PIUs. Each PIU type needs an algorithm to do the actual visualization. This may involve re-positioning selected PIUs, e.g., re-distributing all weak passwords with the same edit distance uniformly on the corresponding circle to make them look better, and moving some PIUs around to avoid conflicts with one or more neighboring PIUs.

5   Semi-structured Interviews

Semi-structured interviews were conducted (by the first co-author of the paper, referred to "the researcher" hereinafter) to investigate the efficacy of our PSV prototype on educating users about password security, compared with three traditional PPCs. Our main goal is to demonstrate PSV as a superior tool for password security education. This user study was reviewed by the University of Surrey's University Ethics Committee (UEC) and a favorable ethics opinion (FEO) was secured.

   To align the UI of our PSV prototype and the three traditional PPCs so that any differences we observed should be only about the PSV and PPCs themselves, we designed a uniform login page with four different variants each of which uses a different password security/checking system. The three traditional PPCs we used include: (1) zxcvbn – a PPC based on the most common 1-D color bar design and the widely-used zxcvbn as the underlying PSM [33], (2) PM – the multi-bar based PPC called "The Password Meter" [24], (3) IFA – the interactive fear appeal based PPC proposed in [28]. We implemented our own versions of the three PPCs to ensure the consistent look of the overall login page. Figure 6 shows UIs of the three PPCs we implemented.

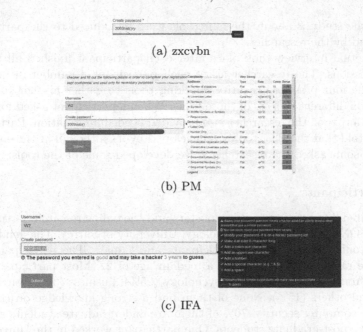

(a) zxcvbn

(b) PM

(c) IFA

Fig. 6. The UI screenshots of the three PPCs used in our user study.

5.1 Interview Design

Although being an interview type user study, participants needed to give subjective opinions on password security/checking tools they might not have any prior knowledge so the user study also involves a short testing session for each tool. We also collected some basic demographic information about participants at the beginning using a questionnaire: age, gender and educational background. The whole session was conducted on a one-to-one basis to avoid interference between participants. The interviews were audio-recorded for further analysis, which later was deleted after being transcribed. Each participant spent around an hour to complete the whole session and was compensated £10 for their time.

In the testing sessions, each participant was asked to play the role of an imaginary security consultant to examine each of the four tools by doing the following for no less than 5 min: (1) trying a number of passwords given by the researcher and of their own choice; (2) paying attention on distinct information shown by each tool; (3) trying to understand the information shown; (4) making notes on different information shown to prepare for the interview with the researcher. Participants were encouraged to interact actively with the researcher during the assessment tests to simulate real-world scenarios where a security consultant will normally interact with the vendor of a candidate tool to get more information about it. Participants were offered to have a break between testing sessions, but none opted to have one. To minimize the bias caused by participants' own prior experience with any of the tested tools and to give participants a big picture of what the study is about, the four tools were introduced to the participants beforehand by the researcher.

The actual interview took place after each participant finished all the four testing sessions. The researcher asked each participant a number of questions around the four password security/checking tools to gather his/her subjective opinions on different aspects of those tools. When a participant asked for clarification on any tool, the researcher also provided needed information. Participants were not told that the PSV tool was developed by us, although at the end of the interview some asked the researcher if we developed some of the tools.

5.2 Participants

We recruited 20 participants using posters and the online research participation system (SONA) of School of Psychology, University of Surrey. The gender ratio was not controlled: we got 14 participants and 7 male. The participants were in the age range of 19 to 45, with a median age of 22. Most participants were students from different subjects: psychology (25%), business (30%), engineering (25%), and others (15%). None of them had a strong knowledge on computer science or computer security. 70% of them are undergraduate students and 25% of them are post-graduate students. One participant worked in the University of Surrey as an administrative assistant.

5.3 Results

PSV as an Educational Tool. In our interview, we collected information about the most educative password checkers perceived by participants. We asked them questions about their newly acquired knowledge after testing the four tools. Figure 7 shows what all participants collectively said about each tool as a word cloud. Many participants found the zxcvbn PPC is the least educative, while the PSV and the PM PPC are the most informative ones. All participants reported that they had gained some new knowledge from PSV and the PM PPC. Many of them found that the PSV directly highlights distinct strategies used for guessing passwords and possible inconsistencies among different PPCs, which they found interesting due to the richer information presented in a visual manner. As a comparison, many felt that they had learned about more concrete new rules to improve password strength from the PM PPC.

At the beginning of the interview, most (18, 90%) participants failed to identify that the PSV as the most informative password checkers according to their understanding of informativity (see Table 1). Although they agreed that the PSV could provide a lot of information but they did not believe such information is all useful, and the majority felt that the PM PPC is the most informative tool. However, after explaining different components of the PSV and the PM PPC with greater details to participants, almost all participants were converted to articulate that the PSV is the most informative tool. A few participants remained their original opinion that the PM PPC is the best, based on the argument that their subjective judgments match the outcomes from the PM PPC better. Note

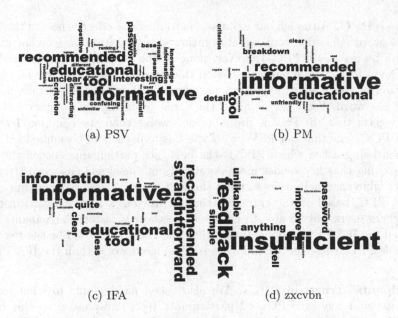

(a) PSV   (b) PM

(c) IFA   (d) zxcvbn

Fig. 7. Mostly highlighted words for the PSV prototype and the three PPCs, each shown as a word cloud (generated by the online tool WordSift [20]).

Table 1. Participants' votes on the most informative tool for password security education, before and after more details on the PSV and the PM PPC were given.

Password tool	Before	After	Converted
zxcvbn	0	0	0
IFA	5	0	−5
PM	13	1	−12
PSV	2	19	17

that no participants asked for more explanation on the zxcvbn and IFA PPCs since they are simpler and more straightforward.

The results on the PM PPC are not totally unexpected since it is indeed the most informative PPC among the three tested. The results should not be interpreted negatively against PSV because as a container of PPCs the PM PPC can also be added to the PSV canvas (which we plan to do in future versions).

We also asked participants which tool (if only one can be selected) they would recommend to their "customers" (average users, normally not security professionals) for self-learning password security. 11 participants (55%) preferred the PSV over the three PPCs, 6 selected the PM PPC, and the remaining 3 selected the IFA PC. None of the participants recommended the zxcvbn PPC as it does not provide enough feedback to users. Some participants explained that they did not recommend the PSV mainly because they felt the PM PPC is easier for average users to understand.

PSV as a PPC. Although our main aim is to measure effectiveness of the PSV as a password education tool, we also gathered information on to what extent PSV can be used as a PPC. However, none of the participants considered the PSV a good PPC. The majority reported that the PSV does not give an overall estimation of the password strength nor direct instructions for improving the current password. Yet, they reported the same problems for the zxcvbn PPC. This suggests that the PSV is probably not worse than the common 1-D bar based PPCs. Note that our PSV prototype has four such PPCs embedded.

When being asked which PPC is the best, six participants chosen the PM PPC, arguing that it provides more details about the single password strength estimate which can help users to trust the PPC more. Three participants chose the IFA PPC, based on the argument that it provides straightforward instructions where users will be able to construct passwords faster. Participants who preferred the IFA PPC also mentioned that the PM PPC would be their second preferable PPC whose user-friendliness is considered worse than the IFA PPC.

Participants' Trust on PPCs. We also asked participants to what extent they trust and rely on PPCs. 12 participants (60%) responded to this question. All except one responded that they have some level of trust on PPCs. One participant argued that such trust can be established only with familiar PPCs. One another participant mentioned he/she always trusts PPCs. Other participants mentioned that they would ignore a PPC if the PPC's password strength estimate is higher than their own subjective judgment. On the other hand, most participants said that they would make serious efforts to improve their passwords if a PPC gives a rating lower than their subjective judgment.

6   Conclusions and Future Work

This paper presents Password Security Visualizer (PSV), a new password security educational system and a prototype developed based on proactive password checkers. We conducted a semi-structured interview based on a number of testing sessions with 20 participants to validate the usefulness of the PSV prototype. The results of the user study showed that the majority of participants agreed that PSV is the most educative tools comparing to three traditional types of PPCs and would recommend it to average users as a self-learning tool on password security. Participants however were not convinced the PSV is a good alternative PPC considering its lacking an password strength estimate and direct instructions for improving passwords. More conversations with participants also revealed that most participants found PPCs useful but their perceptions vary on what PPC is preferred and when they will follow the ratings of a PPC.

Participants' responses revealed that the rich information provided by our PSV prototype was perceived somewhat negatively especially at the very beginning. Some participants seemed confused about what to do with so much information since the PSV does not give them a single piece of information (like what traditional PPCs do) which they can simply focus on. This negative feeling was significantly reduced after we provided clearer instructions on how the PSV should be used and highlighted its conceptual differences from traditional PPCs, thus suggesting that the tool may be better used with instructors. For self-learning purposes, the PSV can be reconfigured to adapt the system's features and its UI to each user's individual preferences and needs.

In our future work, we will study how to improve the current designs and implementation of PSV to make it more useful as both a user education tool and an alternative PPC. For instance, we may redesign the PSV so that fewer PIUs are shown to make the UI less crowded and complicated.

Acknowledgments. Nouf Aljaffan was funded by a PhD scholarship from the King Saud University, Kingdom of Saudi Arabia. Haiyue Yuan and Shujun Li were supported by the UK part of a joint Singapore-UK research project COMMANDO-HUMANS, funded by the Engineering and Physical Sciences Research Council (EPSRC) under grant number EP/N020111/1.

References

1. Beetham, H., Sharpe, R. (eds.): Rethinking Pedagogy for a Digital Age: Designing and Delivering E-Learning. Routledge, Abingdon (2007)
2. Burr, W.E., Dodson, D.F., Newton, E.M., Perlner, R.A., Polk, W.T., Gupta, S., Nabbus, E.A.: Electronic authentication guideline. NIST Special Publication 800–63-2 (2013)
3. de Carné de Carnavalet, X., Mannan, M.: From very weak to very strong: analyzing password-strength meters. In: Proceedings of the NDSS 2014. Internet Society (2014)
4. Carnavalet, X., Mannan, M.: A large-scale evaluation of high-impact password strength meters. ACM Trans. Inf. Syst. Secur. **18**(1), 1:1–1:32 (2015)
5. Ciampa, M.: A comparison of password feedback mechanisms and their impact on password entropy. Inf. Manag. Comput. Secur. **21**(5), 344–359 (2013)
6. Furnell, S.: Assessing password guidance and enforcement on leading websites. Comput. Fraud Secur. **2011**(12), 10–18 (2011)
7. Hanov, S.: Succinct data structures: cramming 80,000 words into a Javascript file (2012). Online document: http://stevehanov.ca/blog/index.php?id=120. Accessed 10 Feb 2017
8. Haque, S.M.T., Scielzo, S., Wright, M.: Applying psychometrics to measure user comfort when constructing a strong password. In: Proceedings of the SOUPS 2014, pp. 231–242. USENIX Association (2014)
9. Hunt, T.: ';-have i been pwned? Check if you have an account that has been compromised in a data breach. https://haveibeenpwned.com/. Accessed 11 Feb 2017
10. Kafas, K., Aljaffan, N., Li, S.: Poster: visual password checker. Presented at SOUPS 2013 (2013). 2-page summary available online at https://cups.cs.cmu.edu/soups/2013/posters/soups13_posters-final19.pdf
11. Klein, D.V.: Foiling the cracker: a survey of, and improvements to, password security. In: Proceedings of the USENIX Security 1990, pp. 5–14 (1990)

12. Komanduri, S., Shay, R., Cranor, L.F., Herley, C., Schechter, S.: Telepathwords: preventing weak passwords by reading users' minds. In: Proceedings of the USENIX Security 2014, pp. 591–606. USENIX Association (2014)
13. Li, Y., Wang, H., Sun, K.: A study of personal information in human-chosen passwords and its security implications. In: Proceedings of IEEE INFOCOM 2016, pp. 1242–1254. ACM (2016)
14. Loge, M., Duermuth, M., Rostad, L.: On user choice for Android unlock patterns. In: Proceedings of the EuroUSEC 2016. Internet Society (2016)
15. Ma, J., Yang, W., Luo, M., Li, N.: Anatomy of a proactive password changer. In: Proceedings of the USENIX Security 1992, pp. 171–184. USENIX Association (1992)
16. Melicher, W., Ur, B., Segreti, S.M., Komanduri, S., Bauer, L., Christin, N., Cranor, L.F.: Fast, lean and accurate: modeling password guessability using neural networks. In: Proceedings of the USENIX Security 2016 (2016)
17. Narayanan, A., Shmatikov, V.: Fast dictionary attacks on passwords using time-space tradeoff. In: Proceedings of the CCS 2005, pp. 364–372. ACM (2005)
18. Navarro, G.: A guided tour to approximate string matching. ACM Comput. Surv. **33**(1), 31–88 (2001)
19. Neil's Toolbox: Password security tester. http://www.neilstoolbox.com/password-tester/. Accessed 11 Feb 2017
20. Roman, D., Thompson, K., Ernst, L., Hakuta, K.: WordSift: a free web-based vocabulary tool designed to help science teachers in integrating interactive literacy activities. Sci. Activities: Classr. Projects Curric. Ideas **53**(1), 13–23 (2016). https://wordsift.org/
21. Shute, V.J.: Focus on formative feedback. Rev. Educ. Res. **78**(1), 153–189 (2008)
22. Solutions Verizon Enterprise: Verizon's 2016 data breach investigations report (2016). http://www.verizonenterprise.com/resources/reports/rp_DBIR_2016_Report_en_xg.pdf
23. Sotirakopoulos, A.: Influencing user password choice through peer pressure. Master's thesis, University of British Columbia, Canada (2011). http://lersse-dl.ece.ubc.ca/record/270
24. Todnem, J.: The password meter. http://www.passwordmeter.com/. Accessed 11 Feb 2017
25. Ur, B., Bees, J., Segreti, S.M., Bauer, L., Christin, N., Cranor, L.F., Deepak, A.: Do users' perceptions of password security match reality? In: Proceedings of the CHI 2016, pp. 3748–3760. ACM (2016)
26. Ur, B., Kelley, P.G., Komanduri, S., Lee, J., Maass, M., Mazurek, M.L., Passaro, T., Shay, R., Vidas, T., Bauer, L., Christin, N., Cranor, L.F.: How does your password measure up? The effect of strength meters on password creation. In: Proceedings of the USENIX Security 2012, pp. 65–80. USENIX Association (2012)
27. Ur, B., Noma, F., Bees, J., Segreti, S.M., Shay, R., Bauer, L., Christin, N., Cranor, L.F.: "I added '!' at the end to make it secure": observing password creation in the lab. In: Proceedings of the SOUPS 2015, pp. 123–140. USENIX Association (2015)
28. Vance, A., Eargle, D., Ouimet, K., Straub, D.: Enhancing password security through interactive fear appeals: a web-based field experiment. In: Proceedings of the HICSS 2013, pp. 2988–2997. IEEE (2013)
29. Wales, M.: How secure is my password? https://howsecureismypassword.net/. Accessed 11 Feb 2017
30. Wang, D., He, D., Cheng, H., Wang, P.: fuzzyPSM: a new password strength meter using fuzzy probabilistic context-free grammars. In: Proceedings of the DSN 2016, pp. 595–606 (2016)

31. Wang, D., Zhang, Z., Wang, P., Yan, J., Huang, X.: Targeted online password guessing: an underestimated threat. In: Proceedings of the CCS 2016, pp. 1242–1254. ACM (2016)
32. Weir, M., Aggarwal, S., de Medeiros, B., Glodek, B.: Password cracking using probabilistic context-free grammars. In: Proceedings of the IEEE S&P 2009, pp. 391–405 (2009)
33. Wheeler, D.L.: zxcvbn: low-budget password strength estimation. In: Proceedings of the USENIX Security 2016, pp. 157–173. USENIX Security (2016). https://github.com/dropbox/zxcvbn
34. Zhang-Kennedy, L., Chiasson, S., Biddle, R.: The role of instructional design in persuasion: a comics approach for improving cybersecurity. Int. J. Hum.-Comput. Interact. **32**(3), 215–257 (2016)

Dear Password, I Know You Too Well
A Congenial Call for Ubiquitous Authentication

Frans F. Blauw[(✉)]

Academy of Computer Science and Software Engineering,
University of Johannesburg, Johannesburg, South Africa
`fblauw@uj.ac.za`

Abstract. Authentication proves the user's identity for a system to authorise access. The traditional process involves some input from the user, be it in the form of a password, a one-time password, biometrics, or all the above. However, all these forms of authentication have their inherent impairment. In this paper, the author fiercely explores archaic authentication methods calling attention to their defects, not only with their security, but also user experience. The idea of abolishing these traditional techniques in favour of ubiquitous approaches – that do not require any user input – is explored.

Keywords: Password · Authentication · Biometrics · Multi-factor authentication · Ubiquitous authentication

1 Introduction

If it's on Facebook, it must have happened. If it's on Twitter, someone will disagree. If it's on Wikipedia, it must be true. Then why, on Wikipedia, is there a section stating that "The Password is Dead" [37], but a password was just used to submit this paper? Claims about the demise of the password have been popping up since 2004, but more than a decade later it is still actively used. And the only victims are the users.

In this paper, we will explore how passwords are used to the detriment of secure systems and actively lead to user error in information systems. Has this been discussed before? Of course, but until the day where we can say that the use of passwords is declining, we should continue advocating for its downfall.

We will start off by seeing where exactly this "password" thing came from. Not surprisingly, humans have been using similar things for authentications for millennia. The value of a password is then determined, but first, we need to determine some way of actually quantifying a "value".

Using this value, we show the huge effort a user must go through to get a "high value" password.

F.F. Blauw—Opinions expressed and conclusions arrived at, are those of the author. Any companies mentioned in this paper are not necessarily endorsed by the author.

© Springer International Publishing AG 2017
T. Tryfonas (Ed.): HAS 2017, LNCS 10292, pp. 212–225, 2017.
DOI: 10.1007/978-3-319-58460-7_14

As we discover that passwords are not all that great, we look at how passwords are generally enhanced, but find those methods lacking too. Finally, we call upon scrapping passwords completely and using proper alternatives.

So, where do passwords come from?

1.1   History of the Password

One of the earliest recollections of a form of a password is described by the Greek historian Polybius, who lived from 264–146 BC. The so-called "watchword" was inscribed on a wooden tablet to be passed around. The only way this watchword could be intercepted would be to physically seize it from the man carrying it [26].

Fast forward to 1961 where MIT introduced a password to a multi-user computer system. The first breach of this security system soon followed where a researcher printed out all the system's passwords in order for him to have more usage time [20].

In this case more than 50 years ago, passwords were inefficient. And today, passwords are still forced on users, making it more difficult for everyone involved.

1.2   Users and Passwords

Humans are lazy. In a sense, this has scientifically been proven [32]. When it comes to passwords, it becomes even more obvious. We could probably fill the pages of this paper with news articles and advisories about password reuse and secure passwords. Security firm, SplashData, keeps track of (mostly stolen) password lists and annually releases a list of that year's top passwords [34]. Every year these lists show that users are blatantly ignoring any advice.

In 2016, the top 5 passwords were:

1. 123456
2. password
3. 12345678
4. qwerty
5. 12345

The password 'password' is "luckily" only #2 on this list, with '1234' only at #8 on the list[1]. At the end of 2017, we should probably not expect this to change much. Ultimately, this list should be shocking, albeit not surprising. But, why do people do this?

---

[1] As an interesting aside, with *Star Wars VII* and *Rogue One: A Star Wars Story* being released in 2015 [16] and 2016 [15], respectively, the password "starwars" moved to #25 on this list, clearly showing a mainstream cultural influence on the choice of passwords.

1.3   Password Psychology

If we want to know why people use such simple passwords, we should attempt to understand the psychology behind passwords. A survey released by LastPass, a well-known password manager app, found a clear cognitive dissonance in our users [19].

The survey showed that 82% of respondents clearly understand that a password that consists of a "combination of letters, numbers and symbols" is more secure, yet 47% still used initials, friends or family names as passwords. Respondents created stronger passwords for systems they deemed to be more important. 69% had strong passwords for financial accounts, yet only 20% had strong passwords for entertainment accounts.

Finally, 91% of respondents knew there was a risk in reusing passwords, but 61% continued to do so (55% fully understanding the risk in doing so).

Why are passwords still being used if users are blatantly brushing off their insecurity? However, we can argue that "not all users" use easy-to-guess passwords; and, that regardless of what they use, information systems should still protect their passwords.

2   Protection of Passwords

It should go without saying that passwords are not supposed to be stored as plaintext in any database. The most common best practice is to store the password as a hash digest. This is not necessarily to protect the information system, but to protect users who reused passwords elsewhere.

Microsoft Research had suggested that systems should stop hashing passwords and rather use (two-way) encryption [14]. They argue that hashing has done more harm than good, and that the decrypted passwords should be available for (offline) analysis in the interest of "social good". Their goal is to study user behaviour in terms of password usage. However, it is understood that this is not the practise in most commercial systems, and so we will look at passwords in their hashed form.

2.1   Cryptographic Hashing

From the first definition of the cryptographic hash function in 1976, it was MD5 (released in 1994) that really took hold as the standard for stored passwords. Since 1997 MD5 was found to be broken and SHA-1 (published in 1995) took over the role of recommended standard. The use of SHA-1 has now been deprecated (due to practical collisions found [12]) and the SHA-2 and SHA-3 suites of cryptographic hashing algorithms are suggested. The recommended algorithm moved to SHA-256 from the SHA-2 set [12,27].

However, even though the use of MD5 and SHA-1 has been strongly discouraged, this hasn't outright stopped its use. Legacy implementations still make use of MD5 and some newer implementations use SHA-1.

Storing the password as a hash digest is not so much to protect the information system, but the user of the password. If a malicious actor has (unauthorised) access to the database to retrieve passwords in the first place, the information system has bigger problems than a couple of leaked passwords. Although users who reuse passwords on different information systems might have a different opinion...

But, as mentioned earlier, we see that the most common passwords are still the same common passwords from a decade ago (well, except it counts to 8 instead of 6). So, hashed or not, it will probably easily be guessed.

Is there a way to put a value on passwords?

2.2   Password Cracking – The Price of a Password

Perhaps if we started giving monetary value to passwords, it would resonate better with users. How snobbish would it be if your password was "worth more" than your neighbour's? But, how can we determine a monetary value of a password? The best way would be to determine how long it would take to guess a user's password. And, as time is money, we should be able to come up with a discernible worth of the password.

When it comes to cracking passwords, malicious actors do not go for the brute force attempt from the get go. The past decade has seen enough large password databases leak to provide a good basis for quickly finding passwords. The best known of these passwords lists was the ROCKYOU list, released between 2009 and 2012. Since then, a variety of large data breaches have added to these password lists [5].

When calculating its worth, if the password can be found in something like the ROCKYOU password list, it should not be worth anything as iterating through the such lists are trivial. But, what if we brute force a password?

For this exercise, we will consider three popular types of hashes (MD5, SHA-1 and SHA-256). Note that these hashes are raw hashed and not seeded, or crypted in any way. As we saw from the top 5 passwords, they only consisted of letters and numbers. So, we will consider a search space of 62 characters (a-z + A-Z + 0-9).

Now we need somewhere to crack these hashes but also determine a monetary value. Amazon's EC2 (Elastic Compute Cloud) can give a value of running an instance per hour. It has been found that cracking hashes on a GPU (as opposed to a CPU) is much faster, so we will take an instance of Amazon's *g2.2xlarge* with access to high performance NVidia GPUs with 1536 CUDA cores. The cost of running a *g2.2xlarge* instance is **$0.65** per hour [2]. That is less than a cup of coffee, per hour.

Finally, we need a tool to do the brute forcing with. The two popular tools are "John the Ripper"[22] and "hashcat"[1]. For the sake of this review, we will use oclHashcat[2]. David Um from the blog Rockfish Sec already did some

---

[2] The **GPU**-based version of hashcat.

benchmarking of hashcat on Amazon's *g2.2xlarge* [35]. The benchmark came down to the following (Table 1):

Table 1. Hash calculations per second on *g2.2xlarge* using "oclHashcat"

	Hashes per second
MD5	2494900000
SHA-1	688300000
SHA-256	296000000

Obviously, MD5 is the easiest and fastest to brute force.

We now have our platform, our hashes, and our search space. The last thing we need for our exercise is a search depth. Since the top 5 passwords were 8 characters or fewer (with the number one being 6 characters), we will use 6 and 8 characters as our search depth. With some number crunching, we calculated the following worst case scenario costs (Table 2):

Table 2. Worst case cost of cracking a hash

	6 Characters		8 Characters	
	Time to crack	Cost	Time to crack	Cost
MD5	23 s	$0.004153	1 d 42 min 29 s	$16.06024
SHA-1	1 min 23 s	$0.014986	3 d 17 h 33 min 36 s	$58.214
SHA-256	3 min 15 s	$0.035208	8 d 16 h 15 min 27 s	$135.3674

We now have a monetary value for our users' passwords. A 6-character word hashed in MD5 will costs less than a cent to crack, whereas an 8-character word hashed with SHA-256 will cost roughly $135.

This should have come as no surprise, and this is why "security experts" advocate for more complex passwords.

3   Password Complexity

Longer passwords. Stronger passwords. Passwords with a mix of uppercase, lowercase, numbers, and symbols (which will effectively give a search space of 94 characters). These passwords will take longer to crack (and increase their value), but how can users be forced to have such intricate passwords? By enforcing password complexity, of course! And it is so easy to do, too.

A couple of clicks in the "Domain Security Policy" in Microsoft Windows Server and a system administrator can enable a plethora of Password Policies.

So, what does Microsoft believe to be the underpinning of strong password management? Let us look at Microsoft Windows Server 2012 [21].

First, one can "enforce password history". The default value for this is 24 passwords. This means that the user must have had 24 unique passwords before an old password can be reused. This sounds legit. The basic rule of anything relating to cryptography is to never reuse the same key (or in this case, password), right?

However, the next policy is that of a "maximum password age". Default setting: 42 days. A user is now forcibly required to change their password to a unique password (that hasn't been used for the previous 23 passwords) every 42 days. Effectively, the user will have to stay employed at the company for 2 years, 9 months and 7 days before they are allowed to reuse the same password (given that they change their password no less than every 42 days).

There is a policy that forces a "minimum password age", but the default for this is 1 day. A user can change their password once a day, if they so desire.

The next policy affecting the user is that of a "minimum password length". As we saw above, a longer password is worth more than a shorter password. The default minimum password length is 7 characters. Which falls in the range of a "cheap" password. However, Microsoft Technet suggests that the "best practise" for a minimum password is 14 characters. Every 42 days, for almost 3 years, the user must remember a new 14-character password.

But, that is not all. The password should not only be long and short-lived. It should also meet a stringent set of "complexity requirements". Default? Enabled. And the definition of this complex password?

- It may not contain the user's account name or display name.
- A password must contain characters from three of the following categories:
  - Uppercase characters,
  - Lowercase characters,
  - Numeric characters,
  - Non-alphanumeric characters (special symbols), or
  - Any Unicode character that does not fall into the above.

As of Unicode 9.0 (released in June 2016) there are 128 172 characters to choose from [36]. However, if we only consider characters that are easily accessible on the English computer keyboard, this brings the number down to 94 characters.

If all the above password policies are enabled with their default or "best practise" setting, we can tally it all up to get the following: A user will be forced to select a unique 14-character password from a space of 4 205 231 901 698 742 834 534 301 696 possible combinations, every 42 days for the next 2 years, 9 months and 7 days.

To the systems administrator this sounds amazing! In the worst-case scenario, (given one hundred trillion guesses per second) it will take 15.67 thousand centuries to guess the password. And considering that the passwords are hashed, even longer! This is turning out to be a very expensive password. Amazing!

Brute force guessing should theoretically not be possible, as the information system should not allow multiple incorrect password attempts. Strangely enough, the default setting on Windows Server 2012 allows for unlimited pass-word attempts before an account is locked. This surely allows the user to try remember their password out of four octillion possibilities. Not only the user, but the malicious actor can try as well. Luckily the "best practice" suggestion is between 4 and 10 attempts before the account is locked and requires human intervention (in the form a helpdesk call) for it to be unlocked.

There are not very many people on this planet who enjoy memorising strings or sentences for fun. Especially if they are forced to do so every 42 days. So, do all these policies all dwindle down to less security?

3.1   More Complexity – Less Security

The first thing a person is taught when remember something complex is to write it down. Students do it in classrooms for examination tips. Waiting staff do it in restaurants for orders placed. Office workers do it to remember their password. Every 42 days a notebook comes out, or a new sticky note is attached to the screen (or more "securely", under the keyboard) containing their newest password.

There is nothing intrinsically wrong with writing down a password. To gain access to the password, the malicious actor will need physical access to the sticky note. In fact, a senior programme manager for security policies at Microsoft, Jesper Johansson, suggests that all users write down their passwords [18] - a suggestion endorsed by crypto-expert Bruce Scheiner way back in 2005 [31]. Yet, we still have security audit companies telling their clients to discourage writing down passwords.

If the note on which the user's password is written happens to be pinched, the system administrator can rest assured that at least the password will become invalid within at most 42 days. If a user discovers the disappearance of their sticky note, they can manually change their password as well (assuming it's after the minimum password age, of course).

To quickly summarise the reasoning behind the complexity and age policies of passwords: they prevent malicious actors from guessing passwords and if a password is revealed, it won't live long thereafter.

Unfortunately, this is not so true. A team of researchers at the University of North Carolina developed a framework that can search for a user's new password using their old password. The reason for this is that users do not choose unique passwords from their four-octillion possibilities [39]. Users tend to use to common techniques to slightly alter their existing password in order to comply with the password complexity policies.

Another study questioned the security of password expiration in a quantifi-able manner. They found that that the benefit of a maximum password age to be miniscule at best [8].

Is there anything that can be done to help the user in their pursuit toward unique, safe passwords, especially when users need to use password authentica-tion for more and more applications?

3.2   Write It All Down!

The password manager is an application that stores multiple passwords in a "password vault" which is protected by a master password. Once the vault is unlocked by the user's master password, any system that requires the user to authenticate will have their credentials automatically completed.

Most password managers come with a feature to generate a unique, secure, and random (a really "expensive") password for each system the user uses. The user is under no obligation to remember this password as it is securely locked up in their vault. The vault can even follow the user between devices. The only requirement for the user is to have a secure master password. At least they do not need to generate and memorise multiple such passwords. However, a user making use of a password manager will probably already know about the security implications and thus have good password management.

This seems like the ultimate answer for secure passwords – as long as the vault (and master password) stay secure. There is a trust in the provider of the password manager. Providers that make use of cloud storage for this password vault need to ensure that their storage is secure. However, some providers use the master password not only as a form of authentication but as the actual key to encrypt and decrypt the password vault. The obvious drawback is that if the user forgets their master password, their password vault is essentially a digital paperweight [23].

But, assuming the user can remember at least one secure password, unfortunately, some applications have gotten it in their minds that the password manager is... insecure.

Although there is a small vector for attack against the password manager, some websites have taken it upon themselves to completely denounce and disallow the use of a password manager. When users question them about this, the customer support will simply utter that it is "for security reasons" [10]. What does this do? It forces the user to manually copy (as in type letter for letter) their secure password, or have a simpler (cheaper) password. Even the United Kingdom Government's National Cyber Security Centre has denounced this action [30].

Luckily, the simplest means of disabling the password manager (by means of setting an **autocomplete = off** tag [33]) can be actively ignored by most modern browsers. However, this does not help corporate users who must create multiple secure passwords in environments where corporate restrictions exists for non-company applications (i.e. password managers). This means these users still have to memorise (or manually write down) their passwords.

However, considering the home user, this could potentially save users from having their cheap password guessed and removes the risk (and time consuming password changing) of a breached password that was used on multiple sites.

From the beginning of this paper to now, it should be clear that passwords can only be secure if they are unique and expensive, but this comes at a premium that most users do not want to pay. If passwords have effectively been a broken authentication system for half a dozen decades, why are they still used? There must be something better!

4   The Enhancements

If you are immediately thinking "use passphrases instead of passwords", please consider that humans are still too lazy... However, as lazy as they are, security experts have found a way to "enhance" password security, by making the entire authentication process even more complex.

4.1   Multi-factor

One of the first alternatives, or rather enhancements, to passwords is the use of Multi-Factor Authentication. The best known additional factor of authentication involves some external (out of band) device while authenticating. This is the infamous "something you have" factor. "Something you have" normally involves some one-time password that is sent via SMS or generated directly on a mobile device (mobile phone or device dedicated to code generation). Users who wish to authenticate to the system will now have to provide use this external device as well. Even if a user's password is compromised, a malicious actor cannot do much with it on the current system without the authenticator.

Remember, password reuse is still remains rampant, and a compromised password might be usable on other systems.

However, to a systems administrator this enhanced security can sound wonderful. However, there are additional costs associated with this.

In a blog by an "Access Control Company", Duo [11], the costs associated with multi-factor authentication can be split into three categories:

- Upfront Costs
- Deployment Costs
- Ongoing Costs

One of the types of costs that fall under all three of these categories involve humans. Essentially, the workforce needs to be trained, encouraged, and supported. The sudden use of a new device can lead to frustration (especially when they keep forgetting the thing at home), and the productivity cost of a lost device (replacement device and administration) can have an impact on the company.

Once again, the human-factor is holding us back in our endeavour for improved security! But, what if we play to the human's strengths using more unconventional authentication methods, that do not directly impact the user.

Graphical passwords rely on the human brain to remember and recognise images (as opposed to words) for authentication. System such as Passfaces™ [24] were explicitly developed for this purpose, but as a second factor of authentication. It requires that the user first remember set of faces (usually between 3–7) and then later, during authentication, select them. However, an investigation showed that using Passfaces™ lead to slower authentication and provoked user resistance [6].

If the human is holding us back, let us involve the human wholly in our search for ultimate security.

4.2   Humans Themselves

Humans and security – if you cannot beat them, use them. Thanks to the proliferation on television and movies, people are no longer stranger to placing their
finger on a pad for a fingerprint scan or staring blankly at a camera to have
their face recognised. These elements, these biometric identifiers, are used as a
means of identifying the person actively providing the biometric. Common place
biometric identifiers include fingerprints, retina scans and voice recognition [29].

Conspiracy theorists aside, there is a belief that the use of biometrics is
completely secure. However, that might ultimately be a false sense of security.
Not only is it possible that fingerprints are not completely unique [17], but even
the way in which biometric systems are designed is flawed [25].

As biometric authentication needs to make a digital decision from some
organic input (fingerprint, etc.) there need to be some decisions made along
the way. This is the biggest failing of a biometric system – its decision policy.

The first of the major decision policies is the "false rejection rate" (FRR).
The FRR describes the number of biometrics that are considered to be incorrect
when in fact they were accurate. That is, the rate at which correct biometrics
will be considered to be incorrect [38]. This could potentially cause a valid user
to be denied access just because their finger is a bit more greasy than normal.
Not a big problem, however, the next of these policies *far* outweighs this.

When any policy contains something called a "false acceptance rate" (FAR),
that should be cause for concern. This FAR describes the number of biometrics
that are considered to be accurate that were in the fact false. In other words,
this is the rate at which fake/incorrect biometrics will be considered to be true
[38]. Yes, the rate at which a malicious actor could potentially breach security
is quantifiable.

These two rates need to be taken into consideration when a decision policy
is decided upon for any authentication system that makes use of biometrics.
A balance needs to be found between the FAR and FRR. Depending on the actual
security required by the system, the policy could rather favour false rejections
(for better security) or false acceptance (for happier users).

While great for false peace of mind, biometrics are inherently fallible [25].
But, because it involves the physical human in the authentication, it feels more
secure.

5   Utopia

Over the course of this paper, we have investigated abhorrent password practises
and how they affect our users; despicable "enhancements" to passwords; and
the contemptible use of parts of humans in our authentication practises. But,
surely, we can do better? What if a user could just sit down and start working
without going through any rigmarole of proving who they are? What if the
system just knew who the user is who is currently dealing it? What if the system
was just... omnipresent[3]?

---

[3] Present everywhere at the same time.

>Could a system know exactly where a specific person is at
>any particular time in order to know their identity?

This idea isn't too *"Big Brother"* and exists in the form of radical "ubiquitous authentication". Fundamentally, a system receives input from a variety of sources (or "informants") regarding the user. These inputs include biographical data, location data, transaction data, and chronographic data. Using this data, the system can construct a digital presence of its users and allow the system to know exactly who is interacting with it at any point in time.

The digital presence can then allow the system to authenticate a user without requiring any input from the user. Yes, the user is ubiquitously authenticated without any express interaction! No passwords, no one-time passwords, no dirty fingerprints. Though utopian sounding, this idea is not very far off.

So, can a simple, everyday task such as typing be made into an authentication method? Keystroke dynamics authentication has been around for more than a decade, but still has not truly found any mainstream proliferation. This involves monitoring the user as they type, and determining which user is doing the typing or if it is still the same user making use of the device [4]. A similar technique can be applied to mouse movements [28].

More extreme approaches have also already been seen. Researchers in Italy have set up an array of detection devices to recognise embedded devices (that is, devices implanted in the user) [9]. Videos have been uploaded to YouTube with instructions on how to implant an RFID chip into someone's hand [3,13].

The reactions to the cited videos have not been overwhelmingly positive. But, that didn't stop a company from Sweden from offering its office employees to have RFID chips (voluntarily) implanted to make their lives at work easier [7]. These examples are undoubtedly taking ubiquitous authentication to... an uncomfortable extreme, and it is positively not something we are advocating at all for our users!

The inputs we propose would come from existing sources such as a mobile device the user *happens to be* carrying with them, Internet of Things devices, and smartspace interactions. All the sources will contribute to a central presence of the user which a system requiring authentication of a user can then query. Sources need to work together, providing information about the user to be useful for the authentication process.

Designing and implementing such a ubiquitous authentication system will be a grand undertaking, will take quite a considerable amount of time to complete, and is well beyond the scope of this paper. The design of such a system should look at, not only the usability, but its own security, as well.

The idea of non-interactive, ubiquitous authentication sounds grand, but it could lead to an Orwellian fear of the system. While it can be argued that users might it unsettling at first, it could very well become a norm. This argument can be lead by the fact that two decades ago the idea of sharing one's everyday menial activities with the world would have seemed laughable. However, thanks to the social infiltration of social media, sharing of the mundane has become a social norm.

We should view ubiquitous authentication in this same light, where users will eventually become "used to it" – especially if it does not require any additional inputs (or implants) from the user.

6   Conclusion

If it has not been clear yet, in this paper we defiantly put our foot down and said "no more" when it comes to passwords, tokens, and biometrics.

Passwords have been weak since its inception, yet more and more information systems rely on them. Authenticators only add deployment costs, high operation costs, along with heightened frustration from users. And, biometrics has never been as secure as the media makes it out to be. But, what do all of these "security mechanisms" have in common? The human!

Instead of looking how these existing technologies can be secured, improved, or enhanced, we should completely "re-examine" authentication, starting with completely cutting out the weakest link – the human. The idea of ubiquitous (omnipresent) authentication is nothing new. But, it will take a new way of thinking about our users to make it useful (and bearable) for them. Ultimately, it will take a big step to completely convert.

Given time and the right technology, the demise of passwords and its ilk will no longer only be a futuristic utopia.

References

1. hashcat. https://hashcat.net/
2. Amazon: Amazon EC2 Pricing (2016). https://aws.amazon.com/ec2/pricing/on-demand/
3. animalnewyork: Watch Artist Implant a Net Art RFID Chip Into His Hand (2013). https://www.youtube.com/watch?v=XECHcbakMIg
4. Bergadano, F., Gunetti, D., Picardi, C.: User authentication through keystroke dynamics. ACM Trans. Inf. Syst. Secur. **5**(4), 367–397 (2002). http://doi.acm.org/10.1145/581271.581272
5. Bowes, R.: Passwords - SkullSecurity. https://wiki.skullsecurity.org/index.php?title=Passwords
6. Brostoff, S., Sasse, M.A.: Are passfaces more usable than passwords? A field trial investigation. In: McDonald, S., Waern, Y., Cockton, G. (eds.) People and Computers XIV – Usability or Else!, pp. 405–424. Springer, London (2000). doi:10.1007/978-1-4471-0515-2_27
7. Cellan-Jones, R.: Office puts chips under staff's skin (2015). http://www.bbc.com/news/technology-31042477
8. Chiasson, S., van Oorschot, P.C.: Quantifying the security advantage of password expiration policies. Des. Codes Crypt. **77**(2), 401–408 (2015). http://dx.doi.org/10.1007/s10623-015-0071-9
9. Conti, V., Vitabile, S., Vitello, G., Sorbello, F.: An embedded biometric sensor for ubiquitous authentication. In: AEIT Annual Conference 2013, pp. 1–6 (2013)

10. Cox, J.: Websites, please stop blocking password managers. It's 2015 (2015). https://www.wired.com/2015/07/websites-please-stop-blocking-password-managers-2015/
11. Duo: comparing the total cost of ownership of two-factor authentication solutions (2016). https://duo.com/blog/comparing-the-total-cost-of-ownership-of-two-factor-authentication-solutions
12. Google: SHAttered. https://shattered.io/
13. Greenberg, A.: RFID chip implantation (2012). https://www.youtube.com/watch?v=sKVj2V4-yPE
14. Herley, C., Schechter, S.: Breaking our password hash habit (2013). https://www.microsoft.com/en-us/research/wp-content/uploads/2016/02/SchechterHerleyWEIS2013.pdf
15. IMDB: Rogue One: A Star Wars Story. http://www.imdb.com/title/tt3748528/
16. IMDB: Star Wars: The Force Awakens. http://www.imdb.com/title/tt2488496/
17. Knapton, S.: Why your fingerprints may not be unique (2016). http://www.telegraph.co.uk/science/2016/03/14/why-your-fingerprints-may-not-be-unique/
18. Kotadia, M.: Microsoft security guru: jot down your passwords (2005). https://www.cnet.com/news/microsoft-security-guru-jot-down-your-passwords/
19. Lauren, V.: Introducing the psychology of passwords. https://blog.lastpass.com/2016/09/infographic-introducing-the-psychology-of-passwords.html
20. McMillan, R.: The world's first computer password? It was useless too (2012). https://www.wired.com/2012/01/computer-password/
21. Microsoft: password policy. https://technet.microsoft.com/en-us/library/hh994572(v=ws.11).aspx
22. Openwall: John the Ripper. http://www.openwall.com/john/
23. Palermo, E.: Should you use a password manager? (2014). www.tomsguide.com/us/password-manager-pros-cons,news-19018.html
24. Passfaces Corporation: Passfaces^{TM}: Two Factor Authentication for the Enterprise. http://www.passfaces.com/
25. Pato, J.N., Millett, L.I.: Biometric Recognition: Challenges and Opportunities. The National Academies Press, Washington, D.C. (2010)
26. Polybius: Daily Orders and Watchwords. www.perseus.tufts.edu/hopper/text?doc=Perseus%3Atext%3A1999.01.0234%3Abook%3D6%3Achapter%3D34
27. Preneel, B.: The first 30 years of cryptographic hash functions and the NIST SHA-3 competition. In: Pieprzyk, J. (ed.) CT-RSA 2010. LNCS, vol. 5985, pp. 1–14. Springer, Heidelberg (2010). doi:10.1007/978-3-642-11925-5_1
28. Pusara, M., Brodley, C.E.: User re-authentication via mouse movements. In: Proceedings of the 2004 ACM Workshop on Visualization and Data Mining for Computer Security, VizSEC/DMSEC 2004, pp. 1–8. ACM, New York (2004). http://doi.acm.org/10.1145/1029208.1029210
29. SANS Institute: Biometrics and User Authentication (2002). https://www.sans.org/reading-room/whitepapers/authentication/biometrics-user-authentication-122
30. Sacha, B.: Let them paste passwords. https://www.ncsc.gov.uk/blog-post/let-them-paste-passwords
31. Schneier, B.: Write down your password (2005). https://www.schneier.com/blog/archives/2005/06/write_down_your.html
32. Selinger, J.C., O'Connor, S.M., Wong, J.D., Donelan, J.M.: Humans can continuously optimize energetic cost during walking. Curr. Biol. **25**, 2452–2456 (2015)
33. Silver, D., Jana, S., Boneh, D., Chen, E., Jackson, C.: Password managers: attacks and defenses. In: Proceedings of the 23rd USENIX Conference on Security Symposium, SEC 2014, pp. 449–464. USENIX Association, Berkeley (2014). http://dl.acm.org/citation.cfm?id=2671225.2671254

34. Titcomb, J.: Do you have one of the most common passwords? They're ridiculously easy to guess (2016). www.telegraph.co.uk/technology/2016/01/26/most-common-passwords-revealed---and-theyre-ridiculously-easy-to/
35. Um, D.: GPU based password cracking with Amazon EC2 and oclHashcat (2015). www.rockfishsec.com/2015/05/gpu-password-cracking-with-amazon-ec2.html
36. Unicode Inc: Unicode 9.0.0 (2016). http://unicode.org/versions/Unicode9.0.0/
37. Wikipedia: Password, December 2016. https://en.wikipedia.org/wiki/Password#.22The_Password_is_dead.22
38. Woodward, J.D., Orlans, N.M., Higgins, P.T.: Biometrics: Identity Assurance in the Information Age. McGraw Hill Professional, New York City (2002)
39. Zhang, Y., Monrose, F., Reiter, M.K.: The security of modern password expiration: an algorithmic framework and empirical analysis. In: Proceedings of the 17th ACM Conference on Computer and Communications Security, CCS 2010, pp. 176–186. ACM, New York (2010). http://doi.acm.org/10.1145/1866307.1866328

Keystroke Inference Using Smartphone Kinematics

Oliver Buckley[1], Duncan Hodges[1(✉)], Melissa Hadgkiss[2], and Sarah Morris[2]

[1] Centre for Electronic Warfare, Information and Cyber,
Cranfield University, Defence Academy of the United Kingdom,
Shrivenham, Swindon SN6 8LA, UK
{o.buckley,d.hodges}@cranfield.ac.uk
[2] Cranfield Forensic Institute, Cranfield University,
Defence Academy of the United Kingdom,
Shrivenham, Swindon SN6 8LA, UK
{m.hadgkiss,s.l.morris}@cranfield.ac.uk

Abstract. The use of smartphones is becoming ubiquitous in modern society, these very personal devices store large amounts of personal information and we use these devices to access everything from our bank to our social networks, we communicate using these devices in both open one-to-many communications and in more closed, private one-to-one communications. In this paper we have created a method to infer what is typed on a device purely from how the device moves in the user's hand. With very small amounts of training data (less than the size of a tweet) we are able to predict the text typed on a device with accuracies of up to 90%. We found no effect on this accuracy from how fast users type, how comfortable they are using smartphone keyboards or how the device was held in the hand. It is trivial to create an application that can access the motion data of a phone whilst a user is engaged in other applications, the accessing of motion data does not require any permission to be granted by the user and hence represents a tangible threat to smartphone users.

1 Introduction

Smartphones are becoming an increasingly significant part of our everyday lives as their popularity continues to grow. Research conducted by the Office of Communications (Ofcom) [1] shows that two thirds of all adults in the UK own a smartphone, compared to only 39% in 2012. The research also highlights how essential smartphones are becoming in our everyday lives as they are now considered to be the most important device for connecting to the Internet, ahead of a laptop. However, this trend of increased smartphone ownership is not limited to the UK as research by the Pew Research Centre [2] shows the global median for smartphone ownership is at 43%.

The increasing popularity of smartphones means that they are now used to manage aspects of our daily lives. A survey conducted by the Pew Research

© Springer International Publishing AG 2017
T. Tryfonas (Ed.): HAS 2017, LNCS 10292, pp. 226–238, 2017.
DOI: 10.1007/978-3-319-58460-7_15

Centre [3] shows that smartphones are being used for a wide variety of sensitive tasks ranging including online banking, education, social interactions, obtaining information about medical conditions, submitting a job application and using key government services.

In this paper we hypothesise that the motion sensors, such as the accelerometer and gyroscope, within a smartphone can be used to infer keystrokes. We posit that it will be possible to infer the keystrokes on a virtual smartphone keyboard based on the movement of the phone, as recorded by the accelerometer and gyroscope.

The remainder of this paper is structured as follows: Sect. 2 provides a review of the related work, focusing on keystroke and swipe analysis in smartphones and the use of motion sensors in user identification. Section 3 details the methodology used to conduct the experimentation. Section 4 provides an analysis of the collected data and the results of the study. Finally, in Sect. 5 we conclude by providing a reflection on our analysis and a discussion of further work in this area.

2   Background

Modern smartphones will typically contain a variety of motion sensors, including a gyroscope that is capable of tracking the rotation of the device and an accelerometer to monitor the movement and orientation of the phone in space. These sensors can be exploited to determine certain information about the user of the phone. For example this includes: recognising the activities that are being performed by the user [4] or identifying an individual based on analysis of their gait [5]. One of the interesting benefits of using these sensors is that they can be run as a background process without the need for explicit approval; therefore it can be possible to covertly capture smartphone motion data without the express permission of the user. In essence, it is entirely possible for a malicious application on a mobile device to be able to freely gather motion data whilst another application is active without first requesting permission from the user. In turn the captured motion data can be used to probabilistically infer the users keystrokes in other applications without their knowledge.

The sensors in smartphones have been used to good effect to infer a wide range of information about an individual solely based on the way that they interact with the smartphone's touchscreen. For example, Bevan et al. [6] used swiping gestures to infer the length of the individual's thumb. The length of the thumb can then be used to infer other physical characteristics such as height. Similarly, Miguel-Hurtado et al. [7] analysed the swiping gestures of users to predict the sex of the individual.

Motion sensors within smartphones have previously been used to attempt to infer a user's keystrokes with promising results. Cai and Chen [8] developed TouchLogger, a smartphone application designed to infer the keystrokes on a soft (or virtual) keyboard based solely on the vibrations recorded by the smartphone's motion sensors. The research was capable of successfully inferring more than 70% of the keys that were typed using only the device's accelerometer. However, the work focused specifically on inferring the keystrokes from a soft keyboard that contained only numbers. The work we present in this paper will look to infer the keystrokes of an individual that use a standard soft keyboard, which contains both numbers and letters.

Owusu et al. [9] extend the work of Cai and Chen to use a smartphone's accelerometer to infer the characters, both letters and numbers, contained within a user's password, although with a relatively small set of only four participants. The work was capable of extracting the 6 character passwords in as few as 4.5 attempts (median). The work of Owusu et al. focused only on the use of accelerometer readings, in contrast to our own work with also includes analysis of rotational data using the smartphone's gyroscope. When a device is being used by an individual it tends to be held in the hand either unsupported or with the wrists resting on a surface, if the device is being held in two hands with the thumbs for typing the device tends to be held loosely and tilted in the palms in order that the relevant keys are closer to the thumb. If a device is held in one hand the same phenomena occurs however the aim tends to be to reduce the amount the 'pecking' digit has to move. Whilst these movements are relatively subtle they are observable both by the human eye and even more so by the smartphone sensor.

3   Method and Experiment

This paper focuses on inferring the keystrokes of individuals as they interact with the virtual keyboard on a smartphone. A data collection framework was created as an Android application, as shown in Fig. 1. The application required participants to type a standard paragraph of text twice and then type a different, and dynamically generated, paragraph of text. The participant was asked to type the text using the standard Android on-screen (or 'soft') keyboard, it is worth noting that the auto-complete or predictive text function was disabled. During this activity the motion of the device was recorded using the rotation, gyroscope and acceleration sensors, the times of the key presses were also record. The standard text that participants were required to type contained 132 characters (less than the length of a tweet) and is shown below:

fly me to the moon and let me play among the stars our freedom of speech is freedom or death we have got to fight the powers that be.

This text was entered twice by all participants of the study, then the final typing activity required the participants to type a paragraph of text that had been dynamically generated. To generate this dynamic text the fixed text, shown above, was segmented into strings of two characters called bigrams. For example, the word *hello* would contain the following bigrams: *he, el, ll, lo.* The dynamically generated text that participants were required to type for the final activity was then generated by searching the Wordnet corpus [10] for words that contained these bigrams. This approach allowed all participants to enter the same set of training data and then the approach would be validated against the third, dynamically generated set of text.

Additionally, the data collection application also asked participants for a number of biographic questions including:

- Age
- Number of hands used to type
- Whether they type with fingers or thumbs
- How comfortable they were with using a smartphone keyboard — this was ranked as 'Very Uncomfortable', 'Uncomfortable', 'Comfortable' or 'Very Comfortable'.

The study collected data from 25 participants, and all of the participants used the same mobile device (a Nexus 5X) in portrait mode. The use of the same device reduces the risk of any anomalous results based on differences in motion sensors across different devices and indeed across different platforms, for a further exploration of this see the future work.

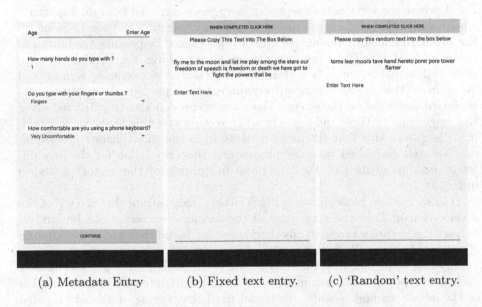

(a) Metadata Entry   (b) Fixed text entry.   (c) 'Random' text entry.

Fig. 1. Android application used in this study

4   Analysis and Results

The experiment reported in this paper explored how 25 different individuals type on smartphone keyboards, the 25 participants were recruited from Cranfield University staff and students and include a mix of age and gender. The distribution of the age is shown in Fig. 2a, as can be seen the majority of participants are in their 30 s and, from the distribution shown in Fig. 2b, consider themselves comfortable with using a smartphone keyboard. Whilst debriefing participants following the experiment it became apparent that a number of participants found that they were in fact less comfortable in using a smartphone keyboard without predictive text. In future work, a supplementary post experiment assessment of the participants comfort would be valuable.

The final factor gathered describing the typing was the method of typing, whether the participant used one hand to hold the device and typed with one finger (or one finger and the thumb of the hand holding the device) or the participant used two hands to hold the device and typed with thumbs. There was an even distribution between these two typing methods amongst the participants as shown in the distribution in Fig. 2c.

The first task in predicting keystrokes from smartphone motion sensors is the detection of keypresses, in order to identify these presses it is intuitive to consider the acceleration sensor. The act of applying a small force to the device to register a press on a solid surface of the screen causes a small acceleration on the phone, in accordance with the simple laws of motion.

An example trace from the acceleration sensors on the device is shown in Fig. 3, where the vertical lines represent keypresses recorded from the keylogger. There are acceleration events caused by initially selecting the box to bring up the keyboard and start typing and other events caused by pressing the button to continue the study. The acceleration traces shown in Fig. 3 are broken down to three orthogonal vectors[1]. It is clear that the greatest acceleration is 'into' and 'away from' the phone, this intuitively maps to the pressing down of the soft-keyboard displayed on the screen. The same graph can also be extracted using the magnitude of these three acceleration vectors and this is shown in Fig. 4, it is clear from this that the measurements from the smartphone's accelerometer are well correlated with key presses and this correlation for the four different measurements (X, Y, Z and the magnitude of the vector) is shown in Fig. 5.

The correlation plots shown in Fig. 5 clearly demonstrate that the use of the acceleration in Z or the magnitude of the acceleration vector can be used to extract the keypress times, in our experiment we found that the acceleration in Z produced marginally better results when using a simple threshold.

In order to be able to predict keystrokes we must first build a model for how each user types in this experiment we were primarily interested in the rotation of the device we first consider the initial fixed text typing, it should be noted that this is less than the size of a tweet and represents a relatively singular event (i.e. the text is only written once). We correlate the keystrokes with the acceleration vector in the Z direction in order to identify the optimal threshold for the accelerometer identification of the keystrokes. Once this is performed we now are interested in the rotation of the device between keypresses — this rotation encodes the movement of the device from one keypress to another and hence encoding the bigram that was typed in the rotation vectors measured by the device.

---

[1] With the phone facing towards the participant X represents left-to-right, Y represents down-to-up and Z represents from behind the phone to the face of the phone.

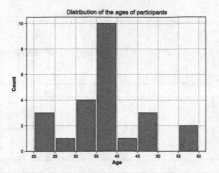

(a) Distribution of participant age.

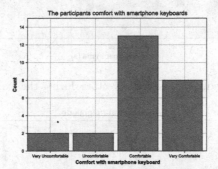

(b) Distribution of self-described comfort with a soft-keyboard.

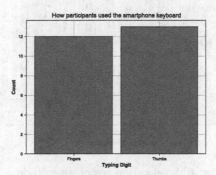

(c) Distribution of digit used to type.

Fig. 2. Distributions of participant information

These rotation vectors are extracted between the keypresses and normalised to a set sample length (in our experiment we chose 1,000 samples), this attempts to remove the effect of an individual not consistently typing a the same pace. These rotation vectors were then further normalised by removing the average from each vector to form the model for each bigram. This normalisation to a

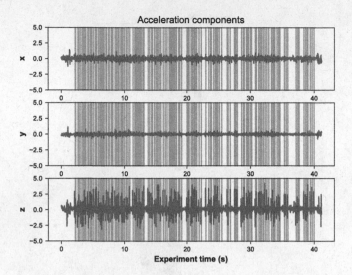

Fig. 3. Individual acceleration vectors during the experiment.

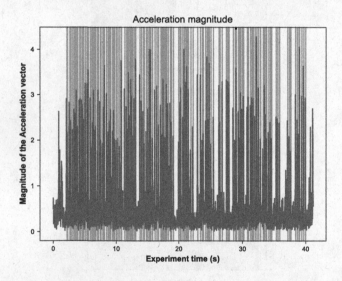

Fig. 4. Acceleration vector magnitude.

mean of zero attempts to reduce the system memory effects from the previous bigrams, as participants do not 'reset' the device to a set position between
bigrams.

In this experiment a model was created for each participant, Fig. 6 shows
the models created for the bigram FL for three different participants, one who
holds in the right hand and types with the left finger, one who holds in the left
hand and types with the right finger and a final participant who holds the phone
in both hands and types with their thumbs. It is not surprising that the two

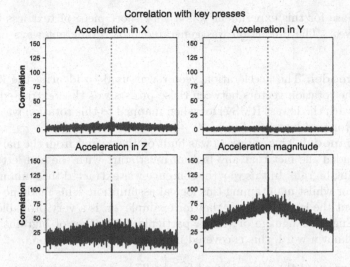

Fig. 5. The correlation of the various accelerometer readings with keypresses as measured by the keylogger. Zero lag is shown by the dotted line.

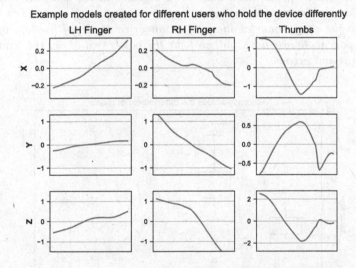

Fig. 6. Example model across three different individuals for the bigram FL

'single-handed' participants result in similar yet inverse models although the extent of the rotation is smaller between two participants. The 'two-handed' participant has a very different trace indicating the centre of rotation closer to the centre of the phone with a more complex rotational vector.

These models were constructed from the fixed text on the first page and then validated against the fixed text in the second page, the model was then used in the final experiment with unseen text. Again it is worth reiterating that the training phase for this experiment was a very short piece of text less than the size of a tweet. The prediction was generated in two different ways using this model:

1. **Naive model:** The acceleration vector was used to identify the key press times, the rotation vectors between these presses was then extracted and the bigram with the lowest RMS error when mapped to this rotation was selected as the proposed bigram.
2. **Bigram model:** This approach was built on the output from the naive model but included the fact that any bigram must start with the end letter of the proceeding bigram. In this way the sentence was extracted that minimised the total error whilst maintaining this logical assumption. This made no assumption about the language used, that for example 'er' is a very probable bigram in the English language or that a particular collection of bigrams actually forms a known word, this is covered in the future work section.

The accuracy of these predictions for the 25 participants is shown in Fig. 7, the accuracy was the measure of the number of bigrams which were correctly identified normalised to the total number of bigrams in the text, an example of one prediction (achieving 83% accuracy) is:

fly t ato ghe moor ang let me play amongowee stars pof freedom of speech isbfreedom por death we have got go fight the powersbed at be, the underlined bigraphs represent errors.

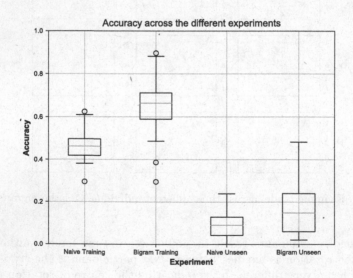

Fig. 7. Accuracy across the experiments.

The average accuracies of the naive and bigram model in predicting the training text was 46.9% and 64.7% respectively and the average accuracies on the unseen text was 9% and 16.7%. Whilst these may be considered low, bear in mind that the training process is very short and even with this short training two participants achieve close to 90% accuracy on the repeated texts and close to 50% on the previously unseen text.

Of interest is whether how the participants used the phone has any effect on the accuracy, in order to explore this question we took the accuracy of the bigram model at predicting the fixed text and compared this to the typing method. This is comparison is shown in Fig. 8, as can be seen there is little difference in the distribution indeed a two-sided Kolmogorov-Smirnoff test resulted in a Kolmogorov-Smirnoff statistic of 0.269 (p-value of 0.683) indicating that, from this sample, the typing method has no effect on the accuracy.

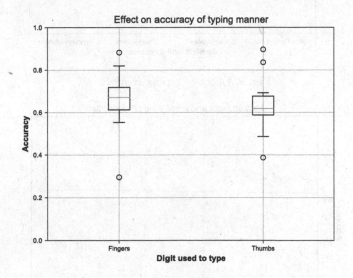

Fig. 8. Effect of typing manner.

We can also explore the effect that comfort with a smartphone keyboard has with the accuracy, a boxplot of the participants self-assessed 'comfort' is shown in Fig. 9. From this experiment, there is a slight decline in performance, but not a statistically significant one, a Pearsons correlation resulted in a correlation of 0.316 and a p-value of 0.124, this is undoubtedly affected by the relatively few participants who considered themselves 'uncomfortable' or 'very uncomfortable' with the smartphone keyboard.

Since the self-assessment of 'comfort' with a soft-keyboard is a qualitative self-assessment, and as discussed previously a number of participants considered the lack of predictive systems reduced their comfort levels we considered the accuracy as a function of a tangible observable typing characteristic. The most illustrative characteristic in our model is that of flight-time and dwell time, this represents the time from a key-up from one key press to the key-up of the next

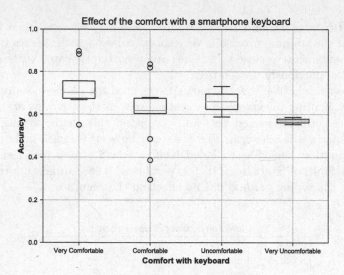

Fig. 9. Effect of typing comfort.

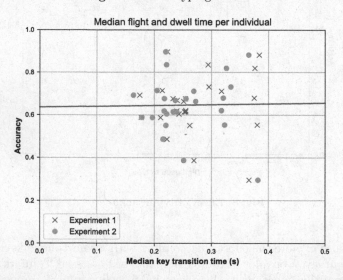

Fig. 10. Effect of typing and timing.

(so includes the time taken to move from one key in addition to the time for which the key is depressed).

In order to remove the effects of long pauses between presses and purely to focus on the measure of typing speed we extracted the median measure of this characteristic across the two fixed text entries, these are then plotted against the accuracy and this is shown in Fig. 10. It is clear from this that for most participants the second attempt was faster than the first attempt and from the linear regression shown in Fig. 10 demonstrates no relationship between typing speed and accuracy.

5   Conclusion and Future Work

In this experiment we have deliberately constrained the experiment to use a single device, a Nexus 5X, in portrait mode. Future work will look to explore different sized devices including different sized phones, 'phablets' and tablets, the different physical size and shapes of devices which we would expect to create different motion patterns. Through pushing the app to the appstore we will also have the opportunity to gather greater numbers of participants across multiple languages and devices. This study focused on the ability to train models for prediction from very small amounts of training data, indeed being able to train this device on a timestamped and publicly observable piece of text is a massive opportunity for exploitation. In order to explore the effect of creating a model with larger ngrams than two characters would require larger training sets, of interest in this study would be the degree to which ngrams of three or more characters could be used to generate specific training data.

In order to improve on the bigram model it is possible to leverage the language used on the device to predict the text that has been entered. The language that the device has been configured to can be requested by an application without explicit permission from the user, this would work in combination with the bigram model to predict not only the sentence with the lowest total error but that maximises the number of valid words in the particular language.

The final piece of future work is to generate generic models for the prediction, from manual observation of the models it is clear that there are similarities between the models produced by individuals who type in similar manners. The ability to create generic models would further reduce the amount of training required and provide an ideal start to a Bayesian approach to predicting keypresses.

We have demonstrated that it is possible to infer the bigrams that are typed on soft-keyboards purely from the rotation of the device, since there is no requirement to ask the user for permission to access the motion sensors of a device this is a covert opportunity for the collection of what is being typed on a smartphone. In our study we trained the models on a small piece of text, shorter than a tweet, even with this limited training data we were able to achieve average performances of 64.7% on text that had been seen before. We have shown that the method that an individual uses to type has no effect on the accuracy of the approach, and whilst how comfortable an individual is using the soft-keyboard does have a small effect it is not statistically significant. In future we look to explore new ways to create the model and inform the predictions to further improve these prediction levels.

References

1. Ofcom. The UK is now a smartphone society (2015). https://www.ofcom.org.uk/about-ofcom/latest/media/media-releases/2015/cmr-uk-2015. Accessed 26 Jan 2017

2. Poushter, J.: Smartphone ownership and internet usage continues to climb in emerging economies (2016). http://www.pewglobal.org/2016/02/22/smartphone-ownership-and-internet-usage-continues-to-climb-in-emerging-economies/. Accessed 26 Jan 2017
3. Pew Research Centre. Smartphone use in 2015 (2015). http://www.pewinternet.org/2015/04/01/us-smartphone-use-in-2015/. Accessed 26 Jan 2017
4. Kwapisz, J.R., Weiss, G.M., Moore, S.A.: Activity recognition using cell phone accelerometers. ACM SigKDD Explor. Newsl. **12**(2), 74–82 (2011)
5. Iso, T., Yamazaki, K.: Gait analyzer based on a cell phone with a single three-axis accelerometer. In: Proceedings of the 8th Conference on Human-Computer Interaction with Mobile Devices and Services, pp. 141–144. ACM (2006)
6. Bevan, C., Fraser, D.S.: Different strokes for different folks? Revealing the physical characteristics of smartphone users from their swipe gestures. Int. J. Hum. Comput. Stud. **88**, 51–61 (2016)
7. Miguel-Hurtado, O., Stevenage, S.V., Bevan, C., Guest, R.: Predicting sex as a soft-biometrics from device interaction swipe gestures. Pattern Recogn. Lett. **79**, 44–51 (2016)
8. Cai, L., Chen, H.: Touchlogger: inferring keystrokes on touch screen from smartphone motion. HotSec **11**, 9 (2011)
9. Owusu, E., Han, J., Das, S., Perrig, A., Zhang, J.: Accessory: password inference using accelerometers on smartphones. In: Proceedings of the Twelfth Workshop on Mobile Computing Systems and Applications, p. 9. ACM (2012)
10. Miller, G.A.: Wordnet: a lexical database for english. Commun. ACM **38**(11), 39–41 (1995)

Live Gaze-Based Authentication and Gaming System

Quan Wang[1], Lelai Deng[2(✉)], Hao Cheng[2], Hualei Fan[3],
Xiaoping Du[2], and Qinghong Yang[2(✉)]

[1] Technology and Innovation Laboratory, Yale Child Study Center,
Yale University, New Haven, CT 06510, USA
quan.wang@yale.edu
[2] Software College, Beihang University, Xueyuan Road no. 37, Haidian District,
Beijing 100191, People's Republic of China
denglelaibh@gmail.com, yangqh@buaa.edu.cn
[3] Beijing Runzhichina Information Technology Co., Ltd., Beijing,
People's Republic of China

Abstract. Face recognition has been widely applied to identification/authentication systems [1–6], however, a considerable drawback of conventional face recognition when used alone lies in its limited ability to distinguish between living human user and 2D photos or pre-recorded videos of the user's face. To address the risk of these systems being easily bypassed by non-living photos or recordings of users, our study proposes an interactive authentication system that requires users to follow a specific pattern displayed onscreen with their gaze. The system uses the subject's eye movement and facial features during viewing for user authentication while randomly generating the displayed pattern in real time to ensure that no prepared video can fake user authentication. Given gaze movement is an inseparable part of the face, our system guarantees that facial and eye features belong to the same human following the pattern displayed. To this its deployment in an eye controlled system, we developed a gaze-controlled game that relies on user eye movement for input and applied the authentication system to the game.

Keywords: Face recognition · Living authentication · Eye-controlled gaming system

1 Literature Review

Face Recognition applications [7] have been widely applied in security systems. With the ever-accelerated development of face recognition technology, more and more identification work has been carried out by face recognition. Common applications include [8]: access control systems for classified departments, login systems for laptops and mobile unlocking systems. For its convenience, efficiency and user-friendliness, face recognition has become one of a most important encryption and decryption methods.

The biggest criticism for face recognition is that the systems are unable to distinguish the liveness of the human face, that is to say, tell apart a real person from photos

© Springer International Publishing AG 2017
T. Tryfonas (Ed.): HAS 2017, LNCS 10292, pp. 239–250, 2017.
DOI: 10.1007/978-3-319-58460-7_16

or videos of that person [9]. Common attacks on face recognition systems are based on users' photos or video recordings. In fact, even when a user is unconscious or asleep, their faces can still be used to pass the authentication. As it was revealed in the famous international conference, Black Hat, a widely recognized face recognition authentication system was easily bypassed with a color image of a user [10].

To overcome this limitation, various adaptations have been made based on the existing face recognition technology. Li [11] proposed a Fourier spectrum analysis method to evaluate the liveness of face that is based on: (1) the face in a photo has less high-frequency components than a real human face and (2) the frequency field changes in time of a face photo is subtle. Kollreider [13] applied a time frame method based on movements, which assumes that real human faces have distinct 3D structure, therefore during the movements, a special 2D movement pattern will be shown on image planes. One main feature of this pattern is that the movement range is wider in the inner area than outer. Kollreider [14] also used mouth movement to carry out the live authentication. Pan [12] gave an aliveness detection method based on different stages of blinks. Bao [15] applied face region light vectors from video series, which prevented the bypass with face images. Nevertheless, a pre-recorded face video with movement of facial organs is still able to bypass Bao's system. In another approach, Kim [16] raised up an infrared face recognition system with 685 nm and 850 nm infrared lights. Then the light intensity information from the face (RGB value and brightness) will be projected to a 2D space, where the real human face and masked face are easier to be distinguished using Linear Discriminative Analysis (LDA). However, Kim's system needs these two conditions for better accuracy: no occluding objects on forehead and having a constant distance between the camera and the user. As a newer study, Tronci [17] implemented a live detection algorithm combining movement information with pattern information (i.e. feature points' location with movement information of these points) using feature points to carry out verification and using movement information to carry out live authentication.

Following the direction of these new developments, we compare the user's eye movement with an interactive visual pattern display, which is unpredictable and therefore impossible to be prepared for, to fulfill a high-precision aliveness detection with face recognition. With the motivation of constructing a gaze controlled system, we applied the live gaze-based authentication first to an eye controlled gaming.

2   Methods

2.1   Construction of the Whole System

We used eye tracking for two applications: live authentication and gaze-controlled gameplay. The whole system works as is shown in Fig. 1. During the live authentication stage, the user is instructed to follow a white dot moving along the trajectory of a circle with their eyes. At the same time, our program uses the video stream to compute the location of user's pupil centers and compares their movement with the trajectory of the displayed moving dot. If the user's eye movement forms a circle-like or ellipse-like ring, the user will be judged as 'Alive'. If not, the access will be denied immediately. In

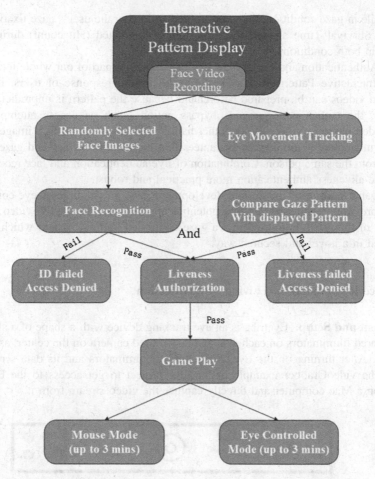

Fig. 1. Interactive authentication system with combination of face recognition live check with gaze pattern.

addition, several images are captured for face-recognition at random time points while the user follows the moving dot. We employed OpenCV [20] to detect faces and employed the Eigenfaces algorithm. The five most similar pictures from video frames of per person were saved in the results folder along with similarity scores. These recognition results were also stored in a log file. Users needed to pass the eye movement with trajectory match, and face recognition to successfully achieve authentication before proceeding to gameplay.

For our second application, we deployed Nightmare, a game that runs on unity3D with the Eyetribe eye tracker and Eyetribe SDK. This SDK can record the trajectory of eyes' movement of users in front of screen. Users were randomly assigned to either the eye or mouse controller input conditions and then switched to the other controller in a counterbalanced sequence. Users played the role of city defenders eliminating zombies in a 3D gaming environment. In the mouse condition, the weapon fired after a mouse click, while in gaze condition, the weapon fired following the user's gaze fixation. We recorded Survival Time and number of zombies eliminated (Hit count) during play sessions in both conditions.

The Authentication and Game Play are both important part of our whole interactive system. Interactive Pattern Display requires the instant response of users, in other words, no videos can be prepared beforehand because the pattern is unpredictable. In this way, the authentication avoids bypass actions such as access attempts with pre-recorded photo or video. On the other hand, randomly selected face images while the gaze movement is monitored, guarantees that the identity of face and gaze movement is from the same person. Combination of live authentication and face recognition makes the aliveness authentication more practical and robust.

The game portion of the current development gave an example of eye-controlled system, providing an interesting and potential application field for the video games. Our goal of this work is to construct a gaze controlled gaming system which can be authorized in a novel and secured way.

2.2 Face Recognition and Living Authentication

Equipment and Setup. Eyetribe is an eye tracking device with a shape of a slim bar, with infrared illuminators on each side and an infrared camera on the center, as shown in Fig. 2. After turning on the EyeTribe camera, illuminators and its data server, we applied the videoGrabber example of the Ofx project to get access to the Eyetribe camera on a Mac computer and directly capture the video stream from it.

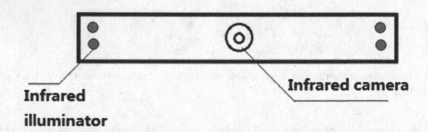

Fig. 2. Structure of our eye tracking device.

When opening the EyeTribe UI, the left area indicates the eye detection, green for detecting eyes while red for not detecting eyes. If not detected, the user needs to change their head angle and position until the screen turns green. This can work as a quality monitoring feature.

The 'calibrate' button (Fig. 3) starts the calibration procedure, several points (up to 16) will show up on the screen. The user needs to focus on these points to finish the calibration work. The quality of calibration is rated into 5 levels: Perfect, Good, Acceptable, Poor and Re-Calibration. Once the user gets the Acceptable (or above) rating, the calibration step is done. We used calibration through EyeTribe UI before the game play.

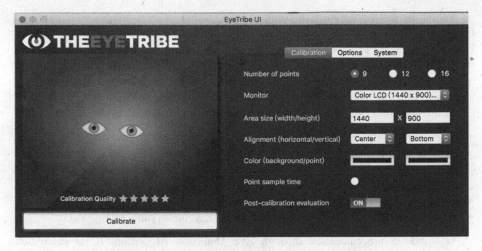

Fig. 3. Screenshot of calibration of EyeTribeUI

Compute the Location of Eyes. During the live authentication stage, the users were instructed to follow a white dot moving along a trajectory with their eyes, in the example here, a circle. The size of screen in this experiment is 15 inches with resolution 1366*768. The radius of circle is set as half of the screen height, with speed at 240 degree/second. The trajectory is shown in Fig. 4(A).

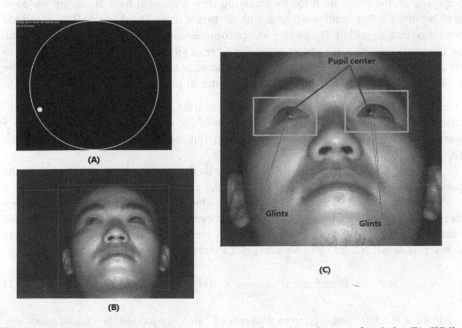

Fig. 4. (A). Interactive display. White dot moving along the trajectory of a circle. (B). While the interactive pattern is displayed, face detection was carried out at the same time on an image from EyeTribe camera. (C). After face detection step, eye tracking process.

While the main program is running in background, several images were captured for face-recognition at random time points while the user followed the moving dot. An Eyetribe was used as an imaging unit to directly output images of the users' faces (Fig. 4(B)). The image sequences from Eyetribe are in gray-scale and have resolution of 1280*768 with 10 frame per second. These images are used for face recognition as well as further calculating of eyes' location from video streaming.

In the meantime, several outputs are extracted from image sequences and recorded:

- Start point of Eye Boxes (SB): Boxes are the region we are interested in, the eye region, red rectangles in Fig. 4. SS is the top left corner location in the picture. In this experiment, boxes are used to compute the center of eyeball so that the track of eye movement is recorded.
- Glints Center (GC): GC is the center of glints points.
- Pupil Center (PC): PC is the center of the eye, yellow points in Fig. 4(C).

GC and SS are calculated through Eye Detection Algorithm, IC is calculated through Starburst Algorithm.

Eye Detection and Tracking. In ideal lighting condition, there should be two glints inside the eye region from the two illuminators. However, in different environmental light settings, sometimes more glints are observed and this can influence the tracking accuracy. We used a chinrest to reduce head movement.

We applied SmartGaze program to compute the geometric center of glints and then crop a 100*80 pixel boxes from the geometric center. Before the computation of eye pupil center, the glints are filled by changing their grey level to 0. By doing so, pupil area becomes a dark continuous area without bright spots. Pupil center (PC) identified with starburst algorithm. By finding an appropriate starting point inside the pupil area, an intensity gradient was used to detect the edge of pupil enabling more edge points to be detected in an iterative way. By fitting the edge of pupil with ellipse so that the center of ellipse can be determined as the center of pupil.

Aliveness Authentication. Parallel to the gaze tracking function, our program compares the eyes' movement with the trajectory of the displayed moving dot. Figure 5 shows the location of left eye when a person following the movement of white dot (A) or not (B).

A Monte Carlo simulation [18] based method was then applied to compare the pattern similarity. As is shown in Fig. 5(C), the similarity comparison process is:

Firstly, to calculate the center of all the location points of eye, the center was taken as point O, O for origin to create a rectangle coordinate system. The points are divided into four regions: I/II/III/IV. Then, the sum of the number of points was calculated in every part as S1, S2, S3, S4. We can get a Percentage (i) through Eq. (1).

$$\text{Percentage (i)} = \frac{s_i}{sum} \times 100\%, i = 1, 2, 3, 4 \tag{1}$$

If there is a Percentage (i) over a threshold value, we judged the task of users' eye movement is not circle-like or ellipse-like. Otherwise, the program will keep running.

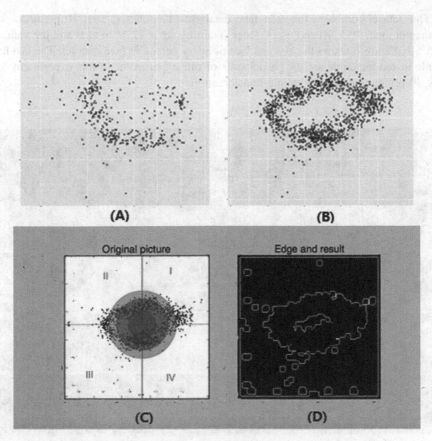

Fig. 5. (A) The track of movement of left eye (Randomly move). (B) The track of movement of left eye (Move following the trajectory). (C) Similarity comparison with displayed moving dot. (D) The edge of the eye movement trace (Color figure online)

Secondly, accounting the distance from every point to the center point O, find the nearest point A_{1near} and the distance of OA_{1near} (to avoid the bias points which are too close to O, OA_{1near} should be longer than a threshold value). Then take the O as center, OA_{1near} as radius, we get the red circle in Fig. 3. If the number of points inside red circle is larger than a threshold percentage of all the points, we judged the tack of users' eye movement is not circle-like or ellipse-like. Otherwise, continue the identifying work.

Finally, if the user's eye movement forms a circle-like or ellipse-like ring, the user will be judged as 'Alive'. If not, the access will be denied immediately. The images were used for face recognition with Eigenface algorithm [19].

Eigenface Algorithm for Face Recognition. The concept of Eigenface algorithm is to transform the face from the initial pixel space to another pixel space and carrying out the similarity comparison in the new space.

The dataset combined the at&t face database (40 persons, each 10 pictures, 400 pictures in total, 40.5 M) and users' faces. Training set is 72 M in total and the validity is 95.5%. Figure 6 shows the average face of every person in face data set. The last five people in red rectangle are the participants of our experiment. In this experiment, we took 40 principal components into consideration.

Fig. 6. Average faces of the face data set (Color figure online)

2.3 Eye-Controlled Gaming

Before the beginning of the game, calibration is strongly suggested in order to have a better experience and higher accuracy in the game. The game starts with the user's character showing on the corner of the map. All the movements are done by the direction keys on the keyboard. When the character is moved to a certain spot, zombies will start appearing and moving towards the user's character (Fig. 7).

In the mouse condition, the weapon fires after a mouse click, while in the gaze condition, the weapon fires following the user's gaze fixation. Living time depends on character's health points (HP, initial HP is 100), once the character is touched by the zombies for more than 3 times, the user loses all his HP and the game ends. We recorded Survival Time and number of zombies eliminated (Hit count) during play sessions in both conditions in the log files of the game.

Fig. 7. In-game screen shots (survive and eliminate more zombies).

3 Results

3.1 Live Authentication Results

For the first tests in the authentication system, the screen was covered so that users could not see the displayed pattern. All users were classified as 'Not Alive' and failed access. Results are listed in Table 1.

Table 1. Live authentication results 1 (5 users, each tests 6 times)

	Condition	Pattern similarity	Face similarity	Authentication result
User 1	No pattern visible	3.7 ± 4%	–	Not alive, denied
User 2		2.0 ± 1%	–	Not alive, denied
User 3		2.7 ± 1%	–	Not alive, denied
User 4		3.1 ± 1%	–	Not alive, denied
User 5		2.1 ± 1%	–	Not alive, denied

The screen was then uncovered for the next tests to clearly display the moving dots, before and after their face has been entered into our face database. Users were able to follow the dots and passed the live authentication. Interactive authentication results are listed in Table 2 (ID failed when their faces not in the database yet) and Table 3 (passed).

Table 2. Live authentication results 2 (5 users, each tests 6 times)

	Condition	Pattern similarity	Face similarity	Authentication result
User 1	Interactive pattern displayed, faces not in the database	70.5 ± 4%	6.3 ± 1.8%	ID failed, denied
User 2		73.3 ± 6%	5.7 ± 4.8%	ID failed, denied
User 3		69.3 ± 4%	6.2 ± 2.2%	ID failed, denied
User 4		74.2 ± 4%	5.9 ± 3.8%	ID failed, denied
User 5		69.7 ± 5%	6.1 ± 4.4%	ID failed, denied

Table 3. Live authentication results 3 (5 users, each tests 6 times)

	Condition	Pattern similarity	Face similarity	Authentication result
User 1	Interactive pattern displayed, faces in database	72.3 ± 4%	87.3 ± 2.3%	Passed
User 2		71.7 ± 4%	85.2 ± 3.8%	Passed
User 3		71.5 ± 6%	91.7 ± 3.3%	Passed
User 4		72.1 ± 4%	87.6 ± 3.5%	Passed
User 5		72.3 ± 4%	88.6 ± 2.7%	Passed

3.2 Eye-Controlled Gaming

After being authorized and having gained access, each user played game for 10 times, 5 in mouse mode and 5 in eye controller mode. Gameplay data is listed in Table 4.

Table 4. Gameplay results

	Average survival time (Mouse)	Average survival time (Gaze)	Average hit count (Mouse)	Average hit count (Gaze)
User 1	94.3 ± 19.2	81.3 ± 19.5	36.3 ± 7.6	20.7 ± 4.5
User 2	91.7 ± 17.0	83.3 ± 16.7	16.3 ± 3.5	18.3 ± 5.0
User 3	95.7 ± 20.3	85.4 ± 11.2	37.7 ± 1.5	31.3 ± 5.8
User 4	93.3 ± 17.9	84.6 ± 13.3	37.5 ± 3.6	24.7 ± 4.4
User 5	94.7 ± 17.3	85.5 ± 17.5	30.3 ± 3.3	20.3 ± 5.7

Average survival time was comparable in mouse (93.6 ± 18.1) and gaze mode (82.6 ± 14.6), with T-test ($t(5) = 3.52$, $p = 0.06$). The average hit count with mouse (34.7 ± 3.5) was higher than with gaze (24.6 ± 5.2), but no significant difference ($t(5) = 3.67$, $p = 0.06$).

4 Conclusion and Discussions

Our goal of this work is to construct a gaze controlled gaming system which can be authorized in a novel and secured way. Gaze interaction was applied in both of the two applications: live authentication and gaze-controlled gameplay. The live authentication with gaze tracking serves as an attractive and natural feature for the eye-controlled game. In the future, we are planning to implement more functionalities in this gaming system by including more gaze controlled interactions.

Preliminary data showed that our system only authorized users who passed both the face recognition and the aliveness test. Given that the users who participated in the study had vastly greater experience with using the mouse as a controller compared to the relative novelty of the gaze-controller, the study suggests that there is considerable potential for gaze-controlled game play.

There are several factors which are related to the function of Live Authentication. Accuracy is an important factor to judge living authentication result. The current pupil detection is unstable in different light conditions, especially for users with glasses. Frequent blinks also reduced the accuracy of pupil detection, about 2% offset from the actual location. The biggest limitation is that eye tracking is sensitive to head movement, so we used a chinrest to reduce head movement. In a future study we will try to improve the pupil detection without the help of the chinrest, to get a stable pupil detection accuracy. Given that most of living authentication systems are used in online applications, efficiency is considered to be one of the most critical factors in the Living Authentication design. In our experiment, living authentication with pattern display takes about 7 s, which is longer than the most of the static face recognition system. Moreover, currently we only used a circle as the interactive pattern. Random pattern and instant judgement is needed improve the robustness of the whole system. In the next step, random pattern with advanced algorithm will be implanted into the liveness authentication to make the pattern not predictable. One of our goals for the next step is to add different types of displayed patterns and shorten the pattern display time, and at the same time continue improving the accuracy in the further work.

For face recognition, we used Eigenface as a classical face recognition method, however, new development of deep learning methods such as Incremental Convolution Neural Network (ICNN) shows an unparalleled efficiency in face recognition. There is no doubt that the implementation of the deep learning method can be a good option for our future work.

This was our first exploration of live gaze-based authentication and its application in a gaze controlled system. Current gameplay still needs the assistance of keyboards for navigation. Eventually, we would like to construct a system which includes live gaze-based Authentication and various keyboard-free and gaze controlled games.

References

1. Daugman, J.G.: Biometric personal identification system based on iris analysis: U.S. Patent 5,291,560. 1994-3-1
2. Piosenka, G.V., Chandos, R.V.: Unforgeable personal identification system: U.S. Patent 4,993,068. 1991-2-12
3. Lanitis, A., Taylor, C.J., Cootes, T.F.: Automatic face identification system using flexible appearance models. Image Vis. Comput. 13(5), 393–401 (1995)

4. Miller, S.P., Neuman, B.C., Schiller, J.I., et al.: Kerberos authentication and authorization system. In: Project Athena Technical Plan (1987)
5. Alfieri, R., Cecchini, R., Ciaschini, V., et al.: VOMS, An Authorization System for Virtual Organizations. Grid Computing, pp. 33–40. Springer, Berlin (2004)
6. Russell, E.A.: Authorization system for obtaining in single step both identification and access rights of client to server directly from encrypted authorization ticket: U.S. Patent 5,455,953[P]. 1995-10-3
7. Ahonen, T., Hadid, A., Pietikainen, M.: Face description with local binary patterns: application to face recognition. IEEE Trans. Pattern Anal. Mach. Intell. **28**(12), 2037–2041 (2006)
8. Yu, H., Yang, J.: A direct LDA algorithm for high-dimensional data—with application to face recognition. Pattern Recognit. **34**(10), 2067–2070 (2001)
9. Kim, Y., Na, J., Yoon, S., Yi, J.: Masked fake face detection using radiance measurements. JOSA A **26**(4), 760–766 (2009)
10. Maatte, J., Hadid, A., Pietikinen, M.: Face spoofing detection from single images using micro-texture analysis. In: International Joint Conference on Biometrics (IJCB), pp. 1–7. IEEE (2011)
11. Li, J., Wang, Y., Tan, T., Jain, A.K.: Live face detection based on the analysis of fourier spectra. In: Defense and Security, pp. 296–303. International Society for Optics and Photonics (2004)
12. Pan, G., Sun, L., Wu, Z., Lao, S.: Eyeblink-based anti-spoofing in face recognition from a generic webcamera. In: IEEE 11th International Conference on Computer Vision, 2007. ICCV 2007, pp. 1–8. IEEE (2007)
13. Kollreider, K., Fronthaler, H., Bigun, J.: Evaluating liveness by face images and the structure tensor. In: Fourth IEEE Workshop on Automatic Identification Advanced Technologies, 2005, pp. 75–80. IEEE (2005)
14. Kollreider, K., Fronthaler, H., Faraj, M.I., Bigun, J.: Real-time face detection and motion analysis with application in "liveness" assessment. IEEE Trans. Inf. Forensics Secur. **2**(3), 548–558 (2007)
15. Bao, W., Li, H., Li, N., Jiang, W.: A liveness detection method for face recognition based on optical flow field. In: International Conference on Image Analysis and Signal Processing, 2009. IASP 2009, pp. 233–236. IEEE (2009)
16. Kim, Y., Na, J., Yoon, S., Yi, J.: Masked fake face detection using radiance measurements. JOSA A **26**(4), 760–766 (2009)
17. Tronci, R., Muntoni, D., Fadda, G., Pili, M., Sirena, N., Murgia, G., Ristori, M., Ricerche, S., Roli, F.: Fusion of multiple clues for photo-attack detection in face recognition systems. In: 2011 International Joint Conference on Biometrics (IJCB), pp. 1–6. IEEE (2011)
18. Mooney, C.Z.: Monte Carlo Simulation. SAGE Publications, Thousand Oaks (1997)
19. Turk, M., Pentland, A.: Eigenfaces for recognition. J. Cognit. Neurosci. **3**(1), 71–86 (1991)
20. OpenCV. OpenCV Version 2.4.13. http://opencv.org/, 2016–05–19/2016–11–01

When Eye-Tracking Meets Cognitive Modeling: Applications to Cyber Security Systems

Haiyue Yuan[1], Shujun Li[1(✉)], Patrice Rusconi[2], and Nouf Aljaffan[1]

[1] Department of Computer Science and Surrey Centre for Cyber Security (SCCS),
University of Surrey, Guildford, UK
Shujun.Li@surrey.ac.uk, hooklee@gmail.com
[2] School of Psychology, University of Surrey, Guildford, UK

Abstract. Human cognitive modeling techniques and related software tools have been widely used by researchers and practitioners to evaluate the effectiveness of user interface (UI) designs and related human performance. However, they are rarely used in the cyber security field despite the fact that human factors have been recognized as a key element for cyber security systems. For a cyber security system involving a relatively complicated UI, it could be difficult to build a cognitive model that accurately captures the different cognitive tasks involved in all user interactions. Using a moderately complicated user authentication system as an example system and CogTool as a typical cognitive modeling tool, this paper aims to provide insights into the use of eye-tracking data for facilitating human cognitive modeling of cognitive tasks more effectively and accurately. We used visual scan paths extracted from an eye-tracking user study to facilitate the design of cognitive modeling tasks. This allowed us to reproduce some insecure human behavioral patterns observed in some previous lab-based user studies on the same system, and more importantly, we also found some unexpected new results about human behavior. The comparison between human cognitive models with and without eye-tracking data suggests that eye-tracking data can provide useful information to facilitate the process of human cognitive modeling as well as to achieve a better understanding of security-related human behaviors. In addition, our results demonstrated that cyber security research can benefit from a combination of eye-tracking and cognitive modeling to study human behavior related security problems.

Keywords: Eye-tracking · Cognitive modeling · CogTool · User interface · Design · Cyber security · Human behavior · User authentication

1 Introduction

Psychologists and computer scientists have developed computational cognitive architectures and models (e.g. ACT-R [1,4], Soar [21,29] and CLARION [30]) to simulate human behaviors using computers to study human cognitive processes such as perception, memory, and attention. Due to their ability to help designers and researchers evaluate human performance and refine user interface (UI)

© Springer International Publishing AG 2017
T. Tryfonas (Ed.): HAS 2017, LNCS 10292, pp. 251–264, 2017.
DOI: 10.1007/978-3-319-58460-7_17

designs more easily without prototyping and user testing [13], cognitive models such as Keystroke-Level Model (KLM) [8] and other more complicated models following the GOMS (Goals, Operators, Methods, and Selection) rules [17] have been widely used in the Human-Computer Interaction (HCI) field. However, such models are relatively less known to and used by cyber security researchers and practitioners, except for some limited work on using human cognitive modeling tools to estimate usability of user authentication systems [19,20,28].

Although human cognitive modeling is less used in the cyber security field, the wider human factors have been actively studied by cyber security researchers. It is well known that many security problems are caused by insecure human behaviors such as weak passwords and poorly-designed/-implemented security policies. In addition, the UI design of a system may lead to insecure human behaviors and thereby compromise the system's security. For instance, as reported in [24,33], for many challenge-response based password systems against observer attacks, human users respond to different challenges differently in terms of the time spent. This allows an attacker to derive the password based on some observable timing differences after seeing a sufficient number of authentication sessions conducted by a target user.

The "standard" approach to identifying insecure human behaviors is to conduct user studies with real human participants. However, this approach is not only time consuming, but also has other issues such as limited/bias samples, ethical concerns, and privacy issues, which could potentially delay the detection of human behavior related security problems and leave systems vulnerable to potential attacks for a longer time. Therefore, it is important and beneficial for both security system designers and end users to discover human behavior related security problems as early as possible ideally at the design stage, which can be considered as a special case of the widely-recognized "security by design" principle [11].

Differently from the above standard approach, cognitive modeling could provide a quicker and sometimes also better solution to study human behavior related security problems. Considering the broad scope of cyber security systems as well as potential security problems related to human behavior, this paper does not aim to provide a comprehensive account of how to model human cognitive tasks for any cyber security systems, instead, we use one advanced user authentication system as a representative example to show how human cognitive modeling can help UI designers and security analysts. Furthermore, some researchers have reported that eye-trackers can provide useful information for cognitive modeling tasks, but the combined use of eye-tracking and cognitive modeling technologies for security-sensitive systems is very rare. We hope this paper will fill this gap as well.

In this paper, we report our work on combining eye-tracking data and Cog-Tool [16], a widely-used cognitive modeling tool, to model human cognitive tasks involved in a relatively complex user authentication system called Undercover [27]. The eye-tracking data proved useful for guiding the modeling process, and helped us to reproduce some *non-uniform* and *insecure* human behavior observed in a previous lab-based user study conducted by Perković et al. in 2011 [24]. The simulation results of the eye-tracking assisted cognitive model led to more insights into the observed non-uniform human behavior and how the UI design may be further refined to improve its security, going beyond what Perković et al. predicted in [24]. Our work suggests that cyber security researchers and practitioners could benefit from a *combined* use of cognitive modeling techniques and eye-tracking data.

The rest of this paper is organized as follows. The next section presents some related work. Then, we describe the authentication system (Undercover) we focused on as a showcase, how we used eye-tracking data to refine the cognitive model of Undercover, and what new insights we learned from the process. The final section discusses the benefits of using eye-tracking data in cognitive modeling of cyber security systems.

2   Related Work

Goals, Operators, Methods, and Selection rules (GOMS) are among the well-established cognitive modeling concepts for analyzing UIs. A number of variants of GOMS models such as KLM, CMN-GOMS [9], and CPM-GOMS [17] have been proposed. Most of these cognitive models can estimate human performance in terms of time needed by an average skilled user to complete a specific task.

Differently from GOMS models, low-level cognitive architectures and models such as ACT-R [1,4] and Soar [21,29] can be used to model broader human cognitive processes, e.g., modeling users' performance on multi-modal UIs such as car navigation systems, which represents a challenge for traditional GOMS analysis [6,26]. ACT-R specifies the time parameters of processes such as the shifting of a user's visual attention, so it can be used to model visual search tasks. For example, Fleetwood and Byrne [12] compared two models representing different strategies of searching for a target icon among distractors.

Cognitive models and related software tools do not normally have built-in support on various UI elements. To fill the gap, a number of software tools (e.g. CogTool [16], SANLab-CM [23], Cogulator [31]) have been developed to make cognitive modeling tasks easier. Such tools often implement a GOMS model from a user-defined UI layout design and then convert that to a model based on one of the lower-level cognitive architectures such as ACT-R. Although these tools are very powerful to support cognitive modeling tasks, it could be difficult for a designer to decide how to model a system involving complicated cognitive tasks, e.g., if they depend on individual characteristics and/or the context. One of the widely-used human cognitive modeling tools in the HCI community is CogTool [16], which is based on KLM and ACT-R and has proven to be a useful tool for predicting and simulating human performance of skilled users to complete computer tasks [18].

Despite the fact that human cognitive modeling has been extensively studied and used in the HCI field, to the best of our knowledge only a few studies in the cyber security community used cognitive modeling to evaluate/design security systems. Kim et al. [19] used CogTool to evaluate the usability of a shoulder surfing resistant mobile user authentication system, and Sasse et al. [28] combined CogTool with a user study to estimate the usability of a user authentication system. Kwon et al. [20] used CPM-GOMS to investigate human shoulder surfers attacking PIN entry methods that rely on the evidence of effective human perceptual and cognitive capabilities.

Although cognitive modeling has not been extensively used in the cyber security field, some cyber security researchers have started considering human cognitive abilities in the design of cyber security systems to achieve a better balance between usability and security. Belk et al. [5] proposed two-step personalized user authentication tasks based on individual cognitive styles of processing textual and graphical information. Galib et al. [2] designed a new user authentication system based on a game of cognitive tasks to capture individual users' implicit cognitive signatures. More recently, Castelluccia et al. [10] developed a new authentication scheme (MooneyAuth) based on using implicit memory to reduce the cognitive load of remembering passwords. Such work also calls for more research on modeling of human cognitive abilities to study usability and the security of such systems.

Eye trackers capture human users' eye movements (fixations and saccades), scan paths, and metrics such as pupil dilation and blinks which provide information about the user's cognitive processes while performing a task. Thus, they have been widely used in studies on cognitive modeling especially on cognitive tasks related to visual objects shown on computer displays [14]. Some researchers also used eye trackers to help validate and compare cognitive models of visual search tasks [7,12,15,25]. There is also research about using eye trackers to better understand human users' cognitive processes when interacting with security-sensitive systems, e.g., recently Miyamoto et al. [22] conducted a study on using eye-tracking data to link UI elements to the detection of possible phishing websites. Alsharnouby et al. [3] used eye trackers to assess the influence of browser security indicators and the awareness of phishing on a user's ability to avoid cyber attacks. While there is quite some work on the combined use of eye tracking and cognitive modeling, to the best of our knowledge, except some general recommendations such as those reported in [15] still limited work has been done on combining the two techniques for cyber security applications. This paper aims to further advance this neglected area.

3   Eye-Tracking Assisted Cognitive Modeling Experiment

In this section, we explain our work in detail. We start with a brief description of the target system Undercover. Then we report our initial cognitive models of Undercover and the simulation results when eye-tracking data were not used. These are followed by an explanation of the eye-tracking experiment we conducted to improve the initial models which were found inaccurate. The last part of the section presents our re-modeling work and the new insights emerged from the eye-tracking assisted cognitive modeling experiment.

3.1 Target System: Undercover

Undercover [27] is an observer-resistant password system (ORPS) developed based on the concept of partially-observable challenges. The password P a user needs to set is a set of five secret pictures called "pass-pictures", selected out of an image pool. To complete an authentication session, the user needs to correctly respond to seven challenge screens, where each challenge screen contains a hidden challenge c_h described below and a public challenge c_p consists of four pictures and a "no pass-picture" icon as shown in Fig. 1(a). The hidden challenge

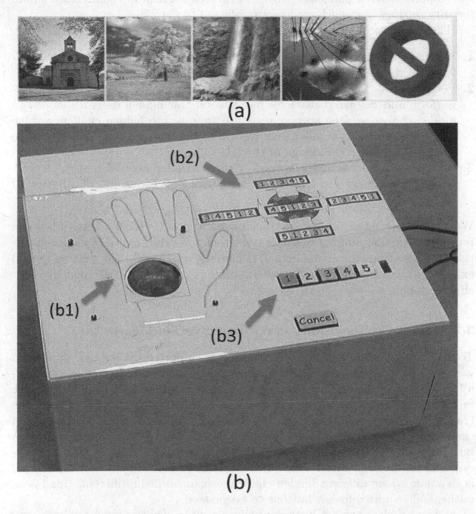

(a)

(b)

Fig. 1. The UI of Undercover [27]: (a) the public challenge panel shown on the computer display; (b) a box composed of the following UI components: (b1) a track ball for transmitting the hidden challenge, (b2) the hidden challenge button layout panel, (b3) the response button panel.

c_h is transmitted via a haptic device (a track ball) covered by the user's palm, as shown in Fig. 1(b1). Five different rotation/vibration modes of the track ball correspond to five different values of c_h: "Up", "Down", "Left", "Right", "Center" (vibrating). As illustrated in Fig. 1(b2), each hidden challenge value corresponds to a specific layout of five response buttons labeled with 1–5. To respond to a challenge screen, the user should firstly obtain a hidden response r_h which is the position index of the pass-picture in the public challenge (1–4 if present and 5 if absent). Then the user looks for r_h in the correct hidden challenge button layout to get a new position index r_h', and finally presses the button labeled with r_h' in the response button panel as shown in Fig. 1(b3). There are some more subtle security settings, for which readers are referred to [24,27].

There are three main reasons why we chose Undercover for our work:

1. Undercover is a relatively complex security-sensitive system that involves different cognitive tasks that are not straightforward to model.
2. Perković et al. [24] conducted a lab-based user study that revealed some *non-uniform* and *insecure* behavioral patterns on how human users responded to hidden challenges (the average response time to the hidden challenge value "Up" is significantly smaller than to other values) which were believed to be caused by an improper design of the UI.
3. How human users actually interact with the Undercover UI remains largely unclear which may lead to other security problems or insights of a better UI design.

We therefore wanted to use eye-tracking data and CogTool to see if we can reproduce the non-uniform behavioral patterns observed and provide some further insights about the actual human behaviors, which will then serve as a good example showcasing the usefulness of combining eye tracking with cognitive modeling techniques.

3.2   Initial CogTool Models (Without Eye-Tracking Data)

To make an adequate comparison with findings reported by Perković et al. [24], we used CogTool to model their Undercover implementation (which is conceptually the same as the original Undercover system reported in [27] but with some minor changes to the UI and the use of an earphone and an audio channel to transmit the hidden challenge instead). The layout of the UI with functionality of each component (which is called the design script in CogTool), and how human interact with the UI (which is called the demonstration script in CogTool) are essential to CogTool. Undercover has a static UI layout, but the user interaction is dynamic where different hidden challenges can result in different visual scan paths, and require different buttons to be pressed.

A key problem we met in the modeling task is how to model human users' visual scan paths for the three separate parts of a challenge screen: the public challenge picture panel, the hidden challenge button layout panel, and the response button panel. Since we did not have any clue about the actual visual scan paths, we decided to make two initial models based on two simple visual scan paths explained below and shown in Fig. 2.[1]

- **A1**: for each part of the challenge screen the user identifies the target without an obvious visual searching process, i.e., the user looks at the pass-picture in the public challenge panel, then moves to the (correct) hidden challenge button layout directly, and finally to the (correct) response button directly.
- **A2**: the same as **A1** but before the user looks at the (correct) hidden challenge button layout (s)he looks at the whole hidden challenge button layout panel first.

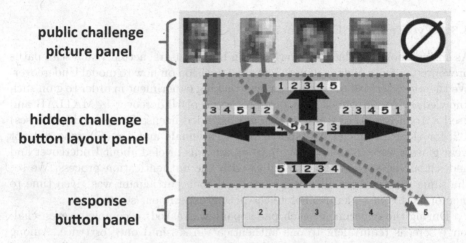

Fig. 2. An illustration of the two visual scan paths when the pass-picture is the second picture in the public challenge and the hidden challenge is "Left": the red dashed and dark green dotted lines show **A1** and **A2**, respectively. (Color figure online)

With the two models, we generated all five possible instances according to the hidden response $r_h = 1, \cdots, 5$ and obtained the average response times as shown in Fig. 3. Comparing the results of **A1** and **A2**, we can see **A2** requires more time due to the added cognitive task, and the hidden challenge value corresponding to the fast average response time differs ("Up" for **A1** and "Center" for **A2**). While the non-uniform response time pattern of **A1** loosely matches the findings reported in [24], the cognitive model is obviously too simplistic, e.g., a proper visual searching process is expected for finding out if a pass-picture is present and where the pass-picture is in the public challenge.

---

[1] We actually built a number of models for each of the two models as CogTool supports only static cognitive tasks but Undercover involves dynamic ones related to varying challenges. We are developing an extension of CogTool to facilitate modeling of such dynamic cognitive tasks, but in this paper we will not focus on this issue.

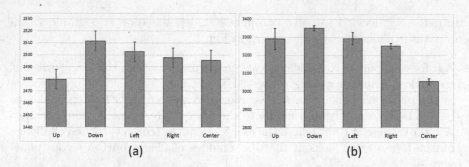

Fig. 3. Average response times for (a) A1 and (b) A2.

3.3   Eye-Tracking Experiment

As shown above, the lack of knowledge on human users' actual visual scan paths prevented us from making a more informed decision on how to model Undercover. We therefore decided to conduct an eye-tracking experiment in order to gain such knowledge. We implemented a fast prototype of Undercover in MATLAB and used a Tobii EyeX eye tracker (with an upgraded license for research purposes) [32] for the experiment. Nine participants (5 female and 4 male), who did not wear glasses were recruited. Each participant was briefed about Undercover and had a training session to get familiar with the authentication process. We set the same password for all participants, and each participant was given time to memorize the pass-pictures before the actual experiment started.

During the experiment, each participant was asked to complete seven challenge screens (equivalent to one authentication session) once or twice. Among the seven challenge screens, each of the five values of the hidden challenge and the hidden response was present at least once. In total, we collected 98 sets of eye-tracking data (each set represents the process of responding to one challenge screen). We removed 12 sets of data due to inaccuracy caused by change of sitting position during the experiment and incomplete tasks. This gave us 86 valid sets of data whose eye-gaze trajectories were manually inspected to identify visual scan patterns. The results revealed four important (not all expected) visual scan patterns explained below and illustrated in Fig. 4.

1. *No obvious searching process for the correct hidden challenge button layout or the correct response button*: For these two parts of the challenge screen, participants identified the targets directly without an obvious visual searching process.
2. *Two searching patterns for the pass-picture*: For 87% cases, participants adopted a searching strategy of center-left-right as illustrated in Fig. 4(a), and for the rest 13% cases, participants searched for the pass-picture simply from left to right.
3. *Confirmation pattern for the pass-picture*: For 59% of all cases, participants showed a confirmation pattern where they went from the hidden challenge

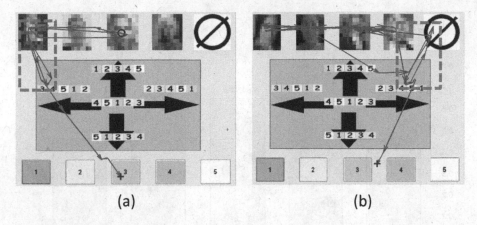

(a)   (b)

Fig. 4. An illustration of observed visual scan patterns where red lines show the eye gaze trajectories, blue circles and blue crosses indicate the starting and ending gazing positions: (a) $r_h = 1$, $c_h = $ Left; (b) $r_h = 5$, $c_h = $ Right. (Color figure online)

button layout panel back to the pass-picture in the public challenge panel before moving to the response button panel, which are highlighted inside the green dash-line rectangles shown in Fig. 4. This pattern is consistent with the findings reported in [25], which suggests that several saccades to the location of the memorized target are typical. We also noticed that the confirmation process rate varies depending on the value of the hidden challenge (see Fig. 5) c_h: 40.91% (Up), 92.31% (Down), 64.71% (Left), 61.9% (Right), 46.15% (Center). Interestingly, the non-uniform confirmation rates partly match the non-uniform response time reported in [24], suggesting they may be one source of the non-uniformity.

4. *Double scanning pattern for absent pass-picture*: When no pass-picture is present in the public challenge, in 66% cases participants double scanned the public challenge picture panel to make sure there was indeed no pass-picture, which is illustrated in Fig. 4(b).

3.4   Re-modeling Undercover (with Eye-Tracking Data)

The four visual scan path patterns learned from our eye-tracking experiment provided additional evidence for us to remodel Undercover in a more complicated (and hopefully more accurate) manner. We firstly constructed four new models named as CLR-C, CLR-NC, LR-C and LR-NC, where CLR represents the (C)enter-(L)eft-(R)ight searching strategy for the pass-picture; LR represents the simpler (L)eft-(R)ight searching strategy for the pass-picture; C after the hyphen stands for the (C)onfirmation process and NC after the hyphen means there is (N)o (C)onfirmation process. As in the case of the two initial models, for each of the above models we also created five instances for the five values of r_h for each model to get the average response time. When $r_h = 5$ (i.e., there is no

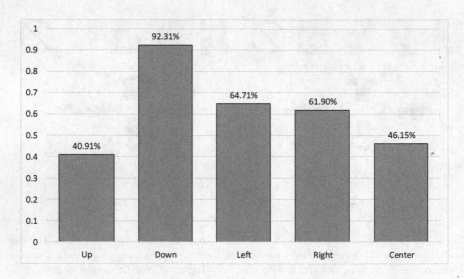

Fig. 5. Confirmation rate for hidden challenges

pass-picture in the public challenge), we also created two further sub-models with and without the double scanning pattern, whose simulation results (response times) are then added up using the weights 0.66 and 0.34 to get the predicted average response time for the case of $r_h = 5$.

The results of the predicted average response time for all the four models are shown in Table 1, from which we can see the hidden challenge value corresponding to the smallest average response time is "Up" (consistently across all models), matching the findings reported in [24].

Table 1. Average response time (in milliseconds) to each hidden challenge value for different models.

Model	Hidden Challenge				
	Up	Down	Left	Right	Center
CLR-C	4148.2	4331.6	4266.2	4229.2	4243.8
CLR-NC	3385.0	3453.2	3445.4	3401.2	3424.6
LR-C	4125.3	4297.5	4232.8	4203.5	4220.3
LR-NC	3362.1	3419.1	3411.9	3375.5	3401.1

Based on the four models, we constructed a mixed probabilistic model where CLR-LR and N-NC patterns are considered based on different probabilities: 87% CLR and 13% LR for all challenge values; 40.9% C and 59.1% NC for "Up", 92.3% C and 7.7% NC for "Down", 64.7% C and 35.3% NC for "Left", 61.9% C and 38.1% NC for "Right", 46.2% C and 53.8% NC for "Center". The predicted average response time for each hidden challenge value of the mixed probabilistic model is shown in Fig. 6(a), where the average response time for the hidden challenge value "Up" is significantly smaller than for other four values, which accords with the finding in [24].

We also looked at the average response times for different values of r_h and the results are shown in Fig. 6(b). The results confirmed another observation in [24], which states that most users tended to respond more slowly when $r_h = 5$ (i.e., there is no pass-picture in the public challenge), and this could be explained by the double scanning pattern we described above. Furthermore, as identified in our eye-tracking experiment, in most cases participants adopted the CLR visual searching strategy for the pass-picture, and thus it is not surprising to observe that $r_h = 3$ (when the pass-picture is right in the middle of the public challenge panel) corresponds to the smallest average response time.

Comparing with the results reported in [24], there are still some noticeable differences. These differences could be caused by some subtle differences between our experimental setup and the one used in [24]. For instance, in the user study reported in [24], participants were allowed to use either mouse or keyboard to click the response button. However, for our models only mouse users are considered because keyboard users are more difficult to model due to various keyboard types and different individual human behaviors of using the keyboard. The smaller and different population of participants used in our experiment may be another source.

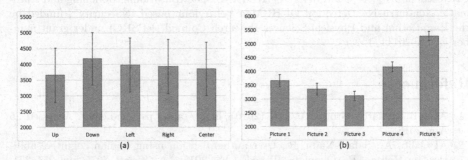

Fig. 6. Average response times (in milliseconds) for different values of (a) the hidden challenge c_h and (b) the hidden response r_h.

Our model could be further refined by considering the additional mental effort of converting r_h to r'_h. This will differ for different values of c_h because this conversion is effectively not needed for "Up" (the hidden challenge response button layout is "12345", which means $r'_h = r_h$). We thus can reasonably hypothesize that there will be less mental efforts for the "Up" case so that the response time is faster, which is also the main hypothesis Perković made in [24]. However, as demonstrated in the above results, the conversion process from r_h to r'_h is not the sole (may not be even the main) factor causing the observed non-uniform human behavior on average response time, which is a new insight obtained from our eye-tracking experiment. In our future work, we plan to investigate the conversion process from r_h to r'_h and see how that can be considered in the cognitive modeling task.

4   Conclusion

Taking Undercover [27] as a relatively complex user authentication system and CogTool as a typical cognitive modeling tool, we demonstrated that the use of an eye tracker can help identify different visual scan patterns which can effectively guide computational modeling of human cognitive tasks. The eye-tracking assisted cognitive modeling approach allowed us to not only reproduce some previously-observed behavioral patterns of human users reported in [24], but also to reveal more unexpected observations of related human behaviors. While our work mainly focuses on a specific system, the insights we learned from the eye-tracking assisted cognitive modeling suggest eye-tracking should be used more widely in cognitive modeling of any cyber security systems with some visual elements in their UIs. We are developing a software tool as an extension version of CogTool, which will cover (semi-)automated fast prototyping and (semi-)automated application of eye-tracking data to adapt cognitive models.

Acknowledgments. This work was supported by the UK part of a joint Singapore-UK research project "COMMANDO-HUMANS: COMputational Modelling and Automatic Non-intrusive Detection Of HUMan behAviour based iNSecurity", funded by the Engineering and Physical Sciences Research Council (EPSRC) under grant number EP/N020111/1.

References

1. ACT-R Research Group: ACT-R (2016). http://act-r.psy.cmu.edu/. Accessed 25 Aug 2016
2. Al Galib, A., Safavi-Naini, R.: User authentication using human cognitive abilities. In: Böhme, R., Okamoto, T. (eds.) FC 2015. LNCS, vol. 8975, pp. 254–271. Springer, Heidelberg (2015). doi:10.1007/978-3-662-47854-7_16
3. Alsharnouby, M., Alaca, F., Chiasson, S.: Why phishing still works: user strategies for combating phishing attacks. Int. J. Hum. Comput. Stud. **82**, 69–82 (2015)
4. Anderson, J.R.: How Can the Human Mind Occur in the Physical Universe?. Oxford University Press, Oxford (2007)
5. Belk, M., Germanakos, P., Fidas, C., Samaras, G.: A personalization method based on human factors for improving usability of user authentication tasks. In: Dimitrova, V., Kuflik, T., Chin, D., Ricci, F., Dolog, P., Houben, G.-J. (eds.) UMAP 2014. LNCS, vol. 8538, pp. 13–24. Springer, Cham (2014). doi:10.1007/978-3-319-08786-3_2
6. Byrne, M.D.: ACT-R/PM and menu selection: applying a cognitive architecture to HCI. Int. J. Hum. Comput. Stud. **55**(1), 41–84 (2001)

7. Byrne, M.D., Anderson, J.R., Douglass, S., Matessa, M.: Eye tracking the visual search of click-down menus. In: Proceedings of 1999 SIGCHI Conference on Human Factors in Computing Systems, CHI 1999, pp. 402–409. ACM (1999)
8. Card, S.K., Moran, T.P., Newell, A.: The keystroke-level model for user performance time with interactive systems. Commun. ACM **23**(7), 396–410 (1980)
9. Card, S.K., Newell, A., Moran, T.P.: The Psychology of Human-Computer Interaction. L. Erlbaum Associates Inc., Hillsdale (1983)
10. Castelluccia, C., Duermuth, M., Golla, M., Deniz, F.: Towards implicit visual memory-based authentication. In: Proceedings of 2017 Network and Distributed System Security Symposium (NDSS 2017). Internet Society (2017)
11. Cavoukian, A., Dixon, M.: Privacy and security by design: an enterprise architecture approach. Online white paper (2013). https://www.ipc.on.ca/wp-content/uploads/Resources/pbd-privacy-and-security-by-design-oracle.pdf
12. Fleetwood, M.D., Byrne, M.D.: Modeling the visual search of displays: a revised ACT-R model of icon search based on eye-tracking data. Hum.-Comput. Interact. **21**(2), 153–197 (2008)
13. Gray, W.D., John, B.E., Atwood, M.E.: Project ernestine: validating a GOMS analysis for predicting and explaining real-world task performance. Hum. Comput. Interact. **8**(3), 237–309 (1993)
14. Hornof, A.J.: Cognitive strategies for the visual search of hierarchical computer displays. Hum.-Comput. Interact. **10**(3), 183–223 (2004)
15. Hornof, A.J., Halverson, T.: Cognitive strategies and eye movements for searching hierarchical computer displays. In: Proceedings of 2003 SIGCHI Conference on Human Factors in Computing Systems (CHI 2003), pp. 249–256. ACM (2003)
16. John, B.E.: CogTool (2016). https://cogtool.com/. Accessed 25 Aug 2016
17. John, B.E., Kieras, D.E.: The GOMS family of user interface analysis techniques: comparison and contrast. ACM Trans. Comput.-Hum. Interact. **3**(4), 320–351 (1996)
18. John, B.E., Prevas, K., Salvucci, D.D., Koedinger, K.: Predictive human performance modeling made easy. In: Proceedings of 2004 SIGCHI Conference on Human Factors in Computing Systems (CHI 2004), pp. 455–462. ACM (2004)
19. Kim, S., Yi, H., Yi, J.H.: FakePIN: dummy key based mobile user authentication scheme. In: Jeong, Y.-S., Park, Y.-H., Hsu, C.-H.R., Park, J.J.J.H. (eds.) Ubiquitous Information Technologies and Applications. LNEE, vol. 280, pp. 157–164. Springer, Heidelberg (2014). doi:10.1007/978-3-642-41671-2_21
20. Kwon, T., Shin, S., Na, S.: Covert attentional shoulder surfing: human adversaries are more powerful than expected. IEEE Trans. Syst. Man Cybern.: Syst. **44**(6), 716–727 (2014)
21. Laird, J.E.: The Soar Cognitive Architecture. MIT Press, Cambridge (2012)
22. Miyamoto, D., Blanc, G., Kadobayashi, Y.: Eye can tell: on the correlation between eye movement and phishing identification. In: Arik, S., Huang, T., Lai, W.K., Liu, Q. (eds.) ICONIP 2015. LNCS, vol. 9491, pp. 223–232. Springer, Cham (2015). doi:10.1007/978-3-319-26555-1_26
23. Patton, E.W.: The stochastic activity network laboratory for cognitive modeling (SANLab-CM) (2012). https://github.com/CogWorks/SANLab-CM/. Accessed 25 Aug 2016
24. Perković, T., Li, S., Mumtaz, A., Khayam, S.A., Javed, Y., Čagalj, M.: Breaking undercover: exploiting design flaws and nonuniform human behavior. In: Proceedings of 2011 7th Symposium on Usable Privacy and Security (SOUPS 2011). ACM (2011)

25. Rao, R.P.N., Zelinsky, G.J., Hayhoe, M.M., Ballard, D.H.: Eye movements in iconic visual search. Vis. Res. **42**(11), 1447–1463 (2002)
26. Salvucci, D.D.: Predicting the effects of in-car interfaces on driver behavior using a cognitive architecture. In: Proceedings of 2001 SIGCHI Conference on Human Factors in Computing Systems (CHI 2001), pp. 120–127. ACM (2001)
27. Sasamoto, H., Christin, N., Hayashi, E.: Undercover: authentication usable in front of prying eyes. In: Proceedings of 2008 SIGCHI Conference on Human Factors in Computing Systems (CHI 2008), pp. 183–192. ACM (2008)
28. Sasse, M.A., Steves, M., Krol, K., Chisnell, D.: The great authentication fatigue – and how to overcome it. In: Patrick Rau, P.L. (ed.) CCD 2014. LNCS, vol. 8528, pp. 228–239. Springer, Cham (2014). doi:10.1007/978-3-319-07308-8_23
29. Soar Research Groups: Soar cognitive architecture (2016). http://soar.eecs.umich.edu/. Accessed 18 Sept 2016
30. Sun, R., Slusarz, P., Terry, C.: The interaction of the explicit and the implicit in skill learning: a dual-process approach. Psychol. Rev. **112**(1), 159–192 (2005)
31. The MITRE Corporation: A cognitive modeling calculator (2014). http://cogulator.io/. Accessed 25 Aug 2016
32. Tobii AB: Tobii EyeX (2016). http://www.tobii.com/xperience/products/. Accessed 25 Aug 2016
33. Čagalj, M., Perković, T., Bugarić, M.: Timing attacks on cognitive authentication schemes. IEEE Trans. Inf. Forensics Secur. **10**(3), 584–596 (2015)

"If It Wasn't Secure, They Would Not Use It in the Movies" – Security Perceptions and User Acceptance of Authentication Technologies

Verena Zimmermann[✉] and Nina Gerber

Faculty of Human Sciences, Technische Universität Darmstadt,
Darmstadt, Germany
{zimmermann,n.gerber}@psychologie.tu-darmstadt.de

Abstract. Whereas the text password is still ubiquitous as authentication scheme, its shortcomings are well-acknowledged within the research community. A plurality of alternatives such as other knowledge-based, token-based or biometric authentication schemes have been developed. Although the usability of these schemes has been analyzed, the results concerning further user perceptions are complex and somewhat ambiguous. Further, most of these results stem from focus groups and surveys where the actual interaction with the systems was not tested. To shine light on this topic we conducted a laboratory study with 35 participants to compare and understand user perceptions of several biometric and non-biometric authentication schemes. We simulated the interaction with authentication schemes to protect our participants' data and to avoid affecting influences of particular implementations. The results showed that the text password is still popular among the participants for reasons of familiarity and due to privacy aspects, namely because no personal information has to be provided. Fingerprint and iris recognition were well liked among the biometrics by many participants due to the perceived security of using a unique feature for authentication. However, the use of personal information also raised privacy concerns in others. This leads to the assumption that there might be two user groups preferring either passwords or biometrics. The assumption along with possible influencing variables such as authentication context or familiarity should be addressed in future research. The simulation of authentication schemes could further be improved by addressing realistic error rates to increase external validity of the study design.

Keywords: Authentication · Biometrics · Security · Perception · Acceptance

1 Introduction

Even though passwords as a classical form of authentication are still wide-spread and well accepted by many service providers and users alike, several short-comings of this mechanism exist: Users tend to create unsafe passwords, forget passwords or use the same passwords for several applications [e.g., 20, 21, 46, 51]. Thus, a lot of research is done to develop and evaluate new forms of authentication technologies [21, 22, 36]. These include for example token-based solutions or graphical passwords [44].

© Springer International Publishing AG 2017
T. Tryfonas (Ed.): HAS 2017, LNCS 10292, pp. 265–283, 2017.
DOI: 10.1007/978-3-319-58460-7_18

The increasing availability of different types of sensors even in mobile devices such as smartphones also made it possible to use biometric authentication technologies. Biometric authentication relies on the recognition of either physical characteristics, like fingerprint, hand geometry, iris, retina, facial characteristics and DNA, or behavioral characteristics, e.g., signatures, keystroke dynamics or voice (which can also be classified as physical treat) [38]. The research in this area however often focuses on the technical aspects of implementing those technologies. Still, user perceptions and user acceptance are not necessarily in line with technical security or robustness of different technologies [2, 5, 18, 23]. The objective of this research was to explore user perceptions concerning security, preference, usage intention, effort, cost-benefit ratio, expected usage problems and privacy concerns using different forms of biometric and non-biometric authentication schemes. The first two research questions therefore were: "How do user perceptions of the interaction with different authentication schemes differ? What are the reasons for users' perceptions and preferences?"

We compared eight different authentication schemes, namely text password and graphical password as well as gesture, fingerprint, face, speech and ear shape recognition in a laboratory study with thirty-five participants. Each participant tested and evaluated each authentication scheme. In a final questionnaire and short interview the participants were asked to rate the tested schemes against each other and provide reasons for their preferences. The interaction with the authentication schemes was tested in a simulation to avoid external influences such as different levels of maturity or different interfaces. Furthermore, we aimed to protect our participants' data.

In context with the study design we were interested in whether the simulation "worked" in that participants didn't see through it. We were also interested in our participants' feedback and in possible ways to further improve the study design. Therefore the third and fourth research questions were: "Does the simulation work? How can the study design be improved further?"

We found that the text password, fingerprint recognition and iris recognition were the most preferred authentication schemes with our participants. The most reported reasons for preferring the biometric schemes fingerprint and iris recognition were the high perceived security due to the uniqueness of the feature and the ease of use. The text password however was not only preferred because of familiarity and perceived ease of use as well. Privacy aspects also played a major role. Several participants stated to prefer text passwords because no personal information had to be given away and couldn't be lifted or stolen. The least liked schemes were ear shape recognition, gesture recognition and the graphical password. Whereas the ear shape recognition was rated as impractical and effortful, participants thought the gesture recognition could be easily copied. The most likely cause for the negative rating of the graphical password were problems with the implementation. Overall, our results indicate that there might be two user groups that either prefer the password due to privacy concerns or biometrics due to the perceived security of using a unique feature for authentication. Earlier research suggests that user preference could further be influenced by context (e.g. newsletter vs. bank account) and familiarity with or knowledge about biometric vs. non-biometric schemes. Future research should address these questions that could have major implications for decision-makers choosing authentication schemes for their systems and services.

2 Related Work

O'Gorman [35] provided an extensive comparison of several knowledge-based, token-based and biometric authentication schemes in terms of security against different kinds of attacks, potential keyspace and entropy, host-side security and also some usability aspects like usage convenience, false nonmatch and false match rates. However, he did not compare the authentication schemes in an empirical study, but partly relied on individual empirical results from previous studies utilizing different study designs and partly based his evaluations merely on theoretical considerations. Bonneau et al. [7] chose a similar approach for rating a broad range of authentication schemes according to several security, usability and deployability criteria. An early literature review about the usability and security of alphanumeric and graphical passwords, token-based and biometric authentication procedures was conducted in 2004 by Sasse [39]. Furthermore, a literature review concerning the security and usability of several biometric authentication schemes can be found at Mayron et al. [34].

Some researchers compared the perceived security, acceptance and usability for a small range of authentication schemes. Bhagavatula et al. [5], for example, focused on smartphone authentication via Android's facial recognition system "Face Unlock" and Apple's fingerprint-based system "Touch ID". Compared to the traditional PIN authentication, two-thirds of survey participants who already used Face Unlock considered it to be more secure. Similar perceptions were found for users of Touch ID. In a corresponding lab study by Bhagavatula et al., seven out of ten participants ranked Face Unlock as their last or second last favored authentication scheme. Touch ID was preferred by six participants, whereas the remaining four described it as their least favorite scheme. Tari et al. [45] assessed the perceived and real vulnerability of the graphical password scheme "Passfaces" [37] to shoulder-surfing compared to alphanumeric passwords in a lab study, with participants trying to shoulder-surf while the experimenter authenticated himself. Both perceived and real shoulder-surfing vulnerability were rather high for Passfaces. Non-dictionary passwords were considered as less vulnerable, but were also found to be easier to shoulder-surf than dictionary passwords. As one of the first, Furnell and Evangelatos [19] conducted a focus group to investigate user perceptions, awareness and acceptance of different biometric authentication schemes, namely fingerprint, hand, signature, voice, keystroke, iris and retina recognition. Behavioral methods (keystroke, voice and signature analysis) were considered as least reliable, whereas fingerprint, iris and retina analysis received the highest ratings. However, iris and retina analysis scored lowest concerning how comfortable respondents would be to use the investigated schemes. Participants were also asked about their preference to use biometric compared to knowledge- and token-based schemes. More than half of the participants (61%) selected biometrics as their first preference, whereas 31% chose knowledge- and 10% token-based procedures.

Dörflinger et al. [14] conducted a focus group along with an online survey to assess the perceived security, goodness and usage intention for a wide range of authentication schemes, namely fingerprint recognition, 2D and 3D gesture recognition, retina scan, activity-based verification, speech recognition, face recognition and a recognition-based graphical password. Participants in the focus group rated retina scan and fingerprint as most secure; the graphical password was considered as the least secure, followed by 3D and 2D gesture recognition. Surprisingly, participants were least likely to use retina scan for authentication in the future, which was also placed second to last in terms of goodness. Fingerprint, on the other hand, was the clear winner according usage intention and perceived goodness. In the online survey, fingerprint, iris and face recognition received the highest security ratings. In another focus group, Sieger and Möller [42] investigated gender differences concerning the perceived security of the same authentication schemes used by Dörflinger et al. [14], except for the graphical password. Though they focused on smartphone authentication, they received the same distribution of perceived security for the investigated schemes as Dörflinger and colleagues. They also found that female users tend to perceive all authentication schemes as being more secure, expect for speech recognition. Ben-Asher et al. [4] also did a survey and focus groups on the perceived security, acceptance, convenience and usage intention of several authentication schemes used on a smartphone. They included fingerprint recognition, gesture recognition, iris scan, voice recognition, face recognition, PIN/password and recognition of one's signature provided on a touch screen. Fingerprint was rated as most secure, followed by iris recognition and PIN/password. Gesture recognition was considered as least secure. Fingerprint and PIN/password also scored highest in terms of convenience, whereas participants clearly preferred PIN/password according to the likelihood of future usage.

While these are very interesting insights about user perceptions of different authentication schemes, the authors relied on more or less sophisticated demonstration of the particular authentication concepts [14] or mere textual presentation [42] and the participants did not actually use the described schemes. Further research is needed to investigate if the reported results can be replicated in a controlled setting based on actual interaction with the evaluated authentication schemes. We aim to contribute to filling that gap by using a controlled laboratory setting with a simulation design to avoid influences of different interfaces and stages of system maturity. Further, participants had the possibility to test and evaluate the actual interaction with eight different schemes. Most of the schemes chosen for this study have also been the object of investigation in the previous studies mentioned above to allow for a comparison of the results in terms of user perceptions.

3   Authentication Schemes

In the following section we describe findings of previous studies regarding user perceptions of the authentication schemes that were compared in the laboratory study.

3.1   Text Password

Text passwords are still the most common form of authentication. Among the shortcomings of text passwords researchers or users respectively list problems with the technical security [7], but also usability issues [27, 43]. The often mentioned poor memorability leads users to apply work-around strategies such as choosing simple and/or guessable passwords, writing passwords on notes or re-using passwords for several accounts [3, 26, 40]. Even though not perfect, the analysis by Bonneau et al. revealed that text passwords still have benefits in terms of deployability and also some usability aspects such as "nothing-to-carry" and "easy-recovery-from-loss" [7]. Users in a survey by Ben-Asher et al. also attested the text password good values in terms of perceived security and convenience. Apart from that, the text password received the highest rating in terms of future intended use [4].

3.2   Graphical Password

Graphical passwords are an alternative to text passwords making use of the fact that people are better in memorizing pictures than words [1]. A range of graphical passwords exist that can broadly be divided into two categories. First, there are recognition-based techniques, where users e.g. have to recognize previously chosen pictures in a particular sequence among other distractors. Examples include Passfaces [37] or Déjà vu [16]. In recall-based variants users often have to recall and draw or click a certain pattern or sequence. Examples for this category are PassPoints [53] and Draw A Secret [28]. Further, some schemes use a combination of recognition-based and recall-based features. Advantages of graphical passwords include a better memorability [8, 16] compared to passwords and the possibility to increase the password space and therefore resistance to dictionary attacks, with a sufficiently large database. Also, some research suggests that graphical approaches might be more joyful for users [49]. On the other side, many graphical schemes come with an increased login-time compared to passwords or PINs [e.g. 31, 52] and, depending on the implementation, can be prone to shoulder-surfing.

3.3   Gesture Recognition

Gesture recognition can either be a non-biometric or a biometric authentication scheme depending on whether one's characteristic dynamics of completing the gesture are measured. Further, 2D gestures e.g. on a touch-screen as well as 3D gestures made in free air in front of a sensor can be used for authentication. In the focus groups conducted by Dörflinger, 2D gestures were rated better and more secure by the participants than 3D gestures. Also, the intention to use 2D gestures was higher [17]. Similar results were found by Sieger and Möller [42]. However, gesture detection in general only received very low ratings in the study by Ben-Asher [4]. User reactions is a study by Trewin et al. were mixed [47].

3.4   Biometric Authentication

The following procedures belong to the group of biometric authentication schemes. After Riley et al. [38] biometric authentication is defined as "the process of establishing an individual's identity through measurable characteristics of their behaviour, anatomy or physiology." Biometric technologies are spreading and already find application in the governmental as well as in private sectors [38]. Whereas some researchers view biometrics as an advantageous approach because they confirm the actual presence of the legitimate user and apply characteristics that cannot be lost, forgotten or stolen, others raise concerns. Critics comprise the inability of a certain percentage of people to authenticate via biometrics, the problems arising for recovery from loss, and privacy issues [12, 46]. For example, in a laboratory study Toledano et al. [46] found that privacy concerns negatively affected confidence in biometrics. In focus groups conducted by Coventry et al. [13] privacy concerns were also raised as a problematic issue. Further, some researchers completely dismiss biometric authentication such as fingerprint because the features used are not per se secret and could be "lifted" [41].

Fingerprint Recognition. Fingerprint authentication is one of the most spread biometric authentication schemes, well-known by users due to the use in films, law enforcement and travel documents. It is also popular because of its high accuracy [32], maturity [12] and relatively low cost of acquisition devices [3]. In several user studies fingerprint recognition was rated as very secure and usable by the participants. For example, in focus groups conducted by Dörflinger et al. [17] fingerprint authentication received the highest acceptance and second highest security ratings compared to other biometric authentication technologies. In a survey by Jones et al. [29], participants perceived fingerprint authentication to be the most suitable biometric authentication technology for the financial and health care area. In a lab study by Holz and Bentley [24], participants experienced an increased sense of security when using fingering authentication in place of passwords to protect their e-mail account. Participants in a survey-based field study by Mare et al. [33] liked fingerprint authentication mainly because it was quick, even if they sometimes encountered failures with the sensors. Results from another survey by Cherapau et al. [10] suggest that besides its speed, participants value the convenience and ease of use of iPhones Touch ID fingerprint authentication. More than half of the participants also perceived it as secure. However, some participants also expressed concerns regarding the privacy of their provided fingerprint, due to uncertainty of whether Apple stores their fingerprints locally or somewhere else. Similar concerns were reported by participants in a survey conducted by De Luca et al. [15].

Face Recognition. Compared to the relatively long-established fingerprint recognition, face recognition is a rather new authentication solution [27]. However, it has recently gained publicity through the implementation of "Face Unlock" in Android phones. Reported user perceptions of this authentication scheme vary across studies: Results from a survey combined with focus groups by Ben-Asher et al. [4], as well as focus groups conducted by Dörflinger et al. [17] suggest a relatively low acceptance and usability of face recognition. A survey conducted by De Luca et al. [15] indicates a problem with perceived security for Android's Face Unlock, along with usability issues like low speed and lack of convenience concerning the correct placement of the smartphone for face scanning. Some participants also mentioned social awkwardness as one factor for not using Face Unlock, due to the fear of looking like they were taking selfies when scanning their face. Participants in a lab study by Bhagavatula et al. [5]

expressed concerns about attackers using a photograph to fool the face recognition system. However, other study results suggest high values for acceptance [47] and perceived security [5].

Iris Recognition. Most users have at least heard about iris recognition as an authentication scheme or seen its application in a movie [4]. Nonetheless, some users express concerns about this authentication approach, including reliability, health issues or misuse of their personal data, for example in a lab study conducted by Tassabehji and Kamala [44]. This is in line with results from another lab study by Crawford and Renaud [14], who found a low acceptance rate for iris recognition. But there are also positive statements from survey and focus group participants [4] in terms of acceptance or usage intention for iris recognition.

Speech Recognition. The recognition of speech can rely on both, behavioral biometric characteristics (i.e. speech pattern) and physiological characteristics (i.e. the individual sound of one's voice). Like for face recognition, users differ in their evaluation of speech recognition as an authentication solution. Some survey studies indicate high values for perceived security and future usage intention [11], but at the same time, results from other survey [4] or laboratory studies [48] suggest relatively low levels of acceptance, and low perceived security values [19].

Ear Shape Recognition. One of the first to investigate ears for identification was Iannarelli [26] who found that all of the more than 10,000 analyzed ears were distinguishable and thus ears provided sufficient unique properties to be used as a biometric. The recognition process is similar to facial recognition with 2D images or 3D models of the ear and does not need direct interaction [50]. Although ear shape recognition is seen as a promising approach by some researchers [25, 40, 50] the literature on the usability or security perception of ear shape recognition seems scarce. Problems might comprise ears covered by hair or hats and religious concerns to uncover ears for authentication [40].

4   Method

In the laboratory study thirty-five participants used and evaluated the eight simulated authentication technologies described above in a within-subject design. The text password as a classical authentication mechanism served as a baseline, whereas the remaining seven technologies were tested in a randomized order. The participants were asked to answer questions concerning the perceived security, effort and cost-benefit ratio, as well as expected usage problems and intention to use the authentication scheme in the future after using each scheme. The preference was rated after testing all schemes, along with possible privacy concerns associated with the authentication procedures.

4.1   Participants

The thirty-five participants that took part in the study were German undergraduates studying either psychology (29) or psychology in IT (6). Eleven participants were male, 24 female. Age ranged between 19 and 47 years with a mean of 23.09 (SD = 5.38).

About half of the participants (17 out of 35) have never used biometric authentication technologies before. All participants completed the study, there were no drop-outs. The participation was compensated with course credit.

4.2   Procedure

After the reception participants were asked to sit in front of a workstation used to simulate the different authentication schemes. The apparatus used for the simulation included an eye and facial expression tracking system called "FaceLAB"[1], a microphone and a built-in fingerprint sensor of a Sony VAIO notebook. The face, iris and ear shape recognition were simulated with the help of the FaceLAB system. For speech recognition, the participant was holding the microphone while saying a given password. We implemented a graphical password similar to PassPoints, where people have to click on predefined areas on a picture in a certain order to authenticate [53]. This procedure dates back to one of the first graphical schemes implemented in 1996, the so-called Blonder scheme [6]. The gesture recognition was implemented as a form of pattern recognition similar to the one used by "SoftKinetic"[2] for the PlayStation. The gesture was completed by moving a pointed finger in front of the FaceLAB camera in the form of the symbol for infinity (∞). Authentication was successful if the correct gesture was shown independent of individual dynamics.

The participant's workstation included two monitors. To one monitor the FaceLAB system was connected, the other monitor displayed instructions on the current authentication task. For reasons of data protection and privacy no biometric data was actually collected or stored. For the simulation, the participants' monitors were remotely controlled by the instructor. The participants' screens were duplicated and displayed on the screens of the instructor which were not visible for the participants. Participants were instead told that the data processing took place on the instructors' computer to provide a credible explanation for the connection between the computers. The experimental set-up is shown in Fig. 1.

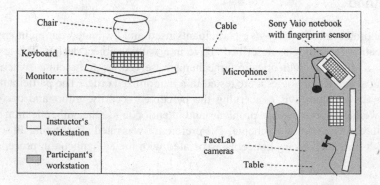

Fig. 1. Illustration of the experimental setup

---

[1] http://www.seeingmachines.com.

[2] https://www.softkinetic.com/products.

Before attending the main task, participants were told that several systems needed to be calibrated beforehand to be able to accurately authenticate the participants during the main task. Again, this was only simulated, but done to allow for a realistic authentication process. Thus, a simulated calibration phase was done for fingerprint recognition, face recognition, iris recognition, speech recognition and ear shape recognition.

After this the participants received the instruction to authenticate with a given text password at their workstation. The instruction was displayed on the screen. The familiar text password served as a baseline and to familiarize people with the procedure. After typing the correct password the participants received textual feedback on their screen indicating the authentication was successful. Participants were then asked to answer several questions on the authentication procedure based on a 5-point-Likert scale with 1 = strongly disagree and 5 = strongly agree, namely:

- Perceived security: "I think this authentication scheme is very secure, that is, it protects me against attacks."
- Expected problems: "I think the use of this authentication scheme generally causes no problems."
- Perceived effort: "How do you rate the effort for using this authentication scheme?" (based on a 5-point Likert-scale with 1 = very low and 5 = very high).
- Perceived cost-benefit ratio: "In my opinion, the effort exceeds the gained benefits for this authentication scheme."
- Intention to use: "If I had the possibility, I would use this authentication scheme."

Afterwards, the procedure was repeated with the other seven authentication schemes in a randomized order. Whenever the instructions were followed correctly, the participants received the "successful authentication"-message on their screen. Questions concerning the instructions were answered, in case of questions concerning technical features or functionality participants just received a general reassuring sentence such as "It works out fine" or "I can see on my computer that the data is processed correctly". After the completion of all authentication schemes participants received some final questions comparing all procedures used:

- Preference: "Please arrange the following authentication schemes according to how much you would like to use them, if all of them were available to you." (based on a ranking from 1 = most preferred to 8 = least preferred)
- Privacy concerns: "I have concerns to disclose the following data for usage of an authentication scheme." (based on a 5-point-Likert scale with 1 = strongly disagree and 5 = strongly agree)

The final part of the study was a half-structured interview asking for the reasons of why people preferred or not preferred certain schemes and why people perceived some procedure as more secure than others. Furthermore, some control variables such as age, gender, familiarity with biometrics and further comments were collected. The last part was the debriefing of the participants. They were told that all authentication schemes were simulated and that no data was stored or processed. Participants were then asked whether they saw through the simulation, and if yes, why that was the case. The participants were finally thanked for their participation, accredited with course credit and provided with contact information should any further questions arise later.

5   Results

In the following section the quantitative results of the questionnaires are presented along with the qualitative results from the interviews. We first describe the participants' perception of the authentication schemes, followed by an evaluation of the study design.

5.1   Preference

The results revealed that most participants preferred to authenticate via text password (11 out of 35), fingerprint (10 out of 35) or iris recognition (9 out of 35). Participants mostly appreciated text passwords due to habit, simplicity and protection of their personal data, for example:

- "I prefer the password, simply out of habit. I suppose it is not the most secure authentication scheme, but I haven't had any negative experiences with it and it is not exactly complex."
- "The question was which scheme I would mostly like to use and I think iris or face recognition are the best schemes, but I just don't want to disclose those [data], hence I chose the password."
- "I know it works well and with a good password you can protect yourself without disclosing personal information. This way, if your account is hacked, it is 'just' your account and not also your fingerprint."

Biometric authentication technologies, on the other hand, were preferred because they were seen as secure and simple and due to the uniqueness of the feature:

- "For me, it is very secure. Our iris is very…everyone has a special iris. It is very unique. Fingerprint is unique and iris too."
- "I think it is exiting, I liked that you could unlock the system with your fingerprint, because only I have this fingerprint. […] and I don't forget that like a password."
- "It is relatively secure, the eye is unique and it is simple once you have scanned it initially. You know it from movies."

The overall rating of the authentication schemes can be found in Fig. 2.

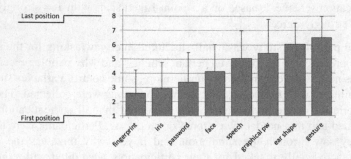

Fig. 2. Preference rating of all authentication schemes; low values indicating high preference

The least popular authentication technologies were the graphical password as well as gesture and ear shape recognition. The negative evaluation of the graphical password is likely to be caused by the rather imperfect technical implementation of the graphical password that manifested itself in the change of the mouse courser every time the mouse was placed in the correct area of the authenticating picture. Another reason for the negative evaluation was that the graphical password and the gesture recognition were viewed as easily copiable and therefore less secure:

- "In my opinion this can be fastest broken through guessing without knowing it."
- "Because of someone knows the gesture he could easily authenticate himself, I would say."

The ear shape recognition was seen as impractical and effortful:

- "I think the ear shape recognition was pointless. [...] if you would employ it in daily life and had to turn your head every time…concerning the practicability and compatibility, I'm not such a great fan."
- "Because I think it's inefficient, it is impractical and I would not be keen to use it."

5.2 Perceived Security

Although there were no significant differences between the authentication technologies concerning the perceived security (F(7, 238) = 0.48, p > .05; see Fig. 3), sixteen out of thirty-five participants rated fingerprint as the most secure technology. The main reasons for this were uniqueness of the authentication feature as well as protection against forgery:

- "Fingerprint is most secure. Iris and face recognition are on the same level. Simply in terms of security…because…fingerprint is unique. Because as far as I now a fingerprint can't be replicated. And the other schemes all provide some opportunity for attacks. And I think the fingerprint scan is difficult to crack from outside the system, you have to get into the system somehow to access the data and copy them."
- "The probability for someone to have the same fingerprint is one billion or so. You can spoof the face with a photo or something like that, but fingerprint is hard [to spoof]."

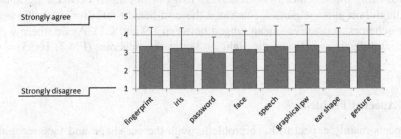

Fig. 3. Perceived security of the tested authentication schemes

Text passwords were also considered as secure "as long as they are applied correctly", i.e. in accordance with common password guidelines:

- "The password is most secure if you apply it correctly. Biometric characteristics can be forged easily, passwords are relatively complex, there are more units to vary."

5.3 Privacy Concerns

However, fingerprint is also the authentication feature for which most participants have concerns to reveal their data, followed by face and iris recognition (differences were significant with $F(4.1, 142.7) = 11.74$, $p < .001$, partial $\eta^2 = 0.25$, see Fig. 4).

The participants also mentioned these concerns in the interviews:

- "It depends on in whose hands it is, if I authenticate myself via fingerprint when entering a country or to identify a delinquent, then I think it's secure, but I still have a bad feeling to disclose this data to the state because I don't know how it is protected."
- "I think it is questionable because the eye is scanned offhandedly. One is just not as familiar with iris recognition as with fingerprint and that stokes fear about digitalization and the 'transparent citizen'."

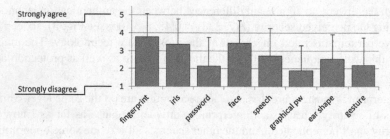

Fig. 4. User concerns to reveal the data necessary for the particular authentication scheme

5.4 Perceived Effort

There were no significant differences concerning the perceived effort for using the authentication schemes ($F(7, 238) = 1.39$, $p > .05$). Overall, participants expected the effort for using the schemes to be relatively low (mean ranged between 2.2 and 2.5). Accordingly, on average participants rated the cost-benefit-ratio for using the authentication schemes as positive (mean ranged between 1.9 and 2.1). Again, there were no significant differences between the eight authentication schemes ($F(4.7, 160.5) = 0.89$, $p > .05$).

5.5 Expected Problems

Participants mainly expect to have problems with the ear shape and face recognition, whereas the other authentication schemes are expected to perform relatively equal, on a moderate, but slightly positive level (see Fig. 5). The differences in the expected occurrence of problems were significant with $F(4.7, 159.5) = 2.91$, $p < .05$, partial $\eta^2 = 0.08$.

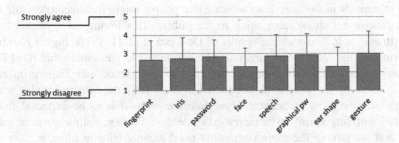

Fig. 5. Expected problems during the usage

5.6 Intention to Use

Although there were also no significant differences in the intention to use the authentication schemes in the future ($F(7, 238) = 1.05$, $p > .05$), the text password still received the highest value, i.e. on average, participants are most inclined to use the text password if they could freely choose between all considered authentication schemes (mean ranged between 2.9 and 3.6).

5.7 Simulation

The majority of participants did not see through the simulation of the authentication schemes. After having been informed about the procedure 22 participants stated they had not been suspicious about the implementation of the authentication schemes. For eight participants, the classification was ambiguous as they mentioned minor concerns only after being informed. Five participants either raised questions during the experiment or clearly stated to have had suspicions after being informed. Some participants stated the authentication process was too "smooth" to be realistic. Of the five, four also had personal experience with biometric authentication.

6 Discussion

The results revealed that even though alternatives are spreading the familiar text password is still popular as authentication method. The text password was the most commonly mentioned preference in the interviews and also ranged among the top three schemes in the list of average preference positions. In accordance with some previous studies fingerprint and iris recognition received the highest values among the biometric schemes. For example, in a survey by Furnell and Evangelatos [19] fingerprint and iris scan were rated the most reliable and Karatzouni et al. [30] found fingerprint to be the most popular choice for the implementation of biometrics on smartphones. Interestingly, none of the schemes investigated in our study differed significantly in terms of their perceived security. Thus, the reasons for the lower ranking of other biometric schemes such as face, speech or ear shape recognition seem to lie in other areas. The rating of expected problems reveals that users expect the face and ear shape recognition to cause more problems than other schemes what might be an explanation. Further, several statements in the interviews indicate that people might feel uncomfortable using speech, face or ear shape recognition in the public. This finding of expected "social awkwardness" is in line with the results of De Luca et al. [15]. The higher ranking of fingerprint and iris recognition might also be connected to the finding that most of our participants who had used biometrics before, had experience with fingerprint recognition. In a survey by Jones et al. conducted in 2007 [29], the fingerprint also was the biometric scheme most participants were familiar with. It is to be expected that the familiarity with fingerprints even increased since then. Further, both fingerprint and iris recognition are among the more commonly used technologies in films, e.g. in crime movies. As a reason for her preference one participant even stated that she knew from films that the iris scan was easy to use and relatively secure.

Another interesting result is that the text password and biometric technologies seem to be preferred for different reasons. The text password is valued not only due to its familiarity but also because no unique, personal information has to be confided to the authentication system and therefore cannot be stolen by an attacker. However, biometrics seem to be valued mainly due to this exact fact. Participants mostly named the uniqueness and unforgeability of the feature as a reason for using biometrics. This leads to the question of whether different user groups exist preferring either the text password due to privacy concerns or biometric technologies for perceived security reasons. The assumption of different user preferences is supported by results of other studies showing that people seem to have complex, somewhat dichotomous opinions about biometrics [9, 38]. In connection with this question one should also consider possible influences of variables that have not yet been tested in the current laboratory study. As mentioned above, the familiarity with biometrics, both personal experience and the familiarity from movies, might influence their assessment. Apart from that, Heckle, Patrick and Ozok [23] found that users were more comfortable using biometrics for personal versus corporate purchases in an online shopping context. The survey results of Jones et al. [29] revealed that in the financial domain the text password was rated as slightly more acceptable than a fingerprint scan, whereas the order changed in the health care sector. In the retail domain again passwords were rated as more appropriate than fingerprint and other biometrics. These results indicate that the authentication context might affect user preference for biometrics versus passwords as well. Future research should address these questions. Due to the short-comings of the implementation of the graphical password it remains open whether the assumption of different user groups is only valid for text passwords versus biometrics or for knowledge-based procedures in general. This question could be addressed in future studies as well.

It is noticeable that the perceived effort did not differ between the different schemes. A reason for this result might be that all our simulated schemes provided a similar interface and were implemented with a zero-error rate to avoid influences of a particular problem on the evaluation of the interaction. On the one hand, the results indicate that the simulation was successful in avoiding theses influences on the participants' assessment. On the other hand, the assessments in a real-life environment with current implementations of the technologies might differ a lot. It is to be expected that errors e.g. due to hand lotion on fingers when using the fingerprint sensor affect users' evaluation of the system. Therefore, to increase the external validity of the results in this regard, future studies should address the problems and error rates of current solutions in the study design. Overall, the simulation worked well for the majority of the participants. Nearly two thirds of the participants were convinced of the functionality of the tested authentication schemes, further eight expressed questions or doubt only after being informed about the simulation. Still, one has to take into account that most of the users were non-experts in terms of information technology and biometric authentication schemes. Only half of the participants had used some form of biometric authentication before. Furthermore, the imperfect implementation of the graphical password might have caused distortions in the participants' assessments. Thus, the inclusion of actual problems and error rates of current solutions as well as the redesign of the interfaces is expected to lead to a further improvement of the simulation in future studies.

6.1   Limitations

Despite the aspects discussed in the context of the study design the research had the following limitations: First, all participants were undergraduate students. Therefore, the sample has been skewed in terms of age, education and technical affinity. About half of the participants already had personal experience with some form of biometrics. This might have been affected the ratings compared to participants who had no personal experience with biometric authentication schemes. Second, the relatively homogenous sample only consisted of thirty-five participants. A larger and more heterogeneous sample would increase the external validity of the results. Third, the tested authentication schemes included several biometric schemes, but for example only one graphical scheme. Token-based schemes were not tested at all. Thus, the inclusion of further knowledge-based and token-based schemes would lead to a more balanced approach. One indication for this effect is that all authentication schemes received a similar rating concerning the expected effort and the perceived cost-benefit ratio. To clarify the influence of the study design on these results it would have been interesting to have the participants provide reasons for their assessments. To increase the degree of realism a future study design should take real world problems and error-rates of the particular authentication schemes into account.

6.2   Conclusion

Concluding, the current research provided valuable insights in user perceptions concerning a broad range of authentication technologies. Whereas some findings were in line with previous studies, such as the high user preference for fingerprint recognition among biometrics, others were a bit surprising in comparison with earlier findings, e.g. the low rating of face recognition or the graphical password. The rating of face recognition can be explained with usage problems expected by the participants. The bad rating of the graphical password is most likely caused by short-comings in the implementation. The combination of user ratings and explanations led to the assumption of different user groups preferring either the password due to privacy concerns or biometrics due to the perceived security of the unique feature used to authenticate. This hypothesis needs to be analyzed further in the future, together with further influencing variables. The simulated study design in general proved effective to compare different authentication schemes in a controlled setting while protecting the data and privacy of our participants. However, to improve the external validity and persuasive power of the simulation, its limitations should be addressed in future studies.

Acknowledgments. This work was supported by the German Federal Ministry of Education and Research (BMBF) as well as by the Hessen State Ministry for Higher Education, Research and the Arts (HMWK) within CRISP. Furthermore, the research reported in this paper has been supported by the German Federal Ministry of Education and Research (BMBF) within MoPPa.

References

1. Abdullah, M.D.H., Abdullah, A.H., Ithnin, N., Mammi, H.K.: Towards identifying usability and security features of graphical password in knowledge based authentication technique. In: Second Asia International Conference on Modelling & Simulation (AMS), pp. 396–403. IEEE Press, New York (2008). doi:10.1109/AMS.2008.136
2. Al-Harby, F., Qahwaji, R., Kamala, M.: The feasibility of biometrics authentication in e-commerce: user acceptance. In: IADIS International Conference WWW/Internet (2008)
3. Alonso-Fernandez, F., Bigun, J., Fierrez, J., Fronthaler, H., Kollreider, K., Ortega-Garcia, J.: Fingerprint Recognition. In: Petrovska-Delacrétaz, D., Chollet, G., Dorizzi, B. (eds.) Guide to Biometric Reference Systems and Performance Evaluation, pp. 51–88. Springer, London (2009)
4. Ben-Asher, N., Kirschnick, N., Sieger, H., Meyer, J., Ben-Oved, A., Möller, S.: On the need for different security methods on mobile phones. In: The 13th International Conference on Human Computer Interaction with Mobile Devices and Services (MobileHCI 2011), pp. 465–473. ACM Press, New York (2011). doi:10.1145/2037373.2037442
5. Bhagavatula, C., Ur, B., Iacovino, K., Kywe, S.M., Cranor, L.F., Savvides, M.: Biometric authentication on iphone and android: usability, perceptions, and influences on adoption. In: Workshop on Usable Security (2015). doi:10.14722/usec.2015.23003
6. Blonder, G.: Graphical password. United States Patent 5559961, Lucent Technologies, Inc., Murray Hill (1996)
7. Bonneau, J., Herley, C., van Oorschot, P.C., Stajano, F.: The quest to replace passwords: a framework for comparative evaluation of web authentication schemes. In: IEEE Symposium on Security and Privacy, pp. 553–567. IEEE Press, New York (2012). doi:10.1109/SP.2012.44
8. Brostoff, S., Sasse, M.A.: Are passfaces more usable than passwords: a field trial investigation. In: McDonald, S., Waern, Y., Cockton, G. (eds.) People and Computers XIV – Usability or Else: Proceedings of HCI, pp. 405–422. Springer, Sunderland (2000). doi:10.1007/978-1-4471-0515-2_27
9. Chen, K.-Y., Chang, M.-L.: User acceptance of 'near field communication' mobile phone service: an investigation based on the 'unified theory of acceptance and use of technology' model. Serv. Ind. J. **33**, 609–623 (2013). doi:10.1080/02642069.2011.622369
10. Cherapau, I., Muslukhov, I., Asanka, N., Beznosov, K.: On the impact of touch ID on iPhone passcodes. In: Symposium on Usable Privacy and Security (SOUPS), pp. 257–276 (2016)

11. Clarke, N., Furnell, S., Rodwell, P., Reynolds, P.: Acceptance of subscriber authentication methods for mobile telephony devices. Comput. Secur. **21**, 220–228 (2002). doi:10.1016/S0167-4048(02)00304-8

12. Clausen, S.: A single-line AC capacitive fingerprint swipe sensor. In: Ratha, N.K., Govindaraju, V. (eds.) Advances in Biometrics. Sensors, Algorithms and Systems, pp. 49–62. Springer, London (2008). doi:10.1007/978-1-84628-921-7_3

13. Coventry, L., DeAngeli, A., Johnson, G.: Honest it's me! Self service verification. In: ACM CHI Workshop on Human-Computer Interaction and Security Systems (2003)

14. Crawford, H., Renaud, K.: Understanding user perceptions of transparent authentication on a mobile device. J. Trust Manage. **1**, 1–7 (2014). doi:10.1186/2196-064X-1-7

15. De Luca, A., Hang, A., von Zezschwitz, E., Hussmann, H.: I feel like I'm taking selfies all day! Understanding biometric authentication on smartphones. In: Conference on Human Factors in Computing Systems, pp. 1411–1414. ACM Press, New York (2015). doi:10.1145/2702123.2702141

16. Dhamija, R., Perrig, A.: Déjà Vu: a user study using images for authentication. In: The 9th USENIX Security Symposium, p. 4. The USENIX Association, Berkeley (2000)

17. Dörflinger, T., Voth, A., Krämer, J., Fromm, R.: "My smartphone is a safe!" The user's point of view regarding novel authentication methods and gradual security levels on smartphones. In: Katsikas, S.K., Samarati, P. (eds.) International Conference on Security and Cryptography (SECRYPT), pp. 155–164. IEEE Press, New York (2010)

18. Eze, U.C., Gan, G.G.G., Ademu, J., Tella, S.A.: Modelling user trust and mobile payment adoption: a conceptual Framework. Commun. IBIMA **3**, 224–231 (2008)

19. Furnell, S., Evangelatos, K.: Public awareness and perceptions of biometrics. Comput. Fraud Secur. **1**, 8–13 (2007). doi:10.1016/S1361-3723(07)70006-4

20. Grawemeyer, B., Johnson, H.: Using and managing multiple passwords: a week to a view. Interact. Comput. **23**, 256–267 (2011). doi:10.1016/j.intcom.2011.03.007

21. Harbach, M., Fahl, S., Rieger, M., Smith, M.: On the acceptance of privacy-preserving authentication technology: the curious case of national identity cards. In: Cristofaro, E., Wright, M. (eds.) PETS 2013. LNCS, vol. 7981, pp. 245–264. Springer, Heidelberg (2013). doi:10.1007/978-3-642-39077-7_13

22. Harbach, M., von Zezschwitz, E., Fichtner, A., De Luca, A., Smith, M.: It's a hard lock life: a field study of smartphone (un) locking behavior and risk perception. In: Symposium on Usable Privacy and Security (SOUPS), pp. 213–230 (2014)

23. Heckle, R.-R., Patrick, A.S., Ozok, A.: Perception and acceptance of fingerprint biometric technology. In: The 3rd Symposium on Usable Privacy and Security, pp. 153–154 (2007). doi:10.1145/1280680.1280704

24. Holz, C., Bentley, F.R.: On-demand biometrics: fast cross-device authentication. In: CHI Conference on Human Factors in Computing Systems, pp. 3761–3766. ACM Press, New York (2016). doi:10.1145/2858036.2858139

25. Holz, C., Buthpitiya, S., Knaust, M.: Bodyprint: biometric user identification on mobile devices using the capacitive touchscreen to scan body parts. In: The 33rd Annual ACM Conference on Human Factors in Computing Systems, pp. 3011–3014. ACM Press, New York (2015)

26. Iannarelli, A.V.: Ear Identification. Paramont Publishing Company, Paramount (1989)

27. International Civil Aviation Organization: Biometric Identification To Provide Enhanced Security And Speedier Border Clearance For Travelling Public (PIO 09/2003). http://www.icao.int/icao/en/nr/2003/pio200309.htm

28. Jermyn, I., Mayer, A., Monrose, F., Reiter, M.K., Rubin, A.D.: The design and analysis of graphical passwords. In: The 8th USENIX Security Symposium, p. 1. The USENIX Association, Berkeley (1999)

29. Jones, L.A., Anton, A.I., Earp, J.B.: Towards understanding user perceptions of authentication technologies. In: ACM Workshop on Privacy in Electronic Society, pp. 91–98. ACM Press, New York (2007). doi:10.1145/1314333.1314352

30. Karatzouni, S., Furnell, S.M., Clarke, N.L., Botha, R.A.: Perceptions of user authentication on mobile devices. In: International Conference for Internet Technology and Secured Transactions (ICITST), IEEE Press, New York (2011)

31. Ma, Y., Feng, J.: Evaluating usability of three authentication methods in web-based application. In: Ninth International Conference on Software Engineering Research, Management and Applications (SERA), pp. 81–88. IEEE Press, New York (2011). doi:10.1109/SERA.2011.18

32. Maio, D., Maltoni, D., Capelli, R., Wayman, J.L., Jain, A.K.: FVC2000: fingerprint verification competition. IEEE Trans. Pattern Anal. Mach. Intell. **24**, 402–412 (2002)

33. Mare, S., Baker, M., Gummeson, J.: A study of authentication in daily life. In: Symposium on Usable Privacy and Security (SOUPS), pp. 189–206 (2016)

34. Mayron, L.M., Hausawi, Y., Bahr, G.S.: Secure, usable biometric authentication systems. In: Stephanidis, C., Antona, M. (eds.) UAHCI 2013. LNCS, vol. 8009, pp. 195–204. Springer, Heidelberg (2013). doi:10.1007/978-3-642-39188-0_21

35. O'Gorman, L.: Comparing passwords, tokens, and biometrics for user authentication. Proc. IEEE **91**, 2021–2040 (2003). doi:10.1109/JPROC.2003.819611. IEEE, New York

36. Paul, C.L., Morse, E., Zhang, A., Choong, Y.-Y., Theofanos, M.: A field study of user behavior and perceptions in smartcard authentication. In: Campos, P., Graham, N., Jorge, J., Nunes, N., Palanque, P., Winckler, M. (eds.) INTERACT 2011. LNCS, vol. 6949, pp. 1–17. Springer, Heidelberg (2011). doi:10.1007/978-3-642-23768-3_1

37. Real User Corporation, Passfaces TM. http//:www.realuser.com

38. Riley, C., Buckner, K., Johnson, G., Benyon, D.: Culture & biometrics: regional differences in the perception of biometric authentication technologies. AI Soc. **24**, 295–306 (2009). doi:10.1007/s00146-009-0218-1

39. Sasse, M.A.: Usability and trust in information systems. In: Mansell, R., Collins, B. (eds.) Trust and Crime in Information Societies, pp. 319–348. Edward Elgar, Cheltenham (2005)

40. Scheuermann, D., Schwiderski-Grosche, S., Struif, B.: Usability of biometrics in relation to electronic signatures. Report, GMD-Forschungszentrum Informationstechnik (2000)

41. Schneier, B.: Secrets and Lies: Digital Security in a Networked World. Wiley, Hoboken (2000)

42. Sieger, H., Möller, S.: Gender differences in the perception of security of mobile phones. In: The 14th International Conference on Human-Computer Interaction with Mobile Devices and Services Companion, pp. 107–112. ACM Press, New York (2012). doi:10.1145/2371664.2371685

43. Stobert, E., Biddle, R.: Memory retrieval and graphical passwords. In: The Ninth Symposium on Usable Privacy and Security, Article 15. ACM Press, New York (2013). doi:10.1145/2501604.2501619

44. Tassabehji, R., Kamala, M.A.: Improving e-banking security with biometrics: modelling user attitudes and acceptance. In: The 3rd International Conference on New Technologies, Mobility and Security, pp. 110–115. IEEE Press, Piscataway (2009)

45. Tari, F., Ozok, A.A., Holden, S.H.: A comparison of perceived and real shoulder-surfing risks between alphanumeric and graphical passwords. In: The Second Symposium on Usable Privacy and Security, pp. 56–66. ACM, New York (2006). doi:10.1145/1143120.1143128

46. Toledano, D.T., Pozo, R.F., Trapote, A.H., Gomez, L.H.: Usability evaluation of multi-modal biometric verification systems. Interact. Comput. **18**, 1101–1122 (2006). doi:10.1016/j.intcom.2006.01.004

47. Trewin, S., Swart, C., Koved, L., Martino, J., Singh, K., Ben-David, S.: Biometric authentication on a mobile device: a study of user effort, error and task disruption. In: The 28th Annual Computer Security Applications Conference, pp. 159–168. ACM Press, New York (2012). doi:10.1145/2420950.2420976

48. Turner, C., Safar, J., Ramaswamy, K.: The effects of use on acceptance and trust in voice authentication technology. Proc. Hum. Factors Ergon. Soc. Annu. Meet. **50**, 718–722 (2006). doi:10.1177/154193120605000522

49. Von Zezschwitz, E., Koslow, A., De Luca, A., Hussmann, H.: Making graphic-based authentication secure against smudge attacks. In: The 2013 International Conference on Intelligent User Interfaces, pp. 277–286. ACM Press, New York (2013)

50. Yan, P., Bowyer, K.W.: Biometric recognition using 3D ear shape. IEEE Trans. Pattern Anal. Mach. Intell. **29**, 1297–1308 (2007). doi:10.1109/TPAMI.2007.1067

51. Wash, R., Rader, E., Berman, R., Wellmer, Z.: Understanding password choices: how frequently entered passwords are re-used across websites. In: Symposium on Usable Privacy and Security (SOUPS), pp. 175–188 (2016)

52. Weiss, R., De Luca, A.: PassShapes: utilizing stroke based authentication to increase password memorability. In: Proceedings of the 5th Nordic Conference on Human-Computer Interaction: Building Bridges, pp. 383–392. ACM Press, New York (2008). doi:10.1145/1463160.1463202

53. Wiedenbeck, S., Waters, J., Birget, J.-C., Brodskiy, A., Memon, N.: Passpoints: design and longitudinal evaluation of a graphical password system. Int. J. Hum. Comput. Stud. **63**, 102–127 (2005). doi:10.1016/j.ijhcs.2005.04.010

Security in Organizations and Infrastructures

Identifying Changes in the Cybersecurity Threat Landscape Using the LDA-Web Topic Modelling Data Search Engine

Noura Al Moubayed[1]([✉]), David Wall[2], and A. Stephen McGough[1]

[1] School of Engineering and Computing Sciences, Durham University,
Durham DH1 3LE, UK
{noura.al-moubayed,stephen.mcgough}@durham.ac.uk
[2] Centre for Criminal Justice Studies, School of Law, University of Leeds, Leeds, UK
d.s.wall@leeds.ac.uk

Abstract. Successful Cybersecurity depends on the processing of vast quantities of data from a diverse range of sources such as police reports, blogs, intelligence reports, security bulletins, and news sources. This results in large volumes of unstructured text data that is difficult to manage or investigate manually. In this paper we introduce a tool that summarises, categorises and models such data sets along with a search engine to query the model produced from the data. The search engine can be used to find links, similarities and differences between different documents in a way beyond the current search approaches. The tool is based on the probabilistic topic modelling technique which goes further than the lexical analysis of documents to model the subtle relationships between words, documents, and abstract topics. It will assists researchers to query the underlying models latent in the documents and tap into the repository of documents allowing them o be ordered thematically.

1 Introduction

Changes in the cybersecurity threat landscape, especially with regard to the impact of cloud technologies on cybercrime are generally very hard to detect and they are made more difficult by the fact that cybersecurity threat reports tend to focus upon proprietary information for which the source information is rarely if ever shared. An alternative method of detecting change in the modern cybersecurity threat landscape is to analyse contemporary news and information sources. Not just a few sources, but tens or hundreds of thousands over a period of time using advanced topic modelling techniques. Such an open source technique is neither exhaustive nor new, but this original take on the technique does provide new prospects for identifying thematic, quantitative and qualitative changes in the cybersecurity threat landscape that can be used to efficiently begin a research enquiry.

Rapidly developing technologies have generated huge benefits to businesses, society and organisations of all sizes. These include technologies such as the world wide web, social media, the internet and Cloud computing. They offer

T. Tryfonas (Ed.): HAS 2017, LNCS 10292, pp. 287–295, 2017.
DOI: 10.1007/978-3-319-58460-7_19

rapid access to information and a mechanism by which people can interact with each other, or with businesses, in a way which has hitherto been unimaginable. However, such an utopian change in the way we interact has brought with it major security threats such as fraud, network infrastructure attacks, and data breaches. Such problems are exasperated by the large volumes of available data. Which provides a greater incentive for the attackers but, more significantly for those who seek to identify such attacks, vastly increases the problem of sifting through all of the available data in order to identify those pertinent facts which are required to understand the situation. For example the UK Crime Statistics Website [1] shows an average of 500,000 reported crimes per month for England and Wales alone. If we seek to identify common attacks, be they against similar victims or similar modes of operation this becomes ever more complicated as no individual could hope to keep abreast of all this data.

Conventional approaches to this problem allow searching of the corpus of collected data for specific words which are likely to relevant. However, as much of the data is collected by many untrained operators who share no common grounding the words which are used to describe things need not be the same. An ontology, where words which can be used to mean the same thing are linked together, can be used to expand the search. Though the effectiveness of this approach is diminished by the fact that these ontologies are rarely complete and require significant effort to compile.

Instead, here, we propose the use of topics as a searching mechanism. Rather than identifying keywords, which are themselves a diminished view of the topic that a searcher is trying to find, we instead allow the searcher to identify information based on the topics that they are interested in. A user may provide a document, or small collection of words, which represent one or more topics. These topics can then be searched for within the corpus. As the construction of what the relevant topics are, and which words would be indicative of a particular topic, would be a time-consuming process for humans to perform we instead use computer software to automatically identify those topics which are present in the entire corpus. This process identifies those words which probabilistically are most likely to form a topic. The same process can then be used to identify the topics present within a new document. This can then be used to identify the other documents within the corpus which are most likely to share similar topics and hence be of interest to the searcher. It should be noted that the size of the document that is used for searching need not be extensive in size.

Each document within the corpus will, in general, relate to more than one topic, with the proportion of the document relating to each exhibited topic being identifiable. Likewise each word which is used, anywhere within the corpus, will have an associated probability for being part of each topic. By this means we can take any new document and obtain the probability of each of the pre-identified topics being present within this new document. Using this we can rank the topics present in the document. It is then a simple mapping exercise to identify those existing documents within the corpus which share the most similar topic make-up as the new document. Likewise we can search on specific topics within the corpus.

As well as identifying other documents within the corpus which are similar to the current document we can also perform topic filtering across the corpus by which topics which we have identified to not be of interest can be removed. In which case any document in the corpus which consists of more than a pre-defined proportion of that topic can be removed. Thus allowing a reduction of the corpus.

This provides a powerful toolkit for the cybersecurity expert allowing them to rapidly track changing information and follow important leads through the ability to search, summarise and understand large volumes of data.

Our work is developed around a novel search engine based on probabilistic topic modelling to help gain an insight and retrieve information from cybersecurity textual datasets. Unlike traditional search engines our tool is customised to train a probabilistic model that fits the dataset. The model transforms the data from the textual space to the more abstract topics' space. This translates into the ability to probe the dataset by the more abstract concepts rather than key words. Each topic within the dataset is colour coded which can be used to categorise and directly access the documents involved. The topic itself is represented as a word cloud – in which the more commonly used words within the topic are displayed in larger sizes – facilitating the understanding of what constituents the concept of that topic. By grouping the documents by relevance the search engine facilitates navigating through large datasets of documents through added functionalities such as finding similar documents, discovering trends, identifying anomalies and finding most/least common topics.

Although our work here is focused on the analysis of cybersecurity and criminal documents this approach is not in any way dependant on the underlying type of data being processed and can therefore be re-applied to any other corpus of data or even applied to non-textual data.

The rest of this paper is structured as follows. In Sect. 2 we discuss the probabilistic topic modelling approach used in this work. Section 3 presents an overview of the framework we have developed for our tool. We conclude the ideas and consider future directions in Sect. 4.

2   Methods

Topic modelling is an established method for text mining that goes beyond the traditional lexical level of text analysis to try to understand the concepts which the text is conveying. These models are usually built as generative probabilistic models within the framework of Bayesian networks [2]. In this framework the model describes how observed variables (words in our case) can be generated by realisation of random variables arranged in a certain network. This allows for the modelling of mixture of models, i.e. each document is assigned a probability of it belonging to a topic, and a document may indeed contain more than one topic. A word can belong to more than one topic and a topic will contain more than one word. The model defines the probabilities governing the relationships between words, documents, and topics.

Latent Dirichlet Allocation (LDA) [3] is the most commonly used method for probabilistic topic modelling. Intuitively, LDA identifies the topic structure in documents using the co-occurance structure of words/terms. LDA assumes that there are k underlying topics responsible for generating the documents in the dataset, and that each topic is represented as a multinomial distribution over the words in the vocabulary. Each document is assumed to be generated by sampling a finite mixture of these topics and then sampling words from each of these topics.

Each document is assigned a feature set where each value in the feature set represents the probability that the document contains a given topic. These features help group and identify the documents and facilitates the ease of use for the end user. To visualise the topic model and to present it in a user-friendly manner to the end user several visualisation systems for topic modelling have been built [4–6,8]. However, these systems focused on browsing the model and demonstrating the inter-connections amongst the documents, topics, and words. The systems, however, are heavily focused on the model or the metadata of the documents in the corpus without any facilities to search, rank, or access the documents within a topic in a direct and accessible manner. LDAVis [7] is a visualisation tool which provides a compact representation of the probabilistic topic model.

In this work we refocus the visualisation effort from the structure of the LDA model to accessibility of information to the end user. The emphasis is then not on how the user navigates the model but rather how the end-user can capitalise on the modelling capabilities of LDA to find efficiently related documents to a topic of interest, which is particularly useful for a cyber-security expert given the size of the data and the urgency to minimise the response time to a given threat. To achieve this goal a (topic modelling) search engine is built to categorise the documents based on their topics. The end users submit their queries to the search engine which in return compares the documents in the dataset with the query based on the topic features extracted from the input. The search engine is built within a web-based framework which provides tools to easily navigate through the entire corpus of documents easily.

3   Framework

The framework starts by colour coding the topics and presenting them as squares on the top of the web page as demonstrated in Fig. 1. By hovering over the coloured topics the framework displays the constituent words as a word cloud with the size of the word representing the probability of it appearing in that topic. The user has the option of either entering a query in the form of free text or uploading a document; alternatively the user may choose to navigate through the topics. For the purpose of demonstrating the functionality of the framework we used a cybersecurity related dataset collected by experts in the School of Law at the University of Leeds.

The framework provides the following main use case scenarios:

- Search: The trained model extracts topic features from the user search query and compares those against the features in the dataset and retrieves the most relevant documents. In the results page, each retrieved document is presented

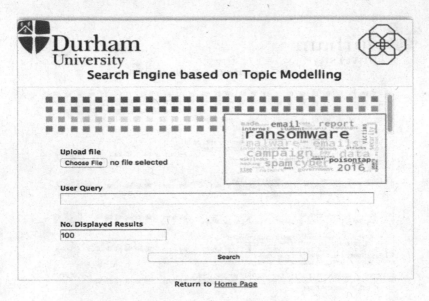

Fig. 1. The home page of the search engine. The topics are colour coded. Each square represents a topic. By hovering over a topic a word cloud is presented to demonstrate the main words within the topic. (Color figure online)

as a link to the original source, similarity measure to the query, colour coded topics that appear in the document, and a pie chart to demonstrate the relative contribution of each topic in the document (Fig. 2).

– Topic Navigation: By clicking on a topic square presented on the top of the page, the framework will display all the related documents ordered by relevance to the chosen topic (Fig. 3). The relevance is measured by the probability of the document being generated by that topic.

– Topic Filtering: to narrow the search space the user can eliminate documents that belong to one or more irrelevant topic(s). Figure 2 demonstrates the results after filtering two topics, which are marked by a red frame around their colour block on the top of the page.

All these scenarios are only possible thanks to the interactive web-based interface of the framework. They allow for direct and easy access to a huge dataset of the corpus collected from a wide range of variable sources. This is particularly interesting for cyber security experts who are dealing with continuously increasing datasets.

The framework also integrates the LDAVis tool [7], which helps visualising the inner contents of a given topic. After building an LDA model, it is passed to a custom webpage where LDAVis is utilised. Figure 4 demonstrate the first view of LDAVis, where the topics are plotted on the left panel as circles with the diameter of the circle is proportional to the probability of the topic to appear in any document. In the right panel the 30 most repeated words (terms) in all the documents are presented. To help navigate the LDA model, by clicking on

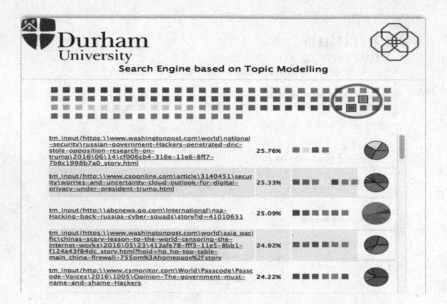

Fig. 2. Demonstration of topic filtering. Each document is associated with coloured squares representing topics. By clicking on a topic, all the associated documents are removed from the page and the topic is marked as deleted. (Color figure online)

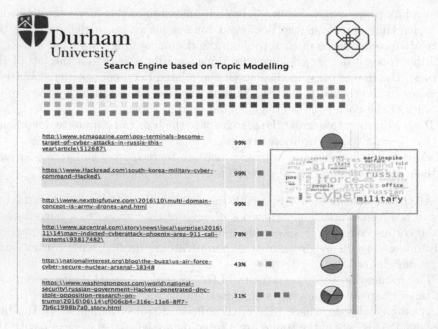

Fig. 3. Demonstration of Topic Navigation. When a topic square is clicked, all the associated documents are drawn. For every document the probability of it belonging to the topic is shown along with the other topics mentioned in the document.

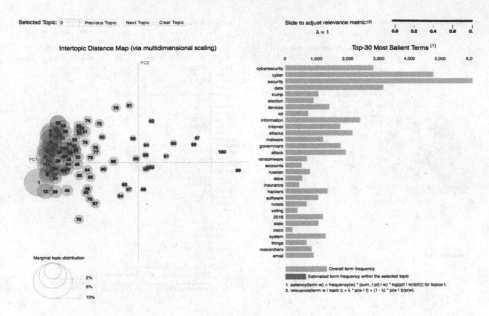

Fig. 4. The layout of LDAVis, with the global topic view on the left, and the 30 most common terms in all the corpus on the right presented as bar charts.

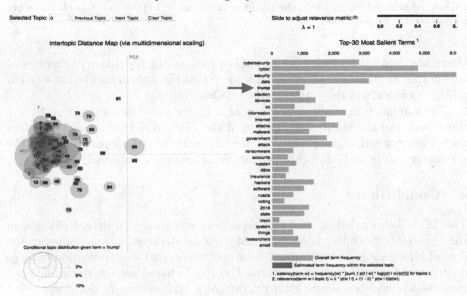

Fig. 5. Once a term is selected on the right panel, all the unrelated topics are removed from the left panel.

a word all the topics which are not related to this word, i.e. the word does not appear in those topics, are removed from the left panel (Fig. 5). By selecting a topic from the left panel the top repeated words in this topic are presented on

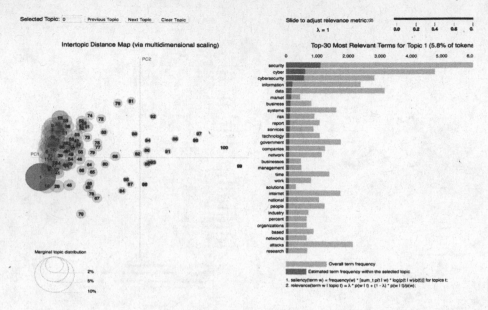

Fig. 6. If a topic is chosen on the left panel, the top 30 words in the topic are plotted on the right panel. The red bar is the number of times the word appeared in the documents within the selected topic, while the blue bar is the overall appearance in all the other topics. (Color figure online)

the right panel but now with added red bar to show the repetition of every word within the documents in the selected topic versus the appearance of the word in all the documents in the corpus – the blue bar (Fig. 6).

The combination of the dynamic search engine capabilities provided by the framework and the static visualisation of the LDA model using LDAVis, gives the security expert a great deal of in-depth knowledge to navigate through the documents easily and efficiently to find the necessary information.

4   Conclusion

The LDA-Web modelling tool technique provides a way to detect changes in the cybersecurity threat landscape, not least by it detecting anomalies in the flow of information. It facilitates the categorisation and summarisation of large unstructured cybersecurity text data. The tool is based on a text mining approach which models complex inter-relationships between words, documents, and abstract topics. The tool aims at providing security experts with full accessibility and functionality and helping them in their investigations.

LDA-Web facilitates the categorisation and summarisation of large unstructured cybersecurity text data. The tool is based on a text mining approach which models complex inter-relationships between words, documents, and abstract topics. The tool aims at providing security experts with full accessibility and functionality and helping them in their investigations.

Topic modelling using Latent Dirichlet Allocation (LDA) is used to model the documents within a large cyber-security related database of unstructured text documents obtained from a wide range of resources. The generated model is presented through our web-based interface and search engine which facilitate easy navigation through the topics and their constituent words. The search engine have the ability to find documents based on keywords, or similarity to an uploaded document. The results are ranked according to their similarity to the queried topic(s).

A third party tool, LDAVis, is also incorporated to provide in-depth understanding of the inner structure of the LDA model. The tool provides easy and user-friendly navigation functinalities to show the words within a topic and the relationship between topics and words. This is a very helpful tool for the security expert to be able to evaluate the quality of the built model and to fine tune their search queries passed to the search engine.

The future work will focus on evaluating the framework by cyber security experts and the feedback will be analysed using the A/B testing methodology. We are also working on collecting more cyber-security related data in order to make our model and search engine more accurate.

We see this as an excellent tool for the analysis of vast corpuses of documents in order to identify interesting and relevant data in a way hitherto difficult to do based on normal searching methods. As such we aim to apply this technique to different datasets in order to identify interesting phenomena which we can then work with subject specific experts in order to identify the significance of the data observed.

Acknowledgment. This work is part of the CRITiCal project (Combatting cRiminals In The Cloud - EP/M020576/1) funded by the Engineering and Physical Sciences Research Council (EPSRC).

References

1. Crime states. http://www.ukcrimestats.com/National_Picture/
2. Blei, D.M.: Probabilistic topic models. Commun. ACM **55**(4), 77–84 (2012)
3. Blei, D.M., Ng, A.Y., Jordan, M.I.: Latent dirichlet allocation. J. Mach. Learn. Res. **3**, 993–1022 (2003)
4. Chaney, A.J.B., Blei, D.M.: Visualizing topic models. In: ICWSM (2012)
5. Chuang, J., Ramage, D., Manning, C., Heer, J.: Interpretation and trust: designing model-driven visualizations for text analysis. In: Proceedings of the SIGCHI Conference on Human Factors in Computing Systems, pp. 443–452. ACM (2012)
6. Gardner, M.J., Lutes, J., Lund, J., Hansen, J., Walker, D., Ringger, E., Seppi, K.: The topic browser: an interactive tool for browsing topic models. In: NIPS Workshop on Challenges of Data Visualization, vol. 2 (2010)
7. Sievert, C., Shirley, K.E.: Ldavis: a method for visualizing and interpreting topics. In: Proceedings of the Workshop on Interactive Language Learning, Visualization, and Interfaces, pp. 63–70 (2014)
8. Snyder, J., Knowles, R., Dredze, M., Gormley, M.R., Wolfe, T.: Topic models and metadata for visualizing text corpora. In: HLT-NAACL, pp. 5–9 (2013)

Secure Peripherals in a Converged Mobile Environment

Jaco du Toit[(✉)] and Ian Ellefsen

University of Johannesburg, Johannesburg, South Africa
jacodt@uj.ac.za

Abstract. Users of computing devices have evolved from a fixed desktop computer environment to a situation where a user not only use one personal computer, but also one or more mobile device for both personal and business purposes. As soon as a user uses multiple computing devices for personal and business purposes, an exchange of data is necessary to ensure that the data is available from the various devices. The mechanisms used to enable data exchange may include potentially insecure cloud storage. Business data stored on cloud storage may also be against company policy. To minimize the dependency on multiple devices, this paper describes a computing environment where a user uses only one computing device, but with multiple input\output peripherals. The communication between the IO peripherals and the Neo device is described in terms of a communications model. The communications model highlight the information security aspects of confidentiality, integrity and authorization. The implementation viability of the model is reviewed against existing technologies. The paper concludes that existing technologies can fulfil most of the requirements for the mdoel, but may require customization to ensure fine-grained access control.

Keywords: Mobile · Wireless · Security

1 Introduction

The history of computing has moved from a centralized, mainframe, computing model to a decentralized, distributed, personal computer and Internet model. This model expanded to include mobile devices in the last few years. It has been observed that many employees own multiple mobile devices for their computing requirements.

Arguably, one of the reasons, why people own and use more than one mobile device is because of the devices' ergonomic nature. Some people prefer the smaller smartphone sized mobile devices in certain environments, while they prefer to use the larger tablet-sized mobile devices in other environments and situations.

As soon as users start using more than one mobile device, one of the ways in which users exchange data between devices is by using potentially insecure cloud storage areas. Previous published work [1, 2] argues that in order to minimize the cloud based storage risk to interchange data between devices, it should be possible to design a mobile based ecosystem where a user has one mobile computing device, called the Neo device, with multiple separate input\output peripherals. These peripherals can be any

© Springer International Publishing AG 2017
T. Tryfonas (Ed.): HAS 2017, LNCS 10292, pp. 296–308, 2017.
DOI: 10.1007/978-3-319-58460-7_20

type of input\output device, such as a smart-phone sized touch screens, or even bigger desktop monitors, with physical keyboard and mouse. An important aspect to understand is that these peripherals do not store any apps or data on them directly.

When a Neo device is used in a mobile environment, with multiple peripherals, the issue of secure communication between the peripherals and the computing device comes into play.

This article describes how input\output (IO) peripherals using various communication channels can securely communicate with a Neo device.

This article is organized as follow: Sect. 2 provides an overview of the Neo device and the basic properties of the Neo device. Section 3 describes existing communication technologies used by peripherals, with the security mechanisms they employ. Section 4 describes the proposed communication model for the Neo device with Sect. 5 providing a bit more detail on how this may be implemented in a prototype or real world device. Section 6 concludes by highlighting the advantages of using the Neo devices with their secure peripherals.

2   Overview of the Neo Device

A short overview is provided at this stage in order to better understand the architecture and ecosystem of the Neo device. [2] introduces the Neo model. The Neo model describes two important properties of a hypothetical mobile operating system. The two properties are a Secure Container Property (SCP) and a Mutual Authentication Property (MAP). These two properties ensure data confidentiality and multiple IO peripheral connections. The Neo model defines a hypothetical mobile device that implements these two properties.

The Neo device is defined as a mobile device. The Neo device does not have any built-in input\output peripherals. The Neo device itself is a hypothetical black box that can easily be carried by a person or docked in a docking station. Any interaction with the device is done using the various peripherals available for the Neo device. These peripherals can be any form factor that the user requires. This means that a peripheral can be as small as a wristwatch, and can be as big as a data projector screen.

The secure communication between the IO peripheral and the Neo device is defined as the MAP. The MAP describes and define firstly the identification of peripherals and Neo devices with each other, and secondly the authorisation of peripherals with the Neo device.

The other important aspect of the Neo device is that it must support usage for both personal and business data and applications. This multi-domain usage requirement is addressed using a SCP.

The SCP ensures personal and business data and apps are isolated and controlled separately in specific secure containers. The boundary definition of a secure container is loosely defined by the ownership of the applications and data. All data and applications owned by the user is grouped in the same container, whereas the data and applications owned by a specific company is grouped inside the same container.

Figure 1 shows the model that describes the MAP and the SCP. The MAP encloses all communications to and from the device. When an IO peripheral communicates with the Neo device, the MAP ensures the identification and authorisation of the peripheral. The property ensures not only identification and authorisation to the device, but also to the various secure containers. A more complete description of the identification and authorisation property is found in section four of this document.

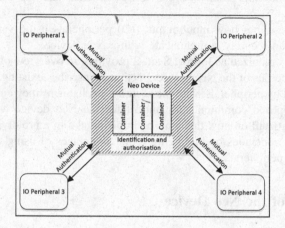

Fig. 1. Neo device with secure containers and identification and authorization service [2]

The SCP describes an isolated computing environment belonging to a specific data and application owner. This property is similar to today's isolation model found in popular mobile operating systems like Android and Apple iOS, except that is it is not based on a per app property, but is applied on a group of applications and their data. The model does not specify the isolation property of apps inside the secure container.

The hypothetical Neo device contains both a MAP and a SCP. The focus of this paper is on how the MAP can be established. The next section provides a literature review on the existing technologies for both wired and wireless IO peripheral security.

3   Security in Today's IO Peripherals

The assurance of Confidentiality, Integrity and Availability of data is an important aspect of data security. Data is provided as input or output through the use of IO peripherals. In both wired and wireless communication models of IO peripherals, a certain amount of risk is associated with the data as it flows between the IO peripheral and the device. This section provides a short discussion on the risks of wired IO peripherals and some of the research and solutions to address some of these risks.

The section then discuss the risks of wireless IO peripherals and in turn summarizes some of the security implementations and research around wireless communications for IO peripherals.

3.1   Risks and Security for Wired IO Peripherals

Wired IO peripherals supply either input to the computer or output from the computer. Input peripherals include typical computer keyboards, while output peripherals include computer screens. Unfortunately, there are risks for both input and output peripherals. The risks for input peripherals are the recording and capturing of keystrokes or mouse movements. The risks for output peripherals are the recording of video while the computer is in use.

The recording of either keystrokes or video can be implemented in either software or hardware. The next two sub-sections provide a brief overview of the risks of software and hardware recorders.

Software Recorders

Software recorders are typically categorized as spyware and many anti-malware products try to detect these types of recorders [3, 4]. These recorders are well documented and described. This paper will not focus on these recorders, but mention them because of the risk that they still provide to Internet connected computers.

The biggest disadvantage for attackers of software recorders are that they can be detected using anti-malware products. The biggest advantage of software recorders for attackers are that an attack is not limit to physical proximity or contact. This proximity negation allows an attacker to attack thousands of Internet connected computers increasing the likelihood that one of the victims will not have the necessary defenses to protect against software recorders.

Hardware Recorders

There are a number of sites that advertise hardware keyloggers [5, 6]. These sites advertise the hardware keyloggers for legitimate purposes that include [5, 6]:

- Monitoring staff productivity.
- Monitor inappropriate use of computers.
- Backing up typed information for authors.
- Computer forensic investigations.

The above purposes may be legitimate, but keyloggers can arguably also be used for malicious purposes.

Hardware keyloggers can be either active or passive [7]. Active keyloggers intercepts a key stroke and retransmits the keystroke to the computer. They are normally connected in-line with the physical keyboard. Figure 2 is an example of an active, in-line, USB keylogger [6].

Passive keyloggers observes the data line or data bus of the keyboard and computer to capture keystrokes. Figure 3 is an example of a passive keylogger that is installed inside a laptop computer [6]. This keylogger observes the data on the PCI bus.

Attackers use hardware recorders to target a specific victim. Hardware recorders are more difficult to distribute and the attacker must have physical access to the hardware of the victim. The challenge to victims of hardware recorders are that you cannot detect them using commonly available software like anti-malware programs.

Fig. 2. Active USB keylogger [6]

Fig. 3. Passive keylogger [6]

Research has shown that hardware keyloggers can be detected by the effect that they have on the data line of the keyboard. Both active and passive keyloggers change the electrical current of the keyboard through their acts of observation. These current fluctuations can indicate the presence of a hardware keylogger [7].

Even though it is theoretically possible to detect hardware keyloggers, the detection mechanisms must be implemented on the computer hardware, with the associated software before a computer can detect a hardware keylogger. None of today's commercial computers has these hardware and software mechanisms.

Wireless IO peripherals exchange data not over a physical bus, but over the air. This increases the likelihood that someone can listen in or intercept the data to or from the IO peripheral. The next section describes these risks and the implementation technology used by today's wireless IO peripherals.

3.2   Risks and Security of Wireless IO Peripherals

IO peripherals that use a wireless signal typically use either Bluetooth [8] or Wi-Fi [9] technology to transmit and receive wireless signals. Consumer electronics usually rely on Bluetooth for input peripherals and limited output peripherals like Bluetooth speakers [10].

Wi-Fi however can easily transmit either input or output signals. Wi-Fi has a specific standard called Miracast [11], which specifies the use of Wi-Fi to stream high definition audio and video between consumer devices easily. The advantage that Wi-Fi has over Bluetooth is that Wi-Fi supports must faster connection speeds and longer ranges [12].

By using the well-known confidentiality, integrity and availability goals for information security as a guideline. Table 1 summarizes the threat model for wireless IO peripherals. The threats do not take into account threats to the many wireless devices, instead the focus is on the wireless network established between IO peripherals.

Table 1. Wireless network threats.

Security goal	Threat
Confidentiality	Unauthorized parties can intercept and disseminate wireless data
	The wireless interface allows access to applications and data
Integrity	Tampering of wireless data by unauthorized parties
	Wireless data sent by unauthorized sources
Availability	The denial of wireless services and data

In order to mitigate these risks both Bluetooth and Wi-Fi standards have implemented certain security mechanisms. The mechanisms aim to minimize the threats during the initial identification and authentication phase, but it also creates a secure channel that ensures data confidentiality and integrity between the sender and receiver.

Bluetooth specification 2.1 introduced simple secure pairing (SSP) that minimized the chances of attackers gaining access to the wireless session, unfortunately it has been proven that even in Bluetooth specification 4.0 that SSP are still vulnerable to man-in-the-middle attacks. SSP uses Elliptic Curve Diffie Hellman cryptography to provide confidentiality of data [13, 14].

Wi-Fi introduced Wireless Equivalent Privacy (WEP) and Wi-Fi Protected Access (WPA and WPA2) as security protocols [15]. Industry and security researchers recommend the use of WPA2 as the more secure protocol [15]. WPA2 uses the concept of pre-shared keys or an authentication server. In situations where WPA2 sessions are established using pre-shared keys, the environment is vulnerable to attacks by getting the handshaking packets and then using brute force or dictionary attacks on the packet data to extract the pre-shared key.

As discussed earlier the risks for wireless communication is significant, because attackers do not have to be physically connected to the peripherals or devices. The security mechanisms in both Bluetooth and Wi-Fi minimizes the risk of attackers gaining access to wireless data or gaining unauthorized access to the devices through the wireless channel. In some cases, IO peripheral data travels across a network, but do not rely on network layer security, but on application layer security. Application-layer security implementations are described next.

3.3   Terminal-Based IO Peripheral Data

In terminal based networking, where users establish a terminal session to a server, the screen, keyboard and mouse traffic is transferred between terminal and server. Some examples of terminal based implementations that was developed for both keyboard and graphical user interfaces include:

- **X Windows System**. The X Windows System has a client, running on a remote system that displays information on the local system using an X Server. Mouse and keyboard input interacts with the X Server and the resulting commands are sent to the client running on the remote system. In this case, the mouse and keyboard settings do not travel across the network, rather the specific action that they cause, travels over the network [16].
- Virtual network computing (**VNC**). VNC is a platform independent open source protocol that allows a VNC Server to run on a computer that is being controlled by another computer that runs a VNC Viewer. Screen information (Output) is sent to the VNC Viewer and Keyboard and Mouse information is sent from the Viewer to the Server (Input) [17].
- Citrix Independent Computing Architecture (**ICA**). As part of the Citrix Terminal services product, Citrix developed ICA. The protocol is proprietary, but is available on multiple operating system platforms [18].
- Microsoft Remote Desktop Protocol (**RDP**). The RDP protocol works in the same principle as VNC and ICA, but is developed to allow remote sessions to Windows operating systems from a number of platforms [19].
- **ITU-T T.128**. The ITU-T T.128 is a standard defined by the International Telecommunications Union that defines multipoint application sharing. The standard does not define any security requirements, instead it relies on the application to implement the security required by the application [20].

These terminal based protocols all run on top of an underlying network protocol, which in turn runs on top of a network architecture, like Ethernet or Wi-Fi. Some of the protocols have built-in encryption protocols, but some also include network level authentication to occur before a session is established. Without network-level authentication, man-in-the-middle attacks are possible [19].

Terminal-based IO peripheral protocols have been developed and has undergone significant upgrades over the years to address network security issues, like confidentiality of data and data integrity. This means that terminal-based IO protocols can allow some level of security even using potential insecure wired or wireless communication channels.

4   Proposed Communications Model

The previous section provided an overview of some of the risks and solutions used by IO peripherals in wired, wireless or terminal based communications. Section 2 described the Neo device, which does not have any built-in IO peripheral, but allows the user to connect different form-factor IO peripherals to the device, either wirelessly or through a wired docking station.

This section discusses the communication model of the Neo device with its IO peripherals in order to address confidentiality of data and integrity. Confidentiality means that the data transferred between the Neo device and IO peripheral must be obfuscated so that only the peripheral and the Neo device understands the data. Integrity means that communication between the IO peripheral and the Neo device has not been changed.

This section breaks up the model by describing how the IO peripheral and Neo device address the following aspects:

- Identification and Authentication.
- Authorization.
- Confidentiality.

4.1   Identification and Authentication

The identification and authentication phase (**Phase 1**) is the initial phase required by any IO peripheral and Neo device that would like to communicate with each other. The outcome of this phase is to establish a shared key between the IO peripheral and the Neo device.

In order to accomplish the above-mentioned goal, both the Neo device and IO Peripheral consists of the following components, as shown in Fig. 4:

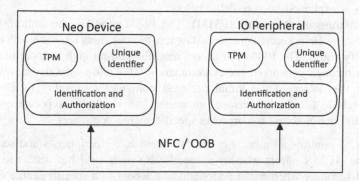

Fig. 4. Components during identification and authentication

- Trusted Platform Module (TPM). The TPM ensures the safe generation and access to the public\private key pairs required for secure communication [21].
- Unique Identifier. The unique identifier is used to ensure that each device is identified and assists in the generation of the shared key.
- Identification and Authorization service. The Identification and Authorization service is the software layer on the device that ensures the successful identification and authentication of devices.

- Near field communication (NFC) [22] or out-of-band (OOB) communication. The initial identification and authorization process occurs only via NFC or OOB. The physical act of either plugging in a device or bringing the devices in close proximity provides another level of authentication.

The most important aspect to understand during Phase 1 is that the secret key that is created between the IO peripheral and the Neo device can only be used between these two devices. Another important aspect is that both devices authenticate with each other. This means the IO peripheral is assured of the identity of the Neo device and the Neo device can be assured of the identity of the IO peripheral, which minimizes the chances of man-in-the-middle attacks.

4.2   Authorization

As soon as both the IO peripheral and the Neo device has been identified, the Neo device authorizes access to the IO peripheral in the Neo device (**Phase 2**). The authorization of the IO peripheral also occurs in the identification and authorization layer (Fig. 4).

Authorization occurs using two specific components:

- **Access control module (ACM)**. The ACM lists the rights of the IO peripherals on the secure containers, as defined by the container owners. The ACM is a complex data structure that defines the low-level rights that the IO peripheral has in both the Neo device and specific container\s. It consists of fine-grained control, which can include settings such as time of day usage and even sensor permissions. These controls is explained in more detail below.
- **Policy management module (PMM)**. The PMM modifies the authorization settings of the various secure containers. Owners of containers interface with the PMM to modify rights. The PMM can accept modification through a custom user interface, or through networked policy commands. This allows the device owner, and thereby the owner of the initial personal container the ability to allow more peripherals to access the personal container, but it allows corporate owners the ability to control access to corporate specific secure containers.

The ACM controls all aspects of the Neo device, IO peripherals and secure containers. The ACM controls whether a specific IO peripheral has access to the Neo device and secondly whether the peripheral has access to a specific secure container. Furthermore, it enforces certain policy requirements that some of the secure containers may have.

These policy requirements defines whether some of the sensors or device features is available to a specific secure container. Example: It may be possible for a specific corporate secure container to not allow access to the microphone or camera.

In addition, a specific policy element controls whether it allows access to other secure containers while some secure container is active or while the device is in a specific area. This allows container owners to ensure only certain containers can be used while in specific areas of a company.

In cases where more than one container requires exclusive access, only the first container starts. More information on the specific access control policy elements can be found in [1].

4.3 Confidentiality

IO peripheral confidentiality is ensured using the secret key that is established during the initial identification and authentication phase. The secret key is established between the Neo device and IO peripheral. This ensures that as peripheral information is transmitted between Neo device and peripheral that the information is encrypted. This type of communication has been briefly introduced in Sect. 3.2.

There is however a concern between confidentiality requirements of the secure containers. The question arises how the system can guarantee confidentiality of peripheral data between containers. How do we ensure that one container cannot access the IO peripheral data of another container?

The simplest solution to the above problem is to implement mutual exclusion for IO peripherals. This means that only one secure container can have access to an IO peripheral at a time.

The communication information between IO peripheral and Neo device is secured using specific identification and authentication phase that establishes a secret key for the peripheral\device combination. This key is used to ensure confidentiality of communication information. Access of peripherals to secure containers are ensured using the ACM. The next section discusses the viability of these model elements using today's known technologies.

5 Viability of Proposed Communications Model Using Existing Technologies

Even though the Neo device is a hypothetical device, it may be possible to implement the requirements defined in the communications model using existing technologies. This section discuss the possibility of using today's communication technology to implement the communications model described for the Neo device.

Table 2 lists the requirements that were identified in Sect. 4 and comments on whether the chosen technologies can be used to fulfill the requirement.

Bluetooth 4.0 fulfills nearly all the requirements in the protocol specification, but it does not specify how the Bluetooth devices should manage access control and how the access control can be modified. Bluetooth also allows a number of SSP association models, which include the insecure "Just works"-association model [14]. The Neo device implementation will not allow this association model, and only allows OOB association to occur.

Bluetooth 4.0 specifies a number of profiles that define the profile specific communication. **Example**: The Video Distribution Profile (VDP) specifies how video is streamed from a master to a slave. The VDP specifications are very different from the Health Device Profile (HDP), which defines how medical devices communicate.

Table 2. Model requirements vs technology

Requirement	Bluetooth 4.0	WPA2
Secure key generation (using TPM)	Yes	Possible using virtual smartcard
Unique identifiers for both IO peripheral and neo device	Yes	Not required
Identification and authorization service	Yes	Yes
Out-of-band initial identification and authentication	Yes	N/A
Access control module	N/A	N/A
Policy management module	N/A	N/A
Encrypted device-to-device communication	Yes	Yes

Bluetooth profiles fit nicely into the principle that the Neo device can also receive not just input signal from an IO device, but potentially also sensor information, like temperature readings, GPS or camera images. When an IO peripheral has a combination of Bluetooth profiles, the access control module can control which profile data is allowed at a specific time, depending on which secure container is currently active.

Bluetooth on its own completes a number of the requirements, but needs extra management software that manages the access control of specific Bluetooth profiles. Some Bluetooth specifications may also be limited to ensure that the OOB requirement is met.

WPA2 defines how devices should identify and authenticate with a WiFi access point and once authenticated ensure encrypted session is established between the device and access point. WPA2 can be extended to ensure that encryption keys are generated using TPM, but relies on higher-level protocols that run over WiFi to ensure authorization. By default, WPA2 does not specify the initial identification to occur using OOB, but technically the implementation stack can be extended to only allow identification and authentication to occur initially OOB.

WPA2 fulfils only some of the requirements for the Neo communication model, but is still a viable option to use for those items that it can fulfill. The other items would need specific implementation extension using higher-level management software. Sensor specific communication would need special application specific implementation.

6 Conclusion

People use multiple mobile devices for the computing needs because of the various form factors available to them. Multiple mobile devices introduce a challenge to ensure that data can safely be transmitted between devices. One solution that addresses the potential insecure data transmission is to use only one device, but with multiple IO peripherals of different form factors.

The use of one device with multiple IO peripherals is not the way in which mobile devices are designed and implemented. The Neo device defines an IO peripheral communication model that ensures IO peripherals and Neo devices are mutually identified, authorized and can securely communicate.

Technologies like Bluetooth or WPA2 can be used as a starting point to implement the communications model that addresses the security requirements for IO peripheral communication.

The challenge with the principle of using one device with multiple IO peripherals allows for many interesting implementation scenarios, but the fact that a user will always need at least two devices may be a big detractor. A possible mitigating action, can be for the Neo device to have at least a built-in touch screen, like today's smartphones. The Neo device will then allow the built-in screen to be switched off in cases where other IO peripherals are communicating with the Neo device.

There are a number of risks when using wired or wireless IO peripherals. Wireless peripherals are particularly at risk because of availability of the wireless channel to potential attackers. One computing device that allows multiple IO peripherals opens up opportunities where the same device can be used for both personal and business use.

To ensure proper isolation and access control of business and personal data a communication model is required that ensures that a data owner has full control over not only who can access the data but must also have the ability to control which peripherals can access the data. The proposed communication model addresses fine-grained access control to not only the computing device, but also the individual secure containers.

References

1. du Toit, J., Ellefsen, I.: Location aware mobile device management. In: 2015 Information Security for South Africa, Rosebank, pp. 1–8 (2015)
2. du Toit, J., Ellefsen, I.: A model for secure mobile computing. In: Science and Information Conference (SAI), London, pp. 1213–1221 (2015)
3. Kaspersky Lab. Spyware Definition and Prevention. http://usa.kaspersky.com/internet-security-center/threats/spyware#.WIxoWUQ2u00. Accessed 28 Jan 2017
4. Trend Micro. Spyware - Threat Encyclopedia. http://www.trendmicro.com/vinfo/us/threat-encyclopedia/malware/spyware. Accessed 28 Jan 2017
5. KeeLog. KeyGrabber - Hardware Keylogger - WiFi USB Hardware Keyloggers. https://www.keelog.com. Accessed 28 Jan 2017
6. KeyCarbon LLC. KeyCarbon Computer Security Hardware. http://www.keycarbon.com. Accessed 28 Jan 2017
7. Gerdes, R.M., Mallick, S.: Physical-layer detection of hardware keyloggers. In: Bos, H., Monrose, F., Blanc, G. (eds.) RAID 2015. LNCS, vol. 9404, pp. 26–47. Springer, Cham (2015). doi:10.1007/978-3-319-26362-5_2
8. Bluetooth SIG, Inc. Bluetooth. https://www.bluetooth.com. Accessed 28 Jan 2017
9. IEEE. In: IEEE-SA -IEEE Get 802 Program - 802.11: Wireless LANs. http://standards.ieee.org/about/get/802/802.11.html. Accessed 28 Jan 2017
10. Bluetooth SIG, Inc. How it Works. Bluetooth Technology Website. https://www.bluetooth.com/what-is-bluetooth-technology/how-it-works. Accessed 2017
11. WiFi Alliance. WiFi Certified Miracast. http://www.wi-fi.org/discover-wi-fi/wi-fi-certified-miracast. Accessed 28 Jan 2017

12. WiFi Alliance. WiFi Certified ac. http://www.wi-fi.org/discover-wi-fi/wi-fi-certified-ac. Accessed 28 Jan 2017
13. Alfaiate, J., Fonseca, J.: Bluetooth security analysis for mobile phones. In: 7th Iberian Conference on Information Systems and Technologies (CISTI 2012), Madrid, pp. 1–6 (2012)
14. Haataja, K., Hyppönen, K., Pasanen, S., Toivanen, P.: Bluetooth Security Attacks: Comparative Analysis, Attacks, and Countermeasures. Springer, Berlin (2013)
15. Khasawneh, M., Kajman, I., Alkhudaidy, R., Althubyani, A.: A survey on Wi-Fi protocols: WPA and WPA2. In: Martínez, P., Thampi, S., Ko, R., Shu, L. (eds.) Recent Trends in Computer Networks and Distributed Systems Security: Proceedings of the Second International Conference, SNDS 2014, Trivandrum, India, 13–14 March 2014, pp. 496–511. Springer, Berlin, Heidelberg (2014)
16. Ts, J.: X window system administration. Linux J. **1998** (1998)
17. Richardson, T., Stafford-Fraser, Q., Wood, K.R., Hopper, A.: Virtual network computing. IEEE Internet Comput. **2**(1), 33–38 (1998)
18. Citrix. In: Citrix. http://www.citrix.com. Accessed 29 Jan 2017
19. Microsoft Corporation. Microsoft Remote Desktop Clients. https://technet.microsoft.com/en-us/library/dn473009(v=ws.11).aspx. Accessed 29 Jan 2017
20. International Telecomunications Union. T.128: Multipoint Application Sharing. https://www.itu.int/rec/T-REC-T.128-200806-I/en. Accessed 2 Feb 2017
21. Trusted Computing Group. TPM Main Specification. https://trustedcomputinggroup.org/tpm-main-specification/. Accessed 2 Feb 2017
22. International Standards Organization: Information Technology – Telecommunications and Information Exchange Between Systems – Near Field Communication – Interface and Protocol (NFCIP-1) ISO/IEC 18092:2013 (2013)

System Dynamics Approach to Malicious Insider Cyber-Threat Modelling and Analysis

Tesleem Fagade[1], Theo Spyridopoulos[2], Nabeel Albishry[1],
and Theo Tryfonas[1(⊠)]

[1] Cryptography Group, University of Bristol, Bristol, UK
{tesleem.fagade,n.albishry,theo.tryfonas}@bristol.ac.uk
[2] Cybersecurity Research Unit, University of the West of England, Bristol, UK
theo.spyridopoulos@uwe.ac.uk

Abstract. Enforcing cybersecurity controls against malicious insiders touches upon complex issues like people, process and technology. In large and complex systems, addressing the problem of insider cyber threat involves diverse solutions like compliance, technical and procedural controls. This work applies system dynamics modelling to understand the interrelationships between three distinct indicators of a malicious insider, in order to determine the possibility of a security breach through developing trends and patterns. It combines observable behaviour of actors based on the well-established theory of planned behaviour; technical footprints from incident log information and social network profiling of personality traits, based on the 'big five' personality model. Finally, it demonstrates how system dynamics as a risk modelling approach can flag early signs of malicious insider threats by aggregating associative properties of different risk elements. Our initial findings suggest that key challenges to combating insider threats are uncertainty, irregular intervals between malicious activities and exclusion of different personality factors in the design of cyber-security protocols. Based on these insights we propose how this knowledge may help with mitigation controls in a secure environment.

Keywords: Malicious insider · Cyber security · Risk modelling · System dynamics · Cyber-risk behaviour · Personality profiling

1 Introduction

An organization's continual effort to reinforce its cyber capabilities and the unique challenge posed by malicious insiders, borders on complex issues that encompass different loosely coupled variables; people, process and technology. Even more so, constructing tools to address this issue often involves diverse controls like technical, procedural, formal and informal solutions, which are difficult to apply in large and complex systems [4]. Organizations' growing reliance on large-scale interconnected information assets and widely available sophisticated attacker tools, suggest that the prevalence and impact of cyber-attacks is set for rapid increase [5]. Insider problem is widely documented in security reports, based on the U.S Secret Service and Verizon reports, of confirmed security breach cases in 2009 alone, insiders are responsible for

© Springer International Publishing AG 2017
T. Tryfonas (Ed.): HAS 2017, LNCS 10292, pp. 309–321, 2017.
DOI: 10.1007/978-3-319-58460-7_21

46% of data breaches, of which 90% were malicious and deliberate acts [3]. Trusted users' elevated access to information utility is a major concern when addressing the problems of insider threat, given that these users already sits behind organizations firewall. Many literature agrees that insiders are the weakest link in organizations defence posture [6, 7], and that insiders are responsible for system exploits more than the failure of technical and procedural measures.

Insider threat manifests when agents' behaviour is contrary to regulatory policies and guidelines. It refers to harmful acts that a trusted employee may carry out to undermine the confidentiality, integrity and availability of information assets. Currently, there is no complete, effective and systemic method developed to address cyber security challenges. The number of attempts to address human factors in cyber security is quite low despite evidence suggesting that a malicious insider exhibits in advance of exploit, an observable 'concerning behaviour' [3]. While the importance of security deterrence investment cannot be completely discounted, the effectiveness against malicious insider is questionable. Deterrence measures can be applied in many ways; for instance, by integrating reward and punishment elements into organisation policies and procedures in order to discourage, remind or compel employees into secure behaviour. However, policies and procedures are behaviour oriented and there is no absolute certainty that people always do as told. What are the key drivers of malicious acts? Are they preventable? It has been shown that security by compliance, as a way to address insider threat problems is a farfetched approach [2], therefore, addressing malicious insider cyber-threat requires a more dynamic approach for analyzing patterns as a precursor to threat.

This work applies system dynamics modelling to understand the interrelationship between three distinct indicators of malicious insider activities. Risk indicators from different domains are aggregated in order to predict the possibility of a security breach, based on how the indicators influence one another. System Dynamics can be used to link hypothesized structure with observed behaviour of systems over a period of time, thereby allowing feedback to uncover certain types of endogenous phenomena [10]. This work combines a behavioural and psychological model of planned behaviour theory; observable personality profiling of actors through social network footprints and system audit trails established from IT resource incident log information. Finally, it demonstrates how system dynamics can flag early signs of malicious insider problems, based on the associative properties of different risk elements. Motivation for this work and relevant literature is covered in Sect. 2. Overview of modelling of the interconnected risk domains is presented in Sect. 3. Methodology and simulation environment including model assumptions is presented in Sect. 4, while Sect. 5 covers discussion and future work.

2 Related Work and Motivation

We review some of the research done in attempt to model insiders' threat behaviour in organisations, but this is by no means an exhaustive list. In terms of understanding the primary driver for malicious behaviour, some of the work in this area [31–36] use decision algorithms to assess the predisposition to malicious behaviour by combining psychometric test scores data and real time technical data obtained from users' information systems. Another literature describes malicious insider threats through a devised taxonomy of attributes; access, risk, knowledge, process and motivation, in order to analyze how each or a combination of these attributes stimulate malicious insiders' behaviour [11]. [9] applies Bayesian network model to study the motivation and psychology of malicious insiders, while [1] evaluates the probability of insider threat detection through a conceptual model that connects real world measurements and a hypothesis-tree, and [28] describes how technical assessment can be combined with information assets categorization and agents behaviour in order to mitigate insider-threat problems through resilience, survivability and security.

In addition, research also shows that employees do not just carry out malicious acts randomly but show some signs of malicious behaviour well in advance of cyber-attacks. In this light, some work emphasize the importance of recognizing early signs of risky behaviour. For instance, [3], described a predictive modelling framework for automated support and detection of high-risk behavioural indicators that may help form risk mitigating decisions. Other research emphasizes the link between personality traits and the tendency to become a malicious insider. Importantly, it is suggested that people's personality can be revealed through the online social media platforms like the Facebook, Twitter and YouTube posts, from which personality types can be mapped to specific job roles, in order to mitigate insider threats [24, 29]. In particular, [32] reveals how it is possible to harvest publicly available information from YouTube video comments, that may identify personality traits through combined dictionary based text classification and machine learning techniques. Similarly, [14] suggests that the personality trait of narcissism is a common characteristics of malicious insiders and that information shared in public domain like Twitter can be utilized to establish predictive actions and deterrence measures against malicious insiders.

It is clear from the relevant literature that detecting insider activities requires more than a single indicator. [19, 27] recommends that there is a need for a framework that encompasses multiple risk indicators for a holistic and predictive threat detection. This paper furthers our previous work on insiders' problem by developing a System Dynamics Model for early detection of insider threat activities, based on personality, behavioural and technical risk indicators. It particularly focuses on malicious insider actions, given that privileged access abuse by malevolent insiders is hard to lock down.

3   Overview of Model Interconnected Risk Domains

For the purpose of this work, we model malicious insider problems by taking into account personality, behavioural and technical risk indicators. Simulating multiple indicators of risk, based on the activities of an employee illustrates a broader implication for collective management of information security. Insider threat detection requires proactive analysis of multiple trigger factors far beyond network analysis alone. Hence, the idea of interconnected domains approach is based on the notion that different elements of risks are inextricably linked, therefore making each contributing factor a function of the malicious insider problem.

3.1 Personality Risk Indicators

Although a personality trait is fairly stable through individuals' lifetimes, the ability to establish a statistically significant relationship between various personality profiles can provide guidelines for implementing security protocols that meet individual needs in a diverse workforce [8]. There are different ways of assessing personality types based on the five psychological construct of Openness, Conscientiousness, Extroversion, Agreeableness and Narcissism (OCEAN). Using publicly available information on Twitter alone, it is possible to predict personality trait to within 11% [23], because certain words tend to be used repeatedly, leading to a pattern that can be correlated with a specific personality trait. Also, through category based textual analysis of browsing behaviour and webpage content, LIWC (Linguistic Inquiry and Word Count) dictionary can be applied to group and link linguistic terms with personality traits [25]; such that, each element of the OCEAN construct can be directly linked to specific malicious activities.

Employees do not only transfer offline behaviour to online social network platforms, there are also evidence to suggest a connection between excessive use of social media and narcissist personality trait [15–17]. Self-promoting contents combined with high level of online activities are also strongly correlated with low self-esteem, malevolent system use, narcissist personality and delinquent behaviour [18]. Personality trait of Openness is linked with susceptibility to phishing, while narcissism, agreeableness and excitement seeking is linked with insider threat and antisocial behaviour [25, 34]. People also reveal certain attributes through social media platforms, relating to psychosocial states like anxiety, debt, adjustment disorder and medical conditions, from which psychosocial risk factors could be drawn.

Although, personality is a direct determinant of intention, individuals with different personality traits are more likely to react differently to the same security scenario, threats and organisation sanctions based on their perception of deterrence, protection motivation or efficacy factors [8]. Consider the generic personality model shown in Figs. 1 and 2,

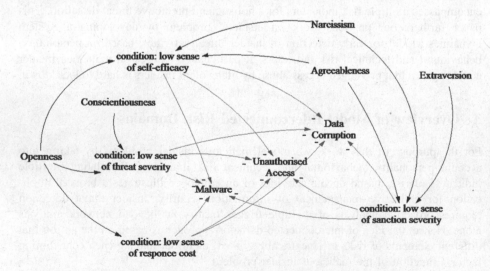

Fig. 1. Cybersecurity risk reduces due to personality traits under specified conditions

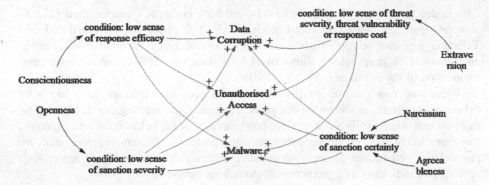

Fig. 2. Cybersecurity risk increases due to personality traits under specified conditions

adopted from [8], it can be seen that an individual with 'Extraversion' personality trait, but with a low sense of sanction severity, is less likely to violate cyber security protocols than an individual with 'Openness' personality trait and low sense of sanction severity. Likewise, an individual with 'Extraversion' personality but with low sense of threat severity, threat vulnerability or response cost is more likely to violate security protocols than an individual with 'Conscientiousness' personality trait with low sense of threat severity or someone with 'Openness' personality trait with low sense of response cost.

3.2   Behavioural Risk Indicators

Theory of planned behaviour has its foundation on a number of constructs and it helps us to understand the reason for deliberate behaviour. It explains why it is hard to change how malevolent insider perceives security protocols. Security managers may provide training, policies and guidelines but users do not necessarily comply, even when mandated. Important aspect of the theory of planned behaviour is that, given a degree of control over events, people are expected to carry out their behaviour, however, intentions can change on the emergence of new information [13]. Previous behaviour and actions of malevolent user can help inform future actions but the challenge is that behaviour may not be easily quantifiable, if there is irregular intervals between malicious activities or no prior established patterns.

Behavioural theories provide guidelines on how behaviour may manifest in different stages of an insider threat scenario through certain indicators. The theory of planned behaviour suggests that a person's intention, perceived behaviour towards crime, subjective norms and attitude are key factors in predicting behaviour [20]. Pre-employment background checks, 360 profiler and other mechanism may help to identify agents that constitute behavioural risk, some of which may be unrelated to employment, like anxiety, breakup, depression, debt and medical conditions [26]. Though some risks may not directly link psychological behaviour to criminal background but may help address psychological factors required to form group homogeneity [12, 14]. Based on 23 cases of insider threat in the banking and finance sector, 33% is due to personal problems that are unrelated to employment, like breakup and anxiety;

23% is due to revenge, 27% is due to debt and 81% is due to financial gains [21]. In another report [22], based on a case study of 52 illicit cyber activities in the IT and Telecommunication sector; 33% is due intolerant to criticism, 57% involves disgruntled employees, 47% is revealed through overt behaviour, and 58% involves direct communication of threat online.

Behaviour and external environmental influences can indicate early signs of cyber-security risks, as shown on the generic system dynamic diagram in Fig. 2. The more an individual exhibits one or more combinations of the behavioural risk elements, the more likely it is to violate cyber security protocols. Human resource staff are particularly well trained to apply observation techniques, recognize and report high scoring risk indicators as a predictor of anomalous behaviour.

3.3 Technical Risk Indicators

There are six categories of critical log information that can be used to identify suspicious activities. These include authentication, system and data change, network activity, resource access, malware activity, failure and critical error logs. Security tools like SIEM/log analysis, data access monitoring, intrusion detection/prevention systems (IDS/IPS) can be leveraged to provide administrators with sufficient information on suspicious activities [30]. Changes to configuration file binaries, network assets authentication and authorization log reports can be tracked to monitor employee activities. For instance, different patterns of system usage based on defined attributes can be combined with log information, job roles and privileges to create a profile for a normal user in a particular role. If there is an irregular pattern in the log information for a particular user compared to the activity of a normal user for the same role, then, that

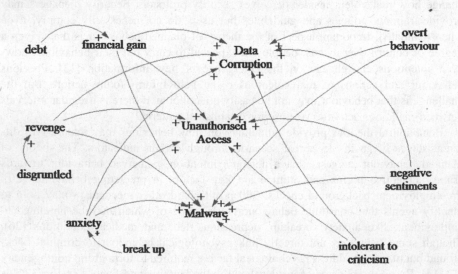

Fig. 3. Cybersecurity risk increases due to individual's behaviour or external influence with negative psychological effects

may suggest potential insider activities. Case study of 52 cyber incidents [22] shows that 57% of incidents are detected through system irregularities; of which 73% involves remote access logs and 57% involves unauthorized file access logs. Based on another study [33] involving 36 illicit cyber activity in the government sector, 24% of incidents is due to unauthorized privilege users and 11% involves installation of backdoors. Figures 2 and 3 shows how technical risk may be influenced by the interplay of other variables like personality traits and behaviour.

4 Methodology and Simulation Environment

4.1 Model Analysis

System Dynamics can be used to link hypothesized structure with observed behaviour of systems over a period of time, thereby allowing feedback to uncover certain types of endogenous phenomena [10]. Ventana Systems (Vensim PLE), a fully functional system dynamics software package, is used to conduct the simulation in this work. We propose that behavioural, technical or personality risk, when considered in isolation is not indicative of the full potentials of malicious insider. Irregular intervals between illicit cyber activities or inconsistent overt behaviour is difficult to apply independently as evidence of malicious insider. In order to prevent false positive triggers, each element of the risk indicators can be inextricably linked and modelled in order to draw more valid inferences. When risk factors are combined and observed as they change over a period of time, developing patterns can provide significant confidence in identifying potential malicious insider.

Consider the high level abstractions for the conceptual model shown in Fig. 4. Organisations can define an employee's 'normal' security profile based on different risk indicators, deterrence, protection motivation, efficacy factors and job roles. Employee activities are then monitored over a period of time e.g. monthly, based on combined data flow from three domain streams. Social network data can be leveraged to determine personality trait for a particular employee. This could be a contentious issue, however we suggest that data from open social networks such as Twitter may be used legitimately and are made available by employees themselves. Human resource (HR) data provides input from constant monitoring and analyzing behavioural risk indicators for that employee, in addition to the employee's psychological state (PS). Monitoring psychosocial behaviour is important because it could be exacerbated by external factors that are not necessarily related to an employee's job. Likewise, incident log data obtained from the IT department is used to determine technical risk indicators. In order to determine the security status for an employee, inputs from external environment that forms PS are combined with behavioural risk factors from HR. Output from this can be influenced by the personality of a user. Then, depending on the personality of an employee and the employee's perception of deterrence, protection motivation and efficacy factors, the likelihood of cyber-security protocol violation can be determined. For instance, someone with 'Narcissistic' personality and low sense of sanction certainty is more likely to cause cyber leakage, espionage or delete system critical files, if associated PS and HR variables are true. Similarly, someone with

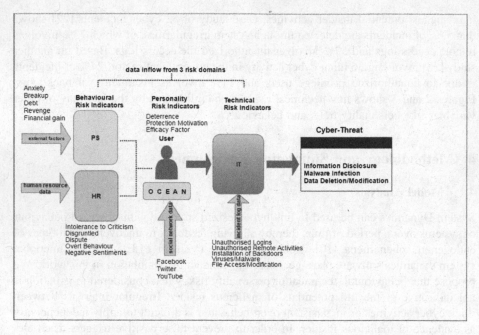

Fig. 4. High level abstraction of our insider threat modelling process

'Agreeable' personality with low sense of sanction certainty is more likely to be susceptible to phishing, if associated PS and HR factors are triggered.

4.2 Model Results and Discussion

The dynamic relationship diagram in Fig. 5 presents the stocks and flows that describes the dynamics between a person's behaviour, personality and the probability of a cyber-security incident (data corruption or unauthorized access), based on the generic system dynamics diagrams provided in Figs. 1, 2 and 3. In particular, we consider behaviour as the combination of a person's psychosocial state (PS), sculptured by external triggers (e.g. breakup or debt), with employee's internal behaviour (e.g. intolerance to criticism or negative sentiments) as observed by the HR department. Negative internal behaviour combined with an unhealthy psychosocial state can increase the probability of a cyber-security incident. On the other hand, personality can play a twofold role; as shown in our generic model (Figs. 1, 2 and 3) depending on specific conditions (e.g. low sense of sanction severity or low sense of response cost) certain personality traits can either increase or decrease the probability of a cyber-security incident. To simplify our stocks and flows diagram we made the assumption that for the employee under consideration, apply the following conditions: "low sense of self-efficacy" and "low sense of threat severity". Under these assumptions and according to our generic diagrams, 'Extraversion' increases the probability of a cyber-security incident while 'Openness', 'Conscientiousness', 'Narcissism' and

'Agreeableness' decreases it. These relationships are captured in Fig. 5, where all personality traits except 'Extraversion' contribute to the decrease of the cyber-security incident risk. All variables in Fig. 5 take values from 0 to 1.

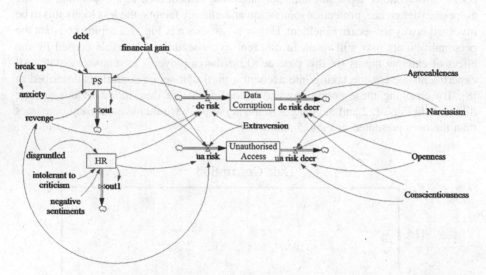

Fig. 5. Dynamic relationship between personality, behaviour and cyber-security incident

Figure 6 shows probability of data corruption in time for different combinations. Before we start the experiment, we set all personality traits to 1 and all internal behaviour and external psychosocial variables to 0. Then we change the following variables:

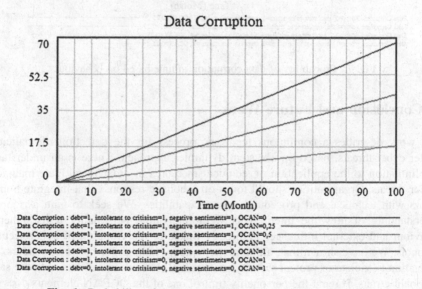

Fig. 6. Probability of data corruption in time based on personality

debt, intolerance to criticism, negative sentiments and O.C.A.N. (Openness, Conscientiousness, Agreeableness and Narcissism) and run the model for various combinations, as shown. As seen, personality plays an important role to cyber-security; the more open, conscientious, agreeable and not narcissist someone is, and depending on the associated deterrence, protection motivation and efficacy factors, the less likely it is to be involved in a cyber-security incident. However, as shown in Fig. 7, keeping constant the personality traits may still result in different cyber-security risk levels caused by the effect of external inputs (in this case debt) on the employee's psychosocial state. All experiments were made taking into account a particular set of conditions described in [8]. By changing these conditions and according to the description of our generic diagrams in Figs. 1, 2 and 3; changes in the personality would have different outcomes than the ones presented in Figs. 5 and 6.

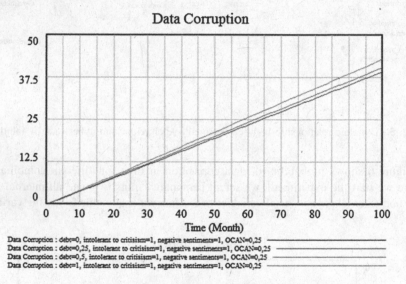

Fig. 7. Probability of data corruption in time based on behaviour

5   Conclusion and Future Work

This work describes a continuous feedback process for the detection of malicious insider cyber-threats, based on a system dynamics approach. There is an understandable limitation to the application of technical measures in order to mitigate malicious insider threats. Organisations should focus on a holistic response that integrate human factors with technical and procedural cyber capabilities. We seek to gain a rigorous understanding of how the interplay between individual personality traits, inherent behaviour and external influences is directly linked to the violation of cyber-security protocols. We have shown that, although personality traits differ between insiders, the motivation to violate or protect security protocols also varies in insiders with the same personality traits. Having the personality trait of one of the OCEAN elements does not make an individual more or less likely to violate a security protocol, but the perception of sanctions, rewards, psychological states and behaviour contributes to the likelihood of acting maliciously.

This study concludes that through combined behavioural analysis (HR) and externally triggered psychological factors (PS), technical footprints (IT) and personality types (OCEAN), the design and implementation of appropriate cyber-security protocols, should be based on a full understanding of insider psychological and security profiles. Providing generic cyber-security training and awareness programs without a deep understanding of employees outlook on deterrence, protection motivation or efficacy factors is simply a one-cap-fits-all approach that rarely ensures compliance. However, by customizing training based on individual personality traits and how they react to deterrence measures, organisation sanctions, threats, motivation and rewards; more positive results can be achieved. This observation is in line with earlier, more practical studies [37]. Based on these findings and a part of future research, we plan to develop a framework for customized cyber-security training that can appeal to different personality types.

References

1. Legg, P.A., et al.: Towards a conceptual model and reasoning structure for insider threat detection. JoWUA **4**(4), 20–37 (2013)
2. Fagade, T., Tryfonas, T.: Security by compliance? A study of insider threat implications for nigerian banks. In: Tryfonas, T. (ed.) HAS 2016. LNCS, vol. 9750, pp. 128–139. Springer, Cham (2016). doi:10.1007/978-3-319-39381-0_12
3. Greitzer, F.L., Hohimer, R.E.: Modeling human behavior to anticipate insider attacks. J. Strateg. Secur. **4**(2), 25 (2011)
4. Dhillon, G.: Violation of safeguards by trusted personnel and understanding related information security concerns. Comput. Secur. **20**(2), 165–172 (2001)
5. Andersen, D.F., et al.: Preliminary system dynamics maps of the insider cyber-threat problem. In: Proceedings of the 22nd International Conference of the System Dynamics Society (2004)
6. Corriss, L.: Information security governance: integrating security into the organizational culture. In: Proceedings of the 2010 Workshop on Governance of Technology, Information and Policies, Austin, Texas, USA, pp. 35–41. ACM (2010)
7. Aurigemma, S., Panko, R.: A composite framework for behavioral compliance within formation security policies. In: Proceedings of the 2012 45th Hawaii International Conference on System Sciences, pp. 3248–3257. IEEE Computer Society (2012)
8. McBride, M., Carter L., Warkentin, M.: Exploring the role of individual employee characteristics and personality on employee compliance with cybersecurity policies. Technical report, RTI International (2012)
9. Axelrad, E.T., et al.: A Bayesian network model for predicting insider threats. In: 2013 IEEE Security and Privacy Workshops (SPW). IEEE (2013)
10. Martinez-Moyano, I.J., et al.: A behavioral theory of insider-threat risks: a system dynamics approach. ACM Trans. Model. Comput. Simul. (TOMACS) **18**(2), 7 (2008)
11. Wood, B.: An insider threat model for adversary simulation. SRI Int. Res. Mitig. Insider Threat Inf. Syst. **2**, 1–3 (2000)

12. Greitzer, F.L., Frincke, D.A.: Combining traditional cyber security audit data with psychosocial data: towards predictive modeling for insider threat mitigation. In: Probst, C.W., Hunker, J., Gollmann, D., Bishop, M. (eds.) Insider Threats in Cyber Security. Springer, US (2010). 85–113

13. Ajzen, I.: From intentions to actions: a theory of planned behavior. In: Kuhl, J., Beckmann, J. (eds.) Action Control. Springer, Berlin (1985). 11–39

14. Kandias, M., Galbogini, K., Mitrou, L., Gritzalis, D.: Insiders trapped in the mirror reveal themselves in social media. In: Lopez, J., Huang, X., Sandhu, R. (eds.) NSS 2013. LNCS, vol. 7873, pp. 220–235. Springer, Heidelberg (2013). doi:10.1007/978-3-642-38631-2_17

15. Mehdizadeh, S.: Self-presentation 2.0: narcissism and self-esteem on Facebook. Cyberpsychol. Behav. Soc. Netw. 13(4), 357–364 (2010)

16. Malik, S., Khan, M.: Impact of Facebook addiction on narcissistic behavior and self-esteem among students. J. Pak. Med. Assoc. 65(3), 260–263 (2015)

17. Skues, J.L., Williams, B., Wise, L.: The effects of personality traits, self-esteem, loneliness, and narcissism on Facebook use among university students. Comput. Hum. Behav. 28(6), 2414–2419 (2012)

18. Shaw, E., Ruby, K., Post, J.: The insider threat to information systems: the psychology of the dangerous insider. Secur. Awareness Bull. 2(98), 1–10 (1998)

19. Schultz, E.E.: A framework for understanding and predicting insider attacks. Comput. Secur. 21(6), 526–531 (2002)

20. US-CERT "Combating the Insider Threat", National Cybersecurity and Communications Integration Center, May 2014

21. Cummings, A., et al.: Insider threat study: Illicit cyber activity involving fraud in the US financial services sector. No. CMU/SEI-2012-SR-004. Carnegie-Mellon Univ Pittsburgh Pa Software Engineering Inst (2012)

22. Kowalski, E., Cappelli, D., Moore, A.: Insider threat study: illicit cyber activity in the information technology and telecommunications sector. Carnegie Mellon University, Software Engineering Institute (2008)

23. Golbeck, J., et al.: Predicting personality from twitter. In: 2011 IEEE Third International Conference on Privacy, Security, Risk and Trust (PASSAT) and 2011 IEEE Third International Conference on Social Computing (SocialCom). IEEE (2011)

24. Back, M.D., et al.: Facebook profiles reflect actual personality, not self-idealization. Psychol. Sci. 21(3), 372–374 (2010)

25. Alahmadi, B.A., Legg, P.A., Nurse, J.R.C.: Using internet activity profiling for insider-threat detection (2015)

26. Ackerman, D., Mehrpouyan, H.: Modeling human behavior to anticipate insider attacks via system dynamics. In: Proceedings of the Symposium on Theory of Modeling and Simulation. Society for Computer Simulation International (2016)

27. Greitzer, F.L., Frincke, D.A., Zabriskie, M.: Social/ethical issues in predictive insider threat monitoring. Inf. Assur. Secur. Ethics Complex Syst.: Interdisc. Perspect 132–161 (2010)

28. Sarkar, K.R.: Assessing insider threats to information security using technical, behavioural and organisational measures. Inf. Secur. Tech. Rep. 15(3), 112–133 (2010)

29. Chen, Y., et al.: Leveraging social networks to detect anomalous insider actions in collaborative environments. In: 2011 IEEE International Conference on Intelligence and Security Informatics (ISI). IEEE (2011)

30. SANS Technology Institute, The 6 Categories of Critical Log Information. http://www.sans.edu/cyber-research/security-laboratory/article/sixtoplogcategories. Accessed 06 Jan 2017

31. Kandias, M., Mylonas, A., Virvilis, N., Theoharidou, M., Gritzalis, D.: An insider threat prediction model. In: Katsikas, S., Lopez, J., Soriano, M. (eds.) TrustBus 2010. LNCS, vol. 6264, pp. 26–37. Springer, Heidelberg (2010). doi:10.1007/978-3-642-15152-1_3

32. Kandias, M., et al.: Proactive insider threat detection through social media: the YouTube case. In: Proceedings of the 12th ACM Workshop on Workshop on Privacy in the Electronic Society. ACM (2013)
33. Kowalski, E., et al.: Insider threat study: illicit cyber activity in the government sector. In: US Department of Homeland Security, US Secret Service, CERT, and the Software Engineering Institute (Carnegie Mellon University), Technical report (2008)
34. O'Connor, B.P., Dyce, J.A.: A test of models of personality disorder configuration. J. Abnorm. Psychol. **107**(1), 3 (1998)
35. Caci, B., et al.: Personality variables as predictors of Facebook usage. Psychol. Rep. **114**(2), 528–539 (2014)
36. Ortigosa, A., Carro, R.M., Quiroga, J.I.: Predicting user personality by mining social interactions in Facebook. J. Comput. Syst. Sci. **80**(1), 57–71 (2014)
37. Styles, M., Tryfonas, T.: Using penetration testing feedback to cultivate an atmosphere of proactive security amongst end-users. Inf. Manag. Comput. Secur. **17**(1), 44–52 (2009)

Developing Usable Interface for Internet of Things (IoT) Security Analysis Software

Seokjun Hong, Youngsun Kim, and Gerard J. Kim$^{(\boxtimes)}$

Digital Experience Laboratory, Korea University, Seoul, Korea
{hong921122, zyoko85, gjkim}@korea.ac.kr

Abstract. In this paper, we present a case study of designing and improving an interface for a web based security analysis software for the internet of things (IoT), called the IoTCube. The objective of the IoTCube is to provide an easy-to-use security vulnerability checking and analysis solution for the IoT related developers and users. The software is consisted and organized of largely three analysis functionalities for the: (1) system/executables, (2) source code and (3) network protocols. The interface design started with the user analysis and deriving of requirements based on usage scenarios, and then went through several iterations of sketches, wire-frames and implementations based on feedbacks from the HCI experts, domain experts and actual users to further improve its usability. The improved usability not only has made the security analysis practice much accessible for the non-experts, but also brought about a concrete understanding of the consequences of identified problems.

Keywords: Usability · Usable security · User research · Interface design · Case study

1 Introduction

Usable security is a field that addresses the issue of improving the interface design for security related software. The underlying thought (and fact) is that, aside from the vulnerability of the core system itself, many security problems can be attributed to the low usability and understandability of the front-end interfaces for security-related settings, configuration and analysis software [1].

In this paper, we outline a case study of designing an interface for a web based security vulnerability analysis software for the internet of things (IoT), called the IoTCube. The objective of the IoTCube is to provide an easy-to-use security analysis solution for the IoT related developers and users [2]. The software is consisted and organized of largely three analysis functionalities for the: (1) system/executables (called the black box testing), (2) source code (called the white box testing) and (3) network protocols.

The interface design started with the user analysis and deriving of requirements based on usage scenarios, and then went through several iterations of sketches, wire-frames and implementations based on feedbacks from the HCI experts, domain experts and actual users to further improve its usability. Figure 1 shows the look of the entry web page for the IoTCube as of February of 2017 [2].

© Springer International Publishing AG 2017
T. Tryfonas (Ed.): HAS 2017, LNCS 10292, pp. 322–328, 2017.
DOI: 10.1007/978-3-319-58460-7_22

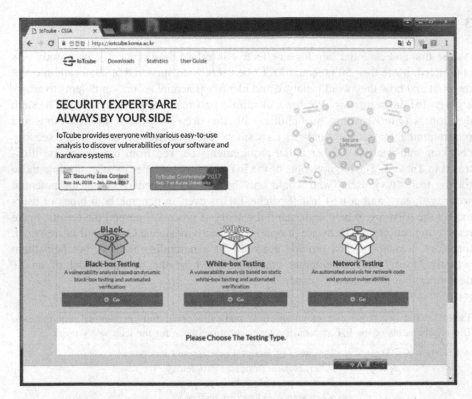

Fig. 1. The look of the entry web page for the IoTCube as of February of 2017 [2] with three clear entry points [7] to the black box, white box and network protocol security analysis options.

2 Related Work

In [1], Payne and Edwards provides a good introduction to the field of the usable security through a few representative case studies such as those for setting password, authentication and email encryption. However, not many studies exist for the security "analysis" software (vs. configuration) which may not necessarily be used only by the domain experts [3, 4]. Payne and Edwards also pointed out that much of the community's work have focused on studying the usability of security controls and interfaces rather than the design process itself. Still, there exist some interface guidelines, mostly for the task of security configuration, some of which should mostly apply to those for analysis as well [5]. For example, the principles of "Expressiveness," "Identifiability," and "Foresight" all point to the need and requirement for the user have a clear understanding and awareness of the current process, and consequences and extent of one's actions. In fact, such principles have originated from the general HCI area [6, 7] but been placed with special emphasis with regards to dealing with information security.

3   User Study

As the first and essential step for an effective interface development, a user study was conducted. More than 50 potential IoTCube users were surveyed at a hackathon event on what and how they would analyze and identify potential security problems to attack a given IoT infrastructure. We have identified two main target users: (1) IoT system developers (who may not be familiar with the deep skills, e.g. for providing and programming for security and (2) tech savvy users (interested only in the security checking and analysis). Other initial requirements derived from the survey are illustrated in Table 1. The requirements of the IoT system developer mostly subsume those for the tech savvy users (who would only be capable of understanding the potential security threats, and at best install patches). However, in general, both types of users expect the software to help understand the analysis process, interpret the results, make remedying actions and be aware of options and activity status. One of our design goal, therefore, was not to just provide guidance in a reminding fashion, but help them actually "learn" the vulnerability analysis, based on the mental model of an IT developer (but not a security expert).

Table 1. The two target user group and their main functional and interactional requirements. The requirements of the IoT system developer subsume those for the tech savvy users.

Iot System developer: *Program and debug for security*	• Be aware of analysis process and its context
	• Filter, isolate, prioritize problems
	• Explore possible solutions
	• Keep status and record history
	• Seek helper functions for development
Tech savvy user: *Patch, upgrade, configure*	• Understand analysis process (mental model)
	• Understand analysis results (e.g. security vulnerabilities, threats, consequences, and severity)
	• Seek helper functions for quick patch/settings

We also derived a task (security analysis) model as shown in Fig. 2. The task model is roughly divided into three distinct parts according to the different analysis techniques, namely the black box, white box and network protocol analyses. Each technique is further broken down into subtasks at a level that is understandable to the target user. Aside from the analysis tasks, there are several miscellaneous or supplementary subtasks to support the requirements listed in Fig. 2, such as results visualization, status monitoring, and process management. The overall task model is "linearly" structured (in three threads according to the types of analysis techniques) for easy understanding of the process.

4   Interface Design Concept

The next phase was to carry out the detailed interface design. The focus was put on providing features to make the target user be aware of one's action and it consequences and comprehend the overall process and analysis results. As such, the step-by-step

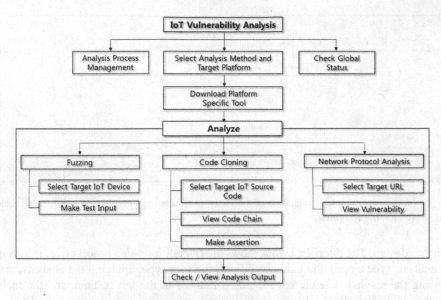

Fig. 2. The overall task model for the vulnerability analysis in the IoTCube software. It is structured as three linear threads according to the analysis types.

linear sequence model was employed once a particular analysis method was chosen. Current status, intermediate results and other guidance information was kept to the minimum and designed to be as informative as possible not to overwhelm the user and elicit confidence in one's work. Figures 3 and 4 show the look and feel of the early

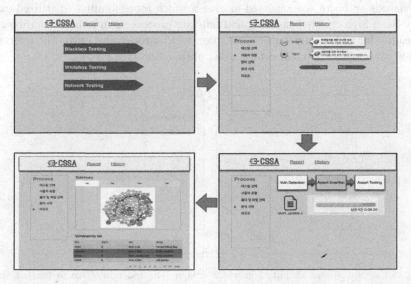

Fig. 3. An early interface design showing the four step analysis process (e.g. selecting of the analysis type, specifying the user type, applying the analysis, and showing the results).

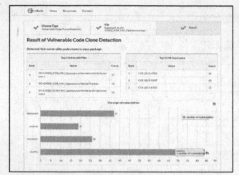

Fig. 4. Easy to understand explanation of the analysis results (e.g. graphs and color coded table entries). (Color figure online)

interface design. The interface layout shows the overall four-step process (e.g. selecting the analysis type among the three, specifying the user type, applying the analysis, and showing the results). The current subtask is marked in the left column, and the main center pane displays the analysis options/parameters, guidance, and test results. The top part of the interface shows buttons for non-analytic support functions.

5 Feedback and Improvement

The initial interface design was continuously analysed, updated and further simplified based on user feedback and expert reviews. Figure 5 shows one notable example in which the old interface simply dumping of difficult-to-understand text output from the core analysis software was changed to give a much more intuitive visualized explanation. Such high comprehensibility and fail-safe process seem to have contributed to the steadily increasing number of users (monitored through the web). The interviews with the users reflect and support the same observation (see Fig. 6).

Fig. 5. An improved and simplified interface design. The older interface in the left simply dumps difficult-to-understand text output from the core analysis software. The improved interface in the right give a much more intuitive visualized explanation.

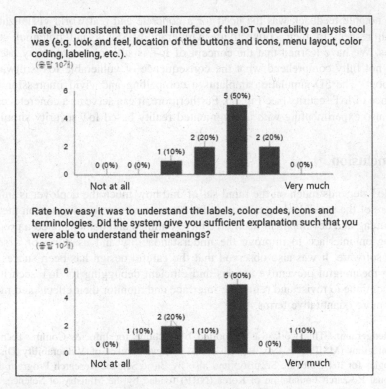

Fig. 6. Samples of results from user surveys on interface consistency and understandability.

Fig. 7. A 3D/realistic illustration of IoT security vulnerability repercussions. An IoT door is opened and lamp is on fire by a simulated outsider attack.

One notable feedback was the need for a concrete and real world visualization of IoT with respect to their connectivity, vulnerability status and potential security problems. We have learned that the concept of IoT is still foreign to many users and they do not fully comprehend what the consequence of vulnerable IoT software can bring about. The 3D simulation implants a compelling and vivid impression of the importance of IoT security (see Fig. 7). Furthermore, it can serve as a concrete test bed. We are also experimenting with an augmented reality based IoT security simulation.

6   Conclusion

Secure IoT depends much on the mind-set of and how much the deployer is informed and aware of the possible danger and needed steps to prevent it, as much on the actual programming and development itself. We have outlined and demonstrated a process of designing an interface to improve the understandability and usability of a security analysis software. It was also observed that the careful design has been successful in inducing meaningful preventive actions and efficient debugging for IoT security. We plan to continue to revise and refine the interface and monitor their effects and measure them in more quantitative terms.

Acknowledgement. This work was supported by Institute for Info. & Comm. Technology Promotion grant (MSIP/IITP, No. R0190-16-2011, Development of Vulnerability Discovery Technologies for IoT Software Security) and also by Basic Science Research Program through the National Research Foundation of Korea (NRF) funded by the Ministry of Science, ICT & Future Planning (No. 2011-0030079).

References

1. Payne, B., Edwards, W.: A brief introduction to usable security. IEEE Int. Comput. **12**, 13–21 (2008)
2. Security experts are always by your side (2016). http:iotcube.korea.ac.kr
3. Birge, C.: Enhancing research into usable privacy and security. In: Proceedings of the ACM International Conference on Design of Communication, pp. 221–226 (2009)
4. Faily, S., Lyle, J., Flechais, I., Simpson, A.: Usability and security by design: a case study in research and development. In: Proceedings of USEC (2015)
5. Yee, K.: User interaction design for secure systems. In: Proceedings of the International Conference on Information and Communications Security, pp. 278–290 (2002)
6. Schneiderman, B.: Designing the user interface for effective human-computer interaction (6th ed.), Pearson (2016)
7. Tidwell, J.: Designing interfaces, O'Reilly Media (2010)

Visualization Technologies of Information Security Support System Using Haptic Devices

Manabu Ishihara[1]([✉]) and Taiki Kanayama[2]

[1] Department of Innovative Electrical and Electronic Engineering,
National Institute of Technology, Oyama College, Oyama, Japan
ishihara@oyama-ct.ac.jp
[2] Advanced Course of Electrical and Computer Engineering,
National Institute of Technology, Oyama College, Oyama, Japan

Abstract. The Internet has become one of the most important tools. A huge amount of data is communicated in the Internet all over the world. The management of data traffic is very important under such a situation, because the computer transmits lots of unnecessary data though it is infected by a computer virus and the network is not well managed. A monitor of data traffic, therefore, should be required for recognizing such a situation. As a result of recent advances in three-dimensional (3D) video technology and stereo sound systems, virtual reality (VR) has become a familiar part of people's lives.

The antivirus software is playing an important role in networking. Additionally, haptic devices have been researched recently and applied in many fields. It is interesting to combine antivirus software and haptic devices. In this paper we experimented on determination criteria of the haptic force and constructed the system for experiment.

Keywords: Haptic device · Antivirus software · Packet

1 Introduction

As a result of recent advances in three-dimensional (3D) video technology and stereo sound systems, virtual reality (VR) has become a familiar part of people's lives. Concurrent with these advances has been a wealth of research on touch interface technology [1], and educators have begun exploring ways to incorporate teaching tools utilizing touch properties in their curriculums [5, 6]. However, when used as teaching tools, it is important that a touch interface provide a "feel" that is as close to reality as possible. This will make replacing familiar teaching tools with digital media incorporating VR seem more attractive.

For example, various learning support systems that utilize virtually reality (VR) technology [7] are being studied. Examples include a system that utilizes a stereoscopic image and writing brush display to teach the brush strokes used in calligraphy [8, 9], the utilization of a robot arm with the same calligraphy learning system [10], a system that uses a "SPIDAR" haptic device to enable remote calligraphy instruction [11], and

© Springer International Publishing AG 2017
T. Tryfonas (Ed.): HAS 2017, LNCS 10292, pp. 329–338, 2017.
DOI: 10.1007/978-3-319-58460-7_23

systems that analyze the learning process involved in piano instruction [12] or in the use of virtual chopsticks [13].

Additionally, since it is a basic rule of pen-drawn characters that even a slight displacement of the pen tip is impermissible, pen-drawn character reproductions must be within 1 mm tolerances and will appear out of balance if drawn too long or too short. In response, support system ems for penmanship instruction and similar applications on tablet PCs have been developed [14], and associated research indicates that both the curriculum and content are important factors for creating VR materials [5]. Penmanship instruction systems and similar applications using interactive haptic devices connected to networks have been devised, and various experiments have been performed into their usage [15]. To facilitate the passing down of technical skills, various operations have been analyzed and the application of those analyses is being investigated. Soldering work by skilled workers and unskilled workers is also being analyzed. (1) For workers having a certain amount of experience, there is diversity of right wrist motions. (2) For beginners, various soldering iron insertion angles and motions of each wrist, and a tendency for instability are observed. (3) For skilled workers, the soldering iron insertion angle and wrist motions are stable, and soldering is completed in nearly a single operation. On the basis of the above, the soldering iron insertion angle, wrist motion stability, and the timing with which to remove the soldering iron are suggested to be three operation characteristics [21].

It can be seen that the number of users who feel a difference in the program begins to increase when, due to delays, the haptic–visual data time difference begins to exceed 10 ms or the haptic–auditory data time difference begins to exceed 40 ms. Visual sense is said to have a greater impact than auditory sense, and that statement is consistent with these findings. Moreover, for visual sense, there exists research showing that people begin to sense network latency when the delay reaches approximately 30 ms, and this is consistent with the finding that 50% of the test subjects began to feel a difference at this level [22].

Cyber attacks use several methods and threaten social infrastracture. Especially, malware is highly sophisticated to steal more valuable information, and the victims are not aware of it's infection. Thus, it is difficult to detect and distinct malware infections by physical sence. Kaneko's paper [16], we geographical visualize malware's attack point with CCC DATAset 2011's Attack-Connection Data and Attack-Source Data, and creates support system for integrate analysis malware to obvious attacker's purpose. The antivirus software, which is one of the security technology, can analyze the network and detect an information leakage and killer virus software. If malware is detected in the network, visualization of security technology enlighten them. Haptization of security technology has most been reported previously. However, no study has been found so far as to the integration of security technology with hapitization and visualization of them. Accordingly, we developed the system which analyze an IP address to cope with an attack to Web and can express the offensive ability from an opponent sensuously in haptic devices.

2 Apparatus

Haptic device is PHANToM Omni (Omni) made by SensAble co., Ltd. The personal computer controlling the system have Intel corei7-2600 CPU@3.40 GHz, 4 GB memory and Windows7 Professional. The system was developed by Microsoft VisualC++ 2008. The library used Open Haptics and WinPcap. Open Haptics control Omni. Figure 1 shows the PHANToM omni.

Fig. 1. PHANToM omni

3 System Overview

The system consists of 4 blocks: ①capture, ②analyze, ③draw and ④provision. The first block captured packets. The system automatically captured packets using WinPcap. The second block analyzed the packets. The captured packets searched an IP addles and time to live (TTL). The third block drew the packet flow image. This image is important for feeling feedback force. The fourth block provisioned a feedback force with user. User touched the image by moving the haptic device. At that time, the user could sense packet volume.

It is known that an IP packet passes through less than 30 routers before it reaches the destination host. According to our observation, some IP packets have an abnormal TTL value that is decreased more than 30 from the initial TTL. These packets are likely to be generated by special software. We assume that IP packets with a strange TTL value are malicious. Yamada's paper investigates this conjecture through several experiments. As a results, we show that it is possible to discriminate malicious packets from legitimate ones only by observing TTL values. The system analyzed the TTL according to the criterion employed in the previous study used [17], which reports that a pop count over 50 is judged as abnormal packet. This paper employs this calculation method.

4 Experiment

We began by modeling images of the surface texture for notebook and other paper types using friction experiments. When creating friction via the haptic display, it was first necessary to determine what level of friction was discernible. Weinstein and Weber [18, 19] report that Weber ratio of the haptic is about 0.2. However, Omni provision

332 M. Ishihara and T. Kanayama

force is not necessarily liner. We apply the function from 0.0 to 1.0 in this paper. The extremes of 0.0 and 1.0 are excluded from the unit of force. The rest is called haptic force level in this report. Thus, this experiment estimated determination criteria of the haptic force by using discriminated packet volume of touch.

Measurements were performed using one test subject at a time. The subject was seated in front of the PHANToM unit and given the pen component to hold. They then followed instructions displayed by the computer and moved their arm to draw a straight line on the model board using an arbitrary amount of force. Subjects were then asked to evaluate a total of 50 randomly presented stimuli combinations comprising five combinations, including an SS pair, each shown 10 times. As the PHANToM only guarantees forces up to 3.0 (kg-m/s^2) (3.0[N]) [2], the unit was restricted because the application of normal force greater than this level would not register.

Figure 2 shows the experiment system window. It has right and left areas. Both areas show difference forces. Taking the stylus of Omni, subjects move in the system window. The one side has a standard stimulus. The other side shows 4 comparative stimuli and a standard stimulus. In total, 5 different stimuli are displayed on the screen. Participants compare right area force and left area force. They answer one of the three choices, "stronger right force", "same" or "stronger left force". The answer data were processed by maximum likelihood method [3, 4].

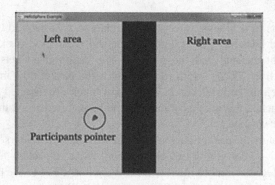

Fig. 2. Experiment system window

5 Experimental Results

The stimulus on which comparisons were based was called the standard stimulus (SS). For frictional forces, the SS was limited to one type of stimulus with a fixed range of physical quantities. The stimulus used for comparison with the SS was called the comparative stimulus (CS). A number of CS types were prepared in incremental quantities centered on the stimulus quantity of the SS.

Measurements were performed using one test subject at a time. The subject was seated in front of the PHANToM unit and given the pen component to hold. They then followed instructions displayed by the computer and moved their arm to draw a straight line on the model board using an arbitrary amount of force.

Fourteen people participated as test subjects, with age ranging from 18 to 21 years. The standard stimulus applied to this experiment was the 0.4 amplitude stimulus, and five types of comparative haptic stimuli ware presented, from 0.0 to 0.8 in step of 0.2. Table 1 shows the measurement example. The horizontal axis indicates the presented stimulus values and the vertical axis indicates the determination probability. Data values are represented with small circles: a green circle is a determination of "weaker than the standard stimulus" (a > xi), a purple circle is a determination of "same as the standard stimulus" (a ≈ xi), and a blue circles is a determination of "stronger than the standard stimulus" (a < xi). The curves show determination probabilities based on parameter values obtained from experimental data.

Table 1. Example of reaction force experiment

Standard stimulus a = 0.4 by 0.2			
Comparison stimuli xi	xi > a	xi ≈ a	xi < a
0.0	0	0	14
0.2	0	0	14
0.4	1	7	6
0.6	13	1	0
0.8	14	0	0

The standard stimulus has an amplitude of 0.4, the point of subjective equality is 0.44. There is little error between the standard stimulus and the point of subjective equality. Moreover, the amplitude threshold for which a test subject can perceive differences in haptic sensation is said to be within the range of 0.395 to 0.485. However, since the change in amplitude was large, there was sufficient width to distinguish the stimuli. Figure 3 shows the Result of maximum likelihood method.

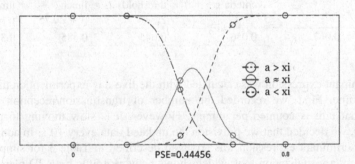

Fig. 3. Analysis results for reaction force experiment (Color figure online)

6   System Prototype

The system can analyze packets and provision user a reaction force. Figure 4 shows the system. The center denotes personal computer to control the system. Lines which lengthen from the center is network image. The blue cone is the pointer which a user

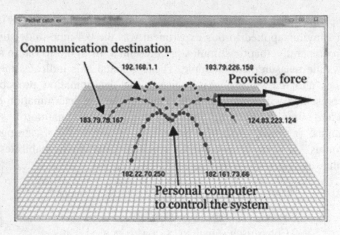

Fig. 4. Basic system by captures packets (Color figure online)

moves. Figure 4 demonstrates the system automatically captures packets. The IP address is represented as numbers near the line.

When a user touch the line and press a button in Omni, the user sense the force like packet volume. Haptic force level and line color are provided in Table 2. Color difference represents the preference about temperature according to the study [20], which states about emotional color. We used technique [17] that a pop count over 50 is regarded as abnormal packet.

Table 2. Parameter values for reaction force experiment

Average μ	Dispersion σ	Determination criteria c	Difference threshold $Z_{0.75}$	Upper limen $\mu + Z0.75$	Lower limen $\mu - Z0.75$
0.44	0.067	0.056	0.045	0.485	0.395

Discriminant expression was calculated with the five-day experiment on the data of packet volume. First, we recorded the number of transmission/reception times of packets. That unit is counted per minute. However, it is slow moving to provision force. Thus, we decided that we provision the updated data every 10 s. In addition, the value of discriminant expression was arranged described in Table 3 for simplicity.

Next step, a visualization tool, which shows network traffic by a 2D plane of days and times, is shown. And we express the degree of threat by color, shown in Fig. 5.

We propose a malware classification method that focuses on the network behavior of malwares. The behavior is translated into reaction force pattern. By modifying two-dimension time-day pattern algorithms, the behavior is analyzed to find out the most similar traffic data. We also performed evaluation by using reaction force traffic collected from the real environment.

Table 3. Discriminant expression, color and force level

Discriminant expression	Color	Force level
10 or less	Blue	0.0
11 to 20	Sky blue	0.2
21 to 30	Green	0.4
31 to 40	Yellow	0.6
41 to 50	Orange	0.8
Over 50	Red	1.0
Pop count over 50	Red	1.0

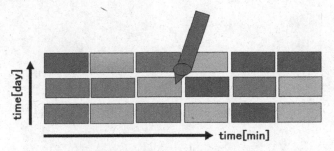

Fig. 5. Color image (Color figure online)

The same system can analyze packets and provision user a reaction force. Figure 6 shows the new system. The center denotes personal computer to control the system. Blocks which lengthen from the center is network image. The blue cone is the pointer which a user moves. Figure 5 demonstrates the system automatically captures packets. The IP address is represented as numbers near the block number and color.

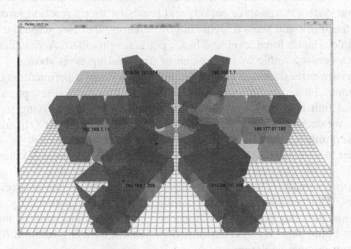

Fig. 6. View of new system image (Color figure online)

When a user touch the block and press a stylus button in Omni, the user sense the force like packet volume. Haptic force level and block color are provided in Table 3 by same. A visualization tool, which shows network traffic by a 2D plane of days and times, is shown.

The unit of system provisioning force should also be newton. We propose about the representation scheme of the relationships between reaction force and functions in a program. Figure 7 shows the experiment results.

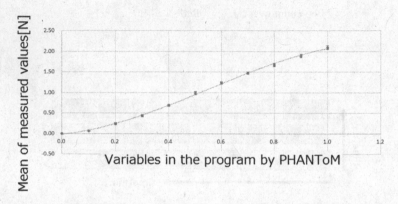

Fig. 7. The relationships between reaction force and functions value in a program

7 Conclusions

In this system can analyze packets and provision user a reaction force. The center denotes personal computer to control the system. Lines which lengthen from the center is network image. The blue cone is the pointer which a user moves. The system automatically captures packets. The IP address is represented as numbers near the line.

The same system can analyze packets and provision user a reaction force. When a user touch the block and press a stylus button in Omni, the user sense the force like packet volume. Haptic force level and block color are provided. A visualization tool, which shows network traffic by a 2D plane of days and times, is shown.

Discriminant expression was calculated with the five-day experiment on the data of packet volume. First, we recorded the number of transmission/reception times of packets. That unit is counted per minute. However, it is slow moving to provision force. Thus, we decided that we provision the updated data every 10 s. In addition, the value of discriminant expression was arranged described in simplicity.

Next step, A visualization tool, which shows network traffic by a 2D plane of days and times, is shown. And we express the degree of threat by color.

We propose a malware classification method that focuses on the network behavior of malwares. The behavior is translated into reaction force pattern. By modifying two-dimension time-day pattern algorithms, the behavior is analyzed to find out the most similar traffic data. We also performed evaluation by using reaction force traffic collected from the real environment.

The system can express packet volume in reaction force. Nevertheless, the present system does not confirm bite size. Therefore, the system provisioned force after assessing packet volume and bite size. Furthermore, discriminant expression was determined under personal experimental environment. It needs to be generalized to other environments. Next step, A visualization tool, which shows network traffic by a 2D plane of days and times, is shown. And we express the degree of threat by color. The unit of system provisioning force should also be newton. These are the issues for our future research.

References

1. Ohnishi, H., Mochizuki, K.: Effect of delay of feedback force on perception of elastic force: a psychophysical approach. IEICE Trans. Commun. **E90-B**(1), 12–20 (2007)
2. Sensable OpenHaptics™ programmer's guide
3. Okamoto, Y.: Psychometrics. Baifukan (2007). (in Japanese)
4. Morgan, C.T., Cook, J.S., Chapanis, A., Lund, M.W.: Ergonomics Data Book. McGraw-HillBook Company, Inc., New York City (1972)
5. Ishihara, M.: On first impression of the teaching materials which used haptic display. In: IEEJ Transactions on Fundamentals and Materials, vol. 129, no. 7, pp. 490–491, July 2009. (in Japanese)
6. Ishihara, M.: Assessment of paper's roughnessfor haptic device. In: Proceedings of Forum Information Technology2011, K-032, Hokkaido, Japan, September 2011. (in Japanese)
7. Hirose, M.: "Virtual Reality," Sangyo Tosho (1993). (in Japanese)
8. Yoshida, T., Muranaka, N., Imanishi, S.: A construction of educational application system for calligrapy master based on virtual reality. In: IEEJ Transactions on Electronics, Information and Systems, vol. 117-C, no. 11, pp. 1629–1634, November 1997. (in Japanese)
9. Yoshida, T., Yamamoto, T., Imanishi, S.: A calligraphy mastering support system using virtual reality technology and its learning effects. In: IEEJ Transactions on Fundamentals and Materials, vol. 123-A, no. 12, pp. 1206–1216, December 2003. (in Japanese)
10. Henmi, K., Yoshikawa, T.: Virtual lesson and its application to virtual calligraphy system. TVRSJ **3**(1), 13–19 (1983). (in Japanese)
11. Sakuma, M., Masamori, S., Harada, T., Hirata, Y., Satou, M.: A remote lesson system for Japanese calligraphy using SPIDAR. IEICE of Japan, Technical report, MVE99-52, pp. 27–32, October 1999. (in Japanese)
12. Otsuka, G., Sodeyama, G., Muranaka, N., Imanishi, S.: A construction of a piano training system based on virtual reality. In: IEEJ Transactions on Electronics, Information and Systems, vol. 116-C, no. 11, pp. 1288–1294, November1996. (in Japanese)
13. Yamaguchi, Y., Kitamura, Y., Kishino, F.: Analysis of learning process of virtual chopsticks. IEICE of Japan, Technical report, MVE2001-3, pp. 11–16, June 2001. (in Japanese)
14. Muranaka, N., Tokumaru, M., Imanishi, S.: The penmanship (script learning) support system: education effect of the animation model for pen strokes. IEICE of Japan, Technical report, ET2005-115, pp. 151–156, March 2006. (in Japanese)
15. Ishihara, M.: Prototype of haptic device and pen tablet collaborative work system. J. Comput. **3**(8), 51–54 (2011)
16. Hirokazu, K.: Integrate analysis malware from geographic visualization. In: CSS2011, Computer Security Symposium, pp. 19–21, October 2011

17. Ryo, Y., Kazuhiro, T., Shigeki, G.: Discriminating malicious packets using TTL in the IP header. IEICE Technical report, pp. 235–240, March 2012. (in Japanese)
18. Weber, E.H.: The Sense of Touch. "De subtilitate tactu", Ross, H.E., Murray, D.J. (Trans), pp. 19–135. Academic Press, London (1834/1978)
19. Weinstein, S.: Intensive and extensive aspects of tactile sensitivity as function of body part, sex, and lateraliry. In: Kenshalo, D.R. (ed.) The Skin Sense, pp. 195–222. Springfiled, Thomas (1968)
20. Masamitsu, I., Tomoko, K., Mieko, A.: Emotion and color(3). Shimane Univ. Educ. Bull. **28**, 35–50 (2001)
21. Ishihara, M.: Haptic device using a soldering test system. In: Stephanidis, C. (ed.) HCI 2015. CCIS, vol. 528, pp. 190–195. Springer, Cham (2015). doi:10.1007/978-3-319-21380-4_34
22. Ishihara, M., Komori, T.: Auditory and visual properties in the virtual reality using haptic device. In: Lackey, S., Shumaker, R. (eds.) VAMR 2016. LNCS, vol. 9740, pp. 135–146. Springer, Cham (2016). doi:10.1007/978-3-319-39907-2_13

Formal Modeling and Analysis with Humans in Infrastructures for IoT Health Care Systems

Florian Kammüller[✉]

Middlesex University, London, UK
f.kammueller@mdx.ac.uk

Abstract. In this paper, we integrate previously developed formal methods to model infrastructure, actors, and policies of human centric infrastructures in order to analyze security and privacy properties. A fruitful approach for discovering attacks on human centric infrastructure models is invalidation of global policies. Invalidating global policies by a complete exploration of the state space can be realized by modelchecking. To counter the state explosion problem inherent in modelchecking, Higher Order Logic (HOL) supported by the interactive theorem prover Isabelle can be used to emulate modelchecking. In addition, the Isabelle Insider framework supports modeling and analysis of human centric infrastructures including attack trees. In this paper, we investigate how Isabelle modelchecking might help to improve detection of attack traces and refinement of attack tree analysis. To this end, we use a case study from security and privacy of IoT devices in the health care sector as proposed in the CHIST-ERA project SUCCESS.

1 Introduction

The expressive power of HOL allows modeling the process of social explanation inspired by Max Weber into an Isabelle Insider Threat framework. We applied this framework to case studies from airplane safety and security [8], insider threats for the IoT [10], and for auction protocols [9]. The CHIST-ERA project SUCCESS [2] will employ the framework in combination with attack trees and the Behaviour Interaction Priority (BIP) component architecture model to develop security and privacy enhanced IoT solutions. A pilot case study from the health care sector, cost-effective IoT-based bio-marker monitoring for early Alzheimer's diagnosis, will enable us to investigate the feasibility of the approach.

The Isabelle Insider framework [14] is used as a basis for a formalisation of an architecture-level description of the infrastructure including human actors, their psychological disposition, and core privacy and security requirements integrated as logical predicates of local security and privacy policies. The modelchecking procedure advocated in the invalidation approach to Insider threat analysis [13] has meanwhile been incorporated into the Isabelle tool [7]. Its applicability has been demonstrated by means of an example on the analysis of an earlier IoT case study [10]. However, in this earlier IoT case study, we originally extended the Isabelle Insider framework by the concept of attack trees to refine known

© Springer International Publishing AG 2017
T. Tryfonas (Ed.): HAS 2017, LNCS 10292, pp. 339–352, 2017.
DOI: 10.1007/978-3-319-58460-7_24

IoT Insider attack vectors. Attack trees allow refining known attack vectors into sequences of state transitions explaining how the attack leads to a state in which the security property is violated. Thus the refined attack corresponds to a path in the state graph of the system model. Similarly, the process of modelchecking produces automatically a sequence of state transition – if the checked property does not hold in the model.

The question we investigate by means of an IoT health care case study is whether the concepts of modelchecking and attack tree refinement correspond. The extension by modelchecking [7] and the embedding of attack trees into the Isabelle Insider framework allow us to examine this correspondence using the mathematical rigour and automated proof support of Isabelle. The results provide important insights on how the methods of modelchecking and attack tree analysis can be fruitfully combined to enhance the verification of attacks on human centric infrastructure models and possibly even the discovery of yet unknown ones.

This paper begins by briefly reviewing the Isabelle Insider framework with a special emphasis on the extensions to modelchecking as well as attack trees. The running example of a simple health care scenario and its privacy and security risks is then introduced followed by the presentation of its formalisation in the Isabelle Insider framework. We reconsider the definition of state transition in modelchecking introducing an adaptation that explicitly shows the attack paths. This allows the transformation of attack traces found by modelchecking into the attack tree refinement process. We show how these processes relate. As illustrated by the case study, we can use the combination of modelchecking and attack trees to guide the attack tree refinement in finding and analysing the attacks in human centric scenarios.

2   Isabelle Insiders, Modelchecking and Attack Trees

In formal analysis of technical scenarios, the motivation of actors and the resulting behaviour of humans is often not considered because the complexity is beyond usual formalisms. The Isabelle Insider framework [14] provides expressiveness to model infrastructures, policies, and humans while keeping up the level of proof automation. In this section, we give a short introduction to this framework for modeling and analysing Insider attacks. We describe its extensions by attack trees and modelchecking. A detailed technical introduction to the framework is given in [14], the extensions are introduced in [7,10] and the Isabelle sources are available online [6].

2.1   Isabelle Insider Framework

The Isabelle Insider framework [14] is based on a logical process of sociological explanation [3] inspired by Weber's *Grundmodell*, to explain Insider threats by moving between societal level (macro) and individual actor level (micro).

The interpretation into a logic of explanation is formalized in Isabelle's Higher Order Logic. This Isabelle formalisation constitutes a tool for proving security properties using the assistance of the semi-automated theorem prover

[14]. Isabelle/HOL is an interactive proof assistant based on Higher Order Logic (HOL). Applications can be specified as so-called object-logics in HOL providing reasoning capabilities for examples but also for the analysis of the meta-theory. Examples reach from pure mathematics [11] to software engineering [5]. An object-logic contains new types, constants and definitions. These items reside in a theory file, *e.g.*, the file `Insider.thy` contains the object-logic for social explanation of Insider threats (see [6,14]). This Isabelle Insider framework is a *conservative extension* of HOL. This means that our object logic does not introduce new axioms and hence guarantees consistency.

The micro-level and macro-level of the sociological explanation give rise to a two-layered model in Isabelle, reflecting first the psychological disposition and motivation of actors and second the graph of the infrastructure where nodes are locations with actors associated to them. Security policies can be defined over the agents, their properties, and the infrastructure graph; properties can be proved mechanically with Isabelle.

In the Isabelle/HOL theory for Insiders, we express policies over actions `get`, `move`, `eval`, and `put` We abstract here from concrete data – actions have no parameters:

```
datatype action = get | move | eval | put
```

The human component is the *Actor* which is represented by an abstract type and a function that creates elements of that type from identities:

```
typedecl actor
type_synonym identity = string
consts Actor :: string ⇒ actor
```

Policies describe prerequisites for actions to be granted to actors given by pairs of predicates (conditions) and sets of (enabled) actions:

```
type_synonym policy = ((actor ⇒ bool) × action set)
```

We integrate policies with a graph into the infrastructure providing an organisational model where policies reside at locations and actors are adorned with additional predicates to specify their 'credentials', and a predicate over locations to encode attributes of infrastructure components:

```
datatype infrastructure = Infrastructure
    "igraph" "location ⇒ policy set" "actor ⇒ bool" "location ⇒ bool"
```

These local policies serve to provide a specification of the 'normal' behaviour of actors but are also the starting point for possible attacks on the organisation's infrastructure. The `enables` predicate specifies that an actor `a` can perform an action `a' ∈ e` at location `l` in the infrastructure `I` if `a`'s credentials (stored in the tuple space `tspace I a`) imply the location policy's (stored in `delta I l`) condition `p` for `a`:

```
enables I l a a' ≡ ∃ (p,e) ∈ delta I l. a' ∈ e
                    ∧ (tspace I a ∧ lspace I l ⟶ p(a))
```

We demonstrate the application of the Isabelle Insider framework in Sect. 5.1 on our running example of an Insider case study from the health care sector.

2.2 Attack Trees

Attack Trees [19] are a graphical tree-based design language for the stepwise investigation and quantification of attacks. They have been integrated as an extension to the Isabelle Insider framework [10, 18]. In this Isabelle framework, base attacks are defined as a datatype and attack sequences as lists over those:

```
datatype baseattack = None | Goto "location"
                     | Perform "action" | Credential "location"
type_synonym attackseq = baseattack list
```

The following definition `attree` defines the nodes of an attack tree. The simplest case of an attack tree node is a base attack. Attacks can also be combined as the "and" of other attacks. The third element of type `attree` is a `baseattack` (usually a `Perform action`) that represents this attack, while the first element is an attack sequence and the second element is the attribute, simply a "string":

```
datatype attree = BaseAttack "baseattack" ("N (_)") |
                  AndAttack "attackseq" "string" "baseattack" ("_ ⊕_^(-) _")
```

The functions `get_attseq` and `get_attack` are corresponding projections on attack trees returning the entire attack sequence or the final base attack (the root), respectively.

The main construction concept for attack trees is *refinement* defined by an inductive predicate `refines_to` syntactically represented as the infix operator ⊑. There are rules `trans` and `refl` making the refinement a preorder; the rule `refineI` shows how attack vectors can be integrated into the refinement process. We will investigate this rule in detail when integrating with modelchecking in Sect. 4.2 because this is where modelchecking and attack tree refinement complement each other nicely.

The refinement of attack sequences allows the expansion of top level abstract attacks into longer sequences. Ultimately, we need to have a notion of when a sufficiently refined sequence of attacks is valid. This notion is provided by the final inductive predicate `is_and_attack_tree`. We will not focus on this here. For details, see [10] or the online formalisation [6]).

Intuitively, the process of refining corresponds to enlarging an attack tree as depicted in Fig. 1.

2.3 Modelchecking

Modelchecking is often advertised as a 'push-button' technique in contrast to automated verification techniques, for example with Isabelle, where the user has to interact with the tool to verify properties. Thus it is in practice very successful mainly due to this full automation. The applications in the Isabelle Insider

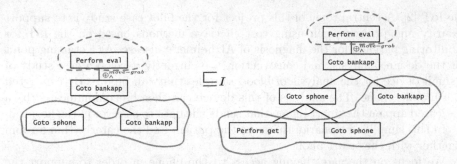

Fig. 1. Attack refinement for healthcare case study (see also Sect. 2.3).

framework that we construct are mostly performed by simple combinations of automatic proof procedures once the theorem and lemmas have been stated. The most well known problem of Modelchecking is the exponential growth of the number of states, the 'state explosion' common in most applications because of infinite data domains. Due to this restriction, models often oversimplify.

Another important advantage of modelchecking is the natural use of temporal logic to express system constraints, e.g., M ⊢AG send -> AF ack to express "on all paths in the model M it is the case that a send request is eventually followed by an acknowledgement ack".

Due to the expressiveness of HOL, Isabelle allows us to formalise within HOL the notion of Kripke structures, temporal logic, and formalise the semantics of modelchecking by directly encoding the fixpoint definitions for each of the CTL operators [7]. To realize this, a change of the state of the infrastructure needed to be incorporated into the Isabelle Insider framework. A relation on infrastructures is defined as an inductive predicate called state_transition. It introduces the syntactic infix notation I →$_i$I' to denote that infrastructures I and I' are in this relation.

```
inductive state_transition ::
        [infrastructure, infrastructure] ⇒ bool ("_  →_i _")
```

The definition of this inductive relation is given by a set of rules. To give an impression of this definition, we show here just the rule for the move action.

```
move: ⟦ G = graphI I; a @_G l; l ∈ nodes G; l' ∈ nodes G;
        a ∈ actors_graph(graphI I); enables I l (Actor a) move;
        I' = Infrastructure (move_graph_a a l l'
                            (graphI I))(delta I)(tspace I)(lspace I)
      ⟧ ⟹ I →_i I'
```

3   Health Care Case Study in Isabelle Insider Framework

The case study we use as a running example in this paper is a simplified scenario from the context of the SUCCESS project for Security and Privacy of the IoT [2]. A central topic of this project for the pilot case study is to support security and privacy when using cost effective methods based on the IoT for monitoring patients for the diagnosis of Alzheimer's disease. As a starting point for the design, analysis, and construction, we currently develop a case study of a small device for the analysis of blood samples that can be directly connected to a mobile phone. The analysis of this device can then be communicated by a dedicated app on the smart phone that sends the data to a server in the hospital.

In this simplified scenario, there are the patient and the carer within a room together with the smart phone.

We focus on the carer having access to the phone in order to support the patient in handling the special diagnosis device, the smart phone, and the app.

The insider threat scenario has a second banking app on the smart phone that needs the additional authentication of a "secret key": a small electronic device providing authentication codes for one time use as they are used by many banks for private online banking.

Assuming that the carer finds this device in the room of the patient, he can steal this necessary credential and use it to get onto the banking app. Thereby he can get money from the patient's account without consent.

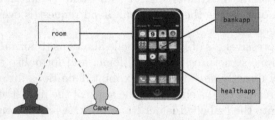

Fig. 2. Health care scenario: carer and patient in the room may use smartphone apps.

4   Combining Modelchecking and Attack Trees

We now show the interaction of the modelchecking and attack tree approaches by introducing the necessary extensions to the Isabelle Insider framework while highlighting the adaptations that manifest the combination. We use the health care case study introduced in the previous section to show how this combination enables the analysis of the Insider risk given by the carer.

4.1   Relation Between State Transition and Attack Sequences

Modelchecking introduces the concept of state transition explicitly into the Isabelle Insider model. The relation $\rightarrow_i$ (see Sect. 2.3) provides a transition between different states of the infrastructure that can evolve into each other through changing actions taken by actors. By contrast, in the attack tree world, we have not explicitly introduced an effect on the infrastructure's state but we have equally investigated and refined attacks as sequences of actions eventually mapping those actions onto sequences of base attacks.

The main clue to combine modelchecking and attack tree analysis is intuitively described as using the Kripke models as the *models* for the attack tree analysis. More precisely, the sequences of attack steps that are eventually found through the process of refining an attack, need to be checked against sequences of transitions possible in the Kripke structure that consists of the graph of infrastructure's state changes.

Technically, this transformation needs a slight transformation between sequences of steps of the infrastructure's state changing relation $\rightarrow_i$ and that same relation but with the actions leading to the exact same state changes annotated at the transitions. Those annotations then naturally correspond to the paths that determine the way through the Kripke structure. They can be one-to-one translated into attack vectors.

Formally, we simply define a relation very similar to $\rightarrow_i$ but with an additional parameter added as a superscript after the arrow.

```
inductive state_step ::
        [infrastructure, action, infrastructure] ⇒ bool ("_ →(-) _")
```

For the definition of this inductive relation we show here again just the rule for the move action which is nearly identical to before just adding the action.

```
move: ⟦ G = graphI I; a @_G l; l ∈ nodes G; l' ∈ nodes G;
       a ∈ actors_graph(graphI I); enables I l (Actor a) move;
       I' = Infrastructure (move_graph_a a l l'
                           (graphI I))(delta I)(tspace I)(lspace I)
    ⟧ ⟹ I →^{move} I'
```

We define an iterator relation `state_step_list` over the `state_step` that enables collecting the action sequences over state transition paths.

```
inductive state_step_list ::
   [infrastructure, action list, infrastructure] ⇒ bool ("_ →(-) _")
where
  state_step_list_empty: I →^{[]} I |
  state_step_list_step : ⟦ I →^{[a]} I'; I' →^l I'' ⟧ ⟹ I →^{a#l} I''
```

Note, how in Isabelle overloading of the operator $\rightarrow^{(-)}$ can be neatly applied.

With this extended relation on states of an infrastructure we can now trace the modelchecking action sequences. Finally, a simple translation of attack sequences from the attack tree model to action sequences can simply be formalised by first defining a translation of base attacks to actions.

```
primrec transform :: baseattack ⇒ action
 where
  transform_move:     transform (Goto l') = move |
  transform_get:      transform (Credential l') = get |
  transform_perform:  transform (Perform a) = a
```

From this we define a function `transf` for transforming sequences of attacks.

```
primrec transf :: attackseq ⇒ action list
where
  transf_empty : transf [] = [] |
  transf_step:   transf (ba#l) = (transform ba)#(transf l)
```

4.2 Improving Attack Refinement

This relative simple adaptation of the modelchecking state transitions to action sequences paired with the transformation from attack traces has a simplifying as well as unifying effect: the attack tree approach necessitated the explicit definition of "attack vectors" that could be used to replace an abstract attack node by a sequence of attacks (see Sect. 2.2). This was manifested by the rule `refineI` which required a predefined list of attack vectors.

```
⟦ P ∈ attack_vectors; P I s l a;
    sublist_rep l a (get_attseq A) = (get_attseq A');
    get_attack A = get_attack A' ⟧ ⟹ A ⊑_I A'
```

An example of an attack vector that had to be replaced for P and provided as premise to the above rule is the example `UI_AV7` of *unintentional Insider attack vectors* [10].

```
⟦ enables I l a move; enables (add_credential I a s) l a get ⟧
⟹ UI_AV7 I s
    (get_attackseq ([Goto l, Perform get] ⊕_∧^{move−intercept} Credential l))
    (Credential l)
```

Previously, such attack vectors had to be defined as inductive rules in an axiomatic fashion. Now, the attack vectors can be *inferred* from the modelchecking process. The new rule in the attack refinement definition is `refineIMC`.

```
⟦ I →^{l'} I'; transf l = l';
    sublist_rep l a (get_attseq A) = (get_attseq A');
    get_attack A = get_attack A' ⟧ ⟹ A ⊑_I A'
```

An application can be seen in the following section.

5 Analysing Carer Attack

5.1 Health Care Case Study in Isabelle Insider Framework

We only model two identities, `Patient` and `Carer` representing a patient and his carer. We define the health care scenario in the locale `scenarioHealthcare`. The syntax `fixes` and `defines` are keywords of locales that we drop together with the types for clarity of the exposition from now on. The double quotes ``s`` represent strings in Isabelle/HOL. The global policy is 'no one except the patient can use the bank app':

```
fixes global_policy :: [infrastructure, identity] ⇒ bool
defines  global_policy I a ≡  a ≠ ''Patient'' ⟶
                          ¬(enables I bankapp (Actor a) eval)
```

The graph representing the infrastructure of the health care case study has the following locations: (0) smart phone, (1) room, (2) bank app, and (3) health app: In order to define the infrastructure, we first define the graph representing the scenario's locations and the positions of its actors. The actors patient and carer are both initially in room. The graph is given as a set of nodes of locations and the actors residing at certain locations are specified by a function associating lists of nodes with the locations.

```
ex_graph ≡  Lgraph
               {(room, sphone), (sphone, healthapp), (sphone, bankapp)}
               (λ x. if x = room then [''Patient'', ''Carer''] else [])
```

In the following definition of local policies for each node in the office scenario, we additionally include the parameter G for the graph. The predicate @$_G$ checks whether an actor is at a given location in the graph G.

```
local_policies G  ≡
  (λ x.  if x = room then {(λ y. True,{get, put, move}) }
     else (if x = sphone then
       {((λ y. has (y, ''PIN'')), {put,get,eval,move}), (λ y. True, {})}
          else (if x = healthapp then
                  {((λ y. (∃ n. (n @$_G$ sphone) ∧ Actor n = y)),
                    {get,put,eval,move})}
                else (if x = bankapp then
                        {((λ y. (∃ n. (n @$_G$ sphone) ∧ Actor n = y ∧
                        has (y, ''skey''))), {get,put,eval,move})}
                      else {}))))
```

In this policy, any actor can move to the room and when in possession of the PIN can move onto the sphone and do all actions there. The following restrictions are placed on the two other locations.

healthapp: to move onto the **healthapp** and perform any action at this location, an actor must be at the position **sphone** already;
bankapp: to move onto the **bankapp** and perform any action at this location, an actor must be at the position **sphone** already and in possession of the **skey**.

The possession of credentials like PINs or the skey is assigned in the infrastructure as well as the roles that actors can have. We define this assignment as a predicate over actors being true for actors that have these credentials. For the health care scenario, the credentials express that the actors **Patient** and **Carer** possess the PIN for the sphone but **Patient** also has the skey.

```
ex_creds ≡ (λ x. if x = Actor ''Patient'' then
                    has (x,''PIN'') ∧ has (x, ''skey'')
                 else (if x = Actor ''Carer'' then
                    has (x, ''PIN'') else True))
```

The graph and credentials are put into the infrastructure hc_scenario.

```
hc_scenario ≡ Infrastructure
                  ex_graph (local_policies ex_graph) ex_creds ex_locs
```

5.2   Modelchecking Supported Attack Tree Analysis

As a setup for the state analysis, we introduce the following definitions to denote changes to the infrastructure. A first step towards critical states is that the carer gets onto the smart phone. We first define the changed infrastructure graph.

```
ex_graph' ≡ Lgraph
              {(room, sphone), (sphone, healthapp), (sphone, bankapp)}
              (λ x. if x = room then [''Patient''] else
                 (λ x. if x = sphone then [''Carer''] else []))
```

The dangerous state has a graph in which the actor Carer is on the bankapp.

```
ex_graph'' ≡ Lgraph
              {(room, sphone), (sphone, healthapp), (sphone, bankapp)}
              (λ x. if x = room then [''Patient''] else
                 (λ x. if x = bankapp then [''Carer''] else []))
```

The critical state of the credentials is where the carer has the skey as well.

```
ex_creds' ≡ (λ x. if x = Actor ''Patient'' then
                     has (x,''PIN'') ∧ has (x, ''skey'')
                  else (if x = Actor ''Carer'' then
                     has (x, ''PIN'') ∧ has (x, ''skey'')
                     else True))
```

We use these changed state components to define a series of infrastructure states.

```
hc_scenario'   ≡ Infrastructure
                   ex_graph (local_policies ex_graph) ex_creds' ex_locs
hc_scenario''  ≡ Infrastructure
                   ex_graph'(local_policies ex_graph') ex_creds' ex_locs
hc_scenario'''≡ Infrastructure
                   ex_graph''(local_policies ex_graph'') ex_creds' ex_locs
```

We next look at the abstract attack that we want to analyse before we see how the modelchecking setup supports the analysis.

The abstract attack is stated as ([Goto bankapp] $\oplus_\wedge^{move-grab}$ Perform eval). The following refinement encodes a logical explanation of how this attack can happen by the carer taking the skey, getting on the phone, on the bankapp and then evaluating.

```
([Goto bankapp] ⊕∧^{move-grab} Perform eval)
⊑_hc_scenario
([Perform get, Goto sphone, Goto bankapp)] ⊕∧^{move-grab} Perform eval)
```

This refinement is proved by applying the rule refineI (see Sect. 4.2). In fact, this attack could be *found* by applying refineI and using interactive proof with the modelchecking extension of the Isabelle Insider framework to instantiate the higher order parameter ?l in the following resulting subgoal.

hc_scenario $\rightarrow^{\mathtt{transf(?l)}}$ hc_scenario'''

This proof results in instantiating the variable ?l to the required attack sequence [Perform get, Goto sphone, Goto bankapp].

So far, we have used the combination of a slightly adapted notion of the state transition from the modelchecking approach to build a model for attack refinement of attack trees. We can further use the correspondence between modelchecking and attack trees to find attacks. To properly employ modelchecking, we first define the Kripke structure for the health case scenario representing the state graph of all infrastructure states reachable from the initial state.

```
hc_states ≡ { I. hc_scenario →*ᵢ I }
hc_Kripke ≡ Kripke hc_states {hc_scenario}
```

Following the modelchecking approach embedded into the Isabelle Insider framework [7], we may use branching time logic CTL to express that the global policy (see Sect. 5.1) holds for all paths globally.

hc_Kripke ⊢ **AG** {x. global_policy x ''Carer''}

Trying to prove this must fail. However, using instead the idea of invalidation [12] we can prove the negated global policy.

hc_Kripke ⊢ **EF** {x. ¬ global_policy x ''Carer''}

The interactive proof of this EF property means proving the theorem

hc_Kripke ⊢ **EF** {x. enables x bankapp (Actor ''Carer'') eval}

This results in establishing a trace l that goes from the initial state hc_scenario to a state I such that enables I bankapp (Actor ''Carer'') eval. This I is for example hc_scenario''' and the action path get, move, move is a side product of this proof. Together with the states on this path the transf function delivers the required attack path [Perform get, Goto sphone, Goto bankapp].

6 Conclusions

Summarizing, we have considered the benefits of relating earlier extensions to the Isabelle Insider framework to modelchecking and to attack trees and illustrated the benefits on a health care case study of an Insider attack.

Clearly relevant to this work are the underlying framework and its extensions [7,9,10,14] but also the related experiments with the invalidation approach for

Insider threat analysis using classic implementation techniques like static analysis and implementation in Java [18] or probabilistic modeling and analysis [1].

We believe that the combination of modelchecking and attack trees is novel at least in the way we tie these concepts up at the foundational level. Considering the simplicity of this pragmatically driven approach and the relative ease with which we arrived at convincing results, it seems a fruitful prospect to further explore this combination. Beyond the mere finding of attack vectors in proofs, the expressivity of Higher Order Logic will allow developing meta-theory that in turn can be used for the transfer between modelchecking and attack tree analysis.

There are excellent foundations available for attack trees based on graph theory [15]. They provide a very good understanding of the formalism, various extensions (like attack-defense trees [16] and differentiations of the operators (like sequential conjunction (SAND) versus parallel conjunction [4]) and are amply documented in the literature. These theories for attack trees provide a thorough foundation for the formalism and its semantics. The main problem that adds complexity to the semantical models is the abstractness of the descriptions in the nodes. This leads to a variety of approaches to the semantics, e.g. propositional semantics, multiset semantics, and equational semantics for ADtrees [16]. The theoretical foundations allow comparison of different semantics, and provide a theoretical framework to develop evaluation algorithms for the quantification of attacks.

Surprisingly, the use of an automated proof assistant, like Isabelle, has not been considered despite its potential of providing a theory and mechanised analysis of attacks simultaneously. The essential attack tree mechanism of tree refinement is relatively simple. The complexity in the theories available in the literature is caused by the attempt to incorporate semantics to the attack nodes and relate the trees to actual scenarios. This is why we consider the formalisation of a foundation of attack trees in the interactive prover Isabelle since it supports logical modeling and definitions of datatypes very akin to algebraic specification but directly supported by semi-automated analysis and proof tools. There have already been attempts at formalising attack trees for specific application domains in the interactive theorem prover Isabelle [10] (for IoT Insider attacks). They are also based on the Isabelle Insider framework but support only the use of axiomatized "attack vectors" derived from real Insider attacks. It is necessary to assume these attack vectors to provide the semantics of attack tree refinement. Clearly, in state based systems, attacks correspond to paths of attack steps. Hence, it is quite obvious to use a modelchecking approach to analyse attack trees. In fact, implementations like the ADTool [17] use modelchecking based on the guarded command language *gal* to analyse scenarios expressed as graphs. Surprisingly, again, it has not been considered to use a logical framework powerful enough to emulate modelchecking to augment this natural approach to modeling and analysing attack trees. The modelchecking approach brings the additional advantage of exploring and thus finding possibilities of attack refinements necessary for the attack tree development. If embedded within an interactive theorem prover, the integration of the formalism can be applied to case studies and meta-theory can be proved with the additional support and safety guarantees of a proof assistant.

The presented foundation of attack trees in Isabelle is consistent with the existing foundations [4,15,16] but instead of providing an on paper mathematical foundation it provides a direct formalisation in Higher Order Logic in the proof assistant. This enables the application of the resulting framework to case studies and does not necessitate a separate implementation of the mathematical foundation in a dedicated tool. Clearly, the Isabelle framework is less efficient and the application to case studies requires user interaction. However, the formalisation in Isabelle supports not only the application of the formalised theory but furthermore the consistent development of meta-theorems. In addition, dedicated proof automation by additional proof of supporting lemmas is straightforward and even code generation is possible for executable parts of the formalisation.

Again in comparison to the existing foundation [4,15,16], the presented attack tree framework is restricted. For example, it does not yet support disjunctive attacks nor attack-defense trees, i.e., the integration of defenses within the attack tree. We are convinced that this is a straightforward future development and will be provided in due course.

Acknowledgement. Part of the research leading to these results has received funding from the European Union (CHIST-ERA 2015) under grant agreement no. 102112 (SUCCESS). This publication reflects only the authors' views and the Union is not liable for any use that may be made of the information contained herein.

References

1. Chen, T., Kammüller, F., Nemli, I., Probst, C.W.: A probabilistic analysis framework for malicious insider threats. In: Tryfonas, T., Askoxylakis, I. (eds.) HAS 2015. LNCS, vol. 9190, pp. 178–189. Springer, Cham (2015). doi:10.1007/978-3-319-20376-8_16

2. CHIST-ERA: Success: secure accessibility for the internet of things (2016). http://www.chistera.eu/projects/success

3. Hempel, C.G., Oppenheim, P.: Studies in the logic of explanation. Philos. Sci. **15**, 135–175 (1948)

4. Jhawar, R., Kordy, B., Mauw, S., Radomirović, S., Trujillo-Rasua, R.: Attack trees with sequential conjunction. In: Federrath, H., Gollmann, D. (eds.) SEC 2015. IAICT, vol. 455, pp. 339–353. Springer, Cham (2015). doi:10.1007/978-3-319-18467-8_23

5. Henrio, L., Kammüller, F., Rivera, M.: An asynchronous distributed component model and its semantics. In: Boer, F.S., Bonsangue, M.M., Madelaine, E. (eds.) FMCO 2008. LNCS, vol. 5751, pp. 159–179. Springer, Heidelberg (2009). doi:10.1007/978-3-642-04167-9_9

6. Kammüller, F.: Isabelle insider framework with attack trees and modelchecking (2016). https://www.dropbox.com/sh/rx8d09pf31cv8bd/AAALKtaP8HMX642fi04Og4NLa?dl=0

7. Kammüller, F.: Isabelle modelchecking for insider threats. In: Livraga, G., Torra, V., Aldini, A., Martinelli, F., Suri, N. (eds.) DPM/QASA -2016. LNCS, vol. 9963, pp. 196–210. Springer, Cham (2016). doi:10.1007/978-3-319-47072-6_13

8. Kammüller, F., Kerber, M.: Investigating airplane safety and security against insider threats using logical modeling. In: IEEE Security and Privacy Workshops, Workshop on Research in Insider Threats, WRIT 2016. IEEE (2016)

9. Kammüller, F., Kerber, M., Probst, C.W.: Towards formal analysis of insider threats for auctions. In: 8th ACM CCS International Workshop on Managing Insider Security Threats, MIST 2016. ACM (2016)

10. Kammüller, F., Nurse, J.R.C., Probst, C.W.: Attack tree analysis for insider threats on the IoT using Isabelle. In: Tryfonas, T. (ed.) HAS 2016. LNCS, vol. 9750, pp. 234–246. Springer, Cham (2016). doi:10.1007/978-3-319-39381-0_21

11. Kammüller, F., Paulson, L.C.: A formal proof of sylow's theorem. J. Autom. Reason. **23**(3), 235–264 (1999)

12. Kammüller, F., Probst, C.W.: Invalidating policies using structural information. In: IEEE Security and Privacy Workshops, Workshop on Research in Insider Threats, WRIT 2013. IEEE (2013)

13. Kammüller, F., Probst, C.W.: Combining generated data models with formal invalidation for insider threat analysis. In: IEEE Security and Privacy Workshops, Workshop on Research in Insider Threats, WRIT 2014. IEEE (2014)

14. Kammüller, F., Probst, C.W.: Modeling and verification of insider threats using logical analysis. IEEE Syst. J. (2016). Special Issue on Insider Threats to Information Security, Digital Espionage, and Counter Intelligence

15. Kordy, B., Pitre-Cambacds, L., Schweitzer, P.: Dag-based attack and defense modeling: don't miss the forest for the attack trees. Comput. Sci. Rev. **13–14**, 1–38 (2014)

16. Kordy, B., Mauw, S., Radomirovic, S., Schweitzer, P.: Attack-defense trees. J. Logic Comput. **24**(1), 55–87 (2014). Oxford Journals

17. Kordy, B., Kordy, P., Mauw, S., Schweitzer, P.: ADTool: security analysis with attack-defense trees (extended version). CoRR abs/1305.6829 (2013). http://arxiv.org/abs/1305.6829

18. Probst, C.W., Kammüller, F., Hansen, R.R.: Formal modelling and analysis of socio-technical systems. In: Probst, C.W., Hankin, C., Hansen, R.R. (eds.) Semantics, Logics, and Calculi. LNCS, vol. 9560, pp. 54–73. Springer, Cham (2016). doi:10.1007/978-3-319-27810-0_3

19. Schneier, B., Secrets, L.: Digital Security in a Networked World. Wiley, Hoboken (2004)

Sharing or Non-sharing Credentials: A Study of What Motivates People to Be Malicious Insiders

Koichi Niihara[1(✉)], Michihiro Yamada[2], and Hiroaki Kikuchi[2]

[1] Meiji University Graduate School, Tokyo, Japan
niihara@meiji.ac.jp
[2] School of Interdisciplinary Mathematical Sciences, Meiji University, Tokyo, Japan

Abstract. The problem of an insider threat is a serious concern within organizations. It has been said that the weakest link in information security is the human element. Various causes of insider threats have been hypothesized. However, because there are so many potential causes of malicious insider threats, which factor has the greatest influence in inducing such threats remains unclear. In this paper, we focus on the most significant factor: *sharing credentials*. The objective of our study is to clarify the influence on the occurrence of malicious activities based on whether a credential is shared and whether a login ID is used. We conducted an experiment on a crowdsourcing service, Crowdworks, Inc., consisting of 198 participants to examine human behavior when attempting to perform malicious activities. Our results show that a non-indicated login ID has a statistically significant effect.

Keywords: Insider threat · Sharing credentials · Information breach

1 Introduction

Today, one of the biggest challenges faced by organizations is system misuse by insiders, and these actions can have a serious impact on organizations. It has been said that the weakest link in information security is the human element because insiders' behaviors rapidly change and are therefore difficult to predict. Insiders have the potential to cause serious damage to, and even threaten the existence of, an organization.

In order to detect malicious behaviors, many studies have been conducted from a human-computer interactive perspective [1–4]. Fagade and Tryfonas conducted a survey of IT professionals, managers and employees selected from a Nigerian bank and proposed ways in which information security could be embedded into security culture [5]. Classifying behaviors into two classes, positive and negative, Hausawi conducted interviews with security experts and identified a total of 21 negative and 15 positive security-related behaviors [6]. These survey-based studies are very useful for understanding insider behaviors and identifying possible features in relation to malicious activities. However, survey and interview responses are not always true, e.g., participants can pretend to be honest

© Springer International Publishing AG 2017
T. Tryfonas (Ed.): HAS 2017, LNCS 10292, pp. 353–365, 2017.
DOI: 10.1007/978-3-319-58460-7_25

and unintentionally protective of their organization. Moreover, it is not feasible to observe every step of a potential insider who intends to perform a malicious action.

To address the drawbacks of survey-based studies, we propose a new experiment-based study to explore key behaviors related to insider threats. Our study allows the risk posed to be quantified by arbitrary conditions. In the present study, we observed all actions made by a set of participants engaging in small pre-defined tasks from a website and counted the number of cheating behaviors they made that might be linked to insider threats.

Among 21 negative behaviors considered to be security concerns [6], we focus on the most significant: *sharing credentials*. For example, suppose a credential (e.g., an ID and password) is shared within a group to access a resource. The members of this group should be considered a more likely potential insider threat than a group whose members do not share such credentials.

It is impossible to observe the details of suspicious behavior, and it is difficult to conduct an experiment in an actual organization because of security policies. If participants are paid for their labor, they might not attempt to perform a malicious action. However, if participants are not paid enough, it is difficult to recruit an adequate sample.

To test our hypothesis, we conducted an experiment in which all participants in one group shared a single credential for logging in and working on a crowdsourcing service, Crowdworks, Inc., while participants in another group were each assigned individual credentials for the same task.

A total of 192 participants were included in the experiment. We compared differences in the number of malicious activities performed between the sharing and individual credential groups. Moreover, we examined the effects of using indicated (visible) vs. non-indicated (hidden) IDs for the website. We assumed that the group using non-indicated IDs would perform significantly fewer malicious activities than the group using non-indicated IDs.

The remainder of this paper is organized as follows. We describe the objectives of the paper and details of our experiments in Sect. 3. We summarize our results and give a discussion in Sect. 4. Our conclusions and plans for future works are presented in Sect. 5.

2   Related Works

For our related works, we consider studies regarding research on insider threats.

Capplli *et al.* classified insider threats into three sections: insider IT sabotage, insider theft of intellectual property, and insider fraud [7]. The present work deals with insider fraud.

Cohen and Felson [1] presented the 'routine activity theory', which argues that most crimes have three necessary conditions: a likely offender, a suitable target, and the absence of a capable guardian. Cressey [2] proposed the Fraud Triangle model to explain the factors present in every fraud situation: perceived pressure, perceived opportunity, and rationalization. Greitzer *et al.* [3,4] provided some indicators of insider threats based on published case studies and discussions with experienced human resources professionals. According to these studies, various hypothesized causes of insider threats exist. However, because there are so many potential causes of malicious insider threats, which ones have the greatest effect on insider behavior remains unclear.

Capplli *et al.* proposed MERIT related to insider threats based on investigations of criminal records [8]. Nurse *et al.* proposed a framework for characterizing insider attacks [9]. Their models are convenient for administrators in solving the problems and analyzing the risks associated with insider threats. We demonstrated experimentally that placing participants in environments with low levels of surveillance is more likely to lead to insider threats [10]. Hausawi conducted an interview study to survey security experts about the behavior of end-users [6]. According to these studies, the most negative behavior is sharing credentials. However, how much sharing credentials increases the risk of insider threats remains unclear.

In this paper, we investigate the relationship between sharing credentials and the risk of malicious insider threats.

3   Experiment to Observe Malicious Activities

3.1   Objective

The objective of our study was to clarify the influence of sharing credentials on the performance of malicious activities. We also aimed to clarify the influence of using indicated IDs for working on a website.

3.2   Hypotheses

We make two hypotheses related to malicious activities. Let H_1, and H_2 be the hypothesized causes of insider threats of sharing credentials and using a non-indicated ID, defined as follows:

H_1 (sharing credentials) states that if an employee shares a common credential with others, then he/she will be a malicious insider.

H_2 (non-indicated ID) states that if an employee finds that no login ID is displayed on the website, then he/she will be a malicious insider.

3.3   Method

In order to test these hypotheses, we conducted an experiment for observing potential insider threats using a pseudo website as the environment. A total of 192 participants were recruited to use a crowdsourcing service, Crowdworks, Inc. They were then divided into four groups, A, B, C, and D, and assigned conditions, as defined in Table 1.

Table 1. Study groups and conditions.

Group	Credentials	Login ID	N
A	Sharing	Non-indicated	45
B	Individual		47
C	Sharing	Indicated	48
D	Individual		52

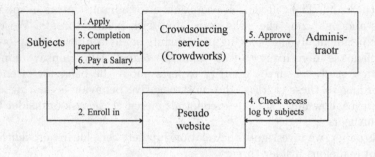

Fig. 1. Flow diagram of the experiment.

Figure 1 shows a flow diagram of the experiment. First, the participants answered a questionnaire composed of 14 items and performed data entry. When the participant finished his/her task, he/she would send a completion report. After we verified and approved the participant's access log, they were paid by the crowdsourcing service.

3.4 Participants

In our experiment, our target population was a set of employees in Japan. An employee subset was sampled from those who had completed the tasks in our experiment and were qualified users of the crowdsourcing service.

To improve the quality of the participants, we recruited only those who had submitted the necessary forms of identification to the company. The participants chosen from the crowdsourcing service were appropriate for our experiment because they had various attributes that were similar to normal employees.

3.5 Groups

In order to test H_1 (sharing credentials), the participants in groups A and C shared a common credential, such as a "guest" account, while those in groups B and D used individual credentials, such as user "93607".

In order to test H_2 (non-indicated ID), we did not indicate credentials to groups A or B, but we did to groups C and D.

In this way, we assigned a different malicious insider condition to participants in each group. We were interested in how many malicious activities would be observed in each group. In this experiment, we attempted to identify the primary causes of malicious activities by insiders.

3.6 Tasks

First, the participants confirmed the terms of use shown in the pseudo website. For details of the terms of service, see the Appendix A. Next, the participants answered a questionnaire composed of six questions, performed data entry, and then answered a questionnaire composed of seven questions. The participants entered text identical to that in two sample PDF documents written in Japanese and English. For details of the survey and the data entry jobs, see the Appendix B. Finally, the participants completed the tasks.

In order to observe the responses of participants who had trouble performing their tasks, we intentionally inserted a fault in the questionnaire in that the website would never accept the response to Question 6. Participants tried to resolve this issue in one of two ways:

- "edit" button prepared for an administrator (prohibited for participants)
- "help" button (correct response)

3.7 Obstacles

Malicious activities were not performed very frequently. Hence, we intentionally included some obstacles that would make participants choose whether to perform their tasks in a prohibited way.

Unacceptable Question 6. After the participants answered 13 questions and carried out data entry, they felt that they had completed all tasks. However, they would then receive the following warning message: 'You have not yet finished Question 6'. The reason for this error is that the system does not ask them Question 6.

To complete their task, the participants could deal with the problem in the following ways:

"Help" Page. If participants accessed the help page, they would be asked to answer 13 questions, after which, they would be regarded as having completed all tasks.

"Edit Button" for Question 6. If participants clicked the "edit" button for Question 6 in an attempt to modify it, this was labeled as a "malicious activity" because it was prohibited in the terms of use.

Synthesized Text of PDF Document. The pseudo business website gives synthesized text to participants who engage in data entry jobs.

For details of the text, see the Appendix B.2. The text looks like meaningless sentences that no one would want to read.

These are aimed at reducing the motivation of the participants and encouraging them to perform more malicious activities than usual.

3.8 Malicious Activities

Malicious activities were detected based on accurate logs that list what activities have been performed, at what time, and by whom. We defined the following malicious activities as prohibited actions:

(1) Violation
    Gaining unauthorized access, e.g., clicking the administrator's edit button.
(2) Copy and paste
    Performing unauthorized activities, e.g., pressing the Ctrl+C or Ctrl+V key.
(3) Sabotage
    Inputting random or wrong text in the data entry website.
(4) Low score
    Answering the questions randomly. To test whether the participants answered the questions honestly, we repeated the same questions twice in random order and then checked the consistency. We evaluated the consistency score S_i, which was defined as follows:
    (a) In the case of a single-response questionnaire, if the first answer is equal to the second, we add 10 points to S_i.
    (b) In the case of a multiple-response questionnaire, if two answers are consistent, we add 25 points to S_i. However, 5 points are deducted for each inconsistent answer.
    Five single-response and two multiple-response questionnaire were provided. The highest possible consistency score S_i was 100.

3.9 Methods of Detection

We used a php script to detect malicious activity. We used javascript to detect malicious behavior such as pressing the Ctrl+C or Ctrl+V key or copying and pasting by right-clicking. We manually analyzed the website log, all survey answers and all input text in the database. Table 2 shows the relationship between malicious activities and methods of detection.

Table 2. Relationship between malicious activities and methods of detection.

Malicious activities	Method of detection
(1) Violation	php script
(2) Copy and paste	javascript
(3) Sabotage	log analysis
(4) Low score	log analysis

4 Result

4.1 Demographic Characteristics of the Participants

Table 3 shows the demographic characteristics of the participants in each group, where N is the number of users in each group. Note that the numbers of participants in a group were not always identical, e.g., there were slightly fewer participants in group A than in group D. This was because we assigned participants to each group in turn, and some participants did not complete the task, resulting in uneven group sizes.

Table 3. Number of users.

Group		A	B	C	D	Total
Sex	Male	18	21	18	21	78
	Female	27	26	30	31	114
Age (years)	under 19	1	1	2	1	5
	20–29	13	14	9	12	48
	30–39	13	16	16	25	70
	40–49	11	12	19	10	52
	50–59	6	4	0	4	14
	60–69	1	0	2	0	3
Job	Office worker	10	16	8	18	52
	Proprietor	11	4	11	10	36
	Student	5	4	4	3	16
	Homemaker	9	7	13	8	37
	Part-time employee	4	9	7	6	26
	None	3	2	4	4	13
	Other	3	5	1	3	12
N		45	47	48	52	192

4.2 Number of Users Who Performed Malicious Activities

Table 4 shows the number of malicious users who performed malicious activities in our experiment. The number of users N is the sum of the two groups in the same category. For example, the number of users sharing credentials are the sum of A and C. In the sharing credentials group, 28 of 93 users copied and pasted text by right-clicking. Surprisingly, more users in the individual credentials group copied and pasted text compared with the sharing credentials group. Similarly, more participants using indicated IDs were found to be performing malicious activities compared with those using non-indicated IDs ($n = 27$). Remarkably, the low scores (4) of some of the malicious participants of increased when they shared credentials within a group.

Table 4. Number of users who performed malicious activities.

Group	N	(1) Violation	(2) Copy and paste	(3) Sabotage	(4) Low score
Sharing credentials ($A+C$)	93	14	28	6	20
Individual credentials ($B+D$)	99	18	35	4	13
Non-indicated ID ($A+B$)	92	18	27	3	21
Indicated ID ($C+D$)	100	14	36	7	12

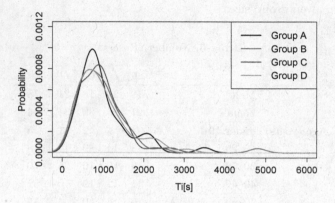

Fig. 2. Probability density function of elapsed time T_i for each group.

Figure 2 shows the probability density function of the elapsed time of the task T_i for each participant i. The elapsed time of task T_i is the difference between the starting and finishing times. A small difference was found between groups. Figure 3 shows the probability density function of the consistency score S_i for each group. Group A had the smallest average consistency.

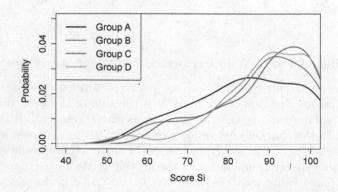

Fig. 3. Probability density function of score S_i for each group.

4.3   Chi-Square Test

To evaluate the confidence of our experimental results, we performed a chi-square test on the number of malicious activities for (1), (2), (3) and (4).

We had the following two hypotheses:

The null hypothesis (H_0): there is no correlation between the groups and malicious activity. Malicious activities are performed independent of the group condition.

The alternative hypothesis (H_1): there is a correlation between the hypothesized causes and malicious activity.

Table 5 shows the results of the chi-square test. The results show that low scores for malicious activities (4) were significantly more frequently observed when the website did not indicate a login ID. However, the P values for activities (1), (2) and (3) were too large to reject the null hypothesis. Therefore, we conclude that only (4), a low score, was dependent on whether IDs were indicated with 90% confidence.

4.4   Discussion

First, we consider the influence of non-indicated IDs on malicious behavior. Based on Table 5, a low score (4) for malicious activities depended on the non-indicated ID condition. If no login ID was shown on the website, more malicious activities were performed. We therefore conclude that people do not stay motivated to work when no login ID is indicated.

Second, we observed that too many malicious activities occurred in terms of clicking the edit button. As we explained in Sect. 3.7, Question 6 was designed to not be answerable in order to tempt potential malicious participants to click the "edit button". However, almost all participants clicked the "edit" button. We therefore believe that the participants clicked the button innocently without realizing that it was a prohibited activity. Alternatively, careless participants simply failed to notice this rule in the terms of use. Since it was useless to identify

Table 5. Chi-square test results

Hypotheses	Malicious activity	χ^2	df	P value
H_1 (Sharing credentials)	(1) Violation	0.1502	1	0.698
	(2) Copy and paste	0.3843	1	0.535
	(3) Sabotage	0.1819	1	0.669
	(4) Low score	1.8108	1	0.178
H_2 (Non-indicated ID)	(1) Violation	0.7054	1	0.401
	(2) Copy and paste	0.6837	1	0.408
	(3) Sabotage	0.7053	1	0.401
	(4) Low score	3.2217	1	0.073*

the hypothesized causes of malicious behavior, we excluded these activities in our analysis.

Finally, we remark on the relationship between individual and temporal credentials. In our experiment, we expected that users who were assigned individual credentials would perform fewer malicious activities. However, they might not have regard themselves as having individual credentials very seriously because they were only for one-time use. If we had assigned more permanent credentials, such as Social Security Numbers, the participants may have viewed them as being more serious.

5   Conclusions

In the present study, based on a survey of research related to insider threats, we focused on the occurrence of malicious activities under the condition of sharing or individual credentials. To clarify the effects, we conducted an experiment involving 198 participants who performed a small task to observe malicious activity. We observed significantly more malicious activity when a user ID was not indicated compared with when it was. However, unexpectedly, users who were sharing credentials did not perform more malicious activities than users who had individual credentials.

In future research, we plan to investigate the reasons underlying the differences seen in the number of malicious activities performed in accordance with the conditions of malicious insiders.

A   Terms of Use

– Terms of use
  A record of your visit and attributes will only be used for research purposes. We do not identify the user, and we will only publish the processed data in a research paper. Appropriate safety control measures have been carried out for all information on this site.
– Things to note
  Please read the questionnaire carefully before answering the survey.
– Prohibited actions
  • In survey tasks
    * Clicking the "back" button
    * Visiting the website by directly specifying the URL
  • In data entry tasks
    * Copying and pasting by right-clicking or pressing the Ctrl+C or Ctrl+V key
  • In both tasks
    * Clicking the edit button intended for the administrator
– Inquiries
  If something is unclear or you experience trouble during the task, please access the inquiry page to contact the administrator.

B Contents of Tasks

B.1 Survey Tasks

- Question 1. How often do you eat curry and rice?
  A.1. 7 or more times per week. A.2. 5–6 times per week A.3. 3–4 times per week A.4. 1–2 times per week A.5. 2–3 times per month A.6. Once per month A.7. Less than once per month
- Question 2. What is your favorite type of curry and rice?
  A.1. Curry and rice cooked by your family A.2. Indian curry served in an Indian restaurant A.3. Curry and rice served in a Japanese curry restaurant A.4. Ready-to-eat curry A.5. Curry and rice served in a family or beef bowl restaurant
- Question 3. What is your favorite ingredient in curry and rice?
  A.1. Pork A.2. Chicken A.3. Beef A.4. Vegetables A.5. Seafood
- Question 4. What is your favorite ingredient related to fruits or vegetables in curry and rice?
  A.1. Potatoes A.2. Onions A.3. Cheese A.4. Apples A.5. Eggplant
- Question 5. How long do you continue eating leftover curry and rice made by your family?
  A.1. The same day only A.2. Until the next day A.3. Up to 3 days after A.4. Up to 5 days after A.5. Up to 7 days after A.6. More than a week after
- Question 6. What is the most important aspect of curry and rice?
  A.1. Spiciness A.2. Sweetness A.3. Fragrance A.4. Depth of flavor (Koku in Japanese) A.5. Deliciousness (Umami in Japanese)
- Question 7. How much do you spend on one curry and rice meal at a restaurant?
  A.1. Less than 500 yen A.2. 500–749 yen A.3. 750–999 yen A.4. 1,000–1,499 yen A.5. 1,500–1,999 yen A.6. 2,000–4,999 yen A.7. 5,000 yen or more

The following questions contain the same contents, but the order of the answers has been changed.

- Question 8. What is your favorite ingredient in curry and rice?
  A.1. Pork A.2. Beef A.3. Vegetables A.4. Chicken A.5. Seafood
- Question 9. What is your favorite ingredient related to fruits or vegetables in curry and rice?
  A.1. Onions A.2. Potatoes A.3. Eggplant A.4. Apples A.5. Cheese
- Question 10. What is the most important aspect of curry and rice?
  A.1. Fragrance A.2. Spiciness A.3. Depth of flavor (Koku in Japanese) A.4. Sweetness A.5. Deliciousness (Umami in Japanese)
- Question 11. How often do you eat curry and rice?
  A.1. Less than once per month A.2. Once per month A.3. 2–3 times per month A.4. 1–2 times per week A.5. 3–4 times per week A.6. 5–6 times per week A.7. 7 or more times per week

- Question 12. How much do you spend on one curry and rice meal at a restaurant?
  A.1. 5,000 yen or more A.2. 2,000–4,999 yen A.3. 1,500–1,999 yen A.4. 1,000–1,499 yen A.5. 750–999 yen A.6. 500–749 yen A.7. Less than 500 yen
- Question 13. What is your favorite type of curry and rice?
  A.1. Indian curry served in an Indian restaurant A.2. Curry and rice served in a Japanese curry restaurant A.3. Ready-to-eat curry A.4. Curry and rice served in a family or beef bowl restaurant A.5. Curry and rice cooked by your family
- Question 14. How long do you continue eating leftover curry and rice made by your family?
  A.1. More than a week after A.2. Up to 7 days after A.3. Up to 5 days after A.4. Up to 3 days after A.5. Until the next day A.6. The same day only

B.2   Data Entry Task

- Please input the following text.
  Saffron is put in a water 1/2 cup, and avails oneself and takes out the color for about 30 min. I sharpen rice, give it to a basket and drain off water for about 20 min. The seafood blanched beforehand is moved to the pot and it's boiled for about 15 min.

References

1. Cohen, L.E., Felson, M.: Social change and crime rate trends: a routine activity approach. Am. Sociol. Rev. **44**(4), 588–608 (1979)
2. Cressey, D.R.: Other People's Money: A Study in the Social Psychology of Embezzlement. Free Press, Glencoe (1953)
3. Greitzer, F.L., et al.: Identifying at-risk employees: modeling psychosocial precursors of potential insider threats. In: 2012 45th Hawaii International Conference on System Sciences, pp. 2392–2401 (2012)
4. Greitzer, F.L., Frincke, D.A.: Combining traditional cyber security audit data with psychosocial data: towards predictive modeling for insider threat mitigation. Insider Threats Cyber Secur. **49**, 85–113 (2010)
5. Fagade, T., Tryfonas, T.: Security by compliance? A study of insider threat implications for Nigerian banks. In: Tryfonas, T. (ed.) HAS 2016. LNCS, vol. 9750, pp. 128–139. Springer, Cham (2016). doi:10.1007/978-3-319-39381-0_12
6. Hausawi, Y.M.: Current trend of end-users' behaviors towards security mechanisms. In: Tryfonas, T. (ed.) HAS 2016. LNCS, vol. 9750, pp. 140–151. Springer, Cham (2016). doi:10.1007/978-3-319-39381-0_13
7. Cappelli, D., Moore, A., Trzeciak, R.: The CERT Guide to Insider Threats: How to Prevent, Detect, and Respond to Information Technology Crimes (Theft, Sabotage, Fraud). Addison-Wesley Professional, Boston (2012)
8. Cappelli, D., et al.: Management and Education of the Risk of Insider Threat (MERIT): System Dynamics Modeling of Computer System. Software Engineering Institute, Carnegie Mellon University (2008)

9. Nurse, J.R.C., et al.: Understanding insider threat: a framework for characterising attacks. In: 2014 IEEE Security and Privacy Workshops (SPW 2014), San Jose, CA, pp. 214–228 (2014)
10. Niihara, K., Kikuchi, H.: Primary factors of malicious insider in e-learning model. In: Stephanidis, C. (ed.) HCI 2016. CCIS, vol. 617, pp. 482–487. Springer, Cham (2016). doi:10.1007/978-3-319-40548-3_80

An Assessment of the Security and Transparency Procedural Components of the Estonian Internet Voting System

Jason R.C. Nurse[1]([✉]), Ioannis Agrafiotis[1], Arnau Erola[1], Maria Bada[1,2],
Taylor Roberts[1,2], Meredydd Williams[1], Michael Goldsmith[1,2],
and Sadie Creese[1,2]

[1] Department of Computer Science, University of Oxford, Oxford, UK
jason.nurse@cs.ox.ac.uk
[2] Global Cyber Security Capacity Centre,
University of Oxford, Oxford, UK

Abstract. The I-Voting system designed and implemented in Estonia is one of the first nationwide Internet voting systems. Since its creation, it has been met with praise but also with close scrutiny. Concerns regarding security breaches have focused on in-person election observations, code reviews and adversarial testing on system components. These concerns have led many to conclude that there are various ways in which insider threats and sophisticated external attacks may compromise the integrity of the system and thus the voting process. In this paper, we examine the procedural components of the I-Voting system, with an emphasis on the controls related to procedural security mechanisms, and on system-transparency measures. Through an approach grounded in primary and secondary data sources, including interviews with key Estonian election personnel, we conduct an initial investigation into the extent to which the present controls mitigate the real security risks faced by the system. The experience and insight we present in this paper will be useful both in the context of the I-Voting system, and potentially more broadly in other voting systems.

Keywords: E-voting · Cybersecurity · Transparency · Procedural controls · Human factors · Practical experiences

1 Introduction

Electronic voting (or e-voting) is widely understood as the use of electronic means to record, process or tally votes. As the use of the Internet has become a central part of modern society, several countries have looked to apply Internet technologies to support the e-voting process. Nations that have utilised some form of Internet voting include the US, Canada, Estonia, and India [1]. The first state to allow online voting nationwide was Estonia, in 2005, via their I-Voting system. This platform is aimed specifically at taking advantage of the numerous

© Springer International Publishing AG 2017
T. Tryfonas (Ed.): HAS 2017, LNCS 10292, pp. 366–383, 2017.
DOI: 10.1007/978-3-319-58460-7_26

benefits of online voting such as increased efficiency and accessibility, but also at providing a secure and reliable voting platform and process.

While some observers hail Estonia's success in Internet voting, their I-Voting system has also come under close scrutiny [2–4]. Security concerns have drawn on in-person election observations, code reviews, adversarial testing on system components, and topics such as the impact of infected voter computers and the lack of end-to-end verification. Some articles have sought to demonstrate these potential problems using simulated examples of attack payloads and patterns to compromise the electoral process [3]. Others point to the fact that integrity should be supported by technological means rather than a complex set of manual checks and procedures [4]. The sum of these assessments has led to some parties concluding that there are multiple ways in which insider threats, sophisticated criminals or nation-state attackers could successfully compromise the I-Voting system.

In this article, we reflect on the Estonian I-Voting system in light of such concerns in order to evaluate how vulnerable it may be to cyber-attacks, intentional or accidental. We limit our scope to *procedural* security components, and thus do not address purely technical issues, such as those pertaining to software engineering or encryption details. Our aim is to consider: firstly, the extent to which procedural controls employed may be adequate to protect against attacks; and secondly the extent to which the existing transparency measures are able to provide confidence in the security of the I-Voting system. This focus on procedural components is guided by the fact that the principles underpinning a secure and democratic online voting system often create conflicting requirements [5]. These conflicts have been deemed impossible to be resolved by software engineering alone [6], hence the need for and importance of broader procedural controls. Such controls are particularly crucial in the Estonian I-Voting system and its processes.

The structure of this paper is as follows: Sect. 2 presents an overview of the I-Voting system, including where key procedures feature and the properties that they seek to guarantee. Next, in Sect. 3, we present the methodology that we adopt. This is heavily based on interviews with key individuals involved in Estonian elections; this is also where our work is particularly insightful as it engages with, and triangulates data from, various officials so as to gain detailed insights into previous elections. Section 4 then presents, reflects on, and discusses our findings regarding the security offered by the procedural components of the I-Voting system, as well as highlighting areas for further improvement. Finally, in Sect. 5, we conclude our report.

2   The Estonian I-Voting System

Estonia is one of the most experienced countries in the world in practising electronic democracy. While there was a slow start in the local elections of 2005 with only 1.9% of votes cast using the I-Voting system, in the 2015 parliamentary elections 30.5% of votes were cast online [7]. The I-Voting system that is used for elections consists of four main components: the I-Voting Client Application (IVCA), the Vote Forwarding Server (VFS), the Vote Storage Server (VSS) and the Vote Counting Application (VCA) [6]. The IVCA is an application released for each election that allows voters to cast their votes using a personal computing device; to vote, citizens must be connected to the Internet and have either their national ID card or a mobile ID. The VFS is the only public-facing server of the system; it is responsible for authenticating voters as they vote via the IVCA, and forwarding the votes to the VSS. The VSS stores all votes which have been cast, including repeated ones. After the close of advance polls, it checks and removes the cancelled votes, and separates the outer encryption envelopes (which hold the voter identity) from inner envelopes (which contain the vote cast).

Finally, the VCA, an offline and air-gapped server, is loaded with the valid votes. This loading is achieved via a DVD which allows votes to be securely passed from the VSS to the VCA. Next, votes are decrypted with the private key possessed by members of the National Electoral Committee (NEC), and the VCA then tabulates the votes and outputs the results. To assist the NEC in the organisation and running of the Internet voting process, in 2011 the Electronic Voting Committee was established.

Security has been a core consideration in the I-Voting system since its inception in 2005. There are a number of reports discussing the security features of the system, but one of the most comprehensive is that of the Estonian NEC [8]. Their report provides descriptions of detailed security measures on: how they ensure that the architectural components of the system will not be compromised; information on audit, monitoring, incident-handling and recovery practices; and operational measures (such as the distribution of tasks and formal procedures on managing risks) that complement technical security tools to ensure that a breach of policies is deterred. There are several key procedures to achieve these measures, including: independent auditors to verify that security procedures are followed by election officials; documented procedures for the generation and management of election keys; procedures for submitting and handling voting-related complaints and disputes; and strategies for responding to incidents or suspicious occurrences detected during online voting [6,8].

While these procedures may go some way to address the security and privacy concerns of the system, as mentioned in Sect. 1 there are still many criticisms of the level of security of the I-Voting's system. To address these concerns, Estonian officials and software developers have made several modifications to the system over its lifetime. For instance, a method to verify that a vote has been cast-as-intended and recorded-as-cast has been implemented [9]. Moreover, facilities for in-depth monitoring of the voting platform have been established to allow detection of attacks on a server and system malfunctions. In addition, this monitoring enables the retrospective study of voter behaviour and issues that may have been encountered in using the system [10].

One of the most notable features of I-Voting is that large parts of the system source code, as well as full documentation on protocols and procedures, have been made publicly available [11]. The various features mentioned here and

those above seek to bring I-Voting closer to fundamental constitutional requirements of the voting process, i.e., generality, freedom, equality, secrecy, direct-
ness and democracy [5], with security added to ensure that these principles are
safeguarded.

3   Methodology for Research Study

Our method to assess the procedures for maintaining security and transparency
in the I-Voting system consists of three main stages. The first stage involves a
reflection on the I-Voting system and related electronic-voting literature. This
includes reviewing all publicly available documentation (e.g., on procedures) on
the system, and its challenges and weaknesses, both self-reported and those identified through independent assessments. This review allows us to gain insight into
the system and also to contextualise the procedural and transparency mechanisms in order to scope our assessment.

The next stage of our methodology involves the planning and conducting of
semi-structured interviews with key individuals involved in Estonian elections.
Our line of questioning is designed specifically to examine many of the issues
identified in our prior review. Questions cover reported voting concerns, unre-
solved challenges, and areas where we believe there might be security or transparency weaknesses. For the interviews themselves, we have recruited seven individuals from Estonia with detailed knowledge of, and insight into, the I-Voting
system, including its design, administration, process aspects, security functions,
and operations in situ; this is the criterion for participation. The majority of
participants possess at least twelve years of experience with Internet voting and
elections in general. This experience and expertise, including each individual's
seniority in their respective organisation, is crucial to ensuring our assessment
is well-informed. While we appreciate that publishing the names and roles of
participants would support the credence and authority of our study, we opt for
anonymous reporting of interview commentaries and findings. The main reason
for this is to encourage honest and open responses, which would lead to more
insightful conclusions.

After conducting interviews with these experts (each lasting approximately
one hour), our final stage involves analysing the data using content analysis
and, more specifically, a mixture of deductive and inductive reasoning [12]. This
analysis leads to the identification of several core response themes related to the
main research areas. We then reflect critically on these themes, triangulate the
responses of individuals, and use these findings to guide the final assessment.

We believe that the pragmatic methodology we adopt – which is based on
primary and secondary data sources – and our emphasis on engaging with those
involved in Estonian elections is where our work has the most value. While
we accept that first-hand (i.e., our own) observation of security during actual
elections would also be ideal, our current method allows us to examine the state
of security via reports from people actually present during elections and those
with knowledge as to why certain security and transparency efforts may not be

in place. Moreover, we are able to uncover nuances in the election system which can help to better understand its apparent success, while also highlighting areas for future improvement. This could help inform future studies, for instance, in exploring the security of the next upcoming election.

4   Assessing I-Voting: Results and Discussion

In what follows, we present and discuss the findings from our analysis and the interviews. As the section progresses, we highlight areas where procedures of the I-Voting system are performing well (i.e., functioning as expected and addressing the targeted risk), and areas which could be improved. This assessment is structured according to the two topics identified in Sect. 1, i.e., procedural components for security and transparency respectively.

4.1   Procedural Security Components

Procedural security controls are core components of the I-Voting system. These controls define the main manual activities and practices that election officials engage in to protect the system from risks. Throughout the course of the interviews, procedural controls were discussed in a variety of contexts, but the following topics were the most salient in our findings: the key role of auditors in the election process; maintaining the security of the devices and equipment used during elections; processes pertaining to handling disputes and incidents; how election knowledge and know-how is maintained and transferred; and procedures to address the risk regarding voters and their context.

The Role of the Auditor: Procedural security controls were referred to directly and indirectly by several interviewees. The primary report documenting these controls is the election manual, and amongst other things, its aims are to ensure: (a) that data integrity between online and offline systems is maintained; (b) that access to election systems is regulated; and (c) that there are mechanisms for dispute resolution and system continuity. These aims would work in conjunction with the variety of technical mechanisms implemented.

Auditors play a key role in ensuring that those various security processes are followed, especially in relation to maintaining data integrity in elections. For instance, there are procedures set within I-Voting to ensure that two professionals serve as auditors to observe core processes. These include when the encryption keys for the election servers are being generated, or when election data is transferred from the online server (where votes are collected) to the offline server (where they are tallied). In these instances, auditors use the election manual to ensure that all tasks relating to the secure treatment of keys and data are followed as prescribed. As one interviewee stated, "... you had to trust... that this private key of the server is not somehow leaked... and making sure that this doesn't happen actually relies quite heavily on organisational measures".

From our analysis of such measures, we found the auditing procedures in place to be well considered, and thus might reduce the potential for malicious attacks (given that such attacks could be detected) and identify instances of human error in the conducting of procedures. This is especially helped by the fact that auditors are required to produce written reports – interim, and at the end of elections – regarding the compliance with procedures, which can be passed to the National Electoral Committee (NEC) for review or further investigation as necessary.

Devices and Equipment Used in the Electoral Process: Devices and equipment used in the electoral process are also governed by a number of procedures to mitigate potential attacks. For example, there are procedures to verify that the hardware is fit-for-purpose and malware-free, since as one interviewee stated, "[it may be] delivered to us deliberately modified to falsify our elections". From our assessment, we found existing procedural controls (such as drawing on an independent pre-voting expert analysis of system security) to be well thought out, but with a few caveats. For instance, while it is important that the experts employed have significant skills and experience in the system and security, a reality is that experts may miss severe problems [13].

An additional suggestion that we would make is for the analysis of the system to be conducted on a regular basis to account for any changes in the software and the changing threat landscape. Firmware-level malware checks are also becoming more important to mitigate the possibility of a sophisticated, and deeply-embedded attack. The concept of Advanced Persistent Threats, i.e., slow-moving and deliberate attacks applied to quietly compromise systems without revealing themselves [14], could be particularly relevant here. We highlight this given that there are increasing concerns about the ability of external parties to influence a country's elections [15].

In order to avoid physical attacks on the system (i.e., servers) and to generally maintain system resilience, we found that several security requirements have been identified for election facilities. For instance, when selecting facilities to host systems, one interviewee mentioned that there are strict "security measures of what this room must [have]" (i.e., security criteria that chosen facilities must fulfil). Given the importance of the server room, access to it is controlled, and in it, all server ports are covered with security seals (to prevent unauthorised server access) and regularly checked for tampering. Here, the tension of balancing transparency (in terms of allowing people to witness from close proximity the electoral process) and security is particularly evident, highlighting the importance of procedural controls, such as sealing the machines, to alleviate the conflict. We must note that while the use of security seals is encouraging, seals themselves are not a panacea and need to be carefully checked and of high quality to stand any chance of being effective [16].

To focus briefly on the individuals who have access to servers and the server room, interviewees mentioned that, "there are very specific people who can go [in] there". This highlights the requirement that only those adequately authorised can enter the server room. In our opinion, this was expected given the room's importance, but we were unable to verify whether any other checks are conducted to ensure that individuals cannot bring potentially malicious devices (e.g., infected pen drives) into the room. While attacks using such devices — whether purposeful or inadvertent — may be unlikely given the relationships and professional trust described by interviewees, the risk should be considered and addressed. For instance, there could be mandatory checks for unauthorised devices prior to entering secure areas and temporary confiscation of devices as required.

A good example of the issue regarding the presence of additional devices in secure areas has already been witnessed in prior elections (e.g., see [3]). In that case, system glitches reportedly prevented the use of DVDs to transfer voting data (votes for tallying) to the VCA, and as a fall-back, officials used a removable device. This behaviour was strictly against documented procedures and protocol, and could easily have resulted in system infection had the device been compromised. Preventing additional devices from entering these areas could act to reduce the likelihood of such attacks, and potentially deter less determined attackers. Moreover, there should be well-vetted (e.g., by the Electronic Voting Committee) and agreed procedures to handle instances where glitches prohibit the usual operations of the system. These procedures should also appreciate the perspective and intentions of observers as they witness deviations from documented protocol.

Handling Disputes and Incidents During the Electoral Period: Two related areas where we found procedures to be crucial were in the handling of disputes and incidents. To comment on dispute-resolution procedures first, we were pleased that there are very clear mechanisms to contest the validity of a vote or to make a complaint about some aspect of the election. According to one interview, in order to reach a speedy resolution of the dispute, the legal time-frames are as follows: three days to file a complaint, five days to resolve the issue, and another three days to contest the decision in the Supreme Court. These procedures have helped to minimise the risk posed by questionable actions, and have provided a formal mechanism for resolving disputes.

While these mechanisms are valuable, a challenge we discovered was that it can be difficult to submit a formal complaint, as the person submitting it would need to have knowledge of legislation regarding the I-Voting. This is due to the fact that complaints that do not follow a very strict structure and do not raise an argument regarding legislative discrepancies in the voting process are not considered. Upon querying this point, interviewees stated that the Electronic Voting Committee also has instituted an informal "notice" procedure that would enable a complaint to be submitted without knowledge of the I-Voting legislation. We view this as a significant addition and one that could increase accessibility and voter confidence in the system. The only other potential improvement that could be made is to encourage increased awareness and education of the legislation regarding I-Voting; but this may not be suitable (or of interest) for a majority of individuals.

With regards to the handling of incidents, we found that a core component of the Estonian voting system is its Incident Report Centre. This centre has two purposes: to address technical glitches reported to the client support centre, and to actively scan for anomalous behaviours in cooperation with the Computer Emergency Response Team (CERT) environment. Given the potential risk from significant threat actors, it is evident that Estonia relies on an effective CERT actively monitoring for attacks on the voting platform. From our interviews, we were especially encouraged to hear that once anomalies are registered, there are specific processes in place to address the issues appropriately, which may result in technicians being dispatched to the area of concern.

For instance, interviewees mentioned a case where a team was dispatched to a house suspected of spreading malware targeting voting applications. Although it transpired to be an elderly lady who knowingly voted more than 500 times, this case clearly demonstrates the capabilities of the incident response team to be deployed rapidly. Once incidents are identified, they are reported based on significance and severity to the NEC. The NEC may then decide to take further action and could ultimately request that affected citizens cast their vote using other means (e.g., paper ballots). This control is somewhat aggressive (i.e., it blocks further I-Voting votes for that election) but ensures that people who are facing problems voting electronically can still participate in a given election. The only other issue this raises is for people that are not within physical reach such as those outside of the country.

Procedural Controls and Knowledge Transfer: While procedural controls can arguably improve security, it is essential that they are properly managed and communicated. This relates to one of our main concerns, i.e., the sustainability of existing security procedures, particularly knowledge definition and transfer. When asked about incorporating lessons-learned from dispute resolution measures for example, one interviewee said, "if you're asking if we have some sort of formalised process for that then, no". Our interactions with interviewees made it clear that such information is generally incorporated in post-election reflections, however, there are few formal mechanisms to guide or ensure that incorporation. This may work well for a close-knit society such as that of Estonia; lack of procedural formality on the other hand does risk some aspects being inadvertently overlooked or forgotten. More broadly, this might also raise concerns about insider attacks, given that if procedures are not formalised and accessible to observers and auditors, that reduces the ability to monitor that they are being followed and that associated risks are being addressed. We would, therefore, strongly recommend that more formal procedures be put in place to facilitate the definition, assessment, transfer and persistence of election knowledge and know-how.

Staffing is another point worth considering in this general context. Given that most of the electoral staff have remained the same over time, in our interviews we noticed a general feeling that everyone already knows what to do. Indeed, one interviewee stated, "they already know what to do, so we don't go on details over it," i.e., some aspects of the system or processes. While it is advantageous to have a core set of professionals to rely upon, in our judgement the extent to which there are formalised procedures for staff training and knowledge sharing was unclear. This could be very important for knowledge-transfer generally and especially if future vote collection is outsourced, as one interviewee suggested it might be. Moving forward therefore, emphasis should be placed on ensuring that all procedures and security knowledge regarding the I-Voting process are fully documented and disseminated to ensure system sustainability.

Voter Technology and the Risks: Human voters and the technology they use to vote (e.g., PC, mobile) have been recognised as the most vulnerable link in the I-Voting system [8]. Interviewees generally agreed with this point, even stating, "e-voting [has been introduced] by accepting the risk that the voter is the weakest link [...] we cannot deny that many things can happen in the voter's computer". This highlights the fact that there is little chance to fully control the voter environment, albeit acknowledging that the system will "still depend on [it] being virus free". Herein lies the challenge therefore.

To avoid potentially malicious code-insertion attempts to compromise the voting system, input from public interfaces (e.g., voters) is thoroughly verified to ensure that "the elements of the digital signature are there, that the zip container is well formed". Moreover, the decrypted ballot is checked for compliance against rules that have been set to define valid ballots. These are commendable practices, as it is of crucial importance that malformed votes are removed before reaching the main systems (e.g., the VSS). In the past, technically-skilled voters have actually engineered the official application code "[to] change the [candidate] number to reflect a non-existent candidate or to write some completely garbled code and then they have encrypted this"; these may be regarded as protest votes. This ability to customise the content sent to the system is why checks on incoming votes are helpful, as they can assist in blocking attacks such as malware injection attempts, and thereby protect the security of the system.

Although a fundamental risk emanates from the voter's device, a large-scale attack affecting voter machines is considered highly unlikely by the NEC [8]. The risk is accepted because of the perceived low likelihood of undetected malware affecting a significant proportion of votes. Looking forward, however, we believe the probability of a large-scale attack to be higher. This is due to the increasing prevalence of malware infections impacting home users [17,18] and the shifting threat landscape towards attacking election systems [15].

Moreover, in the past, citizens in Estonia have used pirated, and thus potentially insecure [19], operating systems. We refer to an incident a few years ago where a significant number of Internet voters had issues voting. It transpired that the reason for this was that they were using the pirated version of Windows. This issue is especially worrying because as one interviewee recounted, "people who did not have official... Windows XP were not able to build up a secure channel between the application and the server. So some layers of security had to be changed on the first day. [...] we didn't expect that so many people would have [problems]". This therefore demonstrates the impact on system security.

If we extend this particular example, one can imagine an attacker exploiting a widespread use of pirated software in two ways. In one way, an attacker may insert malware into a pirated version of Windows (or another popular application), and promote this to Estonian citizens via bit-torrent applications or illegitimate third-party app stores. Or, a simpler way is to disguise malware as a legitimate files (e.g., software, games, apps, etc.) — a common practice as highlighted in [20] — and again, promote it to Estonian citizens. These are, of course, only thought experiments; however, determined attackers may find novel ways to exploit such situations, if only to cause havoc.

Also, while there are warnings on both the voter application and election websites advising voters to install anti-virus software (as seen in [21]), we believe that efforts should focus as well on larger issues including educating users about the perils of pirated or unsupported software. The Windows XP case may not be an isolated incident, and it would be prudent to plan for such potential issues, especially given Estonia's strides towards a digital society.

4.2 Transparency Measures

Transparency measures seek to provide insight into the I-Voting system and the way it functions, with the aim of building public trust and confidence. Our analysis of these measures explores three key areas: the auditing, observation and monitoring of the election process; the broad topic of public awareness of e-voting and secure practices; and the ability for voters to verify their votes.

Auditing, Observation, and Monitoring of the Election Process: The monitoring of the I-Voting process by auditors was one of the main transparency measures cited by interviewees. As discussed in Sect. 4.1, several independent auditors are contracted by the voting committee during an election period to provide feedback on the extent to which critical processes are followed. After elections, they provide a report with their findings, which is then published. Reflecting on this process, it is our opinion that the use of auditors and the publication of subsequent audit reports can act to increase trust in the I-Voting process. The only question that we would raise here is with regards to the extent to which these reports are publicly available and comprehensible to lay readers; the more accessible and easier to understand, the better. Although some reports suggest that they are accessible [3], others speak to the contrary [2].

In addition to auditors, observers drawn from the public are allowed to witness the election process. A press release before the elections invites the public and all political parties to observe the I-Voting process in situ. Anyone can serve as an observer; no formal vetting is undertaken, and the process is such that they can view elections in real-time and comment with suggestions and feedback. In our judgement, and considering earlier findings regarding procedural controls, we were especially interested in how such feedback was used by election officials. We were pleased to discover that there is a method to capture and reflect on this feedback, both during and after elections. One example of this is the change from the use of only formal complaints to less formal 'notice' procedures when issues are identified by observers or voters.

One challenge that we noted, which was also expressed by interviewees, was that observers often do not fully understand the voting system. The electoral committee is obliged to offer a two-day course for observers to learn the technical details, but attendance is low. Moreover, the majority of attendees do not complete the course, due to an overload of (often complex) information. This is an interesting conundrum yet to be addressed, since the manner in which the committee can communicate details to the public is rather restricted, due to political and party complexities. Certain parties believe that the I-Voting system is favoured by the government and influences the outcome of elections, therefore rendering any intervention as a political problem. As pointed out by interviewees, concerns regarding misleading the public may be raised if the technical details are simplified. An outstanding challenge, therefore, is to balance voter interest and political considerations. This is particularly important because some voters may not be interested in technical aspects, but still wish to understand how the system maintains standard voting requirements (as mentioned in [5]).

Publication of the system documentation is one of the most crucial transparency measures [6]. These documents cover topics from preparing the system, to conducting e-voting and final operational procedures. The filming of critical processes (e.g., server software installation) is also conducted for purposes of transparency. Speaking with reference to the server details, one interviewee mentioned, "... the screen of a computer is filmed as key procedures are performed... and 97% of the code used is also made public". Some of these videos have also been released post-election on YouTube for public consumption.

We view the publication of documents, code (particularly for community review) and videos as encouraging transparency measures that should be continued. However, as highlighted by other articles [3], better care must be taken to ensure security despite the pursuit of transparency. A perfect example of this issue is inadvertently exposing sensitive information (e.g., passwords) in published videos, or observers being able to take photos or film passwords themselves. Balancing security and transparency in such cases is not trivial, but careful planning and procedures (e.g., being aware of when sensitive data is being entered and protecting that data-entry) may allow for an adequate balance to be struck. Here, we need to note our finding that further procedural measures have been implemented to prohibit such issues and that videos are now uploaded online only after the elections have concluded.

With regard to the 3% of the code that is not published, we discovered that this is focused on malware detection and avoidance at the voter's machine, and therefore, publication would effectively defeat its purpose. We found two transparency procedures implemented to protect voters here. Firstly, the code is checked and audited by independent and trusted third parties, and secondly, the voting protocol is fully documented online and hence any individual (given the appropriate skills) could create their own compliant voting software. It is our view that these efforts by election officials are well-considered for the assessed risk, and they also demonstrate a notable impetus towards a transparent system. As the threat landscape shifts and adversaries become more determined, however, current practice around unpublished code will need to be revisited as security through obscurity is known to be ineffective [22].

E-voting Security and Awareness: Awareness is another important factor in supporting transparency. At its initial launch, the I-Voting system was heavily promoted to enable the public to understand the online voting process and the core aspects of security. As mentioned above, there is also a significant amount of detail on the system available online (e.g., NEC documents) [8,11]. In this way, trust might be built based on information and understanding. More recently, when the phone-based vote-verification application was released, there were media campaigns and articles explaining to the public how to engage with the new technology.

We noticed, however, that there does not appear to be a comprehensive, ongoing (that is, before and during elections) official campaign to promote secure online voting. Such a campaign should be grounded in best practice [23,24] and focused on raising public awareness of the range of risks as well as how they might be mitigated. For instance, mitigation via secure practices such as updating anti-virus solutions (though the current value of anti-virus might be debatable, it is a still a first line of defence [25]). We note the formal acceptance of the risk present with voter PCs (NEC) [8] and the mention of anti-virus software on the voting page, but still felt that more effort is required.

When we mentioned these points to interviewees, they reported that such campaigns were run in the past and are considered for the future, but there were political challenges with bespoke online voting campaigns. That is, such efforts were seen by some political parties to prefer or give more attention to one form of voting over another. This is a difficult predicament, but we would recommend two potential solutions that are worth exploring. These are: running smaller security-focused campaigns for all voting methods (on and offline); and/or incorporating such information into e-governance campaigns more broadly.

The next municipal elections (scheduled for October 2017) might be an ideal opportunity to explore the suggestions mentioned above. This is because Estonia has lower the local-election voting age to sixteen [26]. This new development will create around 24,000 potential new voters, so a special awareness campaign is expected for them. Having online safety as part of the school curriculum would also build awareness and provide a better understanding of how I-Voting procedures are established, thus benefiting online-voting transparency. We have already witnessed awareness campaigns in Estonia, but these have been promoted via other, non-governmental means [27].

Verification of Votes: Allowing citizens to verify their votes via a smartphone application is another measure used within the I-Voting system to enhance transparency. Procedurally, the verification application performs as expected and appears simple to use. According to one interviewee, "the verification application allows for actual proof of the process and enhances trust". This has also been witnessed through a user study of the system where officials found that even though only around 3% of the voters verified their votes, the availability of the application increased their confidence in the system generally.

In our judgement it was encouraging to witness the separation in devices used for casting and verifying votes. Amongst other aspects, this meant that successful vote-hijacking, particularly on a large-scale, would be challenging, as malicious parties would need to control both users' PCs and smartphones. We do stress, however, that the application will only be truly helpful to the I-Voting process and related security concerns, if it is widely used. There are approaches towards this goal (e.g., the availability of the application on Android, iOS and Windows platforms), and future efforts in information dissemination (e.g., via official government websites) and wider educational campaigns should continue to encourage its use. Another area worth further consideration is whether usability issues, which are common with vote-verification systems [28], might have influenced the uptake of the application. We are yet to find any publications or usability studies of the application, so would recommend this as an imperative area of future research. If it is the case that usability is an issue, designers will need to reconsider the application, as vote-verification is a critical part of transparency in I-Voting.

4.3   Summarising the State-of-Security of the I-Voting System

Reflecting generally on our analysis and interview findings as discussed above, there were many positives, but also some challenges and areas for improvement. We found that procedural security controls are fundamental to the system as designed, and overall they go a long way towards mitigating certain attacks. Procedures that are particularly well considered include: the use of independent auditors to ensure system compliance and monitor for any issues; and the processes by which disputes and incidents are handled by election officials. These procedures enable the prevention and detection of various attacks (intentional and accidental) that may seek to compromise the voting process.

As highlighted in our assessment, there are areas where procedures may be improved. For instance, while crucial procedures are clearly documented, some situations appear to be addressed in more informal ways which rely heavily on staff knowledge. These processes still work well given the close professional relationships between officials, and their vast experience, but this could change if key individuals leave their roles or are unexpectedly unable to participate. Furthermore, if procedures are not always formally defined, observers and auditors have little against which to judge whether actions by election officials are valid or are actually part of an insider attack, whether accidental or intentional.

Another area of potential improvement pertains to procedures on the assessment of devices and equipment. We believe that the security of the system could be enhanced by: conducting a more thorough initial assessment of election servers (e.g., for firmware level malware); engaging in mandatory checks for unauthorised devices prior to allowing persons' entry to secure areas; and having suitable system continuity plans to avoid unauthorised deviations from procedures. It may also be appropriate to revisit the risks originating from the voter's environment given that there are an increasing number of large-scale, sophisticated attacks which make such risks more salient today.

Focusing on the topic of transparency, we found that the measures adopted appear to have had a noteworthy impact on building confidence and trust in the I-Voting system both locally and internationally. The publishing of system documentation, source code and election videos, in addition to the open-door policy on election observers, are crucial initiatives in maintaining such transparency. As such, we would strongly recommend that these continue. With respect to procedural improvements, there are a few areas we identified in our assessment. These particularly relate to the difficulty in educating observers, running voting awareness campaigns and in increasing voter usage of transparency measures (e.g., verification). We have suggested small security-focused campaigns for all voting methods – thus not preferring one over the other – and this may also be used to highlight the benefits of verifying votes as well as generally being secure. It is important that politics does not leave voters at a disadvantage, and that they have the support they need in understanding voting processes to the extent that they feel appropriate and comfortable.

Lastly, we must state that even though the research methodology that we adopted is sound, our research relies heavily on interview reports on voting systems from individuals in Estonia; this is as opposed to direct observation of the I-Voting process in situ. We attempted to counteract this limitation by engaging in a critical reflection on the documented system and existing literature, and also by interviewing a range of experts from across Estonia. In the future, we hope to expand on this study, and further address these issues in two ways. The first way is in terms of participants, and aiming to have named officials engage with us via several rounds of interviews. This would help us delve into greater detail and conduct more critical analyses. Secondly, we would seek to participate in actual election observations (the October 2017 local government elections would be an ideal opportunity).

4.4   The New I-Voting System

With the core topic areas of this article now examined, we briefly expand on our work to discuss the upcoming version of the I-Voting system. Whilst we were aware that there were plans for a new system iteration before our study commenced, it was only during the interview process that we recognised how different it would be. This future system is the result of more than ten years of experience in e-democracy — from laws and regulations to technical and socio-technical aspects. This was a point that interviewees emphasised, i.e., the system was not being overhauled due to concerns about its integrity, but rather it was felt to be the appropriate time to update the full system (including enriching server-side code, as opposed to incremental improvements, as has been done for many years).

One of the most significant changes in the new system will be its structure and focus on returning complete authority to the NEC. In line with this goal, there are a few key modifications worth noting. First, as was mentioned in Sect. 4.1, the vote collection system (i.e., the system that interacts with voters directly) is likely to be outsourced. The benefit of this change is that in order to run an election, the NEC only needs to provide directives, the list of candidates, the cryptography to be used and the key and e-signature methods. Second, given the shift in power, the Electronic Voting Committee is to be dissolved. To accommodate for the technical understanding required to fulfil the new charter of the NEC, an IT auditor will assume a role on the NEC.

To comment on these changes generally, we view the decision to return the power to the NEC as a commendable move for democracy. This is especially the case given that an IT auditor will now be a core part of the election oversight and process. Our main concern with this new approach relates to the selection of companies to implement the vote collection system, and the level of checks on code and processes that will be conducted. It is crucial that any tendering process for the selection of companies to build election systems is monitored for fairness. Furthermore, it is essential that the good practices highlighted in our analyses above (e.g., independent assessments, code reviews, and audits), are continued to avoid placing democracy at risk.

Another finding of interest from interviewees was that the next iteration of the voting system will shift, in part, from procedures to incorporate more technology. This is likely to mean that monitoring will be reduced, and only processes related to encryption of results will be subject to observation. By reducing the amount of monitoring, public trust in the system may be affected. One interviewee noted that, "It is trust in mathematics rather than people," where the shift would occur. We agree that the move to an end-to-end verifiable and formally-proven system is ideal in many ways. The difficulty will come in communicating these details to the general public, when current engagement in courses for the mainly procedural system is low. The very nature of voting and its link to democratic rights means that attempts must be made for more accessible outlets for information about the national e-voting system.

A point related to our reflection above is the goal of the new system to allow for more formal verifiability. This particularly refers to making server-side operations more mathematically transparent and comprehensive as compared to previous years. This is clearly important as any changes in the votes, such as deletion or modification, will be more-easily detected. It is premature to report specifics of the new system, but as one interviewee stated, "[the] tender description suggests that it will include mix-nets, homomorphic encryption and provable decryption, and that the existing double envelop method will remain"; also, the server code will be openly published. These modifications will enable officials to prove that the decryption and tabulation of votes is performed correctly, and give additional assurance to external parties that want to verify election results.

Lastly, there is also the fact that for this new system, there will be a more substantial reliance on voter and client support. If voters notice that the system is not performing as expected, they will require various options for assistance. In the current system, there are several excellent support options and we would hope that this would continue in the future. Moreover, an interviewee pointed out that, "the new system could be used also outside Estonia in the future", as there is the possibility of removing its linkages to the Estonian ID card. This highlights a broader scope, but only time will tell whether such a system would be adopted outside of Estonia.

5   Conclusion

Estonia has been one of the main countries pioneering the adoption of a national Internet voting system. Our aim in this article was to assess the procedures relating to security and transparency in the system, and the extent to which they fulfilled their aims. While we found areas where these procedures performed well, there were also areas that could be improved. Some of these improvements are straightforward, but others (e.g., instituting awareness campaigns) require more delicate handling to avoid political controversy. Overall, we view the I-Voting system as one with many successes, but these arguably rely heavily on the expertise, knowledge and professional relationships between the individuals involved. This works for a close-knit society such as Estonia, but may be problematic in other, larger contexts.

We deem our article to be well-timed since the Estonian system will be changed significantly for the next elections in 2017. It is of paramount importance that the decision on which controls will be discarded will follow a certain procedure and that citizens' feedback will be taken into account. The I-Voting system has established a trust relationship with its citizens, and though mathematical proofs are scientifically justifiable as more secure, they may not necessarily provide the same assurance to citizens. This is especially true considering that citizens currently show little interest in technical system details. Still, with major changes on the horizon, it is essential that procedures are continuously critically reflected on and improved.

Acknowledgements. This research has been funded by the European Social Fund and the Estonian Government. It has been conducted on behalf of the Cyber Studies Programme at the Department of Politics and International Relations, University of Oxford. A much earlier version of this paper is available on the Cyber Studies Programme working paper series website.

References

1. i Esteve, J.B., Goldsmith, B., Turner, J.: International experience with e-voting. International Foundation for Electoral Systems (2012)
2. Organisation for Security and Co-operation in Europe (OSCE): Estonia Parliamentary Elections, OSCE/ODIHR Election Expert Team Final Report (2015). http://www.osce.org/odihr/elections/estonia/160131

3. Springall, D., Finkenauer, T., Durumeric, Z., Kitcat, J., Hursti, H., MacAlpine, M., Halderman, J.A.: Security analysis of the Estonian internet voting system. In: ACM SIGSAC Conference on Computer and Communications Security, pp. 703–715. ACM (2014)
4. Halderman, J.A.: Practical attacks on real-world e-voting. In: Hao, F., Ryan, P.Y. (eds.) Real-World Electronic Voting: Design, Analysis and Deployment (2016)
5. Gritzalis, D.A.: Principles and requirements for a secure e-voting system. Comput. Secur. **21**(6), 539–556 (2002)
6. Estonian National Electoral Committee: Internet Voting in Estonia (n.d.). http://www.vvk.ee/voting-methods-in-estonia/engindex/#Brief_description_of_the_I-voting_system
7. Estonian National Electoral Committee (NEC): Statistics about Internet Voting in Estonia (2005). http://www.vvk.ee/voting-methods-in-estonia/engindex/statistics
8. Ansper, A., Buldas, A., Jrgenson, A., Oruaas, M., Priisalu, J., Raiend, K., Veldre, A., Willemson, J., Virunurm, K.: E-voting concept security: analysis and measures. Technical report EH-02-02, Estonian National Electoral Commitee (2010)
9. Heiberg, S., Parsovs, A., Willemson, J.: Log analysis of estonian internet voting 2013–2014. In: Haenni, R., Koenig, R.E., Wikström, D. (eds.) VOTELID 2015. LNCS, vol. 9269, pp. 19–34. Springer, Cham (2015). doi:10.1007/978-3-319-22270-7_2
10. Heiberg, S., Willemson, J.: Verifiable internet voting in Estonia. In: 6th International Conference on Electronic Voting (EVOTE), pp. 1–8. IEEE (2014)
11. Estonian National Electoral Committee: E-voting system: a general overview (2010). http://www.vvk.ee/public/dok/General_Description_E-Voting_2010.pdf
12. Berg, B.: Qualitative Research Methods for the Social Sciences. Pearson, London (2004)
13. Yee, K.P.: Extending prerendered-interface voting software to support accessibility and other ballot features. EVT **7** (2007)
14. Friedberg, I., Skopik, F., Settanni, G., Fiedler, R.: Combating advanced persistent threats: from network event correlation to incident detection. Comput. Secur. **48**, 35–57 (2015)
15. Schneier, B.: By November, Russian hackers could target voting machines (2016). https://www.washingtonpost.com/posteverything/wp/2016/07/27/by-november-russian-hackers-could-target-voting-machines/
16. Appel, A.W.: Security seals on voting machines: a case study. ACM Trans. Inf. Syst. Secur. (TISSEC) **14**(2), 1–29 (2011)
17. PCWorld: Malicious, large-scale Google ad campaign slams users with malware (2015). http://www.pcworld.com/article/2907492/largescale-google-malvertising-campaign-hits-users-with-exploits.html
18. ZDNet: Mirai botnet attack hits thousands of home routers, throwing users offline (2016). http://www.zdnet.com/article/mirai-botnet-attack-hits-thousands-of-home-routers-throwing-users-offline/
19. TechRepublic: Pirated copies of Windows OS in China prone to security issues (2013). http://www.techrepublic.com/blog/asian-technology/pirated-copies-of-windows-os-in-china-prone-to-security-issues/
20. Cuevas, R., Kryczka, M., González, R., Cuevas, A., Azcorra, A.: Torrentguard: stopping scam and malware distribution in the bittorrent ecosystem. Comput. Netw. **59**, 77–90 (2014)
21. Estonian National Electoral Committee (NEC): Elections and Internet voting (n.d.). https://www.valimised.ee/eng/juhis

22. Hoepman, J.H., Jacobs, B.: Increased security through open source. Commun. ACM **50**(1), 79–83 (2007)
23. Bada, M., Sasse, A., Nurse, J.R.C.: Cyber security awareness campaigns: why do they fail to change behaviour? In: International Conference on Cyber Security for Sustainable Society, pp. 118–131 (2015)
24. Kritzinger, E., von Solms, S.H.: Cyber security for home users: a new way of protection through awareness enforcement. Comput. Secur. **29**(8), 840–847 (2010)
25. Sukwong, O., Kim, H., Hoe, J.: An empirical study of commercial antivirus software effectiveness. Computer **44**(3), 63–70 (2010)
26. Parliament of Estonia: The Riigikogu gave 16 and 17 year olds the right to vote at local elections (2015). https://www.riigikogu.ee/en/press-releases/the-riigikogu-gave-16-and-17-year-olds-the-right-to-vote-at-local-elections/
27. UNITE-IT: Get Online Week (2016). http://www.unite-it.eu/profiles/blogs/get-online-week-2016-in-estonia-raising-awareness-and-contest
28. Acemyan, C.Z., Kortum, P., Byrne, M.D., Wallach, D.S.: From error to error: why voters could not cast a ballot and verify their vote with helios, prêt à voter, and scantegrity II. USENIX J. Elect. Technol. Syst. (JETS), 1–25 (2015)

Application of Work Domain Analysis for Cybersecurity

Hao Wang[1], Nathan Lau[1(✉)], and Ryan Gerdes[2]

[1] Grado Department of Industrial and Systems Engineering,
Virginia Tech, Blacksburg, VA, USA
{drkwh05,nathan.lau}@vt.edu
[2] Bradley Department of Electrical and Computer Engineering,
Blacksburg, USA
rgerdes@vt.edu

Abstract. Cyber Physical Systems (CPSs) are pervasive in businesses and critical infrastructures that are becoming targets of cyber attack by our adversaries. The presence of advanced persistent threats or zero-day attacks suggests that cyber defense must include recovery response from cyber intrusions. Recovery response must rely on adaptive ability of the CPS as the impact of zero-day attacks cannot be anticipated. In unanticipated situations, human adaptive ability can contribute greatly to the recovery from cyber intrusions. This paper presents Work Domain Analysis (WDA) as a human factors engineering tool for evaluating system and identifying solutions supporting operators in their response to cyber threats. The cyber attack on Australian Maroochy Water Services is used as illustrative case study to demonstrate the potential of WDA in enhancing cyber security of CPS.

Keywords: Cyber-physical systems · Cyber security · Work domain analysis · Abstraction hierarchy · Maroochy water breach

1 Introduction

Cyber physical systems (CPSs) are becoming pervasive in our society. CPSs are "engineered systems that are built from, and depend upon, the seamless integration of computational algorithms and physical component" [1], in which embedded computer and network systems monitor and control physical processes [2, 3]. Computer or automated control of physical equipment and process through communication networks is going to be a fundamental aspect for all future systems [4, 5]. Even very small systems such as a family home are becoming "smart" with internet of things.

For today, many of the most significant CPSs still reside in critical infrastructures and heavy industries, such as electric power generation, sewage treatment, petrochemical refineries and steel mills. The systems for these industries and infrastructures are pioneers in computer control of equipment or physical process out of necessity for safety and productivity (e.g., extreme temperature in a steel mill). Further, virtually all of these CPSs critical to our society have a cyber or operational technology (OT) design around the Supervisory Control and Data Acquisition (SCADA) control system

© Springer International Publishing AG 2017
T. Tryfonas (Ed.): HAS 2017, LNCS 10292, pp. 384–395, 2017.
DOI: 10.1007/978-3-319-58460-7_27

architecture [6]. A SCADA system typically consists of supervisory computers, remote terminal units (RTUs) and programmable logic controllers (PLCs), human-machine interface, and a communication infrastructure [7]. The RTUs, preferred for wireless controls, and PLCs, preferred for wired controls, connect to sensors for collecting process information and actuators for controlling the equipment according to the instructions from the supervisory computers. The supervisory computers run software applications that process the sensor data, issue control commands and host the human-machine interface. Finally, the communication infrastructure connects the supervisory computers, PLCs and RTUs while providing an interface for human operators to oversee the physical process and exercise manual controls. Figure 1 depicts a simplified network for a typical SCADA system [8]. In essence, the functions of the SCADA system are essential for the operations of major industries and critical infrastructures.

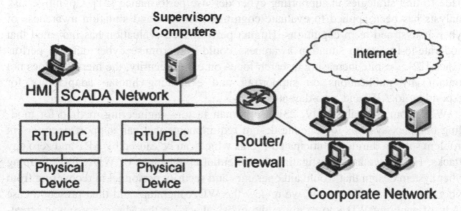

Fig. 1. A simplified SCADA network depicting PLCs, RTUs, supervisory computers, and human-machine interface.

While providing autonomous and complex functions in CPS, SCADA systems have also become the target of cyber attacks for effecting the physical systems. For example, Stuxnet is a malicious worm employing multiple zero-day exploits to penetrate traditional single detection mechanism [9, 10] and to infect PLCs for controlling industrial equipment. As discovered after being deployed to damage about 1,000 centrifuges in the Iran's nuclear program [11], Stuxnet was designed to access the SCADA components for physical sabotage rather than the traditional data theft or denial of service [12, 13]. Other infamous attacks on CPSs have resulted in severe social, economic, and political impacts, such as the 2015 Ukrainian Power Grid cyber attack causing power outages for over 225,000 customers [11].

Cyber attacks, such as Stuxnet, are classified as "Advanced Persistent Threat" (APT), which cannot be mitigated with traditional cyber security tools such as virus scans [14]. APT targeting major industries and critical infrastructures are mostly carried out by well-prepared, well-funded and well-trained adversaries. Current cyber security solutions are mostly perimeter-based such as firewalls and authentication although research has expand to network traffic monitoring, vulnerability modeling, and cyber deception (e.g., honeynet) [15, 16]. Though essential to improve overall security of SCADA, these research, by definition, do not directly address zero-day attacks when intrusion already occurred. To cope with APT, security research must also investigate effective and efficient recovery from cyber intrusions.

Recovery from APT or zero-day attacks must rely on adaptive behaviors built into the CPSs. Human intelligence remains superior to computers or machines in responding to unanticipated events or handling ill-defined tasks [17]; thus operators can play a central role in recovering from cyber intrusions, particularly in formulating and executing mitigation plans [18, 19]. Human factors research has begun investigating how to aid operators in cyber defense. There was an organized panel to identify the human role in cyber defense across professionals from diverse domains [20]. Research has found high demands and low vigilance for cyber defenders, and efforts have been made to find strategies in supporting cyber defense performance [21]. Cognitive task analysis has been applied to evaluate cognitive demands and situation awareness of cyber analyst and team cognitions. Human performance evaluation has indicated that moderate-to-low team situation awareness could compromise cyber defense perfor-mance [22]. Despite increasing research focus on cyber security, the literature does not contain any publications on supporting and evaluating human adaptability for responding to APT and zero-day attacks.

Work domain analysis [17, 23] is a human factors engineering method for mod-eling complex systems to generate design requirements that can support operators in problem solving during unanticipated events which can be caused by APT and zero day attacks. Hence, we are investigating the potential applications of WDA for informing cyber system design that would aid operators and security personnel in recovering from cyber intrusions. In this paper, we review the WDA literature and then present a case study of applying WDA to examine the cyber attack on the Maroochy sewage treat-ment plant. The paper concludes with a discussion on how the WDA can be useful for system design evaluation and coordinate incidence response in the case study.

2   Work Domain Analysis

Work Domain Analysis (WDA) [17, 23] models the functional structure of the system for identifying domain invariants or constraints that workers and automated controllers must respect in order to achieve system goals [24]. By depicting the boundary con-ditions and relationships with respect to goals of the system, WDA stands in contrast to many other human factors analysis methods that focus on eliciting requirements from the user or inferring human limitations from science [25]. That is, WDA studies how system works and thereby informs design requirements for tools that help operators conceive possible actions or trajectories within such operational constraints of the system, thereby supporting adaptive behaviors during unanticipated events.

Abstraction hierarchy [26] is one of the major modeling tools for WDA [24]. The abstraction hierarchy is a knowledge representation framework characterized by structural means-ends links between levels (see Fig. 2) as each level describes the work domain from a different perspective. Between adjacent levels, middle levels represent the structure of the work domain (what), while levels above explain the purpose (why) and levels below describe the means (how). In other words, the lower level represents the system elements to achieve the higher level ends, or what can operators use to accomplish a system function. The upper level describes the goals or functions that can be supported by lower level means, or why operators are provided with various system elements.

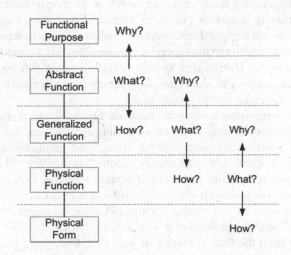

Fig. 2. Typical five-level abstraction hierarchy depicting why-what-how means-ends relationships

A typical abstraction hierarchy has five levels: Function purpose serves as the highest level which describes the primary purpose of the system. Abstract function is the second level which describes the scientific laws or disciplines applied to achieve the functional purpose. Generalized function is the third level which represents the engineering processes derived from applying the scientific laws. Physical functions is the forth level which depicts the physical equipment or components that realize the engineer processes. Physical forms is the lowest level which represents the physical appearance, condition, and location of the system equipment or components to indicate their operating states.

The abstraction hierarchy has demonstrated merits in modeling and supporting human problem solving in many safety critical domains, including algorithm development in computer science [27], automated trading system in finance [28], process control in nuclear power plants [29], flight control in civil aviation [30], and system acquisition in military [31]. Regarding nuclear power plants, WDA has been widely acknowledged as a valid and qualified technique in all stages of system design to accommodate human abilities and limitations [32]. However, the literature does not contain any applications of WDA for cyber security.

To investigate the application of WDA for cyber security, we completed two abstraction hierarchies for analyzing the cyber attack on a sewage treatment plant

(Maroochy Water Services) in Australia. This case study can illustrate whether WDA is a meaningful analysis tool for developing cyber security solutions.

3 Case Study: Australian Maroochy Water Services Cyber Attack

The cyber attack targeted the water sewerage system in Maroochy Shire Council which consists of 142 pumping stations that treats 35 million liters of wastewater per day [33]. All pumping stations are equipped with two-way radios systems to receive commands from and transmit information to the supervisory computers and the main control room. For safety, the Protective Distribution System (PDS) Compact 500 computer devices are installed at each pumping to issue alarms, communicate with main control room, as well as to start or terminate pump operations.

The Maroochy cyber attack occurred between February and April, 2000 during which pumps were not running when they should, alarms were not transmitted to industrial control system and main control room, and communication were lost between pumping stations and supervisory control computers. The initial troubleshooting involved monitoring and recording radio traffic as well as inspection of physical equipment. The troubleshooting indicated that a PDS Compact 500 computer of a particular identification was issuing corrupt electronic messages that led to erratic pump operations. The OT staff devised a workaround that all pumping stations would ignore commands from the PDS computer of that identification.

The workaround was short lived as a PDS computer with another identification began sending corrupted messages. In March, the attack involving remote access of a PDS computer altered the electronic signals and caused erratic pump operations. The OT staff was able to identify the bogus information but the intrusion was not stopped. The sewage facility resorted to mobilizing field workers to operate the pumps manually at a great cost. On one occasion, this costly workaround was deficient, resulting in 800,000 L of untreated sewage overflow, polluting over 500 m of open drain and creek and incurring significant financial losses for the cleanup [34].

Another intrusion occurred in late April resulting alarms being disabled on four pumping stations. At this time, a former contractor of an outsourcing company to the sewage company was under suspicion. This contractor was eventually arrested for the cyber attack with the possession of a PDS Compact 500 computer and a two-way radio set to frequencies of radio systems of the sewage facility. The attack was an act of revenge for failing to secure a job at the sewage facility [35]. Given his knowledge of the sewage facility as a former contractor, the attacker was considered an insider. He used the same radio equipment as the sewage facility to intervene the communication between pumping stations and supervisory computers in central control room. He stole the PDS Compact 500 computer to disable alarms and change pump configurations. Between February and late April, he intruded 46 times through the radio, disguising himself with different identifications.

3.1   Work Domain Model: The Abstraction Hierarchy

The Maroochy cyber attack highlights the physical damages that can incur as a result of deficient OT security. To study this cyber attack from a CPS perspective, we present and integrate two abstraction hierachies representing the physical and cyber/OT design of the sewage plant. Due to limited access to system documentations and restriction on publication lengths, the two work domain models are highly simplified representations of the plant's physical and cyber system. There can be many more elements for each levels of abstraction. However, the simplification should still be sufficient for the purpose of illustrating the application of WDA for system evaluation and coordinated incident response during cyber attacks.

Abstraction Hierarchy of Sewage Treatment Process. Modern sewage treatment plant is a CPS in which a series of complex physical processes to remove contaminants from water is controlled by a network of computers [36]. The abstraction hierarchy provides a multi-level representation of the sewage treatment process and thus can be applied to illustrate the physical impact of the Maroochy cyberattack. The top half of Fig. 3 (in yellow background) presents an abstraction hierarchy of a simplified sewage treatment plant that should be suffice to illustrate the general operations and impact of the cyber attack in Maroochy Shire. This abstraction hierarchy is based on the Australia and New Zealand 1997 guidelines for sewage systems that highlights six major processes – pre-treatment, primary treatment, secondary treatment, disinfection, sludge treatment, and advanced/tertiary wastewater treatment [37].

The abstraction hierarchy depicts that the functional purpose of sewage plant is to ensure sewage throughput and quality as well as environmental safety and public health. These purposes are achieved through the application of several abstract functions: mass transfer and fluid dynamics, conservation of energy, biochemistry balance, discharge and emission regulations. The means to achieve abstract functions are engineering processes at the generalized function level such as transport of liquid/gas and disinfection. For example, environment regulation and biochemistry balance can be fulfilled through disinfection of sewage materials. These engineering processes are realized through several major types of equipment in the physical functions level. Continuing on the means-end example, the disinfection process can be achieved through ultraviolet irradiator and chemicals. Finally, the states of these equipment are described in the physical form level to indicate how the equipment is functioning. For instance, the on/off state and radiation frequency would be indications of whether the UV irradiator is disinfecting wastewater.

Abstraction Hierarchy of OT for Sewage Treatment Plant. To represent the cyber design and impact of the Maroochy sewage plant, an abstraction hierarchy is developed for the OT as shown bottom of Fig. 3 (In reverse order of abstractions). The functional purpose of OT is to ensure efficient, effective, and secure equipment controls as well as personnel communication. Achieving security depends on fundamental principles of information integrity, confidentiality and availability in the abstract function level; whereas, effective and efficient equipment control depends on control theory as well as information availability. Adhering to these fundamental principles requires information transmission, computation and security process to be in place. For example, information

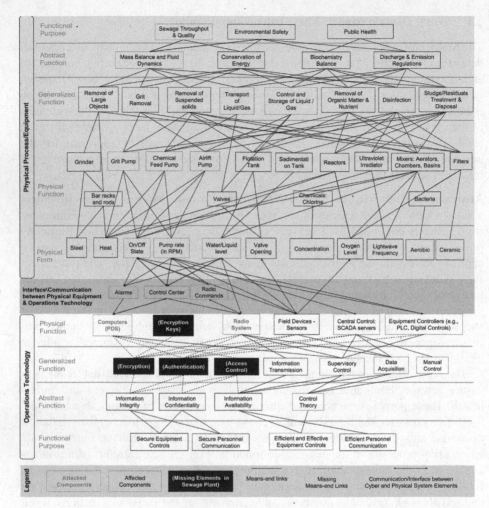

Fig. 3. Abstraction hierarchies representing physical process of a simplified sewage plant (top in yellow background), and corresponding operational technology (bottom in white background). (Color figure online)

integrity and confidentiality are commonly achieved through encryption, authentication and access control. However, the Maroochy sewage plant was lacking in these security processes/protocols. In other words, there are no means to information integrity and confidentiality. The abstraction hierarchy of Fig. 3 denotes missing elements in the Maroochy plant using white texts in parenthesis and black boxes, and missing means-end relationships using dashed lines. On the other hand, the Maroochy sewage plant was able to adhere to control theory through supervisory control, data acquisition and information transmission. These engineering processes are enabled by OT hardware and software. For example, encryption are enabled by computers generating encryption keys and performing decryption. Given the lack of encryption protocol, encryption keys did not exist in the Maroochy OT system. Supervisor control and data acquisition of Maroochy plant was achieved through the SCADA server, equipment controllers and radio transmission system. The physical function level of the OT abstraction hierarchy is omitted because the additional level of details (e.g., packet size) are not necessary to illustrate the merits of WDA for cyber security.

Integrating the Abstraction Hierarchy and Mapping the Cyber Attack. The integration of the abstraction hierarchies for physical and cyber design of Maroochy sewage plant is represented by the interface of OT controllers and sensors with physical states of the equipment as highlighted with green background and arrowed lines in Fig. 3 That is, an OT component can communicate and thus impact the physical state of the process that in turns propagate upwards in the abstraction hierarchy to alter the equipment operations (physical function) which together in turns effect various engineering processes (generalized function). The engineering processes reflect whether scientific principles (abstraction function) are satisfied to achieve system goals (functional purpose). For example, the PDS computers can issue commands to stop pumps when water/liquid level becomes too low or high. Such commands may eventually impact other pumping operations with grit pump, chemical feed pump, airlift pump and thereby affect multiple generalized functions, namely transport of liquid/gas, removal of organic matter & nutrient, disinfection, and sludge/residual treatment and disposal in the generalized function level.

The integration of physical and cyber abstraction hierarchies provides a system map to study the Maroochy cyber attack. The attacker began the intrusion by using a system computer to access the plant control systems wirelessly using the same radio equipment and frequency as depicted with the red boxes with red texts in Fig. 3. Once intruded, the attacker issued radio commands to equipment controllers to cause erratic pump behaviors, affecting transport, control and storage of liquid/gas resulting in mass imbalance for the plant. At the same time, the attacker also used PDS computer and software to access the SCADA system, disabling alarms and overriding messages from or to the control center/room. This intrusion thus propagated upwards in the OT abstraction hierarchy to affect supervisory control, acquisition and manual control, thereby breaking process control fundamentals for the sewage treatment and thus the goal of effective equipment control.

3.2 Work Domain Model in System Evaluation and Design

The Maroochy cyber attack case study illustrates that the abstraction hierarchy can be useful to assess cyber security of CPS and thereby inform system design. Referring the abstraction hierarchy for OT or cyber system design, encryption and authentication are important processes to ensure information integrity and confidentiality. However, none appeared to be implemented for computer devices or wireless system at Maroochy sewage treatment plant, permitting attacker to intrude through the radios and access the SCADA system easily. As shown by the dashed lines in Fig. 3, there are no means or processes to achieve information integrity and confidentiality pointing to cyber design deficiencies that must be mitigate in order to prevent access to OT components by adversaries. In essence, the abstraction hierarchy helps identify potential physical impact from missing security processes.

The abstraction hierarchy also highlights specific engineering process or equipment that should be "hardened" or further defended for cyber security. In this case study, attacker's access in PDS computer led to erratic of pump operations. The OT abstraction hierarchy shows that PDS computers serve as the only interface between the pumps and OT. Given physical pumping stations are essential to so many processes, OT components connected to pumping stations may deserve additional security solutions such as frequency hopping for the radio communication system. The protection provided by frequency hopping itself is limited, so diverse and redundant techniques may also be employed depending on budgets.

3.3   Work Domain Model for Coordinated Incidence Response

Coordination between operations and OT staff is essential in troubleshooting, specifically in deciphering cyber attacks from system malfunctions. The equipment connected to OT components without security features can be the primary target of cyber attacks. In this case study, control room operators were first to experience erratic pumping operation as a symptom of the cyber attack, and field operators were first to rule out physical problems with equipment inspection. Their investigation into erratic pump operations informed OT staff to look for false data, commands, and network address. In addition, the operations staff conceived the workarounds of manual controls at the pumping station to maintain throughputs while the OT personnel identified the compromises in the radio communication and alarm configurations. In essence, the final diagnosis and mitigation response to the cyber attack mandated coordination between operations and OT staff [33].

As cyber attacks are detected, coordination between operations and OT staff plays a critical role in responding to cyber intrusions. The abstraction hierarchies can help to illustrate the interaction between OT components and plant equipment during cyber events. In the Maroochy case study, the unexplained pump operations and pump lock ups were highly observable to operations personnel but the root cause of cyber attack could only be diagnosed by OT personnel.

The joint abstraction hierarchies therefore illustrates that effective incidence response to cyber intrusion must be coordinated between operations and OT staff. For example, when OT personnel detected suspicious network traffic between plant equipment, operations should be informed to monitor specific process area for unusual behaviors. Verification of control room indications with field operators may become temporarily necessary as OT personnel investigate the issue. Similarly, when unusual process behaviors occur, operations personnel may need to troubleshoot the root cause with OT personnel who would be aware of the security levels for different SCADA components.

4 Limitation

The WDA in this case study is solely based on publicly available information on the cyber attack and the Maroochy sewage treatment facility. For this reason, the WDA or the abstraction hierarchies likely contain some discrepancies to the physical and cyber design of the actual sewage facility. Discrepancies may also exist in the details of the actual cyber attack. Further, cyber security technology for SCADA equipment has improved drastically since the 2000 Maroochy cyber attack. Thus, the cyber security findings derived from the WDA specifically for Maroochy sewage facility are for illustration only rather than generating exact solutions.

5 Conclusion

This paper proposes WDA for evaluating and designing CPS through a case study of the Maroochy cyber attack on the sewage treatment plant. The case study illustrates that WDA can help identify system deficiencies and potential solutions to enhance cyber defense. Thus, WDA has demonstrated promise for improving cyber security that is increasingly relevant with advancing digital technology in CPS. As all of our critical infrastructures are becoming CPSs, cyber security is an essential design consideration that has serious economic, social, and financial implications. Given increasing number of insider threats and evolving APT, WDA can be one of many invaluable tools for system design and incidence response in cyber security.

References

1. NSF Program Guidelines: Cyber-Physical Systems (CPS) (2017). https://www.nsf.gov/funding/pgm_summ.jsp?pims_id=503286
2. Lee, E.A.: Cyber physical systems: design challenges. In: 2008 11th IEEE International Symposium on Object Oriented Real-Time Distributed Computing (ISORC). IEEE (2008)
3. Alur, R.: Principles of Cyber-Physical Systems. MIT Press, Cambridge (2015)
4. Baheti, R., Gill, H.: Cyber-physical systems. Impact Control Technol. **12**, 161–166 (2011)
5. Helal, S., et al.: The gator tech smart house: a programmable pervasive space. Computer **38**(3), 50–60 (2005)
6. Kott, A., Aguayo Gonzalez, C., Colbert, E.J.M.: Introduction and preview. In: Colbert, E.J.M., Kott, A. (eds.) Cyber-security of SCADA and Other Industrial Control Systems. AIS, vol. 66, pp. 1–13. Springer, Cham (2016). doi:10.1007/978-3-319-32125-7_1
7. Sridhar, S., Manimaran, G.: Data integrity attacks and their impacts on SCADA control system. In: 2010 IEEE Power and Energy Society General Meeting. IEEE (2010)
8. Bagri, A., Netto, R., Jhaveri, D.: Supervisory control and data acquisition. Int. J. Comput. Appl. **102**(10) (2014)
9. Langner, R.: Stuxnet: dissecting a cyberwarfare weapon. IEEE Secur. Priv. **9**(3), 49–51 (2011)
10. Karnouskos, S.: Stuxnet worm impact on industrial cyber-physical system security. In: 37th Annual Conference on IEEE Industrial Electronics Society, IECON 2011. IEEE (2011)
11. Denning, D.E.: Stuxnet: what has changed? Future Internet **4**(3), 672–687 (2012)

12. Chen, T.M., Abu-Nimeh, S.: Lessons from stuxnet. Computer **44**(4), 91–93 (2011)
13. Farwell, J.P., Rohozinski, R.: Stuxnet and the future of cyber war. Survival **53**(1), 23–40 (2011)
14. Hutchins, E.M., Cloppert, M.J., Amin, R.M.: Intelligence-driven computer network defense informed by analysis of adversary campaigns and intrusion kill chains. In: Leading Issues in Information Warfare and Security Research, vol. 1, p. 80 (2011)
15. Tang, K., Zhou, M.-T., Wang, W.-Y.: Insider cyber threat situational awareness framework using dynamic Bayesian networks. In: 4th International Conference on Computer Science and Education, ICCSE 2009. IEEE (2009)
16. Cai, N., Wang, J., Yu, X.: SCADA system security: complexity, history and new developments. In: 6th IEEE International Conference on Industrial Informatics, INDIN 2008. IEEE (2008)
17. Vicente, K.J.: Cognitive Work Analysis: Toward Safe, Productive, and Healthy Computer-Based Work. CRC Press, Boca Raton (1999)
18. Mancuso, V.F., et al.: Human factors of cyber attacks a framework for human-centered research. In: Proceedings of the Human Factors and Ergonomics Society Annual Meeting. SAGE Publications (2014)
19. Gutzwiller, R.S., et al.: The human factors of cyber network defense. In: Proceedings of the Human Factors and Ergonomics Society Annual Meeting. SAGE Publications (2015)
20. Mancuso, V.F., et al.: Human factors in cyber warfare II emerging perspectives. In: Proceedings of the Human Factors and Ergonomics Society Annual Meeting. SAGE Publications (2014)
21. Finomore, V., et al.: Effects of cyber disruption in a distributed team decision making task. In: Proceedings of the Human Factors and Ergonomics Society Annual Meeting. SAGE Publications (2013)
22. Champion, M.A., et al.: Team-based cyber defense analysis. In: 2012 IEEE International Multi-disciplinary Conference on Cognitive Methods in Situation Awareness and Decision Support (CogSIMA). IEEE (2012)
23. Rasmussen, J., Pejtersen, A.M., Goodstein, L.P.: Cognitive Systems Engineering. Wiley, Hoboken (1994)
24. Naikar, N.: Work Domain Analysis: Concepts, Guidelines, and Cases. CRC Press, Boca Raton (2013)
25. Burns, C.M., Hajdukiewicz, J.: Ecological Interface Design. CRC Press, Boca Raton (2004)
26. Rasmussen, J.: A framework for cognitive task analysis in systems design (1985)
27. Tokadli, G., Feigh, K.M.: Option and constraint generation using work domain analysis. In: 2014 IEEE International Conference on Systems, Man and Cybernetics (SMC). IEEE (2014)
28. Li, Y., Burns, C., Hu, R.: Understanding automated financial trading using work domain analysis. In: Proceedings of the Human Factors and Ergonomics Society Annual Meeting. SAGE Publications (2015)
29. Lau, N., et al.: Ecological Interface Design in the nuclear domain: an empirical evaluation of ecological displays for the secondary subsystems of a boiling water reactor plant simulator. IEEE Trans. Nucl. Sci. **55**(6), 3597–3610 (2008)
30. Ahlstrom, U.: Work domain analysis for air traffic controller weather displays. J. Saf. Res. **36**(2), 159–169 (2005)
31. Jenkins, D.P., et al.: Using cognitive work analysis to explore activity allocation within military domains. Ergonomics **51**(6), 798–815 (2008)
32. Sanderson, P., et al.: Use of cognitive work analysis across the system life cycle: from requirements to decommissioning. In: Proceedings of the Human Factors and Ergonomics Society Annual Meeting. SAGE Publications (1999)

33. Weiss, J.: Industrial control system (ICS) cyber security for water and wastewater systems. In: Clark, R.M., Hakim, S. (eds.) Securing Water and Wastewater Systems, pp. 87–105. Springer, Cham (2014)

34. Abrams, M., Weiss, J.: Malicious Control System Cyber Security Attack Case Study–Maroochy Water Services, Australia. The MITRE Corporation, McLean (2008)

35. Slay, J., Miller, M.: Lessons learned from the Maroochy water breach. In: Goetz, E., Shenoi, S. (eds.) ICCIP 2007. IIFIP, vol. 253, pp. 73–82. Springer, Boston, MA (2008). doi:10.1007/978-0-387-75462-8_6

36. Metcalf, E., et al.: Wastewater Engineering: Treatment and Reuse. McGraw Hill, New York City (2003)

37. Australian Guidelines for Sewerage Systems: Effluent Management. Australian Water and Wastewater Association, Editor (1997)

Using Human Factor Approaches
to an Organisation's Bring Your Own Device
Scheme

Jodie Ward, Huseyin Dogan$^{(\boxtimes)}$, Edward Apeh, Alexios Mylonas,
and Vasilios Katos

Department of Computing and Informatics,
Bournemouth University, Bournemouth, UK
{i7933001, hdogan, e.apeh,
amylonas, vkatos}@bournemouth.ac.uk

Abstract. Bring Your Own Device (BYOD) is an emerging trend that is being adopted by an increasing number of organisations due to the benefits it provides in terms of cost efficiency, employee productivity, and staff morale. However, organisations who could benefit from implementing BYOD remain sceptical, due to the increasing threats and vulnerabilities introduced by mobile technology, which are amplified due to the human element (insider threats, non-security savvy employees). In this context, this paper investigates the application of human factor techniques to the BYOD scheme of an anonymised, real-life organisation (referred to as "Globex"). Questionnaires and Interactive Management are two Human Factor methods used in this case study to help determine areas for improvement. Results from the experiment highlight an issue with employee satisfaction towards their employers' BYOD scheme, which could negatively impact their organisational culture. The paper concludes with recommendations for additional information within the BYOD policy and the review of reimbursement eligibility and entitlements.

Keywords: Bring Your Own Device (BYOD) · Mobile devices · Mobile device management · Security · Interactive Management · Human Factors

1 Introduction

The emergence of smartphones and other mobile devices with advanced capabilities has encouraged organisations to introduce them into the workplace. These devices coupled with high-speed mobile internet increases productivity by enabling employees to work on-the-go. Recently, many organisations are considering the concept of Bring Your Own Device (BYOD), which enables employees to use a personal device of their choice to connect to company resources whenever they like. Besides increased productivity, organisation's also benefit from reduced costs as the responsibility of purchasing and maintaining the device lies with the employee (Ali et al. 2015; Eshlahi et al. 2014). Another potential benefit is increased staff morale as a result of having more flexibility (Downer and Bhattacharya 2015).

© Springer International Publishing AG 2017
T. Tryfonas (Ed.): HAS 2017, LNCS 10292, pp. 396–413, 2017.
DOI: 10.1007/978-3-319-58460-7_28

BYOD is a relatively new domain and comes with various security challenges that must be considered before adoption. Mobile security is not as advanced as computer security, and research has found attacks typically aimed at computers are increasingly targeting smart devices (Clay 2015; Eslahi et al. 2012). Additionally, by shifting the responsibility of purchasing and maintaining a mobile device to employees, the company relinquishes control over the device making security mechanisms harder to enforce. If BYOD implementations are not properly secured the organisation risks leaking sensitive information and damaging their reputation.

There are multiple trust and privacy issues acting as barriers to the uptake of BYOD. Employees must be able to trust their employer not to use technical security mechanisms to access or monitor their personal information, but in the same respect the employer must be able to trust their employees to follow company policy and safeguard corporate information. This research contributes to cyber security policies and user behaviour domains by applying human factor approaches to investigate information confidentiality and privacy issues that tend to arise between corporations and their employees from the adaptation of BYOD.

This paper critically evaluates an organisation's BYOD scheme and makes recommendations for improvement based on research and experimental case study results. This paper is ordered as follows: Sect. 2 elaborates on BYOD security threats and challenges. Section 3 discusses Human Factors as a discipline and how various approaches can be used to improve security. Section 4 presents the case study results i.e. information gathered about the organisation's security solution in addition to questionnaire and IM results. Section 5 discussed the research with final remarks and recommendations and proposes future work.

2 Bring Your Own Device

2.1 BYOD Security Threats

Attacks aimed at mobile devices are heavily increasing (Wang et al. 2014). A report published by Symantec show mobile vulnerabilities rose by 214% in 2015 compared with 2014 (Symantec 2016). It is therefore important to understand the types of attacks to defend against them.

Loss or Theft. Mobile devices present an increased risk of compromise due to their size and mobility as it makes them susceptible to loss and theft (Souppaya and Scarfone 2013). Globex should therefore assume an attacker will gain access to a lost or stolen device in the future, and think about what tools they want in place to prevent access corporate information.

Malicious Applications. In 2011, it was estimated that 11,000 malicious applications were residing in Google's Play store, which hosts a multitude of applications for downloading to devices running the Android operating system (Miners 2014). This number quadrupled by 2013. Such applications contain malicious code commonly designed to steal the user's data for committing fraud. A recent example of a malicious application involves WhatsApp, Uber, and Google Play (Kan 2016). The malware spread through an SMS prompting victims to click a link which then downloads the malware. The malware then creates an overlay to spoof a trusted application and requests credit card information. Once the victim submits the information, it is sent to the attackers.

Phishing and Smishing. A phishing attack is a form of social engineering designed to trick recipients into divulging sensitive information, such as credit card details, by masquerading as a legitimate and trustworthy entity. The attack comes through various channels such as email and malicious applications. A phishing attack in the form of a text message is referred to as 'smishing'. Phishing is difficult to defend against as attackers are constantly changing their techniques to evade security mechanisms (Wu et al. 2016). There are many technical solutions available for phishing, however many researchers agree the most effective solution is staff education, training, and awareness (Dodge et al. 2007; Symantec 2016).

Mobile Botnets. A botnet is an interconnected network of infected computers used to spread malware. It is fully controlled by an attacker through a command and control server. A botnets potential for inflicting damage increases as more machines are infected and become a part of the zombie network (F-secure labs 2016). Botnets are considered one of the most dangerous cyber threats as they can be difficult to detect and shut down due to their dynamic nature and complexity. In recent years' researchers have discovered botnets operating on mobile devices. The lack of security knowledge of many mobile users and less advanced security solutions has motivated botmasters to migrate (Eshlahi et al. 2012). While the threat of mobile botnets is not as prevalent as traditional botnets, security experts expect it to grow (Winder 2016). Table 1 lists some well-known examples and their attack vectors (Eshlahi et al. 2012; Winder 2016).

Table 1. Examples of mobile botnets

Name	Attack(s)	Mobile OS
Zeus (Zitmo)	Fraud Private data theft (mobile banking) Illegal transactions	Symbian Windows BlackBerry Android
DroidDream	Private data theft Malicious applications	Android
Android.Bmaster	Revenue Private data theft	Android
Viking Horde	Fraud DDoS Revenue generation	Android
Ikee.B	Revenue Private data theft	iPhone

Disgruntled Employees. Employees can leave an organisation feeling disgruntled for a variety of reasons: being made redundant, having a poor relationship with their managers or colleagues, or feeling unappreciated for their work. A disgruntled employee is more likely to have motive for an attack or data leakage over one who left amicably (Kumar 2015). Therefore, it is vital to ensure corporate data is removed from personal devices before every employee's termination date.

Unsecured Wireless Networks. Most organisations encourage staff to use Wi-Fi wherever possible to save on costly data usage bills. This means staff may connect to unsecured public wireless networks whilst travelling, which is an easy target for attackers to gain access to sensitive information.

2.2 BYOD Challenges

There are many other challenges involved in BYOD besides security threats. The National Cyber Security Institute (2014) and Information Commissioners Office (2016) divide BYOD challenges into eight main categories, namely:

Limiting Information Shared by Devices. Personal devices are often set-up for easy or automatic sharing of data such as backing up to the cloud or automatically connecting to nearby wireless hotspots. Appropriate consideration should be made into how to protect data from unlawful access, regardless of storage location. Additionally, organisation's must also think about how personal applications may interact with company applications and what methods are available to keep them separate.

Creating an Effective BYOD Policy. A BYOD policy clarifies the responsibilities of the employer and employee for protecting corporate information on mobile devices. A policy is only fully effective when it is enforced and regular compliance checks are carried out. This is because people tend to forget over time or are not made aware of changes (Downer and Bhattacharya 2015). An effective BYOD policy is also realistic and flexible. Employees who strongly disagree with a policy may ignore it or actively seek loopholes if there is a benefit for them (Thomson 2012; Mathias 2013).

Technical Controls. There are a range of technical controls available to help organisations remotely manage, secure, and support BYOD devices. Such controls may support compliance and policy enforcement, password enforcement, a remote wipe facility, locate device function, containerization and more. While technical controls provide measures for protecting corporate data on personal devices, they do not come without their limitations. The limitations for various tools are explored in the next section.

Planning for Security Incidents. Mobile devices can be easily lost or stolen. It is vital for an organisation to plan for such incidents to protect corporate data. An organisation must be able to act immediately to limit losses, prevent the spread of any compromise, and learn lessons from the incident (NCSC 2014).

Technical controls are useful in events such as the loss or theft of a device as it will enable the organisation to remotely wipe corporate data. Although this will only work if the server is able to establish communication with the device over a network connection. It is crucial that staff understand the process of reporting such incidents to the organisation and the importance of doing so in a timely manner for technical controls to be effective.

Alternative Ownership Models. The National Cyber Security Centre (2014) advise considering alternative ownership models before jumping into BYOD. A 'choose your own device' policy is one where the company purchases the device and maintains control over it, but the employee can choose from a selection of models that best suits them. There is also a 'corporately owned, personally enabled' policy that allows staff to use corporately owned devices for personal use. An option that gives the organisation full control but allows flexibility to the employee. The main problem with the afore-mentioned policies is the organisation remains responsible for expenditure of devices and so would not appeal to one looking to cut costs.

Encouraging Staff Agreement. Some staff may resist BYOD as it transfers the costs of purchasing and maintaining the device over to them. Some will likely have privacy concerns with technical controls the organisation enforces and sharing their personal contact number to clients or colleagues. Moreover, staff may not receive the same level of technical support from IT services as they did for corporate liable devices as it widens the scope for technical issues.

The National Cyber Security Centre (2014) advise communicating BYOD policies through employee training and education to ensure staff understand their responsibil-ities and the decision-making processes behind the company's decision. Organisation's should consider how they present training materials to staff depending on their local organisational culture. To ensure maximum impact, the right information needs to be presented in the right way through the right communication channels (Lacey 2009). Sources of influence play an important role in changing attitudes and behaviour in staff. Three sources of influence include:

- Hierarchical: those that respond well to authoritative figures such as the CEO;
- Democratic: those that respond better to peer discussions;
- Sophisticated: those that respond better to thought leaders.

Increased Device Support. A BYOD policy invites the use of a wider range of mobile devices, which increases demand for device support. Technicians may have to keep multiple operating systems compliant and up-to-date, support a greater number of device types, and respond to security incidents across a variety of devices (NCSC 2014). For a successful BYOD approach organisation's must have sufficient support capability and expertise to support a growing range of devices. Increased device support is likely to come with an associated cost for training or hiring additional support staff.

Understanding Legal Issues. There are myriads of legal issues surrounding BYOD, many of which are ill-defined and do not yet have solid solutions. Laws and regulations are continuously evolving as technology grows, so policies and standards must be regularly maintained to demonstrate good practices (Mavretich 2012). Additionally, legal issues will present various constraints for IT managers implementing a BYOD policy, so it is important to prepare for changes and allow room for flexibility.

A BYOD policy is largely influenced by local government laws and regulations, and so organisation's looking to implement BYOD on a global scale should customise their policy for each country (Absalom 2012). A comprehensive policy constructed around local laws is a strong way of ensuring legal compliance. It ensures that employees are fully aware of the implications of using their own device and understand their responsibilities.

3   Human Factors Approaches Adopted: Questionnaire and Interactive Management

Human factors (HF) is a scientific discipline also referred to as ergonomics. It combines knowledge from various fields of research to design systems that complement the natural abilities of people to improve efficiency and safety at work (Chartered Institute of Ergonomics 2016). The term 'ergonomics' is mostly used to describe human interactions with physical environmental factors at work, whereas HF covers the broader aspects such as interaction with systems, processes, and products. HF has contributions from such fields as psychology, engineering, physiology, cognitive science, human computer interaction (HCI), and more. BYOD is centred on managing the way humans interact with their devices and corporate systems. Human error and malicious intent are the most common causes of security breaches (Greenberg et al. 2015; PWC 2015), so considering HF is essential for a strong scheme.

There are various human factor approaches available to help see a broader picture of the problem, which presents a wider range of solutions. Applying HF helps to design a system for people that is user-friendly yet effective. One approach is Heuristic Evaluation, which is used to identify usability issues in the design of a user interface (Nielsen and Molich 1990). Another approach is Soft Systems Methodology (SSM), which is a decision support tool typically used to help develop a better understanding for a problem to prevent premature solutions that do not work or are not effective enough (Wilson 2001). Focus groups is another methodology which is used to gather qualitative research from a group of people, usually based on their thoughts, perceptions, and attitudes towards a certain product or system (Lindlof and Taylor 2011). As another example, there is also Cognitive Walkthrough which is typically used to evaluate the usability of a system by asking participants to work through a series of tasks while answering questions posed by the researcher (Wharton et al. 1994).

This paper utilises questionnaires and an approach called Interactive Management (IM), and applies them to an organisation's BYOD scheme with the aim of identifying areas for improvement. These approaches are discussed next.

3.1   Questionnaires

The most commonly used technique for gathering information from people is questionnaires. They are useful for obtaining large amounts of information because they can be distributed widely and therefore can get more response. However, due to the lack of social cues from respondents and the inability to ask for clarification, the validity of the data received is always questionable (Wickens et al. 2003). For this paper, questionnaires were used to gather information from IT managers regarding what BYOD solutions Globex have in place as the information required is purely factual and does not require human interaction. This information helps to recognise if and where Globex's solutions need improvement.

3.2   Interactive Management

Interactive Management (IM) is a system designed to manage complex situations through structured group discussions between a group of people knowledgeable to the problem. Focusing on the problem in detail and building a deeper understanding of it prevents premature solutions that are not fit for purpose (Warfield 2002).

IM supports consensus decision-making where group members reach an agreement on a solution together rather than voting and leaving some members unhappy with the outcome. It promotes effective communication, participation, and is an efficient use of participants' time. IM can also be considered as a 'soft' systems approach that helps to capture the stakeholder requirements in order to better contextualise the problem space (Dogan and Henshaw 2010). To support consensus decision-making there must be a facilitator, participant group, a set of methods for reaching decisions, a computer or flip chart for organisation of ideas, and a decision support room (Broome and Keever 1986). IM is made up of three phases:

The Planning Phase. The first and most important step in this phase is to make sense of the situation at hand. This is achieved with scope and context statement writing, actor identification, and definition of the state. These methods encourage members to think about who and what is involved, and how it is effecting them to gain a broader picture of the problem. Defining the state of the problem helps to reveal questions that if answered, may significantly contribute towards an effective solution (Warfield 2002).

The Workshop Phase. The workshop is where participants come together to answer any questions derived from the planning phase and put consensus decision-making into action. The workshop is largely focused on three key concepts: Context, content, and process (Warfield 2002). Discussions are led by the facilitator, who provides the group with context derived from the planning phase. The group provides content based on the contextualisation through discussion and idea sharing. The facilitator manages the process of the workshop to ensure discussions remain on topic and members are making the best use of their time.

The IM workshop will consist of three methods: Idea Writing, Nominal Group Technique, and Interpretive Structural Modelling. In idea writing, a trigger question is presented to participants to silently write down ideas for. The written ideas are then exchanged with others and additional ideas are added. Everything is then collated and divided into categories, and presented to the group. Next is the Nominal Group Technique, where participants generate further ideas after a more holistic view of the problem is gained from idea writing. This also allows for clarification and editing of problem statements. Participants then rank each idea based on importance. The final part of the workshop is to transform idea statements into objectives and then create an interpretive structural model (ISM) to identify relationships amongst various items surrounding the problem (Attri et al. 2013). To gather participants for the group discussion, an email was sent to a group of people either enrolled in BYOD or likely have a good understanding of it due to their role and responsibilities. Five participants were selected in total.

The Follow-Up Phase. This phase puts into action the objectives derived from the workshop and begins the planning phase of solution implementation. If, during this stage it is realised that the issue had been misunderstood or new issues arose afterwards that were not taken into consideration before, a new planning phase would be entered (Warfield 2002).

4   Case Study Results

This section examines Globex's BYOD security solutions and assesses them based on professional guidelines from the previous section. Findings contained within this section were obtained by analysing Globex's BYOD policy, and conducting questionnaires and informal interviews with IT management staff. The information gathered from this helped to form a deeper understanding of the company's current set-up and future plans for their BYOD scheme. As an example, one question posed to IT management was "what policies are enforced through MDM?" In total three participants were asked to fill out the questionnaires: one being the line manager of IT, one being the senior manager of IT, and the last one was an IT engineer who is mainly responsible for the company's BYOD technical controls.

4.1   Company Profile

Globex is a global company exercising BYOD in various countries. They began rolling it out to employees earlier this year. The deciding factors for Globex adopting BYOD were to reduce costs, allow employees to choose their own device, and to keep up with modern technology trends. New hires are enrolled in BYOD by default, and employees with corporate liable devices before the introduction of BYOD are allowed to remain on a corporate liable plan until further notice. Employees can opt in to BYOD at any time, subject to managerial approval. Users can expense a capped amount of their network service costs to Globex for business-related usage.

4.2   BYOD Policy

As Globex is a global company, it would not have been possible to analyse every policy. This section focuses only on the BYOD policy for the UK. Globex's BYOD policy is very detailed and quite clearly communicates the responsibilities of the employee for both BYOD and corporate liable devices. It covers reimbursement and eligibility, device selection, corporate applications, separation upon termination, maintenance and repair, technical support, invoicing, and more. The employee's responsibilities are clearly conveyed followed by a best practices guide for avoiding additional costs and using mobile devices safely.

Corporate Responsibilities. One of the first aspects of this policy that stood out is how it lacks a clear definition of Globex's responsibilities. The employee's responsibilities are clearly illustrated in a sizeable list, but the company's responsibilities appear to be lesser and are embedded in text. From the employee's perspective the policy may be interpreted as a set of rules telling them what to do rather than a policy that represents both the interests of the company and the employee.

On-Boarding Process. Results from the questionnaire found that the BYOD policy is not currently a part of HR's on-boarding process for new hires. This is concerning since the majority of new hires are not entitled to corporate liable devices and would have no choice but to enrol in BYOD if they needed a mobile device for their role. Imposing BYOD on an employee's first day may come as a surprise and give an unprofessional first impression of the company.

Policy Enforcement and Compliance. At present, employees are not required to re-read and sign the BYOD policy at regular intervals, which makes it easy for them to forget about.

Social Media Policy. Globex should consider writing a social media policy to prohibit the disclosure of confidential information on social media (ICO 2016). Such a policy will aim to clearly define the types of information that must not be shared with each one supported by an example. This helps to cover the Globex's liability should a situation arise where corporate information is accidentally leaked due to inadequate care.

Encryption. Globex's policy makes no mention of device encryption for additional security for data at rest. It might be deemed too inconvenient for a lot of Android users due to the fact it enforces a strong password rather than a passcode, but for security conscious staff, the mention of device encryption may encourage some.

Anti-malware. The policy does not advise employees to install anti-malware solutions. Research presented earlier in the paper shows that mobile malware is on the rise, particularly on devices that install open source applications from Google's Play Store.

4.3   Technical Controls

AirWatch MDM. AirWatch is a mobile device management (MDM) application used by Globex which employees must enrol in before being accessing corporate resources. AirWatch has many features and supports multiple platforms, making it an easy choice. Of the many features included with AirWatch, Globex use: passcode enforcement, containerisation, device visibility excluding GPS tracking, and remote wipe.

To enrol in AirWatch, employees are provided with documentation with step-by-step set-up instructions. Globex have documentation for Android, Windows 8, Windows 10, and Apple iOS devices. Once enrolled in AirWatch, the user can access their corporate emails. The user is also given access to an AirWatch portal that they can sign into from their PC to manage their device. Users can still access their corporate OneDrives without AirWatch enrolment.

As highlighted by Eshlahi et al. (2014) and Ali et al. (2015), BYOD security models like MDM only provide a basic security solution and focuses mainly on management of the device. Because MDM is a reactive solution, it's effectiveness is only as good as the reaction time in the event of a security breach (NCSC 2014). MDM is a controversial model because of employees' privacy concerns and the inconvenience of security protocols enforced on the device (Downer and Bhattacharya 2015). MDM solutions like AirWatch can also be high maintenance due to regular updates and the number of devices connecting is constantly changing.

Alternative Solutions. An alternative solution to MDM is mobile information management (MIM), where corporate information is secured rather than devices and stored in a central location for secure access. The problem with MIM is it requires an internet connection to access resources which is inconvenient to staff who travel a lot (Eshlahi et al. 2014). This limitation is also shared by the VPN-based access model (Ali et al. 2015). Similarly, there is mobile application management (MAM), which is used to install, manage, and audit enterprise applications. Since MAM requires unique coding for each enterprise application to work properly, it is not a popular option (Steele 2013). Finally, another option is kernel modification, but employees may feel uncomfortable allowing the organisation to make changes to their devices operating system (Ali et al. 2015).

It is evident that more work is needed to address BYOD challenges. However, as it stands at the time of writing, MDM is the most feasible option for Globex to manage personal devices.

Improvement of MDM. Globex could use more of Airwatch's features to their advantage. The use of encryption enforcement would provide an extra layer of security for data at rest and should be considered in the future when BYOD develops. Training and awareness methods can be utilised to win employees over for such security protocols if done correctly. Blacklisting is another feature currently not in use that prevents jailbroken devices from connecting to corporate resources.

4.4 Planning for Security Incidents

As mentioned in the previous section, organisation's must be able to act quickly in the event of a lost or stolen device. AirWatch MDM is a good tool for this, but it's only effective with quick reaction time and a network connection to the device.

Globex's BYOD policy states it is the employee's responsibility to report a lost or stolen device to IT immediately. Globex have a dedicated 24-hour helpdesk that can be reached via telephone or email. However, if an employee doesn't have a spare phone or has lost all of their contact information, the reporting process might be delayed. Helpdesk staff have administrative privileges to the AirWatch portal so they can perform a remote wipe quickly in a security event. Employee's also have access to the AirWatch portal to perform a remote wipe, but only on their own device. Research discovered that IT are meant to perform remote enterprise wipe for terminated BYOD users, but there is currently nothing within in their leavers process that communicates this.

4.5   Encouraging Staff Agreement

Globex communicated the shift to BYOD primarily through line management and email newsletters from the CIO (chief information officer). The introduction newsletter outlined basic policy information and expected time of introduction to each region. Subsequently, Globex held a series of Q&A webinars.

Training and awareness is provided in several documents available on the corporate intranet. These documents were also included in the email newsletter. The problem with email communication is it is easy to miss and removes the human element from communication, which makes it easy to be misinterpreted.

Communication and change management is a complex task requiring in-depth knowledge of the company, as well as advanced planning techniques.

4.6   Increased Device Support

The policy reads that IT support will not support mobile devices unless the issue is related to AirWatch. From a cost and resources perspective this makes sense because it would impose an increased demand on IT staff, but BYOD users may feel abandoned by company. In the long term this may negatively contribute to the organisation's culture and attitudes.

The policy also states employees are responsible for maintaining and repairing their own device, which makes sense as they hold the warranty information.

4.7   Understanding Legal Issues

Exploring legal issues surrounding Globex's BYOD policy is out of the scope of this experiment as it requires background information from the Legal team and Human Resources. However, it is worth mentioning the value of employing risk management techniques to identify legal risks and develop strategies to outsource, mitigate, or transfer them.

4.8   Interactive Management (IM) Results

One of the authors acted as the facilitator for the IM session. The session took place in a meeting room situated in one of Globex's offices for the participants' convenience. Five participants were selected in total to participate in the IM workshop. Two of five participants are enrolled in BYOD, one by choice and the other as part of their on-boarding process to the company. One participant is from the legal department, another from the facilities department, and the final three participants are from customer support. All participants but one has been with the company for 10 years or more.

As explained in the previous sections, idea writing requires a trigger question which participants can write down ideas for and then exchange them. However due to the limits set by the participants' schedules, it was not possible to spend much time on this phase so ideas were exchanged aloud from the beginning. Ideas were recorded on a computer connected to a projector. The trigger question presented was:

"What are the issues with Globex's BYOD scheme?"

Table 2 presents the ideas generated from the trigger question. The ideas are numbered for ease of referring to, they do not represent the order of importance.

Table 2. Results of idea generation

1	Privacy of personal information being accessed by AirWatch
2	Lack of control over what information Globex can and can't see
3	Users have to accept permissions for AirWatch to access the device in but it states on the set-up document Globex does not monitor it
4	Don't understand why higher level executives are entitled to corporate liable devices
5	The standard cap is not enough for some users and should be flexible depending on the employee's role
6	The principle is a good idea but it needs more work
7	There's no clear definition of where the office ends and begins. Employees can end up bringing work on holiday
8	Sharing your personal number with customers and/or colleagues
9	It seems like IT are able to wipe your device and control your personal data
10	Clients may still be contacting people after leaving the company
11	Getting the workers council to approve it
12	It's not clear what BYOD leavers do in terms of wiping their device when they leave and cutting contact
13	There's nothing in the mobile policy about insuring the mobile devices
14	There's no advice about what to do if your device breaks. Will IT provide you with a temporary one in that situation?
15	The admin work involved in separating business and personal usage involves time. People may end up not bothering
16	Most people nowadays take out a package of minutes, texts, and data with their network supplier and don't necessarily get a break down of their usage which is covered under their contract so you can't expense it. In the mobile device policy, it states no contribution will be made to packages

Table 3 presents the categories in which each idea falls into. The categories are ranked based on how many ideas belong to each category. Based on this data, the biggest concerns for BYOD are to do with privacy and lack of communication. The next most occurring concerns are for the inconvenience presented to BYOD users and monetary issues. Following on from that is the users lack of understanding. Finally, the least concerns fall under culture and other. 'Other' represents ideas that are too generic to fall under any category.

Next is the nominal group technique, where participants were asked to pick their top five issues from the list of ideas and rank each one between the numbers one and five, with one being the most important. Table 4 displays the results.

Table 3. Categorization of ideas

Category	Ideas	Ranking
Privacy	1, 2, 3, 8, 9	1
Culture	4, 7	4
Monetary	5, 13, 15, 16	2
Lack of communication	3, 7, 9, 12, 14	1
Lack of understanding	2, 3, 9	3
Inconvenience	7, 10, 14, 15	2
Other	6, 11	4

Table 4. Participant's ranking of ideas

Idea	P1	P2	P3	P4	P5
1	3	5	1	3	1
2	2		4	2	2
3		3			
4			1		
5				5	
7	4		2		4
8	5		5		5
10		2			
12				4	
15	1	4			3
16		1		1	

Based on this data, ideas that were ranked most important are privacy of personal information, the additional administrative work, and not being able to get re-imbursement for network packages. Interestingly, one participant ranked higher-level executive's eligibility to corporate liable devices as their most important issue. During idea generation one participant commented that they 'were used to senior level executives getting more out of the company'. This could indicate an organisational culture issue that Globex's BYOD scheme is contributing to. It also shows a lack of understanding for security from the participant. The reason Globex may have implemented this rule is because senior executives handle more sensitive information in their roles and therefore the company requires complete control over the device to protect corporate data. On the contrary, it could be argued that the responsibility of ensuring employees understand this lies with Globex.

The final part of the workshop involves transforming idea statements into objectives and creating an interpretive structural model to demonstrate the relationships. Table 5 displays the objective statements from ideas deemed important enough by participants to rank in their top five.

To make ISM simpler, objectives from Table 5 are grouped by similarity to derive more generic objectives. The numbers grouped in the bottom right-hand corner of the boxes in Fig. 1 represent the objectives from Table 5 in their new group.

Table 5. Objective statements

1	Elucidate what personal information corporate installs like AirWatch can and cannot access through training and awareness methods
2	Improve employee's awareness of the control they have over corporate installs through training and awareness methods
3	Improve employee's awareness of how application permissions to personally owned devices work and what they really access through training and awareness
4	Provide clarity as to why higher level executives are entitled to corporate liable devices
5	To implement a flexible re-imbursement cap for employees based on their role and travel frequency
6	Include a section in the BYOD policy that covers the employees right to separate work from their personal life with tips on how to practice it in BYOD
7	Include an advice section in the BYOD policy on how to manage sharing your personal number with customers and colleagues
8	Include an advice section in the BYOD policy on how to manage client contacts upon termination from the company
9	Advise users on how to wipe corporate information from their device upon termination with tips on how to detach
10	Minimise the administrative work to make it as easy as possible for users to expense network usage
11	Look at allowing employees with a bundled network package to expense a certain percentage back, perhaps based on their role

Figure 1 shows the interpretive structural model derived from the objective statements and their relationships.

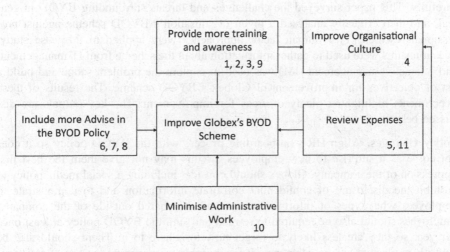

Fig. 1. Interpretive structural model

To conclude the workshop, participants were asked to rate their overall satisfaction with Globex's BYOD scheme on a scale of one to five, with one being very unsatisfied and five being very satisfied. Figure 2 shows the ratings.

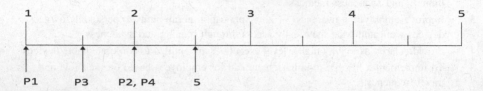

Fig. 2. Participants satisfaction with BYOD

The overall result of the IM session shows that all of the participants are unhappy with Globex's BYOD scheme to some extent. Of course this only represents a miniscule percentage of Globex as a whole. The participants all belonged to the same office, which will have its own unique culture to other offices. It could also be coincidence that brought five people together who share similar feelings towards Globex's BYOD scheme. In spite of having a small study group, some interesting points were made which are used to produce a clear list of objectives that Globex can use to improve employee satisfaction with BYOD.

5 Conclusion and Discussion

Bring your own device provides many benefits for an organisation and its employees. It is cost effective, increases productivity, and can improve staff morale if planned carefully. This paper surveyed the challenges and threats surrounding BYOD in general, and then critically analysed a given organisation's BYOD scheme against professional research. Two human factor approaches were applied to this case study: questionnaires were used to gather information about the scheme from IT management; and interactive management (IM) was used to explore the problem scope and build a list of objectives for improvement of Globex's BYOD scheme. The results of these experiments highlighted plenty of areas for improvement. The key outputs are discussed below.

Policy Changes. Align HR's on-boarding process with the BYOD policy so it does not come as a surprise to new employees, as this may not give them the best first impression of the company. Globex should consider including a social media policy to prohibit the disclosure of confidential corporate information and to demonstrate to employees what types of information must not be shared outside of the company. Employees should also be required to re-read and sign the BYOD policy at least once per year so they are less likely to forget how to adhere to it. There should also be controls in place to ensure adherence. It is advisable to encourage the use of anti-virus software for mobile devices as many people are unaware of threats transferring to mobile devices. Device encryption should also be recommended to protect data at rest.

It would not be a good idea to enforce encryption until employee satisfaction towards BYOD improves as this may cause more resistance and negative feelings. There should be an additional section in the policy with separation advise for cutting ties with the company upon termination. Finally, the policy could be re-worded to sound less like a set of rules and cover more of the employer's responsibilities to 'even the scales' between the company and employee. This will make the policy appear more friendly.

Technical Controls. The use of mobile device management (MDM) as a technical control is the most feasible solution for the company at this time, but some features are not being used to their full potential. For example, additional policies could be set to prevent jailbroken devices connecting to corporate resources, ensure an up-to-date anti-malware solution is installed, and device encryption enforcement could be considered for the future. In addition, the set-up instructions for configuring AirWatch on mobile devices need to be reviewed and updated more regularly as it quickly becomes outdated with updates to the graphical user interface. Interestingly, results obtained from the questionnaire state IT staff are meant to performing remote wipes upon an employee's termination, but there is no formal documentation on this in the leavers process. This means there might be staff leaving with company with corporate information still on their device. This item should be actioned immediately.

Encouraging Staff Agreement. It is clear from the experiments that there is bad energy amongst the employees about the Globex's BYOD scheme. Certain aspects are still misunderstood by employees and will have easily been forgotten since they were made to read and sign the policy. Therefore, more creative methods of training and awareness should be developed rather than using email newsletters and Q&A sessions. People are less likely to speak out in large groups and people can often miss email communications. Role-playing activities, games, and demonstrations are proven to be more effective in the long-term (Lacey 2009). Of course this will come with additional costs, but it would be incomparable to the potential losses of a security breach. The re-imbursement caps should be reviewed on an individual basis depending on the employee's role and recent travel requirements. Two participants from the IM session felt it was unfair of Globex to send them to a country with high data roaming charges where they could not expense it all back. Moreover, employees with network bundles should be able to expense some of their usage to the company without a breakdown of the business and personal costs. Particularly if they are someone who uses their mobile device for business on a daily basis. Globex should consider awarding employees with a one-off contribution to their employee's mobile devices in order to improve staff morale and encourage the shift. If Globex issued £50 to each user, they would feel less disgruntled and resentful. Doing this would still significantly reduce IT costs because corporate liable devices are purchased above £100, and that's not including the monthly network usage plan. Finally, the company should try to find ways to reduce the amount of administrative work involved in expensing business usage so staff are not discouraged from doing so.

Device Support. The final note for improvement to this case study is, not to rule out device support completely. No additional training will be required from IT, nor will they be under any obligation to the support BYOD devices, but if they have previous experience with the device in question, it should be down to the engineer's discretion to help the user.

This work could be expanded upon in the future with the use of other Human Factor approaches, as mentioned in Sect. 3. One area of particular interest is the use of Cognitive Walkthrough.. Cognitive walkthrough could be used in this case study to evaluate the usability of the AirWatch set-up. By identifying problem areas in the set-up of devices, the company might save a lot of time that employees spend in IT support and improve overall efficiency in the configuration.

References

Absalom, R.: A guide for BYOD policies. Int. Data Priv. Legis. Rev. **1**, 1–23 (2012). http://www.webtorials.com/main/resource/papers/mobileiron/paper5/Guide_for_BYOD_Policies.pdf. Accessed 2 Nov 2016

Ali, S., Qureshi, M., Abbasi, A.: Analysis of BYOD security frameworks. In: 2015 Conference on Information Assurance and Cyber Security (CIACS). The Military College of Signals (MCS), Pakistan (2015)

Attri, R., Dev, N., Sharma, V.: Interpretive Structural Modelling (ISM) approach: an overview. Res. J. Manag. Sci. **2**(2), 3–8 (2013). ISSN: 2319-1171

Broome, B.J., Keever, D.B.: Facilitating group communication: the interactive management approach (1986). http://files.eric.ed.gov/fulltext/ED273997.pdf. Accessed 6 Nov 2016

Chartered Institute of Ergonomics: What is ergonomics? Chartered Institute of Ergonomics & Human Factors (2016). http://www.ergonomics.org.uk/what-is-ergonomics/. Accessed 6 Nov 2016

Clay, J.: Continued rise in mobile threats for 2016. Trend Micro (2015). http://blog.trendmicro.com/continued-rise-in-mobile-threats-for-2016/. Accessed 12 Oct 2016

Dodge, R., Carver, C., Ferguson, A.: Phishing for user security awareness. Comput. Secur. **26**, 73–80 (2007)

Dogan, H., Henshaw, M.J.D.: Transition from soft systems to an enterprise knowledge management architecture. In: International Conference on Contemporary Ergonomics and Human Factors, 13–15 April 2010. Keele University, UK (2010)

Downer, K., Bhattacharya, M.: BYOD security: a new business challenge. In: 2015 IEEE International Conference on Smart City/SocialCom/SustainCom (SmartCity). IEEE, Australia (2015)

Eshlahi, M., Salleh, R., Anuar, N.: MoBots: a new generation of botnets on mobile devices and networks. In: 2012 International Symposium on Computer Applications and Industrial Electronics (ISCAIE 2012). IEEE, Malaysia (2012)

Eshlahi, M., Var Naseri, M., Hashim, H., Tahir, N.M., Mat Saad, E.: BYOD: current state and security challenges. In: 2014 IEEE Symposium on Computer Applications & Industrial Electronics (ISCAIE). IEEE, Malaysia (2014)

F-secure labs: Botnets. A quick guide to botnets - what they are, how they work and the harm they can cause (2016). https://www.f-secure.com/en/web/labs_global/botnets. Accessed 14 Oct 2016

Greenberg, A., Reporter, S., Colón, M.: Human error cited as leading contributor to breaches, study shows. SC Magazine US (2015). https://www.scmagazine.com/study-find-carelessness-among-top-human-errors-affecting-security/article/535928/. Accessed 8 Nov 2016

Information Commissioners Office: Bring Your Own Device (BYOD) Guidance (2016). https://ico.org.uk/media/for-organisations/documents/1563/ico_bring_your_own_device_byod_guidance.pdf. Accessed 4 Oct 2016

Kan, M.: This malware pretends to be WhatsApp, Uber and Google play. PCWorld (2016). http://www.pcworld.com/article/3089514/security/this-malware-pretends-to-be-whatsapp-uber-and-google-play.html. Accessed 12 Oct 2016

Kumar, R.: A proactive procedure to mitigate the BYOD risks on the security of an information system. ACM SIGSOFT Softw. Eng. Notes **40**(1), 1–4 (2015)

Lacey, D.: Transforming organisation attitudes and behaviour. In: Managing the Human Factor in Information Security. Wiley, West Sussex, pp. 237–240 (2009)

Lindlof, T.R., Taylor, B.C.: Qualitative Communication Research Methods, 3rd edn. SAGE, Thousand Oaks (2011)

Mathias, C.: Potential BYOD legal issues you may not have thought of. SearchMobileComputing (2013). http://searchmobilecomputing.techtarget.com/tip/Potential-BYOD-legal-issues-you-may-not-have-thought-of. Accessed 7 Nov 2016

Mavretich, R.J.: Legal Issues within Corporate "Bring Your Own Device" Programs, Sans Institute (2012). https://uk.sans.org/reading-room/whitepapers/legal/legal-issues-corporate-bring-device-programs-34060. Accessed 14 Oct 2016

Miners, Z.: Report: malware-infected Android apps spike in the Google play store. PCWorld (2014). http://www.pcworld.com/article/2099421/report-malwareinfected-android-apps-spike-in-the-google-play-store.html. Accessed 12 Oct 2016

NCSC: BYOD guidance: executive summary. GOV.UK (2014). https://www.gov.uk/government/publications/byod-guidance-executive-summary/byod-guidance-executive-summary#create-effective-byod-policy. Accessed 4 Oct 2016

Nielsen, J., Molich, R.: Heuristic evaluation of user interfaces. In: Proceedings of the SIGCHI Conference on Human Factors in Computing Systems. ACM (1990)

PWC: 2015 Information Security Breaches Survey. HM Government (2015)

Souppaya, M., Scarfone, K.: Guidelines for Managing the Security of Mobile Devices in the Enterprise. National Institute of Standards and Technology (NIST), Gaithersburg (2013)

Steele, C.: Mobile device management vs. mobile application management. Search Mobile Computing (2013). http://searchmobilecomputing.techtarget.com/feature/Mobile-device-management-vs-mobile-application-management. Accessed 6 Nov 2016

Symantec: Internet Security Threat Report, vol. 21. Symantec (2016)

Thomson, G.: BYOD: enabling the chaos. Netw. Secur. **2012**(2), 5–8 (2012)

Wang, Y., Wei, J., Vangury, K.: Bring your own device security issues and challenges. In: The 11th Annual IEEE EENC- Mobile Device, Platform and Communication. IEEE, Las Vegas (2014)

Warfield, J.N.: A Handbook of Interactive Management, 2nd edn. Ajar Publishing, Palm Harbor (2002)

Wharton, C., Rieman, J., Lewis, C., Polson, P.: Usability Inspection Methods, 1st edn. Wiley, New York (1994)

Wickens, C., Lee, J., Liu, Y., Gordon-Becker, S.: An Introduction to Human Factors Engineering, 2nd edn. Pearson, Upper Saddle River (2003)

Wilson, B.: Soft Systems Methodology. Wiley, Chichester (2001)

Winder, D.: Viking horde: are mobile botnets a thing now? SC Magazine UK (2016). http://www.scmagazineuk.com/viking-horde-are-mobile-botnets-a-thing-now/article/496002/. Accessed 14 Oct 2016

Wu, L., Du, X., Wu, J.: Effective defence schemes for phishing attacks on mobile computing platforms. IEEE Trans. Veh. Technol. **65**, 6678–6691 (2016)

A Case Study: Heartbleed Vulnerability Management and Swedish Municipalities

Shao-Fang Wen[✉] and Stewart Kowalski

Faculty of Information Technology and Electrical Engineering,
Norwegian University of Science and Technology, Gjøvik, Norway
{shao-fang.wen, stewart.kowalski}@ntnu.no

Abstract. In Sweden, the use of open source software (OSS) in public sectors has been promoted by the government in recent years. A number of Swedish municipalities forms interest communities to share OSS information and work together with OSS issues. However, it lacks of studies and evidences that these municipalities have adequate routines for managing warnings and advices from the communities on OSS security incidents. The Heartbleed vulnerability that occurred in April 2014 was a sudden case for these municipalities to take remedial actions to protect their information assets in a timely manner. This work aims to take a socio-technical study of how Swedish municipalities utilizes information channels to handle the OSS security incident and their security posture before, during and after the incident. We conducted a case study for Heartbleed incident management in Swedish municipalities, where three municipalities located in different regions of the country were studied. This study used a qualitative research method combining with Security-by-Consensus (SBC) analytical model as a research paradigm for data collection, and processing and analysis. The result suggests that the socio-technical aspects of open source security should be taken into account in Swedish municipalities for OSS adoption and security incident management.

Keywords: Open source software · Heartbleed · Security incident · Socio-technical · Swedish municipalities · SBC model

1 Introduction

On April 7, 2014, news of the Heartbleed bug hit the world. The Finnish company Codenomicon and Google had independently [16] discovered a bug present in the open source software (OSS), OpenSSL. The vulnerability allowed attackers to remotely get sensitive data, possibly including user authentication credentials and secret keys, through incorrect memory handling from both clients and servers [12, 17]. In Sweden, the use of open source software in the public sector has been promoted by the government [39]. Several municipalities in different parts of the country formed interest organizations to work together with OSS and issue around it. The Heartbleed vulnerability required these municipalities to take remedial actions to protect their information assets in a timely manner. Because of the great impact of the bug, there were also many different information sources to resort to when solving the problem with the

T. Tryfonas (Ed.): HAS 2017, LNCS 10292, pp. 414–431, 2017.
DOI: 10.1007/978-3-319-58460-7_29

bug, both official and unofficial The Computer Emergency Response Team-Sweden, CERT-SE, helps Swedish organizations with security issues. CERT-SE sent out security warnings when serious incidents like the Heartbleed bug occurs [7]. On April 4, 2014, rumors about the Heartbleed bug started to spread across the open source community. Codenomicon published a website, www.heartbleed.com, which contained detailed information about the bug; how to update the software and how to update certificates [16]. Swedish media sources started to disseminate information about the Heartbleed bug to the Swedish population, three days after the Heartbleed website was actually released. The majority of the Swedish newspapers did not share any recommendations to the public [11, 13, 22]. Aftonbladet was the only newspaper that actually recommended the public not to visit any servers that might be using OpenSSL and recommended people not to send any secrets on the net [35]. The Swedish Television (SVT) and the Swedish radio (SR) did recommend people to change their passwords [10, 48]. When it comes to Social Media, on 7th of April Facebook announced a message reassuring Facebook users that protection had been implemented and that they continue to monitor the situation closely [16]. The first tweet about the bug came out on April 7, which was made from Adam Langley. The tweet that was about the bug also referred to the Heartbleed website [26].

The problem is that research shows that half a year after the Heartbleed incident the necessary precautions against Heartbleed from various information sources had not been taken by many users of OpenSSL [50]. This work studied how Swedish municipalities handled the Heartbleed incident and their security posture before, during and after the incident. Specifically, this case study will focus on exploring and describing what procedures surround security incidents with OSS and which sources of information are consulted in the process.

1.1 Heartbleed Bug

The naming of Heartbleed is based on Heartbeat, while the Heartbeat is an extension for the Transport Layer Security (TLS) and Datagram Transport Layer Security (DTLS) protocols, it was proposed as a standard in February 2012 by RFC 6520 [8, 12].

The Heartbeat Extension allows either end-point of a TLS connection to detect whether its peer is still present, and was motivated by the need for session management in DTLS [12]. In 2011, one of the RFC's authors, Robin Seggelmann implemented the Heartbeat Extension for OpenSSL. OpenSSL failed to notice a bug in Seggelmann's implementation and introduced the flawed code into OpenSSL's source code repository on December 31, 2011. The vulnerable code was adopted into widespread use with the release of OpenSSL version 1.0.1 on March 14, 2012. Heartbeat support was enabled by default, causing affected versions to be vulnerable by default [46].

The feature, introduced by Seggelmann, enables arbitrary data to be sent from one end of a connection to another. The receiving end would then ping back an exact copy of that same data to prove that the connection is secure, according to a detailed breakdown by The Register [47]. After the initial Heartbeat message is sent, however, the bug tricks the recipient server into spilling out data from its memory instead of just sending back an exact copy of the original data. In short, it enables the server to "bleed" out extra information after receiving a Heartbeat message. The sensitive information that may be retrieved using this vulnerability includes primary key material contains secret keys, secondary key material contains usernames and passwords used by vulnerable services, protected content contains sensitive data used by vulnerable services, and collateral contains memory addresses and content that can be leveraged to bypass exploit mitigations [19, 46].

The Heartbleed vulnerability was originally found by Neel Mehta, a Google computer security employee, in March 2014 [16]. Upon finding the bug and patching its servers, Google notified the core OpenSSL team on April 1. Independently, a security-consulting firm, Codenomicon, found the vulnerability on April 2 and reported it to National Cyber Security Centre Finland (NCSC-FI). After receiving notification those two groups independently discovered the vulnerability, the OpenSSL core team decided to release a patched version.

The public disclosure of Heartbleed started on April 7, 2014, at 17:49 UTC with the version 1.0.1g release announcement [37], followed by the public security advisory [36] released at 20:37 UTC; both announcements were sent to the OpenSSL mailing list. At 18:55 UTC, National Vulnerability Database (NVD) of NIST (National Institution of Standard and Technology, USA) released a Vulnerability Summary for CVE-2014-0160 [33], which is the official reference to this Heartbleed bug.

1.2   About CERT-SE

In Sweden, the Computer Emergency Response Team (CERT-SE), an organization within the Swedish Civil Contingencies Agency (Myndigheten för samhällskydd och beredskap; MSB), deals with and works preemptively with IT-security incidents that affect society [31]. Their assignment is to deliver information of security incidents to those organizations who sign up their mail services. They also communicate and cooperate with other CERT organizations around the world. CERT-SE aims to work for both the private and public sector such as municipalities. At the occurrence of a major IT-incident CERT-SE sends out a warning to organizations who have subscribed to receive an e-mail "flash warning" about serious incidents. For the Heartbleed incident, CERT-SE, in their "flash warning", recommended users of OpenSSL to upgrade to the new OpenSSL version 1.0.1g. Later in their newsletter, they also instructed users to exchange the certificates for the updated software, and other secret data that could have been disclosed due to the bug [6].

2   Related Works

Most of the recent research in Open Source/Heartbleed incident management has largely technology driven. Wu [49] identified the technical procedures and findings of Heartbleed incident management through a real case analysis in a medical school, including sever inventory audit and risk assessment. The difficulties of detecting the Heartbleed vulnerability by a static or a dynamic analysis technique alone have been identified and discussed in [25]. To address such vulnerabilities, some research works focus on building feasible mechanisms for the detection of Heartbleed vulnerability [23, 27, 44].

Other studies have been conducted in the area of OSS adoption and security management. Ramanathan and Iyer [38] identified the influence of outsourcing on OSS and further investigated the factors that impact the adoption of OSS in global Information Technology outsourcing organizations serviced by Indian IT services providers. Their study adopted positivism research philosophy and qualitative approach. Tosi et al. [45] studied the adoption of OSS in the Public Administration in Italy, including the obstacles of their adoption and willingness of stakeholders to proceed with their introduction. Lundell et al. [28] studied the state of practice with respect to OSS in Swedish companies across the small and medium enterprises and large company sectors that have adopted OSS. They analyzed its implications from a number of perspectives, including business motivations and rationale, individual and organizational motivations, and tensions concerning different values (community vs. corporate values).

There is another study on OSS and its use in Swedish municipalities from the Högskolan in Skövde [3]. Focus in that work was on the risks and possibilities during the transfer from proprietary software systems to introduction of OSS in municipalities. The subject of how to deal with security vulnerabilities in OSS is only fleetingly touched upon in this work. The discussion then concerns support and a worry at the municipalities that the support from OSS providers is not as good as for proprietary software. Focus in the study is on risks during the actual migration of software and not management and daily support of OSS.

In our research work, we aim to use a socio-technical analysis approach to form a view on both technical and social aspects of handling Heartbleed incident and obtain an better understanding of the events and causes of action during this incident.

3   Research Approach and Data Collection

The objective of this research is to study security incident management of OSS in Swedish municipalities. The study attempts to answer the following research question: *How does the socio-technical security posture of Swedish municipalities affect the use of official and unofficial sources' warnings and advice concerning Open Source security vulnerabilities?* Swedish municipalities are the unit of analysis in this case study. The study used an exploratory qualitative and the case study approach, which provides a rich and in-depth analysis of OSS incident management of organizations. Qualitative research method is a field of scientific inquiry that crosscuts various disciplines and subject matters. Usually, it uses qualitative data and involves interviews, observations, and document reviews in order to understand human behavior (social and cultural) and the entire environment [5, 32].

In this case, study the problem statement covers areas of IT-security within open source software at municipalities. The focus was on the IT-department, a particular group of people from the chosen municipality. As we wanted to get input from the users, while still allowing for them to think freely to some extent, we chose to use a

418   S.-F. Wen and S. Kowalski

semi-structured interview as described by May [30]. With a semi-structured interview, the questions are prepared in advance, but the researcher can ask complimentary questions and have a dialogue with the subject. In order to facilitate elaboration, certain possible follow-up questions were prepared beforehand. As we suspected that the subjects would be unwilling to consider themselves behaving insecurely, we also asked about what their colleagues would do. This also has the benefit of covering more subjects.

3.1   Socio-Technical Framework

In order to create questions on the social element of security, we needed a framework describing security that covered both social and technical issues. In this case study, we adopted a socio-technical framework provided by Stewart Kowalski [24], which contains two basic models: a dynamic model of socio-technical changes, called the socio-technical system (Fig. 1), and a static one, called the security-by-consensus (SBC) model or stack (Fig. 2). At the abstract level, the socio-technical system is divided into two subsystems, social and technical. Within a given sub-system, there are further sub-systems. The former (social) has culture and structures, and the latter (technical) has methods and machines. From the system theory/s point of view, inter-dependencies between system levels make a system adjust for attaining equilibrium. The process is referred to as homeostasis state. For instance, if new hardware is introduced into one of the technical sub-systems, for instance, the machine sub-system, the whole system will strive to achieve homeostasis. This suggests that changes in one sub-system may cause disturbances in other sub-systems and consequently to the entire system.

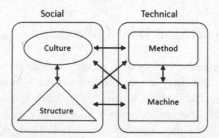

Fig. 1. Socio-technical model (Kowalski [24], p. 10)

Reflecting the static nature of the socio-technical systems, the SBC stack is a multi-level structure that divides security measures into hierarchical levels of control. The social sub-system includes following security measures: ethical and cultural norms, legal and contractual documents, administration and managerial policies, and operational and procedural guidelines. Similarly, the technical sub-system consists mechanical and electronic, hardware, operating systems, application systems, and data. Other aspects are store, process, collect, and communication.

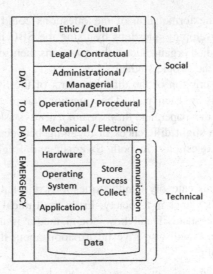

Fig. 2. The SBC model (Kowalski [24], p. 19)

In the socio-technical framework, each system interacts with other systems rather than being an isolated system. Internal and external changes—both social and technical—will affect system security. Therefore, systematic deployment of security measures is required. In particular, this framework has been applied to evaluate threat modeling in software supply chain [1], business process re-engineering [4], a framework for securing e-Government services [19] and an information security maturity model [20]. The application of the socio-technical framework to software analysis is an appropriate and legitimate way of understanding the intrinsic context in open source phenomenon. It provides a way to perform system analysis through a systemic–holistic perspective [21].

3.2 Data Collection

Interview Questions. The interview template that has been made covers specific areas or themes from the problem section to collect data for the research question. Since the research tends to adopt a specific analytical approach called the SBC-model, the interview questions were separated into different categories. Each question is unique and asked only once depending on the respondent. To formulate the questions for the interviews the categories according to the SBC-model were used: Ethical and Cultural, Legal and Contractual, Administration and Managerial, Operational, and Technical. The different categories of questions were not disclosed to the interviewed persons during the interview to prevent the participants from being influenced by them in their answers.

A preliminary test was done on the interview questions, after which slight changes were made on the order in which the questions were asked and how the questions were formulated. By listening to the recording, the researcher became more aware about how the wording and how the formulation of the questions could influence the subject. While the process of developing questions by using the SBC model as a background can be used for most studied organizations, the questions themselves should be adapted to the organization and the people studied.

Below follows a description of the different parts of the SBC-model and a motivation for the questions in each part. The questions were asked in Swedish but translated to English for this paper, and they were not always asked exactly as the same phrases. There might be slight differences in meaning between the languages lost in translation. The actual questions (in both Swedish and English) can be found in Appendix A.

Ethical and cultural: This category handles questions of what is considered morally right and wrong people's values in a society. From the Ethical interview questions, it will be possible to understand if and how social media is a possible tool for the IT-administrators to use. It will also give information about the general handling of IT-risks in the municipality.

Political and legal: Handles questions with regard to how society implements its own laws and rules and its awareness of them. The political and legal interview questions will disclose how well the governments' intent on increasing the use of OSS has been implemented. It will also show if it is political or legal influences of OSS adoption or if it is used on the recommendation from the employees at the IT-department.

Administrative and managerial: Actions aims at creating policies/rules to obtain a high-security level and to ensure activities that facilitate the implementation of policies/rules are in place. The organizational management is important to have for comparison to other municipalities and to show generality for the study. Some of these questions try to clarify the management activities during the Heartbleed incident to understand when and how different information sources were used and how the organization will act in a similar situation in the future.

Operational: This category aims to understand how Heartbleed was handled by concrete security activities at the operational levels.

Technical: This includes computer hardware and software applications. The hardware interview questions will reflect the organization's use of OSS and in what state the applications are in today.

Data Collection

There are 290 municipalities in Sweden [43]. For this case study, the selection of municipality had to be based on certain specific attributes [9]. The criteria were: (1) Municipalities that use OSS. (2) Municipalities that have been affected by the Heartbleed bug; and (3) Municipalities that manage system administration in-house. Sambruk is an organization consisting of Swedish municipalities, formed 10 years ago, with 100 members. Their focus is to coordinate and work together with organizational development and e-governance using open source software and platforms in the municipalities [42]. Because of the use of open source code in the Sambruk interest organization, it was considered a good source to find a suitable candidate for this study within that organization. A selection of Sambruk members around the Stockholm area was contacted to try to convince one or some of them to participate in the case study. The Stockholm area was chosen due to closeness to the interview subjects.

When recruiting municipalities for participation in the study a letter describing the project was sent out to several municipalities, which were known from the Sambruk organization to use OSS. The letter also contained bullet points on subjects that was going to be studied to give the recipient an opportunity to understand the content of the case study.

Three municipalities (M-1, 2, 3) have been considered good candidates for this study because they met the three criteria stated above and the organizations were active on social media like Twitter and Facebook. The result from the case was expected to be representative of other municipalities that meet the three criteria. An investigation of municipalities from and around the Mälardalen region showed that five of eleven municipalities manage their system administration in-house. Municipalities geographically close to each other and belonging to the same County Council (sv. "landsting") have been found to meet and discuss IT-security. Speculatively, they can indirectly be influenced by each other to embrace the other municipalities' safety routines and behavior. From the reasons mentioned in this section, results from this report should be possible to generalize to other municipalities that use OSS. Factors that limits how much the findings in the study can be generalized are primarily if the municipalities outsource their IT-administration or not. If they are outsourcing, it can be difficult to know how the security incidents are dealt with. There are a large number of municipalities, judging from collaborations like Sambruk, should encounter the same problems with how to deal with OSS bugs as the studied municipality

The Interviews

The interviews all started with an explanation of the study, ethical aspects etc. During the interviews, other questions than the pre-developed were asked, which was expected in advance. The interviews lasted between 35 and 55 min. They were taped and later transcribed and then sent to the subjects in order to see that there were no major misunderstandings or misquotes after which the interviews were analyzed using qualitative methods. This was sent using e-mail due to practical reasons but it is notable that poor e-mail security might danger the anonymity of the subjects. Different themes and categories in the answers were apparent, and in some cases, the subjects answered in such a way that the answers could easily be compared; in those cases, a comparative analysis was made.

3.3   Ethical Aspects

During the study, the participants were introduced to the subject and the authors. None of the participants were forced to take part and signed the form of consent. At the start of the interview, the subjects were informed again about the aim and method of the study, both orally and in a written document. They were also informed that the interviews would be taped and the tapes stored, but that they would remain anonymous in the study and on the tapes, how the material would be published and also that they could abort the study at any time, without needing to give a reason. Both the subject and the researcher then signed the document. The subjects were also offered a chance to see the transcriptions from their own interviews to ensure that there were no misunderstandings or misquotes.

All the interviews were recorded and the participants were informed about that. After transcription, the results of the interviews were sent to the interviewees for correction of misinterpretation. One ethical concern was that it would be discovered during the study that the studied organizations had not dealt with the Heartbleed bug in a proper way. To be on the safe side, all the organizations were informed about the proper procedure to deal with Heartbleed after the interviews if it was not apparent during the interview that they had updated their systems in a proper way.

4   Findings: Data Analysis and Results

Eight interviews were done. The interviewees all came from IT department: three was female and five were male. The ages were between 25 to 50 years. They had been in IT fields for 4 to 15 years. Below is a summary of the results and analysis in this study. The form used for the analysis is set by the SBC categories.

Ethical/Cultural: All subjects expressed the security awareness of adoption of open source software. Each OSS had a dedicated system administrator, who was responsible to overlook the system and make sure that the patches were applied routinely and effectively. There was no restriction in the use of social media in these three municipalities. Despite that social media delivered the quicker news about Heartbleed than CERT-SE [16], municipalities still relied on the information source of CERT-SE. where they believe they can find trustworthy information. While the Heartbleed occurred, IT departments took most actions in dealing with the vulnerability. There was no information sent out to the users about the bug during and after the incident in M-1 and M-2. M-3 had a simple description of IT measurements in their system maintenance notice, but also did not mention Heartbleed bug in this announcement.

Legal/Contractual: There were no known political or legal pressures or incitements to use OSS in respondent units. It is interesting to note that the promotion of OSS in the public sector by the Swedish government [39] had not fully reached some organizations. There was also no known knowledge about political strategies to implement OSS in the organizations. While there was information on OSS adoption, the documents were not known by most of the subjects, and their actual influence on the day-to-day security work was probably very slight.

Administrational/Managerial: In Swedish municipalities, the IT manager worked on the strategic, tactical, and operational levels. There was an established practice to manage IT systems and OSS products, including audited IT systems periodically, identified people to be responsible for keeping track of OSS products and assessed risks of IT systems. The chain of command at each municipality with regard to report hierarchy was clear. IT managers in the county met up regularly and exchange information about e.g. security incidents like Heartbleed and how to deal with security problems in general that were encountered in their organizations. It helped municipalities network with each other and learn from experiences.

Operational/Procedure: People in charge of maintaining OSS subscribed themselves to respective mailing list from CERT-SE. They would check the threads posted in social media in day-to-day operations, however, when emergency incidents came in, it was thought that they would take longer time for them to filter through all information sources of social media to deal with the security incident. Compared to proprietary software support where they called customer support and know whom they talk to and trust that the support person can solve the problem that they have. There seemed to be a reluctance to contact OSS support even though they thought that they probably would obtain the same service.

Technical: There was a good security coverage on open source products in IT departments, such as installed OSS in intranet only, enabled firewall and updating the patch routinely. However, employees at each municipality that has a municipality owned computer can download any software to that computer. There was no specific policy or technical mechanism for the control of downloading OSS in personal computers.

Using the data acquired in the interviews, we made a judgment on the readiness of the areas surveyed based on frequency of answers, and the impact of the vulnerabilities. It can be seen in Fig. 3 below. On a scale from 0–10, the answers were rated on impact on security. The higher the rating the better influence on security.

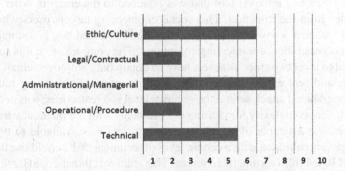

Fig. 3. Result of SBC interpretation

To make it easier to discuss both technical and social aspects of a security incident we use a coordinate system proposed by Alsabbagh and Kowalski [2] which aims to visualize the relationship between operational environment threat metrics and organizational security posture. Using the result from the study, the coordinate system is presented in Fig. 4. In the right-hand part of the graph, the severity of the security incident is displayed, from a social and technical aspect. The left-hand side of the graph shows the perceived posture of the organization towards the security threat studied. The range is set from 1 to 5 on all axis, where the low numbers corresponds to low threat/posture on the x-axis and from less to more complex problems on a social and technical level on the y-axis [2].

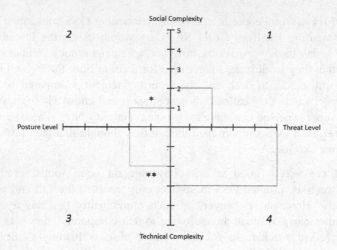

Fig. 4. IS warning coordination system

According to Symantec Security Response [15], by the time of Heartbleed vulnerability announcement, a spam campaign was uncovered using Heartbleed as a way to scare users into installing malware onto their computer. The spam requested that the user run the Heartbleed bug removal tool that was attached to the email in order to "clean" their computer from the infection. This social engineering targets users who may not have enough technical knowledge to know that the Heartbleed bug is not malware and that there is no possibility of it infecting computers. The complexity of this social threat was estimated to level two since attackers have to obtain only employee email addresses, and compose and sent email. This kind of attack is more a discrediting rather than a financial or operational attack so that the severity level suggested here was deemed level two. The technical complexity for causing the problems with the incident was judged to be level 3 because a sample of proof-of-concept scripts was available to be retrieved [14, 29]. Attackers equipped with a certain level of technical skills could use the script to dump a bit of RAM from a vulnerable server. This technical threat could have been very critical if confidential information were disclosed which puts the threat level at four.

The social security posture of the organization was to be medium-low (level 2), since the responsibility and ownership of system administrators were high, however, there was no enough information revealing to users in order to enrich their knowledge and raise security awareness. The complexity of social posture was estimated heuristically to a level 1 because only one official information source was used to find information about how to deal with Heartbleed vulnerability, and there was no political or legal knowledge in implementation OSS in organizations. Both the levels of technical posture and complexity were set to two since the standard countermeasures have been made only within IT systems.

To be able to resolve the potential threat, the posture level should be on the same level as the threat to be able to deal with the problem. If the solution of the threat is less than the actual threat the capability of the organization is not enough to deal with the potential security problem. In this research, the threat level was a lot higher than the low posture level of the organization. This gap between threat and posture is represented by the stars in the Fig. 4. To bridge the gaps (*social, **technical) and be better prepared for security incidents like Heartbleed the municipality would have to take preventative measures that are discussed in the next section.

5 Discussion

The purpose of this study is to investigate whether the socio-technical security posture of Swedish municipalities affects the use of official and unofficial sources' warnings and advice concerning open source security vulnerabilities. It can be shown that even though the municipalities in this study used social media when keeping track of problems with OSS-security incidents they still follow the recommendation that CERT-SE gave. The reason for this seems to be a trust in the official information from CERT-SE in combination with an insecurity of how truthful information from unofficial sources like social media sources on the internet are.

However, several sources in social media conveyed the right course of action to deal with Heartbleed from the start and was faster to publish the news than CERT-SE. To avoid a situation where only one official source of information is trusted it would be beneficial to track other alternative sources when seeking solutions to security vulnerabilities which would mitigate the gap of social complexity in Fig. 1 (*social improvement). Another important aspect is to also follow up on incidents to both make sure that proper preventative measures against the vulnerability has been taken and also improve management of open source downloading and patching (**technical improvement). With the large amount of municipalities using OSS and the government, promoting its use there could also be a national policy on how to deal with OSS in organizations. In March 2015, almost a year after the Heartbleed incident, the Swedish "Riksrevisionen" handed in a petition to the government in which they wanted to have better rules implemented for security management; supervision of security management in the public sector and sanctions for those who don't comply with the regulation should be introduced [41]. These requests are in line with a European Union (EU) directive to ensure a high level of internet- and information security (IS) throughout the EU [40]. The Government also wants to start a national incident report system [41]. An incident report system, from a general Safety, Health, and Environment perspective, used right, will be able to pick up on small "not so dangerous"-events and by learning from those more severe incidents can be avoided [31].

The SBC model result shows a low rating in the Legal/Contractual and Operational categories. This rating could be remedied by the government when they propose a transfer from proprietary software to OSS to reflect over what kind of risks the municipalities run when doing so and make sure that proper policies are in place for operational employees to follow. The security problem that can be seen in connection to the use of OSS in the public sector, stem from a lag in development in method, culture, and structure compared to machine from a socio-technical perspective. The technology is implemented as the software but the method for dealing with a security incident due to a software bug is not robust when the user doesn't have clear methodology for solving the problem i.e. the user doesn't know where to find information about a security incident [24]. A strong culture in an organization forms when the employees follow the rules that are set up for the work processes. In the Heartbleed case, the studied municipalities had to change their routines after the incident, which is a sign of that the original rules were not adequate to deal with the new process of dealing with OSS vulnerabilities. The municipality management in question took the experience with Heartbleed to heart and improved their routines. That type of behavior is evident of good leadership and improves on the structure in the organization [31].

6 Conclusion and Recommendation

In this study, we use conducted a socio-technical study for Heartbleed incident management in Swedish municipalities and used qualitative research method combining with SBC analytical model as a research paradigm. Findings in this study compares to the study from Högskolan in Skövde by Andersson [3] in which the municipalities also were under the impression that OSS support is inferior to support from proprietary software providers. This belief is contradicted by O'Reilly [34] who claims that many OSS has a proven track record of support over many years. The Sonatype survey [18] showed that many of the private organizations didn't have an OSS policy. This study indicates that it might be true for the municipalities, but a larger study needs to be made to confirm that. In the Sonatype study, the general perception was that it is difficult to know how much of the software used in the organization actually contains OSS. A societal consequence of this work could be that municipalities look into how they handle OSS vulnerabilities, which will lead to better policies on OSS bug management. Better OSS security will also derive more secure systems for employees at the municipalities and municipality residents.

The research area could benefit from a more extensive survey into how OSS is managed in the Swedish municipalities with a higher number of municipalities involved. Such a study would give a better understanding of the extent of the problem with OSS management. In such a project, it might be difficult to verify specific information sources to deal with OSS bugs since different incidents would need to use various information sources. It is probably more interesting to develop a process on how to act in the discussed situation and make sure that policies are well founded in the organization. The problem with OSS bugs is not exclusive to the public sector and research, on this subject, into the private sector is just as interesting.

Acknowledgement. The authors would like to thank Katinka Ruda and Armina Arazm for their assistance in this study and doctoral candidate Vasileios Gkioulos for his comments and suggestions.

A Appendix

Annex I: Interview Questions (Swedish)

- På en skala från 1–10 hur beroende är ni av OSS? (Ethical, Managerial)
- Hur många kritiska applikationer har OSS i er organisation? (Managerial, Technical)
- Hur hanterar ni uppdateringar av OSS? (Ex. vilka som ska göras, när, av em)...vem meddelar om uppdateringar? (Managerial, Operational, Technical)
- Hur vet ni när ni ska göra uppdateringar? (Ethic, Operational)
- Gör ni alla uppdateringar? (Ethic, Operational)
- Har alla tillgång till social media på arbetsplatsen? (Ethic, Operational)
- Hur används social media generellt i kommunen? (Ethic, Operational)
- Varför använder ni OSS? (Ethic, Managerial)
- Görs det en riskanalys av säkerhetsläget på kommunen varje år? Har risken med OSS inkluderats i analysen? (Managerial)
- Behövde ni gå ut med information till användarna av systemen som drabbats av Heartbleed I samband med incidenten? (Managerial, Operational)
- Finns det några politiska eller lagstadgade påtryckningar för användningen av OSS? (Legal)
- Hur hanterar ni IT? (Internt, outsourcing, annan lösning) (Managerial)
- Hur ser organisationen ut? (Vem rapporterar IT-ansvarig/du till? Taktisk/Operationell)
- Hur skulle du placera dig själv i en Strategisk, taktisk och operationell modell?
- Vad hände vid Heartbleed-incidenten? (Ethic, Managerial, Operational)
- Hur får ni den informationen of Heartbleed? (Operational)
- Använder ni sociala medier för att få information lite snabbare? (Ethic, Operational)
- Var det någon specifik sida ni var inne på under Heartbleed-incidenten? (Ethic, Operational)
- Skulle du se någon fördel med att ha örat mot sociala medier också? (Ethic, Managerial, Operational)
- Ändrade ni eller skapade nya rutiner/policies efter Heartbleed-incidenten? (Managerial)
- Har ni några speciella regler eller policys som bara rör OSS och inte proprietär mjukvara? Vilka? Vet ni hur andra kommuner hanterar IT? (Legal, Managerial)
- Använder ni några varningssystem för säkerhetsincidenter? (Technical)
- Tycker ni att det är lätt att hitta information om öppen källkod och dess brister? (Ethic, Operational)
- Om man jämför med proprietär mjukvara? (Ethic, Operational)
- Känns det som att det är svårare att få ansvarstagande från OSS-leverantörerna? (Ethic, Operational)

428 S.-F. Wen and S. Kowalski

Annex II: Interview Questions (English)

- On a scale from 1–10 how dependent are you on OSS? (Ethical, Managerial)
- How many critical applications has OSS in your organization? (Managerial, Technical)
- How do you handle updates of the OSS? (e.g. What should be done, when, by whom) (Managerial, Operational, Technical)
- How do you know when to make updates? (Ethic, Operational)
- Do you perform all updates? (Ethic, Operational)
- Can anyone use social media at your office? (Ethic, Operational)
- How do you use social media in general in the municipality? (Ethic, Operational)
- Why do you use OSS? (Ethic, Managerial)
- Is there a risk analysis of the system security in the municipality every year? Has the risk of OSS included in the analysis? (Managerial)
- Which information did you give the users of your systems in connection to Heartbleed? (Managerial, Operational)
- Is there any political or legal influence to use OSS? (Legal)
- How do you manage IT? (Internally, outsourcing, another solution) (Managerial)
- How does the organization look like? (Managerial)
- How would you place yourself in a strategically, tactical or an operational model? (Managerial)
- What happened during the Heartbleed incident? (Ethic, Managerial, Operational)
- How do you receive the information about Heartbleed bug? (Operational)
- Do you use social media to obtain information more quickly? (Ethic, Operational)
- Was there any specific page you visited during the Heartbleed incident? (Ethic, Operational)
- Can you see any advantages with keeping an eye on social media too? (Ethic, Managerial, Operational)
- Did you create or change any new routines/policies after the Heartbleed incident? (Managerial)
- Do you have any special rules or policies that concern OSS, not proprietary software? Do you know how other municipalities manage IT? (Legal, Managerial)
- Do you have any warning systems for security incidents? (Technical)
- Do you think it is easy to find information about open source and its deficiencies? (Ethic, Operational)
- If compared with proprietary software? (Ethic, Operational)
- Do you feel that it is harder to get accountability from OSS suppliers? (Ethic, Operational)

References

1. Al Sabbagh, B., Kowalski, S.: A socio-technical framework for threat modeling a software supply chain. In: The 2013 Dewald Roode Workshop on Information Systems Security Research, 4–5 October 2013, Niagara Falls, New York, USA. International Federation for Information Processing (2013)

2. Alsabbagh, B., Kowalski, S.: A cultural adaption model for global cyber security warning systems. In: 5th International Conference on Communications, Networking and Information Technology Dubai, UAE (2011)
3. Andersson, C.: Öppen källkod inom kommuner-Analys av risker och möjligheter. Bachelor. Skövde Högskola, Sweden (2014)
4. Bider, I., Kowalski, S.: A framework for synchronizing human behavior, processes and support systems using a socio-technical approach. In: Bider, I., Gaaloul, K., Krogstie, J., Nurcan, S., Proper, H.A., Schmidt, R., Soffer, P. (eds.) BPMDS/EMMSAD-2014. LNBIP, vol. 175, pp. 109–123. Springer, Heidelberg (2014). doi:10.1007/978-3-662-43745-2_8
5. Bryman, A., Bell, E.: Business Research Methods. Oxford University Press, New York (2015)
6. CERT-SE: BM14-001 - Allvarlig sårbarhet i bash. Blixtmeddelande. 25 September 2014. https://www.cert.se/2014/09/bm14-001-allvarlig-sarbarhet-i-bash
7. CERT-SE: CERT-SE's newsletter v. 17. CERT-SE, 25 April 2014. https://www.cert.se/2014/04/cert-se-s-veckobrev-v-17
8. Datatracker: TLS and DTLS Heartbeat Extension. Datatracker, February 2012. https://datatracker.ietf.org/doc/rfc6520/
9. Denscombe, M.: The Good Research Guide for Small-Scale Research Project, 4th edn. Open University Press, Maidenhead (2010)
10. Dickson, Å.: Buggen visar allt du vill skydda utan att det märks. SVT, 10 April 2014. http://www.svt.se/nyheter/buggen-visar-allt-du-vill-skydda-utan-att-det-marks
11. Drevfjäll, L.: Information från din e-port kan läcka ut. Expressen, 8 April 2014. http://www.expressen.se/nyheter/information-fran-din-e-post-kan-lacka-ut/
12. Durumeric, Z., Kasten, J., Adrian, D., Halderman, J.A., Bailey, M., Li, F., Weaver, N., Amann, J., Beekman, J., Payer, M.: The matter of Heartbleed. In: Proceedings of the 2014 Conference on Internet Measurement Conference. ACM (2014)
13. Eriksson, G.: Nätets "största säkerhetsläcka någonsin" upptäckt. Metro, 8 April 2014. http://www.metro.se/teknik/natets-storsta-sakerhetslacka-nagonsin-upptackt/EVHndh!Wcv38F6U6n8Es/
14. Github: OpenSSL heartbeat PoC. gist.github.com (2014). https://gist.github.com/takeshixx/10107280
15. Graziano, J.: Spam Campaign Spreading Malware Disguised as HeartBleed Bug Virus Removal Tool. Symantec Official Blog, 27 May 2014. http://www.symantec.com/connect/blogs/spam-campaign-spreading-malware-disguised-heartbleed-bug-virus-removal-tool
16. Grubb, B.: Heartbleed disclosure timeline: who knew what and when. Sydney Morning Herald, 15 April 2014. http://www.smh.com.au/it-pro/security-it/heartbleed-disclosure-timeline-who-knew-what-and-when-20140414-zqurk.html
17. Heartbleed: The Heartbleed bug (2014). http://heartbleed.com/
18. Jackson, W.: Sonatype Open Source Development and Application Security Survey. Electronic document (2014). http://img.en25.com/Web/SonatypeInc/%7B138a2551-edac-46a3-bfcb-240352a42fed%7D_2014SurveyResults_july-14-14.pdf
19. Karokola, G., Kowalski, S., Yngstrom, L.: Secure e-government services: towards a framework for integrating it security services into e-government maturity models. In: Information Security South Africa (ISSA). IEEE (2011)
20. Karokola, G., Kowalski, S., Yngström, L.: Towards an information security maturity model for secure e-government services: a stakeholders view. In: HAISA (2011)
21. Karokola, G.R., Kowalski, S., Mwakalinga, G.J., Rukiza, V.: Secure e-government adoption: a case study of Tanzania. In: European Security Conference (2011)
22. Kihlström, S.: Bugg öppnade hål i Krypteringsprogram. Dagens Nyheter, 8 April 2014. http://www.dn.se/ekonomi/bugg-oppnade-hal-i-krypteringsprogram/

23. Kiss, B., Kosmatov, N., Pariente, D., Puccetti, A.: Combining static and dynamic analyses for vulnerability detection: illustration on heartbleed. In: Piterman, N. (ed.) HVC 2015. LNCS, vol. 9434, pp. 39–50. Springer, Cham (2015). doi:10.1007/978-3-319-26287-1_3
24. Kowalski, S.: IT insecurity: a multi-discipline inquiry. Ph.D. thesis, Department of Computer and System Sciences, University of Stockholm and Royal Institute of Technology, Sweden (1994). ISBN: 91-7153-207-2
25. Kupsch, J.A., Miller, B.P.: Why do software assurance tools have problems finding bugs like heartbleed? Continuous Software Assurance Marketplace, 22 April 2014
26. Langley, A.: Time to update all OpenSSL 1.0.1 to 1.0.1g to fix CVE-2014-0160. Twitter, 7 April 2014. https://twitter.com/agl_/status/453235260520542208
27. Lee, C., Yi, L., Tan, L.-H., Goh, W., Lee, B.-S., Yeo, C.-K.: A wavelet entropy-based change point detection on network traffic: a case study of heartbleed vulnerability. In: 2014 IEEE 6th International Conference on Cloud Computing Technology and Science (CloudCom). IEEE (2014)
28. Lundell, B., Lings, B., Lindqvist, E.: Open source in Swedish companies: where are we? Inf. Syst. J. 20(6), 519–535 (2010)
29. Lyne, J.: Heartbleed Roundup: Hacking Made Easy, First Victims Come to Light and Heartbleed Hacker Arrested. forbes.com, 17 April 2014. http://www.forbes.com/sites/jameslyne/2014/04/17/heartbleed-roundup-hacking-made-easy-first-victims-come-to-light-and-heartbleed-hacker-arrested/#3f8fe3e01fe6
30. May, T.: Social Research. Open University Press, Buckingham (2011)
31. MSB: Att lära stort från små incidenter, July 2012. https://www.msb.se/RibData/Filer/pdf/26272.pdf
32. Myers, M.D.: Qualitative Research in Business and Management. SAGE, Thousand Oaks (2013)
33. NIST: Vulnerability Summary for CVE-2014-0160. NVD, 7 April 2014. https://web.nvd.nist.gov/view/vuln/detail?vulnId=CVE-2014-0160
34. O'Reilly, T.: Ten Myths About Open Source Software (1999). http://archive.oreilly.com/lpt/a/2019
35. Persson, I.: Skatteuppgifter stulna i Kanada efter Heartbleed. Omni, 15 April 2014. http://www.aftonbladet.se/nyheter/article18688985.ab
36. Project, O.: OpenSSL Security Advisory. Mail-Archive, 7 April 2014. http://www.mail-archive.com/openssl-users@openssl.org/msg73408.html
37. Project, O.: OpenSSL Version 1.0.1g Released. Mail-Archive, 7 April 2014. http://www.mail-archive.com/openssl-users@openssl.org/msg73407.html
38. Ramanathan, L., Iyer, S.K.: A qualitative study on the adoption of open source software in information technology outsourcing organizations. In: Damiani, E., Frati, F., Riehle, D., Wasserman, Anthony I. (eds.) OSS 2015. IAICT, vol. 451, pp. 103–113. Springer, Cham (2015). doi:10.1007/978-3-319-17837-0_10
39. Regeringen: Från IT-politik för samhället till politik för IT-samhället. Digital document (2004). http://www.regeringen.se/rattsdokument/proposition/2005/07/prop.-200405175/
40. Riksrevisionen: NIS-direktivet. NIS-direktivet (2013). http://www.riksdagen.se/sv/Dokument-Lagar/EU/Fakta-PM-om-EU-forslag/NIS-direktivet_H006FPM68/
41. Riksrevisionen: Riksrevisionens rapport om informationssäkerhet i den civila statsförvaltningen, March 2015. https://data.riksdagen.se/fil/BE7AD878-9C78-4756-95B0-F1617EAB2241
42. Sambrk: Municipalities for Joint Development of e-Services. http://www.sambruk.se/ovrigt/inenglish.4.72ebdc8412fd172bb7480001338.html
43. SKL: Kommuner och Landsting. http://skl.se/tjanster/kommunerlandsting.431.html

44. Torres, G., Liu, C.: Can data-only exploits be detected at runtime using hardware events? A case study of the Heartbleed vulnerability. In: Proceedings of the Hardware and Architectural Support for Security and Privacy 2016. ACM (2016)
45. Tosi, D., Lavazza, L., Morasca, S., Chiappa, M.: Surveying the adoption of FLOSS by public administration local organizations. In: Damiani, E., Frati, F., Riehle, D., Wasserman, Anthony I. (eds.) OSS 2015. IAICT, vol. 451, pp. 114–123. Springer, Cham (2015). doi:10.1007/978-3-319-17837-0_11
46. Wikipedia: Heartbleed. CERT-SE, 25 April 2014. https://en.wikipedia.org/wiki/Heartbleed
47. Williams, C.: Anatomy of OpenSSL's Heartbleed: just four bytes trigger horror bug. TheRegister, 9 April 2014. http://www.theregister.co.uk/2014/04/09/heartbleed_explained/
48. Winter, J.S.: Upphandlare missar inlåsningseffekter. Upphandling24, 18 June 2014. http://sverigesradio.se/sida/artikel.aspx?programid=83&artikel=5834048
49. Wu, H.: Heartbleed OpenSSL vulnerability: a Forensic Case Study at Medical School. NJMS Advancing Research IT, May 2014. http://research.njms.rutgers.edu/m/it/Publications/docs/Heartbleed_OpenSSL_Vulnerability_a_Forensic_Case_Study_at_Medical_School.pdf
50. Zhang, L., Choffnes, D., Levin, D., Dumitras, T., Mislove, A., Schulman, A., Wilson, C.: Analysis of SSL certificate reissues and revocations in the wake of Heartbleed. In: Proceedings of the 2014 Conference on Internet Measurement Conference. ACM (2014)

Usable Security Management for Network Access Rules of Critical Infrastructure

Jeong-Han Yun[1(✉)], Seungoh Choi[1], Woonyon Kim[1],
Hwasun Kang[2], and Sung-Woo Kim[2]

[1] National Security Research Institute, Daejeon, Korea
{dolgam, sochoi, wnkim}@nsr.re.kr
[2] Interaction Design, Graduate School of Techno Design,
Kookmin University, Seoul, Korea
kmdesignmediator@gmail.com, caerang@kookmin.ac.kr

Abstract. The security problem of the national critical infrastructure is constantly occurring. In recent years, penetrating into the closure network of the critical infrastructure and attack from the inside frequently occur, so that detecting and managing the internal threat is also a very important security issue. Thus, we developed F.Switch, a network switch that can monitor all traffic without installing a software agent in a controlling system and remotely apply a white-list based access control list (ACL), and we designed F.Manager, which is an integrated management system that can monitor, control and manage multiple F.Switch at the same time, so that the internal security network can be efficiently controlled and managed. In this case, F.Manager, which is an integrated management system, is designed by applying usable security viewpoints and methodologies from the planning period to prevent the decrease of productivity of operator's work due to the manager system which is not user friendly, and we have secured usability that was essential for the control and management of security system by inducing the use of the full function of the program, and discovered the value and role of new usable security in the security area.

Keywords: Integration of security management system · Usable security · Internal network security monitoring · Usability of security management system

1 Introduction

The security problems of the critical infrastructure facility control system that can shake the foundation of the industry such as power, nuclear power, water resource, railroad and traffic system, continuously occur, and the number of occurrences increases every year. To prevent cyber-attacks, most infrastructures consist of closed networks that are disconnected from the outside. But, even in such closed networks, it is difficult to prohibit the entry of external equipment by external personnel for the processing of maintenance or operation of the control system. There are cases of attacks from inside through USB memory penetrating air-gap, so the management of the threat from inside to the control system became a very important security issue.

© Springer International Publishing AG 2017
T. Tryfonas (Ed.): HAS 2017, LNCS 10292, pp. 432–447, 2017.
DOI: 10.1007/978-3-319-58460-7_30

The control system's performance and functionality are optimized for the purpose of security only, so the security agent software might not be available on the system. Due to the stability of systems, the price of tapping equipment and complex cabling reasons, the existing monitoring technique (e.g. mirroring, tapping) on the control system has been reluctant to use (Realistically impossible).

Thus, we developed F.Switch, a network switch, that can monitor all traffics inside the internal network without installing software agent in the control system of the critical infrastructure and apply white list based access control list (network access control list, hereinafter, ACL) remotely.

As described above, F.Switch, was developed to solve various internal security threats, can log all source (IP, MAC, port) - protocol - destination (IP, MAC, port) information of all packets that occurred per the user set unit time, and, unlike sampling based monitoring (e.g. netflow), it monitors all traffics that go through F.Switch to generate log, and can block the traffic that violates ACL and generate alarm, so it solved several problems of the control system security. Also, F.Manager, an integrated management system that can efficiently manage multiple F.Switches installed in the control system network, is designed since there was a problem of the practical security staff having to control and manage multiple F.Switch installed in the control system at once. Figure 1 is the overall concept diagram of F.Manager, the integrated management system.

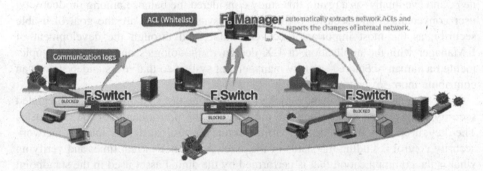

Fig. 1. The overall concept diagram of F.Manager

On this paper shows the contents of the design on the integrated management system, which is F.Manager, through user friendly perspective, that is, the perspective of usable security, during the development of F.Switch, a new concept network security switch that effectively blocks the threat from inside the critical infrastructure control system.

The description of the overall configuration of this paper, which is a development study of the integrated management system F.Manager, in terms of usable security, is as follows.

Section 1 explained the background and purpose of the study on the development of the national key industries control system security integrated management system in terms of usable security, and Sect. 2 introduced the detailed research methods in the development of F.Manager and explained the secured values through UI screens. Section 3 presented the main functions of the developed F.Manager, Sect. 4 introduced the whole work procedure and integrated information structure diagram designed based on user scenarios, and evaluated the improvement of usability through efficient information design. In Sect. 5, it evaluated the value and role of new usable security in the security area through the system with improved usability and mentioned about the future research.

2 Usable Security Value-Based Security Management System

2.1 Reflection of UX and Usable Security Values to F.Manager

Usable Security is a study that breaks the convention of the security researchers so far that maintaining high security technology and increasing user convenience, that is the security technology and user convenience conflict with each other, Since the interest in the development of user-oriented security technology has been increased by combining human computer interaction (HCI) and user experience (UX) design into information security, it is in 2013 that full-scale research has started in Korea. This study tried to explain that the emphasize on the importance of security shall change from 'Human for System' to 'Human-centered System' and high usability system is not vulnerable to security but is consideration for the users, who are the operators of the security business, and eventually, as a result, this study considered the balance among productivity, user convenience, and security of the security system, which are the goal of usable security, as the most important discovery value, and through the development of F.Manager with the application of UX design methodologies and processes, implemented a human - centered security management system so that users and systems can contribute more to security.

For such purpose, this study looked at the core tasks of the current integrated security management system and the problems in the performance of the core tasks. The key tasks of current critical infrastructure control system's internal network security control is finding the status of the asset at a glance in real time, and verifying what is the communication that is performed by the digital asset used in the standpoint of the security policy to quickly report to the person in charge who can solve the problem when a problem occurs in the verified items, but as in Fig. 2, it is difficult to quickly synchronize hundreds and thousands of assets and security policy to the site situation, and it is very difficult to monitor the changes in the network that continuously occur.

In addition, many changes are occurring continuously but non-regularly during the operation of the control system, such as usage time point, temporary suspension of certain service, starting of new services, introduction of new equipment, and replacement of main-sub system, etc. Security personnel should monitor such status of ACL operations on a daily basis to identify changes in the operating environment as well as identification of assets and services, and continuously analyze these changes to ensure that they are suitable for the security policies and are consistent with actual operation status. On Fig. 2 the graph below, the lower graph shows whether traffic is generated

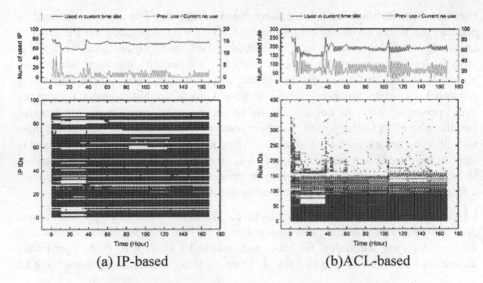

(a) IP-based   (b)ACL-based

Fig. 2. IP per hour, communication usage (Color figure online)

by IP and ACL per time, and the above graph shows the number of IPs and ACLs currently in use (Black line). It shows the number of unused IPs and ACLs (Blue line). Such work requires continuous analysis of large amounts of data as shown in the above figure, and it cannot be carried out manually, so even if equipment such as F.Switch that can effectively control such status is introduced and F.Manager, integrated management program for integrated management of multiple F.Switch, is developed, if the functions suitable for the work of the security personnel are not provided according to the user's usage frequency or the order of usage, there have to be many limits in the improvement and enhancement of actual work capability at the site, so F.Manager is designed for the users and system to focus more on the value proposition of security from the planning stage.

2.2   Research Method for User Centered Design of F.Manager

For the user-centered design of F.Manager, we developed F.Manager, a new user-centered security management system, through four major research methods as follows. First, we classified the users of the F.Manager, the national key infrastructure control system operators, in terms of UX design and usable security, and analyzed the control system network traffic in real operation and interviewed the related personnel to characterize the security tasks they perform. Secondly, user interface (UI) concept required for UI design of integrated management system was discovered through the derived contents, and integrated information structure (IA) was designed by summarizing all work processes. Third, the work-flow of the functions was summarized through the user scenario based integrated user itinerary map, and the screen design diagram (Wire-Frame) of the entire system functions is developed. Finally, we completed UI/GUI design through wireframes.

Persona Classification and Integrated Needs Analysis. The users who need to perform the works on the system mentioned above vary depending on the level of knowledge related to security and the tasks to be performed. Operational experts (e.g. team leader, system manager, network manager, and security manager) are divided according to information access levels and responsibilities, and simple monitoring personnel also exist. Some users have security knowledge, but in general, there are many personnel who are not the experts in security, and some users are also not familiar with IT technology itself. For these reasons, it is important to classify the main and sub users according to their level of security knowledge and scope of work, and to identify their needs, and it can be said that it is essential to analyze their work processes on the systems, to design efficient work processes through it, and to list up the information during the design of the management system.

UI Concept and Information Architecture. The needs required by the users were derived by analyzing the tasks and paint points in the course of performing the tasks by the users who use the system the most, and system UI concept of F.Manager finally summarized through this is as in Table 1. Once the needs are identified through the UI

Table 1. System UI concept for F.Manager

UX, usable security oriented strategy	Research & analysis			Ideation & define
				User/system/design UI concept
User goal: easy, fast, and convenient	System task analysis / System analysis / User needs analysis / User scenario (key task & features finding)	Minimize risk / Rapid recovery	Error handing	**Relief: relief, relaxation, reduction, alleviation** Alleviate many worries on the handling and operation of the system to help comfortable system operation by users
			Stability	
			Error-less	
			Predictability	
			Secure	
System goal: optimized information system		Simple procedure / Easy to control / Easy to understand / Easy to manage / Customizing-information-classification	System simple	**Easy: easy, simple, soft, hand-down** Function operation and procedure through system's information system and information is designed to be as simple as possible to help the easiest understanding, handling, and management of the system by users
			UI simple	
			Operation simple	
			Managing simple	
			Perception simple	
UI design goal: interface design that most effectively shows the optimized information and business design			Procedure simple	**Convenience: efficiency, convenience, comforts, optimization** It is the same context as the above easy, but, through the display of the situation and information in the system, it minimized the information, process, and operation system compared to the supplied effort and partially permitted personalization to provide the optimized system handling to the users
			Information architecture simple	
		Current state check / Customization	Efficiency	
			Economization	
			Optimization	

concept, it is necessary to integrate the analysis of various tasks and the execution procedures of the tasks, and the information architecture of F.Manager was designed by concentrating on the organization and structure of the contents so that the users are well guided on the structure. As such, it shows that making useful contents structure beyond the complexity of information through the analysis of entire tasks matching the context and the scenarios of the tasks is the most important task of IA. A more advanced and detailed F.Manager IA will be mentioned in Sect. 4.

Workflow, Wireframe of F.Manager. Figure 3 shows Workflow and Wireframe of batch registration of non-registered IP in Whitelist creation wizard page. Which will fix inconvenient tasks of finding non-registered IP list and manually registering one by one were summarized as minimized process through the writing of Workflow, and it was designed to check non-registered IP list in one screen and to complete the batch registration. As such, the functions suitable for the work of the security personnel were designed using experience design methodology to improve the productivity.

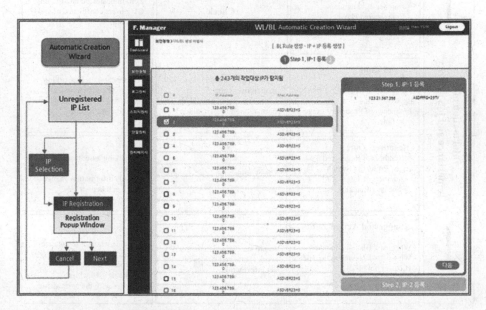

Fig. 3. Workflow, Wireframe of Whitelist/Blindlist automatic creation wizard

3   F.Manager's Main Functions

3.1   F.Manager's Main Functions and UI from the Perspective of UX, Usable Security

One of the most core tasks when a user performs internal network security control is first to understand the status of assets in real time. And secondly, it is to verify the communication performed by the digital assets in use in terms of security policy, and if problem occurs, quickly reporting to the person in charge who can solve the problem, and this section briefly introduces the main function of F.Manager designed with sufficient considerations of user task characteristics, and tries to explain by presenting the system screen designed with maximum consideration of the user experience.

Dashboard. F.Manager's dashboard is a page that verifies the view of various information in a single page in order to look at system management and control at a glance, and it is designed by analyzing the tasks that shall be performed by the user in the order of the importance of the information and priority of the works.

Figures 4 and 5 are the dashboard information design through the analysis of the importance of the information and work priority and actual UI designed through it.

	Menu of Dash Board	Goal	Task Performance
High ↑	**Alarm Zone** - Number of violation - Unregistered Device Protocol / Switch - System Error	**Check Unusual Condition**	**Make all states as '0'.** Zero indicates no abnormality. Give users confidence of system control.
	Trend Zone - Frequency of Whitelist / Blacklist usage over time - Frequency of Resources usage over time	- Check operational information over time - Notification of normal/abnormal operating condition	-Understand user's working time zone characteristics - Utilizing the user's additional intuition and abilities
	Resource Zone - Numbers of Registered Device / Protocol / Switch - Numbers of Registered Whitelist / Blacklist	Check registered asset changes	- Checking asset management status - Status information change check at takeover
↓ **Low**	**Suggested Action Zone** - Whitelist / Blacklist to add - Whitelist / Blacklist to be deleted (Lists of not used) - Resources to delete (Lists of not used)	Rapid synchronization of network status and statues of asset information	- Decide whether to take recommended work - '0' means the current Whitelist / Blacklist matches with the asset status

Information of Importance and job priority

Fig. 4. Information & task priority on dashboard

Client-Sever Relationship Automatic Creation Wizard. There are already many network switches that provide traffic control functions using ACL even if they are not F.Switch. However, as we have seen in the previous section, in order to manage a single control network, it is necessary to create and manage hundreds of IPs and ACLs, and if the user has to manually create all these rules, the user experience has to be bad naturally.

- **NOT easy:** It is difficult to gather information of all devices in SCADA network.
- **NOT convenience:** It is inefficient to manually generate ACL regarding not only service oriented control system but also default service provided by operation system.
- **NOT relief:** It is anxious to make and apply ACL due to the possibility of human error.

Fig. 5. F.Manager dashboard

F.Switch generates a source-destination type log for all traffic in real time and sends it to F.Manager. F.Manager provides the function to automatically generate server-client type ACL rule using algorithm from collected log information while storing and managing it. This allows users to easily and efficiently extract all communication relationships. The automatically generated result is the server-client relationship that occurred during the user-specified period, and in order to use it as a security policy, the user needs confirmation. Thus, for users to be able to systemically check the generated result and feel safe, and for users to be able to first check the asset information (IP, MAC) and information on the service in use, which can be easily identified at the site, screen providing ACL information is composed as in Fig. 6.

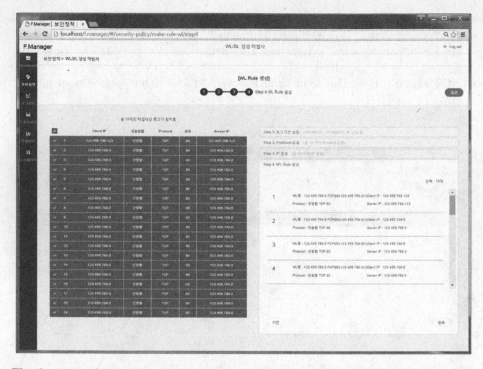

Fig. 6. Automatic generation rule list requiring the decision on whether to apply to the system

Integrated Management Function for Security Rules. Security rules integrated management function. If several F.Switch are introduced and used in one network, the following pain points exist if you need to separate and manage ACLs applied to F.Switch individually.

- **NOT easy:** It is not easy to divide the ACLs required for individual F.Switch exactly based on auto-generated ACL.
- **NOT convenience:** If you need to apply the divided ACL to individual F.Switch, and if you need to change ACL information, such as introducing a new system, the process of finding F.Switch that requires change of ACL at every time is inefficient.
- **NOT relief:** There is an anxiety over whether all ACL corresponding to F.Switch are well divided and correctly applied.

The integrated security rules management function is provided to the user as an integrated form of ACL. Users can manage ACL as if one firewall was introduced in the internal network area where F.Switches was applied. As shown in Fig. 7, the integrated management function automatically distributes the ACL for the monitored traffic for each F.Switch and you can check the application status in real time. Users can feel relieved since they can check that the security policy is well applied to all F.Switches.

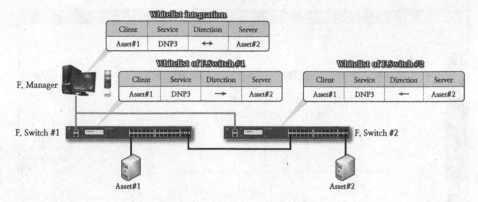

Fig. 7. Whitelist management

Blindlist Feature. It is the main task to help most of the users who check the alarms in real time for prompt response by notifying the information to the relevant person in charge, rather than taking the countermeasures directly. At this time, in order to inform the alarm to the related personnel, firstly, it is necessary to be able to distinguish the type of the alarm, and it is necessary to find the person corresponding to the alarm and quickly transmit the alarm information. That is, it is the first task to identify and distinguish the notifications that have not yet reported, and the second task is to confirm the follow-up of the alarms after the report has been made. The difficulties in performing security tasks with Whitelist based security alarms are as follows.

- **NOT easy:** When an attack or anomaly signal occurs, many alarms related to this occur. It is difficult to distinguish many alarms that occur in real time, so that it is difficult for the user to accurately report to the persons in charge of the alarms.
- **NOT convenience:** Existing systems often show redundant alarms together, but most of the time, the alarms are combined and recognized with the previous input attack pattern. If the user cannot manage the filtering of the alarm suitable for the characteristics of the user according to the relationship by abnormality signal and reporting system, even if the function is excellent, it is inefficient for the user's task.
- **NOT relief:** If alarms are continuously generated, it is difficult to confirm whether the report has been completed to all the related persons, and there is an anxiety that the user cannot be sure of the start and end of the work.

If the persons to whom the information is to be transmitted are determined by the characteristics of the alarm, the user should be able to immediately check the only alarms that he/she should newly report in addition to the alarms that have completed the reporting. For this purpose, Blindlist function was designed and inserted into F.Manager as Fig. 8. Blindlist function does not generate alarms with user defined characteristics in real time alarm window, so that user can easily input characteristics of alarm that need not to be seen at present. This allows you to easily see the alarms that need to be reported by removing alarms from the real-time alarm window as described above.

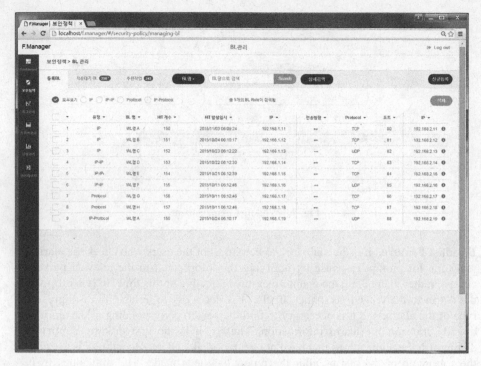

Fig. 8. Blindlist management UI

Alarms of Unused Rules. The user creates the security policy with Whitelist and manages alarms using the Blindlist. The rules written as such are meaningful for the corresponding traffic to occur. The absence of traffic corresponding to the rule may indicate that the rule does not properly reflect the characteristics of the site. If there is remaining security policy for communication and equipment that are not used currently, or if there is remaining blind list rule for alarm that does not occur any more, it is not just favorable for the security, but also, it may cause several adverse effects such as causing confusion for the information recognition by the user (Fig. 9).

In the control system site, there is a separate process for discarding and stopping the equipment, and when the request is received, the related security rules are often manually deleted. Similar things also happen to Blindlist. There are the following problems when rule removal must be performed manually. If the works are carried out as such, there are the following problems.

- **NOT easy:** When an application for deletion due to the disposal of equipment is received, the user should search all relevant rules based on the information and operation status. And the user has the inconvenience of continuously checking the log and operation information in order to determine when Blindlist rules created for temporary use by the user are unnecessary and need to be deleted.

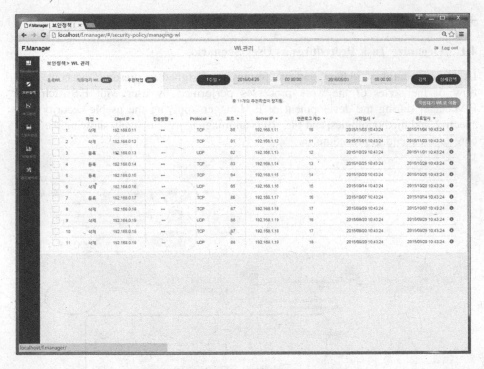

Fig. 9. Suggested actions of unused rules

- **NOT convenience:** The process of manually synchronizing the off-line information such as the report of the relevant personnel and the security rules of the F.Switch monitoring the network in real time, or performing the "automatic generation of the server-client relationship" every time for several information updates are also inefficient.
- **NOT relief:** It is difficult to confirm whether the reporting information of relevant personnel is being performed quickly and accurately and clearly reflected in the security policy, so the security officer may always feel anxiety about the synchronization between the current operation status and the security policy.

We have added the function in F.Manager to tell users if there are rules for Whitelist based ACL and blind list that are have not been used for more than the user specified period. The F.Manager notifies the users of unused rules (no traffic corresponding to the rules) for user specified period of time. This allows the user to more quickly synchronize the status of the site and the security policy. Also, this function can identify and recognize the phenomena that the equipment and service that are to be continuously operated are temporarily stopped.

4   Improved User Experience on F.Manager

4.1   Organize Task Procedures as User Scenarios

IA, user scenario, workflow, and wireframe are designed to preserve the contextual flow of the series of the work processes performed by user with F.Switch and F.Manager during the development of F.Manager applying the usable security perspective and methodologies, and Fig. 10 is an image representatively showing the most core task execution procedure.

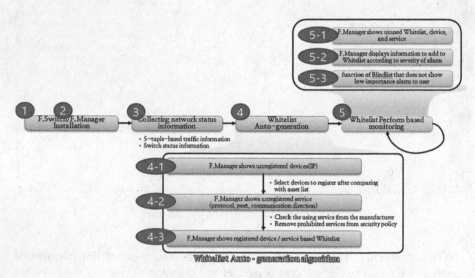

Fig. 10. F.Manager task procedures

It is the process of 1. Installation of F.Switch, 2. Installation of F.Manager, 3. F.-Switch collects network communication log and status information in real time and sends it to F.Manager, 4. Creates and applies Whitelist. 5. Based on this monitoring/observing, 5.1 Recommending of unused rules continuously and repeating the process of checking, deleting unnecessary rules, 5.2 periodically update the Whitelist information using "Whitelist auto generation function [1]" to match asset management status with Whitelist information. 5.3 In case of Whitelist violation alarm, it shows only the alarm that the security officer should perform the corresponding task using the Blindlist.

With this process, it is possible to quickly acquire, control, and manage the program by minimizing the screen switching frequency, touch frequency, and job input frequency naturally on the system.

4.2   Integrated Information Architecture of F.Manager

Figure 11 is the information architecture of newly designed integrated F.Manager through analysis from UX and usable security perspective. Dashboard, terminal

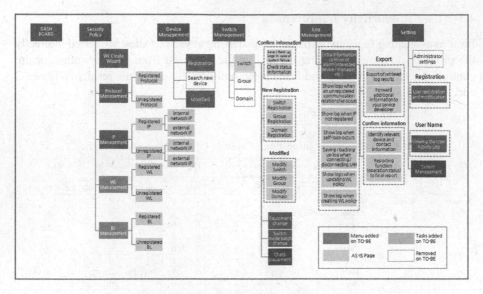

Fig. 11. Integrated F.Manager information architecture

management, switch management, and manager pages, which existed in the past, have been upgraded to reflect the needs of users as much as possible in terms of functions, tasks, and procedure in the tasks. Through personal analysis and entire system analysis, the tasks that improve the manager's business productivity were newly developed, and essential functions are added. They are the functions that are intensively mentioned, including automatic server-client relationship generation wizard security rule integrated management function, Blindlist function, and alarms for unused rules. These functions are intensively applied and designed to the second menu which is security policy and the fifth menu of analysis. In the security policy menu, functions of checking Whitelist security policy information, checking Whitelist security policy violation information, and checking Whitelist security policy change information are added, so that the manager can check asset information easily and quickly. When creating a security policy, the new registration became easier and the task of manual creation became simplified. Furthermore, the automatic generation function added, so after the generation of Whitelist, it can be applied to all F.Switch automatically in batch. Security policy modification and update functions have been also added, and Whitelist update work procedure for F.Switch to add, replace, and remove has become easier and more convenient because of recognition and execution tasks with security policy check and update application. In terms of security management, observing people direct access to network devices or servers is as important as monitoring network traffic. To this end, F.Switch generates an event when the LAN cable is physically connected to/disconnected from the connection point (self-looping), and the security manager can check the alarm and log management function in F.Manager of those events.

4.3   User Productivity Improvement

Prior to evaluating usability through on-site testing at various sites, we tested indirectly the usability improvement using network traffic collected from the key infrastructure control system for F.Switch and F.Manager, and you can check the results in Tables 2 and 3.

Table 2. Usability inspection of system UI through network traffic

Main page	Sub page	Action	Use frequency		Information accessed		Human error		Memorability		Feedback	
			Prev.	Proposed	Prev.	Proposed	Prev.	Proposed	Prev.	Proposed	Prev.	Proposed
Security policy	Whitelist	Add	6	6	1	0	4	0	1	0	0	5
		Modify	6	6	1	0	4	1	1	0	0	0
		Delete	2	2	0	0	0	0	0	0	0	1
		Detail	1	1	0	0	0	0	1	0	0	0
		Confirm	2	3	0	0	0	0	1	0	0	2
	Protocol	Add	11	9	1	0	9	3	1	0	0	3
		Modify	1	10	1	0	0	3	1	0	0	0
		Delete	2	2	0	0	0	0	0	0	0	1
		Detail	1	1	1	0	0	0	1	0	0	0
		Confirm	2	4	0	0	0	0	1	0	0	1
	IP	Detail	2	1	0	0	0	0	1	0	0	0
		Confirm	2	3	0	0	0	0	1	0	0	2
	Whitelist wizard	Protocol	11	1	1	1	9	0	1	0	0	1
		IP	14	1	1	1	5	0	1	0	0	1
Switch	Switch	Add	12	8	1	0	4	3	1	0	0	0
		Modify	12	9	1	0	4	3	1	0	0	0
		Delete	2	2	0	0	0	0	1	0	0	1
		Detail	1	1	1	0	0	0	1	0	0	0
	Switch group	Add	7	7	0	0	5	5	1	0	0	0
		Modify	7	6	0	0	5	3	1	0	0	0
		Detail	1	1	1	0	0	0	1	0	0	0
Device	Device	Add	14	14	1	0	5	5	1	0	0	0
		Modify	14	14	1	0	5	5	1	0	0	0
		Delete	2	2	0	0	0	0	1	0	0	1

Table 3. Summary of usability comparison

Features	Existing F.Manager	New F.Manager
No. of user touch (handling)	135	114
No. of screen conversions	13	2
No. of direct user inputs	59	31
No. of hindrance to information recognition	22	0
No. of providing feedbacks	0	19

First of all, Table 2 shows the results of the frequency of occurrence of representative needs attributes of managers in operation of F.Manager such as accessibility of the information, user error, easiness of remembering, and providing feedback, etc. through the security policy with the highest frequency of usage and menu of switch and terminal management page, and information accessibility is increased, user error is significantly decreased, and required feedback and guideline are provided at the right time to greatly improve overall productivity [2].

Table 3 is a comparison table of existing F.Manager and the new F.Manager advanced through UX and usable security perspective, it measured the user experience improvement by comparing the number of screen switching times, the number of user manipulations, and the number of direct user input, and the reason that the operation frequency of new F.Manager is remarkably lower is because of the result of achieving process execution through semi-automatic input on the system and minimizing page switching with the consideration of efficiency in UI design. In addition, the number of hindrances of information recognition has been reduced from 22 to 0, and the number of feedbacks has been increased from 0 to 19, so it can be evaluated as that, it maximized productivity and usability together in system management and control as a result of eliminating human errors by the users.

5 Conclusion

We developed F.Switch, a network switch equipped with security function such as a firewall, to prevent cyber accidents by promptly responding to cyber threats while monitoring the entire internal network of the national key infrastructure control system. Internal network monitoring information from F.Switch can be cooperated with various security analysis solutions such as SIEM, etc., so it can be widely used in many ways. However, if the functions appropriate to the user and the characteristics of the user's business are not provided, the user cannot utilize F.Switch effectively and it is judged not as effective to improve the security, so we designed F.Manager, the integrated management system for F.Switch, and we designed the system from usable security perspective so that users could easily and efficiently utilize F.Switch to perform security work. With F.Switch and F.Manager, it can be used not only for rapid asset management, efficient internal network security control, and security policy information management and application, but also for the proper management of service companies, and we expect that it will be a big help for security policy synchronization of individual sites. Since F.Switch and F.Manager are only indirectly tested using network traffic collected from key infrastructure control system, it is difficult to verify 100% improvement of usability of system, but we will test in various sites and continue the study of upgrading of programs that include the needs of the sites.

References

1. Choi, S., Chang, Y., Yun, J.-H., Kim, W.: Traffic-locality-based creation of flow whitelists for SCADA networks. In: Rice, M., Shenoi, S. (eds.) ICCIP 2015. IAICT, vol. 466, pp. 87–102. Springer, Cham (2015). doi:10.1007/978-3-319-26567-4_6
2. Hornbaek, K.: Current practice in measuring usability: challenges to usability studies and research. Int. J. Hum Comput Stud. 64(2), 79–102 (2006)

Cyber Security Policies

Are the Current System Engineering Practices Sufficient to Meet Cyber Crime?

Ahto Buldas[1,2](✉) and Märt Saarepera[3]

[1] Tallinn University of Technology, Akadeemia tee 15a, 12618 Tallinn, Estonia
ahto.buldas@ttu.ee
[2] Cybernetica AS, Mäealuse 2/1, 12618 Tallinn, Estonia
[3] Tallinn, Estonia

Abstract. During the last decades, we have witnessed an explosive growth of computer-technology and the Internet. Due to the growing role of computers and Internet in important business and state-related activities, investments to computer security and the security industry have also been growing fast. In spite of that, we also see the growing trend of cyber crime and losses due to security incidents. We predict that these three growing trends will continue in the future the main reasons being that: (1) as more and more assets will be connected to the Internet, the number of potential targets and stimuli for attackers grow; (2) fundamental (and hard to change) design decisions made in early development stages of todays Internet- and computer technology guarantee persistent technical vulnerabilities in Internet-based systems due to which attackers will always be one step ahead of defenders; (3) growing role of Chief Security Officers (CSOs) in organisations, who do not necessarily have to understand the detailed purpose and functionality of the system but whose duty is still to make the ITC system of the organisation secure. These reasons guarantee the continuous growth of the security industry but also the continuous growth of losses through cyber crime.

Keywords: Computer security · Cyber crime · System engineering

1 Introduction

The importance of computer technology in our everyday life and also its strategic importance are growing fast. Nowadays, digital communication networks are almost inevitable in both private and public sector organisations. Due to the growing role of computers and Internet in important business and state-related activities, investments to computer security have also been growing fast. Computer security as a subject is as old as the computer technology but during the explosive growth of computer industry and the Internet, Computer Security has become a rapidly growing industry. Many companies offer security products and security services, international standards organisations develop standards on best security management practices, etc.

© Springer International Publishing AG 2017
T. Tryfonas (Ed.): HAS 2017, LNCS 10292, pp. 451–463, 2017.
DOI: 10.1007/978-3-319-58460-7_31

In spite of the growth of the security industry, we also have been witnessing a fast growing trend of the losses through cyber crime. In this paper, we go through some fundamental reasons that suggest us to predict that both these rapid growth trends will probably continue in the future. The reasons we refer to are related to historical design decisions made during the development of the frameworks, protocols and formats that todays computers and the Internet are based on, but also on the current system engineering practices and the role of security industry in these practices. There are three main observations that justify our prediction.

The first observation is that the Internet itself continues to grow fast. Not only in terms of the number of users but also in terms of the amount of available data (cloud computation), as well as in terms of the types of devices connected to the Internet (e.g. Internet of Things). More and more assets will be connected to the Internet which increases the motivation for potential attackers. Internet is not only used for inter-organisational communication but also for internal communications at very high level. For example, while ten years ago only dedicated communication lines were used for the government's internal mail exchange, today, the Internet mail is used. The known security incidents, like the Hillary Clinton's mailbox scandal [10], seem not to decrease the optimism of companies and countries to use Internet in the most sensitive areas.

The second observation is related to fundamental technical design choices during the development of computers and engineering that, one the one hand, enabled rapid growth of the computer industry and the Internet, but which on the other hand, have caused numerous fundamental vulnerabilities in systems that are very hard to eliminate. For example, one of the main design decision is Open Systems Interconnection (OSI) framework that can be considered as the main reason why the rapid growth of computers and Internet was possible. This framework proposed a modular layered design approach such that the information exchange formats and protocols between the layers are standardised, while inside the layers the producers have full freedom to implement the desired functionality. On the one hand, such an approach guarantees scalability of the production of computer- and Internet technology. On the other hand, as the information exchange between different layers is limited, the layers are not able to cooperate in a way that is sufficient for effectively meeting denial of service attacks.

The third observation is related to the growing role of Chief Security Officers (CSOs) in organisations. Nowadays, they are even higher in the hierarchy than Chief Technical Officers (CTOs) and Chief Information Officers (CIOs). The mainstream approach today for developing a secure application is that CTO and CIO present a functional solution of the system and the role of CSO is to make and keep it secure by applying security measures to the system by following a general rules (given in security management standards and best practices) that do not assume understanding the functionality of the system. This guarantees that there will always exist vulnerabilities in systems that attackers can abuse and hence, there is a reason to apply more security measures and buy more security products.

The paper is organised as follows. In Sect. 2, we discuss the reasons and mechanisms behind the rapid growth of computer technology and the Internet and the reasons why such growth will continue in the future. In Sect. 3, we discuss the role of Security as a separate discipline and characterise its branches. In Sect. 4, we discuss the reasons behind the persistent vulnerabilities in today's and future systems. In Sect. 5, we discuss the role of todays system engineering and management practices in the existence vulnerabilities in systems.

2   Computers and Networks

Billions of personal computers are in use today and most of them are interconnected via computer networks. Novaday's computers and the networks have *modular design*, which means they are built using mutually compatible macrocomponents that are easy to interconnect and make computers and networks easy to assemble.

The modularity is achieved due to conventions and standards that specify the physical parameters and the data formats used in interfaces between the components. This means that the components will fit together independent of their producers and can be produced anywhere in the world, which means that the components are widely accessible.

The modularity also means *specialisation*. Engineers who interconnect the macro components of a computer do not have to know how to produce such components. Computer engineers are not necessarily electronic engineers. Electronic engineers do not necessarily know enough solid state physics to understand how the basic components of electronic circuits (such as transistors, diodes, etc.) are built. Similar specialisation happens in higher levels. Application programmers do not necessarily know the details of the operating systems. Systems programmers do not necessarily know the physical details of computers. This makes the education and training of specialists much easier and together with standardisation enables efficient industrial mass production of complex computer systems, such as personal computers, computer networks, supercomputers, etc.

In addition to general purpose computers there are many different types of special-purpose computers and controllers with various internal architectures. Similarly, there are many different computer networks but nowadays most of them are connected to the Internet that has become the world-wide infrastructure for information exchange. Compared to 1985 the number of Internet hosts in the world has grown about one million times: from thousands to billions.

Both the companies and states use and trust the Internet more and more. Their everyday functions have become almost impossible without Internet communication. Therefore, the Internet has become a critical infrastructure for both the companies and the states. Numerous services for private and legal persons are offered through the Internet such as electronic banking, web shops, citizen services offered by states, etc.

In addition, Internet has become an entertaining system and a communication environment for private persons. Today, most of the TV-sets and phones are connected to the Internet and use the Internet as a communication channel.

3   Security

All this makes Internet a potential target of attacks and we have witnessed an increasing trend of attacks and crime through the Internet, and also an increasing trend of losses through cyber crime. This has created a Security industry, the obvious goal of which should be decreasing these losses. Nowadays, security is a popular topic among the users and designers of information technology. Several forms and notions of security have been discussed, like Computer Security, Network Security, Information/Data Security, as well as Cyber Security. In this section we just observe what are branches of Security as a discipline and what has been written about them.

Five-minute science project (a joke): we searched Amazon bookstore with these keywords and got the following numbers of matches: Computer Security (145,000), Network Security (70,000), Information/Data Security (68,000), Cyber Security (7,000). The funny thing here is that $70,000 + 68,000 + 7,000 = 145,000$, which suggests that Computer Security is the form of security which is as important as all the other forms altogether.

A far more practical implication from these figures is that we have so many textbooks on security that no-one is able to have a complete picture of the subject. Security has become an independent (of the systems' engineering) discipline with its own specialists who do not necessarily know the details of other systems' engineering disciplines. In the following, we briefly describe what is meant about these different areas of security.

3.1   Computer Security

Computer security deals with protecting all components of computer systems (and the information stored in them) from threats such as backdoors, denial-of-service (DOS) attacks, direct access attacks, eavesdropping, spoofing, tampering, privilege escalation, phishing, clickjacking, etc. Computer security is the most general term about security. It is also the oldest security area which became important once computers became widely used in banks and other organisations.

3.2   Network Security

Network security is focused on protecting computer systems from network-related attacks, such as wiretapping, port scanning, denial-of-service (DOS), DNS spoofing, buffer- and heap overflow attacks, as well as the forms of man in the middle attacks, and many other attacks. Sometimes, also the phishing attacks are considered as a subject of network security. Hence, Network Security deals with both the attacks targeted against the network as an infrastructure and the attacks targeted to the computers and the users through the network. In addition to the Internet, all other kinds of networks (public and private) are also covered by Network Security.

3.3   Information/Data Security

Information Security is very close to Computer Security but the threats it considers are focused on information, not the physical components of computer systems. It considers general threats like information *leakage* (secrets become known to unauthorised persons), information *modification* (existing data is modified in unauthorised way), information *forgery* (falsified data is added to the system), information *destruction* (all data that encodes the information has been accidentally lost or intentionally deleted).

Threats in such an abstract general form suggested to define "security" in positive terms by using three abstract properties of information, the so-called *CIA-triad*:

- *Confidentiality*: no leakage
- *Integrity*: no modifications or forgeries
- *Availability*: no destruction

Such abstract goals are not self-explanatory and do not give any hints how they can be achieved in particular computer systems. Therefore, the CIA triad has been constantly criticised and there have been many proposals of extending the triad with new features [3], like for example *accountability* [14], *awareness*, *responsibility*, *ethics* [11], *auditability*, *non-repudiation*, and *privacy* [4], etc.

In 1998, Parker [12] proposed and alternative six-component list of properties called the *Parkerian hexade* that consists of *Confidentiality*, *Control*, *Integrity*, *Authenticity*, *Availability*, and *Utility*. Some systems have a relatively large number of different properties. For example, the system proposed by NIST [14] has 33 properties!

These principles of Information Security have the main responsibility why the Security tends to become an independent technical discipline. As some of the claims about information security tend to be neither verifiable nor falsifiable, such a discipline is claimed to be non-scientific [8].

3.4   Cyber Security

Cyber security is a relatively young form of security that pays more attention to the homeland-security aspects of computer security and fight against *cyber terrorism* and the strategies of *cyber war* between countries. Cyber Security as a discipline started to develop rapidly in 2007 after the massive DOS attacks against Estonia [5,15]. After that several massive cyber attacks have been witnessed, like the DOS attack against elections in Burma [16] or the *Stuxnet* [9], a malicious computer worm against Iran's nuclear program.

3.5   Security-Providing Methods

There are several methods that describe how the security-related decisions have to be made in organisations. The methods can be divided into two categories: *risk-oriented* methods and *baseline* methods.

Risk-oriented methods (such as FAIR [6]) try to estimate the risks in monetary terms and approach the security from economic perspective. Potential threats that produce loss to the organisation have to be identified, their likelihood estimated, and possible countermeasures applied, considering their economic feasibility, i.e. the reduced risk must outweigh the cost of the measures. Risk-oriented methods have often criticised for the hardness of estimating risks in a reasonable precision.

Baseline methods (such as BSI IT-Grund-schutz [7]) try to define a hierarchy of *security-levels* described by sets of mandatory security measures that the organisations are obliged to take if they decided or have to belong to a certain security level. Baseline methods do not require risk calculation. After having decided which level of security is suitable, it only remains to apply the security measures of that particular level. Baseline methods have been criticised for too course-grained view to the protected systems which may lead to over-secured systems or insufficient protection.

4   Fundamental Vulnerabilities

As so far we have been witnessing a growing trend of real monetary losses from security incidents, it would be reasonable to analyse the causes of the security incidents. We can identify three types of general vulnerabilities:

 I. *Non-technical*: System is abused without breaking any intended business rules of the system.
 II. *Fundamental technical*: Well known general vulnerabilities that exist due to the global design choices made in the computer- and network design.
 III. *Non-fundamental technical*: Vulnerabilities caused by the systems' developer (improper design), builder (improper implementation), or holder (improper maintenance).

Meeting the attacks that abuse type I vulnerabilities require traditional crime fighting or cyber-defense strategies. Type III vulnerabilities can be avoided by proper design practices. We will focus on them later in Sect. 5. In this section, we focus on some of the causes of type II vulnerabilities that cannot be avoided without changing the technical standards that are followed today.

The have been many important design choices made during the development history of nowadays computers and networks the positive effect and the impact of which have been thoroughly studied and taught in universities. A topic that is much less covered is the negative effect of these studies for the security of today's systems. Security threats and incidents point to undesired features of computer systems that are there due to these historical design choices. In this section, we observe some of the design choices that influence today's security situation. We do not claim that the list we provide is even close to being complete. We divide the design choices into three classes: (1) Internet design, (2) operating systems design, (3) computer hardware design, and (4) applications/services design.

4.1   Internet Design

Internet has been designed to allow any user A to send any data X to any other user B at any time. Among the main drivers for the design decisions have been: (1) the robustness of the Internet, (2) the communication efficiency, and (3) the modular design.

Packet Switching Instead of Circuit Switching. Circuit Switching and Packet Switching are two different methods for establishing a connection between network nodes A and B. *Circuit switching* establishes a dedicated communication channel (a multi-link path in the network graph) before A and B start to communicate. This channel remains connected for the duration of the whole communication session. Old telephone networks were connected this way. If one phone calls another, a continuous electrical circuit between the two phones is established and the phones stay connected until the end of the call.

Packet switching divides data into packets that are then transmitted through the network independently. All packets have a payload (used by applications) and header (used by the networking hardware). Headers are added to the payload before transmission and are removed by the networking hardware when the packets reach their destinations. The connections between the communicating pairs of nodes are logical (not physical) and may have common links, i.e. links are not occupied by just one connection and can be used to transfer packets from many different logical connections. This may cause the loss of quality compared to circuit switching. On the one hand, packet switching may cause potentially arbitrarily large transfer delays, while in circuit switching the transfer delay is constant. On the other hand, it enables more efficient use of channel capacity because in circuit switching all the links (wires) of the connection stay occupied by the connection and cannot be used by other connections even if no actual communication is taking place (for example, silence periods during a phone call). Packet switching increases the robustness and efficiency of the network and enables simultaneous interaction of many network applications.

The packet switching technology is the method used in todays Internet. It was invented and developed by American computer scientist Baran during a research project funded by the US Department of Defense [1,2]. The name "packet switching" came from British computer scientist Donald Davies due to whose works the concept of packet switching was engaged in the early ARPANET in the US [13].

Though the design decision of using packet switching instead of circuit switching in the Internet was essential for robust and efficient communication, it also created the possibility of efficient co-operative denial of service (DOS) attacks against any Internet node.

Layered Design of Data Transfer, OSI Stack. The Open Systems Interconnection (OSI) model fixes interconnection standards of communication and computing devices, so that their connection is possible independent of their internal structure and technology. By providing standard communication protocols it creates interoperability between diverse computer/communication systems.

The model partitions systems into a hierarchy of abstract layers, the so-called *OSI stack*. Each layer serves the layer above it. For sending a message obtained from the layer above, a new header is added to the message and the message with the new header is given to the lower layer, until in the lowermost (physical) layer the data is converted to physical signals on the transmission medium (wire, radio-waves, etc.). When the message is received from the lower layer, the corresponding header is removed and the rest of the message is given to the upper layer until the highest (application) layer is reached. There are seven layers in the original version of the OSI stack:

7. Application layer: APIs for resource sharing, remote file access, etc.
6. Presentation layer: Converts the data between applications and networking services (character encoding, compression, enciphering)
5. Session layer: Organises continuous exchange of information between two nodes by using multiple transport-layer transmissions
4. Transport layer: Transmission of data segments between network nodes (TCP and UDP protocols). Segments data and forms packets from the segments
3. Network layer: Organising a multi-node network (addressing, routing, packet traffic control, etc.)
2. Data link layer: Transmission of data frames between two nodes
1. Physical layer: Transmission and reception of bits encoded into physical signals.

The protocols of the OSI framework enable two same-level entities at two nodes to communicate, i.e. to exchange messages by using the lower layers as a transport mechanism.

The OSI framework was developed during the Open Systems Interconnection project in late 1970s at the International Organization for Standardization (ISO) and was published in 1984 as the standard ISO/IEC 7498-1.

OSI framework supports specialisation and fair market of products. As the input/output and the basic functionality of the tools at every layer is specified by the standard, industrial competitors can implement such functionality in the best possible and economically efficient way. This guarantees that best products win and a high quality communication can be achieved.

Every layer (taken separately) specifies a universal data exchange framework which does not depend on what happens at lower layers, i.e. the protocols and formats of the layer can potentially stay the same even if the standards of lower layers will change.

In spite of its extremely positive role in the fast development of the Internet and computer systems, the OSI framework is not flexible enough for an efficient strategies against massive denial of service (DOS) attacks. The formats and protocols of ISO/IEC 7498 do not enable higher layers to give complex options about transmission strategies at the lower levels. Much more cooperation between the layers would be needed for fighting against organised DOS.

4.2   Operating Systems Design

In this subsection, we provide some examples of design choices in the field of operating systems design that, while being reasonable and economically feasible at their time, are responsible for the most important universal technical vulnerabilities that todays cybercrime abuses.

Code and Data Mixed. Compared to nowadays computers, early computers had very little memory which was tried to be used flexibly. For example, programs at certain stage could modify the part of memory where their own code was held, in order to reuse the memory under the segments of the code which will no more be executed. Some of the early general purpose operating systems did not distinguish between the memory intended for running code and the memory for storing data.

This enables viruses that already run to easily modify other programs in computer's memory and devices and use it for subsequent infections and damage.

Loadable Operating Systems. The code of operating system of a personal computer is uploaded and executed from the same memory (e.g. hard disk) that is used for storing ordinary data by the computer. Such an option is good for flexible update and bug-fixes in the operating system.

The problem with such a choice is that a virus that already runs has no obstacles to rewrite the operating system stored on the hard disk and will thereby get a full control over the computer.

4.3   Computer Hardware Design

Shared Interfaces for Loadable Code and Loadable Data. Bootstrapping is done with the same type (an shape) of disks than those used to store data and even the same interfaces. For example, early personal computers even had a default option that if at the time of computer's restart a floppy disk is in a disk-drive, then the computer automatically uploads a segment of code on the floppy disk (the so-called *boot-sector*). Computers with a hard disk upload and run a piece of code that is stored on a certain part of the hard disk (*master-boot-sector*). Such options provided a flexible mechanisms of upgrading computer's operating system and also using your own operating system (that is saved on your floppy disk) in any other computer of the same type.

At the same time, such design choices provided an efficient infection mechanism for computer viruses.

Bus Architecture. Buses transfer data between components of a computer as well as between a computer and its external devices. Buses in early computers were collections of parallel electrical wires with many connections but the nowaday's meaning of a bus is wider and engages any solution with the same logical function as a bus with electrical wires. Buses may use parallel or serial bit-connections and use several ways of connection and topology. The *external bus* (or *expansion bus*) connects the different external devices (e.g. printers) to the computer.

Mostly, operating systems do not handle the external buses completely and hence viruses may use the external devices for hiding themselves and being very hard to detect.

4.4   Applications'/Services' Design

Global Identities. Many Internet applications are related to identities that are used to take (define) real contractual responsibilities. For example, in some countries, personal digital signatures must be used, in spite of the fact that their owners have almost no control over the corresponding devices and supporting infrastructures. Global identities also have risen the increasing topic of privacy. The foundation of the privacy problem are provable relations between data and identities.

Though, global identities give us many convenient options in electronic services, the public trust on them seems to be too optimistic. The best example is voting over the Internet (i-voting), universal and for everybody to use! Are we indeed ready to handle the case where someone gains power through a falsified i-voting?

Clouds. Cloud storage/computing is an Internet-based data-storage and computing platform that provides shared computational power and data to computers and other devices. Clouds enable on-demand access to a shared configurable computing resources (e.g. computer networks, servers, storage, applications, services) that can be handled with minimal management effort. It provides users and enterprises with various capabilities to store and process their data in privately owned or third-party data centres across the world. Clouds help organisations to lower the computer- and network-related infrastructure costs. They also enable organisations to more rapidly adjust the resources in case the business demands change unpredictably. Via clouds, companies can easily increase the used memory and computational power in case their business needs increase, and also decrease the used memory and power if business demands decrease.

Clouds have many negative aspects too. For example, there is no way for users to detect how carefully their valuable data is held, i.e. what are the likelihoods of losing the data, and modifying or using the data in unintended and unauthorised way. Possible privacy violations is one of the main concerns regarding clouds. We find more and more references to claims that public data can be used more efficiently than any intelligence agencies have been done in the past.

5   Systems Development and Security Management

The historical design decisions described above and specialisation have supported a systems' design approach where system development engineers build universal platforms which are later "secured" by security engineers.

Numerous security specialists in the World understand the direct causes of losses via security incidents and try to take measures against these causes. For example, to fight against computer viruses, security specialists recommend using virus detection/protection software. After discovering a new computer virus, the virus scanners are updated for being able to recognise the new virus in the future, so the security specialists recommend frequent updating of virus-detection software. They also recommend using Virtual Private Network software/hardware to prevent attackers from eavesdropping secret communications going on via otherwise non-protected communication channels. Pairing vulnerabilities with the corresponding measures creates *security practices* many of which are standardised, and which contain lists of security measures that are necessary to fight against vulnerabilities. Security specialists know (standard) security practices, can follow them and make systems "secure" by applying measures and installing numerous security-oriented products. In some cases, measures mean significant redundancy, which means one has to install several copies of a functional component instead of one.

Often, security specialists do their job without having sufficient knowledge about the initial (business) intention of the system they secure. So they automatically follow their security practices even if the system is actually *secure by design*. Security standards and best practices support such an approach. Some of them even claim that security risks are fundamentally different from ordinary business risks. There is a huge number of organisations that offer security-related certified education. Most of the education is dedicated to technical staff and to middle-level executives, not much to top-level executives. Certified security courses mostly teach security engineers how to buy security products and explain their necessity to their management staff. This all makes it very hard for Chief Executive Officers (CEOs) to have technical decisions under control, i.e. to make sure that technical decisions always support rational business decisions of the company.

In companies, Chief Technical Officers (CTOs) are responsible for the whole computational platform of the company. For more than 15 years, companies also have Chief Information Officers (CIOs) who are responsible about all the information the company produces/processes and also about how this is done. Just about 10 years, companies also have Chief Security Officers (CSOs) who are positioned even higher than CIO and Chief Financial Officer (CFO), i.e. CSO receives a functional solution from CIO and CTO and makes it secure.

One the one hand, such an approach may enable faster and modular development of the systems. On the other hand, all the additional security-related equipment may make the system many times more expensive. Another drawback of such a development practice is that the security specialists who try to protect the systems are always behind the attackers.

Though there exist more systematic approaches to systems' design, where the specifications include both the functionality and the restrictions and which may significantly reduce the overall costs of designing, building and maintaining a system, for some reasons, such approaches are not practiced.

For obvious reasons, security equipment sellers are interested in such a situation. Also the producers of ordinary computer equipment gain from the situation because due to redundancy required by security standards they can sell more products. This is one probable reason why such a practice is very hard to change.

It is also very hard to come out with scientifically proved arguments against such practice because there is no general theory of systems' security [8]. One cannot prove that the security measures one applies are justified, and no one can either prove that they are not. Systems' security is not yet an engineering practice (such as we have in Civil Engineering), it is just a *technician practice* that has no sufficient support from science.

6   Conclusions

We predict that the growing trend of the losses via cyber crime will continue in the future the main reasons being that: (1) as more and more assets will be connected to the Internet, the number of potential targets and stimuli for attackers grow; (2) fundamental (and hard to change) design decisions made in early development stages of todays Internet- and computer technology guarantee persistent technical vulnerabilities in Internet-based systems due to which attackers will always be one step ahead of defenders; (3) growing role of Chief Security Officers (CSOs) in organisations, who do not necessarily have to understand the detailed purpose and functionality of the system but whose duty is still to make the ITC system of the organisation secure. These reasons guarantee the continuous growth of the security industry but also the continuous growth of losses through cyber crime.

References

1. Baran, P.: Reliable Digital Communications Systems Using Unreliable Network Repeater Nodes. RAND Corporation P-1995 (1960). https://www.rand.org/content/dam/rand/pubs/papers/2008/P1995.pdf
2. Baran, P.: On Distributed Communications. RAND Corporation P-2626 (1962). https://www.rand.org/content/dam/rand/pubs/papers/2005/P2626.pdf
3. Cherdantseva, Y., Hilton, J.: Information security and information assurance. The discussion about the meaning, scope and goals. In: Almeida, F., Portela, I. (eds.) Organizational, Legal and Technological Dimensions of Information System Administrator, pp. 167–198. IGI Global Publishing, Hershey (2013). http://www.igi-global.com/chapter/information-security-and-information-assurance/80717
4. Cherdantseva, Y., Hilton, J.: A reference model of information assurance and security. In: Proceedings of ARES 2013, pp. 546–555 (2013). doi:10.1109/ARES.2013.72
5. War in the fifth domain. Are the mouse and keyboard the new weapons of conflict? Econ., 1 July 2010. http://www.economist.com/node/16478792
6. http://www.fairinstitute.org
7. https://www.bsi.bund.de/EN/Topics/ITGrundschutz/itgrundschutz_node.html

8. Herley, C.: The unfalsifiability of security claims. In: Proceedings National Academy of Sciences, May (2016). https://www.microsoft.com/en-us/research/wp-content/uploads/2015/09/unfalsifiabilityOfSecurityClaims.pdf
9. Nakashima, E.: Stuxnet was work of U.S. and Israeli experts, officials say. The Washington Post, 2 June 2012
10. Caldwell, L.A., Winter, T.: FBI Releases Notes From Interview With Hillary Clinton Over Emails. NBCNews, 3 September 2016. http://www.nbcnews.com/politics/2016-election/fbi-releases-documents-hillary-clinton-s-interview-n642126
11. OECD's Guidelines for the Security of Information Systems and Networks: Towards a Culture of Security. OECD (2002). http://www.oecd.org/internet/ieconomy/15582260.pdf
12. Parker, D.B.: Fighting Computer Crime. Wiley, New York (1998). ISBN 0-471-16378-3
13. Roberts, L.G.: The evolution of packet switching. Proc. IEEE **66**(11), 1307–1313 (1978). http://www.packet.cc/files/ev-packet-sw.html
14. Stoneburner, G., Hayden, C., Feringa, A.: Engineering Principles for Information Technology Security (A Baseline for Achieving Security), Revision A. NIST Special Publication 800–27 Rev A (2004). http://csrc.nist.gov/publications/nistpubs/800-27A/SP800-27-RevA.pdf
15. Traynor, I.: Russia accused of unleashing cyberwar to disable Estonia. Guardian (2007). https://www.theguardian.com/world/2007/may/17/topstories3.russia
16. Internet out hits tourism sector. Myanmar Times, 2 November 2010. http://www.burmanet.org/news/2010/11/02/myanmar-times-internet-out-hits-tourism-sector/

Walking the Line: The Everyday Security Ties that Bind

Lizzie Coles-Kemp[1](✉) and René Rydhof Hansen[2]

[1] Royal Holloway, University of London, Egham, UK
Lizzie.Coles-Kemp@rhul.ac.uk
[2] Aalborg University, Aalborg, Denmark
rrh@cs.aau.dk

Abstract. In this paper we argue that in contemporary society a form of security emerges that is qualitatively neither technological nor social but that is truly sociotechnical. We argue that everyday security is a form of sociotechnical security co-constituted of both technological protection mechanisms designed to protect assets and of relational social practices that enable people to build and maintain trust in their daily interactions. We further argue that the complexity of real-world information security problems requires security models that are able to articulate and examine security as a sociotechnical phenomenon and that can articulate and examine the results of interaction between these two security constructions. Security must be modelled to acknowledge, at least, the connection between an individual's security needs and the protection of assets if it is to help design secure services with which citizens can safely engage. We exemplify these attributes from case studies conducted as part of two sociotechnical research projects: the UK government and research council funded Cyber Security Cartographies (CySeCa) project and the EU FP7 funded project TREsPASS. These are introduced to discuss the potential for a family of modelling techniques. In this paper we examine the attributes of everyday security problems and reflect upon how such a modelling family might influence both academic research and practice in contemporary information security.

1 Introduction

The subtleties of secure human-computer interaction are often hard to pin down. The design of security technologies focuses on the protection of data and the usability requirements for that technology. Rarely does the security technology design process address the human security needs of the individual where human security needs fundamentally address a sense of confidence to achieve well-being e.g. financial well-being and emotional well-being. In security theory, protection from harms is sometimes termed negative security whilst the freedom to achieve human security needs such as financial security or well-being is termed positive security [23,31]. Whilst security technology design is well-established in terms of protecting data and by extension, the owners and dependents of that data, from harm, security technology design is less well-established in enabling the freedom

© Springer International Publishing AG 2017
T. Tryfonas (Ed.): HAS 2017, LNCS 10292, pp. 464–480, 2017.
DOI: 10.1007/978-3-319-58460-7_32

to use that data in a way that enables individuals to meet their other human security needs. For example, when a granddaughter helps her grandmother conduct important on-line activities [21], e.g., by conducting on-line banking or interacting with the on-line welfare system on her grandmother's behalf, the granddaughter is acting as a so-called social proxy, a position of power that can be either supportive or abusive. In a supportive situation, the grandmother may want to have the freedom to share her access with her granddaughter as a means of enabling financial security through the receipt of care from her granddaughter. Similarly, when a grandmother gives her granddaughter advice on which friends to block or whether to respond to a social media post, the grandmother is acting as a type of gatekeeper that in a supportive situation enables the granddaughter to maintain her social relationships.

Although such usage scenarios are not uncommon and have obvious consequences for the security of the system and the safety of the actors, it is a very rare digital service design that takes such scenarios into account and even rarer that the underpinning system has an underlying security model that can capture the many subtle aspects of such scenarios. In this scenario the sharing of passwords, the incorporation of those typically considered to be non-users of a system is often built around the human security need to build and maintain trust relationships to engender confidence and a sense of well-being, rather than the focus on protecting data on a system. For this reason, standard technical responses of delegated authority and role-based access control do not fully suffice because these technological responses focus on the data and system protection needs, with an assumption that these fully correspond to the human security needs.

In the example outlined above, the technological problem is one of ensuring managed access, the human problem is one of preventing outsiders from gaining access and of enablement to meet the fundamental need of a sense of well-being through the receipt of care and support from family members. The technological controls respond to the former human security problems but not the latter ones. The technological support needed for the latter human problem is one of building and maintaining care relationships and managing the trust relationships needed to support those care relationships.

The focus of information security practice and academic study has traditionally been squarely aimed at IT security [14]. IT security can be explained as the protection of computer produced data and information and the associated protection of the infrastructure that makes possible the production, circulation, protection and curation of that data. However, the protection of data is not solely a question of IT security. The widespread adoption of digital technology across all strata of society and the increasing reliance by governments and industry on engagement with citizens through digital media brings data protection into the realm of everyday life for citizens. If data protection is to make sense to citizens as they go about their everyday lives, IT security must clearly link to human security needs such as those related to an individual's financial, health, physical well-being and stability. This paper asks how might we model data protection in this everyday realm, how this model might improve understanding of everyday security practices and how it might help broaden IT security.

2   Security: A Divided Field of Study

The separation that we can see in information security between the human security needs of the actors and the data security needs of the infrastructure is
common to many studies of security, not only technological ones. As McSweeney
highlights in the introduction to "Security, Identity and Interests: A Sociology of International Relations" [23] security is a term that is used in a wide
range of contexts in all aspects of life and it can refer to people, things, practices, external events and innermost feelings. The study of security is equally
broad and is studied from many different perspectives [26] across many different
disciplines including Politics and International Relations e.g. [27], Geopolitics
e.g. [1,8], Critical and Social Geography e.g. [11], Psychology e.g. [4,7], Sociology e.g. [10,24], Computer Science e.g. [18,19] and Maths e.g. [3]. These different
perspectives of security often influence each other. For example, Security Studies
focuses on the protection of the State and is often located within Politics and
International Relations but also crosses over into Geopolitics in order to examine
the security of boarders and of populations e.g. [1]. Regardless of the focus of
security study, there is a tendency to focus on the materiality of security using
epistemologies related to positivist forms of knowledge [23]. Materials of security
range from battlefield technology to surveillance technologies and information
access control systems. Just as traditional international relation security theorists emphasise the use of the military, traditional computer security theorists
emphasise the use of cryptography and access control protocols. In pursuing
this focus on the materiality of security, traditional security studies across all
disciplines tend to focus on the externalising of security problems and ignore
the question of the internalising of security problems within the individual and
the central question of how the individual conceptualises security [23]. However,
the relationship between the externalisation of security problems (how they are
articulated and framed) and how an individual conceptualises security is an
important dimension to secure human-computer interaction.

Studies of security do, however, differ in the families of referent objects that
are the focus of each type of study [23]; a separation often motivated by academic rather than governmental politics. In the case of information security, the
primary referent object is the computer generated data or information with a secondary referent object being the computational infrastructure that supports the
generation, storage, circulation and curation of the data, e.g. [2,3,15,19,22,32].
When humans are introduced into this picture of information security by way
of sociotechnical security modelling, they are typically subjugated to the needs
of the protection of data and their actions are analysed in terms of their contribution to or detraction from the protective act. The implicit assumption in this
type of modelling is that the protection of data and the concomitant protection
of the technological infrastructure is a human security need. Examples of this
genre of security modelling include: [9,29]. Traditional models of information
security extended to include human action therefore reflect this assumption that
human actions related to the needs of data protection are modelled. However,
human-centered studies of information security consistently demonstrate that

the relationship between data protection and the needs of individuals is complex [17, 28]. In order to achieve this the perspective of information security needs to be broadened to include a focus on the connection between human security needs and IT security needs and the development of a meaningful connection between the two.

3 The Case for Broadening the Focus of Information Security

Over the last two decades there has been a growing call for the broadening of security studies in the international arena [23]. Sociologist Bill McSweeney argued that security in a broader context should be regarded as both protection *from* (negative freedoms) and the freedom *to* (positive freedom) [23]. In terms of negative freedom there is a freedom from threat and is, as McSweeney argues, characterised in objects such as locks, doors, walls etc. that protect things and prevent things from happening. However, there is another form of security, this is adjectival rather than normative — "secure" rather than "security" — a quality that conveys the essence of making things possible. This related form is "freedom to" rather than "freedom from" and should not be seen as an alternative to the more traditional conceptualisation of security as freedom from threat but should be seen as an interrelated concept. From this perspective access control to a particular data file, for example, should not only be seen as a mechanism for the protection of the data but also as the granting of access to data that empowers an individual to build and sustain relationships as they go about their daily activities. In this case the human security need is focused on the relational use rather than on the material protection of data. If the need for the material protection of data is to be understood, the protection mechanisms must support, and be understood to support, the building and maintenance of relationships in order to capture the co-constituted nature of the negative security protection of the data (data protection need) and the positive security enablement of a sense of security derived from trusted human relationships (human security need). This broader view of information security that more fully captures the relationship between data and human security needs is highly relevant to the understanding of secure human-computer interaction.

In the following two sections we examine how information security is traditionally modelled when the primary referent object is data and how relational security might be modelled. We start with a description of Bell/LaPadula, Role Based Access Control and Harrison/Ruzzo/Ullmann modelling and explain the focus of these classic access control models. We explore the security goals that can be expressed through such models. We then move to a description of two rich-picture based modelling attempts to articulate patterns of relational security within a scenario.

4 Modelling the Granddaughters and Grandmothers Case Using Traditional Security Models

From the granddaughter and grandmother example in the introduction section, it is clear that the (strategic) security needs of the grandmother and grand-daughter example is quite different from the kind of security formalised in the classic access control models such Bell/LaPadula (BLP) [3], Role-Based Access Control (RBAC) [32], and Harrison/Ruzzo/Ullmann (HRU) [15]. In the following sub-sections we explore how such access control models can be applied in the granddaughter and grandmother example and, in particular, to what extent they are able to capture and support (and possibly enforce) the grannies' security goals.

4.1 Bell/LaPadula (BLP)

The Bell/LaPadula access control model, also called the multi-level security (MLS) model, was originally proposed as a solution to the problem of Trojan horses stealing information in classified military systems. In the BLP model, every information source (called an object in the BLP terminology) is assigned a security level, e.g., secret or top secret (security levels are assumed to be totally ordered), and every user or user-process of the system (called a subject in the BLP terminology) is assigned a corresponding clearance level, indicating the level of information the user is allowed to access. The BLP model then defines (and enforces) security by preventing users from reading information above their own level (no read-up) and from writing information below their own level (no write-down). In other words, a user with a "secret" clearance level can only read information that is classified as secret or lower and can only write information at level secret or higher.

In order to apply the BLP model in the context of the granddaughter and grandmother scenario, we must first identify the relevant objects (information sources) and subjects (information sinks, e.g., users). In the interest of readability, we shall use the terms "user(s)" and "subject(s)" as well as "information (sources)" and "objects" interchangeably. An obvious first choice is to let grannies and granddaughters be subjects and then define the information provided by on-line services, e.g., Facebook, to be objects. Even with this simple modelling, we have captured essential security features/requirements for typical on-line services: the login process and the privacy/security settings of the service. In principle, a grandmother could classify information and/or activities meant to be shared with a granddaughter, such as games provided by the on-line service, at a low security level and other, more sensitive information as at a high security level. In this way, the grandmother could make a "low level" login when sharing the on-line account with a granddaughter, e.g., for playing games or simply sharing information, and a "high level" login when using the on-line service for private/personal purposes. Using the framework of the BLP model, the set of security/clearance levels is subject to very few constraints (technically they must form a lattice) and can be constructed with arbitrarily high granularity and thus cover most use cases occurring in practice.

Of course, for the above access control to work, grandmothers would have to manage on-line identities with several security/clearance levels and, potentially, several completely different digital identities with different levels of authorisation and access and, not least, with different login credentials — a daunting task for even the most tech-savvy granny. One traditional way of solving or at least alleviating the problem of managing multiple identities, or roles, is to use the role-based access control model which we will discuss next.

4.2   Role-Based Access Control (RBAC)

The notion of security that underpins and motivates the RBAC model is the same as for the BLP model discussed above: essentially preventing users with a given clearance level from accessing information at a higher security level. However, in addition, the RBAC model explicitly acknowledges that *(1)* a user may interact with the system in several different capacities, e.g., both as an administrator as well as a "normal" user; *(2)* some system activities may be performed by any user in a group of users, e.g., any user belonging to the "auditors" group may perform certain system audit functions. In the RBAC model this is captured by introducing *roles* that can be assigned to users in such a way that a user may have several roles and a role may be assigned to several users. Roles are typically defined by the collection of functions (on the system) that a user performing that role must have access to. This approach has several advantages over "raw" BLP: it makes administration of access control policies much easier (at least for large systems with many users and security levels) and more robust since the required access rights for specific items of information can now be specified "abstractly" based on what the information should be used for rather than on an individual basis. This also makes it easier to manage when a users' access rights should be expanded/revoked.

For grandmothers wanting to play on-line games or share on-line information with their granddaughters, the RBAC model offers a cleaner and easier way to mange security than the BLP model. Instead of managing different identities and several on-line accounts and their concomitant access control policies, it is a matter of specifying the different roles a user (grandmother) can perform in a given on-line service. As an example, a grandmother could specify a "sharing" or "public" role and a "private" role where the latter is obviously used for interactions the grandmother does not necessarily wish to share with her granddaughter, and the former for the kind of shared on-line experience(s) mentioned above, e.g., playing games or watching video clips together. The notion of roles can be refined almost endlessly, facilitating a very granular approach to access control: the grandmother could specify roles to use with each of her grandchildren or specify roles based on age intervals (of her grandchildren or, indeed, any other family member or friend) ensuring that even the youngest grandchildren will not accidentally see or access information intended for an older audience.

Although RBAC offers simpler management of access control policies, it is important to note that the underlying security notions of the RBAC model are equivalent to those of the BPL: everything that can be (conveniently) specified in the RBAC model could (much less conveniently) be encoded in the BLP model.

4.3 Harrison/Ruzzo/Ullmann (HRU)

The Harrison/Ruzzo/Ullmann model [15] of access control significantly extends the previous access control models by allowing access control rights to be changed *dynamically*, i.e., during operations, and also makes it possible to *delegate* authority to other subjects. Unfortunately, the increased expressivity of the HRU model also makes it much more difficult to reason about the security of a given system, since it is not generally possible to adequately account for all the dynamic behaviour of a system. In fact, determining the security of a given system in the HRU model has been shown to be *undecidable* in the general case [15].

With the HRU model a grandmother can, dynamically and temporarily, grant her granddaughter access rights to information and authority to perform certain functions on behalf of the grandmother, e.g., in order to play on-line games, all *without* letting the granddaughter use grandmother's login credentials. Another use of the HRU model would be for a grandmother to *delegate* authority over certain aspects of an on-line service to, e.g., a granddaughter. The granddaughter (with delegated authority) would then be able to both act on behalf of the grandmother, but also potentially to *further delegate* authority, e.g., to a carer or another family member.

Although the HRU model solves (part of) the problem of a grandmother sharing login credentials with her granddaughter in order to play (on-line) games and engage in on-line activities, it also introduces a much more complex dynamic (security) behaviour that is potentially even different on-line accounts. Even more to the point, the formal access control models discussed above, i.e., BLP, RBAC, and HRU, all miss the important point that maybe a grandmother deliberately *wants* to share her login credentials with her granddaughter in order to form a stronger bond, i.e., strengthen her *relational security*.

5   Modelling the Relational Security Aspects of Granddaughters and Grandmothers

The granddaughter and grandmother study was conducted as part of a UK research council funded research project titled Visualisation and Other Methods of Expression (VOME) that gathered everyday security narratives in the context of digital services from communities that hitherto had not been part of the digital service debate. In particular, the project focused on digital service use and the associated security needs of underserved communities, including: lower socio-economic groups, long-term unemployed, use of digital services within families and families separated by prison. The project developed methods of engagement that were designed to elicit everyday security narratives and develop an articulation of human security needs in the context of digital service use [5]. One of the project findings was that human security needs were related in large part met through the management of relationships and the development of new relationships [6,30]. In two follow-on projects, the UK research council funded research project titled Cyber Security Cartographies (CySeCa) and the EU FP7 funded project TREsPASS, methods of visualising and modelling human security needs were developed. In both projects methods of data elicitation and abstraction were developed that used techniques to gather narratives of everyday security and then to abstract relationship networks from the narratives. The approaches were based on a soft systems modelling technique known as rich picturing [25].

The goal of the CySeCa project was focused on understanding the intersection between digital data protection mechanisms and relational security practices. There were two work streams within the project, one that examined relational security practices from the perspective of human social networks and one that examined data protection mechanisms at the digital network level. Both work streams developed analytical methods to identify and analyse the information sharing and protection activities taking place within each type of network. They also developed visualisations to communicate the security practices and mechanisms in operation within each network. In this paper, we use an example of the relational security work from CySeCa to illustrate how the modelling of relational security might be undertaken. In one case study in the CySeCa project, the relational security work stream examined the sharing and protection of information flows within a community centre providing digital service support for essential service such as housing, welfare, food, health, education etc. [20]. The analytical goal of this study was to explore how people feel about using the centre and the different roles that the centre plays in their lives. In particular, in this study we wanted to understand how people felt about sharing information while at the centre — both as part of the process of obtaining the practical assistance they need in accessing on-line services and also as part of the socialising and social network building that takes place at the community centre. In this study we developed visual and written narratives to show how people experienced information sharing and protection within the community centre and then used social networking techniques to show the trust bonds between people in the community centre and the information that flows through and is protected by those bonds.

This type of approach could be used to produce visual and written narratives as shown in Fig. 1 to describe the interaction between grandmother and granddaughter. In particular, these narratives show the role of the "non-users" or the social proxy who is helping the service user to carry out a task. For example, such a narrative might show the granddaughter logging on to on-line banking on behalf of her grandmother or the grandmother giving advice as to how the granddaughter might respond to a conflict on Facebook. These narratives could then be abstracted using social network analysis to show the trust relationships between grandmother and granddaughter.

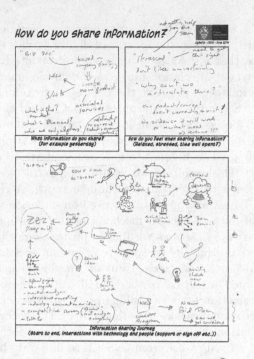

Fig. 1. A storyboard of everyday information sharing

Whilst the CySeCa work was successful in depicting the relational security practices and the relationship of those largely positive security practices to the human social network, the modelling work did not articulate the interaction between the relational security practices and the digital security practices which largely reflect negative security of data protection. The EU FP7 project, TREsPASS [33] developed methods and tools to quantify, analyse and visualise sociotechnical information security risks in dynamic organisations. The TREsPASS project included a work stream to explore the visualisation of sociotechnical information security risk. The goal of this work stream was to extend the state of the art in cyber security risk tools by developing visualisations that combine information visualisations with techniques from critical cartography and digital humanities to articulate different sociotechnical dimensions of risk and provide tools through which to explore these dimensions. A form of participatory diagramming and physical modelling [16] was deployed in TREsPASS using physical modelling tools such as LEGO as shown in Fig. 2. The modelling approach places social data gathered directly from case-study participants at centre-stage which has the effect of broadening the traditional process of information risk assessment, accessing social data as a starting point for identifying and then scoping the issues that are of paramount interest to the stakeholders in a risk scenario.

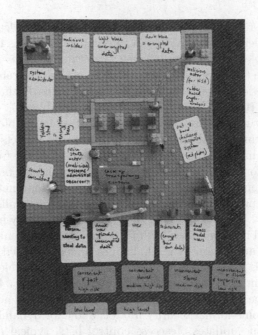

Fig. 2. LEGO model of a data sharing and protection scenario

The physical modelling process uses the following steps to brainstorm risk scenarios: *(1)* A context or scenario for information sharing and protection is agreed with a participant group. *(2)* Participants identify their core values and the basis on which they share and protect information. *(3)* Participants are given physical modelling material, for example LEGO building bricks of given types and colours, selected so as to encode the movement of shared information and data, actors, and devices. *(4)* Participants collaboratively model the chosen context or scenario in the physical modelling medium and, during this collaborative process, discuss the types of information generation and flows that occur within this space. *(5)* Participants identify information sharing and protection narratives relevant to the context.

Open questions and provocations are used by the modelling session facilitators to encourage participants to focus on a particular sociotechnical information security risk theme and thereby draw out both the positive and negative security responses to the scenario. This type of approach could be used to show where the emphasis of control is in the granddaughter and grandmother scenario and to enable analysis of where both the human and data security needs might not be met.

6 Modelling Information Security's Broader View

The TREsPASS' physical modelling approach, whilst it combines the positive and negative security perspectives, is still focused on human security needs as the referent object rather than data security needs as is the case for the traditional security models. This difference in referent object focus makes combining the models a complex task. The challenge that then emerges is how to enable interaction between the formal data security models and the relational models of human security needs. In everyday terms this is particularly challenging because the referent object (the individual) is inherently unstable [23].

Formal security models are typically regarded as incapable of capturing or modelling the proximity and relational attributes and aspects of human security needs. Indeed, much of the terminology and many of the fundamental ideas and concepts in information security originate from military needs and military thinking with a strong focus on "asset protection" and automated (or automatable) technological protection mechanisms e.g., network firewalls and access control models [3,15,22,32]. Even though the traditional security models have been successfully applied in many cases both to design and reason about the security of a system, there are a number of challenges and pitfalls with this approach. First of all, there is an implicit assumption that it is possible to identify and define all the relevant assets and authorised entities in a system. Furthermore, the security goals (of the authorised entities) must be aligned and non-contradictory. Finally, although some formal security models allow for dynamic changes in the model, e.g., dynamic updates of access control lists, typical (formal) security models assume that the underlying security goals of a system do not change (too often) and that such changes are handled "out of band". This traditional asset-based approach to information security contrasts with a focus on human security needs where security is a property of relationships and enables a form of security located in how we build relationships within our kin and friendship networks. In order to understand this type of security a different type of knowledge is developed from a socially-constructed knowledge paradigm where formal mathematical models are replaced by patterns of connections forming and re-forming over time and space.

One approach might be to combine the two types of security goals but as the granddaughter and grandmother example shows, this requires the modelling of contradictory goals. Another possibility is to articulate a complex scenario such as the grandmother and granddaughter case using a family of models where the data security and relational security models are separate and a third type of model is introduced which captures the negotiation and navigation between the two. This third type of model would be a model of everyday negotiation and serves to shine a light on the important practices undertaken by individuals to marry data security needs with their human security needs in order to achieve the most effective co-construction of positive and negative security in a given context. In the following sections below we introduce the notion of the everyday into positive and negative security and conclude with a short discussion of the potential for modelling such everyday security interactions.

7   Introducing the Everyday

One of the touch points between the computer security models and the relational security models is the individual. The individual has to manage the computer security requirements inscribed into the computer security models with the relational security requirements inscribed in the relational security model. For example in our scenario the grandmother has to manage the banking requirement to use a username and password for her on-line banking account alongside her practice of sharing technology use with her granddaughter as part of the grandmother's approach to managing her fear of losing financial security. This social practice is based on her trust relationship with her granddaughter. This is a complicated negotiation between the two types of security models. It requires the grandmother to, amongst other things, judge the trustworthiness of the granddaughter, be aware of any potential changes in her granddaughter's behaviour and to understand the purpose of the username and password controls and agree a course of action with her granddaughter. This is an everyday security problem that requires negotiation between the granddaughter and grandmother.

In recent years there has been a move to develop a scholarship that explores, theorises and develops an understanding for security in the everyday. The everyday has become a category of security studies where the focus is "the 'everyday' as a category of analysis — with its alternative temporal stress on rhythm and repetition and scalar emphasis on the micro and proximate" [34]. For example, we can see in the grandmother and granddaughter example that there are information sharing routines between the granddaughter and grandmother that are both frequent, small and happen in close proximity blending on- and off-line information sharing.

This direction of study is driven by the perspective that the individual is the ultimate referent object in security studies [23,31]. The focus of the social sciences in studying the everyday has largely been developed from a critical position. Critical theorists argue citizens have not been engaged with in order to understand their security needs and concerns [34]. In HCI and usable security studies, the focus has been on describing security practices found in the wild [12,35] but with little fundamental discussion as to the security goals that these practices support. In this paper we use the critical theory perspective to augment our understanding of security practices in the wild by taking a closer look at the interaction between the traditional information security goals related to the protection of data and human security needs. This augmented understanding is needed if the grandmother's and granddaughter's security practices are to be understood. In the scenario we have sketched in this paper, both grandmother and granddaughter need guidance on their security responsibilities to each other and approaches for ensuring that the trust bonds between them are sufficiently strong as well as guidance to develop their technical know-how.

8   Security and the Everyday

Human security needs are the primary referent object of everyday security as patterns of practice are, in part, routinised and repeated to develop an individual's ontological security, a form of security founded on basic trust within relationships [13]. Croft and Vaughan-Williams [34] citing Croft 2012 describe ontological security as follows: "the key elements of an ontological security framework are a biographical continuity, a cocoon of trust relations, self-integrity and dread, all of which apply at the level of the individual, and all of which are constructed intersubjectively." In our example we can see that as family members the granddaughter and grandmother are embodiments of each other's biographical continuity, which help to foster strong and deep trust bonds. Each provides the other with trust relations that insulates or cocoons the other from unwelcome events using digital services. The self-integrity of both the grandmother's and granddaughter's identity is seemingly intact in the sense that both grandmother and granddaughter are willing to share different parts of their lives with each other, fostering a sense of security and safety in the other. Both granddaughter and grandmother routinise each other's lives and help to give structure which helps to manage the dread of insecurity (for example the dread of financial or social insecurity).

As we can see from the above examples, ontological security therefore manifests itself in the everyday practices that are designed to build and maintain routines that enable an individual to use trust relationships to cope with complex and uncertain situations. The main focus of ontological security practice is to routinise life to prevent it from tipping into chaos and to enable individuals to have the confidence to go about their daily activities. In a digitally-mediated society, an individual's everyday security is characterised by combining positive and negative security techniques in order to maintain an individual's sense of ontological security.

In our example of granddaughters and grandmothers the following aspects of everyday security need to be navigated. The scenario is everyday in the sense that it is composed of proximate, close, micro relationships between family members. These close relationships are founded on a repetition of micro interactions. It is also co-constituted by positive and negative security practices because the relationship between the granddaughter is in part strengthened by sharing access to essential on-line services and supporting each other in the use of those services. The close relationship between granddaughters and grandmothers make possible the sharing of access and the flow of personal information, equally the sharing of access and the flow of personal information serve to further strengthen those bonds meeting the human security need of being confident to engage with the on-line services and achieve financial security (on-line banking) and relationship security (mediated through social media).

9   Modeling the Everyday

Everyday security can not be reduced to a simple model and to encompass the different views and the interactions between those views make models too complex to construct and interpret. An alternative approach is to introduce a family of security models, where computer security models and relational security models are linked by everyday security models that capture the interaction between positive and negative security techniques and which show the outcomes of the negotiation between human security and data security needs.

Models of everyday security need to capture the relationship between positive and negative security techniques. As our grandmother and granddaughter example shows, positive and negative aspects of security are concomitant of each other; the negative protection of username and password protects the grandmother and granddaughter as service users from attacks from outside the family and also give each the positive freedom to engage in services that help each to meet their human security needs of economic stability (on-line banking) and relational security (social media). Equally granting the other access to their on-line accounts, either through login credentials or by allowing the viewing of account activity, provides the positive security of further building trust bonds through sharing and also the negative security of an additional person to check the integrity of the on-line transactions. The negative security aspects of this example can be modelled using standard security modelling techniques such as BLP and RBAC. The relational aspects of this example can be modelled using social network analysis. However, neither of these modelling approaches capture the concomitant nature of positive and negative security and in particular the different ways in which the individual has to navigate and bring together these two forms of security to construct an everyday security strategy for a given situation.

Models of everyday security also need to capture the ontological security position. Traditional and relational security models also do not explicitly take into account the ontological security position of both grandmothers and granddaughters. Furthermore, current modelling techniques do not enable security goals to be understood from multiple perspectives. In order to understand the security goals of the granddaughter and grandmother scenario, the security positions of both the granddaughter and the grandmother has to be taken into account as well as the perspective of the digital service provider and as well as the perspectives of other family members.

Everyday security models also need to capture the issues arising from emotional, physical and social proximity. These issues include: the negotiation of proximity and the evaluation of what to share and what to keep private and an on-going assessment of the motivations of the other in maintaining the trust relationship.

In summary, a family of models that include the computer security and relational modelling approaches linked by models of everyday security is one possible approach to responding to the complexity of everyday security. By introducing a linked family of models, the security knowledge becomes less fragmented and, importantly, is brought together without denying the different epistemologies in which each security knowledge is grounded. In this section we have sketched some of the requirements for models of everyday security. Such models make visible the positive security goals arising from fixed-space interaction which is traditionally invisible to the service security design. Whilst these interactions are outside of the realm of technological security mechanisms, they have an important bearing on the meaning and the significance of such mechanisms and can be used to shape technological security mechanism design.

10 Conclusion

Information security practitioners and scholars have long understood the importance of context when defining and responding to information security problems. It is also understood that in real world security multiple perspectives need to be worked with in order to understand both the problem and the most appropriate responses. However, as the grandmother and granddaughter scenario shows, information security is not solely about protection, it is also a story of enablement and achievement that result in the meeting of an individual's human security needs as well as data protection needs. A modelling approach that relates human security needs with data protection needs and shines a light on the negotiation process between the two, enables us to connect these two families of security need and identify how each can support the other. Such a modelling approach also contributes to the reunification of the field of security, something that is needed for an effective response to complex real-world everyday security problems.

References

1. Adey, P.: Facing airport security: affect, biopolitics, and the preemptive securitisation of the mobile body. Environ. Plan. D: Soc. Space **27**(2), 274–295 (2009)
2. Anderson, J.P.: Computer security technology planning study. Technical report ESD-TR-73-51, Electronic Systems Division, Hanscom Airforce Base, Hanscom, MA, USA, October 1972
3. Bell, D.E., LaPadula, L.J.: Secure computer systems: mathematical foundations. Technical report ESD-TR-73-278, ESD/AFSC, Hanscom AFB, Bedford, MA, November 1973. Also appears as MTR-2547, vol. 1, Mitre Corp., Bedford, MA. Digitally reconstructed in 1996
4. Briggs, P., Jeske, D., Coventry, L.: Behavior change interventions for cybersecurity. In: Behavior Change Research and Theory: Psychological and Technological Perspectives, p. 115 (2016)
5. Coles-Kemp, L., Ashenden, D.: Community-centric engagement: lessons learned from privacy awareness intervention design. In: Proceedings of BCS HCI Workshops: Designing Interactive Secure Systems, pp. 4:1–4:4, September 2012
6. Coles-Kemp, L., Kani-Zabihi, E.: Practice makes perfect: motivating confident privacy protection practices. In: Proceedings of the IEEE Third International Conference on Privacy, Security, Risk and Trust (PASSAT 2011) and the IEEE Third International Conference on Social Computing (SocialCom 2011), pp. 866–871. IEEE (2011)

7. Coventry, L., Briggs, P., Jeske, D., Moorsel, A.: SCENE: a structured means for creating and evaluating behavioral nudges in a cyber security environment. In: Marcus, A. (ed.) DUXU 2014. LNCS, vol. 8517, pp. 229–239. Springer, Cham (2014). doi:10.1007/978-3-319-07668-3_23

8. Crampton, J.W.: Cartographic rationality and the politics of geosurveillance and security. Cartogr. Geogr. Inf. Sci. **30**(2), 135–148 (2003)

9. David, N., David, A., Hansen, R.R., Larsen, K.G., Legay, A., Olesen, M.C., Probst, C.W.: Modelling social-technical attacks with timed automata. In: Proceedings of the 7th ACM CCS International Workshop on Managing Insider Security Threats (MIST 2015), pp. 21–28. ACM (2015)

10. Denney, D.: Risk and Society. SAGE, Thousand Oaks (2005)

11. Dodds, K.: Jason bourne: gender, geopolitics, and contemporary representations of national security. J. Popul. Film Telev. **38**(1), 21–33 (2010)

12. Dourish, P., Grinter, R.E., Flor, J.D., Joseph, M.: Security in the wild: user strategies for managing security as an everyday, practical problem. Pers. Ubiquit. Comput. **8**(6), 391–401 (2004)

13. Giddens, A.: Modernity and Self-identity: Self and Society in the Late Modern Age. Stanford University Press, Palo Alto (1991)

14. Hansen, L., Nissenbaum, H.: Digital disaster, cyber security, and the Copenhagen school. Int. Stud. Q. **53**(4), 1155–1175 (2009)

15. Harrison, M.A., Ruzzo, W.L., Ullman, J.D.: Protection in operating systems. Commun. ACM **19**(8), 461–471 (1976)

16. Heath, C.H.P., Coles-Kemp, L., Hall, P.A., et al.: Logical Lego? Co-constructed perspectives on service design. In: Proceedings of the 10th Biannual Conference on Design and Development, pp. 416–425 (2014)

17. Inglesant, P., Sasse, M.A.: Information security as organizational power: a framework for re-thinking security policies. In: 2011 1st Workshop on Socio-Technical Aspects in Security and Trust (STAST), pp. 9–16. IEEE (2011)

18. Jeske, D., Briggs, P., Coventry, L.: Exploring the relationship between impulsivity and decision-making on mobile devices. Pers. Ubiquit. Comput. **20**(4), 545–557 (2016)

19. Lampson, B.: Protection. In: Proceedings of the 5th Princeton Conference on Information Sciences and Systems. Princeton (1971). Reprinted in ACM Oper. Syst. Rev. **8**(1), 18–24 (1974)

20. Lewis, M.M., Coles-Kemp, L., Siganto, J.: Picture this: tools to help community storytelling. In: Presented at the CHI 2014 Workshop on Tactile User Experience Evaluation Methods (2014). https://www.riscs.org.uk/?p=832

21. Light, A., Coles-Kemp, L.: Granddaughter beware! An intergenerational case study of managing trust issues in the use of Facebook. In: Huth, M., Asokan, N., Čapkun, S., Flechais, I., Coles-Kemp, L. (eds.) Trust 2013. LNCS, vol. 7904, pp. 196–204. Springer, Heidelberg (2013). doi:10.1007/978-3-642-38908-5_15

22. McLean, J.: Security models. In: Marciniak, J. (ed.) Encyclopedia of Software Engineering. Wiley, Hoboken (1994)

23. McSweeney, B.: Security, Identity and Interests: A Sociology of International Relations. Cambridge Studies in International Relations. Cambridge University Press, Cambridge (1999)

24. Molotch, H.: Everyday security: default to decency. IEEE Secur. Priv. **11**(6), 84–87 (2013)

25. Monk, A., Howard, S.: Methods & tools: the rich picture: a tool for reasoning about work context. Interactions **5**(2), 21–30 (1998)

26. Neocleous, M.: Critique of Security. Edinburgh University Press, Edinburgh (2008)
27. O'Loughlin, B., Gillespie, M.: Dissenting citizenship? Young people and political participation in the media-security nexus. Parliam. Aff. **65**(1), 115–137 (2012)
28. Pfleeger, S.L., Sasse, M.A., Furnham, A.: From weakest link to security hero: transforming staff security behavior. J. Homel. Secur. Emerg. Manag. **11**(4), 489–510 (2014)
29. Probst, C.W., Kammüller, F., Hansen, R.R.: Formal modelling and analysis of socio-technical systems. In: Probst, C.W., Hankin, C., Hansen, R.R. (eds.) Semantics, Logics, and Calculi. LNCS, vol. 9560, pp. 54–73. Springer, Cham (2016). doi:10.1007/978-3-319-27810-0_3
30. Reddington, J., Coles-Kemp, L.: Trap hunting: finding personal data management issues in next generation AAC devices. In: Proceedings of the Second Workshop on Speech and Language Processing for Assistive Technologies, pp. 32–42. Association for Computational Linguistics (2011)
31. Roe, P.: The 'value' of positive security. Rev. Int. Stud. **34**(04), 777–794 (2008)
32. Sandhu, R.S., Coyne, E.J., Feinstein, H.L., Youman, C.E.: Role-based access control models. Computer **29**(2), 38–47 (1996)
33. The TREsPASS Project. Project web page. http://trespass-project.eu. Accessed 10 Feb 2017
34. Vaughan-Williams, N., Stevens, D.: Vernacular theories of everyday (in)security: the disruptive potential of non-elite knowledge. Secur. Dialogue **47**(1), 40–58 (2016)
35. Vines, J., Blythe, M., Dunphy, P., Vlachokyriakos, V., Teece, I., Monk, A., Olivier, P.: Cheque mates: participatory design of digital payments with eighty somethings. In: Proceedings of the Conference on Human Factors in Computing Systems (CHI 2012), pp. 1189–1198. ACM (2012)

Radicalization, the Internet and Cybersecurity: Opportunities and Challenges for HCI

Joanne Hinds[(⊠)] and Adam Joinson

Information, Decisions and Operations, School of Management,
University of Bath, Bath, UK
{J.Hinds,A.Joinson}@bath.ac.uk

Abstract. The idea that the internet may enable an individual to become radicalized has been of increasing concern over the last two decades. Indeed, the internet provides individuals with an opportunity to access vast amounts of information and to connect to new people and new groups. Together, these prospects may create a compelling argument that radicalization via the internet is plausible. So, is this really the case? Can viewing 'radicalizing' material and interacting with others online actually cause someone to subsequently commit violent and/or extremist acts? In this article, we discuss the potential role of the internet in radicalization and relate to how cybersecurity and certain HCI 'affordances' may support it. We focus on how the design of systems provides opportunities for extremist messages to spread and gain credence, and how an application of HCI and user-centered understanding of online behavior and cybersecurity might be used to counter extremist messages. By drawing upon existing research that may be used to further understand and address internet radicalization, we discuss some future research directions and associated challenges.

Keywords: Radicalization · Cyber security · Online behavior

1 Introduction

The role of the Internet in radicalization has been the topic of considerable debate since the widespread adoption of the web in the mid to late 1990s. As far back as 1999, David Copeland, a right-wing extremist, detonated nail bombs in London using expertise gained from books downloaded from the internet [1]. Although early discussions e.g. [2] primarily focused on the use of the internet to conduct, co-ordinate or prepare for terrorist acts, more recently much of the discussion has been around propaganda and the use of the internet to mobilize support [3–5]. Not surprisingly, much of the discussion of Internet radicalization has been conducted in the security and terrorism studies field. For instance, in the years 2001–2016, the term 'radicalization' (or 'radicalisation') was used 21 times in the titles of articles in the journal "Security and Conflict Studies", and mentioned in the text of 232 papers. During the same period,

The original version of this chapter was revised: A Funding Disclosure Statement has been inserted. The correction to this chapter is available at https://doi.org/10.1007/978-3-319-58460-7_51

© Springer International Publishing AG 2017, corrected publication 2020
T. Tryfonas (Ed.): HAS 2017, LNCS 10292, pp. 481–493, 2017.
DOI: 10.1007/978-3-319-58460-7_33

the term was used zero times in papers in ACM CHI, CSCW, or indeed HCII. However, it is our contention that researchers in human-computer interaction (HCI), and cyber security more generally, have investigated a number of phenomena and topics that we believe are directly relevant to understanding (and addressing) internet radicalization.

The goal of the present paper is to highlight ongoing challenges faced by security researchers in understanding 'internet radicalization', and to suggest where HCI and cybersecurity researchers might fruitfully contribute. We begin by outlining what is meant by the term 'radicalization', before considering the nature of 'online radicalization', and then the potential links between cybersecurity, HCI and radicalization.

1.1 Definition of Radicalization

In general, the term 'radicalization' is a poorly understood concept, with considerable disagreement over not only its definition, but also whether or not it serves a meaningful purpose in understanding politically motivated violence [6]. Whilst there is no universal, agreed-upon definition, radicalization is broadly acknowledged to be a process in which an individual willingly moves towards more extremist views e.g. [7]. Importantly, radicalization is not necessarily negative or a precursor to terrorism, as many people who accept radical ideas do not participate in violent behavior as a result of their beliefs [8]. Further, radical ideas are not necessarily anti-social as radicalism can give rise to positive change (e.g. universal suffrage), and the categorization of an individual or group as 'radical' or 'radicalized' is not a politically neutral activity. More recently, discussions of radicalization have also become entwined with concerns about safeguarding vulnerable young people (e.g. to stop teenage girls traveling to war zones).

Violent radicalization (or violent extremism) is usually argued to be when an individual adopts 'extreme political, social and/or religious ideas and aspirations, and where the attainment of particular goals justifies the use of indiscriminate violence. It is both a mental and emotional process that prepares and motivates an individual to pursue violent behavior.' [8] (p. 38). Many individuals holding radical beliefs and opinions will not commit extremist or violent acts and, conversely, many terrorists are often not deep believers and have limited knowledge of their motivating ideology [9].

There are myriad potential causes for radicalization toward violent extremism (e.g. social inequality, poverty, violation of basic rights; [6]), a detailed description of which is outside the remit of the present paper. Rather, in the following section we briefly summarize the main approaches, before moving to consider how these might relate to work within HCI and cybersecurity.

1.2 Radicalization: Theories and Models

Most theories of radicalization propose a combination of individual and social factors that, in combination, can both push and pull individuals towards violent action [10]. Typically, not one factor is assumed to be sufficient on its own to trigger radicalization, but rather is assumed to operate in conjunction with other factors and vulnerabilities to lead an individual towards violent radical action. Research suggests that there is not a specific psychological profile or vulnerability that might pre-dispose individuals to violent radicalization [10]. For instance, *relative deprivation*, the notion that a person comes to feel deprived as a result of comparing their situation with others, has been consistently linked with radicalization, e.g. [11–14]. A sense of relative deprivation can drive people to join movements e.g. [15], the intention being that joining a movement will bring about social change and put an end to their grievances [10]. Other 'triggers' for radicalization may be the tendency of (some) people to adopt religious beliefs or join religious groups after experiencing some form of crisis e.g. [16–18].

Whilst a definite, agreed-upon process of radicalization has not been established, a number of models have outlined some proposed stages of radicalization, a summary of which are outlined as follows:

1. **Social/economic deprivation or a personal crisis** – An individual experiences relative deprivation or some form of crisis, which can be personal or group-based [19–22]. The individual views their situation as unfair/unjust.
2. **Resentment and information seeking** – The perception of relative deprivation causes an individual to feel increasing resentment towards others who they perceive as being more fortunate. An individual may seek answers to their situation and in doing so becomes receptive to new ideas and possibly new religious beliefs [22, 23].
3. **Attributing blame and justification of violence** – Individuals blame others for their perceived injustice [19] and socialize with likeminded others, which strengthens these new beliefs [20]. Violence is viewed as a legitimate means to rectify perceived injustices [19, 23].
4. **The violent act** - An individual embraces and fully commits to the group's beliefs and mission [23, 24].

While none of these models directly incorporates the role of the internet in radicalization, it seems plausible that it could be utilized at any stage as a source of information or communications mechanism that could help to develop/reinforce feelings of hardship and justified violence. In the following section, we discuss some of the more specific aspects of the internet (referred to as 'affordances') that may contribute towards an individual's radicalization.

2 Online Radicalization

At a fundamental level, the internet allows rapid access to vast amounts of information as well as the opportunity to connect to others through social networks, fora, messaging systems etc. Each of these mechanisms has an associated set of 'affordances', a term commonly used in HCI to describe how technology functions and thus how it should be used. This idea of objects *affording* certain types of behavior was adopted by human-computer interaction researchers, most notably Norman [25], following the introduction of the term by cognitive psychologist Gibson [26]. Norman argues that affordances are the "perceived and actual properties of the thing, primarily those fundamental properties that determine just how the thing could possibly be used" [25]

(p. 9). We would argue that the notion of affordances – while valuable in highlighting the links between design, the user, and action – does not fully represent the ways in which design and behavior interact. Taylor et al. [27] argue that:

> 'Research on the 'social shaping' of technology ... suggests that we shape technology as much as we are in turn influenced by the decisions made by designers, or the content it provides ... this means that use of the Internet needs to be considered from neither a simple 'technologically deterministic' standpoint (e.g. the Internet causes radicalisation), nor simply as a socially neutral 'tool' (p. 4).

Gibson [28] describes how affordances can be both perceivable and straightforward (e.g. Facebook allows people to keep in touch with friends) or more hidden/camouflaged (e.g. a person can use Facebook to portray themselves in a more positive light by only posting attractive photographs). It is therefore possible to speculate how similar affordances may apply to online radicalization. For instance, ideologues have become proficient at using social media, online communities etc. to disseminate their radical ideologies, gain support [29, 30] and to provide instruction in terrorist activity. Online magazines such as Dabiq and Inspire along with other internet resources can equip an individual with everything they need to know to commit a terrorist attack, from assembling a bomb to breaching security in an airport [31].

It is indisputable that such resources available online (including via the dark web) provide ample support for violent extremists in terms of attack planning, as well as (potentially) the opportunity to gather information in relative anonymity. However, in this respect the internet is nothing more than a conduit for the provision of information and communications, with little or no influence on the process itself. A RAND report [32] surveyed 15 cases of mostly Islamic terrorist activities, where the internet was implicated in radicalization and actual attacks in the UK. They concluded that while the internet provided more opportunities for radicalization, it did not necessarily increase the speed at which individuals became radicalized, or replace face-to-face contact or kin and peer influence. A more recent study by Gill et al. [33] studied the use of the Internet by 223 convicted terrorists in the UK. They conclude that patterns of use differ according to the requirements of the terrorist (e.g. to gain expertise in explosives, recruit co-conspirators or gain ideological justification), also stating that, "The Internet is largely a facilitative tool that affords greater opportunities for violent radicalization and attack planning". In other words, these findings suggest that certain affordances of the internet can potentially fuel different aspects of radicalization (although it is not possible to decipher exactly how this is achieved). This suggests that technology in itself is not enough to radicalize individuals to take action, but rather that the internet acts as an enabler *once* an individual is radicalized, or when specific hurdles need to be addressed (e.g. how to choose a target, build an improvised explosive device etc.).

Another aspect to consider is that radicalization encompasses a broad spectrum of people with different needs, motives and goals, ranging from lone actors to individuals seeking belonging from group membership. Thus, this is likely to be reflected in different uses and approaches toward using information disseminated online. In the following section, we move to explore some ways in which certain affordances may enable certain types of behavior/transformations in the context of group behavior, echo chambers, offline action and self-presentation online.

2.1 Group Behavior

The internet allows people to communicate rapidly to masses of people online, as well as seek out and develop new relationships with different people and different groups. In doing so the internet may help individuals to develop and maintain an identity through joining an online community, forum, social media group etc. Being part of a group can provide an individual with a sense of belonging [34, 35] and the internet can provide an opportunity for individuals to seek out and connect with likeminded others with whom they may not have the opportunity to meet offline. Classic studies of group behavior have demonstrated that groups have the potential to change behavior – individuals exert less effort as they feel less accountable for their actions e.g. [36], individual attitudes and opinions can become more extreme through group polarization [37], individuals can favor consensus through groupthink [38] and groups can increase a person's inclination to conform, e.g. [39]. Therefore, by extension, can similar effects underpin or play a role in radicalization?

Research on computer-mediated communication demonstrates how some group effects can be exaggerated online. The SIDE model (social identity model of deindividuation effects) for instance, explains how anonymity can enhance people's identification with a group [40, 41], leading to group polarization e.g. [42]. Taken together, the ability to change and strengthen an individual's opinions and behavior, combined with an individual's search for belonging may increase the potential for radicalization online.

2.2 Echo Chambers and Identity Demarginalization

Related to the notion that the internet can foster group polarization is the idea that the internet can fuel echo chambers, where particular opinions can easily start to be recirculated and reinforced, which could have the gradual effect of causing someone to experience a change in mindset. There are numerous design aspects that can serve to fuel this, for instance much of the content an individual is exposed to is a result of content that has been filtered by certain algorithms. For example, social media is a primary news source for over 60% of US internet users [43], which means that most news consumed is filtered by both algorithms and 'friends' [44], and is consumed in the context of others' reactions. As seen in the 2016 US Election, this 'filter bubble' and 'echo chamber' can lead to the rapid spread of false news stories and creation of ghettos of information with little transfer across ideological boundaries [45]. Since radicalization often relies on a sense of injustice and unfairness, an unintentional outcome of the design of online systems may well be that individuals are exposed to increased amounts of material that fuels such grievances. Furthermore, most social media services not only create echo chambers, but also provide validation to content through the positive reactions of others and supportive comments and sharing. Thus, even 'fake' news can gain additional credence by being shared and supported by large numbers of other people. According to principles of social comparison and herding (e.g. [46]) people look to others for guidance on how to act and respond, particularly when uncertain. If a large number of people are also sharing and supporting radical content, it is likely that for any one individual, such views will be more likely to be adopted.

Simultaneously, a relatively large number of people sharing the same content and opinions serves to demarginalize a previously socially anti-normative set of beliefs or actions. Early work by McKenna and Bargh [47] found that participation in online newsgroups by people with stigmatized identities led to increased self-acceptance, likelihood of 'coming out' to family and friends, and less social isolation. Similar findings emerge from qualitative work on the Stormfront extreme right wing forum [48], with respondents stating that participation helped express an identity that was stigmatized and hidden in face-to-face dealings. There is further evidence that identities expressed online – particularly those publicly affirmed and responded to – later transfer to offline action [49]. It is not that much of a stretch then to predict that the combination of in-group homogeneity, echo chambers, public expression of usually hidden identities or beliefs and supportive comments from others would be enough to encourage increased radicalization.

2.3 Online Action and Offline Acts

Computer-mediated communication has also been found to influence how a group behaves offline. For instance, social media applications (in particular microblogging applications such as Twitter) can be extremely useful for sharing information and reaching large numbers of people when events unfold rapidly and other forms of communication may fail, e.g. [50, 51]. Further, the freedom to publish information publicly enables people to bypass official media censorship and inform a global audience. Subsequently, this surge of online collective information exchange can cause 'mobilizing' effects where groups assemble and combine their efforts offline e.g. [52, 53]. These mobilizing effects typically occur at the onset of major news events, disasters and crises. For instance, during the Arab Spring, a series of political protests and demonstrations that occurred across the Middle East in 2011, many people on the ground in Cairo used Twitter to communicate meeting times, coordinate actions and gather support [54, 55]. We also see similar mobilizing activities in the 'shaming' of individuals via social media [56], where large numbers of people mobilize online to express outrage and condemn an individual judged to have transgressed.

Whilst there is clear evidence for the power of social media to fuel and support social unrest (and hence similar situations that may lead to violent extremist activity), none of these examples provide ample evidence that the people participating were radicalized (e.g. the people participating in the London riots in 2011 were not hailed as 'radicalized'). There has also been heavy criticism over the extent of the effectiveness of social media to actually promote and fuel offline action. For instance, whilst Twitter was used heavily during the London riots, there was little evidence to suggest that Twitter was used to promote illegal activities at the time, rather it served as a tool for spreading information (and misinformation) about subsequent events and showing support for beliefs in others' commentaries [57]. The ability for users to provide cheap and easy support via social media has been referred to as 'slacktivism' [58, 59], where low-risk, low investment actions such as signing a petition or 'liking' a Facebook page can lead them to feel their contribution is enough [60, 61]. These online activities therefore provide little insight for online radicalization, as those that may appear to hold strong beliefs and even encourage or threaten violent extremism online may have no intention of taking offline action.

2.4   Deception and Self-presentation

In addition to changing how individuals behave when immersed in a group, computer-mediated communication can affect how individuals present themselves and interact with others online. Social contextual cues such as body language, facial expressions, intonation etc. that are visible in face-to-communication are absent, e.g. [62]. This can mean that information can more easily be misinterpreted or individuals may 'fill in the blanks', that is, they make assumptions about information that is unclear or is not communicated explicitly.

The absence of cues can make it easier to lie and deceive others online, especially when communicating with others whom an individual has never met before, e.g. [63, 64]. For instance, extensive research of online dating demonstrates that deception is frequently observed when people exaggerate details of their physical attributes (height, weight, age) in attempt to enhance their attractiveness online, e.g. [65, 66]. The style of deception that is demonstrated in online dating highlights numerous techniques that ideologues could use in radicalization. For instance, ideologues can pose as someone else by using an identity more appealing to the victim in terms of how they appear or what they represent. Private conversations can be used to develop intimacy, which can be extremely persuasive as messages can be personalized and cannot be viewed by others, who may attempt to intervene. These tactics mirror grooming attempts, which have in some cases appeared to have lured young people into joining radical groups, for example the three teenage girls who left the UK for Syria in 2015 after interacting with extremists online [67].

Unlike dating, many of the interactions that occur through these media will continuously occur publicly with (potentially) many others. A number of studies have suggested that the awareness of an audience causes individuals to present themselves more favorably to avoid embarrassment, shame or unfavorable impressions, e.g. [68–70]. Because individuals now have many opportunities to present themselves online (and spend significant amounts of time doing so), some research has suggested that they may alter their identity offline as a result, an effect commonly referred to as 'identity shift' [49]. In a study where participants were instructed to present themselves in an extraverted manner online, Gonzales and Hancock [49] found that participants subsequently began to demonstrate extraverted behavior offline. By extension, these findings may imply that similar shifts in identity may occur for individuals who start to present themselves as dedicated followers of radical groups in any of their online profiles.

The potential for identity shift is not only a factor in terms of how one presents themselves online, but also how their audience responds to and reinforces that identity. Walther's hyperpersonal model [71], for instance explains how the combination of reciprocal interactions and selective self-presentations over time lead to exaggerated levels of affect and intimacy which in turn can make an individual feel more committed to the identity they have created or developed online. The internet provides many opportunities for others to provide feedback (likes, retweets, comments, etc.) which may prove to be conducive to an individual exploring new aspects of their identity online. Further, feedback from others can serve as cues (referred to as 'warrants' [72]) that can help to verify or increase someone's inclination to believe that an individual is being truthful.

3   HCI Opportunities and Challenges

Throughout this article we have outlined the complex nature of radicalization and how such affordances provided by the design of social media applications, fora etc. may help to foster mechanisms that may, over time cause someone to change their opinion, identity or even conduct violent action offline. However, the lack of real understanding about radicalization, (which is in turn reflected in our lack of ability to truly measure or detect whether it is happening) means that is incredibly difficult to make any specific recommendations for how to address these issues with persuasive design in an online arena. At best, we can speculate how certain affordances may bring about certain types of behavior (e.g. rapid real-time communication on Twitter can provoke offline activity). In this respect, approaches to tackle this could lead toward attempting to counter or diffuse such behavior should it be anticipated or when it occurs.

One particular challenge in addressing these issues is that behavior often evolves from people's use of technology in a way that was unintended or unanticipated from the original design. For example, the design of social media was not expected to increase the spread of misinformation – rather it was hailed as a unique opportunity for a business to 'lose its chains' e.g. [73]. Many of the same processes that enable radicalization online also have socially beneficial outcomes - ranging from the ability of people to seek help and guidance for health problems in a pseudonymous environment to providing important methods for alternative news to spread outside of oppressive regimes. Therefore, this raises the question of what equivalent unintended types of behavior would result from attempts to address radicalization online.

Another consideration is that different groups will likely use the internet in different ways, in order to meet varied motives. It is therefore unlikely that a one-size-fits-all solution could address all the nuances between these different groups. Further, given that not all radical groups are problematic (indeed in many instances radical groups are harmless or even beneficial), there would be a danger in trying to counter certain opinions or behaviors online. Flexible approaches towards design are therefore needed, that consider radicalization as a multivariate problem. In spite of this, we discuss a number of light suggestions that may act as potential steps towards addressing radicalization online. However, because most of these approaches could be applied in both good and bad contexts, we acknowledge the potential pitfalls associated with each one.

First, an obvious, simplistic solution would be to block, or re-direct users from viewing (potentially) radicalizing content. This poses the immediate benefit of preventing them from possibly being influenced by propaganda or other radicalizing material. However, such content may have already been viewed/shared and it is likely that it could merely be re-posted elsewhere. Likewise, this approach is far too unrealistic and restrictive to apply so broadly across the web as it runs the risk of constraining opportunities for positive influence and interaction.

Second, although individual's generally have control over the content they consume, much of the information they are exposed to is determined by algorithms and the content shared by their contacts [44]. This can create the potential for internet echo chambers to emerge, which (in certain contexts) may create the impression that specific ideological views are shared by a larger proportion of people than is the case, as well as demarginalizing more extreme views. Changes to algorithmic design that aim to steer individuals away from or block suspicious content could attempt to diffuse or hinder the formation of echo chambers. However, this approach also runs the risk of wrongly disrupting beneficial content.

Third, in a similar vein, counter-messaging strategies could be employed in attempt to directly neutralize or diffuse extreme opinions or attempts to influence online. Counter-messaging is an emerging area of research, which has examined how targeted responses to hateful or opinionated online speech can effectively inhibit or end it. For instance, presenting counter-messages *may* be effective, particularly if combined with evidence of social proof (i.e. the number of people sharing/supporting a particular viewpoint). Some strategies for tackling this have already been suggested, for instance, the US based Anti-Defamation League [74] recommend that certain techniques such as responding to the original speaker, using comedy/satire and correcting falsehoods can be useful. At present, there is little evidence that indicates how successful these strategies are, so further research would benefit from attempts to establish effective messaging strategies online.

Fourth, the speculation that individuals can experience an identity shift as a result of their online interactions suggests that particular cues or warrants in social media applications (such as likes, comments, retweets etc.) could be used in attempt to reinforce or influence behavior. In other words, if an individual is suspected to be vulnerable to a potential identity shift, targeted efforts could seek to dissuade potentially radicalizing elements (e.g. not liking or commenting on a post which displays a support of violence) and instead reinforcing more positive behaviors (e.g. retweeting a post about sport). Such approaches would need to be cautious in order to ensure that the right kind of behaviors were reinforced.

Fifth, similar approaches could be used to set behavioral norms in forums. Some existing HCI/cybersecurity research has described how moderators can shape how people behave online by removing, re-directing or rating posts. This can encourage lurkers to contribute [75], set the standard for new users who may not know how to behave when they enter a community [76], discourage bad behavior and manage conflicts (e.g. trolls or flame wars). Certain design aspects such as reputation systems/rewards can also reinforce good/bad behavior, for instance, moderators on Slashdot (a social news website) assign labels and ratings to posts which causes the highest rated comments to appear at the top [77].

It seems likely that online communities could be a place where people experiencing relative deprivation may seek out like minded others for support. Preece [78] describes how designing communities to foster empathy are crucial for empowering people to discuss their problems and provide support to others. It therefore seems that encouraging and rewarding behavior through skillful moderation, rewards etc. may be an effective way to allow people to obtain the support they need, whilst motivating compliance within online communities. Of course, the potential for this to effectively disrupt radicalization would be dependent on the type of community and the moderators' motives.

Overall, these suggestions provide numerous approaches that may contribute towards tackling radicalization online. Whilst no method is without limitation, further research would benefit from exploring if and how behavior can be shaped in the context of radicalization online.

4 Conclusion

In summary, whilst is seems possible that an individual may become radicalized online, there is little evidence to suggest it actually occurs. Unfortunately, the lack of understanding about what radicalization actually is makes the task of recognizing it with any real accuracy impossible. By extension, it is therefore unrealistic to assume that this problem can be solved entirely by a technological solution. However, by drawing upon prior research from HCI and cybersecurity we have highlighted numerous avenues that may contribute towards designing systems and shaping behavior in ways that attempt to (at least) steer individuals in a more positive direction. Taken together, we hope these ideas may encourage HCI and cybersecurity researchers to think about new approaches towards tackling radicalization online.

Funding Disclosure Statement. This research was funded by the Centre for Research and Evidence on Security Threats (ESRC Award: ES/N009614/1), which is funded in part by the UK security and intelligence agencies. The funders had no role in study design, data collection and analysis, decision to publish, or preparation of the manuscript.

References

1. Conway, M.: Terrorism and the internet: new media—new threat? Parliam. Aff. **59**(2), 283–298 (2006)
2. Conway, M.: Terrorist use of the internet and the challenges of governing cyberspace. In: Power and Security in the Information Age: Investigating the Role of the State in Cyberspace, pp. 95–127 (2007)
3. Aly, A., Macdonald, S., Jarvis, L., Chen, T.M.: Introduction to the special issue: terrorist online propaganda and radicalization. Stud. Terror. Confl. 40, 1–9 (2016)
4. Conway, M.: Determining the role of the internet in violent extremism and terrorism: six suggestions for progressing research. Stud. Confl. Terror. **25** (2016)
5. Gendron, A.: The call to jihad: charismatic preachers and the internet. Stud. Confl. Terror. **40** (1), 44–61 (2017)
6. Schmid, A.P.: Radicalisation, de-radicalisation, counter-radicalisation: a conceptual discussion and literature review. ICCT Res. Pap. **97**, 22 (2013)
7. Fraihi, T.: Escalating radicaliastion: the debate within muslim and immigrant communities. In: Jihadi Terrorism and the Radicalization Challenge in Europe. Ashgate, Hampshire (2008)

8. Wilner, A.S., Dubouloz, C.J.: Homegrown terrorism and transformative learning: an interdisciplinary approach to understanding radicalization. Glob. Chang. Peace Secur. 22(1), 33–51 (2010)
9. Borum, R.: Radicalization into violent extremism I: a review of social science theories. J. Strateg. Secur. 4(4), 7–36 (2011)
10. Horgan, J.: From profiles to pathways and roots to routes: perspectives from psychology on radicalization into terrorism. Ann. Am. Acad. Polit. Soc. Sci. 618(1), 80–94 (2008)
11. Runciman, W.G.: Relative deprivation and social justice: study attitudes social inequality in 20th century England (1966)
12. Gurr, T.R.: Why Men Rebel. Routledge, Abingdon (2015)
13. Korpi, W.: Conflict, power and relative deprivation. Am. Polit. Sci. Rev. 68(04), 1569–1578 (1974)
14. Walker, I., Pettigrew, T.F.: Relative deprivation theory: an overview and conceptual critique. Br. J. Soc. Psychol. 23(4), 301–310 (1984)
15. Gunning, J.: Social movement theory and the study of terrorism. In: Critical Terrorism Studies: A New Research Agenda, pp. 156–177 (2009)
16. Lofland, J., Skonovd, N.: Conversion motifs. J. Sci. Stud. Relig. 20, 373–385 (1981)
17. Moscovici, S.: Toward a theory of conversion behavior. Adv. Exp. Soc. Psychol. 13, 209–239 (1980)
18. Rambo, L.R.: Theories of conversion: understanding and interpreting religious change. Soc. Compass 46(3), 259–271 (1999)
19. Borum, R.: Understanding the terrorist mindset. FBI Law Enforc. Bull. 72(7), 7–10 (2003)
20. Moghaddam, F.M.: The staircase to terrorism: a psychological exploration. Am. Psychol. 60(2), 161 (2005)
21. Sageman, M.: A strategy for fighting international Islamist terrorists. Ann. Am. Acad. Polit. Soc. Sci. 618(1), 223–231 (2008)
22. Wiktorowicz, Q.: Joining the cause: Al-Muhajiroun and radical Islam. In: Devji, F. (ed.) The Roots of Islamic Radicalism conference, Yale. Landscapes of the Jihad: Militancy, Morality and Modernity. C Hurst & Co Publishers Ltd., London (2004)
23. Silber, M.D., Bhatt, A., Analysts, S.I.: Radicalization in the West: The Homegrown Threat, pp. 1–90. Police Department, New York (2007)
24. Precht, T.: Home grown terrorism and Islamist radicalisation in Europe. From conversion to terrorism (2007)
25. Norman, D.A.: The Psychology of Everyday Things. Basic Books, New York (1988)
26. Gibson, J.J.: The theory of affordances. In: Shaw, R., Bransford, J. (eds.) Perceiving, Acting, and Knowing (1977)
27. Taylor, P.J., Holbrook, D., Joinson, A.: Same kind of different. Criminol. Public Policy 16(1), 127–133 (2017)
28. Gibson, J.J.: The theory of affordances. In: The Ecological Approach to Visual Perception, pp. 127–143 (1979)
29. Ashour, O.: Online de-radicalization? Countering violent extremist narratives: message, messenger and media strategy. Perspect. Terror. 4(6) (2011)
30. Chen, T., Jarvis, L., Macdonald, S.: Cyberterrorism. Springer, Heidelberg (2014)
31. Torok, R.: "Make A Bomb In Your Mums Kitchen": Cyber Recruiting and Socialisation of 'White Moors' and Home Grown Jihadists (2010)
32. Von Behr, I.: Radicalisation in the digital era: the use of the Internet in 15 cases of terrorism and extremism (2013)
33. Gill, P., Corner, E., Conway, M., Thornton, A., Bloom, M., Horgan, J.: Terrorist use of the internet by the numbers. Criminol. Public Policy 16(1), 99–117 (2017)
34. Tajfel, H.: Social psychology of intergroup relations. Ann. Rev. Psychol. 33(1), 1–39 (1982)
35. Taylor, D.M., Moghaddam, F.M.: Theories of Intergroup Relations: International Social Psychological Perspectives. Greenwood Publishing Group, Westport (1994)

492   J. Hinds and A. Joinson

36. Latane, B., Williams, K., Harkins, S.: Many hands make light the work: the causes and consequences of social loafing. J. Pers. Soc. Psychol. **37**(6), 822 (1979)
37. Myers, D.G., Lamm, H.: The polarizing effect of group discussion: the discovery that discussion tends to enhance the average prediscussion tendency has stimulated new insights about the nature of group influence. Am. Sci. **63**(3), 297–303 (1975)
38. Janis, I.L.: Victims of Groupthink: A Psychological Study of Foreign-Policy Decisions and Fiascoes. Houghton Mifflin, Boston (1972)
39. Asch, S.E.: Studies of independence and conformity: I. A minority of one against a unanimous majority. Psychol. Monogr.: Gen. Appl. **70**(9), 1 (1956)
40. Lea, M., Spears, R.: Computer-mediated communication, de-individuation and group decision-making. Int. J. Man Mach. Stud. **34**, 283–301 (1991)
41. Postmes, T., Spears, R., Lea, M.: Breaching or building social boundaries? SIDE-effects of computer-mediated communication. Commun. Res. **25**, 689–715 (1998)
42. Sia, C.L., Tan, B.C., Wei, K.K.: Group polarization and computer-mediated communication: effects of communication cues, social presence, and anonymity. Inf. Syst. Res. **13**(1), 70–90 (2002)
43. Gottfried, J., Shearer, E.: News Use Across Social Media Platforms 2016. Pew Research Centre (2016). http://www.journalism.org/2016/05/26/news-use-across-social-media-platforms-2016/. Accessed 10 Feb 2017
44. Bakshy, E., Messing, S., Adamic, L.A.: Exposure to ideologically diverse news and opinion on Facebook. Science **348**(6239), 1130–1132 (2015)
45. Baer, D.: The 'Filter Bubble' Explains Why Trump Won and You Didn't See It Coming (2016). http://nymag.com/scienceofus/2016/11/how-facebook-and-the-filter-bubble-pushed-trump-to-victory.html. Accessed 10 Feb 2017
46. Cialdini, R.B.: Influence, vol. 3. A. Michel (1987)
47. McKenna, K.Y., Bargh, J.A.: Coming out in the age of the internet: identity "demarginal-ization" through virtual group participation. J. Pers. Soc. Psychol. **75**(3), 681 (1998)
48. De Koster, W., Houtman, D.: Stormfront is like a second home to me: on virtual community formation by right-wing extremists. Inf. Commun. Soc. **11**(8), 1153–1175 (2008)
49. Gonzales, A.L., Hancock, J.T.: Identity shift in computer-mediated environments. Media Psychol. **11**(2), 167–185 (2008)
50. Qu, Y., Huang, C., Zhang, P., Zhang, J.: Microblogging after a major disaster in China: a case study of the 2010 Yushu Earthquake. In: Proceedings of CSCW 2011, pp. 25–34 (2011)
51. Starbird, K., Palen, L., Hughes, A., Vieweg, S.: Chatter on the red: what hazards threat reveals about the social life of microblogged information. Proceedings of CSCW **2010**, 241–250 (2010)
52. Conway, M.: From al-Zarqawi to al-Awlaki: the emergence and development of an online radical milieu. CTX: Combat. Terror. Exch. **2**(4), 12–22 (2012)
53. Gleason, B.: # occupy wall street: exploring informal learning about a social movement on Twitter. Am. Behav. Sci. **57**(7), 966–982 (2013)
54. Starbird, K., Palen, L.: (How) will the revolution be retweeted? Information diffusion and the 2011 Egyptian uprising. In: Proceedings of the ACM 2012 Conference on Computer Supported Cooperative Work, pp. 7–16. ACM, February 2012
55. Wulf, V., Misaki, K., Atam, M., Randall, D., Rohde, M.: 'On the ground' in Sidi Bouzid: investigating social media use during the tunisian revolution. In Proceedings of the 2013 Conference on Computer Supported Cooperative Work, pp. 1409–1418. ACM, February 2013
56. Cheung, A.S.: China internet going wild: cyber-hunting versus privacy protection. Comput. Law Secur. Rev. **25**(3), 275–279 (2009)
57. Tonkin, E., Pfeiffer, H.D., Tourte, G.: Twitter, information sharing and the London riots? Bull. Am. Soc. Inf. Sci. Technol. **38**(2), 49–57 (2012)

58. Christensen, H.: Political activities on the Internet: slacktivism or political participation by other means? First Monday **2** (2011). http://firstmonday.org/ojs/index.php/fm/article/viewArticle/3336
59. Schumann, S., Klein, O.: Substitute or stepping stone? Assessing the impact of low-threshold online collective actions on offline participation. Eur. J. Soc. Psychol. **45**(3), 308–322 (2015)
60. Morozov, E.: The brave new world of slacktivism [Weblog post] (2009). http://neteffect.foreignpolicy.com/posts/2009/05/19/the_brave_new_world_of_slacktivism
61. Gladwell, M.: Small change: why the revolution will not be tweeted [Weblog post] (2010). http://www.newyorker.com/reporting/2010/10/04/101004fa_fact_gladwell
62. Sproull, L., Kiesler, S.: Reducing social context cues: electronic mail in organizational communication. Manag. Sci. **32**(11), 1492–1512 (1986)
63. Ellison, N., Heino, R., Gibbs, J.: Managing impressions online: self-presentation processes in the online dating environment. J. Comput.-Mediat. Commun. **11**(2), 415–441 (2006)
64. Toma, C.L., Hancock, J.T., Ellison, N.B.: Separating fact from fiction: an examination of deceptive self-presentation in online dating profiles. Pers. Soc. Psychol. Bull. **34**(8), 1023–1036 (2008)
65. Guadagno, R.E., Okdie, B.M., Kruse, S.A.: Dating deception: gender, online dating, and exaggerated self-presentation. Comput. Hum. Behav. **28**(2), 642–647 (2012)
66. Hancock, J.T., Toma, C., Ellison, N.: The truth about lying in online dating profiles. In: Proceedings of the SIGCHI Conference on Human Factors in Computing Systems, pp. 449–452. ACM, April 2007
67. McVeigh, T., Reidy, T.: Families who fear Isis is targeting their children urged to lock up their passports. Guard. (2015). https://www.theguardian.com/society/2015/feb/21/syria-isis-uk-families-warned-lock-up-passports-daughters
68. Kelly, A.E., Rodriguez, R.R.: Publicly committing oneself to an identity. Basic Appl. Soc. Psychol. **28**, 185–191 (2006)
69. Tice, D.: Self-concept shift and self-presentation: the looking glass self is also a magnifying glass. J. Pers. Soc. Psychol. **63**, 435–451 (1992)
70. Schlenker, B.R., Dlugolecki, D.W., Doherty, K.: The impact of self- presentations on self-appraisals and behavior: The power of public commitment. Pers. Soc. Psychol. Bull. **20**, 20–33 (1994)
71. Walther, J.B.: Computer-mediated communication impersonal, interpersonal, and hyperpersonal interaction. Commun. Res. **23**(1), 3–43 (1996)
72. Walther, J.B., Parks, M.R.: Cues filtered out, cues filtered. In: Handbook of Interpersonal Communication, pp. 529–563 (2002)
73. Kaplan, A.M., Haenlein, M.: Users of the world, unite! The challenges and opportunities of social media. Bus. Horiz. **53**(1), 59–68 (2010)
74. Anti-Defamation League: Best practices for responding to cyberhate (2014)
75. Harper, F.M., Frankowski, D., Drenner, S., Ren, Y., Kiesler, S., Terveen, L., Riedl, J.: Talk amongst yourselves: inviting users to participate in online conversations. In: Proceedings of the 12th International Conference on Intelligent User Interfaces, pp. 62–71. ACM, January 2007
76. Kiesler, S., Kraut, R., Resnick, P., Kittur, A.: Regulating behavior in online communities. In: Building Successful Online Communities: Evidence-Based Social Design. MIT Press, Cambridge (2012)
77. Lampe, C., Resnick, P.: Slash (dot) and burn: distributed moderation in a large online conversation space. In: Proceedings of the SIGCHI Conference on Human Factors in Computing Systems, pp. 543–550. ACM, April 2004
78. Preece, J.: Empathic communities: balancing emotional and factual communication. Interact. Comput. **12**(1), 63–77 (1999)

Its Not All About the Money: Self-efficacy and Motivation in Defensive and Offensive Cyber Security Professionals

Duncan Hodges$^{(\boxtimes)}$ and Oliver Buckley

Centre for Electronic Warfare, Information and Cyber,
Cranfield University, Defence Academy of the United Kingdom,
Shrivenham, Swindon SN6 8LA, UK
{d.hodges,o.buckley}@cranfield.ac.uk

Abstract. Two important factors that define how humans go about performing tasks are self-efficacy and motivation. Through a better understanding of these factors, and how they are displayed by professionals in different roles within the cyber security discipline we can start to explore better ways to exploit the human capability within our cyber security. From our study of 137 cyber security professionals we found that those in attack-focussed roles displayed significantly higher-levels of self-efficacy than those in defensive-focussed roles. We also found those in attack-focussed roles demonstrated significantly higher levels of intrinsic motivation and significantly lower levels of externally regulated motivation. It should be noted we found no correlation with age or experience with either the focus of the practitioners task (whether offensive or defensive focussed) or their levels of motivation or self-efficacy. These striking findings further highlight the differences between those performing tasks that are self-described as offensive and those that are self-described as defensive. This also demonstrates the asymmetry that has long existed in cyber security from both a technical and opportunity viewpoint also exists in the human dimension.

1 Introduction

Cyber security is an important concern to organisations, with increasing numbers of cyber security decisions being moved from the technical domain to the boardroom. Whilst organisations continually consider the technical solutions to managing their cyber risk, few are building on these technical solutions through investing in people.

Whilst people are often considered the biggest risk [1] it is clear that people, specifically staff, represent the biggest defence against cyber attack [2]. People design defensive systems, processes and procedures; during an attack people triage the effects and staff the network operations centre; and post-attack people manage recovery and the lessons-learned phases. Whilst all staff in an organisation have a responsibility to help manage the security posture and within their

© Springer International Publishing AG 2017
T. Tryfonas (Ed.): HAS 2017, LNCS 10292, pp. 494–506, 2017.
DOI: 10.1007/978-3-319-58460-7_34

daily activity all staff have the opportunity to weaken or strengthen this posture, this is a secondary effect from their business function, for example, a HR
manager may weaken the posture of an organisation by opening a phishing email
but the primary focus of their business function is not securing the organisation.
This paper will focus on the staff who are explicitly tied to cyber security as
it is these individuals whose primary focus of their daily tasks can be directly
attributed to ensuring the secure operation of an organisation.

The tasks individuals employed in cyber security are varied and diverse from
those employed in strategic-level risk management through to the technical
security analysts ensuring the operational-level of the organisation is running
securely. This paper considers how these individuals go about their daily tasks
and what characteristics they typically exhibit performing these tasks. Through
understanding the characteristics displayed by individuals we hope to start to
better understand how staff can differ in their ability to perform tasks and,
through this better understand how individuals can be better able to perform
their tasks.

In order to explore the tasks that cyber security professional typically perform
we can break typical tasks into offence-focused (or adversarial) tasks and defence-
focussed tasks. Whilst the author acknowledges the over-militarisation of the
cyber discussion [3], it is useful at this stage to break typical tasks in cyber
security down into attack-focussed and defence-focussed tasks.

Defence-focussed tasks are those such as writing policy, managing and designing networks under attack. These represent tasks that are largely pro-active and
are designed to reduce either the likelihood of an attack being successful or
reduce the impact of a successful attack. These are often a mixture of technical
and management tasks.

Attack-focussed tasks include tasks such as red-teaming and penetration testing – where a team has been given suitable legal authority to attempt to compromise an organisation or system. These clearly represent an attack-focussed task
– however there are a number of other offensive-focussed tasks which are less
obvious, an example would be exploit development where a researcher is looking to prove that a vulnerability can be exploited and the degree to which that
vulnerability can compromise a system (e.g. remote code execution, privilege
escalation, etc.).

How successful we are at performing tasks in the workplace is a function of
a number of different variables related to both the task and our own skills and
attributes. The workplace can also have an effect on the efficacy of individuals
in their work [4]. This work focusses on two particular factors that are related
to how an individual performs tasks as part of their daily lives [5], these are
self-efficacy and motivation.

In this paper we focus on these two particular characteristics individuals
display in the workplace that have a tangible effect on how individuals go about
these tasks, namely self-efficacy and motivation. The ability to believe in ones
own ability and persist longer on a task, twinned with the inherent motivation to
continue with the task are clearly important whether its balancing the risk and

business requirements of an organisation whilst working with a security policy, exploring a piece of malware or red-teaming an organisation. Hence, motivation and self-efficacy are both important factors in the ability of security professionals to perform the tasks required of them, or more importantly to be creative and innovative in their approaches to their tasks.

This paper continues with a discussion of both self-efficacy and motivation before outlining the study presented in this paper. The paper continues to present the results from the study before closing with a final discussion.

1.1   Self-efficacy

Self-efficacy is the extent or strength of one's belief in one's own ability to complete tasks and reach goals [6], those with higher self-efficacy are more likely to make efforts to complete a task, and to persist longer in those efforts, particularly in the face of adversity, than those with lower self-efficacy.

However, at very high self-efficacy, some individuals may feel overconfident and reduce their efforts [7], Assuming that individuals feel efficacious about surmounting problems, holding some doubt about whether one will succeed can mobilize effort and lead to better use of strategies than will feeling overly confident [8].

In many cyber security roles there are clearly 'hard' tasks which require persistence notably under adversity, whether this adversity is a tangible actor or the task itself.

1.2   Motivation

Work motivation can be defined as the '... *a set of energetic forces that originates both within as well as beyond an individual's being, to initiate work related behaviour'* [9] or '... *the process of instigating and sustaining goal-directed behaviour.'* [10]. However, clearly it is not just the degree of motivation that is important but how that motivation is orientated (i.e. how the motivation manifests itself). This orientation of motivation is also a function of the individual and the activity, for example an academic may be internally motivated to perform research tasks yet externally motivated to complete marking.

The orientation of motivation is aligned along a continuum representing the degree to which goals or tasks have been internalised [11], this is shown in Fig. 1.

The most internal type of motivation is Intrinsic Motivation, which is defined as the doing of an activity for it's inherent satisfactions. When intrinsically motivated an individual is moved to act for the fun or challenge entailed rather that from external rewards. In contrast the lowest level of internal orientation is amotivation, which is a state of lacking an intention to act, this typically results from the lack of personally valuing an activity [12].

Extrinsic motivation is another orientation of motivation that is important for work-based activities. Extrinsic motivation is the construct that pertains when an activity is done in order to attain some separable outcome [13]. However, extrinsic motivation can be modulated in a number of different ways as

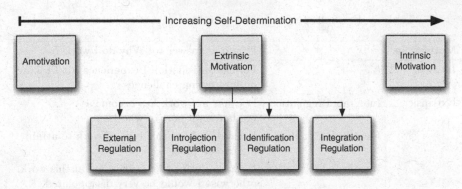

Fig. 1. A scale of human motivation

an individual translates or internalises the external motivation. For example a member of staff who is motivated by not wanting to be reprimanded and a member of staff who is motivated by wanting a promotion and better career prospects are both externally motivated but have internalised this motivation in different ways. To capture this extrinsic motivation is typically broken down into four different categories as shown in Fig. 1.

The least autonomous form of extrinsic motivation is external regulation, this involves engaging in an activity only in order to satisfy an external demand or obtain an externally imposed reward.

Introjected regulation is another form of external regulation; this involves the internalisation of external controls that are then applied through self-imposed pressures in order to avoid guild or anxiety or to attain pride. In this case although the regulation is internal the locus of causality is still external [13].

Identified regulation involves a conscious acceptance of the behaviour as being important in order to achieve an outcome that is personally valued, for example a life goal.

The most autonomous form of extrinsic motivation is integrated regulation, this occurs when the identified regulation has been fully assimilated within the self. This shares many qualities with intrinsic motivation, however since the behaviour is still measured against some external outcome which is separate form the behaviour itself [13] (e.g. because this job is part of my life).

Examples of statements associated with these differing regulations with respect to work are shown in Table 1. These motivations can be combined to create a work self-determination index [14] which can be particularly useful for representing the individuals level of self-determination [15].

It is clear that motivation twinned with self-efficacy is key to complex problem solving indeed '... *creative solutions are not found unless the individual is motivated to apply his or her skills*' [16].

Table 1. Example statements for each level of motivation from [5]

Motivations		Example answer to 'Why do I work ?'
Intrinsic		For the satisfaction I experience from taking on interesting challenges
Extrinsic	Integrated regulation	Because my work has become a fundamental part of who I am
	Identified regulation	Because I chose this type of work to attain my career goals
	Introjected regulation	Because I want to be very good at this work, otherwise I would be very disappointed
	Externalregulation	For the income it provides
Amotivation		I don't know why, we are provided with unrealistic working conditions

1.3 Creativity

Whilst some have argued that creativity is simply a function of self-efficacy and motivation [5,17], we believe that whilst creative individuals will typically display high levels of self-efficacy and, generally, will have a more internal motivation there are other factors that cause individuals to display high levels of creativity. In addition to these personal factors, creativity can be encouraged by the organisation and the fundamental environment in which individuals work [4].

In a similar vein to that explored in this paper understanding the difference in creativity between attack-focussed and defence-focussed cyber professionals would be an exciting prospect and it is clear that this research on self-efficacy and motivation are the early steps to a more complete understanding of the differing factors between employees.

2   Method

In order to explore the current levels of self-efficacy and motivation in cyber security professionals a simple study was performed which looked to survey those in cyber security and attempt to find evidence of these factors.

A survey was created that used well-regarded scales to measure motivation [18] and self-efficacy [19] in addition to biographic questions regarding age and experience in cyber security. The participants were also asked to estimate the '... *ratio between the amount of 'defence-focused' work (defending networks, writing process and policy, etc.) and 'attack-focused work (red teaming / penetration testing, exploit development, etc.)*' where the answer was a seven point Likert scale 'all defensive-focussed', 'mostly defensive-focussed', 'some defensive-focus', 'even-split', 'some attack-focus', 'mostly attack-focussed' and 'all attack-focussed'.

This survey followed the Cranfield University Research Ethics (CURES) process and achieved full permission before being deployed; the participants were sampled using snowball sampling in social networks. This resulted in 137 respondents who completed the entire survey.

3   Results

The demographics of the respondents are shown in Fig. 2 as can be seen there is a relatively even spread over both the age range 18–44. The respondents had a spread of experience, just over a third had experience of between 0–3 years and 3–5 years with slightly under a third having more than 5 years experience.

A Pearsons Chi-squared test resulted in a p-value of 0.02486 indicating there was some dependence between the experience and age of the respondents[1]. We could expect to see some correlation between age and experience, particularly given approximately a third of respondents were aged between 18–24 and hence unlikely to have more than 3 years experience.

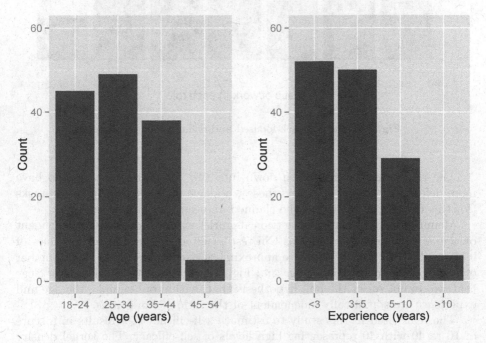

Fig. 2. Age and experience of respondents.

The self-declared offensive/defensive ratio of the respondents tasks are shown in Fig. 3, this shows that the largest group are entirely defensively focussed with

---

[1] Although this is approximate given the small number of respondents in the higher age brackets.

another large group consider themselves to have an even split between defensive and offensive tasks. There is also another large group who have 'some offensive-focus' to their tasks.

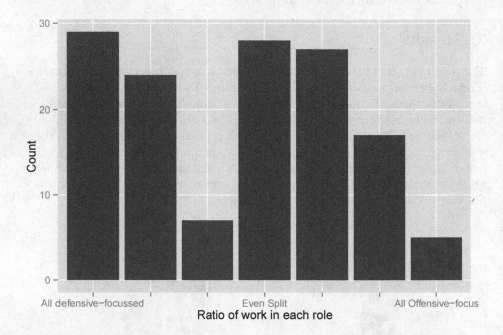

Fig. 3. Ratio of attack-focused and defence-focused work.

The respondents were broken down into two categories – those who have more defensive focussed tasks and those who have more offensive focussed tasks (for this initial analysis those who claimed an even split were discarded).

Membership of either of these two categories was not found to be dependent on age or experience; a Pearsons Chi test resulted in approximate p-values of 0.887 and 0.218. Whilst these are approximate (since there are a small number of respondents in the higher age and higher experience categories) it is clear that we cannot reject the null hypothesis that, within our sample, the age and experience are statistically independent of the ratio of work tasks.

The scale used in this study to estimate self-efficacy [19] results in a score of 10 to 40 with 40 representing high levels of self-efficacy. The kernel density estimate (KDE) of the self-efficacy estimates and a boxplot is shown in Figs. 4 and 5 for the attack-focused and defence-focused groups.

In general there are high-levels of self-efficacy amongst all respondents, yet there is a tendency for the attack focussed individuals to have a higher level of self-efficacy. A bootstrapped two-sample Kolmogorov-Smirnov test confirms the two distributions are drawn from different underlying distributions (p-value of 8.54e-4). A Pearsons correlation between the full ordinal scale representing the

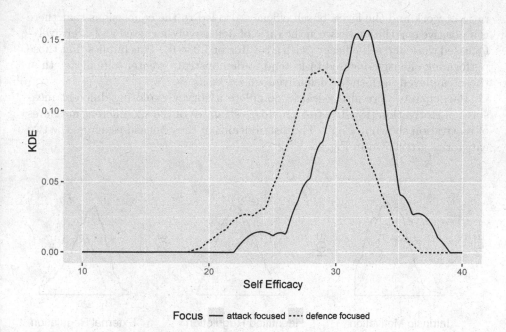

Fig. 4. Self-efficacy associated with the respondents.

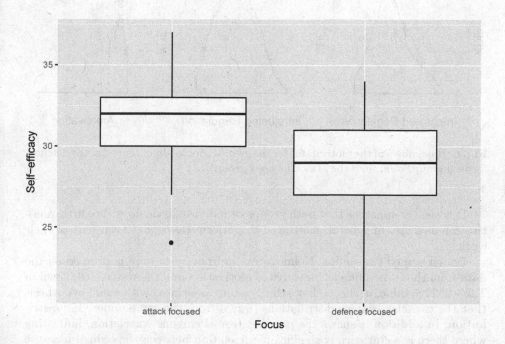

Fig. 5. Self-efficacy associated with the respondents.

ratio of work and the levels of self-efficacy also led to the conclusions that there is a positive correlation between the ratio of defensively-focussed and offensively-focussed work and self-efficacy (with a p-value of 5.23e-6). This implies that those performing offensive-focused tasks tend to demonstrate greater self-efficacy than those employed performing defensive-focused tasks.

Participants were also asked to complete a survey exploring different measures of motivation [18]. The test provides estimates of the six different measures of motivation shown in Fig. 1. The distributions of these measures across the two categories are shown in Fig. 6.

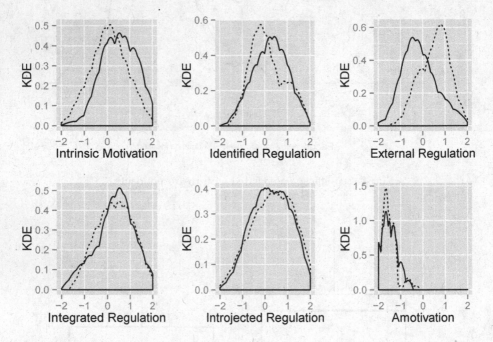

Fig. 6. Breakdown of the motivations for the groups (dotted-lines represent the defence-focused group, solid lines the attack-focused group).

It is clearly apparent that both groups of individuals demonstrate little amotivation and are, in general, motivated to perform tasks that form part of their work.

Bootstrapped two-sample Kolmogorov-Smirnov tests were performed on the data from these six different measures of motivation and the results are shown in Table 2. This table, in effect, shows the p-values associated with a null hypothesis that the two classes have distributions drawn from the same underlying distribution. In addition it shows the p-values from Pearsons correlation, indicating where there is a statistically significant correlation between the ordinal measure of the work ratio and the measures of motivation.

Table 2. Comparison of the various motivations between groups.

Motivations		Average score (defence-focussed)	Average score (attack-focussed)	p-value from K-S test	p-value from Pearson's correlation
Intrinsic		0.00889	0.5510	0.0190	0.0027
Extrinsic	Integrated regulation	0.3611	0.3605	0.8790	0.7651
	Identified regulation	0.1278	0.2449	0.1190	0.2204
	Introjected regulation	0.3333	0.2653	0.7450	0.7056
	External regulation	0.5500	−0.1361	<0.0000	<0.0000
Amotivation		−1.5556	−1.5170	0.6230	0.5317

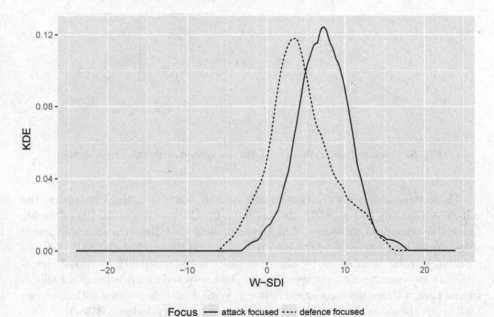

Focus —— attack focused ···· defence focused

Fig. 7. Work self-determination index associated with the respondents.

From the results shown in Fig. 6 and Table 2, we can clearly see that there are similar degrees of amotivation, integrated regulation and introjected regulation between the groups. However, there are statistically different distribution between the two populations when considering externally regulated external motivation; with those engaged in defensive-focussed roles being significantly more externally regulated than those in offensive-focussed roles. It is also note-worthy that those in defensive-focus roles are statistically less intrinsically moti-vated (whilst this is less clear it is still statistically at a 0.02 confidence level).

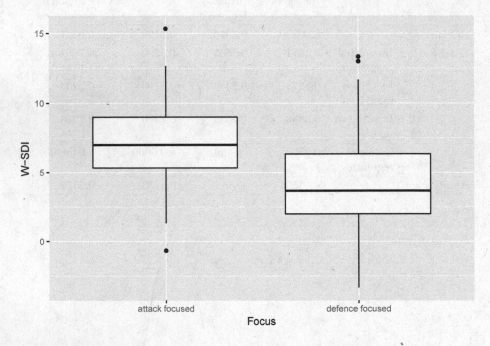

Fig. 8. Work self-determination index associated with the respondents.

These measures of motivation can be broken down to a single measure, the self-determination index (SDI), this is shown for the two classes in Figs. 7 and 8. Since the individual measures of motivation show that those in attack focussed roles would be more self-determined it is not surprising that the SDI of those working in roles dominated by offensive tasks are statistically more self deter-mined (a two-sample Kolmogorov-Smirnov test resulted in a p-value of 8.104e-5). In addition, a Pearsons correlation between W-SDI and the ordinal ratio between task types shows a statistically significant correlation (p-value 7.927e-5).

4   Conclusion and Further Work

From this study of 137 cyber security professionals it is clear that those whose work is more biased towards offensive cyber tasks are more internally moti-vated, less externally motivated with a higher self-determination index and have a higher self-efficacy than those employees who are focussed on defensive cyber tasks.

This leads to a very interesting question – are those who are more internally motivated drawn to offensive tasks whilst defensive tasks are structured to be more externally motivating? Or alternatively are those in defensive tasks poorly managed and organisations are unable to support the staff in ways that maintains both their self-efficacy and motivation?

In this research we have focussed on those attack-focussed and defence-focussed cyber security professionals within the workplace. Within the cyber security domain there are clearly very important and influential actors who exist outside the workplace—particularly partaking in offensive actions in cyberspace. This varies from individual hobbyists, through to well-resourced cyber crime groups and nation-states. To contrast similar measures between these cohorts would prove very interesting.

Future work will look to build on this platform with a more complex picture of creativity. Creativity has been identified as increasingly important within cyber security [20], however there is little discussion or evidence of the degrees to which organisations are being creative at present and the potential observable differences increased creativity would make to an organisation.

The striking findings in this paper highlight the differences between those performing tasks that are self-described as offensive and those that are self-described as defensive. This also demonstrates the asymmetry that has long existed in cyber security from both a technical and opportunity viewpoint [21] also exists in the human dimension.

References

1. Choo, K.K.R.: The cyber threat landscape: challenges and future research directions. Comput. Sec. **30**(8), 719–731 (2011)
2. Caldwell, T.: Plugging the cyber-security skills gap. Comput. Fraud Sec. **2013**(7), 5–10 (2013)
3. Lawson, S., Putting the war in cyberwar: Metaphor, analogy, and cybersecurity discourse in the United States. First Monday **17**(7) (2012)
4. Andriopoulos, C.: Determinants of organisational creativity: a literature review. Manag. Decis. **39**(10), 834–841 (2001)
5. Malik, M.A.R., Butt, A.N., Choi, J.N.: Rewards and employee creative performance: moderating effects of creative self-efficacy, reward importance, and locus of control. J. Organ. Behav. **36**(1), 59–74 (2015)
6. Bandura, A.: Self-efficacy mechanism in human agency. Am. Psychol. **37**(2), 122 (1982)
7. Salomon, G.: Television is 'easy' and print is 'tough': the differential investment of mental effort in learning as a function of perceptions and attributions. J. Educ. Psychol. **76**(4), 647 (1984)
8. Schunk, D.H.: Self-efficacy for reading and writing: Influence of modeling, goal setting, and self-evaluation. Read. Writ. Q. **19**(2), 159–172 (2003)
9. Pinder, C.C.: Work Motivation in Organizational Behavior. Psychology Press, Hove (2014)
10. Schunk, D.H.: Learning Theories. Printice Hall Inc., New Jersey (1996)
11. Deci, E.L., Ryan, R.M.: Handbook of Self-determination Research. University Rochester Press, Rochester (2002)

12. Ryan, R.M.: Psychological needs and the facilitation of integrative processes. J. Pers. **63**(3), 397–427 (1995)
13. Ryan, R.M., Deci, E.L.: Intrinsic and extrinsic motivations: classic definitions and new directions. Contemp. Educ. Psychol. **25**(1), 54–67 (2000)
14. Vallerand, R.J.: Toward a hierarchical model of intrinsic and extrinsic motivation. Adv. Exp. Soc. Psychol. **29**, 271–360 (1997)
15. Green-Demers, I., Pelletier, L.G., Ménard, S.: The impact of behavioural difficulty on the saliency of the association between self-determined motivation and environmental behaviours. Can. J. Behav. Sci./Rev. Can. Sci. Comportement **29**(3), 157 (1997)
16. Runco, M.A.: Motivation, competence, and creativity. In: Handbook of Competence and Motivation, pp. 609–623 (2005)
17. Prabhu, V., Sutton, C., Sauser, W.: Creativity and certain personality traits: understanding the mediating effect of intrinsic motivation. Creativity Res. J. **20**(1), 53–66 (2008)
18. Tremblay, M.A., Blanchard, C.M., Taylor, S., Pelletier, L.G., Villeneuve, M.: Work extrinsic and intrinsic motivation scale: its value for organizational psychology research. Can. J. Behav. Sci./Rev. Can. Sci. Comportement **41**(4), 213 (2009)
19. Schwarzer, R., Jerusalem, M., Generalized self-efficacy scale. In: Measures in Health Psychology: A User's Portfolio. Causal and Contrl Beliefs, pp. 35–37 (1995)
20. Patrick, H., Fields, Z.: A need for cyber security creativity. In: Collective Creativity for Responsible and Sustainable Business Practice, pp. 42–61. IGI Global (2017)
21. Colbaugh, R., Glass, K.: Asymmetry in coevolving adversarial systems. In: IEEE International Conference on Software Quality, Reliability and Security Companion (QRS-C), pp. 360–367. IEEE (2016)

Behavioural Profiling in Cyber-Social Systems

Jason Perno[1] and Christian W. Probst[2(✉)]

[1] Utica College, Utica, NY, USA
jwperno@utica.edu
[2] Technical University of Denmark, Kongens Lyngby, Denmark
cwpr@dtu.dk

Abstract. Computer systems have evolved from standalone systems, over networked systems, to cyber-physical systems. In all stages, human operators have been essential for the functioning of the system and for understanding system messages. Recent trends make human actors an even more central part of computer systems, resulting in what we call "cyber-social systems". In cyber-social systems, human actors and their interaction with a system are essential for the state of the system and its functioning. Both the system's operation and the human's operating it are based on an assumption of each other's behaviour. Consequently, an assessment of the state of a system must take the human actors and these interactions into account. However, human behaviour is difficult to model at best. While socio-technical system models promise the inclusion of human actors into a basis for system assessment, they lack the modelling mechanisms for human behaviour. Existing behavioural models, on the other side, mostly aim at explaining actions after an event. In this paper we discuss, how behavioural models can be used to profile actor behaviour either online or in simulations to understand the potential motivation and to test hypotheses.

1 Introduction

In many computer systems, human actors and their interactions with the system are essential for the state of the system and its functioning. Consequently, an assessment of the state of a system must take the human actors and these interactions into account. This need results from computer systems evolving from standalone systems, over networked systems, to cyber-physical systems. In all stages, human operators have been essential for the functioning of the system and for understanding and interpreting system messages. These recent trends make human actors an even more central part of computer systems, resulting in what we call "cyber-social systems".[1]

Explaining human behaviour is – in principle – easy: all we need is a concise model of human behaviour that integrates dependencies on surroundings, a precise surveillance system, and an evaluation system to draw conclusions from

---

[1] As discussed in Sect. 3, we consider cyber-social systems at the system level, opposed to Stanford University's Cyber-Social Systems [24].

© Springer International Publishing AG 2017
T. Tryfonas (Ed.): HAS 2017, LNCS 10292, pp. 507–517, 2017.
DOI: 10.1007/978-3-319-58460-7_35

input. Of course, such a model and its components are neither "easy" to realise, nor desirable, and many aspects depend on legal regulations. As a result, human behaviour is difficult to model at best, be it at the societal or the individual level. While socio-technical system models promise the inclusion of human actors into a basis for system assessment, they lack the modelling mechanisms for human behaviour. Existing behavioural models, on the other side, mostly aim at explaining actions after an event, for example, to help analysts understand and explain, what has happened.

In this paper we discuss, how cyber-social systems can be represented as a combination of socio-technical systems and behavioural models, and how they can be used to profile actor behaviour. This profiling can be performed online or in simulations to understand the potential motivation.

The rest of this article is structured as follows. The next section introduces some background material about socio-technical systems, attack representations, and behavioural models, followed by a discussion of cyber-social systems and behavioural trees, which are our behavioural model, in Sect. 3. In Sect. 4 we discuss, how these systems can be used to perform behavioural profiling. Finally, Sect. 5 concludes this article, and discusses future research directions.

2   Background

The work presented in this paper builds upon findings and developments in three main areas: socio-technical system models, attack representations, and models for explaining insider threats.

2.1   System Models

Recently, several system models have been introduced that inspire our work. ExASyM [17,19], Portunes [3] and ANKH [15] models follow similar ideas - the modelling of infrastructure and data, and analysing the modelled organisation for possible threads. The semantics of both ExASyM and Portunes is formalised using a variant of the Klaim family of process calculi [13]. However, Portunes supports mobility of nodes, instead of processes, and represents the social domain by low-level policies that describe the trust relation between people. The latter is used to represent social engineering. In contrast to the above two models, ANKH has a flat structure and the formal representation is a hyper-graph where the hyper-edges represent containment. The modelling formalism heavily depends on policies, which must be well defined in order to avoid unrealistic cases.

Pieters *et al.* consider policy alignment to address different levels of abstraction of socio-technical systems [16], where policies are interpreted as first-order logical theories containing all sequences of actions (the behaviours) and expressing the policy as a "distinguished" prefix-closed predicate in these theories. In contrast to their use of refinement for policies we use the security refinement paradox, *i.e.*, security is *not* generally preserved by refinement, in order to discover attacks.

2.2   Attack Representations

Attack trees [21,22] specify an attacker's main goal (or a main security threat) as the root of a tree; this goal is then disjunctively or conjunctively refined into sub-goals. This refinement is repeated recursively, until the reached sub-goals represent basic actions that correspond to atomic components. Disjunctive refinements represent alternative ways of how a goal can be achieved, whereas conjunctive refinements depict different steps an attacker needs to take in order to achieve a goal [10,20]. Techniques for the automated generation of attack graphs consider computer networks only [14,23], or general policies [7,8].

2.3   Behavioural Models

Legg *et al.* [12] address the complex and dynamic problem posed by insiders against organisations. Their three-tier model incorporates a tier representing the real world, a tier representing measurements or observables, and a tier representing hypotheses. The goal of the model is to support the analyst in detecting potential insider threats. On the real world tier, a large set of elements exist that correlate with insider threats, for example, activities, physical behaviour, and psychological mindset. Since most of these elements can not be observed directly, the analyst and the hypothesis tier must rely on measurements provided by the middle tier of the model. The confidence in observations made by elements in this layer depends on how directly they are able to observe the real world: the technical ones probably have high confidence in the associated values, whereas the psychological and behavioural ones can only be observed indirectly through a small set of indicators, and consequently provide a much lower level of confidence.

System dynamics models represent complex systems in order to understand their nonlinear behaviour. Models contain flow, feedback loops, and time delays, and can model complex interaction between different actors. System dynamics has been used to model and analyze the dynamic nature of the insider threat problem [2,5], especially with focus on modelling human behaviour.

3   Cyber-Social Systems

Cyber-social systems result from cyber-physical systems by integrating human actors into the system and the reasoning about it. Computer systems have evolved from standalone systems, over networked systems, to cyber-physical systems. In all stages, human operators have been essential for the functioning of the system and for understanding system messages. Recent trends make human actors an even more central part of computer systems, resulting in what we call "cyber-social systems". As mentioned above, we consider cyber-social systems at the level of the actual system and actors interacting with it. This complements the work by, *e.g.*, the Stanford Cyber Initiative, which investigates how cyber-technologies interact with existing social systems to understand cyber-social systems [24].

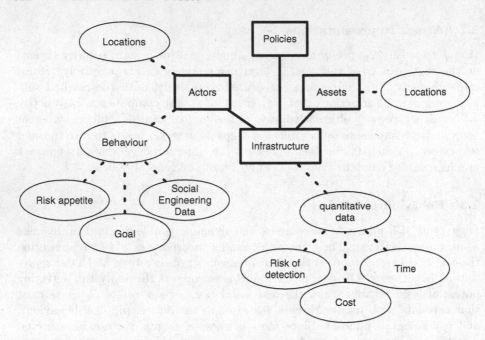

Fig. 1. A system model structure with explicit behaviour and quantitative data [6]. Together, these components form a cyber-social system, which is parameterised with the underlying system model and behavioural model.

In cyber-social systems, human actors and their interaction with a system are essential for the state of the system and its functioning. On a societal level, these may be influenced by markets, political systems, and policies. We are interested in instances of such systems, and the processes at the system and actor level. Decisions and behaviour at this level may be influenced by more abstract concepts, but that is currently beyond the scope of our work.

To reason about cyber-social systems, we represent them as a combination of a *socio-technical system model*, which represents the context of the system being analysed, and a *behavioural model* for the human actors in that system. Cyber-social systems thus enhance socio-technical systems with components for the actors' behaviour similar to approaches for externalizing behaviour in system models [6]. The models for systems and behaviour are parameters of a cyber-social system. Based on the application and the goal, these components can be chosen as needed. In the remainder of this section, we briefly present candidates for each of these.

It is important to note that the techniques described in this paper are independent from the underlying models, similar to earlier developments by Ivanova *et al.* [6]. Figure 1 shows their system model, which extends actors with individual behaviour. The main contribution of the current work is the development of behavioural trees and their embedding in cyber-social systems.

3.1   The Socio-Technical System Model

The socio-technical system model is closely related to existing models [17,26]. It is based on a process calculus that represents the three layers of socio-technical models – the physical, the virtual, and the social layer – as parts of a graph-based representation with processes for describing functionality at the virtual and social layer.

The socio-technical system model represents the system infrastructure as nodes in a directed graph [17], representing rooms, access control points, and similar locations. Processes also represent actors and can possess data and items that are relevant in the modelled scenario. Elements in the model can be annotated with values, *e.g.*, the likelihood of being lost. Data and items can be attached to locations or processes; those attached to processes move around with that actor. Processes perform actions on locations, including physical locations or other processes. These actions are restricted by policies, which consist of required credentials and enabled actions. Credentials represent the data or assets an actor needs to provide in order to enable the actions in a policy, and the enabled actions describe the gained rights by doing so [25]. Policies are used both for access control and for organisational policies.

3.2   Behavioural Trees

Behavioural trees capture two components: they structure larger behavioural patterns into sub-actions, and they include dependencies that represent how the actor's disposition towards certain actions changes based on events. A behavioural tree extends the embedding of behaviour in system models [6] by encoding an analyst's experience and strategy. In structure, behavioural trees are similar to attack trees and attack templates [27].

Attack trees as described in Sect. 2.2 are a very flexible and loosely defined tool to represent steps in possible attacks. Their success is to a large extent due to their loose definition. Behavioural trees follow a similar strategy by offering a simple structure for defining human behaviour and enabling factors. Just like for attack trees, however, extensions will be needed to model, *e.g.*, prohibiting events, which could be represented similar to attack-defense trees [9].

Behavioural trees contain similar nodes as attack trees [1]:

- Disjunctive nodes represent options of which one must be present,
- Conjunctive nodes represent options, which all must be present, but may appear in arbitrary order,
- Temporal disjunctive nodes represent options that are tried from left to right, and of which one must be present, and
- Temporal conjunctive nodes represent options that must occur in that order from left to right.

In attack trees, leafs usually describe basic actions, and inner nodes are mostly used to label the "meaning" of the sub-tree rooted in these nodes. In behavioural trees, both leafs and inner nodes describe actions, events, and decisions taken

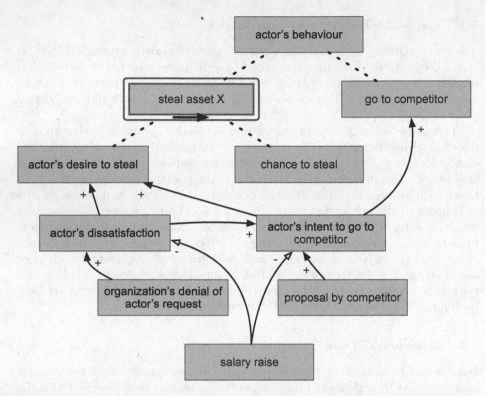

Fig. 2. An example for a behavioural tree that represents two possible actions: stealing an asset and going to a competitor, which both are influenced by parts of the system dynamics overlay [2]. The dashed lines connect nodes in the behavioural tree, the solid arrows connect nodes in the system dynamics model, and describe direct or opposite changes in the value of the target node based on changes at the source node. The node with the double frame represents a temporal conjunctive node.

by an actor. Both leafs and inner nodes may also be part of one or more system dynamics overlays, which describe, how the events and actions of the actor or the environment influence the actor's behaviour and disposition towards certain behaviour.

Figure 2 shows an example for a behavioural tree that represents two possible actions: stealing an asset and going to a competitor, which both are influenced by parts of the system dynamics overlay [2]. The node with the double frame represents a temporal conjunctive node: in order to steal an asset, the actor must first have the desire to steal, and then get the chance. The dashed lines connect nodes in the behavioural tree, the solid arrows connect nodes in the system dynamics model, and describe direct or opposite changes in the value of the target node based on changes at the source node. Nodes may be part of either the behavioural tree, the system dynamics model, or both.

It is noteworthy that the changes induced to one node in the system dynamics model based on changes at another node do not need to be constant, but can vary based on time, the current value, or other factors influenced by the overall state of the system. Also, the threshold at which the action at a node is enabled is usually not binary, but changes continuously.

Behavioural trees need not and cannot be complete, since it is impossible to predict all aspects of human behaviour, its dependencies on inside and outside events, and the relevant events influencing behaviour. However, some of the quantitative measures can be initiated based on personality testing and lifestyle polygraphs, as are often performed as part of job interviews.

Furthermore, parts of the behavioural trees are similar for all actors, probably with different factors, and thus can be shared across populations. Furthermore, behavioural trees can be extended during the behavioural profiling with newly observed actions. While these actions initially do not have quantitative properties, they can be initialised with heuristic values to feed the analysis and simulation, which in turn will refine the initial values to more sensible ones.

4   Behavioural Profiling

Legg *et al.* [12] discuss two applications of their model: *bottom-up* and *top-down*, where the top tier is the hypothesis, as described above, and the bottom layer is the real world.

Based on direct observations (measurements) of the real world, bottom-up reasoning begins with making indirect observations, for example, based on statistical profiles for each individual, and profiles capturing their traits and behaviours. These indirect observations then feed into hypotheses, which are the building blocks for the analyst to formulate more complex hypotheses, triggering alerts, for example, if the collected measurements of an indicator exceed the expected values [12].

On the other hand, top-down reasoning begins from a concrete concern, for example based on input from a whistle blower or from a trigger-based alert from the bottom-up analysis. In this case, the analyst will formulate a hypothesis, and the model would attempt to "fulfil" this assumption given possible observations from the measurement tier.

In this section we describe how behavioural trees can be applied to model this workflow in automatic analyses in two different cases: the backward-looking analysis explaining observed events, and the forward-looking analysis predicting future events. Finally, we discuss methods for refining the values in behavioural trees by combining these two analyses, and how to refine values through statistical model checking.

All analyses described in the following can be applied in general on a population of actors, in which case they result in conditions that potential actors must fulfil, or on a specific actor, in which case they confirm or invalidate a hypothesis with respect to that actor.

4.1 Explaining Past Behaviour

Explaining past behaviour is equivalent to the top-down reasoning described above. In this setting, the analyst has a concern and tries to understand, what happened and how, and which observations to look out for.

In this application scenario, behavioural trees are traversed top down, from behaviour to actions. At transitions to the system dynamics model, this part is explored backwards. This exploration provides the analysis with possible reasons, why a certain action was performed, and with events that can be expected to have occurred. At transitions to the behavioural tree, the top down exploration continues from the nodes that are triggered by the system dynamics model.

In the tree in Fig. 2, for example, if the theft of an asset has been observed, the analysis will identify the desire to steal and the chance to steal as necessary pre-conditions. The desire is influenced positively by the actor's dissatisfaction and an intent to go to a competitor, but negatively by a possible salary raise.

4.2 Predicting Future Behaviour

Predicting future behaviour is equivalent to bottom-up reasoning, which builds hypotheses that the analyst can use to setup surveillance mechanisms.

As before, also in this application scenario we traverse behavioural trees top down, but with a different goal: now we aim at identifying the actions and events to look out for, and possibly also actors who are likely to perform these actions or trigger these events. The system dynamics model is now explored *in both* directions: backward to identify possible reasons and triggering events for actions, and forward to identify possible followup events and actions to lookout for. The backward events must be handled with care, since some of them are likely to have occurred before the analysis started; this must be accounted for in the reasoning.

In the behavioural tree presented in Fig. 2, for example, the type of asset defines the applicable actions for obtaining it, *e.g.*, logging in remotely, the use of flash drives, or emails. The analysis may use this information to suggest where to set up surveillance mechanisms to alert a human operator or online surveillance mechanisms [18]. Especially the notification of the organisation is promising, since many events influencing behaviour are difficult to formalise and measure, *e.g.*, that an actor might be on the verge of leaving the organisation.

4.3 Combining Past and Future

Executing either of the two analyses described above after the other, as well as iterations alternating between the two phases, is beneficial to understanding and profiling behaviour:

- Results of an analysis of past behaviour provide the analysis with input to make better predictions of the future behaviour, and similarly,

– Results of an analysis of future behaviour, that is which events and actions to look out for, guide the analysis of past events towards those parts of the behavioural tree that may influence this future behaviour.

Typically, we expect several changes of direction in such an analysis: based on results for the future, the analysis of the past is refined, and vice versa, providing more input for explaining future events, or extending the possible set of future events and trying to identify more supporting data from the past.

Another dimension are combinations of behavioural trees for different actors, which extend the search space for possible motivations. Also here, the observed past events or identified future events help the analysis to limit exploration to those actors that potentially may perform the actions or perform relevant actions that may influence the behaviour of an actor under scrutiny.

4.4 Refining Values

As mentioned before, precise models of human behaviour cannot be built, and consequently behavioural trees are incomplete and the values and factors in the trees will not be precise. However, behavioural trees describe possible behaviour of actors, and as such can be used together with the socio-technical system model for simulations of this behaviour in statistical model checking [11].

Simulations through statistical model checking provide the behavioural profiling of cyber-social systems, and they provide the means to verify computed and observed likelihoods of actions and events. The simulation applies the analysis results for past behaviour to future behaviour, by simulating the behaviour of actors. This simulated behaviour can be predetermined, randomised, or follow more involved strategies [6].

5 Conclusion and Future Work

In this article, we have described how to perform behavioural profiling for cyber-social systems, which combine socio-technical systems and behavioural trees. Cyber-social systems are the next step in integration of computer systems by making human actors an even more central part of these systems, which have evolved from standalone systems, over networked systems, to cyber-physical systems. In all stages, human operators have been essential for the functioning of the system and for understanding system messages. Now, human actors and their interaction with a system are essential for the state of the system and its functioning. Both the system's operation and the human's operating it are based on an assumption of each other's behaviour. Consequently, an assessment of the state of a system must take the human actors and these interactions into account.

Behavioural profiling based on a combination of behavioural trees and socio-technical system models promises the simulation of analysts' workflows [12], and the verification of results using statistical model checking. Behavioural trees are by definition incomplete, but can be extended during the analysis with newly observed actions. While these actions initially do not have quantitative properties, they can be initialised with heuristic values to feed the analysis and simulation, which will refine them to more sensible values.

We are currently working on a theory for cyber-social systems and their application to behavioural profiling. This involves refining behavioural trees and relevant properties, as well as heuristics for choosing new actions and events to add to the tree. Especially psycho-analytical based profiling models, as well as studying personality traits, are interesting to benchmark and refine the profiling in cyber-social systems. In automated approaches it is in general impossible to observe the context and circumstances that dictate and predict criminal behaviour, let alone to understand them. However, there are many similarities between Weber's sociological explanation of the social situation and the collective explanandum [4], and abstraction and realisation applied in the computation of fix points in formal methods.

References

1. Aslanyan, Z., Nielson, F., Parker, D.: Quantitative verification and synthesis of attack-defence scenarios. In: Proceedings of the 29th Computer Security Foundations Symposium (CSF) (2016)
2. Cappelli, D.M., Moore, A.P., Trzeciak, R.F.: The CERT Guide to Insider Threats: How to Prevent, Detect, and Respond to Information Technology Crimes. Addison-Wesley Professional, Boston (2012)
3. Dimkov, T.: Alignment of Organizational Security Policies - Theory and Practice. University of Twente, Enschede (2012). http://eprints.eemcs.utwente.nl/21578/
4. Esser, H.: Soziologie Allgemeine Grundlagen, Campus (1993)
5. Gonzalez, J.J., Sawicka, A.: A framework for human factors in information security. In: Proceedings of the WSEAS International Conference on Information Security (2002)
6. Ivanova, M.G., Probst, C.W., Hansen, R.R., Kammüller, F.: Externalizing behaviour for analysing system models. In: 5th International Workshop on Managing Insider Security Threats (MIST 2013) (2013)
7. Kammüller, F., Probst, C.W.: Invalidating policies using structural information. In: 2nd International IEEE Workshop on Research on Insider Threats (WRIT 2013). IEEE, co-located with IEEE CS Security and Privacy 2013 (2013)
8. Kammüller, F., Probst, C.W.: Combining generated data models with formal invalidation for insider threat analysis. In: 3rd International IEEE Workshop on Research on Insider Threats (WRIT 2014). IEEE, co-located with IEEE CS Security and Privacy 2014 (2014)
9. Kordy, B., Mauw, S., Radomirović, S., Schweitzer, P.: Attack-defense trees. J. Log. Comput. 24(1), 55–87 (2014)
10. Kordy, B., Piètre-Cambacédès, L., Schweitzer, P.: DAG-based attack and defense modeling: don't miss the forest for the attack trees. Comput. Sci. Rev. 13–14, 1–38 (2014). http://www.sciencedirect.com/science/article/pii/S1574013714000100
11. Legay, A., Delahaye, B., Bensalem, S.: Statistical model checking: an overview. In: Proceedings of the First International Conference on Runtime Verification (2010)

12. Legg, P., Moffat, N., Nurse, J.R., Happa, J., Agrafiotis, I., Goldsmith, M., Creese, S.: Towards a conceptual model and reasoning structure for insider threat detection. J. Wirel. Mob. Netw., Ubiquitous Comput., Depend. Appl. **4**(4), 20–37 (2013)

13. de Nicola, R., Ferrari, G.L., Pugliese, R.: KLAIM: a kernel language for agents interaction and mobility. IEEE Trans. Softw. Eng. **24**(5), 315–330 (1998). http://dx.doi.org/10.1109/32.685256

14. Phillips, C., Swiler, L.P.: A graph-based system for network-vulnerability analysis. In: Proceedings of the 1998 workshop on New security paradigms NSpPW 1998, pp. 71–79 (1998)

15. Pieters, W.: Representing humans in system security models: an actor-network approach. J. Wirel. Mob. Netw., Ubiquitous Comput., Depend. Appl. **2**(1), 75–92 (2011)

16. Pieters, W., Dimkov, T., Pavlovic, D.: Security policy alignment: a formal approach. IEEE Syst. J. **7**(2), 275–287 (2013)

17. Probst, C.W., Hansen, R.R.: An extensible analysable system model. Inform. Sec. Tech. Rep. **13**(4), 235–246 (2008)

18. Probst, C.W., Hansen, R.R.: Analysing access control specifications. In: 2009 Fourth IEEE International Workshop on Systematic Approaches to Digital Forensic Engineering, pp. 22–33 (2009)

19. Probst, C.W., Hansen, R.R., Nielson, F.: Where can an insider attack? In: Dimitrakos, T., Martinelli, F., Ryan, P.Y.A., Schneider, S. (eds.) FAST 2006. LNCS, vol. 4691, pp. 127–142. Springer, Heidelberg (2007). doi:10.1007/978-3-540-75227-1_9

20. Qin, X., Lee, W.: Attack plan recognition and prediction using causal networks. In: 20th Annual Computer Security Applications Conference, pp. 370–379, December 2004

21. Salter, C., Saydjari, O.S., Schneier, B., Wallner, J.: Toward a secure system engineering methodology. In: Proceedings of the 1998 Workshop on New Security Paradigms (NSPW 1998), pp. 2–10. Charlottesville, Virginia, United States, September 1998

22. Schneier, B.: Attack trees: modeling security threats. Dr. Dobb's J. Softw. Tools **24**(12), 21–29 (1999). http://www.ddj.com/security/184414879

23. Sheyner, O., Haines, J., Jha, S., Lippmann, R., Wing, J.M.: Automated generation and analysis of attack graphs. In: Proceedings of the 2002 IEEE Symposium on Security and Privacy (S&P 2002), vol. 129, pp. 273–284 (2002)

24. Stanford Cyber Intiative: Understanding "cyber-social systems". https://cyber.stanford.edu/sites/default/files/stanford_cyber_initiative_.pdf. Accessed 10 Mar 2017

25. The TRE$_S$PASS Project: Deliverable D1.2.2: The Final TRE$_S$PASS Policy-Specification Language (2015). https://www.trespass-project.eu/node/222. Accessed 10 Mar 2017

26. The TRE$_S$PASS Project: Deliverable D1.3.4: The TRE$_S$PASS Socio-technical Security Model and Specification Languages (2016). https://www.trespass-project.eu/node/302. Accessed 10 Mar 2017

27. The TRE$_S$PASS Project: Deliverable D5.4.2: The Integrated TRE$_S$PASS Process (2016). https://www.trespass-project.eu/node/315. Accessed 10 Mar 2017

The Impact of Changing Technology on International Cybersecurity Curricula

Huw Read[1,2]($\boxtimes$), Iain Sutherland[1,4], Konstantinos Xynos[5],
Tom Drange[1,3], and Ernst Sundt[1]

[1] Noroff University College, Kristiansand, Norway
{iain.sutherland,tom.drange,ernst.sundt}@noroff.no
[2] Norwich University, Northfield, VT, USA
hread@norwich.edu
[3] University of Sunderland, Sunderland, UK
[4] Edith Cowen University, Perth, Australia
[5] Darkmatter LLC, Dubai, United Arab Emirates
konstantinos.xynos@darkmatter.ae

Abstract. Cyber Security degree programs vary in scope; from those that are constructed around traditional computer science degrees with some additional security content, to those that are strongly focused on the need to develop a dedicated cyber security professional. The latter programs typically include a grounding in computer science concepts such as programming, operating systems and networks to specialised security content covering such disparate areas as digital forensics, information assurance, penetration testing and cryptography. The cyber security discipline as a whole faces new challenges as technology continues to evolve, and therefore significant changes are being faced by educators trying to incorporate the latest technological concepts into courses. This presents cybersecurity educators with a number of related challenges to ensure that changes to degree programs reflect not only the educational needs of students, but of the needs of industry and government. The evolving use of technology therefore presents both opportunities and problems, in how these changes are demonstrated in the curriculum. This paper highlights the accreditation, standards and guidelines (from three of the countries where the authors of this paper have sought accreditation) that shape the way educators are encouraged to develop and structure degree courses and considers these in lieu of factors relating to incorporating new technology in cybersecurity curriculum, particularly in the presentation of technical exercises to students.

Keywords: Standards · Education · Curriculum

1 Introduction

Bachelor programs in the area of computer security and in particular computer forensics started to gain traction around 2006 with some of the earliest UK courses being taught in Royal Holloway and the University of Glamorgan (now University of South Wales). Currently universities across the UK and further afield now offer degrees

© Springer International Publishing AG 2017
T. Tryfonas (Ed.): HAS 2017, LNCS 10292, pp. 518–528, 2017.
DOI: 10.1007/978-3-319-58460-7_36

in computer security and related crime investigation programmes (Keystone Academic Solutions 2017). There is a need for differentiation and specialisation although the drive for certification and accreditation limits the potential curriculum. In addition to increasing competition in this area, universities have had to deal with a continued rapid expansion in technology. Furthermore if courses are to remain current, there is a need to investigate and incorporate the impact of the changing environment and changing technologies into the degree itself.

2 Changing Environment

Technology continues to develop with the inclusion of processing power and data storage into a continuing wide variety of end-user devices. These devices are oft described as being part of systems such as 'smart cities', 'smart' houses, 'smart clothing' and other 'smart' devices. At the present it could be argued that these so-called smart devices are providing little more than additional automation and not intelligent processing and decision-making functions, although these features are gradually being added to different systems. One example of this type of technology is the Verisure alarm company (Verisure 2016) in Norway provides alarm systems with additional functionality including flood senses and the ability to monitor temperature and humidity in addition to intrusion warnings. Technology is now being incorporated into a variety of devices; examples include wearable devices and clothing (Hexoskin 2016), drinking containers (Disney Food Blog 2016, Glassify 2016) and smart housing (Amazon 2017). This now provides a challenging and information rich environment for capture, analysis and presentation in the classroom or via online laboratories. Universities therefore have to respond to these changes to train graduates that are ready for these future workplace challenges. A question is how to respond to the challenges in the way in which courses and degrees are designed and structured; which topics to focus and prioritise and how to best integrate these into taught content, in particular how to provide exposure to new systems and technologies. Consultation of nationally recognised accreditation schemes, in particular those recognising Universities as centres of national excellence in the Cyber discipline should be used to identify challenges in adopting subject matter into courses.

3 Accreditation, Standards and Guidelines

There are a number of accreditation schemes and guidelines that attempt to address the specific needs of the discipline that can be used as an indication of the types of topics that should be addressed at a technical level in university courses. These vary considerably both in terms of the prescribed content required to achieve the accreditation or standard and in terms of the level of detail required. The authors have explored accreditation options in three countries; Norway, USA and the UK.

One of the most comprehensive and detailed systems is that used in the USA. The National Security Agency (NSA 2016) has been recognising higher-education institutions in cyber since 1998 with the Centre of Academic Excellence (CAE) in Information Assurance Education (IAE). Originally open only to 4-year universities, the NSA (later joined by the Department of Homeland Security in 2004), in 2008 began recognising postgraduate universities by awarding the Information Assurance Research (IAR) certification. Furthermore in 2010, 2-year institutions could also apply for the IAE designation.

Today, the process has been updated considerably with the gradual phasing out of the IAE designation, being replaced with Cyber Defence Education (CDE) to reflect the more active component in defending against threat actors in addition to focusing on the assuring of information security (IAE). There are 214 accredited institutions (NIETP 2017a) out of 4,700 (NSF 2016) across the United States, or 4.5% penetration at the time of writing. With a shortfall of 209,000 employees in the US (Morgan 2016) and with higher-education producing about 10,000 skilled graduates per year any designation programme needs to ensure the right practical skills are being given to undergraduates so they can make an effective transition into the workforce. To assist with this, the CAE application process has 17 specialist designations (NIETP 2017b), or focus areas, including cyber investigations, health care security, digital forensics, secure software development and systems security administration to name a few. Of the 214 accredited, it has been said about 20% of institutions have been designated as a CAE with a defined focus area, the rest achieving the general CAE-CDE.

The application process is comprehensive, the actual programme path/degree path being assessed had to meet certain Knowledge Units (KUs) which themselves contain a number of topics that academic institutions must provide evidence for. Evidence can be a reference to chapters of a book, an academic product such as a lecture or tutorial or an assessment exercise. A large part of the evidence must demonstrate technical, practical, hands-on experience in different cyber areas. Considering the high-cost of entry into the cyber-education market for a University, it is no small feat. For example, specialist software, hardware, complex real/virtual network configuration for red/blue team vulnerability assessment scenarios, disparate wide-ranging vulnerable devices found in the market (e.g. Internet of Things (IoT)) and understanding how students should interact with specialist cybersecurity subjects (i.e. KUs) is the best way to ensure effective use of University resources.

For the generic NSA cybersecurity designation, CAE-CDE, 4 year institutions must collect evidence for a minimum of 22 of these KUs. Many cover core cyber principles in the degree curriculum but others relate to special focus areas. For a specialist focus area, the number of KUs can change, for example the digital forensics designation requires 20 KUs but many of these courses are specialisms in the discipline. For example, those seeking a designation of CAE-CDE with a focus area of digital forensics, the following KUs are required in the degree.

Basic Scripting or Introductory Programming, IA Fundamentals, Intro to Cryptography, IT Systems Components, Networking Concepts, Policy Legal Ethics and Compliance, System Administration, Networking Technology and Protocols, Operating Systems Concepts, Data Structures, Device Forensics, Digital Investigations, Forensic Accounting, Hardware Reverse Engineering, Host Forensics, Media Forensics, Network

Forensics, Operating Systems Theory, Software Reverse Engineering and Vulnerability Analysis.

The combination of Topics comprising the different KUs provides robust definition of a Cyber curriculum in the USA. However, the impact of new technology can make such curricula age rapidly. A recent development in the process has been the addition of a Wiki whereby academics can propose changes to the KUs that, if accepted, will be required when an institution seeks designation (Cyberedwiki 2017). It is not yet known the timeframe in which changes in the Wiki will be reflected in the CAE requirements, however if successful, this may be an opportunity to ensure programs are dynamically updated during each NSA redesignation cycle (5 years) to more effectively keep up with the changing threat landscape.

In terms of practical advice on actual procedures, standards like those proposed by NIST (NIST 2016) are a useful indicator of skills and knowledge required by those working in this area. The NICE Cybersecurity Workforce Framework (NCWF) is, at the time of writing, in draft stage and is currently open for comment and contributors are encouraged to "…ensure it applies to all cybersecurity workforce needs" (NIST 2016). In particular, it seeks to identify and more clearly articulate the Knowledge, Skills and Abilities (KSAs) required by industry. Of particular importance to educators is how it is anticipated to become a "cybersecurity workforce dictionary that will allow employers, educators, trainers, and those in the workforce to use consistent terms to describe cybersecurity work" (NIST 2016). The implications will be felt by those teaching cyber security who will need to ensure that common terminology is used for consistency; this is not a bad thing considering what was known as computer forensics several years ago became digital forensics to highlight that evidence is not limited to what is found on the PC. Now the term also includes the non-device specific elements of acquisition (e.g. Cloud storage or automated sensor networks, etc.).

Where the NCWF is emphasising the workforce, the CSEC2017 (CyberSecurity Curricula 2017) Curriculum task force (comprising of ACM, IEEE-CS, AIS SIGSEC and IFIP WG 11.8) represents an expansion of the ACM's education initiative to provide the "…first set of global curricula recommendations in cybersecurity educa-tion". The knowledge area comprises of six categories; data security, software security, system security, human security, organisational security, and societal security. The first three are technical in nature, whilst the latter are in areas significant to cybersecurity but not commonly taught in such programmes. CSEC2017 is working towards imple-menting a roadmap to achieve parity with the NCWF. The intention appears to provide course roadmaps that demonstrate a pathway for knowledge acquisition between the two.

Such guidelines may be one way for those countries that have not yet developed standards to use as a starting point. For example, Norway has no explicit governmental requirements for cyber security education, however there are several organisations that have provided advice or influence to academia. The Norwegian Educational Quality Assurance Agency (NOKUT) prescribes some aspects of IT curricula. However for other subjects such as engineering, a more detailed approach is taken. There are several organisations that have developed broader advice or policy relating to cyber security.

The Norwegian Business and Industry Security Council (NSR) serves the Norwegian business sector in an advisory capacity on matters relating to crime, and works actively to prevent losses. One aspect they address is that professional competence should contain three factors; Academic foundation, Practical skillset and Authorisation or Certification. These parts can act as guidelines for security programs (Stranden 2010).

In addition the governmental Norwegian Center for Information Security (Norsis) state in their publication (Malmedal and Røislien 2016), the need for a holistic approach. The public and private sector need a common methodology to establish a culture of incorporating all the aspects of cybersecurity (Norsis 2016).

The UK has an approvals system that the EPSRC and Government Communication HeadQuarters (GCHQ 2011) issues for research, recognising Academic Centres of Excellence in Cyber Security Research (ACE-CSR). There was discussion of recognising contributions by education-focused institutions with the Academic Centre of Excellence in Cyber Security Education designation (ACE-CSE (GCHQ 2014)), but there is little mention of ACE-CSE on the GCHQ website at the present time.

However, as mentioned in (GCHQ 2014), ACE-CSE will require certified postgraduate Master's degrees. To this end, courses already certified include Cyber Security, Cyber Defence, Digital Forensics and Information Security (GCHQ 2016). An initial call for certifying undergraduate Bachelor's was issued in November 2016 (GCHQ 2016b), the closing date of which has only recently passed at the time of writing. Whereas the NSA identifies 17 different cybersecurity focus areas, GCHQ recognises 4 distinct areas (GCHQ 2016c). Each area comprises of security disciplines/principles/ computer science subject areas, which contain skills groups. These skills groups contain a number of indicative topics. These topics provide the institution with the level of detail as to what should be covered in a cybersecurity degree to attain certification.

Additionally in the UK, the Chartered Society of Forensic Sciences (CSFS) has a scheme for approving the content of a wide range of courses within the forensic science domain. It is interesting to note that out of 31 universities that have gained approval for programs, so far only two have been in the cyber-realm (digital forensics) the vast majority has been focused in the area of traditional forensic methods (Chartered Society of Forensic Sciences 2016).

One issue with standards and both commercial/government accreditation is that they tend to trail new development due to the length of time required to create and agree on a standard. The NSA-CAE, as of Nov 2016, has a wiki where changes can be updated by the academic community, However participation is voluntary, and it remains to be seen how this might be adopted by those who drive the research in the area, the academic community. Furthermore, how Universities choose to adopt new recommendations, in lieu of cost, remains to be seen.

Table 1 below summarises the different accreditation and standardisation programs outline above, highlighting in which country the program is located, for whom the program will ultimately assist, and a brief summary.

Table 1. Summary of accreditation, standards and guidelines influencing cybersecurity education by region

Standard	Country	Subject focus area	Summary
National Security Agency, Centre of Defence Excellence	U.S.A.	Government	Gov't centric knowledge units identify topics to be covered, skills required by NSA
NICE Cybersecurity Workforce Framework	U.S.A.	Workforce	Skills identifiable and referenceable by employers
ACM, Cybersecurity Curricula 2017	Global	Academia	Topics should be included in cyber degrees
Nasjonalt organ for kvalitet i utdanningen (NOKUT) The Norwegian Agency for Quality Assurance in Education	Norway	Academia	Academic Quality assurance
Norsk senter for Informasjonssikring (Norsis) The Norwegian Center for Information Security	Norway	Industry	Serves as an advisory body on matters relating to a security, focussing on preventable loss
Næringslivets Sikkerhetsråd (NSR) Norwegian Business and Industry Security Council	Norway	Industry	Industry related security body
Government Communication HeadQuarters (GCHQ)	UK	Government	Gov't centric topic areas
The Chartered Society of Forensic Sciences (CSFS)	UK	Industry	Four key objectives including providing opportunities for education, training and development

4 Current Educational Methods

The idea of universities and other institutions of higher learning teaching cyber-related curricula is not new; the first undergraduate degree to feature the term "hacking" appeared in 2006 (University of Abertay 2017), whilst many programmes and courses in information security were available as far back as the 1990s (Kessler and Ramsay 2013). The typical forms of teaching cyber within higher-education has aggressively moved away from the more traditional forms of teaching (lectures, reading literature, understanding concepts in principle, often referred to colloquially as "the sage on the stage") as they have been identified to not be adequate enough for cyber security training as the student cannot apply the academic principles they have learnt to a realistic environment (Willems and Meinel 2012). Available literature in the public domain shows that the "Capture The Flag" (CTF) genre, whereby a specific aim or goal is set typically for an offensive exercise such as obtaining a particular file from a system, has remained very popular as an educational tool to help students understand how to configure, respond, defend, attack and exploit networked systems. Indeed, many organisations have taken to using this model as a recruiting tool in recent years

(NSA 2016b, GCHQ 2011b, Telegraph 2011). Others encourage a team-based model; Conklin (2007) describes an information security practicum course whereby students, working as part of a team, make amendments in a simulated small business environment. Changes are issued via memos deliberately sent outside of assigned student class contact hours, such as introducing malware or the "accidental" deletion of a file. The real world simulation is kept by maintaining system states between classes providing the sense of continuity and by incorporating the input of industry professionals whom can prevent the instructor from doing the "same old thing" (Conklin 2007). By focusing on business aspects (business processes, business continuity, etc.) students are prevented from treating the simulations like their "personal playgrounds" (Conklin 2007), i.e. taking risks and performing actions that would not be considered during a real exercise. Rege (2015) recognises other issues with the prevailing CTF model, namely novice encouragement, temporal constraints, and skewed experiences (barriers to entry based on prior knowledge). Furthermore the focus of the paper is on applying cyber curricula, taught traditionally to those with a strong background in computing to those in criminal justice majors.

Similar practical educational exercises have been developed for other, more focused areas within the cyber-realm. Sitnikova et al. (2013) discuss their experiences taking the experiential model in cybersecurity learning and applying it to the realm of Supervisory Control and Data Acquisition (SCADA) systems. Practical exercises were designed, which help to maximise a student's education of cyber within this area whilst minimising the amount of time needed overseas at specialist training facilities.

Those courses typically focusing on a more investigative angle such as forensics tend to focus analytical and investigative challenges. These are commonly in the form of smaller practical exercises.

Dopplick (2015) summarises up these worldwide trends in experiential cybersecurity learning; technical project-based activities, competitions, training and research are becoming commonplace as are universities "…teaming with companies to provide structured programs on an ongoing basis".

5   Educational Challenges to Changes in Technology

Universities needed to respond to the changing environment as education/training and certification has been highlighted as a key issue in the discipline for a number of years (Rodgers et al. in 2004).

A number of the standards outlined above indicate the need for students to develop specific skills that can only be achieved in depth with hands on experience of hardware, which will continue to be a challenge in cybersecurity. As discussed in the Current Educational Methods section, it is clear that there are established hands-on practical exercises in areas such as CTF (Capture The Flag) competitions, which have been particularly successful at interfacing between subject matter and the student's ability to learn. However, within the specialisms of cybersecurity, such as digital forensics, there are a vast array of skills that a future investigator may be expected to have upon leaving university. Knowledge of the acquisition process and how it applies to disparate evidence sources e.g. encrypted computers, mobile phones, tablets, embedded systems such as games consoles, IoT, SCADA systems, network traffic, malware acquisition, live vs. dead acquisition, data recovery from deliberately damaged devices, etc. Knowledge of the analysis process, different operating system artefacts, file systems, root cause analysis, structured vs. unstructured data, and so on. Knowledge of the presentation process, developing concise expert witness reports, the courtroom process, public speaking, giving expert testimony under oath or affirmation, etc. The fact that many cases involving digital evidence contain all of these areas does not make for an easy task in creating effective teaching interfaces to transmit such knowledge to students.

The analysis process lends itself rather well to the virtualised lab environment. Using the "here's-one-I-made-earlier" approach, devices and hardware can be acquired forensically prior to the lab exercise and easily copied into pre-configured virtual machines with appropriate forensic software (commercial offerings such as Access-Data's FTK, Guidance Software's EnCase or open source alternatives such as Autopsy/The Sleuth Kit or the Digital Forensics Framework). Such exercises can be conducted remotely as part of online course offerings rather well. However, a large part of digital forensics is in understanding the importance of evidence seizure and data acquisition and the practical challenges that go with these areas. This requires students to adequately explore and experience some of the problems and challenges with actual equipment and devices.

Universities then have to respond to both the need to incorporate new technologies and to do so in a way that gives students an appropriate interface to obtain the practical skill set required to meet learning objectives and outcomes.

In terms of meeting the demands of the subject specialisation, one route is to develop a broader range of specialised electives to enable students to focus in particular technologies. However while it is desirable to have, for example, digital forensics investigators or penetration testers with a common understanding and knowledge of core concepts, there is the question as to how much additional specialist content is required. The cost of implementing advanced forensic data recovery or advanced kernel exploitation for classes require specialist staff training, specialist equipment, at a considerable additional cost.

An alternative to developing several specialised courses covering the breadth of cybersecurity is the development of degree programmes that concentrate on specific focus areas. This approach is inline with the current NSA method of evaluating higher education institutions. As mentioned previously, universities may seek certification as an academic centre of excellence in 17 different areas of specialization. The advantage of this approach is that there is a core set of transferrable cyber security skills that are common across all the specialisations, whilst allowing individual universities to play to the strengths of their academics. Further advantages of the specialist centre model are that, as new and novel ways of implementing practical learning into tutorials, labs and other exercises are developed by a specialist institution, the university can share the material with others whilst continuing research, development and investment in the focus area. As centres of excellence are expected to engage in outreach activities (considering both the NSA and GCHQ certifications), there is also the impetus to disseminate the specialist knowledge beyond enrolled college students, to make the subject matter accessible for those of school-going age, for other university cyber-programmes and to the general populace as a whole (e.g. Continuing Professional Development).

This will enable many other universities to rapidly adapt to a changing environment (as it is far easier to develop courses for existing programs and incorporate ideas and suggestions from these specialist centres) and better keep par with changes in technology. Therefore this will enable universities to put individuals into the workplace that have a broader understanding of cyber with a common understanding of key concepts that are developed early on in the degree program before students seek specialisation, perhaps at a defined centre of excellence in a particular discipline.

6   Summary and Conclusions

It is clear that the expansion in the adoption of technology is presenting a number of challenges in terms of the breath of new technologies that need to be incorporated into cybersecurity courses. Universities have a number of options to look towards for guidance as to what to include in cyber security programmes, whether generic or in a specific focus area. Such guidance covers content for academic programmes directly, what universities should be addressing in terms of the workforce or the needs of Government organisations or industry.

Two ways of responding to the challenges are discussed - new specialisation courses for existing degree programs - and the need for new degree programs. Clearly both approaches are equally valid and will depend on existing specific university provisions and resources. Perhaps both approaches are required as the specialism develops. A number of educational challenges to incorporating new technology were also presented; the cost barrier to entry for incorporating specialist courses may be too high for smaller institutions and that existing models for incorporating technical teaching material (e.g. virtualised capture-the-flag exercises) may not translate well to new technologies.

There is much to be done in this field. With several types of accreditation/guidance available for academic institutions focusing on different categories of industry, further work needs to be conducted into how specific subject/topic areas can be delivered to students in a way that facilitates hands-on experiential learning with the appropriate technological tools.

Acknowledgements. This project was supported by work funded by the Senter for internasjonalisering av utdanning (SIU), project no. PNA-2015-10010, Forensics and Security Teaching Educational Resources (FASTER).

References

ACM: Cybersecurity Curricula 2017, Curriculum Guidelines for Undergraduate Degree Programs in Cybersecurity (2017). http://www.csec2017.org/csec2017-v-0-5

Amazon: Smart Home (2017). https://www.amazon.com/smart-home/b?node=6563140011. Accessed 18 Apr 2017

Chartered Society of Forensic Sciences: Component Standards (2016). http://www.csofs.org/Digital-Forensics. Accessed 10 Nov 2016

Conklin, A.: The design of an information security practicum course. In: Proceedings of the AIS SIG-ED IAIM 2007 Conference (2007)

Cyberedwiki: 2017. http://cyberedwiki.org/mediawiki/index.php?title=Welcome_to_CyberEd_Wiki. Accessed 31 Jan 2017

Disney Food Blog: Disney Refillable Mugs (2016). http://www.disneyfoodblog.com/disney-refillable-mugs/. Accessed 12 Nov 2016

Dopplick, R.: Experiential cybersecurity learning. ACM Inroads 6(2), 84 (2015). http://dx.doi.org/10.1145/2743024

GCHQ: Scheme to Recognise Academic Centres of Excellence in Cyber Security Research (2011). https://www.epsrc.ac.uk/files/funding/calls/2011/scheme-to-recognise-academic-centres-of-excellence-in-cyber-security-research/. Accessed 15 Nov 2016

GCHQ: Can you crack it (2011b). http://www.canyoucrackit.co.uk/. Accessed 15 Nov 2016

GCHQ: Working with academic to increase the UK's capability in cyber security (2014). http://www.nationalarchives.gov.uk/documents/information-management/cesg-aces-partnerships.pdf. Accessed 31 Jan 2017

GCHQ: GCHQ certifies six more Masters' degrees in Cyber Security (2016). https://www.gchq.gov.uk/news-article/gchq-certifies-six-more-masters-degrees-cyber-security.   Accessed   15 Nov 2016

GCHQ: New call to certify Cyber Security Degrees (2016b). https://www.gchq.gov.uk/news-article/new-call-certify-cyber-security-degrees. Accessed 31 Jan 2017

GCHQ: Certification of Bachelor's and Master's Degrees in Cyber Security… is your degree in scope? (2016c). https://www.ncsc.gov.uk/content/files/protected_files/article_files/degrees-at-a-glance.pdf

Glassify: The Smart Glass (2016). http://www.glassify.me/. Accessed 12 Nov 2016

Hexoskin Wearable Body Metrics (2016). http://www.hexoskin.com/collections/all. Accessed 13 Nov 2016

Kessler, G.C., Ramsay, J.: Paradigms for cybersecurity education in a homeland security program. J. Homel. Secur. Educ. 2, 35–44 (2013). http://www.journalhse.org/v2-kesslerramsay.html

Keystone Academic Solutions (2017). https://www.bachelorstudies.com/BSc/IT/Cyber-Security/. Accessed 18 Apr 2017

Malmedal, B., Røislien, H.E.: The Norwegian Cyber Security Culture, Norsk senter for informasjonssikring (Norsis) (2016). https://norsis.no/wp-content/uploads/2016/09/The-Norwegian-Cybersecurity-culture-web.pdf

Morgan, S.: One Million Cybersecurity Job Openings in 2016, Forbes (2016). http://www.forbes.com/sites/stevemorgan/2016/01/02/one-million-cybersecurity-job-openings-in-2016/#209e17d77d27. Accessed 11 Nov 2016

National Science Foundation: https://www.nsf.gov/statistics/seind14/index.cfm/chapter-2/c2s1.htm. Accessed 11 Nov 2016

NCSC: GCHQ Degree Certification - Call for New Applications (2016). https://www.ncsc.gov.uk/articles/gchq-degree-certification-call-new-applicants. Accessed 31 Jan 2017

NIETP: Current CAE Designated Institutions (2017a). https://www.iad.gov/nietp/reports/current_cae_designated_institutions. Accessed 11 Nov 2016

NIETP: NSA/DHS National Centers of Academic Excellence for Cyber Defense (2017b). https://www.iad.gov/NIETP/documents/Requirements/CAE-CD_Focus_Areas.pdf. Accessed 11 Nov 2016

NIST: DRAFT NICE Cybersecurity Workforce Framework (NCWF): National Initiative for Cybersecurity Education, SP 800-181 (2016). http://csrc.nist.gov/publications/PubsDrafts.html#SP-800-181

NSA: National Centers of Academic Excellence in Cyber Defense (2016). https://www.nsa.gov/resources/educators/centers-academic-excellence/cyber-defense/. Accessed 10 Nov 2016

NSA: 2016 NSA Codebreaker Challenge (2016b). https://codebreaker.ltsnet.net/home. Accessed 10 Nov 2016

Rege, A.: Multidisciplinary experiential learning for holistic cybersecurity education, research and evaluation. In: Proceedings of the 2015 USENIX Summit on Gaming, Games and Gamification in Security Education, Washington DC, 11 August 2015 (2015)

Rodgers, M., Siegfried, K.: The future of computer forensics: a needs analysis survey. Comput. Secur. **23**(1), 12–16 (2004). http://www.sciencedirect.com/science/article/pii/S016740480 4000100

Sitnikova, E., Foo, E., Vaughn, R.B.: The power of hands-on exercises in SCADA cyber security education. In: Dodge, R.C., Futcher, L. (eds.) WISE 2009. IAICT, vol. 406, pp. 83–94. Springer, Heidelberg (2013). doi:10.1007/978-3-642-39377-8_9

Stranden, R.: Sikkerhet – en profesjon? Næringslivets Sikkerhetsråd (NSR) (Norwegian Business and Industry Security Council (2010). https://www.nsa.gov/resources/educators/centers-academic-excellence/cyber-defense/

The Telegraph: GCHQ spy recruitment code solved (2011). http://www.telegraph.co.uk/news/uknews/defence/8928088/GCHQ-spy-recruitment-code-solved.html. Accessed 11 Nov 2016

University of Abertay: Ethical Hacking Degree (2017). http://www.abertay.ac.uk/studying/undergraduate/bsc-ethical-hacking/

Verisure: 2016. https://www.verisure.no/. Accessed 11 Nov 2016

Willems, C., Meinel, C.: Online assessment for hands-on cybersecurity training in a virtual lab. In: Proceedings of the 3rd IEEE Global Engineering Education Conference (EDUCON 2012). IEEE Press, Marrakesh, Morocco (2012)

Towards a Conceptualisation of Cloud (Cyber) Crime

David S. Wall[(✉)]

Centre for Criminal Justice Studies, School of Law, University of Leeds,
Leeds, UK
d.s.wall@leeds.ac.uk

Abstract. The term 'Cloud' is a misnomer that diverts attention from the level of conceptual clarification that is needed to understand the implications of cloud technologies upon criminal behavior, crime analysis and also law enforcement. Cloud technologies have increased computing power and storage capacity whilst reducing the cost of computing; all are qualities that have not been lost on criminals who have been using them to commit DDoS attacks, Data theft, mass spam attacks and other mass cyber-dependent crimes. This paper offers a framework for conceptualising cybercrimes in the cloud (cloud crimes) and for understanding how they drive offenders and affect victims. It also outlines the key challenges for law enforcement.

Keywords: Cybercrime · Cloud crime · Policing cybercrime in the cloud · DDoS · Data theft · Mass spam attacks

1 Introduction[1]

The 'Cloud' is a term that is frequently misused and often obfuscates attempts to understand its implications for criminal behavior. Some commentators refer to it as a 'thing', an object, whereas others see it as simply a technological method of increasing computer storage and power. Of course, there are also those who either see it as both, or neither, with the latter vehemently denying its existence at all. Yet, despite contradictory views about cloud technologies, it is clear that they have had a significant impact upon increasing computing power, increasing storage and generally making computing much cheaper than before. Cloud technologies provide an up-scale in criminal activity that is not lost on criminals who have already exploited the digital and networked technologies of the internet to commit high volume cybercrimes that greatly challenge preventative, investigative, and prosecution processes. They both facilitate and escalate cybercrimes. Furthermore, this 'cloud' lift also brings into play a range of new forms of (cyber) crimes against the machine; crimes that use the machine and crimes that are in the machine. All are crimes that need to be further understood in terms of their offending behaviors and their impact on victims. Such understanding will

---

[1] Paper delivered at the Human Dimensions of Cybersecurity panel of the 5th International Conference on Human Aspects of Information Security, Privacy and Trust, Vancouver Convention Centre, Vancouver, Canada 9-14 July 2017.

© Springer International Publishing AG 2017
T. Tryfonas (Ed.): HAS 2017, LNCS 10292, pp. 529–538, 2017.
DOI: 10.1007/978-3-319-58460-7_37

inform policy debates and help resolve legal and law enforcement challenges in order to restore and maintain public confidence in the internet. This paper will suggest a framework for understanding cybercrimes and the way that they have been impacted upon by cloud technologies.

2   Methods

This paper draws upon previous work into the conceptualisation of cybercrimes (Wall 2017) (EPSRC CeRes EP/K03345X/1), including 'cloud', to begin a dialogue that seeks a more informed and workable conceptualisation of cloud crime and criminal behavior in the cloud? It forms an essential basis for the EPSRC funded CRITiCal project (Combatting cRiminals In The Cloud - EP/M020576/1) and the paper effectively outlines the structure and thinking behind the first work package. This conceptual paper also draws upon a couple of decades of my own work into technology and crime before and after the introduction of cloud technologies. It attempts to synthesize my own work and that of others on cybercrime and consider it as a platform for understanding cloud crime (see further the references cited in this paper and then the references that those works are based upon). The data requirements for this paper are therefore mainly library based, plus some secondary data to be re-analysed for the CRITiCal project that will feed into a later version of this paper. Later in the project cycle, work completed on the work packages will be fed back into the conceptualisation.

3   Framework

The conceptualisation of cybercrimes and the 'cloud' will be the focus of this paper and also the challenges they raise for law and law enforcement. They are challenges and conceptualisations that will need to be approached from an interdisciplinary perspective because different stakeholders' experience cloud technologies in different ways. Computer scientists, on the one hand, need to explore changes in cloud technologies and criminal behavior and they also need to understand the 'difference' between before and after cloud. Yet, police officers, on the other hand, for various reasons linked to the reporting, recording and investigating processes, will be unlikely to see any major direct impacts of cloud technologies in reports they receive of cybercrimes. Yet, a broader and more accurate conceptual understanding of cloud technologies and cloud crimes is vital if new predictive and investigative tools are to be created that will not only meet evidential legal standards where cybercrimes are investigated and prosecuted, but also to prevent them from happening in the first place.

The first part of this paper explores what is and is not a cybercrime. The second part then looks at the conceptual differences between cyberspace and the cloud (and also the Internet of Things). The third part explores the new criminal opportunities that the cloud adds to the cybercrime landscape and also raises questions as to whether, or not, the cloud changes patterns of criminal organisation online? The fourth and final part of the paper will consider the key challenges being faced by policing agencies who police cloud crimes.

3.1 What Is and What Is Not a Cybercrime

Over the past quarter century Cybercrime has changed from little more than a cyber-punk fantasy into a matter of national priority and international policy. Research and teaching programs have proliferated alongside a large and sophisticated cybercrime security industry with investments being counted in the $billions. Yet, whilst there is no doubt that everyone agrees that the problem exists, there is still considerable dis-agreement as to what cybercrime exactly is and how to deal with it, even so far on in time from the early 1990s.

Before exploring what is or what is not a cybercrime it is important to first outline the changing technological environment which has transformed criminal behavior. The following are observations about that transformation drawn from my own work and that of others (found in the references of those works). The first is that cybercrime takes place in a cyberspace; an 'imaginary' space created by the social reaction to the combination of Digital and Network technologies and culturally shaped by social science fiction (Wall 2012). Social behavior online has been transformed by digital and networked technologies across networks of communication, which has created behaviors that are *global*, *informational*, and *distributed* (see the references to Castells 2000 in my 2007 book). Important here is the fact that whilst this space may be imaginary, the consequences of criminal actions in cyberspace have very real conse-quences in the physical world.

The second observation is that cybercrimes are enabled by the same technologies that create cyberspace. The same technologies that create cyberspace have also trans-formed criminal behavior in much the same ways to make crime global, informational and distributed (Wall 1997, 2007). This virtual world has not only had a massive impact upon our everyday lives, but it has also created new criminal opportunities, causing victimizations that have very real consequences for individuals. Originating in 1980s cyberpunk literature, the term cyberspace and cybercrime causes much confu-sion, even conflict, between different commentators. But, cybercrime and cyberspace are here to stay because they have become so culturally embedded in the common parlance - despite attempts to avoid them by using the term 'digital' or some other word instead (see further, discussion in Wall (2002, 2007, 2012)).

The third observation is that cybercrimes become more and more automated as digital and networked technologies become advanced and more sophisticated. Net-worked and digital technologies do what other advanced technologies do, they deskill and then re-skill labor - this deskilling and reskilling process also applies to the crime labor that commits cybercrime (for offending is a form of labor) (see Wall 2007). As with many aspects of ordinary work (labor) over time, technology and the ideas behind it have tended to separate out work tasks and automate them; usually to make them cheaper to perform and improve efficiency. In so doing, many skills have been absorbed by an automation process, but this deskilling has also created new skills to control the technology that controls those new processes (re-skilling). The fact that one or two people can now control an entire criminal process that once required many people and with specialist skill sets has profound implications for our understanding of the organization of cybercrime. In a rather cynical way, the internet has effectively democratized crimes such as fraud that were once seen as the crimes of the powerful and the privileged. In a nutshell, networked and digital technologies have created an environment in which there is no longer any need for criminals to commit a large crime at great risk to themselves, because one person can commit many small crimes with lesser risk to themselves. The financial criminal no longer needs to commit a single $50 million robbery with its complex collection of criminal skill sets and high levels of personal risk when he or she can, for example, commit 50 million X $1 low risk thefts themselves from the comfort and safety of their own home (Wall 2007: 3, 70). If not a bank robbery, then criminals can commit a major hack, a DDOS (Distributed Denial of Service) attack, a hate speech campaign, or suite of micro-frauds; see for example, the case of Lomas in the UK who scammed 10,000 victims out of £21 million or the 15 year old hacker who, with three others, allegedly hacked the TalkTalk database and stole personal information on 1.2 million customers (Wall 2015).

At the far end of this automation process, some forms of malware can operate totally by itself (see for example, fake anti-virus scams and Ransomware). Or it can run crime portals that can rent out bespoke malware via crimeware-as-a-service (Wall 2015). In such circumstances, the scientific entry level required of cybercrime offenders has fallen and the technology effectively 'disappears' because its operation becomes intuitive and offenders no longer require the high-end programming skills that they once needed. Another significant development has been the drop in the cost of technologies, which has dramatically reduced the start-up costs of crime, thus increasing the level of incentive. The impact of these transformations upon cyber crime is that the average person can, in theory, now commit many crimes simultaneously in ways not previously imagined possible, and on a global scale. These three observations set out the basic differences between online and offline crime as well as outlining the changes in the technological environment in which cybercrimes take place. But what they do not do is explain the differences in cybercrime and the many competing explanations of them that exist in the literature. There are two differentiating factors here:

The first differentiating factor is that cybercrime accounts often confusingly address different victim groups, which each proscribe different security debates. Although there may be similarities in 'crime type' used, individual victims are quite different from business and organizational victims, who in turn are different from nation state victims (national infrastructure) (see Wall 2015). Each has different motivations, offender groups and also attack tactics, different stakeholders and agencies. In addition, we also need to separate the cybersecurity debates over risk and threats from the cybercrime debates (cybersecurity) over *actual* harms to individuals, businesses and nation states (policing). These two sets of issues are often confused, sometimes deliberately, when in fact they each represent different actions. As in the offline world, not all threats and risks manifest themselves as harms to the individual, and not all harms are crimes. But some do and how do we make sense of them?

The second differentiating factor is that cybercrime should be understood as a process of transformation rather than a thing or things. One of the problems with contemporary explanations of cybercrime is that they often attempt to button hole online actions into a definition; which never seems to explain satisfactorily the complete phenomenon - only parts of it at any one time.

3.1.1   Understanding Cybercrime as Transformational Rather than Definitional

Instead of taking a definitional approach, I have suggested that cybercrime really describes a transformational process from one state (offline) to another (online) (see Wall 2007) - a process that is continuing into the future with the development of cloud technologies and the internet of things. By using this approach the multiple layers of cybercrime offending can be understood, not just in legal terms, but also the different acts and different motivations. The most important characteristic is that cybercrime disappears if you take away digital and networked technologies. This is possibly the most significant of all observations when understanding cybercrime. If it does not disappear, then it is not a 'true' cybercrime. By applying this 'transformation test' (Wall 2007), either scientifically or metaphorically, then the possibility arises that in addition to 'true' cybercrimes there are a range hybrids, which might explain some of the rather confusing definitions. It also helps explain what the 'cyber-difference' is. This test also helps reflect upon how the crime was committed and the levels to which networked and digital technology have impacted upon the criminal behavior. We can use this 'transformation test' to understand how crimes have been transformed in terms of their mediation by technologies. At one end of the spectrum are 'cyber-assisted' crimes that use the internet in their organization, but which would still take place if the internet was removed (e.g. a murderer web searching 'how to kill someone' or 'dispose of the body'). At the other end of the spectrum are 'cyber-dependent' crimes which are the spawn of the internet, such as DDoS attacks, spamming, piracy etc. If the internet (networked technology) is taken away, then they simply disappear. In between the cyber-assisted and cyber-dependent crimes are a range of hybrid 'cyber-enabled' crimes. These include most types of frauds and deception, but not exclusively, and are existing crimes in law, but are given a global reach by the internet, see for example the Ponzi frauds and pyramid selling scheme scams. Take away the internet, and these crimes still happen, but at a much more localized level, and they lose the global, informational and distributed lift that is characteristic of 'cyber' (see further discussion in Wall (2007, 2015)).

In addition to mediation by technologies, cybercrime offending has a number of different *modus operandi* (objectives and intents). This is a difference that is rarely commented upon systematically in the literature. We therefore need to distinguish '*cybercrimes committed against the machine*', such as hacking and DDOS attacks etc., from '*cybercrimes that use the machine*', such as frauds etc. Both of these also differ from '*cybercrimes in the machine*', such as extreme pornography, hate speech, offensive imagery and social networking originated offences and others. Yet, the distinction between them is rarely made in practice, even though the three types of *modus operandi* each relate to different bodies of law in most jurisdictions. Each of the three dimensions of cybercrime (influence of technology; *Modus Operandi*, victim group) can also be checked against each other in a matrix, see example in Fig. 1, to illustrate the different implications for understanding the levels of victimization experienced, but also the offenders and the way that they organize cybercrimes.

Technology by *Modus Operandi*	Crimes against the machine	Crime using the machine	Crimes in the machine
Cyber-assisted	Social engineering password theft	P2P fraud	Informational crime – terror handbook
Cyber-enabled		Mass Frauds	
Cyber-dependent	DDoS attacks, mass hacks	Phishing, Ransomware,	SNM, Hate speech

Fig. 1. Developing a cybercrime matrix (Mediation by technology v *modus operandi*)

3.2   What Are the Conceptual Differences Between Cyberspace and the Cloud (and the Internet of Things)

Mapping out cybercrime in the way described above enables cybercrime to be differentiated from offline crime and also in terms of different *modus operandi*, plus, also important for this discussion, levels of mediation by technology. The key question arises, what, therefore, happens when the technologies transforming or mediating criminal behavior change? Do the crimes change, does the criminal behavior change? These are essentially some of the objectives of the CRITiCal research project which this paper briefs. Early observations suggest that cloud technologies are impacting upon criminal behavior online in three transformational ways; by *increasing computing power*, they *increase storage capacity* and *reducing the cost of computing power*. This means that (cyber) criminals can commit a larger volume of more complex crimes at a reduced cost. So, cloud technologies are yet another form of force multiplier and one that helps to facilitate 'the internet of things' which greatly increases the number of devices that can be accessed by the internet and also potentially be exploited by criminals.

As stated earlier, cloud technologies both facilitate and enable cloud cybercrimes (cloud crime). They facilitate cloud crimes via Botnets, Crime-ware-as-a-service and also via ancillary procedures such as password decryption which requires the massive computing power that only cloud technologies can bring to the table. Cloud technologies also greatly escalate the scale of DDoS (Distributed denial of service) attacks, frauds and deception through spam transmission, and even the theft of complete clouds (mass data storage facilities). In a nutshell, the difference is that whereas networked and digital technologies meant that criminals no longer needed to commit a high risk $50 million robbery when they could commit 50 million low risk $1 robberies using a networked computer (see earlier example). The changes of scale that cloud technologies bring to the table now enable the same criminals to commit 50 billion robberies of, say, 0.1 cent, to achieve a greater yield and reduce the risk of prosecution even further.

In reality, cybercrimes have been gradually facilitated by cloud based technologies for about 15 years now and are part and parcel of cybercrimes already. But, whilst the differences mapped out here between cybercrime and cloud (cyber)crime are largely conceptual, they still need to be established in order to understand the technological aspects of crime for this project. Also, to refine the model or framework for understanding cybercrime outlined above. Furthermore, it also suggests that a further conceptual level could be related to the impact of cloud technology on the facilitation of cybercrime. Using the 'transformation' test or logic outlined above, we could hypothetically consider what would happen if the cloud technologies were to be removed. So, in this *cloud mediation model*, some cybercrimes are, for example, *cloud-assisted*, in that the underlying facilitating technologies assist them but, were the cloud aspect to be removed, they would still take place. At the other end of the spectrum, *cloud-dependent* cybercrimes would disappear if the cloud technologies were to be removed. In between, *cloud enabled* cybercrimes would lose the cloud lift (as described above) and crime volumes would return to their pre-cloud state.

3.3 What New Criminal Opportunities Are Facilitated and Enabled by Cloud Technologies?

This discussion raises the question as to what sort of cloud cybercrimes are emerging and what new cybercrimes can we expect in the future. As mentioned earlier cloud technologies facilitate cybercrimes via botnets, crimeware-as-a-service etc. They also enable a large volume of more complex crimes to take place etc. To understand this change, we can follow through the cloud mediation model outlined earlier. People will always source physical products from the internet so whilst these purchases are *cloud assisted* – assisted by cloud technologies - they would still take place regardless of the cloud. In contrast, a *cloud dependent* cybercrime would include, for example, some forms of data-theft, especially the theft of, or manipulation of a complete cloud. Take away the cloud aspect and the crime disappears. In between are *cloud enabled* cybercrimes; mass scam spams, for example, would (in estimation) reduce from 10 billion every 10 seconds to 10 million every 10 minutes if the cloud technologies were removed.

This cloud 'lift' has potential implications for changes in the organisation of cybercrime and the organisation of (cyber)criminals. The organisation of cybercrime and cybercriminals is very different to the organization of crime offline. Whilst there has been a tendency by media to sensationalize cybercrime by linking it with mafia groups, the literature covering this issue suggest that the nature of cybercrime and conceptualizations of traditional organized crime groups are highly incompatible (see Wall 2015). Indeed, the literature points to new forms of organization online that follow the distributed (networked), globalized and informational patterns of cybercrime. So, using the transformation terminology once again, we can talk about cyber-assisted forms of organization, where crime groups use technologies to assist their existing operations, including some traditional organized crime groups taking their existing areas of crime business online. There are also examples of cyber-enabled organization, where new groups of criminals use the internet networks to organize themselves to commit financial crimes. They obtain personal information online (say, though Phishing), then give it to offline money mules to monetarize the information. Take away the internet and they would commit the same crimes more locally and in much smaller volumes. Finally there are cyber-dependent organized crime groups, who commune online and commit crimes online. They are likely never to have met and are often unlikely to know each other's identity other than by pseudonym. They are also very ephemeral, even fluid because they tend to be a collaboration of ideas. Their organization is disorganized by comparison to other criminal groups and if you could take away the internet they would vanish.

To understand the potential for the growth of new forms of organized crime groups online in a cloud technology environment an economic model of cybercrime developed for the CeRes project (EP/K03345X/1) is combined with an analysis of organized crime online (Wall 2015). One of the potentially most obvious aspects of the force multiplier effect of cloud technologies' is the increased impact of cybercrimes upon mass victims. Because of the 'cloud lift' the financial or political yield of cybercrime (depending upon motivation) would be theoretically be much the greater, especially without any strong and effective organized crime groups online controlling the market for victims – as they do offline. Once a cybercrime is successful, however, then many other cybercriminals copy and try to commit the same form of cybercrime. This means that particular cybercrime types have a very short active life because, on the one hand, the victim market is diluted as other cybercriminals want to capitalise and there is no one preventing them from doing so. On the other hand, however, the potential victims (the victim market) become risk averse to cybercrime quite quickly through the words of mouth and warnings from the internet itself. The first generation of each cybercrime is therefore always the most successful in terms of yield from cybercrimes. But, the yield potential means that the stakes are high and it also means that organized crime groups are paradoxically incentivised to police other criminals in order to control their own share of the market.

Whilst there is little evidence to date of traditional organized crime groups moving activities online (as stated above), some have developed an online capacity to some of their more conventional criminal activities such as gambling. The concern is that there is now a strong incentive and means for online organized crime groups to develop and establish themselves online, especially as yields from crime grow, for example, as with Ransomware and extortion crimes more generally online.

3.4   What Are the Key Challenges Being Faced by Policing Agencies and the Criminal Justice System by Cloud Crimes

Cybercrime continues to challenge the criminal justice processes because of its very nature. One of the most distinctive characteristics of 'true' cybercrimes (cyber-dependent) is that they tend to be small-impact bulk-victimizations. So, cyber-frauds are micro-frauds and DDOS attacks and hacks of data are, with some exceptions, all individually small and most significant in their aggregate. This means that they are often *de minimis non curat lex*, too small to prosecute, and police and the criminal justice system find it hard to act on them individually. Police can only really act when a perpetrator is found, along with the aggregated proceeds of the crime as evidence. Furthermore, for reasons linked to the reporting, recording and investigating processes, police officers will be unlikely to see any major direct impacts of cloud technologies in reports they receive of cybercrimes. Because of their globalized nature, cybercrimes are also jurisdictionally problematic, unless the perpetrator is found and the evidence is strong enough to warrant an extradition order-if a treaty exists between the countries involved. Finally, there is also the need for policing expertise in cyber-crime to be able to collect the relevant forensic evidence, build a case and present it to the court for prosecution – also to instruct a specialist when needed, say, a criminal psychologist. The final challenge is the 'reassurance' problem in policing cybercrime. A 'culture of fear' exists around cybercrime which, for various reasons, exaggerates its impacts and causes a 'reassurance gap' between levels of security demanded by the public which policing agencies that cannot deliver. This 'gap' broadly shifts the policing focus towards answering those demands, highly publicized arrests, visible actions, which often shifts resources from essential cybercrime policing functions. The 'cloud lift' will widen this shift and potentially cause the 'reassurance gap' to increase.

4   Conclusion

In this paper I have observed that Cybercrimes take place in a cyberspace and are therefore enabled by the technologies that create cyberspace, including cloud tech-nologies. Cybercrimes are also becoming increasingly automated and they address a series of quite different victim groups. They should also be understood as techno-social-behaviors in a process of transformation rather than as a thing or things. So, adding these up, if you take away digital and networked technologies, then 'true' cybercrime disappears, but there are actually a range of cybercrime types. They differ according to the level of technological transformation and different *modus operandi*. Their organization also differs to that of crime offline. Furthermore, cybercrime creates immense challenges for the criminal justice system and its processes, which impacts upon public opinion. Finally, cybercrime is not going to go away as the internet cannot be switched off and there is no silver bullet solution.

The best we can do is mitigate their impact as new forms of cybercrime and threats arise. For this we need to keep on top of developments, design out some weaknesses and mitigate issues as they arise, however, over the next 5–10 years three key types of technological developments could further challenge law enforcement and keep crimi-nologists and colleagues awake at night. Mesh technologies will probably join our digital 'devices' to develop lateral networks; self-deleting communications, such as Tiger texts or Snapchat will eradicate evidence before it can be captured, and crypto-currencies such as Bitcoin, Robocoin, Dodgecoin, Litecoin and especially Zerocoin, which claims to be anonymous will create alternative value-exchange sys-tems. All three will potentially challenge existing forms of governance in different ways. Collectively, these three technologies, further amplified in time by cloud tech-nologies that will make more computing power available to criminals at a cheaper cost and the 'internet of things' which will expand the scope of devices connected to the internet and also the volume of data flows which will provide new criminal opportu-nity. Most worrying is the fact that the technology will become so intuitive that it will tend to disappear as we will not notice it any more.

One final point to make is that the solutions to cybercrime are not always simply high tech. On the one hand, cybercrimes are a product of the social reaction to new (criminal) opportunities created by networked and digital technologies, so some technical solutions are needed. But on the other hand, there is a need to also respond to the social impacts of cybercrime, especially where young and other vulnerable people are either not understanding the gravity of their own actions. Or their actions are being misunderstood by significant others (parents, teachers, police), particularly the transgressive behaviors which drift into serious crime without the offender leaving their bedroom!

Acknowledgements. I must acknowledge the various inputs and inspiration of my interdisciplinary colleagues on the various research projects I am working on: the CeRes, CRITiCal, TAKEDOWN and BITCOIN projects. First are the many co-Is who are mentioned on the proposals and also the research assistants who came along later, more specifically, those who were with me at Durham; Ladan Cockshut, Noura Al-Moubayed, and those at Leeds, Laura Connelly, Yanna Papadodimitraki, Alena Connolly, Roberto Musotto and Maria Porcedda. I also value greatly my many conversations with members of the National Crime Agency who are both a strategic partner and also stakeholder on the CRITiCal project and also the members of the police forces who helped with the CeRes project (please note that the views expressed here are my own).

There are also a number of authors in my field of study who I would like to acknowledge and who have over the years helped me develop my thinking on the subject in my particular area of the field (Criminology and Criminal Justice) and I apologize to those whom I have accidentally omitted. There are the old school who are still writing and refining their work. They are Susan Brenner, Rod Broadhurst, Dorothy Denning, Andrew Goldsmith, Peter Grabosky, Yvonne Jewkes, Mike Levi, Sam McQuade, Russell Smith, Maggie Wykes, Majid Yar. There is also an exciting new school of scholars such as Adam Bossler, Tom Holt, Mike McGuire and Matt Williams. Plus on the horizon there is an emerging inter-disciplinary cadre of authors such as Russell Brewer, Lennon Chang, Raymond Choo, Alice Hutchings, Natalia Garcia, Grainne Kirwan, Rutger Leukfeldt, Anita Livorgna, Jonathan Lusthaus, Fernando Miro, Anna Sergi, Lisa Sugiura, Michael Yip and others. I recommend that you Google their names along with the term 'cybercrime'.

References

Wall, D.S.: Policing the virtual community: the internet, cyber-crimes and the policing of cyberspace. In: Francis, P., Davies, P., Jupp, V. (eds.) Policing Futures, pp. 208–236. Macmillan, London (1997)

Wall, D.S.: Insecurity and the policing of cyberspace. In: Crawford, A. (ed.) Crime and Insecurity, pp. 186–209. Willan, Cullompton (2002)

Wall, D.S.: Cybercrime: The Transformation of Crime in the Information Age. Polity, Cambridge (2007)

Wall, D.S.: The devil drives a lada: the social construction of hackers as cybercriminals. In: Gregoriou, C. (ed.) Constructing Crime: Discourse and Cultural Representations of Crime and 'Deviance', pp. 4–18. Palgrave Macmillan, London (2012)

Wall, D.S.: Dis-organized crime: towards a distributed model of the organization of cybercrime. Eur. Rev. Organ. Crime **2**(2), 71–90 (2015)

Wall, D.S.: Crime, security and information communication technologies: the changing cybersecurity threat landscape and implications for regulation and policing. In: Brownsword, R., Scotford, E., Yeung, K. (eds.) The Oxford Handbook on the Law and Regulation of Technology. Oxford University Press, Oxford (2017)

How Might Crime-Scripts Be Used to Support the Understanding and Policing of Cloud Crime?

Steve Warren[1(✉)], Gavin Oxburgh[1], Pam Briggs[2], and David Wall[3]

[1] School of Psychology, Newcastle University, Newcastle, UK
{steve.warren,gavin.oxburgh}@ncl.ac.uk
[2] Department of Psychology, Northumbria University, Newcastle, UK
p.briggs@northumbria.ac.uk
[3] Centre for Criminal Justice Studies, School of Law,
University of Leeds, Leeds, UK
d.s.wall@leeds.ac.uk

Abstract. Crime scripts are becoming an increasingly popular method for understanding crime by turning a crime from a static event into a process, whereby every phase of the crime is scripted. It is based on the work relating to cognitive scripts and rational-choice theory. With the exponential growth of cyber-crime, and more specifically cloud-crime, policing/law enforcement agencies are struggling with the amount of reported cyber-crime. This paper argues that crime scripts are the most effective way forward in terms of helping understand the behaviour of the criminal during the crime itself. They act as a common language between different stakeholders, focusing attention and resources on the key phases of a crime. More importantly, they shine a light on the psychological element of a crime over the more technical cyber-related elements. The paper concludes with an example of what a cloud-crime script might look like, asking future research to better understand: (i) cloud criminal fantasy development; (ii) the online cultures around cloud crime; (iii) how the idea of digital-drift affects crime scripts, and; (iv) to improve on the work by Ekblom and Gill in improving crime scripts.

Keywords: Crime scripts · Cloud-crime · Cyber-crime

1 Introduction

Cloud computing is a relatively new term – estimated to be first used in the mid-2000s [6] - with the first cloud-type services offered as early as the late 1990s [14]. Since then, cloud computing has grown exponentially and continues to become a central part of consumer and business computing. Seventy-six percent of businesses make use cloud computing [24] with a prediction that by 2020, over half of mobile devices will rely on the cloud. The National Institute of Standards and Technology [32] have defined cloud computing as:

'*A model for enabling convenient, on-demand network access to a shared pool of configurable computing resources (e.g., networks, servers, storage, applications, and services) that can be*

© Springer International Publishing AG 2017
T. Tryfonas (Ed.): HAS 2017, LNCS 10292, pp. 539–556, 2017.
DOI: 10.1007/978-3-319-58460-7_38

rapidly provisioned and released with minimal management effort or service provider interaction.'

They continue to state that cloud computing is composed of five essential elements: (i) *on-demand self-service* (an individual can alter the computing capabilities in an instant); (ii) *broad access network* (access via a network and standard mechanisms); (iii) *resource pooling* (multiple resources – physical and virtual - and multi-tenant design); (iv) *rapid elasticity* (resources can instantly scale up or down), and; (v) *measured service* (automatic control and optimization of resources).

The exponential growth of cloud computing has brought with it a steep rise in crime involving the cloud. The reasons are obvious, especially when considering the five elements listed above which allow criminals to commit crimes in a multitude of ways to both improve the effectiveness of the crime itself and lessen their chance of getting caught. Some examples of cloud crime include criminals who buy cloud computing resources (with stolen credit cards) to host computational resources to break passwords on databases (brute force), or use these cloud resources to launch a Distributed Denial of Service (DDoS) attack (in this case using the cloud-virtual machines as a botnet – see appendix for definitions of computer science terms). The fact that many businesses and individuals use the cloud to store private information allows criminals easier access to that data. Criminals may even use the cloud to store illegal data, such as child exploitation material. In one example of fraud, criminals used phishing emails (created on the cloud) which installed malware that mimicked a bank website, meaning that when an individual went to transfer money (using what they thought was their bank's website), it went direct to the criminals. The interesting facet of this was the malware was located on a cloud server.

The complexities of these cloud crimes are such that it is important for policing/law enforcement agencies to better understand both the crime event and the criminal in one easy to understand, yet complete, framework. One of the ways academia has put forth is a systematic framework called *crime scripts*. Crime scripts were first put forward by Cornish [13] as a way to understand a crime with a more psychological edge. Crime scripts essentially turn a crime from an *event* into a *process*. This means that rather than a crime being a confusing and singular episode, we are now able to see every step the criminal takes leading up to the crime, followed by the crime itself, then after the crime. This includes any resources, locations, actors, activities, and even motivations (if known). Once constructed, a crime script forms a cognitive script – an organised and structured pattern of thought presented as a script where every element has a relationship with each other - that includes any decision a criminal will make, therefore creating a sequence of the pragmatic knowledge about their *modus operandi*.

Whilst the growth of cloud computing is undoubtedly useful in many positive ways, it brings with it an extra and potent dimension to cybercrime. Already, policing/law-enforcement agencies are struggling to keep up with all the crimes committed using digital and networked technologies [27]. The authors of this current paper believe that the creation of crime scripts is an essential element in understanding, and therefore tackling, cloud crime.

2 Cyber-Crime and Cloud-Crime

Cybercrime is continuing to grow at a high rate because of the potential that new digital and networking technologies affords criminals. For example, real world drug dealers are taking to the dark net to sell their goods because of the lack of face-to-face interactions (thereby decreasing the chances of getting caught), increase in security around selling (*PGP encryption* and the *TOR network* – see appendix) and increase in potential buyers' market share. The ever-increasing growth in crime-as-a-service is another issue, where a select few programmers create the viruses/spam/Trojans/DDoS (see appendix) capabilities and sell them to a layperson online, thereby distancing themselves from a 'crime scene'.

Westlake and Bouchard [47] believe that the Internet has affected crime on websites in three main ways. First, in terms of sexual exploitation, social networking sites have been used to groom victims [49–51] and have also been used for phishing [2], for the spread of malware [53] and spam [54], and financial institutions' websites are used to acquire private financial information of customers [30]. Second, both the Internet and the dark net (see appendix) are all used as a platform to buy and sell illegal goods/services [38]. Third, the Internet, deep web, and dark net are also used as a communal space to exchange ideas and provide social support to other criminals [52].

Wall [44] simplifies even further what the advent of digital and networked technologies has meant for criminals. It now allow criminals to commit over 50 million, £1 thefts (at a lower risk) rather than a single £50 million theft at an obviously far higher risk. Wall [45] believes that this transformation means that, in theory, the average person can now commit many crimes simultaneously on a global level. This is an entirely new, and somewhat terrifying, concept to deal with for policing/law-enforcement agencies. Thus, there is an urgent need for digital and networking forensic experts to better understand the process by which these crimes take place. Without this understanding, international policing/law-enforcement agencies have little hope of successfully making an impact. The UK has a strategy for impact through their 'Four Ps Strategy' - Protect, Prevent, Pursue, and Prepare:

> 'Existing [UK] Government strategy... has four components (the 'Four Ps Model') and involves a multiplicity of national and transnational organisations intervening both before ('Protect' and 'Prevent') and after ('Pursue' and 'Prepare') criminal activity.' (p.11 Implications of Economic Cybercrime for Police)

However, despite these defined strategies and the growth of cybercrime, the definition of cybercrime itself is still under debate because whilst everybody agrees that it exists, not everybody agrees what it is [44]. Wall [44] argues that there are three main types of cybercrime based on his transformation test. A transformation test in this case means removing the impact of the Internet is removed from the equation. First, there are *cyber-assisted crimes* – crimes that would, and could, still take place without digital or networking technologies (Wall uses an example of 'Googling' how to dispose of a dead body). Second, is *cyber-enabled crimes* which are crimes previously committed on a local level but now can take place on a much larger scale through the Internet (e.g., fraud). Third, and the purest form of cybercrime, is *cyber-dependent crimes*. These are crimes that if you took away the Internet, the crime itself disappears completely. This type of crime is completely dependent on the digital and networking technology – an example would be DDoS (distributed denial-of-service) attacks or spam e-mails. This paper will lean on the work of Wall and concentrate not only on *cyber-dependent* crimes, but what is now a subsection of that definition - *cloud-dependent* crimes.

Cloud-crime brings with it its own set of issues that differ from cyber-crime. Cloud crime can be defined as any crime committed with the assistance of the cloud, with this paper particularly focusing on cloud-dependent crimes. Traditional cybercrime forensic investigations involve collection of data or evidence from the location of the computer or device, followed by validation, analysis, interpretation, documentation, and presentation of results to a Court. Cloud-computing distorts this process as investigators must deal with multi-tenant hosting (same server serves multiple tenants), synchronisation problems, non-localised data, and jurisdiction issues (amongst others). Finding where the data is kept and retrieving it can be very problematic - in most cases, the user may not even know. With the exponential growth of cloud-computing, it is therefore essential to better understand the *behaviours* and *procedures* involved in cloud-dependent crime. This means understanding the criminal and their actions, something crime scripts do in a systematic way.

3   The Importance of Crime Scripts

It is well known that members of the public, in general, struggle to understand the science behind cybercrime and cybersecurity and this problem is exacerbated by the different regulatory frameworks associated with cybercrime, thereby resulting in a confusing array of issues for the average citizen [41]. One key issue in setting-up an effective and robust evidence-chain that might lead to successful prosecution in the cloud crime arena concerns the way in which the underlying crimes may be communicated to key stakeholders and to the general public. At present, there are real challenges in communicating effectively across stakeholders with an interest in cybercrime, where, for example, understanding the use of advanced machine learning and AI techniques – which will help automate the identifying and remedying of a cyber-crime – demand a level of computational expertise that is well beyond the non-expert. How much more difficult, then, will the task of convincing a court that such techniques have demonstrated criminal culpability beyond reasonable doubt. To address such issues, we take inspiration from literature around science communication [15, 34] where recently, the more traditional approaches to information delivery has given ground to participatory methods that actively seek the involvement of various communities in the science process. In other words, this problem is not simply one of, "How shall we simplify a message", but becomes one of, "How can we collectively construct a common language with which to discuss key issues". Such a 'common language' would bring benefits, not only to the research process (facilitating the ability of researchers to involve key stakeholders more directly), but would also allow the different stakeholders throughout the criminal justice process to talk to each other more meaningfully. It would also help to raise public awareness and allow public input to the process more directly (e.g., by facilitating the rapid identification and reporting of cloud-crime as it happens).

The use of scenarios to understand the complexities of a particular situation (or set of tasks) have been in evidence for a long time, although their context of use has changed considerably in recent years. For example, scenarios were introduced as design tools to aid disaster planning where they were found to be powerful tools to support the visualisation of a range of possible outcomes [10]. Go and Carroll [23] described two kinds of scenarios: (i) 'problem scenarios' that could illustrate the complexities and difficulties with known systems, and; (ii) 'activity scenarios' that facilitate the process of reasoning about uncertainties and supported the creation of sets of alternative realities that could stimulate the design process. It is now recognised that one of the principal contributions of scenarios in the design process is the creation of a common language that can span different communities. The construction and use of scenarios evolved, however, and came to be more widely recognised as 'stories' with settings, actors and plots, capable of describing existing situations, but also of describing future and emerging situations. Not surprisingly, scenarios started to be played out in a form of a design theatre, where particular situations could be dramatised with actors and props in order to understand just how innovative tools and systems could be effectively introduced [5]. In addition to the script-based scenarios and a variety of techniques for describing the actors or personas involved in the script [12], some researchers have argued that good personal development is essential for the generation of a rich and credible script [35]. More recently, new tools for the scripting of highly ambiguous scenarios have been developed that allow the interpersonal elements of a scenario to be fore-grounded and allow the audience more flexibility in considering a range of possible variants or outcomes [9].

Consequently, one important technique in overcoming these issues is the creation of crime scripts [7, 14]. Crime scripts are schemata that guide our understanding of a criminal's behaviour and routines. Once this logical and cognitive sequence of events are known, policing/law enforcement agencies know where to focus their resources to investigate and prevent crime, with both researchers and practitioners adopting this method as an analytic tool for looking at rational and goal-orientated behaviour [37]. Levi [31] suggests that crime scripts can be important in improving understanding of complex crimes, such as *cloud-dependent* crime.

4 Crime Script Analysis

Cornish [13] was the first person to create a systematic approach to creating these scripts – the work based on the concept of rational choice and cognitive scripts [1, 37]. The rational choice perspective examines a crime from the perspective of the offender [14] and takes a present-centred look at the interaction between the offender and their environment. The cognitive script approach is used extensively in psychology whereby a sequence of behaviours or decisions are 'scripted' for a specific situation.

In order to create a crime script, a crime script analysis must be undertaken. This is a systematic methodology [7, 13, 24] that generally relies on qualitative data and behavioural decision-making. It classically involves breaking down the actions of the criminal into four main stages - *preparation*, *pre-activity*, *activity*, and *post activity* [7]. However, crime scripts have been further broken down by other researchers into *preparation*, *pre-condition*, *instrumental pre-condition*, *instrumental initiation*, *instrumental actualisation*, *post-condition*, and *exit* [13, 18] – different types of crime developing different sequences. These stages are created by concentrating on the main elements of a crime (e.g., who, what, when, where, why, and how). Classically, the most important information gathered is how the offender goes about the crime and what decisions s/he makes along the way. This includes how *'they accessed the crime scene, the skills they required, the effort involved, information about the crime opportunity, the financing required to carry out the crime, facilitators (tools, transport, weapons, communication), and technical expertise'* [43, p. 7]. This information will be almost impossible to gather from a single source, thus, drawing on multiple sources is a salient point to remember when undertaking a crime script analysis. The information needed can be gained from various sources such as interviews with criminals, police notes, police investigative interviews/interrogations, CCTV footage, or from anyone intimate with the crime, etc.

In order to create these scripts, some form of qualitative or quantitative analysis must take place on the data. Qualitative analysis, particularly content analysis, is a popular choice [11] with a process of data categorisation allowing the researchers to develop the scripts. The exact type of analysis conducted seems less important than making sure the chosen analysis (whether it be content, conceptual, thematic, or a mix) allows for categories of themes to emerge, thereby lending understanding to the process and sequence of the crime. Script analysis can create high-order scripts - more generalised, over-arching scripts - or individual tracks - where every decision a criminal makes (or could make) is mapped. Crime scripts highlight the procedural nature of crime [7, 13] and should be able to reveal an overall picture of the sequence of actions a criminal undertakes before, during, and after a crime has occurred.

The script outlined in Table 1 highlights the process of how a robbery takes place, mapping out the sequence in which the event occurs, giving policing/law enforcement agencies multiple phases to explore in regard to either preventing the crime taking place or apprehending the offender - this is a salient point often forgotten in the creation of crime scripts. Surely the purpose must be for such agencies to carry out their job more efficiently, therefore ensuring crime scripts are more driven towards practitioners is important [22]. One paper that creates a crime script with possible interventions at every stage is on the activities involved in drug manufacturing in clandestine laboratories [11]. This paper divided up potential interventions into three categories: (i) *manager-place*; (ii) *guardian-target*, and, (iii) *handler-offender*. For every stage, they had potential interventions for policing/law enforcement agencies that apply to these categories.

Despite a diversity of papers employing crime scripts for real world crimes [18, 20, 22, 33, 43], the literature contains almost no cyber-crime scripts, with specific cloud-crime scripts an, as of yet, unresearched area. One paper that explores the creation of cyber-crime scripts relates to the online stolen data market [30]. In it, the authors found six universal stages, with each stage containing a mix of behaviours and events:

Table 1. An example crime script of a robbery given by Cornish in his original paper [13].

Script scenes	Script actions
Preparation	Meet and agree on hunting ground
Entry	Entry to underground system
Pre-condition	Travel to hunting ground
Pre-condition	Circulating/waiting at ground
Instrumental Pre-condition	Selecting victim and circumstances
Instrumental Initiation	Closing-in/preparation
Instrumental Actualisation	Striking at victim
Instrumental Actualisation	Pressing home attack
Doing	Take money, etc.
Post-condition	Escape from scene
Exit	Exit system

Stage 1: Preparation (setting up the necessary client software and creating accounts, steps towards anonymity and security, marketplace location, and learning specialist knowledge);
Stage 2: Entry (learning marketplace language and rules);
Stage 3: Pre-condition (obtaining and manufacturing products to sell, instrumental pre-condition, advertising products and services, instrumental initiation, exchanging law enforcement information, negotiating and communicating, instrumental actualisation, sending and receiving payment);
Stage 4: Doing (packaging goods, transporting goods);
Stage 5: Post-condition (reputation management, exchanging currency);
Stage 6: Exit (laundering proceeds).

One of the biggest challenges in creating cyber-crime scripts will be to understand how different they are to real-world crime scripts. The Internet is a fluid space – something we discuss in detail in the next section - so do we expect cyber-crime scripts to be so fluid, so lacking in concrete stages, as to be worthless? Hutchings and Holt argue that human behaviour is *human behaviour*, thus, wherever a human is involved, we are able to understand and map their behaviour and decisions.

5   What Elements Might We See in a Cloud-Crime Script?

The inherent nature of the cloud means that committing a crime can be committed from any location in the world, with preparation and pre-activity phases now a more complex and expansive phase due to increased elasticity and access. The activity itself is, by definition, a far more elusive crime, and the traditional post-crime period can now involve a more active monitoring period - where the criminal can monitor the effect of the crime at a more intense frequency (be it participating in forums, contacting the victim for ransom, sharing the data multiple times over a long-time period, etc.). Disengagement and exit from a crime scene is also now more fluid and less concrete, which means that the process of a cloud-crime may be less formal and concrete than a real-world crime.

An important element that should appear throughout most cloud-crime scripts should be the role of the online community. Research in both the psychological and sociological literature has shown that online communities are very powerful and effective spaces, just as much as real world communities and even real world social interactions. The breaking-down of communication barriers by the Internet [36] have allowed communities to transform into global social networks [49] rather than local ones. Hillman, Procyk, and Neustaedter [26] argue that these online communities allow the easier conduct and targeting of illegal activities and potential victims. The Internet, they argue, brings crime from a solitary business into a globally communal business, where anyone with an Internet connection can take part, or indeed be a victim.

Holt [28] explored online criminal communities and found that crimes that would normally be categorised as solitary crimes (e.g., hacking) are in fact a communal effort, where the tools, resources and knowledge required are shared within these communities. The growth of cybercrime has made it a necessity to further explore these communities – through both quantitative, but more importantly, qualitative methodologies such as ethnography - that play a major role in facilitating these cybercrimes.

One of the most important elements, or stages, of a cyber-crime is the criminals' access to a like-minded online community. Westlake, Bouchard, and Frank [48] looked at how child exploitation communities are built and found that these websites play a crucial role in facilitating criminal activities. Henson, Swartz, and Ryns [25] decided to better understand the relationship between offline and online, and looked at the concept of street-orientated beliefs [3, 4] in the context of online culture. Anderson [3, 4] examined an inner-city community (in Philadelphia, USA), and found that the widespread feeling of isolation and mistrust in 'the system' stemmed from the endemic poverty, unemployment, and perceived discrimination. Because of this, some people in that community created their own notions of success, a more achievable notion than the 'white, middle class version'; in other words, respect through toughness. Anderson called this the "code of the street", which is an informal set of violence-orientated rules as a means to achieve and maintain respect.

These findings show that, as hypothesized by Henson et al. [25], codes of the street exist and play out in online settings. The second finding is an equally important one. It was found that individuals who were off-line criminals were more likely to commit a cybercrime than those who were not. These findings suggest that there is a strong relationship between the off-line and on-line criminal world, that real world strategies and known criminal psychology can be applied with potential success. Henson et al. [25] called for a greater exploration of these relationships to confirm the findings in their study. They believe that these online street codes might be the single greatest factor in driving cybercrime participation. This tends to indicate that *cloud-dependent* crime scripts will fundamentally be the same as a *normal* crime script. They will be more similar in behaviours, emotions, learning curves, planning, amount of trial and error etc., than the complexity of cloud-crime hints. This means, and corroborates the work of Ekblom and Gill [20], that cloud-crime scripts will be more psychological than event-driven. Therefore, cloud-crime scripts will be, and should be, just as much as a journey into the mind of the offender as other non-technical crime scripts.

One important facet of this new type of crime, especially cloud crime, is the concept of *digital drift*. This is defined in the work of Goldsmith and Brewer as *"individuals [who] can gain access to criminal associations, networks and resources in ways that see them drift in (and out) of related illicit activities facilitated by the medium of the Internet itself"*. They argue that the increasing ubiquitousness of technology, along with the increasing networking power of technology, means technology now acts as cognitive extensions - things that augment not only our cognition but our lived experience. They argue that the networking technologies can substitute for other interaction partners, making a crime potentially easier. What Goldsmith and Brewer warn of is a new form of 'bad guy', not one that is unambiguously a criminal, but those that move in and out of doing bad things. This fluidity of criminal is something we must understand better, according to Goldsmith and Brewer, if we are to tackle cyber-crime.

6 Limitations of Current Crime Scripts

One major criticism of using a rational choice perspective in crime scripts is that it fails to explain irrational behaviour – examples including when the offender is drunk, is unaware of how his/her actions will affect the situation, having to change plans on the spot, etc. Cornish and Clarke [14] have argued that the rational choice perspective is only to create a focused framework in which to assess criminal decision-making. If we are to make crime scripts a more systematic and successful tool, the work of Ekblom and Gill [20] is of paramount importance. They argue that with the rise in the use of crime scripts, *"...rather than tinkering with the concept [of crime scripts], a fundamental rewrite was indicated" (p.321)*. They list some grievances they have with the current crime-script analysis, including:

- The universal script (with its preparation stage, pre-activity stage, etc.) can be difficult to apply, with more work than may be rewarded required to assign actions to the universal stages;
- There is a dilemma in how scripts can be generalised and yet accommodate variation;
- There is confusion between declaratory and procedural knowledge;
- It is unclear whether scripts describe behaviour or events.

Ekblom and Gill want to scrutinise the underlying concepts of crime-scripts to help develop more accurate scripts. One of the major issues they see with the current crime-scripts in use is the conceptual foundation on which they are based - the 'cognitive script' from Abelson [1], and Schank and Abelson [37]. Ekblom and Gill found this approach to be unclear and too narrow for what is needed in this situation. In general, they felt crime scripts were too loose, with a definition dependent upon who was creating it. They see differentiating *behaviours* and *events* as key to a crime script. For them, behaviour focuses on the perpetrator, while the event focuses on the interaction between perpetrator and their environment. They view scripts as, *"Abstracted descriptions of a particular kind of behavioural process, namely, structured sequences of behaviour extended over time and perhaps space, which could be considered functionally self-contained units or subunits of longer sequences" [p. 323].* They clarify that the behaviour they speak of may be individual or group. By concentrating on the behaviour, and then its consequence on events, we get to see a more consistent script.

Two of the example crime scripts they present in their paper offer some interesting thoughts, the first being *empirical scripts.* These, *"...are simple descriptions of recurrent sequences of behaviour in situ" [p. 324].* In these, goals must be evidenced and never should an assumption be made about the inner thoughts of a possible offender. The second is called an *explanatory script.* They borrow from Tinbergen [42] four stages of explanation for animal/human behaviour: (i) function; (ii) causation; (iii) development, and; (iv) evolutionary history. Because crime scripts deal with agents' perception, knowledge, and experience, Ekblom and Gill [20] added a fifth stage - phenomenology (the subjective experience of the offender). All stages need to be taken into account when creating explanatory scripts; a salient point we take from the paper - that crime scripts should be vital for understanding the offender in a broader way. Specifically, crime-scripts need to include goals, emotions, planning, learning, and errors. This is something we find vitally important, and have applied it to the cloud/crime script found in the final section of the current paper.

7   Potential Universal Cloud-Crime Script

Whilst Ekblom and Gill [20] question the usefulness of universal scripts, here we use one as an example to allow discussion on some potential stages in committing a cloud-crime. Using a crime script analysis (involving thematic analysis) on information found in online articles, including clippings in the UK (found on LexisNexis, a search engine for newspaper articles) relevant to cloud crime, a universal crime script was created (see below). Themes were then categorised using a mix of the classic universal stages (preparation, pre-initiation, instrumental initiation, exit), with the induction stage and monitoring stage newly created through the thematic analysis. This should not be seen as a fully completed cloud crime script due to the lack of hardened data, such as transcripts of police investigative interviews, interviews with cloud criminals, Court proceedings, etc. Rather, it should be viewed as a starting point for future discussions.

Our crime-script analysis found two main types of cloud criminal based on two skillsets: (i) **creators** and (ii) **purchasers**. The *creators* are those that actually create and distribute the malicious content - they are the individuals with the programming skillset needed to either be actively involved from day one, or just create the content for personal reasons and have no more to do with an actual crime. The *purchasers* are the mainly everyday individuals who primarily purchase the malicious content – malware, etc. – for profit or for chaos. They may have the skillset needed, but instead decide to purchase for sake of ease. They can also be (and this is common) an average person with no programming skillset who can only operate via instructions. We also found three main types of cloud criminal based on motivations: (i) **profiteers**; (ii) **jokers**, and; (iii) **hacktivists**.

In terms of motivations, we found those who would take part in a cloud crime for moral or ethical reasons, a *hacktivist* - an example being the group Anonymous. which is a collective of moral or ethical hackers, joined under the umbrella term Anonymous, often working separately but with no set goals. The *jokers* are those that like nothing more than to cause chaos for self-interests, and take part just for their own personal enjoyment. The most common motivation for cloud crime (it appears) is for profit with the majority of purchasers of malicious cloud malware using it for ransomware purposes (*profiteers*). As Wall [45] argued, the cloud now allows many small crimes to take place instead of one large crime – and this extends to average individuals holding one person ransom via purchased, cloud-based content. Turning now to what sort of social 'being' a cloud criminal is, we found that there were unsurprisingly three types: (i) **collectivists**, (ii) **lurkers**, and; (iii) **lone-wolfs**. A *collectivist* is someone who relies on, and participates in, the community, learning, teaching, boasting, etc. The *lurker* is the individual who is a member of a community but does not actively participate. They watch and read, and if it is an online community, are never seen. The *lone-wolf* is the criminal who acts outside of any community but does not enter any communities and acts completely alone.

The recent development, and alarming growth, of cyber/cloud crime-as-a-service makes for a very different type of crime-script. Those criminals that purchase malicious malware (or otherwise) with criminal intent, but are not actively involved in the creation of it, will have a different overall process to their crime. They may have the same fantasies, but lack some psychological element (e.g., determination, motivation, intelligence) or situational element (e.g., time, age) to create their own content. A criminal fantasy is the psychological growth of ideas and wants that to take place before any action, and have been linked with deviant behaviour in offenders. The induction phase (and subsequent phases) for these will involve less community involvement, etc. It is for these reasons that the current crime script is based on those who are actively engaged in the creation and distribution of cloud-crime. It is imperative that further work focuses on each type of cloud-crime and criminal - the more accurate a script, the more successful an investigation.

7.1 Example Crime Script

The following example cloud/cyber-crime script was created using a crime script analysis on newspaper articles, and based in the previous work on crime scripts. It differs in parts from pervious crime scripts due the analysis gleaning different phases due to the cyber-cloud factor.

Preparation

Phase 1 - Induction. This includes the development of cybercrime fantasies – those psychological ideas and wants that grow over time - learning about technical aspects, feelings of a political nature (whether experienced by oneself, or learnt in a community – see 'The Silk Road', the first Dark Net market place for selling illegal goods and services. The apparent creator and moderator, Ross Ulbrict, painted the project as a political act, fighting the increasingly oppressing nature of governments). These will include how they interact in online communities dedicated to passing-on knowledge – the formation of a criminal identity. The creators will be technically aware, who will mostly engage with each other online about technology-related matters. There are many communities specifically for cyber-crime available via the Internet, the dark net or some IRC chat group (a text-based communications software) or 4chan thread (an online forum that is infamous for its anonymity of use and therefore darker subjects discussed). This phase holds two areas of high importance to the current paper in: (i) the development of criminal fantasies, and; (ii) the involvement in online communities – such participation could come before, during, or after the development of criminal fantasies. These are two main areas in which psychology can add a strong understanding, so that less cybercrime occurs, and cyber crime reports to policing/law enforcement agencies are reduced, meaning that valuable resources can be devoted to other areas.

Phase 2 - Pre-conditions. It could be that an opportunity arises due to a system update or a weakness is discovered via some newly created content. It could also be participation in a community where an opening will appear (someone might mention hacking a business cloud, and the community, as a collective whole, take it upon themselves to figure out how to do that). What seems to be the most common is a member of a community will succeed in discovering an opportunity, and will post about it (e.g., to show off), thereby opening the door for others to continue. In terms of a *lone wolf*, this phase will revolve around ideas in their head based on the induction phase. We suggest that a true *lone wolf* requires their own crime script, as their behaviours, emotions, thoughts and experiences will be very different to someone involved in a community.

Pre-activity

Phase 3 - Instrumental Initiation. This phase relates to the planning of the crime, the learning of exact knowledge, the finding of weaknesses in a similar system, testing what they have - an iterative phase of 'getting ready' for their planned cyber-crime. The practicing of the crime may be conducted in legal or illegal ways in the first instance. For some cloud-crimes, the instrumental initiation and crime initiation are one and the same, but usually, one would expect to see a testing period, no matter how small, using maybe sqlmap to test for SQL (Structured Query Language) flaws. An sqlmap is a testing tool that automates the process of exploiting SQL flaws and taking over of database servers. Cloud-criminals were found to prey on a number of poorly written content management systems, poorly thought out authentication management processes, and even plain poor passwords that were found during this 'testing' period. While cloud crime can be complex, at times we found better public understanding is vital.

Entry to Crime Setting

Phase 4 - Crime Initiation. This phase is the enactment of the planned crime. Given the wide differences in cloud crimes, this stage will be different in detail on each occasion. For example, differences exist between hacking the iCloud and infecting users with malware for ransom via cloud resources. This phase should be split into the main types of cyber-crime based on the role of the cloud (e.g., target, tool, distributor) but should also be based on Wall's (2007) crimes against, crimes with, and crimes using the computer categorisation. Phases 3 and 4 can be iterative as they plan and test (and re-plan and re-test) while attempting hacks. Whilst it is important to define this phase in terms of the technology, it is vital for any successful crime script to contain as much information about the psychology of the suspect as possible. It is, therefore, essential to describe this phase in terms of the person undertaking the crime.

Phase 5 - Monitoring. This phase will depend on the type of cloud crime that has been committed. For example, an attack like the iCloud hack may be carried out once, then disengaged from the server for good with a monitoring of the result via community or other online means. In contrast, a ransom by malware might be monitored for responses, etc. Thus, there are subtle differences in the type of monitoring conducted before and after disengagement, but what is clear is that cyber-criminals will monitor the crime in all its different meanings. The monitoring stage is important as digital and networked technologies allow crime to happen easier than crime in the non-digital world, with some of the crimes requiring constant engagement and monitoring before disengagement (e.g., ransom). This, potentially, means it is easier to uncover evidence, and therefore the suspect, involved. This is, of course, offset by the Internet's ability to hide the 'footprints' of an offender – it does, however, open-up avenues of investigation.

Post-crime

Phase 6 - Disengagement. This relates to 'leaving' the scene of the crime. Dependent on the type of cloud-crime committed, this may mean different things. However, a 'behaviour' will take place (the crime) and then the 'behaviour' will cease thereby ending the role of the perpetrator in the crime (disengagement).

We believe that because crime scenes can be very fluid and fast-moving, it is not as simple as having definitive phases one after another. We believe our phases outlined above are capable of 'blending' and 'being fluid'. This is something that academic researchers and policing/law enforcement agencies need to be aware of - with flexibility of the Internet comes flexibility and potential erratic criminal behaviour.

8 Discussion

It is hoped we can now start to see how crime scripts can potentially be an essential element in tackling cloud-crime. They act as a common language between different stakeholders, focusing attention and resources on the key phases of a crime. Perhaps, more importantly, they shed light on the psychological elements of a crime as opposed to the more technical elements. The offender's mind seems to be of the greatest importance in the creation of crime scripts - to better understand the behaviours, motives, feelings, decisions within the process of a crime. The most pressing questions going forward, in our opinion, are those brought up by Ekblom and Gill [20] on the accuracy and fundamental makeup of crime scripts. Are crime scripts event driven or behaviour driven (Ekblom and Gill believing it should be behaviour driven)? How do we define and describe the behaviours? What type of crime script is best and in what situation? These are all fundamental questions and although the current crime scripts are focused enough to guide our thinking, we agree with Ekblom and Gill that it is now time to create a better (more accurate) definition of a crime script.

One of the big questions that cloud/cyber-crime scripts may help with is within the criminal justice system when decisions are being made about the correct policing strategy to tackle cyber-criminals. Should the law be strictly enforced with hackers given harsh prison sentences, or will sending them to prison make the situation worse, by allowing the criminals to socialise with one another, with the potential to develop links with other hackers? Conversely, perhaps they have all the connections they need from their own online communities, given the scope of these communities? What about young hackers that are harder to prosecute because they do not show full criminal intent? One of the major advantages of accurate crime scripts is that they guide intervention policy by policing/law enforcement agencies. A good crime script should not only describe the behaviour and psychology behind the crime/criminal, but also have anchor points for clear interventions to tackle the crime.

Finally, if we look at the example cloud-crime script we presented above, we can see similarities to the Darknet crime script created by Hutchings and Holt [30], as well as the more classic crime-scripts depicted by Cornish and Clarke [14]. The example crime script also has some key differences - mainly in how iterative and flexible the phases look to be, with the addition of a monitoring phase. While the Darknet actors tend to follow a tried and tested formula, the crime script presented here is more fluid. Future, more specific, cloud crime scripts created should continue to show that, this is especially so when we take into account the effect of *digital drift*. Our crime script analysis found many categories of cloud-crime offenders, all of them widely different both psychologically and situationally. It will be interesting to see how these types of cyber/cloud criminal both hold up in future research and how they relate to each other in terms of behaviour during the crime and interactions beforehand through online channels, as well as the influence of digital drift.

8.1   Future Research

We feel that there are four main areas for academic researchers to focus on to give better structure to policing/law enforcement agencies in their investigation of cloud-crime:

1. The role of 'fantasy'

Understanding not just the individual who fantasizes about a criminal life or a crime, but the fantasies themself. There is a dearth of research in this area but is an area that is central to understanding the potential profile of a cyber-criminal, or at the very least, how agencies can stop a potential criminal before they act. For example, why does a certain teenager fantasize about being a Ross Ulbricht (Silk Road creator) over a Paul Thomas Anderson (a filmmaker)? We all evolve different fantasies and motivations, and understanding why individuals are drawn to cyber-crime over other popular pastimes is vitally important in tackling it. In this example, there may well be a simpler reason, as Ulbricht painted himself as a political rebel. But in other cases, it will not be as easy to understand the qualitative elements that create a potential criminal's mind. There have been many papers exploring this idea of criminal fantasy, but the vast majority relate to sexual predators [15] or homicide [7], with more quantitative rather than qualitative research methodologies employed. We need to understand the subjective qualities of these cybercrime fantasies and their formation during adolescence, and so we call on future work to qualitatively explore these issues.

2. The role of 'communities'

It is clear from the literature [25–28, 30, 36, 47–50] that online communities play a major role in inspiring, organising, and implementing online crime. Future research needs to focus on how cloud criminals (and/or potential criminals) are able to access the resources they need to undertake a cloud-crime – this will more than likely mean entering spaces of ethical divisiveness, such as the Dark Net or 4chan (or whatever new installment they have access to [e.g., 8chan]). Both qualitative and quantitative research methodologies must be employed to provide a richer understanding of all the elements Ekblom and Gill discuss.

3. Understanding digital 'drift'

We need to advance the previous work of Goldsmith and Brewer relating to digital drift and in understanding the creation of cloud/cyber crime-scripts. They *"...propose the concept of digital drift to capture some of the mediated effects of the Internet upon criminal commitments, particularly his [Matza, 1964] idea that drift into and out of criminal pathways can often be 'accidental or unpredictable' [p. 113].* In short, the Internet has now allowed what we would consider everyday citizens to either drift (or drift deeper) into criminal spaces, much more easier than before. However, what does this fluid nature of cybercrime now mean for a crime script?

4. Creation of crime-scripts

Precise crime scripts need to be created for all types of cloud (or cyber-crime) that can take place. All types of cloud criminal behaviour needs to be mapped out which will allow policing/law enforcement agencies the opportunity to be ahead of the game, rather than falling behind.

8.2   Conclusion

We believe that the creation of cloud-crime scripts is an essential activity to be undertaken in the battle against cyber-crime. The exponential growth of cyber (and cloud) crime means policing/law enforcement agencies are struggling to have an effect, and while computer science works on machine learning and data collection automation, psychology and criminology can help policing agencies better understand the mind of a cloud criminal – and not just a static picture, but the process and evolution of behaviours before, during and after a cloud crime.

Acknowledgments. This work is part of the CRITiCal project (Combatting cRiminals in The Cloud - funded by the Engineering and Physical Sciences Research Council (EPSRC; EP/M020576/1).

Appendix

Term	Meaning
Botnet	A number of geographically separate networked computers controlled by some master (for nefarious purposes)
Cloud-crime	Crime undertaken using the cloud (see below)
Cyber-crime	Crime undertaken using a computer and network
Dark net	A series of networks that can be only accessed using specific software and configurations
DDoS	Distributed Denial of Service – making a network service unavailable by flooding the server with requests
Deep web	The un-indexed, or hidden, parts of the Internet
Malware	**Mal**icious soft**ware**
PGP encryption	PGP (Pretty Good Privacy) encryption allows messages to be sent so only the sender and receiver have the 'keys' to read it
The cloud	A network of networked computers or servers used to store, manage, and process data instead of local computers
TOR network	Free software used to connect to the dark net
Trojans	Malicious software that misleads a user into using it

References

1. Abelson, R.P.: Psychological status of the script concept. Am. Psychol. **36**(7), 715 (1981)
2. Aggarwal, A., Rajadesingan, A., Kumaraguru, P.: Phishari: automatic realtime phishing detection on twitter. In: eCrime Researchers Summit (eCrime), pp. 1–12. IEEE, October 2012
3. Anderson, E.: The code of the streets. Atl. Mon. **273**(5), 81–94 (1994)
4. Anderson, E.: Code of the Street, pp. 107–141. Norton, New York (1999)
5. Aoki, P.M.; Woodruff, A.: Making space for stories: ambiguity in the design of personal communication systems. In: Proceedings of the CHI 2005, pp. 181–190. ACM (2005)
6. Bogatin, D.: Google CEO's new paradigm: 'cloud computing and advertising go hand-in-hand'. ZDNet, 23 August 2006
7. Borrion, H.: Quality assurance in crime scripting. Crime Sci. **2**(1), 6 (2013)
8. Burgess, A.W., Hartman, C.R., Ressler, R.K., Douglas, J.E., McCormack, A.: Sexual homicide a motivational model. J. Interpers. Violence **1**(3), 251–272 (1986)
9. Briggs, P., Olivier, P., Blythe, M., Vines, J., Lindsay, S., Dunphy, P., Nicholson, J., Green, D., Kitson, J., Monk, A.: Invisible design: exploring insights and ideas through ambiguous film scenarios. In: Designing Interactive Systems Conference (DIS 2012), 11–15 June 2012, Newcastle-upon Tyne (2012)

10. Carroll, J.: Scenario-Based Design: Envisioning Work and Technology in System Development. Wiley, New York (1995)
11. Chiu, Y.N., Leclerc, B., Townsley, M.: Crime script analysis of drug manufacturing in clandestine laboratories implications for prevention. Br. J. Criminol. **51**(2), 355–374 (2011)
12. Cooper, A.: The Inmates Are Running the Asylum. SAMS Publishing, Indianapolis (1999)
13. Cornish, D.B.: The procedural analysis of offending and its relevance for situational prevention. Crime Prev. Stud. **3**, 151–196 (1994)
14. Cornish, D.B., Clarke, R.V.: The rational choice perspective. In: Environmental Criminology and Crime Analysis, p. 21 (2008)
15. Cormick, C.: Ten big questions on public engagement on science and technology. Int. J. Delib. Mech. Sci. **1**(1), 3550 (2012)
16. Daleiden, E.L., Kaufman, K.L., Hilliker, D.R., O'neil, J.N.: The sexual histories and fantasies of youthful males: a comparison of sexual offending, nonsexual offending, and nonoffending groups. Sex. Abuse: J. Res. Treat. **1**(1), 195–209 (1998)
17. Desisto, R.P., Plummer, D.C., Smith, D.M.: Tutorial for understanding the relationship between cloud computing and SaaS. Analysis **2**(2) (2008)
18. Deslauriers-Varin, N., Beauregard, E.: Victims' routine activities and sex offenders' target selection scripts: a latent class analysis. Sex. Abuse **22**(3), 315–342 (2010)
19. Ekblom, P.: Talking to offenders: practical lessons for local crime prevention. In: Urban Crime Statistical Approaches and Analyses. International Seminar Held Under the Auspices of Ajuntament de Barcelona Forum des Collectives Territoriales Europeenes pour la Securit6 Urbaine. Institut d'Estudis Metropolitans de Barcelona, Barcelona (1991)
20. Ekblom, P., Gill, M.: Rewriting the script: cross-disciplinary exploration and conceptual consolidation of the procedural analysis of crime. Eur. J. Crim. Policy Res. **22**(2), 319–339 (2016)
21. Ekblom, P., Tilley, N.: Going equipped: criminology, situational crime prevention and the resourceful offender. Br. J. Criminol., 376–398 (2000)
22. Gavin, H., Hockey, D.: Criminal careers and cognitive scripts: an investigation into criminal versatility. Qual. Rep. **15**(2), 389 (2010)
23. Go, K., Carroll, J.: The blind men and the elephant: views of scenario-based system design. Interactions **11**(6), 44–53 (2004). ACM
24. Haelterman, H.: Crime Script Analysis: Preventing Crimes Against Business. Springer, Heidelberg (2016)
25. Henson, B., Swartz, K., Reyns, B.W.: # Respect: applying Anderson's Code of the street to the online context. Deviant Behav., 1–13 (2016)
26. Hillman, S., Procyk, J., Neustaedter, C.: Tumblr fandoms, community & culture. In: Proceedings of the Companion Publication of the 17th ACM Conference on Computer Supported Cooperative Work & Social Computing, pp. 285–288. ACM, February 2014
27. HMIC Report: Real lives, real crimes: a study of digital crime and policing (2015)
28. Holt, A.: (En) Gendering responsibilities: experiences of parenting a 'young offender'. Howard J. Crim. Justice **48**(4), 344–356 (2009)
29. Holt, T.J., Turner, M.G.: Examining risks and protective factors of on-line identity theft. Deviant Behav. **33**(4), 308–323 (2012)
30. Hutchings, A., Holt, T.J.: The online stolen data market: disruption and intervention approaches. Glob. Crime, 1–20 (2016)
31. Levi, M.: Organized fraud and organizing frauds Unpacking research on networks and organization. Criminol. Crim. Justice **8**(4), 389–419 (2008)
32. Mell, P., Grance, T.: The NIST definition of cloud computing. Natl. Inst. Stand. Technol. **53**(6), 50 (2009)

33. Morselli, C., Roy, J.: Brokerage qualifications in ringing operations. Criminology **46**(1), 71–98 (2008)

34. Powell, M., Collin, M.: Meaningful citizen engagement in science and technology. What would it really take? Sci. Commun. **30**(1), 26–36 (2008)

35. Pruitt, J., Grudin, J.: Personas: practice and theory. In: Proceedings of the DUX 2003, pp. 1–15. ACM Press (2003)

36. Rheingold, H.: Social networks and the nature of communities. In: Purcell, P. (ed.) Networked Neighbourhoods, pp. 47–75. Springer, London (2006)

37. Schank, R.C., Abelson, R.: Scripts, goals, plans, and understanding (1977)

38. Scotford, E., Yeung, K. (eds): The Oxford Handbook on the Law and Regulation of Technology. Oxford University Press, Oxford

39. Somer, T., Hallaq, B., Watson, T.: Utilising journey mapping and crime scripting to combat cyber crime and cyber warfare attacks. J. Inf. Warfare **14**, 39–49 (2016)

40. Steinmetz, K.F., Tunnell, K.D.: Under the pixelated jolly roger: a study of on-line pirates. Deviant Behav. **34**(1), 53–67 (2013)

41. Sanquist, T., Morris, F., Mahy, H.: An exploratory risk perception study of attitudes toward homeland security systems. Risk Anal. **28**(4), 1125–1133 (2008)

42. Tinbergen, N.: On aims and methods of ethology. Zeitschrift für Tierpsychologie **20**, 410–433 (1963)

43. Tompson, L., Chainey, S.: Profiling illegal waste activity: using crime scripts as a data collection and analytical strategy. Eur. J. Crim. Policy Res. **17**(3), 179 (2011)

44. Wall, D.: Cybercrime the Transformation of Crime in the Information Age, vol. 4. Polity, Cambridge (2007)

45. Wall, D.S.: Crime, security and information communication technologies: the changing cybersecurity threat landscape and implications for regulation and policing. In: Brownsword, R., E (2017)

46. Wellman, B., Boase, J., Chen, W.: The networked nature of community: online and offline. IT Soc. **1**(1), 151–165 (2002)

47. Westlake, B., Bouchard, M.: Criminal careers in cyberspace: examining website failure within child exploitation networks. Justice Q. **33**(7), 1154–1181 (2016)

48. Westlake, B.G., Bouchard, M., Frank, R.: Finding the key players in online child exploitation networks. Policy Internet **3**(2), 1–32 (2011)

49. Whittle, H.C., Hamilton-Giachritsis, C.E., Beech, A.R.: "Under His Spell": victims' perspectives of being Groomed Online. Soc. Sci. **3**(3), 404–426 (2014)

50. Whittle, H.C., Hamilton-Giachritsis, C.E., Beech, A.R.: In their own words: young peoples' vulnerabilities to being groomed and sexually abused online. Psychology **5**, 1185–1196 (2014)

51. Whittle, H., Hamilton-Giachritsis, C., Beech, A., Collings, G.: A review of online grooming: characteristics and concerns. Aggress. Violent. Beh. **18**(1), 62–70 (2013)

52. Wortley, R., Smallbone, S.: Internet child pornography: causes, investigation, and prevention. ABC-CLIO, Santa Barbara (2012)

53. Yang, C., Harkreader, R., Zhang, J., Shin, S., Gu, G.: Analyzing spammers' social networks for fun and profit: a case study of cyber criminal ecosystem on twitter. In: Proceedings of the 21st International Conference on World Wide Web, pp. 71–80. ACM, April 2012

54. Yardi, S., Romero, D., Schoenebeck, G.: Detecting spam in a twitter network. First Monday, **15**(1) (2009)

Modelling Trust and Trust-Building Among IT-Security Professionals

How Do Practitioners Find Out Whom to Work With?

Laurin B. Weissinger$^{(\boxtimes)}$

Nuffield College, University of Oxford, Oxford, UK
Laurin.weissinger@nuffield.ox.ac.uk

Abstract. By analysing cyber-security as a private protection market, and linking it with technological aspects and the dominating risk-environment, valuable insights into its workings can be gained, particularly when it comes to non- or semi-technical factors. Using high-granularity, empirical interview data ($n = 140$) as input, this paper presents insights about trust, signalling and cooperation among practitioners in the context of a complex field. At the moment, trust-building in the cyber-protection business is very personalised. Due to complexity and uncertainty, cooperation is based on social networks and reputation, while institutional signals are less significant than in other high-risk areas. While more research is necessary to unpack this issue, the analysis provides some understanding of how the field and technological aspects shape protection-market conditions, and how preferences regarding signalling and assessment change in practice according to the actors and organisations involved in a given situation. Evaluating other actors is generally based on above-mentioned personal factors, rather than institutional signalling.

1 Protection and Cooperation in IT-Security

IT-Security is complex, decentralised, and predominantly privately ordered [1, p. 13], [2, p. 272]. This makes judging other actors, human and organisational, an important aspect of IT-Security provision. This paper draws from analytical sociology [3–5], signalling theory [6–8], and studies about protection-markets [9–11] to contribute an understanding of trust-building in cyber-protection that is focussed on the human side of the equation. If tasks are diverse and actors depend on each other to ensure overall functionality, both within and across organisations, *organic* conditions are given [12, chap. 3], [13, pp. 315ff], [14, pp. 19ff]. This means that different centres of expertise must cooperate to keep the system running. Information technology and security are a prime example for such conditions: Actor A, Alice, requires her machines and networks to run smoothly, and consequentially must be confident that other actors, e.g. Bob (B), behave as promised or expected. Alice has two ways to build confidence: control or trust [15, p. 4].

© Springer International Publishing AG 2017
T. Tryfonas (Ed.): HAS 2017, LNCS 10292, pp. 557–566, 2017.
DOI: 10.1007/978-3-319-58460-7_39

The *traditional* strategy in modernity has been control-focussed and bureaucratic, *guaranteeing* compliance through audits and standardisation [13, pp. 14ff], [16, pp. 6–8]. Institutional trust, embodied in rules [13, p. 68], is given to regulators, which govern a certain *domain* by testing, auditing, and certifying products and people [15, p. 32], [16]. This top-down system is based on uniformity and non-dyadic *system trust* [14, pp. 16–17]. Control-strategies increase predictability by reducing individual agency and expectable errors [17, p. 128], which helps to mitigate anticipatable risks [18]. Yet, rigid regimes struggle with *Unknown Unknowns* [19, p. 335] that are common in IT-Security due to the complexity of interconnected components and systems: Alice is confronted with a nearly unlimited number of (potential) threats and weaknesses. With third party enforcement – e.g. by states – currently lacking, cybersecurity is defensive and specific: cyber-protectors use counter-measures that are difficult to test and never perfect [20, p. 208]. The strongest security solution wins, while the weakest link, if human or technological, defines system security [20, p. 114].

To succeed in building and maintaining a functional security architecture, cyber-protectors, i.e. those individuals actively trying to prevent harm by ensuring confidentiality, availability, and integrity,[1] and their clients must cooperate [21, p. 239], [22, pp. 27ff]. This setup demands interpersonal or intra-organisational trust between high-level experts. Generally, managing and anticipating risks, securing systems, and evaluating people are uncertain processes, based on *internalised learning processes* and *heuristics* [18], [23, p. 24], [24, p. 40], [25] but in IT-Security, the trust game is particularly difficult: First, cyber-attacks and vulnerabilities are usually harder to detect than physical ones. Second, networks grow and evolve quickly, escaping standardisation. Inappreciable disparities can compromise networks, while one vulnerable component can affect millions of machines and users (e.g. *Hearthbleed* bug). Third, alongside networks and systems, attack- and defence-strategies change rapidly, causing ever-unfolding imbalances [20, pp. 73ff, p. 89]. Last but not least, cyber-protection is necessarily multi-dimensional. Various resources and types of expertise are needed to establish protection.

In consequence, collaboration and using other people's work is the only rational option to reach an acceptable level of security: trusting Bob reduces the scenarios Alice must take into account. For example, if Alice is sufficiently confident that Bob's code is error-free, she will discard some attack-scenarios. To gain this sufficient confidence in Bob's abilities and trustworthiness, Alice, as assessor, interprets signals emitted by Bob, signals emitted by others about Bob, and recorded past signals to form her beliefs about him. Based on this imperfect information and the given situation, Alice judges if Bob is sufficiently unlikely to defect or fail in future cooperation, i.e. she forms

a hypothesis of future behaviour that is located between knowing and not knowing, but an assumption held with enough confidence to base practical action on. [26, p. 346]

---

[1] e.g. Analysts, Penetration Testers, Security Architects.

Yet, as Alice starts trusting, her dependence becomes a risk; and while trustworthy entities do not fail, failing trusted entities compromise security [27, p. 13]. In consequence, Alice will try her best to cooperate with actors that are both trustworthy and sufficiently skilled. Much work has been done in the security field about managing trust but trust and trust-building, particularly in the social realm, have remained black boxes [3, pp. 27ff]. This paper discusses one important aspect, namely how signalling and assessment-processes feed into beliefs [24, p. 29]:

How can an agent, the receiver, establish whether another agent, the signaller, is telling or otherwise conveying the truth about a state of affairs or event, which the signaller might have an interest to misrepresent? And, conversely, how can the signaller persuade the receiver that he is telling the truth, whether he is telling it or not? [28, p. 168]

In line with the theory [13, 14, 23, 29–31], it seems that market conditions and technological aspects in cyber-security increase the importance of trust vis-à-vis control. Cooperation-ties with autonomous experts in critical fields are always hazardous [32, p. 214], but particularly so in security, where protectors need a lot of privileges and insights. In IT-Security, testing prowess is difficult for a variety of reasons, as institutional signalling or embeddedness are usually deficient [33]: many cyber-protectors lack official certifications and there are no strong associations with signalling power between officially sanctioned certifications or memberships, and the individual, hidden properties of sufficient skill and particularly trustworthiness. Thus, this paper hypothesises:

H_{1a} A more individually-focussed process than in other high-security, high-discretion sectors is expected.

H_{1b} Actors will prefer personal and network-based assessment over institutionally-based signals.

H_{1c} Homophily, continued interaction and reciprocity will strengthen ties.

H_2 Reputation is central, as demonstrating fundamental qualities is costly (skill) or impossible (trustworthiness).

2 Methodology

This paper is based on 140 research interviews with cyber-protectors, whose identities cannot be revealed. Individuals were sampled from a variety of industries and countries. In terms of experience and skill, the main focus was on people with considerable experience (five years or more) and/or expertise. Nevertheless, some less experienced individuals were interviewed to avoid an overly biased sample. In terms of geography, most interviewees were either European or from North America, with some people from Latin America, and fewer Asians and Africans. Most people in the sample work for smaller employers, particularly penetration testers and consultants, while some, for example security architects, predominantly worked for large corporations. Interviews were in-depth and comprehensive, usually taking between 45–70 min.

Due to the aims of this paper, expert interviews were the most suitable data source. Yet, the interviewees represent a small, potentially non-random sample of the target population [34, pp. 56–59], [35, p. 124] and thus external validity is difficult to establish. Due to misrepresentation and misunderstandings, the findings could therefore be affected by *systematic measurement errors* [35, p. 156]. On the other hand, expert interviews are most appropriate. Firstly, personal contact was necessary to establish trust and legitimacy [34, pp. 64–65]. Second, the *microanalysis of processes* [36, pp. 58–59] requires dialogue, like the use of examples and hypothetical scenarios. Third, as this study tries to develop a model and understanding [17, p. 4], [32], empirical evidence directly feeds into the model, requiring interactivity and flexibility [36, p. 98]. Fourth, the research problem is multi-faceted [37, p. 190], which, at the outset, is best approached qualitatively [34, see p. 8]. Internally, conclusions seem valid: people in different positions, companies, and fields from a variety of different backgrounds presented similar interpretations of the field, which were also in line with the sociological and security literatures [38, see pp. 312–315].

The interviews focussed on the questions of trust and cooperation. The main goal was to grasp the way the interviewees tried to ensure that they were working with trustworthy contacts, and exploring how they would go about finding individuals with specific skills. For example, how would they try to get a feel for another person, what would they do to avoid being manipulated or conned, what types of information would they focus on, and where would they acquire this information? The main focus of the analysis was then to understand the perceptions and preferences of the interviewees but also to develop a basic, yet functional model of how these perceptions influence decision-making when it comes to hiring and cooperation. This was achieved using a *Content Analysis* methodology, i.e. by systematically interpreting, coding, systematising, and finally quantifying the interpretations and preferences expressed in the interviews.

3   Model and Findings

3.1   Main Assessment Factors and Decision Model

Cyber-security is a complex market with little external enforcement, which influences what actors consider *subjectively rational* [32, p. 136]. As in Spence [39, pp. 360–361], [40, p. 455], non-cooperation is an option per individual evaluation process but actors must choose *someone* and determine their trustworthiness correctly. Decisions result from belief-based, rationalising thought-processes [41, p. 4], within the limits imposed by empirical reality. The data indicate that cyber-security experts do actively research and weight different kinds of evidence and signals to decide if they want to cooperate. Formally, the decision to cooperate (D) is based on the believed probability p of success times the expected benefits, minus the probability $(1-p)$ of failure multiplied by the expected costs [42, see p. 394], and [32, chap. 9]. As this is a decision making process, p is not equivalent to the real probability, but represents beliefs. The assumed probability of success is based on a function (f) of the assessment of skills and trustworthiness, with C denoting confidence-levels. Both confidence levels, C_{Skill} and $C_{Trustworthiness}$, are based on beliefs resulting from signals received.

$$D_{Cooperation} = (p \times Benefits) - (1 - p \times Costs)$$

with

$$p = f(C_{Skill} \times C_{Trustworthiness})$$

The interviews show that C_{Skill} and $C_{Trustworthiness}$ are dependent on eight main factors, of which some are more decisive than others, yet further research is needed to understand and analyse their relative importance in different situations.

- Intentional Signalling, i.e. what actors tell others openly through speech, written text, or otherwise.
- Unintentional Signalling, i.e. signals sent out unwillingly, e.g. signs of stress, accent, habitus.
- Interpersonal Histories, i.e. a shared past with the assessee.
- Official Qualifications, e.g. degrees, certifications.
- Artefacts, i.e. remainders of activity on the internet, e.g. published papers, blogs, or code on github.
- Professional Associations, e.g. membership in the $(ISC)^2$.
- Group Affiliations, e.g. ex-hacker, ex-criminal, nationality, etc.
- Social Networks, e.g. shared professionals contacts, or friends.

The interviews further indicate that the weighting of these factors is variable: personal preferences (α) regarding different signalling types (δ_x), organisational preferences or rules (β), and situational factors (γ) influence the way the assessment is made. While input signals and evaluation procedures differ, the function is the same for both C_{Skill} & $C_{Trustworthiness}$.

$$C = (\alpha_1 + \beta_1 + \gamma_1) \times \delta_{Intent.Sig.} + (\alpha_2 + \beta_2 + \gamma_2) \times \delta_{Unintent.Sig.}$$
$$+ (\alpha_3 + \beta_3 + \gamma_3) \times \delta_{Interpers.Hist.} + (\alpha_4 + \beta_4 + \gamma_4) \times \delta_{Qualifications}$$
$$+ (\alpha_5 + \beta_5 + \gamma_5) \times \delta_{Artefacts} + (\alpha_6 + \beta_6 + \gamma_6) \times \delta_{Prof.Assoc.}$$
$$+ (\alpha_7 + \beta_7 + \gamma_7) \times \delta_{Group Aff.} + (\alpha_8 + \beta_8 + \gamma_8) \times \delta_{Soc.Netw.Sig.}$$

The outcome C would be an assumed trustworthiness- or skill-level, ranging from absolute confidence to none.[2] How strongly preferences and external factors, α, β & γ, influence the overall multiplicator depends on the relative power of their source: bigger organisations are more influential in rule-setting, while powerful individuals have more discretion.

Unlike in other domains, usually influential aspects, like demographic factors, locality, and nationality[3] are not salient. However, interviewees note that it is

---

[2] With $\sum \alpha_{1-8} = \alpha_{total}$.

[3] With some exceptions.

easier for them to judge socially similar actors [43, p. 435]. Dyadic homophily increases inter-personal understanding but also the likelihood of having access to triadic relationships, which directly or indirectly, passively or actively *vouch* for the other party. Second, market-conditions and interactions are formative, unlike nationality or geographical location. Generally, cyber-protectors prefer evidence-based trust, or at least an approximation thereof; a *lack of contrary evidence* [6, p. 234] is not enough. As hypothesised, the process among experts is very individualised and specific. Someone doing general website-security can accept higher risks than cyber-protectors of a defence company; the latter's confidence, C, must be much higher to accept cooperation.

3.2   Illustrative Example

Let it be assumed that Alice is an IT-Security professional who requires Bob's services, specifically his expertise in cryptography. Alice herself is specialised in computer networking and does not have the needed expertise, nor the time and resources to obtain them. Alice who works in a small security consultancy will try to find suitable candidates within her close social network, preferably someone she already knows personally and has worked with in the past. That failing, Alice will try to find Bob within her wider social network, i.e. asking her contacts for recommendations and ideas, with a preference for those colleagues and friends that she knows best and trusts the most. Based on these recommendations from the social network, Alice could then draw up a short-list, again with a strong preference for people she already knows, or people that her most trusted contacts know and can vouch for.

In all likelihood, Alice will try to gain insight into Bob's work; e.g. if he has published papers or code online, scanning these artefacts for evidence of Bob's skill. In addition, she may read and analyse his communications, say on an online forum to get a better *feel* for him. Interviews are likely to be significant to Alice, both to listen to what Bob has to say, and to test him as much as she can. As the interviewees report, good questions and challenges will provoke insightful answers that allow them to get a good grasp of candidates and potential partners. Face-to-face encounters are also important to Alice. These create many unintentional signals that Alice can analyse. What Alice would be looking for specifically depends on the situation (γ) and preferences (α, β) but she will likely focus on signs of betrayal, on the (in-)ability to work under stress, and on inconsistencies in what is being said and Bob's non-verbal signalling, i.e. his behaviour more generally. Group affiliations are usually less important as signals but may be relevant, particularly if Bob has a background that could be associated with criminality or foreign powers.

All these signals and factors would also play into the selection of doctors, pilots, or lawyers. The main difference is that in these cases, there would be an *un-circumventable* pre-selection rule-set related to officially sanctioned qualifications like degrees, and professional associations, e.g. boards, which are based on testing and/or other conditions of membership. Cyber-protectors often struggle to demonstrate their prowess in the way that other professions can.

Unlike cyber-protectors, surgeons can refer to photographic evidence, pilots can show their service and training record, and lawyers can refer to cases they have won. This lack of powerful signalling devices in IT-Security is due to strong secrecy specifications and non-disclosure agreements, and because there are no general pre-selection rule-sets as in areas like medicine or law.

While it is true that some positions require certain credentials, commonly the CISSP, the interviewees did not discuss this aspect in much detail. Rather, they expressed the opinion that a CISSP can be held by individuals with little skill, due to its high-level, theoretical nature. Another aspect that was only discussed in passing were security clearances and background checks. Firstly, most interviewees were or are employed in private industry, and those that had been cleared or checked did not consider this an important element of assessing other people when it comes their *trustworthiness* or *skill*. Rather, they saw this as a necessary step after their selection had been made to confirm eligibility, satisfy requirements, and mitigate risks going forward.

Last but not least, it is important to note that Alice's preferences may be overwritten by her organisation, or the situation. Due to the regulative environment, compliance likely trumps security in an organisational context. While such requirements were often considered to have only limited impact on actual security and trustworthiness, they do increase the salience of certifications in the selection process. If problems arise, the ability to present credentials and demonstrate *due diligence* may be more important than a functional security environment. Thus, the objectives of security actors are potentially in-congruent with the aims of their employer. Alice's situation is also crucial to the evaluation process: the more pressing the circumstances and the higher the payout vs. the potential losses, the more leeway she will – or be ordered to – allow. Particularly in combination with above-mentioned organisational requirements, this can lead to incentives and strategies that are unaligned with the goal of increasing security.

3.3   Hypotheses and Empirical Insight

It is nearly impossible to unequivocally signal trustworthiness or skill in the professional sphere of IT-Security, as cheating is comparatively easy and because there is little enforcement in general. With institutional signals that dominate other professional fields being largely absent, the evaluation of alters is mainly individual and specific, on a case-by-case basis ($H_{1a\&b}$). Having, and retaining, a good reputation is immensely important (H_2) and security professionals strongly prefer using their social networks and contacts to find new colleagues or partners. As expected in more or less any social network, homophily (H_{1c}) facilitates trust-building. The sources indicate that they have an easier time gauging individuals from backgrounds similar to their own. Yet, they claim – and appear – to not exclude individuals based on their nationality, past, or other types of group belonging. In contrast to other high-risk domains, assessment appears to be more thorough and personalised, while control efforts appear less useful. Yet, more research is necessary to explain and link the factors presented above.

The reasoning behind interviewees' preferences appears to be associated with the uncertainties experts face due to the lack of trusted institutions or enforced regulation regimes.

4 Conclusion

At this time, protection in cyberspace is necessarily private, defensive and particular, as there are no authoritative institutions that can settle disputes and enforce decisions. Technology and the cyber-protection market condition the importance of trust and reputation, and strongly influence the way trust is assessed and signalled in the field. When hiring an accountant or doctor, the foremost criterion is official recognition. For most IT-Security professionals in the sample, this pre-selection criterion is usually absent.

In the technological realm, confidence-building is based on control and trust. Yet, socially and among experts in particular, control is often difficult to employ as a guarantor for compliance. Trust can hardly be replaced, due to IT-Security's complexity and interconnectedness: there is no other way but to trust complex technical systems, contractors, one's own team or employees, as well as the general infrastructure. The interviews are congruent in supporting the hypotheses: the evaluation and *testing* of other actors is based on personalised processes, reputation seems to matter a lot, and the eight factors described are considered central. As underlined, further research is necessary to unpack the concepts, their relationships, and interconnectedness, as well as their relative importance in different situations. In many ways, trust-building in cyber-security appears to be procedurally similar but more extreme than trust-building elsewhere. In a nutshell, cyber-protectors prefer and are compelled by the IT-security domain to find out whom to work with by thoroughly looking into every possible co-operator, their past, their available work and skills, as well as their social networks. However, fully understanding how assessment in the sector could be streamlined or improved would necessitate further research into this area.

References

1. Kobayashi, B.K.: Private versus social incentives in cybersecurity: law and economics. In: Grady, M.F., Parisi, F. (eds.) The Law and Economics of Cybersecurity. Reissued, pp. 13–28. Cambridge University Press, Cambridge (2011)
2. Trachtman, J.P.: Global cyberterrorism, jurisdiction, international organization. In: Grady, M.F., Parisi, F. (eds.) The Law and Economics of Cybersecurity. Reissued, pp. 259–296. Cambridge University Press, Cambridge (2011)
3. Hedström, P.: Dissecting the Social: On the Principles of Analytical Sociology, 188 p. Cambridge University Press, Cambridge (2005)
4. Elster, J.: Explaining Social Behavior: More Nuts and Bolts for the Social Sciences, 1st edn., 496 p. Cambridge University Press, Cambridge (2013)
5. Hedström, P., Bearman, P.: The Oxford Handbook of Analytical Sociology, 800 p. Oxford University Press, Oxford (2009)

6. Gambetta, D.: Trust: Making and Breaking Cooperative Relations, 1st edn., 280 p. Wiley-Blackwell, New York (1988)
7. Gambetta, D.: Codes of the Underworld: How Criminals Communicate, 368 p. Princeton University Press, Princeton (2009)
8. Goffman, E.: Behavior in Public Places: Notes on the Social Organization of Gatherings. Reissued, 258 p. Free Press, New York (2008)
9. Varese, F.: The Russian Mafia: Private Protection in a New Market Economy. New edition, 306 p. Oxford University Press, Oxford (2001)
10. Varese, F.: Mafias on the Move: How Organized Crime Conquers New Territories. Reprint, 284 p. Princeton University Press, Princeton (2011)
11. Gambetta, D.: The Sicilian Mafia: The Business of Private Protection, New edition, 346 p. Harvard University Press, Cambridge (1993)
12. Durkheim, E.: The Division of Labour in Society, New edition, 412 p. Palgrave Macmillan, Basingstoke (1984)
13. Fox, A.: Beyond Contract: Work, Power and Trust Relations, 408 p. Faber & Faber, London (1974)
14. Lane, C., Bachmann, R.: Trust within and between Organizations, 334 p. Oxford University Press, Oxford (1998)
15. Cofta, P.: Trust, Complexity and Control: Confidence in a Convergent World, 1st edn., 310 p. Wiley-Blackwell, Chichester (2007)
16. Power, M.: The Audit Society: Rituals of Verification, New edition, 208 p. Oxford University Press, Oxford (1999)
17. Weber, M.: Wirtschaft und Gesellschaft, 868 p. Mohr, Tübingen (1922)
18. Hutter, B.: Anticipating Risks and Organising Risk Regulation, 320 p. Cambridge University Press, Cambridge (2010)
19. Beck, U.: Living in the world risk society: a Hobhouse Memorial Public Lecture given on Wednesday 15 February 2006 at the London School of Economics. Econ. Soc. **35**(3), 329–345 (2006)
20. Schneier, B.: Beyond Fear: Thinking Sensibly About Security in an Uncertain World, 2nd edn., 296 p. Copernicus, New York (2003)
21. Cofta, P., Furnell, S.: Understanding Public Perceptions: Trust and Engagement in ICT-mediated Services, 262 p. International Engineering Consortium, Chicago (2008)
22. Schneier, B.: Liars and Outliers: Enabling the Trust that Society Needs to Thrive, 366 p. Wiley, Indianapolis (2012)
23. Luhmann, N.: Vertrauen: Ein Mechanismus der Reduktion sozialer Komplexität, 140 p. Lucius & Lucius, Stuttgart (2000)
24. Ostrom, E.: Towards a behavioral theory linking trust, reciprocity and reputation. In: Ostrom, E. (ed.) Trust and Reciprocity, pp. 19–79. Oxford University Press, New York (2003)
25. Hamill, H., Gambetta, D.: Streetwise: How Taxi Drivers Establish Customers' Trustworthiness, 256 p. Russell Sage, London (2005)
26. Simmel, G.: Soziologie. Untersuchungen über die Formen der Vergesellschaftung, 804 p. Duncker and Humblot, Leipzig (1908)
27. Anderson, R.J.: Security Engineering: A Guide to Building Dependable Distributed Systems, 2nd edn., 1080 p. Wiley, New York (2008)
28. Gambetta, D.: Signalling. In: Hedström, P., Bearman, P. (eds.) The Oxford Handbook of Analytical Sociology, pp. 168–194. Oxford University Press, Oxford (2009)
29. Beck, U.: Risikogesellschaft. Auf dem Weg in eine andere Moderne. Suhrkamp, Frankfurt (1986)

30. Giddens, A.: The Consequences of Modernity, New edition, 200 p. Polity Press, Cambridge (1991)
31. Ostrom, E.: Trust and Reciprocity, 409 p. Oxford University Press, New York (2003)
32. Goldthorpe, J.: On Sociology: Numbers, Narratives, and the Integration of Research and Theory, 337 p. Oxford University Press, Oxford (2000)
33. Weesie, J., Buskens, V., Raub, W.: The management of trust relations via institutional and structural embeddedness. In: Doreian, P., Fararo, T.J. (eds.) The Problem of Solidarity: Theories and Models. Taylor & Francis, Boca Raton (1998)
34. Arksey, H., Knight, P.: Interviewing for Social Scientists, 224 p. Sage Publications Ltd., London (1999)
35. King, G., Keohane, R., Verba, S.: Designing Social Inquiry: Scientific Inference in Qualitative Research, 300 p. Princeton University Press, Princeton (1994)
36. Corbin, J.M., Strauss, A.: Basics of Qualitative Research: Techniques and Procedures for Developing Grounded Theory, 3rd edn., 400 p. Sage, Los Angeles (2008)
37. Silverman, D.: Doing Qualitative Research, 3rd edn., 472 p. Sage, London (2009)
38. Miles, M., Huberman, M., Saldana, J.: Qualitative Data Analysis - A Methods Sourcebook. Sage, London (2014)
39. Spence, M.: Job market signaling. Q. J. Econ. **87**(3), 355–374 (1973)
40. Spence, M.: Signaling in retrospect and the informational structure of markets. Am. Econ. Rev. **92**(3), 434–459 (2002)
41. Battigalli, P.: Rationalization in signaling games: theory and applications. Int. Game Theory Rev. **8**(1), 67–93 (2006)
42. Jonsson, J.O.: Explaining sex differences in educational choice an empirical assessment of a rational choice model. Eur. Sociol. Rev. **15**(4), 391–404 (1999)
43. McPherson, M., Smith-Lovin, L., Cook, J.M.: Birds of a feather: homophily in social networks. Ann. Rev. Sociol. **27**, 415–444 (2001)

Law Infringements in Social Live Streaming Services

Franziska Zimmer$^{(\boxtimes)}$, Kaja J. Fietkiewicz, and Wolfgang G. Stock

Department of Information Science, Heinrich Heine University Düsseldorf,
Düsseldorf, Germany
{Franziska.Zimmer,
Kaja.Fietkiewicz}@uni-duesseldorf.de,
Stock@phil.uni-duesseldorf.de

Abstract. Over the past few years, the popularity of Social Live Streaming Services (SLSSs) like Periscope, Ustream, or YouNow, has been on the rise. The services offer their users the opportunity to interact with the viewers in real time while broadcasting themselves. With this kind of human-computer interaction legal dangers are a possibility. We performed an empirical investigation on law infringements on YouNow, Periscope, and Ustream. To this end, a content analysis of live-streams was applied. We developed a codebook based on literature regarding the usage of social media and on the conducted observations of streams. Based upon the most restrictive law (German law), researchers defined categories on potential law infringements while using SLSSs which were the following: copyright violations regarding music, video and picture, violation of personality rights with an additional focus on data protection and insults, committed road traffic acts, the violations of the sports broadcasting rights, as well as violations of the Health Insurance Portability and Accountability Act. In a time span of four weeks we observed 7,621 streams from SLSSs in Japan, Germany, and the U.S. We further examined if there are differences regarding law infringements between age groups, genders, motivations, contents, countries, and platforms.

Keywords: Social Live Streaming Service (SLSS) · Social Networking Service (SNS) · Periscope · Ustream · YouNow · Law infringement

1 Introduction: HCI Research on SLSSs

Social Live Streaming Services, in short SLSSs, allow their users to broadcast themselves to everyone who wants to watch, all over the world. The streamer films himself with a camera, depending on the service, either on his mobile phone or from a webcam. The spectator sees everything what the user does in real time. This could be watching him just talking or drawing a picture, attending a concert or whatever the person is doing at that moment. The user can also interact with the streamer while he is streaming [26].

Critics and newspapers warn parents of the potential dangers of SLSSs. One major concern is the disclosure of personal information [17]. It is impossible to know every viewer personally. There could be people who gain the trust of the victim and misuse the data. Furthermore, younger users feel they have control over the disclosed information on

© Springer International Publishing AG 2017
T. Tryfonas (Ed.): HAS 2017, LNCS 10292, pp. 567–585, 2017.
DOI: 10.1007/978-3-319-58460-7_40

social network services [1], which can potentially be harmful. People also stream while they are outside, which could result in personality rights violations (for example, when a third person is shown in the stream without her or his permission) [8]. Some people even stream themselves while driving, which could possibly be dangerous, since some streamers engage with their viewers, thus ignoring the traffic [31]. Even the spectators can commit criminal offences by bullying or sexually harassing the streamer [29].

A possible solution to avoid those dangers is to educate teenagers and children as well as their parents about potential threats of SLSSs. With this study, we will investigate if the concerns of the critics and parents are to be justified.

Figure 1 shows our research model. A stream generates content, which in turn can include potential law infringements. A platform is the basis to broadcast a stream, in our case it is an SLSS. The investigated SLSSs are Ustream, YouNow, and Periscope. Streams have (in most cases) an audience. In the center of the streaming process we find the streamer, who has a certain age, a gender, and a motivation to stream. A streamer broadcasts from a country, which in our study is Japan, Germany, or the Unites States of America. The data for the different aspects was collected by observation of live streams in a span of four weeks.

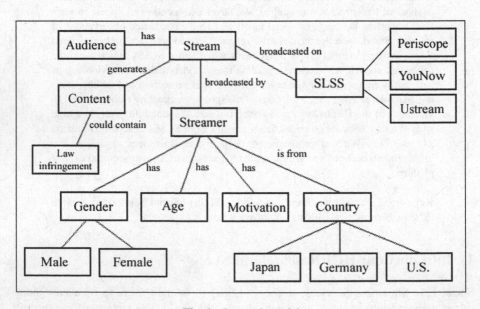

Fig. 1. Research model

A previously conducted study analyzed law infringements on YouNow in Germany and the U.S. [11]. On this basis, our analysis will expand the range of law infringements which will be evaluated and include another country, namely Japan, and two more services, Periscope and Ustream.

Different aspects of the law infringements on SLSSs will be investigated. According to the research model, our research questions (RQs) are:

- RQ1: Are there any law infringements on SLSSs and, if yes, which ones?
- RQ2: At what age do the users commit law infringements more often?
- RQ3: Are groups of people or rather single persons more likely to commit law infringements, and if it is a single person, which gender?
- RQ4: Are there relations between the motivation of a person to use an SLSS and law infringements?
- RQ5: In which content categories are the most law infringements committed?
- RQ6: Are there differences between the countries regarding the law infringements?
- RQ7: Are there differences between the SLSSs regarding the law infringements?

In the following section, the different SLSSs Periscope, Ustream, and YouNow will be introduced.

Periscope can be used on a mobile phone and has no website. It was developed by Kayvon Beypour and Joe Bernstein and acquired by Twitter, Inc. in 2015 [4]. Ten million people have an account on Periscope, which Twitter stated on August 2015 [25], 58% of these accounts belong to citizens of the United States. After downloading the Periscope App for iOS or Android, the user can sign up with his Twitter account or mobile phone number. The service is free to use. While being logged in, the user can zoom in on a map of the world and choose an active streamer he wants to watch. Then, the stream along with a little screen window to chat with the streamer appears (Fig. 2).

Fig. 2. Live stream on Periscope with its chat panel

After sending a chat message, it disappears in a few seconds. Other users cannot see all the text messages that were sent a few minutes before. By tapping on the phone, hearts will appear on the screen for the streamer, showing him appreciation of his content. The users can be followed by clicking on their profile. One can see the newest streams, the own followers, and the followed people. Especially Periscope was criticized because people use it to live-stream sport events, for which the sports industry tries to keep their distribution monopole [4]. This even led the service to be banned from several events [25]. However, it is hardly realizable to prosecute the offenders who violated copyright or personality rights [27]. Another aspect of Periscope is its adoption by professional journalists and usage for citizen journalism and civic streaming to live-broadcast breaking news, crisis, riots, or natural disasters [6, 25]. Periscope also has its place in neurosurgery and other science education. For instance, it can be used to live stream operations so that more students follow the procedures done by the neurosurgeon and thus supports the learning process. However, this way it is also possible to share critical protected health care information (PHI) [21]. This can be avoided, if the appropriate administrative, technical, and physical measures are taken to protect this information.

Ustream was founded in 2007 by Brad Hunstable, John Ham, and Gyula Feher and was acquired by IBM in 2016 [13]. 80 million viewers per month use it to see live videos or videos on demand [22]. Ustream offers not only its service for the public, but also for the employees of a company who bought Ustream Align, which can be used for internal video communication. Ustream also distinguishes between two kinds of broadcasting. The user can either choose the free "Basic" broadcast, which means the viewer will see ads before the stream starts and only 50 people per country can watch a broadcast, or the fee-based "Pro Broadcasting." By choosing "Pro Broadcasting" the streamer must pay between 99$ to 999$ per month, depending on what features he wants to add to his channel. This could be showing no ads before the stream starts, channel password protection, Facebook and Twitter integration and so on. A third category, "Enterprise," can also be booked. This includes custom plans which are especially adjusted to each individual business. The live-streams can be watched without being registered to the site, unlike the other two services. When creating a channel, the user gives his channel a title, chooses a category and writes a description or adds tags to make it easier for other people to find the channel. Each broadcast gets a new title. A chat panel is available while the stream is broadcasted; this way the spectators who are logged in are able to communicate with the streamer or other viewers (Fig. 3). Each broadcast shows the spectators that are watching the stream at the moment, total views, followers of the channel, and, whether the broadcast is a live-stream or was recorded a while ago. Since Ustream has a focus on more scientifically oriented content, it has the potential to be used in educational contexts [5].

YouNow as a website was founded in 2011 by Adi Sideman and since then an Android and iOS app is available. 100 million user sessions per month are happening on YouNow. The biggest user group, according to Alexa (as of January 2017) originates from the U.S. with 36.6%, followed by Germany with 12.3%, and Turkey with 6.6%. Teenagers and young adults are the most welcomed target group on YouNow [26]. When a user watches a stream, YouNow will grey out the screen after two minutes to make the viewer register to, or log in onto the site. To sign up for YouNow, one needs a Twitter, Facebook, Google+, or Instagram account. YouNow is free to use.

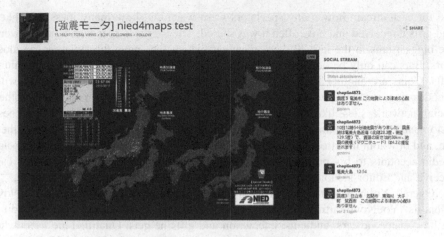

Fig. 3. Live stream on Ustream with its chat panel

When starting a stream, a hashtag needs to be assigned to the channel so other users can find it. On the left side of the website popular hashtags are displayed. Each broadcast shows the number of likes the streamer received for all his broadcasts combined, how often the current stream was shared, how many screenshots were taken, how long the stream is broadcasting and how many spectators are currently watching (Fig. 4). The user also has a level assigned to his or her profile, which is shown beside the user name. The level rises with activities on YouNow. This includes receiving gifts, likes, chatting, and getting new fans. Beside the broadcast panel a chat panel is available for logged in users, where the spectators and guests are shown, as well as the "#1 Fan" and "#2 Fan." After the stream ends, the streamer and other people who visit the streamers profile can

Fig. 4. Live stream on YouNow with its chat panel

see for each stream how many spectators were watching, how many messages, likes and gifts it received and how often it was shared. The user also sees which people were the biggest fans in the last 30 days, meaning, which fans gave the streamer the most Bars. Bars can only be bought with real money and can also be used to buy premium gifts. Coins are another form of currency on YouNow. Those can be obtained with broadcasting, watching, voting, and chatting, logging in or sharing YouNow on other social network sites like Facebook or Twitter. The profile also shows the best "Moments" of the streamer, some old streams, a discussion panel, fans and who they are, and of whom the streamer is a fan. Furthermore, the streamer can link all his social media accounts to his profile like Instagram, Facebook, or Twitter. A streamer can receive an "Editor's choice" mark on his profile to push his site into prominence.

Overall, YouNow puts a big emphasis on building a brand for a streamer. YouNow offers its "YouNow Partner Program," which means the streamer gets paid depending on how many viewers, audience interaction and gifts he gets. Qualified are users who garner an average of 500+ viewers per stream and conform to the Terms of Service and to the Digital Millennium Copyright Act Notification Guidelines. It is also possible to apply to the program with a YouTube, Vine, Twitter or Instagram account if one has 75,000+ Subscribers or Followers and 25,000+ average views per video on there. Some formal analyses of YouNow were conducted [28], in which it was stated that 93% of streaming sessions last less than 100 min. Furthermore, there are very few streams with a lot of spectators, 80% of the viewer traffic is garnered by 10% of the streamer. There are many streams that have very few spectators, 5% even have no viewers at all. Boredom, community acceptance, and the need to represent oneself are the main motivations to use YouNow [26].

Two other SLSSs were considered for this research but were disregarded because of different reasons. *Meerkat* was the competitor of Periscope but could not stand against it and has since then abandoned its live streaming service [32]. *Nico Nico Douga* is a popular streaming service in Japan, but due to the possibility that not enough streams could be investigated for Germany and the U.S., this service was also excluded from the study.

2   Law Infringements

In this section, the possible law infringements and how they could take place on SLSSs will be discussed. For the investigation, the German law was applied, because it is the strictest one of the three countries. An exception was made for the Copyrights regarding music. Here, the aspect of 'fair use' from the U.S. law was incorporated.

The German Act on *Copyright* and Related Rights (Copyright Act) states that only the author has the right to determine, if and how his work should be published. Furthermore, the author has the exclusive right of reproduction, the right of distribution and the right of exhibition of his work, even in non-material form, which includes broadcasting (Copyright Act § 15(II), § 20). Therefore, the live streamer needs the explicit permission to use the copyrighted content in a stream. An exception marks the case of reporting on current events, the reproduction and public distribution of those news (Copyright Act § 50). It is also permitted to quote other authors intellectual property as stated in § 51 of the German Copyright Act. For this study music in the background was handled as incidental work (Copyright Act §57). In the U.S., it is permitted to use copyrighted material in case of news reporting or commenting because it falls under the doctrine of "fair use" (§107 U.S. Copyright). It was only marked as a copyright violation if the music was clearly the content of the stream, meaning it was played without someone talking over it. Violation of copyright is a big problem on the internet and on SLSSs in particular [25]. It could be argued that violating the copyright act has, of course, legal consequences, but economically, it could potentially help to make a product more popular and even raise the number of sales [19].

The *Personality Rights* are established by Art 1 and Art 2 of the German Basic Law, which state that the human dignity shall be indefeasible. The personality rights are protected according to § 823 (I) of the German Civil Code (BGB). This also means that a person has the right to not be filmed or streamed to the public, even if they are only standing in the background. If this scenario was observed, it was marked as a potential personality rights violation. Also, further individual cases of personality rights violations were investigated. Those are data protection, and insults. According to § 1 of the Federal *Data Protection Act*, every person has the right to be protected against violations of their privacy resulting from mishandling of their personal data. This could include giving away information about the home address of a person, their phone number or reading private messages from someone without his or her consent. Streamers chat about varying kinds of topics so it is likely that this law may be violated. *Insults* will be punished with imprisonment up to one year or a fine, according to § 185 of the German Criminal Code. Insults happen in everybody's life and the internet is no exception. This potential law violation needs to be assessed in context of the respective stream, because an insult is not necessarily linked to a specific insulting word, but rather situation-dependent. For example, potentially insulting words can be used in a jokingly manner between friends and not be perceived as an insult.

Regarding *Road Traffic Act*, it is not permitted to hold or pick up a mobile phone or a car phone while operating a vehicle. Only exclusions are if the vehicle is standing with the motor turned off (§ 23 of the German Road Traffic Act). Since Periscope, YouNow and Ustream can be used on a mobile phone, it is possible that road traffic violations are committed.

Law does not regulate the *broadcasting of sport events*, but there are still rules and related laws that apply. But for all those laws, counter arguments could be exercised, which will not be listed here [24]. For this study, sports' broadcasting was marked as a potential law infringement if the stream was either broadcasted from a stadium via a mobile phone or streamed off a TV, with the following reasoning. For instance, if a person attends a Bundesliga soccer match of Borussia Mönchengladbach, he would be able to stream the match via his mobile phone. Now, following laws could potentially be applicable. Per §4 of the German law against unfair competition (UWG), someone is acting unfair, if he imitates the services of others and uses them for his own gain or impairs the gain of the services' owner. The organizer of the event could be unfairly impaired because he is not able to use it for his commercial gain in the same scope as he would be without someone else broadcasting the event (§ 3 UWG). Furthermore, every host can use his domestic authority to prohibit streaming of the event (German Civil Law Code § 823 Abs.1, § 1004, § 862), which also applies to the organizer of professional sport events. This grants them the security to receive the commercialization income. If the person streams a broadcast of the match off his TV, the act becomes a potential Copyright Violation (§ 87 UrhG), because the person streams material the TV station has paid for. The same rules do not apply to most amateur sports, though (German Federal Supreme Court, D. f. 10.28.2010 – I ZR 60/09). Edelmann [4] states that the sports industry could suffer losses because of live streaming. But on the other hand, this kind of behavior could also help to raise attention for an event.

The *Health Insurance Portability and Accountability Act* (HIPAA) regulates the use of information about the health status of a person in the U.S. That kind of information is protected under the Federal Data Protection Act in Germany, but we decided to observe violations of the data concerning health information separately since Periscope and maybe other SLSSs are used to live stream surgical operations.

The *age limit* is regulated by each service and their terms and conditions. YouNow sets its minimum age at 13, Ustream at 18. Periscope does not state a minimum age. The age limit was also marked if a minor was seen in the stream, even if the person was not the streamer.

3   Method

This section will describe how the empirical data was collected. A team of researchers assessed, evaluated and compared SLSSs' users' streaming behavior as well as the content of a stream and motives of a streamer to produce a live stream.

The empirical procedure of the content analysis was implemented as follows. A codebook [16] was developed, which was based on already existing literature regarding the usage of social media in order to create standardized data sets. Two different approaches were applied to ensure a qualitative content analysis with a high reliability. The directed approach was implemented with assorted literature to get guidance for the research categories. Additionally, the conventional approach via observation was used to get a general idea of what people stream about [12].

Several steps are necessary to guarantee a good outcome while analyzing the content. According to McMillan [23], the steps are: first, a draft of the research questions or hypotheses needs to be done. This is followed by selecting a sample. Step three is to define categories which include a period; in this case it was a time span of four weeks. Content units need to be identified as well as facets that are necessary for the research question. A spread sheet with four different categories was generated from this. The categories are:

Content. For the content of the stream, a tally chart was made. The different kinds of streaming content were: to chat; make music; share information; news; fitness; sport event; gaming; animals; entertainment media; spirituality; draw/paint a picture; 24/7; science, technology, and medicine (STM); comedy; advertisement; nothing; slice of life; politics; nature; food; business information.

Potential Law Infringements and Violations of Terms and Conditions. Norm entries were used for the possible law infringements and violations of the terms and conditions. Those were: copyright violations regarding music, video, and picture (Pic.); violation of personality rights (Pe.Ri.) with an additional focus on data protection (D.P.), and insults; committed road traffic acts (R.T.A.); the violation of the sports broadcasting rights (S.B.R.); Health Insurance Portability and Accountability Act (HIPAA) violations. For the violation of terms and conditions the contempt of the age limit (Age Li.) was investigated.

Motivation. A tally chart was used for the motives of the streamer [15, 18, 20], which were: boredom [26]; self-expression [33]; to reach a specific group [3, 10]; to make money; need to belong; to become a star [2, 9]; socializing [1]; relationship management [30]; need to communicate [3, 14]; loneliness [2]; hobby; sense of mission [9]; fun; exchange of view; self-improvement; troll; no comment. "No comment" was marked if the streamer did not state a motivation or no person could be reached via chat, for example if an animal was shown or a 24/7 stream (e.g. from a webcam) was broadcasted.

Formalities. Norm entries were used for the formalities. Those were: gender (male, female, group, other); age of the streamer.

The data about the streams was collected from three different countries, namely Germany, Japan, and the United States of America, to see if there were differences in distant cultural areas. To ensure that the streams originated from those countries the declaration of the country for a broadcast on each platform was checked for every stream. Additionally, the data collectors had the required language skills for those countries.

The fourth step is to train the coders to ensure the reliability of their coding skills. Twelve research teams consisting of two persons per team were formed. The teams were evenly distributed between the three countries. The last step is the analysis and interpretation of the data [23]. Every coder received a spread sheet and coded the data in it when any of the investigated aspects was applicable to the stream.

For collecting the data, the 'four eyes principle' was applied. Each stream was observed simultaneously but independently by two people for two to a maximum of ten minutes. Communication always happened between the two observers to guarantee a 100% intercoder reliability, which sometimes resulted in discussions, but a consensus was always reached. Usually the streams were observed in two phases. First, the stream was watched and the data collected. In phase two, if some aspects were not clear, for example the motivation of the streamer, the streamer was asked via the chat system of the service.

The streams were not recorded, since this would require an agreement with the streamer, which would not be always possible, as not every streamer communicates with the viewer. Recording without streamer's consent would result in personal right violations. Some streamers even denied the permission to record them.

In the end, a data set of a total of 7,621 streams in a time span of four weeks, from April 26 to May 24, 2016, was collected. The results of those streams were statistically analyzed and compared following the questions of our research model.

4 Results: Law Infringements on SLSSs

4.1 Law Infringements (RQ1)

In the following section the general results (RQ1) and the findings on law infringements regarding different generations (RQ2), genders (RQ3), motivations (RQ4), content categories (RQ5), countries (RQ6), and services (RQ7) will be examined. Total 1,364 out of 7,621 streams were identified with potential law infringements and breaches of terms and conditions. This means that 17.9% of all streams are concerned. The most potentially violated law is the Copyright Act, especially regarding music (53.5%) and videos (25.4%), followed by personality rights violations (9.2%) (Table 1), which was observed in another study as well [11]. Since music was only treated as incidental work, the total number of potential infringements as well as the number of music copyright violations measured on the German Copyright Act is potentially even higher, because it was observed that nearly every streamer had music playing in the background while broadcasting.

Table 1. Distribution of law infringements on SLSSs (all streams: N = 7,621; streams infringing law: N = 1,364)

Infringement	Amount	Relative Frequency
N	1,364	100.0%
Copyright – Music	730	53.5%
Copyright – Video	347	25.4%
Personality Rights	125	9.2%
Sports Broadcasting Rights	50	3.7%
Road Traffic Act	31	2.3%
Insult	27	2.0%
Data Protection	23	1.7%
Age Limit	19	1.4%
Copyright – Picture	12	0.9%
HIPAA	-	-

4.2 Law Infringements by Generations (RQ2)

The comparison of different generations regarding the potential law infringements first requires to define the concerned age groups. Generation Z (Gen. Z) defines the youngest users born after 1996. Generation Y (Gen Y.) was born between 1980 and 1996, Generation X (Gen. X) includes people born between 1960 and 1980. Baby Boomers (Baby B.) were born between 1946 and 1960 [7].

When looking at the distribution of the potential law infringements and breaches of the terms and conditions, the percentage of those infringements relative to the number of streams per generation, rises from Gen. Z (15.7%) to Gen. Y (16.3%), but then declines and reaches the lowest percentage with the Baby Boomers (12.1%).

Table 2. Distribution of law infringements by generation (N = 7,621)

	Gen. Z	Gen. Y	Gen. X	Baby B.
N	1,821	2,553	493	33
Infringement amount per generation	285	415	70	4
Relative frequency of infringements per generation	15.7%	16.3%	14.2%	12.1%
Infringement (N = 1,364)				
Copyright – Music	77.2%	77.6%	62.9%	50.0%
Copyright – Video	3.9%	4.3%	4.3%	25.0%
Personality Rights	5.3%	7.5%	10.0%	25.0%
Sports Broadcasting Rights	0.4%	2.9%	2.9%	-
Road Traffic Act	0.7%	2.9%	12.9%	-
Insult	3.9%	3.1%	4.3%	-
Data Protection	3.9%	0.7%	1.4%	-
Age Limit	4.9%	0.5%	-	-
Copyright – Picture	-	0.5%	1.4%	-
HIPAA	-	-	-	-

Even though older generations are usually less tech-savvy than younger ones, they appear to be more cautious when it comes to law infringements (Table 2). Younger people growing up with the internet perceive it as having no limitations or regulations, so they may be more prone to ignore the legal restrictions. The most potentially violated law for all generations is the copyright regarding music. Furthermore, all generations were responsible for personality rights violations. This shows that sensibility for this matter does not increase with age. Especially for Gen. Z (5.3%) and Gen. Y (7.5%) personality right is the second most violated law. Generation Z as compared to other generations, exhibits a high number of data protection violations (3.9%), which demonstrates that some teenagers act more careless than the other generations when it comes to the personal data of other people. A remarkable result is the relative frequency of violations of the road traffic act of Gen. X (12.9%), which is much higher than the values for all other generations.

4.3   Law Infringements by Groups and Gender (RQ3)

The frequency of the law infringements per groups and gender were split in different categories. First, a distinction was made between streams in which people streamed themselves (People), and streams without a streamer (No Person). For example, if an animal or a TV show was broadcasted. The category "People" was further split into groups, single male, and single female streamers.

The overall percentage of the potential violations does not differ by more than 2% between the genders and groups (Table 3). Nonetheless, groups were more often responsible for potential violations than single male and female streamers. The streams in which no person could be seen had the highest share of potential law infringements.

Table 3. Distribution of law infringements among people (group, single male, single female) and streams without people (N = 7,621)

	No Person	People	Group	Male	Female
N	2,036	5,585	1,072	2,759	1,754
Infringement amount per group/gender	458	906	186	450	270
Relative frequency of infringements per group/ gender	22.5%	16.2%	17.4%	16.3%	15.4%
Infringement (N = 1,364)					
Copyright – Music	18.1%	71.4%	58.1%	71.6%	80.4%
Copyright – Video	63.5%	6.2%	11.3%	5.8%	3.3%
Personality Rights	9.6%	8.9%	16.1%	8.0%	5.6%
Sports Broadcasting Rights	5.9%	2.5%	1.6%	4.0%	0.7%
Road Traffic Act	-	3.4%	0.5%	5.6%	1.9%
Insult	-	3.0%	4.8%	2.7%	2.2%
Data Protection	0.9%	2.1%	4.8%	0.9%	2.2%
Age Limit	-	2.1%	2.7%	1.1%	3.3%
Copyright – Picture	2.0%	0.3%	-	0.4%	0.4%
HIPAA	-	-	-	-	-

First, the streams for which a gender (including groups) and for which no gender could be determined will be compared. Obviously, all age limit violations, road traffic acts and insults can only happen when groups, men or women were seen. When it comes to potential copyright infringements, music was more often played when people were streaming (71.4%) and videos when no streaming person could be determined (63.5%), which could be explained with the rather socially motivated reasons for people to listen to music rather than streaming videos while they are broadcasting themselves. Potential data protection violations happened more often when people were streaming (2.1%) than when no gender could be determined (0.9%).

Now, the streams for which a gender or a group could be determined will be compared. Overall, groups have the highest percentage of violations in five categories, namely the age limit, copyright regarding videos, data protection, insults, and personality rights. Groups may be more careless than a single streamer when it comes to regulations on the internet, because people often feel more protected in a group. Another explanation could be peer-pressure, making children feel the need to ignore the age limit and sign up, for example, on YouNow. It was observed that groups were more often outside than single persons, which could explain the high percentage of personality rights violations in contrast to single men and single women streaming more from inside. Men potentially commit more road traffic acts and violate sports broadcasting rights more often than women and groups. Women have the highest percentage of potential violations in the music copyright category. Lin and Lu [18] observed that women care about the opinion of the members using the SNSs whereas men do not. This could be one of the reasons why women commit the least law infringements.

4.4 Law Infringements by Streamers' Motivations to Stream (RQ4)

In the following, the law infringements and the streamer's motive will be further analyzed. Since one streamer could name more than one motivation to stream, the overall number of infringements will be higher as well. If we were able to correctly identify the streamer's motivation to stream (Table 4), the highest absolute number of law infringements (with 311 cases out of 1,659; 18.7%) was committed while the streamer was bored, which was followed by the streamers need to socialize (221 cases out of 1,245; 17.8%). The highest relative frequency of violations was observed when the motivation of the streamer was to make money (137 cases out of 479; 28.6%), followed by the streamers need to belong with 23.7% or 74 cases out of 312. The third highest percentage of infringements (23.0%, 43 cases out of 187) was observed when the streamer felt lonely.

Table 4. Distribution of law infringements by motivations (N = 7,621); Pe.Ri = Personality Rights, S.B.R. = Sports Broadcasting Rights, R.T.A. = Road Traffic Act, D.P. = Data Protection, Age Li. = Age Limit. Pic. = Copyright Picture

Motivation	N	Offenses	Rel. freq.	Law infringement								
				Music	Video	Pe.Ri.	S.B.R.	R.T.A.	Insult	D.P.	Age Li.	Pic.
Money	479	137	28.6%	11.0%	73.7%	8.8%	5.1%	-	-	0.7%	0.7%	-
Need to belong	312	74	23.7%	73.0%	5.4%	2.7%	-	4.0%	2.7%	2.7%	9.5%	-
Loneliness	187	43	23.0%	62.8%	2.3%	20.9%	-	7.0%	-	2.3%	4.7%	-
Troll	84	19	22.6%	31.6%	-	10.5%	-	-	36.8%	21.0%	-	-
No Comment	2,245	451	20.1%	35.5%	39.9%	11.1%	7.3%	2.0%	2.0%	1.1%	0.2%	0.9%
Fun	1,022	195	19.1%	76.4%	5.1%	10.3%	-	3.1%	1.0%	1.5%	2.0%	0.5%
Boredom	1,659	311	18.7%	74.9%	4.2%	8.7%	0.3%	2.9%	3.2%	1.3%	3.5%	1.0%
Self-Expression	840	152	18.1%	80.3%	1.3%	8.5%	-	5.9%	2.0%	-	2.0%	-
Socializing	1,245	221	17.8%	72.8%	3.2%	9.1%	-	5.9%	2.7%	1.8%	3.6%	0.9%
Relationship mgmt	270	48	17.8%	75.0%	-	6.2%	-	4.2%	4.2%	4.2%	2.1%	4.2%
Sense of mission	331	52	15.7%	36.5%	32.7%	17.3%	1.9%	3.9%	3.9%	-	3.9%	-
Reach specific group	1,163	175	15.0%	55.4%	18.3%	12.0%	3.4%	1.7%	0.6%	2.9%	0.5%	5.1%
Need to communicate	1,112	166	14.9%	62.7%	5.4%	12.6%	4.8%	3.0%	3.0%	5.4%	1.8%	1.2%
Hobby	676	100	14.8%	69.0%	9.0%	9.0%	1.0%	3.0%	-	-	1.0%	8.0%
Become a star	301	42	13.9%	76.2%	2.4%	11.9%	-	-	4.8%	2.4%	2.4%	-
Exchange of view	495	68	13.7%	55.9%	-	26.5%	1.5%	4.4%	7.3%	2.9%	1.5%	-
Self-Improvement	245	31	12.6%	87.1%	-	9.7%	-	3.2%	-	-	-	-

For music copyright infringements, the motivations with high percentages seem to be socially motivated (boredom, socializing, fun, need to belong), whereas videos seem to be broadcasted because of the desire to make money or because the streamer has a sense of mission. Especially exchanges of view provoke infringements of personality rights (26.5%). Some children seem to ignore the age limit (9.5%) because they have a need to belong. The highest relative frequencies for music copyright infringements are self-improvement (87.1%), self-expression (80.3%), and the desire to become a star (76.2%). Data protection violation has the highest percentage if the streamer was a troll (21.0%), which makes it potentially dangerous since trolls usually want to harm others.

4.5   Law Infringements by Content Categories (RQ5)

In the following, the law infringements and the stream content categories will be further analyzed. Since one stream can produce more than one content category, the overall number of infringements will be higher. Since chatting was the most produced content overall (3,349 streams), the number of infringements will be high as well (556 streams; 16.6%) (Table 5). But the highest relative frequency happened in the entertainment media category with 51.2%, which also had the second highest number of infringements overall (458 cases). Remarkable is the fact that even though there were four times as many streams in the "to chat" than in the "entertainment media" category, the number of infringements is just about 20% higher. The second highest percentage of violations (27.9%) happened in the category drawing, with 17 cases out of 61. The category sport event had the third highest relative frequency (25.6%) with 77 cases out of 301.

Table 5. Distribution of law infringements by content categories (N = 7,621); Pe.Ri = Personality Rights, S.B.R. = Sports Broadcasting Rights, R.T.A. = Road Traffic Act, D.P. = Data Protection, Age Li. = Age Limit. Pic. = Copyright Picture

Content	N	Offenses	Rel. freq.	Law infringement								
				Music	Video	Pe.Ri.	S.B.R.	R.T.A.	Insult	D.P.	Age Li.	Pic.
Entertainment media	894	458	51.2%	40.8%	56.1%	0.7%	0.4%	-	0.4%	0.7%	0.4%	0.4%
Drawing	61	17	27.9%	88.2%	-	-	-	-	-	-	-	11.8%
Sport event	301	77	25.6%	23.4%	13.0%	3.9%	58.4%	-	1.3%	-	-	-
24 / 7	1,151	279	24.2%	28.3%	54.1%	12.6%	1.1%	-	2.1%	1.8%	-	-
Gaming	415	98	23.6%	30.6%	56.1%	2.0%	-	-	3.1%	-	2.0%	6.1%
Slice of life	1,084	227	20.9%	58.6%	2.6%	23.8%	0.9%	6.2%	2.2%	4.0%	1.3%	0.4%
Make music	734	141	19.2%	87.9%	2.8%	2.8%	-	3.6%	0.7%	0.7%	1.4%	-
To chat	3,349	556	16.6%	77.0%	2.7%	7.7%	0.2%	4.7%	3.2%	1.3%	2.7%	0.5%
Advertisement	222	34	15.3%	82.3%	2.9%	-	5.9%	-	2.9%	2.9%	-	2.9%
Share information	1,299	195	15.0%	69.7%	2.6%	12.8%	0.5%	2.6%	1.5%	8.2%	1.5%	0.5%
Fitness	110	16	14.5%	50.0%	6.2%	31.2%	-	6.2%	-	-	6.2%	-
Comedy	116	15	12.9%	40.0%	46.7%	6.7%	-	-	-	6.7%	-	-
Food	176	22	12.5%	77.2%	4.6%	13.6%	-	-	4.6%	-	-	-
Nature	421	43	10.2%	20.9%	2.3%	67.4%	-	4.7%	2.3%	2.3%	-	-
STM	72	7	9.7%	42.9%	57.1%	-	-	-	-	-	-	-
Business information	105	10	9.5%	60.0%	10.0%	10.0%	-	-	-	20.0%	-	-
Politics	105	8	7.6%	50.0%	25.0%	12.5%	-	-	-	12.5%	-	-
Spirituality	239	16	6.7%	68.7%	-	18.7%	-	6.3%	6.3%	-	-	-
News	261	17	6.5%	58.8%	11.8%	23.5%	5.9%	-	-	-	-	-
Animals	516	20	3.9%	65.0%	15.0%	20.0%	-	-	-	-	-	-

When entertainment media is broadcasted, one can expect copyright violations in both, music (40.8%) as well as videos (56.1%). In the sport event category, every second streamer (58.4%) ignored broadcasting rights. Potential personality rights violations were observed when the streamer was outside (nature, slice of life, animals, and fitness), for example, when he or she accidentally streamed other people being in the background.

4.6   Law Infringements by the Streamer's Country (RQ6)

Germany had the highest absolute as well as relative numbers of potential law violations with overall 614 out of 2,586 streams. This means that 23.7% of all streams in
Germany were concerned. Japan has the second most potential violations with 390
streams out of 1,919 (20.3%), and the U.S the least with only 360 out of 3,116 streams
(11.6%).

There are recognizable differences between the three countries (Table 6). Concerning relative frequencies of law infringements, music copyright, age limit and data
protection was violated more often in the U.S. compared to the other two countries. In
Germany, video copyright violations have an over twice as large relative frequency as
Japan and the U.S. Sports broadcasting rights were more often potentially violated in
Germany as well. In Japan, no one was insulted, the age limit was not ignored, and the
data protection act was never violated. However, they committed a comparably high
percentage of potential personality rights violations, committed the most road traffic
acts and showed the highest number of copyrighted pictures.

Table 6. Distribution of law infringements by countries (N = 7,621)

	Germany	Japan	U.S.
N	2,586	1,919	3,116
Infringement amount per coun-try	614	390	360
Relative frequency of infringe-ments per country	23.7%	20.3%	11.6%
Infringement (N = 1,364)			
Copyright – Music	44.0%	54.4%	68.9%
Copyright – Video	43.0%	12.8%	9.2%
Personality Rights	2.0%	23.6%	5.8%
Sports Broadcasting Rights	5.5%	2.8%	1.4%
Road Traffic Act	1.1%	3.6%	2.8%
Insult	2.4%	-	3.3%
Data Protection	0.8%	-	5.0%
Age Limit	1.1%	-	3.3%
Copyright – Picture	-	2.9%	0.3%
HIPAA	-	-	-

4.7   Law Infringements by SLSSs (RQ7)

Ustream had the highest relative frequency of observed law violations with 20.6% (553
out of 2,681 streams), followed by Periscope with 18.7% (546 out of 2,927 streams),
and YouNow with 13.2% (265 out of 2,013 streams). We were able to identify differences among the platforms in relation to the potential law infringements (Table 7).

Concerning music copyright violations, there is a clear ranking: on YouNow, you
find the highest number of relative frequency (81.5%), followed by Periscope (69.7%),
and Ustream (only 24.8%). The ranking of SLSSs by video copyright infringements is

Table 7. Distribution of law infringements by SLSSs (N = 7,621)

	Ustream	Periscope	YouNow
N	2,681	2,927	2,013
Infringement amount per SLSS	553	546	265
Relative frequency of infringements per SLSS	20.6%	18.7%	13.2%
Infringement (N = 1,364)			
Copyright – Music	24.8%	69.1%	81.5%
Copyright – Video	57.0%	4.6%	2.6%
Personality Rights	9.9%	11.7%	2.3%
Sports Broadcasting Rights	4.9%	3.8%	0.8%
Road Traffic Act	-	4.9%	1.5%
Insult	0.2%	3.1%	3.4%
Data Protection	1.6%	2.0%	1.1%
Age Limit	0.2%	-	6.8%
Copyright – Picture	1.5%	0.7%	-
HIPAA	-	-	-

reverse: Ustream (57.0%) followed by Periscope (4.6%), and YouNow (2.6%). We could observe personality rights violations primarily on Periscope and Ustream, but seldom on YouNow. Problems with sports broadcasting rights occur mainly on Periscope and Ustream as well, while on YouNow there are more insults and age limit violations. The last fact is not surprising since many very young streamers use You-Now [26]. Since Periscope was used outside more often than the other two services, the most potential infringements of road traffic acts happened on this platform.

5   Discussion

The study showed that there are indeed many potential law infringements happening on SLSSs. Furthermore, the number of those infringements could possibly be even higher since music was handled as incidental work and many streams were observed in which music was playing in the background.

The question arises, should parents and critics be concerned? Yes and no. It depends on where they look at and what they are worried about. First, Generation Z had the second highest percentage of potential law infringements in contrast to the other generations. If parents are concerned about their children committing copyright act violations, then they are right, since 77% of all potential infringements committed by Generation Z were related to it. But there is another, more concerning aspect about the law infringements committed by Generation Z. They committed 4% of data protection violations, which was three times higher than for the other generations. This clearly shows that the younger streamers do not act sensible when the data of other people is concerned and which, potentially, can be very harmful. Furthermore, 4% of all potential violations of Generation Z were related to insults, which is the highest percentage in contrast to the other generations as well. Those insults could potentially be linked to serious bullying and have traumatic consequences for the victim. Should parents have a special focus on a specific platform or even country? Interestingly, yes. In Japan, not one instance of data protection violation or insult happened, regardless of generation, so the parents do not need to worry about those potential infringements there. Unfortunately, potential data protection violations happened on all three platforms. It is advisable to help children understand that they need to act more careful with the personal data of other people.

Other general observations can be made about the video copyright and sports broadcasting rights. Those potential violations usually happened when no age or gender of the streamer could be determined, meaning, anonymous people committed them. If a person could be contacted, they usually stated that the motivation to broadcast entertainment media or sport events was to make money. Especially on Ustream and in Germany a high amount of video copyright violations was observed. Even though Periscope was criticized for live streaming sport events, Ustream has a higher percentage of streamers doing so than Periscope.

When the personality rights are concerned, which is another problematic factor on SLSSs, as this was observed by another study [11] and witnessed in this research as well, every generation and gender or group was responsible for this kind of potential violation. On Periscope, 12% of all violations and 10% on Ustream were related to personality rights. But the execution and how they happened was different on the platforms. On Periscope, the violations were committed when the streamer (or group) just wanted to chat because he was bored and streamed while he was outside with people in the background. This kind of streaming was especially popular in Japan, where the streamer broadcasted himself being in nature or when he was out with friends. On Ustream it was not a person, but a fixed camera which broadcasted a city or nature 24/7. Therefore, the potential violations on Periscope happened because of social reasons. On Ustream there is presumably no person having an eye on the stream all the time. Periscope is especially designed for mobile phones so it is not surprising that the highest percentage of this violation happened on there.

This study's approach is a quantitative one. In further research, it should be completed by qualitative interviews with streamers on their awareness of law infringements while streaming. Only users on YouNow, Periscope and Ustream were studied; other general SLSSs as Nico Nico Douga, YouTube Live or Facebook Live have to be investigated in the future as well.

References

1. Beldad, A.D., Koehorst, R.: It's not about the risks, I'm just used to doing it: disclosure of personal information on Facebook among adolescent dutch users. In: Meiselwitz, G. (ed.) SCSM 2015. LNCS, vol. 9182, pp. 185–195. Springer, Cham (2015). doi:10.1007/978-3-319-20367-6_19
2. Brandtzæg, P.B., Heim, J.: Why people use social networking sites. In: Ozok, A.A., Zaphiris, P. (eds.) OCSC 2009. LNCS, vol. 5621, pp. 143–152. Springer, Heidelberg (2009). doi:10.1007/978-3-642-02774-1_16

3. Cheung, C.M.K., Chiu, P.Y., Lee, M.K.O.: Online social networks: why do students use Facebook? Comput. Hum. Behav. **27**, 1337–1343 (2011). doi:10.1016/j.chb.2010.07.028

4. Edelmann, M.: From meerkat to periscope: does intellectual property law prohibit the live streaming of commercial sporting events? Colum. J.L. Arts **39**(4), 469–495 (2015)

5. Educause Learning Initiative: 7 Things You Should Know About Ustream (2008). https://library.educause.edu

6. Fichet, E., Robinson, J., Dailey, D., Starbird, K.: Eyes on the ground: emerging practices in Periscope use during crisis events. In: Tapia, A., Antunes, P., Bañuls, V.A., Moore, K., Porto, J. (eds.) ISCRAM 2016, Conference Proceedings – 13th International Conference on Information Systems for Crisis Response and Management, pp. 1–10. Federal University of Rio de Janeiro, Rio de Janeiro (2016)

7. Fietkiewicz, K.J., Lins, E., Baran, K.S., Stock, W.S.: Inter-generational comparison of social media use: investigating the online behavior of different generational cohorts. In: Proceedings of the 49th Hawaii International Conference on System Sciences, pp. 3829–3838. IEEE Press, Washington (2016). doi:10.1109/HICSS.2016.477

8. Görmann, M.: YouNow: Wo sich Teenies über Spanner freuen (2015). http://www.rosenheim24.de

9. Greenwood, D.N.: Fame, Facebook, and Twitter: how attributed about fame predict frequency and nature of social media use. Psychol. Pop. Media Cult. **2**(4), 222–236 (2013). doi:10.1037/ppm0000013

10. Hollenbaugh, E.E., Ferris, A.L.: Facebook self-disclosure: examine the role of traits, social cohesion, and motives. Comput. Hum. Behav. **30**, 50–58 (2013)

11. Honka, A., Frommelius, N., Mehlem, A., Tolles, J.N., Fietkiewicz, K.J.: How safe is YouNow? An empirical study on possible law infringements in Germany and the United States. JMSS **1**(1), 1–17 (2015)

12. Hsieh, H.F., Shannon, S.E.: Three approaches to qualitative content analysis. QHR **15**(9), 1277–1288 (2005)

13. Kehn, D.: IBM Acquires Ustream (2016). https://www.ibm.com

14. Kim, D., Kim, J.-H., Nam, Y.: How does industry use social networking sites? An analysis of corporate dialogic uses of Facebook, Twitter, YouTube, and LinkedIn by industry type. Qual. Quant. **48**(5), 2605–2614 (2014)

15. Kim, Y., Sohn, D., Choi, S.M.: Cultural differences in motivations for using social networking sites: a comparative study of American and Korean college students. Comput. Hum. Behav. **22**, 365–372 (2010)

16. Krippendorff, K.: Content Analysis: An Introduction to Its Methodology, 2nd edn. Sage, Thousand Oaks (2004)

17. Kühl, E.: Seht her, ich bin beliebt! (2015). http://www.zeit.de

18. Lin, K.-Y., Lu, H.P.: Why people use social networking sites: an empirical study integrating network externalities and motivation theory. Comput. Hum. Behav. **27**, 1152–1161 (2011)

19. Linde, F., Stock, W.G.: Information Markets. A Strategic Guideline for the I-Commerce. De Gruyter Saur, Berlin, New York (2011). doi:10.1002/asi.22619

20. Marwick, A.E., Boyd, D.: I tweet honestly, I tweet passionately: Twitter users, context collapse, and the imagined audience. New Media Soc. **13**(1), 114–133 (2010)

21. Maugeri, R., Giammalva, R.G., Iacopino, D.G.: On the shoulders of giants, with a smartphone: periscope in neurosurgery. World Neurosurg. **92**, 569–570 (2016). doi:10.1016/j.wneu.2016.03.019

22. McLain, T.: IBM cloud video services: a revolution in streaming video (2016). http://www.ustream.tv

23. McMillan, S.J.: The microscope and the moving target: the challenge of applying content analysis to the World Wide Web. JMCQ **77**(1), 80–98 (2000). doi:10.1177/107769900 007700107

24. Pötters, S.: EUGH-Urteil zu Exklusivlizenzen für TV-Sportübertragungen. JuraExamen. Online Zeitschrift für Jurastudium, Staatsexamen und Referendariat, 21 October 2011. http://www.juraexamen.info

25. Rugg, A., Burroughs, B.: Periscope, live-streaming and mobile video culture. In: Geo-blocking and Global Video Culture (Theory on Demand; 18), pp. 64–73. Institute of Network Culture, Amsterdam (2016)

26. Scheibe, K., Fietkiewicz, K.J., Stock, W.G.: Information behavior on social live streaming services. JISTP **4**(2), 06–20 (2016). doi:10.1633/JISTaP.2016.4.2.1

27. Stewart, D.R., Littau, J.: Up, Periscope: mobile streaming video technologies, privacy in public, and the right to record. JMCQ **93**(2), 312–331 (2016)

28. Stohr, D., Li, T., Wilk, S., Santini, S., Effelsberg, W.: An analysis of the YouNow live streaming platform. In: IEEE 40th Local Computer Networks Conference Workshops, pp. 673–679. IEEE, New York (2015). doi:10.1109/LCNW.2015.7365913

29. Tempesta, E.: New live streaming app Periscope is already on its way to becoming a parent's worst nightmare following numerous reports of sexual harassment and bullying. Daily Mail/MailOnline, 3 April 2015. http://www.dailymail.co.uk

30. Tosun, L.P.: Motives for Facebook use and expressing "true self" on the internet. Comput. Hum. Behav. **28**, 1510–1517 (2012)

31. Vallance, C.: The danger with streaming and driving. BBC Magazine, 31 March 2016. http://www.bbc.com

32. Wagner, K.: Meerkat is ditching the livestream – and chasing a video social network instead. Recode, 4 March 2016. http://www.recode.net

33. Zota, V.: Me, myself & YouNow. YouNow – finde das Talent im Heuhaufen. c't **13**, 81 (2015)

HCI and Privacy Issues

Privacy Decision-Making in the Digital Era: A Game Theoretic Review

Kallia Anastasopoulou[1(✉)], Spyros Kokolakis[1], and Panagiotis Andriotis[2]

[1] Department of Information and Communication Systems Engineering,
University of the Aegean, Samos, Greece
{k.anastasopoulou,sak}@aegean.gr
[2] Cyber Security Research Unit, University of the West of England,
Frenchay Campus, Bristol BS16 1QY, UK
panagiotis.andriotis@uwe.ac.uk

Abstract. Information privacy is constantly negotiated when people interact with enterprises and government agencies via the Internet. In this context, all relevant stakeholders take privacy-related decisions. Individuals, either as consumers buying online products and services or citizens using e-government services, face decisions with regard to the use of online services, the disclosure of personal information, and the use of privacy enhancing technologies. Enterprises make decisions regarding their investments on policies and technologies for privacy protection. Governments also decide on privacy regulations, as well as on the development of e-government services that store and process citizens' personal information. Motivated by the aforementioned issues and challenges, we focus on aspects of privacy decision-making in the digital era and address issues of individuals' privacy behavior. We further discuss issues of strategic privacy decision-making for online service providers and e-government service providers.

Keywords: Information privacy · Decision-making · Human behavior · Strategic interactions · Game theory

1 Introduction

Information privacy is a multi-disciplinary and crucial topic for understanding the digital world [4,65]. Information privacy mainly relates to personal data stored in information systems, such as medical records, financial data, photos, and videos. In this research, we focus on online privacy where personal data are shared over the Internet.

Current research on information privacy highlights issues such as privacy concerns of online users [8,17,74], the so-called "privacy paradox", referring to the inconsistency of users' privacy-related behavior and their privacy concerns [40,44,81]. Another main strand of research includes Privacy-Enhancing Technologies (PETs) [58].

In the information age, privacy has become a luxury to maintain as data privacy can be violated on the internet through technical tools such as cookies

© Springer International Publishing AG 2017
T. Tryfonas (Ed.): HAS 2017, LNCS 10292, pp. 589–603, 2017.
DOI: 10.1007/978-3-319-58460-7_41

or tracking online activities [11,57]. However, the rapid growth of the Internet and what it has brought to people's lives (especially during the past ten years) are truly astonishing. The Internet makes people's lives incredibly convenient and websites will probably remain an important communication channel, along with direct messaging applications.

Privacy, however, is not just an Information Technology (IT) problem, although it could be in many cases. Many psychological, social and cultural factors play a significant role in the field of privacy. Human behavior is a considerable variable as individuals interact with others in online environments exchanging private information and making decisions about their privacy [15].

The variety of information that individuals share online can potentially characterize them [13,54]. The mechanisms that individuals use when making online sharing decisions are the main focus of this research.

The individual decision process with respect to privacy is affected by multiple factors. Incomplete information bounded rationality, and systematic psychological deviations are considerable variables that influence individual's privacy behavior [2,10]. First, incomplete information refers to privacy decision-making, where third parties share personal information about an individual without her being part of the transaction. How personal information will be used might be known only to a subset of the parties making decisions (information asymmetry); thus, risk could be hard to calculate, as it may dependent on unknown random variables. Benefits and costs associated with privacy intrusions and protection are complex, multifaceted, and context-specific. They are frequently bundled with other products and services (e.g., a search engine query can prompt the desired result but can also give observers information about the searcher's interests), and they are often realized only after privacy violations have taken place. They can be monetary but also immaterial and, thus, difficult to quantify.

Second, individuals would be unable to act in an optimal way, even if they had access to complete information. Especially when individuals have to manage huge volumes of data and make decisions about the protection or disclosure of personal information, bounded rationality limits their ability to process and memorize all their actions. They rely on simplified irrational models, strategies, and heuristics [6].

Third, individuals might deviate from the rational strategy, even if they had access to complete information and could successfully calculate optimization strategies for their privacy-sensitive decisions. A vast body of economics and psychology literature has revealed several forms of systematic psychological deviations from rationality that affect individual decision-making [36,76]. For example, in addition to their cognitive and computational bounds, individuals are influenced by motivational limitations and misrepresentations of personal utility. Research in psychology also documents how individuals mispredict their own future preferences or draw inaccurate conclusions from past choices [5]. In addition, individuals often suffer from self-control problems, in particular, the tendency to trade off costs and benefits in ways that damage their future utility in favor of immediate gratification. Individuals' behavior can also be guided by social preferences or norms, such as fairness or altruism. Many of these deviations apply naturally to privacy-sensitive scenarios. Any of these factors might influence decision-making behavior inside and outside the privacy domain, although not all factors need to always be present. Empirical evidence of their influence on privacy decision-making would not necessarily imply that individuals act recklessly or make choices against their own best interest. It would, however, imply bias and limitations in the individual decision process that we should consider when designing privacy public policy and PETs.

2   Privacy Trade-Offs in the Digital Age

What are the privacy implications of behavioral decision-making in online transactions? To answer this question we should notice what privacy stands for. For decades a long-lasting debate exists among scholars to define exactly what that right entails [61]. Undoubtedly, privacy is a fundamental human right [79], but also a "chameleon" that changes meaning depending on context [37]. Looking for a privacy definition in literature we found clear disarray. Nobody seems to have a very clear idea what the right to privacy is [53]. As Solove [72] points out, privacy means different things to different people.

Warren and Brandeis [79] in 1890 described Privacy as the protection of individuals space and their right to be left alone. Other authors have defined privacy as the control over personal information [80], or as an aspect of dignity, integrity and human freedom [68]. Nonetheless, all approaches have something in common: a reference to the boundaries between private and public.

Privacy in the modern world has two dimensions. First, it has to do with the identity of a person and, second, it has to do with the way personal information is used. Individuals during their daily online transactions as consumers of products and services have many topics to consider and decisions to make related to privacy. Consumers seek for maximum benefits and minimum cost for themselves. Firms, on the other hand, can benefit from the ability to learn so much about their customers. Under the above prism scientists working on behavioral decision-making focus their research on the trade-offs and the protection (or sharing) of information [4].

Privacy transactions nowadays occur in three different types of markets [3]. First, we have transactions for non-privacy goods where consumers often reveal personal information, which may be collected, analyzed and processed some way. In this case, the potential secondary use of information should be considered as a possibility. The second type of privacy-related transactions occurs where firms provide consumers free products or services (e.g. search engines, online social networks, free cloud services). In these transactions, consumers provide directly personal information, although the exchange of services for personal data is not always visible. The third type of privacy-related transactions occurs in the market of privacy tools. For example, consumers may acquire a PET tool to protect their transactions or hide their browsing behavior [7].

Consumers' personal data analysis can improve firms' marketing capabilities and increase revenues through targeted offers. Consequently, firms employ innovative strategies in order to allure consumers to easily provide more personal information and shape preferences [60]. By observing consumers' behavior, firms can learn how to improve their services and turn to price discriminations strategies for clear profit [9]. On the other hand, consumers benefit from targeted advertisement strategies, since advertisements are tailored to consumers' interests. Firms and consumers can both benefit from such targeting; the former reduce communication cost with consumers, and the latter gain easily useful information [75].

Finally, a more intangible but also important form of indirect consumers' costs is related to the fact that the more an individual's data is shared with other parties, the more those parties gain a bargaining advantage in future transactions with that individual. While consumers receive offers for products, data holders accumulate information about them over time and across platforms and transactions. This data permits the creation of a detailed dossier of the consumers' preferences and tastes, and the prediction of her future behavior [29].

Results from literature about privacy transactions show that decision-making for the collection and diffusion of private information by firms and other third parties will almost always raise issues for private life. Consumers seem to act shortsightedly when trade-offs apply short term benefits and long term costs for privacy invasions. This suggests that consumers may not always behave rationally when facing privacy trade-offs. Current research talks about the privacy paradox phenomenon, where individuals face obstacles in making privacy sensitive decisions because of incomplete information, bounded access to the available information, and plenty deviations and behavioral biases suggested by behavioral decision research [2,6].

3   Information Privacy in Cloud Computing: A Game Theory Approach

In the literature, the adoption and implementation of cloud computing technology have become an important milestone for modern organizations and inseparably connected with the protection or disclosure of personal information. Four-factor analysis of the human component, technology, organization, and environment is used to understand cloud computing technology adoption [43,46,51]. Cloud computing adoption by the organizations can be considered as a utopia if individual users are not familiar with the cloud technology. Sharma et al. [70] point out studies from the field of information systems where behavioral constructs are key factors influencing the individual user to adopt a new technology [12,24,41,77]. Sharma et al. [70] examine if and to what extent factors such as perceived usefulness, perceived ease of use, computer self-efficacy and trust can affect individual users to adopt cloud technologies and indicate that the above factors were found to be important indeed.

A major inhibiting factor has to do with the loss of control over storage of critical data and the service's outsourced nature. The challenge for cloud providers is to identify and understand the concerns of privacy-sensitive stakeholders and adopt security practices that meet their requirements [19]. Misunderstanding the privacy concerns of end-users may lead to loss of business, as they may either stop using a perceivably insecure or privacy-abusing service, or falsify their provided information, hence minimizing the potential for profit via personalized advertising. An end-user can give fake data if she believes that the service provider is going to abuse the privacy agreement and sell personal data derived from a cloud based subscription to a third party [16].

Di Vimercati et al. [78] underline that the significant benefit of elasticity in clouds appealed companies and individual users to adopt cloud technologies. At the same time, this benefit is proved harmful for users' privacy, as security threats and a potential loss of control from data owners exists. In this case, the adoption of the cloud computing paradigm is diminished. European Network and Information Security Agency (ENISA) [1] lists the issue of loss of control over data as a top risk for cloud computing. Also, in 2013 the "Cloud Security Alliance - CSA" lists data breaches and data loss as two of the top nine threats in cloud computing [14,32]. The new complexity of the cloud paradigm (e.g. distribution and virtualization), the class of data (e.g. sensitive data) or the fact that CSPs might be not fully trustworthy are topics that increase security and privacy obstacles for cloud adoption.

Game theory in these cases emerges as an interesting tool to explore the aforementioned issues, as it can be used to interpret stakeholder interactions and interdependencies across the above scenarios. For example, Rajbhandari and Snekkenes [62] implemented a game theory-based approach to analyze risks to privacy, in place of the traditional probabilistic risk analysis (PRA). Their scenario is based on an online bookstore where the user has to subscribe in order to have access to a service. Two players take part in this game: the user and the online bookstore. The user could provide either genuine or fake information, whereas the bookstore could sell user's information to a third party or respect it. A mixed strategy Nash equilibrium was chosen for solving the game, with user's negative payoffs, in order to describe quantitatively the level of privacy risk.

Snekkenes [71] applies Conflicting Incentives Risk Analysis (CIRA) in a case where a bank and a customer are involved in a deal. Snekkenes attempts to identify who is to take the role of the risk owner in case of data breach incidents and what are the utility factors weighted on the risk owner's perception of utility. The CIRA approach identifies stakeholders, actions, and payoffs. Each action can be viewed as a strategy in a potentially complex game, where the implementation of the action amounts to the participation in a game. CIRA shows how this method can be used to identify privacy risks and human behavior.

Also, according to Hausken [33], the behavioral dimension is a very important factor in order to estimate risk. A conflict behavior, which is recorded on individuals' choices, can be integrated into a probabilistic risk analysis and analyzed through game theory. Resnick [66] worked on providing the use of "cheap pseudonyms" as a way to measure reputation in Internet interaction between stakeholders. This was a game of multiple players where users provided pseudonyms during an interaction in the Internet world and they had the option either to continue playing with the current pseudonym or find a new one, at each period of time. A suboptimal equilibria is found, as a repeated prisoner's dilemma type of game, while methods of limiting identity changes are suggested.

Cai et al. [20] insert a game-theory approach to managing decision errors, as there is a gap between strategic decisions and actions. They study the effects of decision errors on optimal equilibrium strategy of the firm and the user. Cavusoglu and Raghunathan [22] propose a game theory for determining if a provider should invest on high or low-cost ICT and compare game theory and decision theory approaches. They show that in cases where firms choose their action before attackers choose theirs (sequential game), firms gain the maximum payoff. Also, when firms adopt knowledge from previous hacker attacks to estimate future hacker effort, then the distance between the results of decision theory and game theory approaches is diminishing.

Gao and Zhong [31] address the problems of distorted incentives for stakeholders in an electronic environment, applying differential game theory in a case where two competing firms offer the same product to customers and the one can influence the value of their information assets by changing pricing rates. To assure consumers that they do not risk losing sensitive information, and also, increase consumer demand, firms usually integrate their security investment strategies. Researchers reveal that higher consumer demand loss and higher targeted attacks, avert both firms from aggressive defense policy against hackers and would rather prefer to decrease the negative effect of hacker attacks by lowering their pricing rates.

Concluding, game theory research in online privacy-related decision-making has shown that it can give credible results in understanding privacy-related behavior.

4 Impact of Consumer Trust in Cloud Services

Sato [67] refers that 88% of consumers, worldwide, are worried about the loss of their data. Who has access to their data? Where consumers' data is physically stored? Can cloud service providers (CSPs) find ways to gain consumers' trust? Is the CSPs attempt towards consumer trust, a value for money strategy? These are typical questions that consumers and CSPs make about trust in clouds and online environments.

Ramachandran and Chang [63] highlight key issues associated with data security in the clouds. One key factor for cloud adoption is building trust when storing and computing sensitive data in the cloud. Trust related to e-services offered in virtual online environments is a major topic for both consumers and cloud service providers, as well as for cloud researchers. Trust is strongly tied to online security. McKnight et al. [49] indicate three significant trust components: ability, integrity and good will as prominent factors for a new ICT adoption.

Ability is equal to CSPs efficiency in resources and skills that will not deter consumers from adopting cloud technologies. Integrity refers to CSPs obligations to comply with regulations, and good will means that CSPs assure priority to consumers' needs.

Sharma et al. [70] suggest that trust in clouds has a positive and significant relationship with individual's decision to adopt cloud computing services. In clouds, users often want to share sensitive information and CSPs should ensure their privacy [39]. Svantesson and Clarke [73] suggested that CSPs should apply such policies to ensure users that their data are safe and allure them to use clouds.

Consumers trust CSPs only to the extent that the risk is perceived to be low and the convenience payoff for them to be high. Pearson [59] argues that when customers have to decide about trusting CSPs for personal data exchange services, they should consider organization's operational, security, privacy and compliance requirements and choose what best suits them.

5   Asymmetric Information and Strategic Stakeholders Interaction in Clouds

Asymmetric information is a concept encountered often in commercial transactions between sellers and buyers, end-users and service providers where one party has more information compared to the other. Potentially, this could lead to a harmful situation as one party can take advantage of the other party's lack of knowledge. Information asymmetries are commonly met in principal-agent problems where misinforming is caused and the communication process is affected [23].

Principal-agent problems occur when an entity (or agent) makes decisions on behalf of another entity: Principal is "a person, who authorizes an agent to act with a third trusted party" [18,27]. A dilemma exists when the agreement between participants is not respected and the agent is motivated to act for his own personal gain and in contrary to the "principal". Principals do not know enough about whether an agreement has been satisfied and, therefore, their decisions are taken under some risk and uncertainty and involve costs for both parties. The above information problem can be solved if the third trusted party provides incentives in order the agents to act appropriately and in accordance with the principals. In terms of game theory, rules should be changed so that the rational agents are confronted with what principal desires [18].

McKinney and Yoos [48] argue that information is almost always unspecified to an unbounded variety of problems and the involved agents (so-called stakeholders) almost always act without having full information about their decisions. Whilst literature on information risk is adequately studied in the last decades, there is no risk premium for information asymmetry [34]. Easley and O'hara [26] argue that information asymmetry creates something called information risk and their model showed that additional private information from consumers receives higher expected returns to the involved agents.

For an agent, a risk premium is the minimum economic benefit by which the expected return from decision-making under risk must exceed the known return on a risk-free decision where full information is provided to the involved stakeholders. A rational agent is risk averse. He attempts to reduce the uncertainty when exposed to information asymmetry. The utility of such a strategic movement expected to be high in many cases. For such risky outcomes, a decision-maker adopts a criterion as a rule of choice, where higher expected value strategic movements are simply the preferred ones [55].

From a game theory perspective, uncertain outcomes exist where potential preferences with regards to appropriate risky choices coincide. In cases where the above-expected utility hypothesis is satisfied, it can be proved useful to explain choices that seem to contradict the expected value criterion. Asymmetric information in clouding introduces scenarios where stakeholders (consumers and service providers) interact strategically. A game theory approach based on trust is regarded as a useful tool to explain the conflict and cooperation between intelligent rational decision-makers.

Njilla et al. [52] introduce a game-theoretic model for trust in clouds suggesting that risk and trust are two behavioral factors that influence decision-making in uncertain environments like cloud markets, where consumers seem they do not have full control over their stored data. They adopt a game theoretic approach to establishing a relationship between trust and factors that could affect the assessments to risk. The scenario refers to three players: end-users, service providers, and attackers. The provider defends the system's infrastructure against attackers, while end-users tempt not to trust an online service in case of data privacy breaches. Njilla et al. [52] propose a game model which mitigates cyber attack behavior. They analyze different solutions obtained from the Nash Equilibrium (NE) and find that frequent attacks with contemporary providers' ability to mitigate the loss, might cause the attacker to be detected and caught. Thus, it is possible, in this case, the attacker not to attack because of high risk and penalties. But what about the gain and the loss when the provider invests in security and the attacker decides to attack and succeeds his target with users' private data compromised? What are the payoffs of each player in this case? These remain open questions.

Maghrabi and Pfluegel [47] use game theory by an end-user perspective to assess risk pertaining to moving to public clouds. While previous works focus on how to help the cloud provider to assess risk, they developed a model for benefits and costs associated with attacks on the end user's asset in order to help the user decide whether or not adopt the cloud. The end-user is conformed to a Service Level Agreement (SLA), which promises protection against external attacks.

Douss et al. [25] propose a game trust model for mobile ad hoc networks. Assuring reputation and establishing trust between collaborating parties is indirectly a way to provide the secure online environment. The authors suggest an evaluation model for trust value. They applied computational methods and developed a framework for trust establishment.

Li et al. [42] study price bidding strategies when multiple users interact and compete for resource usage in cloud computing. The provided cloud services are available to end-users with a pay-as-you-go manner [38,56]. A non-cooperative game model is developed with multiple cloud users, where each cloud user has incomplete and asymmetric information about the other users. They work on utility functions with the "time efficiency" parameters incorporated to calculate net profit for each user, in order to help them to decide whether to use the cloud service. For a cloud provider, the income is a number of money users pay for resource usage [50]. A rational user will maximize his net reward by choosing the appropriate bidding strategy $(= U_{of\ choosing\ the\ cloud\ service} - P_{ayment})$; U stands for utility and P stands for payment. However, it is irrational for a cloud provider to provide enough resources for all potential requests in a specific time. Therefore, cloud users compete for resource usage. The above stakeholders' strategic interactions are analyzed from a game-theoretic perspective and the existence of Nash equilibrium is also confirmed by a proposed near-equilibrium price bidding algorithm. For future research, a good idea is to study the cloud users' choice among different cloud providers or determine a properly mixed bidding strategy.

Fagnani et al. [28] consider a network of units (e.g., smartphones or tablets) where users have decided to make an external backup for their data and, also, are able to offer space to store data of other connected units. They propose a peer-to-peer storage game model and design an algorithm which makes units interact and store data backup from connected neighbors. The algorithm has been converged to Nash equilibrium of the game, but several challenges have arisen for future research analysis related to stakeholders' interactions in a more trusted environment.

Moreover, the resource allocation problem in cloud computing where users compete for gaining more space to run their applications and store their data is analyzed by Jebalia et al. [35]. They develop a resource allocation model based on a cooperative game approach, where cloud providers provide a great number of resources in order to maximize profit and combine the adoption of security mechanisms with payoffs maximizing.

Security and privacy are often located as opposite concepts. Much of focus is on reducing cost during the establishment of a trustworthiness infrastructure in cloud computing, which gradually requires disclosing private information and proposing a model of trading privacy for trust [52,69]. Also, Lilien et al. [45] indicate the difference between maintaining a high level of privacy and establishing trust for transactions in cloud environments. Users, who display a particular interest in concealing private information intensively, request from cloud providers a set of corresponding credentials which establishing trust for these users. The tradeoff problem exists where the assurance for the minimum user's privacy loss meet the choice of revealing the minimum number of credentials for satisfying trust requirements.

Raya et al. [64] suggest a trust privacy tradeoff game-theoretic model that gives incentives to stakeholders to build trust and at the same time assure privacy loss at a minimum level. Individual players do not trust cloud providers unless they received an appropriate incentive.

Gal-Oz et al. [30] introduce a tradeoff approach studying the relationship between trust and privacy in online transactions. They suggest that pseudonyms constitute a necessary component for maintaining privacy since pseudonyms prevent association with transaction ID and ensure a level of reputation. The more pseudonyms used, the more reputation is succeeded.

Mentioning the above major issues, we indicate that any application relying upon an emerging cloud computing technology should consider the different possible threats. The problem is a lack of a clearly defined meaning of such a risk that benefits the cloud users to make proper choice and cloud service providers to avoid threats efficiently.

6   Conclusions

A game theory approach is adopted as a very general language for modeling choices by agents in whom the actions of other agents can affect each player's outcome. Game theory assumes players choose strategies which maximize the utility of game outcomes given their beliefs about what others will do.

The most challenging question is often how beliefs are formed. Most approaches suggest that beliefs are derived from what other players are likely to do. Game theory focuses on preferences and the formation of beliefs. Equilibrium specifies not only a strategy for each of the players but also a belief for each of the players. Each belief is the probability of the other players having particular types, given the type of the player with that belief. The way players specify reasonable beliefs is by equating choices.

However, some limits arise. First, many games that occur in social life are so complex, which means that at a specific time, players cannot form accurate beliefs about what other players would choose and therefore they cannot choose equilibrium strategies. So, what strategies might be chosen by players with bounded rationality, or how a repeated game helps players to improve their strategic choices? Second, in empirical works, only received payoffs are easily measured (e.g., prices in auctions). A huge variety of experiments show that game theory sometimes explains behavior adequately, and sometimes is badly rejected by behavioral and process data [21]. The above inference can be used to create a more general theory which matches the standard theory when it is accurate, and explains the cases in which is badly rejected. This emerging approach is called "behavioral game theory" which uses the analytical game theory to explain observed violations by incorporating bounds on rationality.

Game theory is the standard theory to analyze cases where individuals or firms interact; for example, strategic interaction of privacy-sensitive end-users' use of cloud-based mobile apps, e-commerce transactions between sellers and consumers, and many other social dilemmas such as the provision of public goods. Behavioral game theory introduces psychological parameters which amplify a rational scenario and give a motivational basis for players' behavior. Representation, social preferences over outcomes, initial conditions and learning are the basic components for a precise analysis [21].

In this work, we focus on Information Privacy in Cyberspace Transactions. Cyberspace is a synopsis for the web of consumer electronics, computers, and communication networks that interconnect the world. The potential surveillance of electronic activities presents a serious threat to information privacy. The collection and use of private information have caused serious concerns about privacy invasion by consumers, creating a personalization-privacy tradeoff. The key approach to addressing privacy concerns is via the protection of privacy through the implementation of fair information practices, a set of standards governing the collection and use of personal information. We take a game-theoretic approach to explore the motivation of firms for privacy protection and its impact on competition and social welfare in the context of product and price personalization. We find that privacy protection can work as a competition-mitigating mechanism by generating asymmetry in the consumer segments to which firms offer personalization, enhancing the profit extraction abilities of the firms. In equilibrium, both symmetric and asymmetric choices of privacy protection by the firms can result, depending on the size of the personalization scope and the investment cost of protection. Further, as consumers become more concerned about their privacy, it is more likely that all firms adopt privacy protection strategies. In the perspective of welfare, we show that autonomous choices of privacy protection by personalizing firms can improve social welfare at the expense of consumer welfare. We further find that regulation enforcing the implementation of fair information practices can be efficient from the social welfare perspective, mainly by limiting the incentives of the firms to exploit the competition-mitigation effect.

References

1. Cloud Computing Risk Assessment, ENISA (2009). https://www.enisa.europa.eu/publications/cloud-computing-risk-assessment. Accessed 10 Feb 2017
2. Acquisti, A.: Privacy in electronic commerce and the economics of immediate gratification. In: Proceedings of the 5th ACM Conference on Electronic Commerce, pp. 21–29. ACM (2004)
3. Acquisti, A.: The economics of personal data and the economics of privacy (2010)
4. Acquisti, A., Brandimarte, L., Loewenstein, G.: Privacy and human behavior in the age of information. Science **347**(6221), 509–514 (2015)
5. Acquisti, A., Grossklags, J.: Privacy and rationality. In: Strandburg, K.J., Raicu, D.S. (eds.) Privacy and Technologies of Identity, pp. 15–29. Springer, Heidelberg (2006)
6. Acquisti, A., Grossklags, J.: What can behavioral economics teach us about privacy. Digit. Priv.: Theory Technol. Pract. **18**, 363–377 (2007)
7. Acquisti, A., John, L.K., Loewenstein, G.: What is privacy worth? J. Legal Stud. **42**(2), 249–274 (2013)
8. Acquisti, A., Taylor, C., Wagman, L.: The economics of privacy. J. Econ. Lit. **54**(2), 442–492 (2016)
9. Acquisti, A., Varian, H.R.: Conditioning prices on purchase history. Mark. Sci. **24**(3), 367–381 (2005)
10. Adjerid, I., Peer, E., Acquisti, A.: Beyond the privacy paradox: objective versus relative risk in privacy decision making (2016)

11. Aguirre, E., Roggeveen, A.L., Grewal, D., Wetzels, M.: The personalization-privacy paradox: implications for new media. J. Consum. Mark. **33**(2), 98–110 (2016)
12. Al-Somali, S.A., Gholami, R., Clegg, B.: An investigation into the acceptance of online banking in Saudi Arabia. Technovation **29**(2), 130–141 (2009)
13. Alberts, J.K., Nakayama, T.K., Martin, J.N.: Human Communication in Society. Pearson, Upper Saddle River (2015)
14. Almorsy, M., Grundy, J., Müller, I.: An analysis of the cloud computing security problem. arXiv preprint arXiv:1609.01107 (2016)
15. Andriotis, P., Takasu, A., Tryfonas, T.: Smartphone message sentiment analysis. In: Peterson, G., Shenoi, S. (eds.) DigitalForensics 2014. IAICT, vol. 433, pp. 253–265. Springer, Heidelberg (2014). doi:10.1007/978-3-662-44952-3_17
16. Andriotis, P., Tryfonas, T.: Impact of user data privacy management controls on mobile device investigations. In: Peterson, G., Shenoi, S. (eds.) Advances in Digital Forensics XII. IAICT, vol. 484, pp. 89–105. Springer, Cham (2016). doi:10.1007/978-3-319-46279-0_5
17. Andriotis, P., Tzermias, Z., Mparmpaki, A., Ioannidis, S., Oikonomou, G.: Multi-level visualization using enhanced social network analysis with smartphone data. Int. J. Digit. Crime Forensics (IJDCF) **5**(4), 34–54 (2013)
18. Bosse, D.A., Phillips, R.A.: Agency theory and bounded self-interest. Acad. Manag. Rev. **41**(2), 276–297 (2016)
19. Brunette, G., Mogull, R., et al.: Security guidance for critical areas of focus in cloud computing v2. 1. Cloud Secur. Alliance 1–76 (2009)
20. Cai, C.X., Mei, S.E., Zhong, W.J.: A game-theory approach to manage decision errors. In: MATEC Web of Conferences, vol. 44. EDP Sciences (2016)
21. Camerer, C.: Behavioral Game Theory: Experiments in Strategic Interaction. Princeton University Press, Princeton (2003)
22. Cavusoglu, H., Raghunathan, S., Yue, W.T.: Decision-theoretic and game-theoretic approaches to it security investment. J. Manag. Inf. Syst. **25**(2), 281–304 (2008)
23. Christozov, D., Chukova, S., Mateev, P.: Informing processes, risks, evaluation of the risk of misinforming. Found. Informing Sci. 323–356 (2009)
24. Davis, F.D.: Perceived usefulness, perceived ease of use, and user acceptance of information technology. MIS Q. 319–340 (1989)
25. Douss, A.B.C., Abassi, R., El Fatmi, S.G.: A trust management based security mechanism against collusion attacks in a MANET environment. In: 2014 Ninth International Conference on Availability, Reliability and Security (ARES), pp. 325–332. IEEE (2014)
26. Easley, D., O'hara, M.: Information and the cost of capital. J. Financ. **59**(4), 1553–1583 (2004)
27. Eisenhardt, K.M.: Agency theory: an assessment and review. Acad. Manag. Rev. **14**(1), 57–74 (1989)
28. Fagnani, F., Franci, B., Grasso, E.: A game theoretic approach to a peer-to-peer cloud storage model. arXiv preprint arXiv:1607.02371 (2016)
29. Farrell, J.: Can privacy be just another good. J. Telecomm. High Tech. L. **10**, 251 (2012)
30. Gal-Oz, N., Grinshpoun, T., Gudes, E.: Privacy issues with sharing reputation across virtual communities. In: Proceedings of the 4th International Workshop on Privacy and Anonymity in the Information Society, p. 3. ACM (2011)
31. Gao, X., Zhong, W.: A differential game approach to security investment and information sharing in a competitive environment. IIE Trans. **48**(6), 511–526 (2016)
32. Group, T.T.W., et al: The notorious nine: cloud computing top threats in 2013. Cloud Secur. Alliance (2013)

33. Hausken, K.: Probabilistic risk analysis and game theory. Risk Anal. **22**(1), 17–27 (2002)
34. Hirshleifer, D.A., Huang, C., Teoh, S.H.: Information asymmetry, market participation, and asset prices (2016)
35. Jebalia, M., Ben Letaïfa, A., Hamdi, M., Tabbane, S.: An overview on coalitional game-theoretic approaches for resource allocation in cloud computing architectures. Int. J. Cloud Comput. 22 **4**(1), 63–77 (2015)
36. Kahneman, D., Tversky, A.: Choices, Values, and Frames. Cambridge University Press, Cambridge (2000)
37. Kang, J., Shilton, K., Estrin, D., Burke, J.: Self-surveillance privacy. Iowa L. Rev. **97**, 809 (2011)
38. Kaur, P.D., Chana, I.: A resource elasticity framework for QoS-aware execution of cloud applications. Future Gener. Comput. Syst. **37**, 14–25 (2014)
39. King, N.J., Raja, V.: Protecting the privacy and security of sensitive customer data in the cloud. Comput. Law Secur. Rev. **28**(3), 308–319 (2012)
40. Kokolakis, S.: Privacy attitudes and privacy behaviour: a review of current research on the privacy paradox phenomenon. Comput. Secur. **64**, 122–134 (2017)
41. Kumar Sharma, S., Madhumohan Govindaluri, S.: Internet banking adoption in India: structural equation modeling approach. J. Indian Bus. Res. **6**(2), 155–169 (2014)
42. Li, W., Huang, Z.: The research of influence factors of online behavioral advertising avoidance. Am. J. Ind. Bus. Manag. **6**(09), 947 (2016)
43. Lian, J.W., Yen, D.C., Wang, Y.T.: An exploratory study to understand the critical factors affecting the decision to adopt cloud computing in Taiwan hospital. Int. J. Inf. Manag. **34**(1), 28–36 (2014)
44. Liang, H., Shen, F., Fu, K.: Privacy protection and self-disclosure across societies: a study of global twitter users. New Media Soc. 1461444816642210 (2016)
45. Lilien, L., Bhargava, B.: Trading Privacy for Trust in Online Interactions. Idea Group, Hershey (2008)
46. Low, C., Chen, Y., Wu, M.: Understanding the determinants of cloud computing adoption. Ind. Manag. Data Syst. **111**(7), 1006–1023 (2011)
47. Maghrabi, L., Pfluegel, E.: Moving assets to the cloud: a game theoretic approach based on trust. In: 2015 International Conference on Cyber Situational Awareness, Data Analytics and Assessment (CyberSA), pp. 1–5. IEEE (2015)
48. McKinney Jr., E.H., Yoos, C.J.: Information about information: a taxonomy of views. MIS Q. 329–344 (2010)
49. McKnight, D.H., Choudhury, V., Kacmar, C.: The impact of initial consumer trust on intentions to transact with a web site: a trust building model. J. Strateg. Inf. Syst. **11**(3), 297–323 (2002)
50. Mei, J., Li, K., Ouyang, A., Li, K.: A profit maximization scheme with guaranteed quality of service in cloud computing. IEEE Trans. Comput. **64**(11), 3064–3078 (2015)
51. Morgan, L., Conboy, K.: Key factors impacting cloud computing adoption. Computer **46**(10), 97–99 (2013)
52. Njilla, L.Y., Pissinou, N., Makki, K.: Game theoretic modeling of security and trust relationship in cyberspace. Int. J. Commun. Syst. **29**(9), 1500–1512 (2016)
53. Nofer, M., Hinz, O., Muntermann, J., Roßnagel, H.: The economic impact of privacy violations and security breaches. Bus. Inf. Syst. Eng. **6**(6), 339–348 (2014)
54. Nosko, A., Wood, E., Molema, S.: All about me: disclosure in online social networking profiles: the case of Facebook. Comput. Hum. Behav. **26**(3), 406–418 (2010)

55. O'Brien, M.K., Ahmed, A.A.: Rationality in human movement. Exerc. Sport Sci. Rev. **44**(1), 20–28 (2016)
56. Pal, R., Hui, P.: Economic models for cloud service markets: pricing and capacity planning. Theoret. Comput. Sci. **496**, 113–124 (2013)
57. Pan, Y., Zinkhan, G.M.: Exploring the impact of online privacy disclosures on consumer trust. J. Retail. **82**(4), 331–338 (2006)
58. Parra-Arnau, J., Rebollo-Monedero, D., Forné, J.: Measuring the privacy of user profiles in personalized information systems. Future Gener. Comput. Syst. **33**, 53–63 (2014)
59. Pearson, S.: Privacy, security and trust in cloud computing. In: Pearson, S., Yee, G. (eds.) Privacy and Security for Cloud Computing. CCN, pp. 3–42. Springer, Heidelberg (2013). doi:10.1007/978-1-4471-4189-1_1
60. Pitta, D.A.: Jump on the bandwagon-its the last one: new developments in online promotion. J. Consum. Mark. **27**(2) (2010)
61. Post, R.C.: Rereading warren and brandeis: privacy, property, and appropriation. Case W. Res. L. Rev. **41**, 647 (1990)
62. Rajbhandari, L., Snekkenes, E.A.: Mapping between classical risk management and game theoretical approaches. In: Decker, B., Lapon, J., Naessens, V., Uhl, A. (eds.) CMS 2011. LNCS, vol. 7025, pp. 147–154. Springer, Heidelberg (2011). doi:10.1007/978-3-642-24712-5_12
63. Ramachandran, M., Chang, V.: Towards performance evaluation of cloud service providers for cloud data security. Int. J. Inf. Manag. **36**(4), 618–625 (2016)
64. Raya, M., Shokri, R., Hubaux, J.P.: On the tradeoff between trust and privacy in wireless ad hoc networks. In: Proceedings of the Third ACM Conference on Wireless Network Security, pp. 75–80. ACM (2010)
65. Regan, P.M.: Privacy as a common good in the digital world. Inf. Commun. Soc. **5**(3), 382–405 (2002)
66. Resnick, P., et al.: The social cost of cheap pseudonyms. J. Econ. Manag. Strategy **10**(2), 173–199 (2001)
67. Sato, M.: Personal data in the cloud: a global survey of consumer attitudes. Minato-u, To yo, pp. 105–7123 (2010)
68. Schoeman, F.D.: Privacy and Social Freedom. Cambridge University Press, Cambridge (1992)
69. Seigneur, J.-M., Jensen, C.D.: Trading privacy for trust. In: Jensen, C., Poslad, S., Dimitrakos, T. (eds.) iTrust 2004. LNCS, vol. 2995, pp. 93–107. Springer, Heidelberg (2004). doi:10.1007/978-3-540-24747-0_8
70. Sharma, S.K., Al-Badi, A.H., Govindaluri, S.M., Al-Kharusi, M.H.: Predicting motivators of cloud computing adoption: a developing country perspective. Comput. Hum. Behav. **62**, 61–69 (2016)
71. Snekkenes, E.: Position paper: privacy risk analysis is about understanding conflicting incentives. In: Fischer-Hübner, S., Leeuw, E., Mitchell, C. (eds.) IDMAN 2013. IAICT, vol. 396, pp. 100–103. Springer, Heidelberg (2013). doi:10.1007/978-3-642-37282-7_9
72. Solove, D.J.: A taxonomy of privacy. Univ. Pa. Law Rev. 477–564 (2006)
73. Svantesson, D., Clarke, R.: Privacy and consumer risks in cloud computing. Comput. Law Secur. Rev. **26**(4), 391–397 (2010)
74. Tsai, J.Y., Egelman, S., Cranor, L., Acquisti, A.: The effect of online privacy information on purchasing behavior: an experimental study. Inf. Syst. Res. **22**(2), 254–268 (2011)
75. Tucker, C.E.: Social networks, personalized advertising, and privacy controls. J. Mark. Res. **51**(5), 546–562 (2014)

76. Tversky, A., Kahneman, D.: Advances in prospect theory: cumulative representation of uncertainty. In: Arló-Costa, H., Hendricks, V.F., Benthem, J. (eds.) Readings in Formal Epistemology. SGTP, vol. 1, pp. 493–519. Springer, Cham (2016). doi:10.1007/978-3-319-20451-2_24
77. Venkatesh, V., Morris, M.G., Davis, G.B., Davis, F.D.: User acceptance of information technology: toward a unified view. MIS Q. 425–478 (2003)
78. Vimercati, S.D.C., Foresti, S., Samarati, P.: Data security issues in cloud scenarios. In: Jajodia, S., Mazumdar, C. (eds.) ICISS 2015. LNCS, vol. 9478, pp. 3–10. Springer, Cham (2015). doi:10.1007/978-3-319-26961-0_1
79. Warren, S.D., Brandeis, L.D.: The right to privacy. Harv. Law Rev. 193–220 (1890)
80. Westin, A.F.: Privacy and freedom. Wash. Lee Law Rev. 25(1), 166 (1968)
81. Young, A.L., Quan-Haase, A.: Privacy protection strategies on Facebook: the internet privacy paradox revisited. Inf. Commun. Soc. 16(4), 479–500 (2013)

A Comparative Study of Android Users' Privacy Preferences Under the Runtime Permission Model

Panagiotis Andriotis[1]([✉]), Shancang Li[1], Theodoros Spyridopoulos[1], and Gianluca Stringhini[2]

[1] Cyber Security Research Unit, University of the West of England,
Bristol BS16 1QY, UK
panagiotis.andriotis@uwe.ac.uk
[2] University College London, London WC1E 6BT, UK

Abstract. Android users recently were given the ability to selectively grant access to sensitive resources of their mobile devices when apps request them at runtime. The Android fine-grained runtime permission model has been gracefully accepted by the majority of users, who also seem to be consistent regarding their privacy and security preferences. In this paper we analyse permission data collected by Android devices that were utilising the runtime permission model. The reconstructed data represent apps' settings snapshots. We compare behavioural insights extracted from the acquired data with users' privacy preferences reported in our previous work. In addition, compared with the responses received from another group of mobile device users, users' privacy settings seem to be affected by the functionality of apps. Furthermore, we advise visual schemata that describe users' privacy settings and point out a usability issue regarding the installation process of Android apps under the runtime permission model.

Keywords: Runtime · Permissions · Android · Settings · Apps · Marshmallow · Privacy · Security · Usability · Profile

1 Introduction

Mobile device sales are increasing every year [1] and consequently, more people are nowadays able to use smartphones and tablets. Contemporary portable devices are usually equipped with numerous sensors and advanced storage capacity. Hence, provided software (apps) can nowadays perform complex tasks and, therefore, produce large amounts of highly personalised data. This type of pervasive technology has been widely criticised in the past, with criticism focusing particularly on the privacy issues it accumulates [8].

Until recently (i.e., autumn 2015), Android users could not control which resources should be available to apps during runtime. However, modern versions of the most popular operating systems (Android and iOS) are now equipped

© Springer International Publishing AG 2017
T. Tryfonas (Ed.): HAS 2017, LNCS 10292, pp. 604–622, 2017.
DOI: 10.1007/978-3-319-58460-7_42

with permission control management systems. One common characteristic of these systems is that when an app needs to access for the first time specific components of the system, e.g. the microphone, the user has to explicitly grant (or deny) permission for this action. Thus, users' privacy and security awareness can be, theoretically, increased.

We can categorise Android versions in two generations, regarding their permission system. The old generation devices (until version 5.1.1) do not allow users to permit or deny access to sensitive resources during runtime, when apps make such requests. The permission model used on devices that run old generation versions requires the user to accept, before installation, all permissions an app might request. In other words, when users want to install an app via the Google Play app store, which is the official Android marketplace, they will see a list of requested permissions before they install the app. Then they have two choices; either accept and continue the installation process (granting thus access to all requested resources), or cancel the installation. Users of the new generation versions might also see a similar list of requested permissions before installing an app. Then, they also need to accept or deny the app installation. The major difference with the old generation versions is that, if an app requests access for the first time to sensitive resources (during runtime), the system will issue a dialogue message requesting from the user to deny or grant access to the specific resource. According to the Android Developer documentation [2], as of February 2017 there exist nine groups of dangerous permissions: Calendar, Camera, Contacts, Location, Microphone, Phone, Sensors, SMS, Storage.

Runtime permissions are increasing users' security and privacy awareness and, in theory, allow them to handle more efficiently the personal data they share. Users can revoke granted permissions anytime using the *Settings* app. Thus, if for example we assume that users do not prefer to share their SMS list with other ecosystems (i.e., apps), they are given the ability under the current permission model to install apps that function properly, but at the same time, they cannot access restricted areas of the device; these areas are set by the users.

We recently conducted a study aiming to examine how Android users adopted to this change [4]. The study demonstrated that users make in general consistent choices regarding the resources they are more willing to grant access. In this paper, we compare previous results with the analysis of a new dataset that came from a different group of Android users. We report similar trends on the way these two different user groups handle permission requests from social (and messaging) apps. Additionally, the current study demonstrates that although people have specific perceptions when asked which resources would be more reluctant to allow an app to access, they eventually overlook their priorities when they need to benefit from functionalities that various apps offer. Also, we stress the luck of sufficient information on the official marketplace regarding the *least required permissions*, which are needed in order an app to function properly. Finally, we conclude this paper by proposing visual schemes that could be used to represent users' security profiles.

The rest of this paper is organised as follows: we discuss related work in the next section and present the methodology we used to gain our dataset in

Sect. 3. Section 4 demonstrates our data analysis method and Sect. 5 presents our results. We further discuss the outcomes and limitations of our work in Sect. 6 and conclude this paper in Sect. 7.

2   Related Work

Over-privileged applications introduce security threats to mobile device ecosystems and pose various reputational risks to online markets such as the Android marketplace [13]. Such threats, according to [13], often derive from the use of advertising libraries. Additionally, users are often not aware of the context of the permissions they granted to installed applications in the past [3]. As a matter of fact, a recent study demonstrated that the majority of users would prevent at least one requested permission from an experimental application, if they knew beforehand the purpose of this request [14]. Furthermore, mobile device users are often astounded by the capabilities of various apps to collect personal data and share them with third-party entities [11]. If an app, for example, is able to gain access to personal data, such as the device's list of incoming or outbound SMS, it is even possible to acquire information about the emotional state of the entities that exchange these messages [5].

Consequently, previous research studies proposed extension mechanisms that would allow to overcome privacy and security constrains of the old permission model [9]. Researchers also introduced in the past fine-grained access control methodologies for Android apps using explicit policies [12]. FlaskDroid [9] for example, offers a flexible fine-grained access control system. Other systems were designed to protect only specific streams of data, such as users' location [7]. A popular technique used for location data protection is obfuscation [10]. The concept of obfuscation is simple; the system feeds with shadow or fake data any application that requests access to location services [6].

Fine-grained access control has been introduced to mobile device users in the past, when the iOS 6 was launched. However, Android users became familiar with the runtime permission model when the sixth version was presented (Marshmallow). In our previous work [4], we presented the first study that was focused on Android Marshmallow users. The study suggested that Android users were comfortable with the runtime permission model. Moreover, data derived from 50 participants demonstrated that Android users make consistent choices regarding their privacy preferences. In the current work we aim to compare responses and permission data from a different group of users with the previous study.

3   Methodology

We developed an Android app, targeting users of the 'Marshmallow' or 'Nougat' versions. In order to apply this limitation, the app was compiled utilising the `android:minSdkVersion` attribute of the `AndroidManifest.xml` file of the app; this attribute was set to API level 23 (Marshmallow). This app was used in our previous work [4], but for the needs of the current experiments we included additional fractions of code to get the timestamps of the first installation of each installed app and its latest update. At a later version, we also included in the collected data the `targetSDKVersion` attribute of each app, aiming to figure out if the installed apps in each device were compiled following the standards of the newest Android version (currently API 25, as on February 2017).

Participants could download the app via the official Android app marketplace (Google Play); the app was named *"Permissions Snapshot"*. After installing the app, participants had to launch our survey-app and read the Information Sheet and Consent Agreement. If they were satisfied with the terms of use, they had to click on a check box; then the data collection procedure succeeded. The respondents were asked to provide some basic demographic data and then they had to answer 6 questions related to the use of the runtime permission model. As described in our previous work [4], the app was also collecting data about the permissions that were granted to the installed apps at the given time. This was achieved utilising the `PackageManager` class. At the end of this procedure the participants had to upload to a server the collected data by clicking a button. They also had the opportunity to read a very brief tutorial, which reminded them that they could check and control app permissions anytime, using the *Settings* app of their devices.

The questions (also described in our previous work [4]) can be summarised as follows: The participants were asked: (1) how long they were using the current Android version; (2) if they had noticed any changes at the permission model; (3) if they believed that using the runtime model they had gained additional control over the data they were sharing; (4) if they knew that they could grant, deny or revoke permissions using the Settings app; (5) if they found the runtime permission model irritating, "because it asks too many questions" and (6) if they prefer the runtime permissions model or the previous one. Note that this study was approved by the UCL Research Ethics Committee *(Project ID Number: 8945/001)*.

As a second step to our experiments, we were aiming to highlight how users would probably react when an app requested access to sensitive resources of their devices. Without a doubt, the act of granting permissions to apps to allow them to access specific resources of a mobile device, relates primarily to the apps' functionality. However, it is also interesting to see how users prioritise the resources they consider as more sensitive. To this end, we asked the following question to 4 groups of undergraduate students, using an online tool *("poll everywhere")*: "Assume an Android app requests access to your phone's resources. Rank them according to the possibility to allow the app to access them. On the top of the stack you should place the group that you are more keen to permit access: Calendar, Camera, Contacts, Location, Microphone, Phone, Sensors, SMS, Storage". The students were given five minutes to answer the question. They could rearrange the groups of dangerous permissions using the interface provided by the online tool. The groups were shown as a stack and the participants could use the mouse and rearrange the stack. We eventually collected anonymous responses from 25 unique participants. We refer to this group of participants as the "online questionnaire respondents". The results of this experiment are presented at Sect. 5.

4   Data Collection and Analysis

"Permissions Snapshot" collected anonymous permission data from participants' mobile devices. The app was using the `PackageManager` class to accumulate information about the installed apps (packages) on each device. We made use of its `getInstalledApplications` method with the `GET_META_DATA` flag to acquire access to the packages; then we invoked the method `getPackageInfo` with the `GET_PERMISSIONS` flag to get information about the packages. The requested permissions were acquired using the `requestedPermissions` and `requestedPermissionsFlags` attributes of the `PackageInfo` data types. The `PackageInfo` data type also returned information about the first installation time, the last update time, and the target SDK version of each installed app, i.e., `firstInstallTime`, `lastUpdateTime`, `targetSdkVersion`. Note that we excluded system apps from the data collection process.

Granted permissions for each installed app were obtained using the correlation of data received from the following data types: `packageInfo.requested Permissions` and `packageInfo.requestedPermissionsFlags`. The former is an array of `Strings` and the latter is an array of `ints`. These data types describe users' settings related to the permissions granted to each app at the given time. Assuming that we are interested to see if a user granted permission to the Facebook app to access the Camera group, we need to see which flag *(int)* is associated with the permission `android.permission.CAMERA`. As suggested in [4], when this flag is equal to 1 this means that the permission was not granted. On the other hand, if the permission was granted, then this number would be equal to 3.

The permission data we analysed and present in this paper are complimentary to the data presented in our previous work [4]. They were collected from 13 participants using the same app ("Permissions Snapshot") that was used in [4]. These participants do not belong to the group of Android users that participated in our previous work. Also, the responses presented in this paper were basically collected during the last three months of 2016. Users' anonymity was maintained by calculating a hashed value of the `ANDROID_ID` of each device. This hexadecimal number describes uniquely a device; we used a hashed value of it to conceal the real identity of the user and, at the same time, to avoid having duplicate entries from the same device.

The collected responses from the 13 participants also contained demographic data and the answers to the aforementioned questions (Sect. 3). The participants provided basic demographics (Gender, Age, Area of Residence) and then were asked to answer six multiple-choice questions. Each question was presented sequentially having a predefined answer to allow us identify any users that where just skipping the questions by clicking the "Next" button. Two responses contained the predefined answers to all multiple-choice questions and were thus excluded from this presentation. However, their permission data were included in our analysis since users cannot manipulate them; these are device-dependent data. Moreover, two files did not contain demographic data; they only contained permission data. Hence, the following demographic information was extracted from nine participants.

Most of the respondents were males (88.88%) and they were between 18 to 30 years old (77.78%) or 31 to 46 years old (22.22%). We got valid responses from Europe (66.67%), Asia (22.22%) and the Americas (11.11%). Additionally, one third of the participants claimed they were using the current Android version for 0–6 months, one third said they were using it for 7–12 months, 22.22% chose the "More than 1 year" option and 11.11% selected "I Don't Know". According to the replies to the second question, most participants (77.78%) had noticed the changes to the permission model. Also, the majority of users (88.89%) agreed that under the new permission model they felt they could control the data they share more efficiently. In the fourth question, 66.67% of the participants knew that they could revoke, or grant access to installed apps using the *Settings* app of their devices (tapped the "Correct" option); 22.22% chose the "Wrong" option and 11.11% replied "I Don't Know". Furthermore, 55.56% suggested that they were not frustrated by the fact that the system interacts with the user frequently, asking them to grant permissions. Finally, users' preference for the runtime model is evident (77.78%). The rest 11.11% preferred the previous model and 11.11% chose the "I don't have any preference" option.

Compared to the responses from our previous work, we identify similarities in most cases. The only difference we noticed here (in question 5) is that 44.46% of the respondents believed that under the runtime permission model, the system interacts very frequently with the users, requesting from them to grant permissions to the app that runs at the foreground. This is quite interesting considering the fact that in our previous study only 15% of the respondents expressed the same belief. However, the responses demonstrate that the participants were knowledgeable and felt they have more control on the data they share under the runtime permission model. Thus, they eventually prefer the runtime permission model against the old one.

Considering the replies from the group of 25 respondents, who prioritised the dangerous groups according to the possibility to allow an app to access them, we can see that these users are keener to allow access to the Calendar or the Sensors of their devices and are more hesitant to grant permission to the SMS or the Microphone groups. The dangerous groups that participants would be more willing to allow an app to access (in descending order) are as follows: Calendar, Sensors, Storage, Location, Contacts, Camera, Phone, SMS, Microphone. In the next section we will further discuss these responses. The next section presents results obtained from the analysis of the collected permission data from 13 Android devices.

5   Results

The results presented in this section derive from data received from 13 unique Android devices. Note that this sample might not be large enough to provide clues about particular behavioural characteristics of Android users. However, in this paper, we refer to this group of users in order to compare previous results and eventually confirm our findings, presented in [4].

5.1 General Information

The devices of the 13 participants contained a variety of data. On average, 46 apps were installed in each device (we do not consider system apps in this study). This is a rough estimation because there were some outliers in our sample. For example, device No4 contained 197 apps and, on the other hand, devices No5 and No9 contained only 4 and 2 apps, respectively. If we do not consider the latter, the average number is 54 apps per device. The participants' devices contained 523 unique apps. As already mentioned, the maximum number of installed apps on a device was 197 and the minimum was only 2. The app that declared the maximum number of permissions (83) is the tool com.sec.android.easyMover, which transfers data across different devices. Moreover, com.quickheal.platform and org.thoughtcrime.securesms were the apps that declared the maximum number of dangerous permissions (20).

Figure 1 shows the number of permissions declared in each installed app on device No1. In addition, the same figure shows the number of dangerous permissions included in these apps. Roughly, one can estimate that almost one third of the declared permissions per app belong to dangerous groups. Furthermore, Fig. 2 demonstrates the average number of declared and the average number of dangerous permissions per device. Again, the same trend is evident in the specific figure. Finally, we calculated the declared and the dangerous permissions of the apps that constitute our sample. The average number of declared permissions per app is 15.92 and the average number of dangerous permissions is 4.61. This means that 28.96% of the declared permissions in each device belongs to dangerous groups. Compared to our previous study, where we reported (on average) approximately 12.39 declared and 3.85 dangerous permissions per app, we can see that the same trend exists in the current work; nearly 30% of the requested permissions belong to dangerous groups.

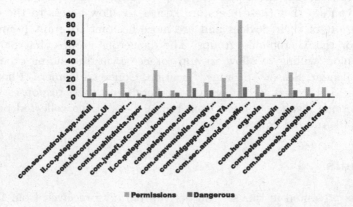

Fig. 1. Number of declared permissions (blue colour) and dangerous permissions (orange colour) in installed apps on device No1. (Color figure online)

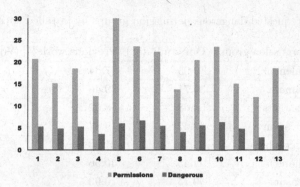

Fig. 2. Average number of declared permissions (blue colour) and dangerous permissions (orange colour) per device. (Color figure online)

5.2 Dangerous Permission Groups

Figure 3 demonstrates the percentage of apps per device that request access to sensitive resources, according to the declared permissions in their AndroidManifest.xml files. The figure illustrates that most apps request access to the devices' Storage group. Contacts, Phone, Location and Camera are also the most requested resources. Table 1 shows on average which are the most requested dangerous permission groups by the installed apps. The last column indicates the results of our previous work [4]. The comparison between the two groups of participants shows that Storage, Contacts, Location or Phone, and Camera are the most requested dangerous groups per device (considering permissions requested in the AndroidManifest.xml file).

Android's runtime permission model was introduced in order to make the user aware that an app needs to access resources that deemed to be sensitive. Hence, Fig. 3 indeed provides insightful information about the most requested dangerous groups. However, it does not actually show which permissions were

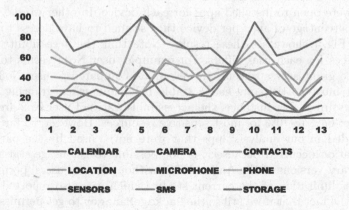

Fig. 3. Percentage of apps per device that request access to sensitive resources.

Table 1. Most requested dangerous permission groups by installed apps (on average).

Permission groups	Our study (%)	Previous work [4] (%)
Calendar	9.05	7.34
Camera	34.71	30.46
Contacts	58.68	58.02
Location	42.42	49.67
Microphone	25.78	21.63
Phone	44.45	40.56
Sensors	0.75	0.93
SMS	24.12	16.51
Storage	75.82	76.64

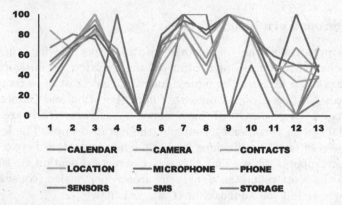

Fig. 4. Percentage of apps that were granted access to dangerous permissions per device.

granted when participants completed our survey. Thus, using information gathered from the `PackageManager` (as discussed in Sect. 4), we estimated which resources were open to installed apps for each device. In other words, we calculated the percentage of apps per device that seemed to have access to sensitive resources; Fig. 4 showcases these results. Note that the accessibility of sensitive resources for each user differs. For example, user No11 seems to be more reluctant to grant access to sensitive resources, compared to user No3. Also, it seems that most participants had a stable behaviour when granting access to sensitive resources. For instance, the accessibility rates of user No2 are between the range of 64% to 70% for most sensitive resources. However, so far we might have included in our analysis apps that were never used by the participants. This limitation occurred because it is not possible to get usage statistics from contemporary versions of the Android OS, without having users' permission.

Another limitation of the current study (which was also reported in [4]) is related to the fact that if we utilise the `PackageManager` to get permission information for apps that were compiled with parameter "targetAPIVersion" < 23, then the `packageInfo.requestedPermissionsFlags` variables will always return the integer 3. This means that we consider that permissions were granted by default to all dangerous groups for these specific applications.

5.3   Fine-Grained Permissions

To overcome the former limitation, we continued our analysis considering data generated from apps that contained only fine-grained user preferences. Thus, for the rest of this section we consider fine-grained permission data from the following users: 2, 3, 4, 6, 10, 11, 13. The numbers of apps with fine-grained permission settings considered from each device respectively are: 12, 6, 11, 7, 6, 6, 22. We will refer to this group as the *"f-g" group*.

Figure 5 shows the percentage of apps in the f-g group that requested access to sensitive resources. The most requested resources on average are as follows: Storage 95.67%, Contacts 85.82%, Location 67.56%, Phone 61.94%, Camera 53.40%.

Figure 6 demonstrates the accessibility to sensitive resources focusing on the participants with fine-grained permission settings. These results are also provided in Table 2. Table 2 shows that the most accessible resources (in descending order) in the f-g group were: Sensors, Camera, Storage, Location, Phone, Contacts, SMS, Microphone, Calendar.

Furthermore, we compared the responses from the two groups of our study (the 'online questionnaire respondents' and the 'f-g group participants') and compiled resulted preferences in Table 3. The first column lists the permissions that respondents were more willing to allow an app to access; the second column lists on average the accessibility to sensitive resources in the devices of our f-g participants, as shown in Table 2 (both in descending order). Interestingly, we can see common trends in these two groups; first, Sensors appear to be more accessible in both groups. This means that if an app requests access to the device's sensors, it is very possible that the user will grant this permission. In addition, SMS and Microphone groups are located at the bottom of both

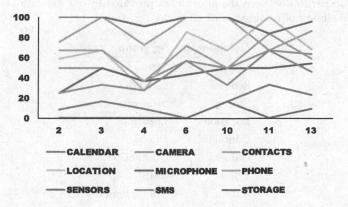

Fig. 5. Percentage of apps in the *f-g* group that requested access to sensitive resources.

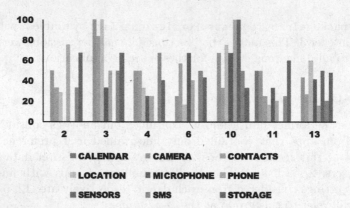

Fig. 6. Percentage of accessible resources per device in the *f-g* group.

Table 2. Percentage (%) of accessible resources in the *f-g* group.

Groups	No2	No3	No4	No6	No10	No11	No13	Average
Calendar	0	0	0	N/A	0	50.00	0	8.33
Camera	50.00	100.0	50.00	25.00	66.67	50.00	42.86	54.93
Contacts	33.33	83.33	50.00	57.14	33.33	25.00	26.32	44.06
Location	28.57	100.0	33.33	16.67	75.00	16.67	60.00	47.18
Microphone	0	33.33	25.00	66.67	66.67	33.33	41.67	38.09
Phone	75.00	50.00	25.00	40.00	100.0	20.00	15.38	46.48
Sensors	N/A	N/A	N/A	N/A	100.00	N/A	50.00	75.00
SMS	33.33	50.00	66.67	50.00	50.00	25.00	20.00	42.14
Storage	66.67	66.67	40.00	42.86	33.33	60.00	47.62	51.02
Average	35.86	60.42	36.25	42.62	58.33	35.00	33.76	

Table 3. Comparison between the priority list provided by questionnaire respondents and the accessibility of resources noticed in the f-g group.

Questionnaire	f-g group
Calendar	Sensors
Sensors	Camera
Storage	Storage
Location	Location
Contacts	Phone
Camera	Contacts
Phone	SMS
SMS	Microphone
Microphone	Calendar

columns. On the contrary, Camera appears to be the second most accessible resource in the f-g group and Calendar the least accessible. These results might indicate that even though users believe they should not provide access to the Camera when requested by an app, they are more keen to do so when this request is actually made. Additionally, despite that questionnaire respondents replied they would allow an app to access their Calendar, we see that the f-g group accessibility to the Calendar resources received the lowest percentage. This phenomenon may have occurred as a result of the fact that some apps request access to the Calendar as a secondary feature of their functionality, thus users did not have the chance to grant or deny access to it.

5.4 Messaging and Social Media Apps

The latter finding urged us to focus on specific apps, aiming to identify connections between functionality and users' privacy settings. The most popular (social) apps in our dataset were the following: Facebook Messenger, Twitter, WhatsApp, Skype, Facebook, Instagram, Snapchat and Slack. Given the small number of participants in this study we will only present comparative results between the current and our previous work for the following apps: Facebook Messenger, Twitter, WhatsApp, Skype, Facebook.

Figures 7 and 8 illustrate the percentage of users that allowed access to sensitive resources after the aforementioned apps requested it. First, we should notice that, in general, the rates of accessibility to the various resources seem to follow the same patterns. For example, WhatsApp users allow access to Camera, Contacts, Microphone, and Storage in both studies. Also, the rates of accessibility to the Storage group for all apps are very high in the current and our previous work. Hence, we conclude that it is very possible an app to get access to the storage of a device when such a request has been made.

Other common characteristics can be highlighted when we examine Skype users; Camera, Contacts, Microphone and Phone are the most accessible resources. Moreover, Facebook Messenger is a similar app, having the same

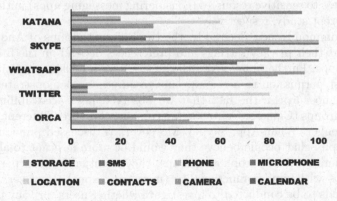

Fig. 7. Percentage of users that allowed access to sensitive resources (previous study).

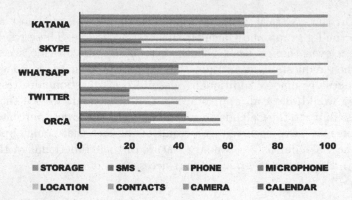

Fig. 8. Percentage of users that allowed access to sensitive resources (current study).

Table 4. Percentage of users that allowed access to sensitive resources (previous study).

Groups	Orca	Twitter	WhatsApp	Skype	Katana
Calendar	0	N/A	N/A	N/A	6.67
Camera	73.68	40.00	83.33	100.0	33.33
Contacts	47.37	33.33	94.44	80.00	33.33
Location	26.32	80.00	22.22	20.00	60.00
Microphone	84.21	6.67	77.78	100.0	20.00
Phone	5.26	6.67	5.56	100.0	20.00
SMS	10.53	6.67	66.67	30.00	6.67
Storage	84.21	73.33	100.0	90.00	93.33

functionality with WhatsApp and Skype. One can notice that the most accessible dangerous groups for Messenger are: Camera, Contacts, Microphone and Storage. In addition, the use of Location services was found to be popular among Twitter and Facebook users. Tables 4 and 5 show the percentage of users that allowed access to sensitive resources (considering messaging apps) in the previous and the current study, respectively.

Those common trends, derived by the two different groups of Android users, indicate that their privacy settings and preferences depend on the functionality of certain apps. Furthermore, given that users have a consistent attitude when apps request permission to access specific resources, as demonstrated in [4], it comes with no surprise the fact that we observed high accessibility to three dangerous groups (Camera, Contacts, Microphone) for three different messaging apps (Messenger, WhatsApp, Skype). Moreover, as discussed previously in this section, despite that people believe they would be more hesitant to allow access to the Camera or the Microphone groups, they eventually grant permission to specific apps with similar functionality (messaging apps). However, additional research needs to be conducted to investigate whether users' privacy preferences are related with their trust on specific apps.

Table 5. Percentage of users that allowed access to sensitive resources (current study).

Groups	Orca	Twitter	WhatsApp	Skype	Katana
Calendar	0	N/A	N/A	N/A	66.67
Camera	42.86	40.0	100.0	75.00	66.67
Contacts	57.14	20.00	80.00	50.00	66.67
Location	28.57	60.00	40.00	25.00	100.0
Microphone	57.14	20.00	80.00	75.00	66.67
Phone	42.86	20.00	40.00	75.00	66.67
SMS	42.86	20.00	40.00	25.00	66.67
Storage	42.86	40.00	100.0	50.00	100.0

6   Discussion

Section 3 discussed the methodology we used to acquire data from participants' devices. We also mentioned that additional metadata were included in the gathered information, i.e., the timestamp of the last update of installed apps and, in some cases, the API version that was used to compile these apps. The latter information was not collected from all devices because we incorporated this feature in later versions of our app.

6.1   App Updates and API Status

Figure 9 illustrates our findings. Blue bars indicate the percentage of apps per device that had been updated at least once (either manually or automatically). Orange bars show the percentage of apps per device compiled with

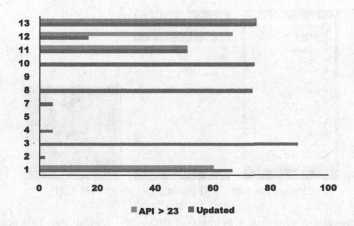

Fig. 9. Percentage of installed apps per device that had been updated at least once (blue colour) and percentage of installed apps compiled with `targetSDKVersion` > 23 (orange colour). (Color figure online)

`targetSDKVersion` greater that API 23. Analysis showed that 50% of the participants did not update their apps or, they selectively updated a small number of apps (up to 17% of the apps were updated in some cases). Additionally, Fig. 9 demonstrates that 50% of the users in our sample updated at least 50% of their apps sometime in the past. Hence, we can deduct that in our small sample of users, only half of them regularly update their apps. Thus, one can suggest that 50% of the users are more vulnerable to malware, given that the updated version of an app can be considered more secure from its previous version.

Additionally, considering data collected from devices No1, No11, No12, No13 (see Fig. 9), we deduce that, approximately 63% of the installed apps (per device) were designed to be compatible with APIs 23, 24 and 25 (API 25 was the most modern version as of February 2017). This means that these apps were fully utilising the capabilities of the runtime permission model. Hence, we can consider that behavioural trends noticed in this study are not substantially skewed by the existence of older apps in some devices. Moreover, as mentioned earlier, we did not collect app usage statistics to avoid engaging our volunteers (Android users) in going through additional steps, such as manually turning on the usage statistics feature for our app. Thus, results presented in Sect. 5.2 might contain information about apps that were never used.

6.2 Privacy Profiles

The usual (and preferred) app installation procedure on an Android device is as follows: Users navigate to the Google Play app store (or any other third-party marketplace), where they can search for their preferred app. Before downloading the app, users have the chance to see a list of permissions that might be requested (Fig. 10a). After installation, and during runtime, if a sensitive resource needs

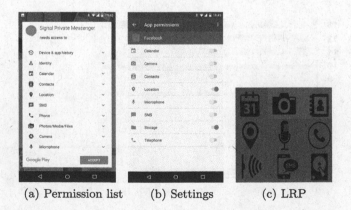

(a) Permission list   (b) Settings   (c) LRP

Fig. 10. Screenshots showing a permission list before installation (a), granted permissions to an installed app (b), and a visual schema describing the *least required permissions* (LRP) for an app. (Color figure online)

to be accessed, the system will issue a message dialogue to get user's approval to access the resource. Users can review and revoke the granted permissions via the Settings app (Fig. 10b).

Section 5.4 showcased privacy settings that seem to be common among users. For example, we noticed that all WhatsApp users allowed access to the Storage. Thus, one could suggest that the app will not be functional if permission to the Storage is not granted. However, users do not have a priori knowledge of this information before they download the particular app. Such information is not provided by the official (or third-party) app marketplaces. Hence, we can state that there exists a gap in the installation procedure, which needs to be filled. In other words, we suggest that users should be able to get basic information about the permissions they need to grant to apps in order to get the minimum functionality they can offer. For instance, the popular messaging app "Google Allo" will not function if access is not granted to (at least) the Contacts, SMS and Storage groups. Another example could be the "Google Duo" video app, which cannot function, unless the user grants access to (at least) the Camera or the Microphone group.

Google Duo is a video app and, indeed, the use of camera is obviously needed, but we believe that users would benefit from schemes that would inform them about the basic requirements of an app. In Fig. 10c, we propose a visual scheme that aims to concisely indicate the minimum permission requirements needed by Android apps in order to function properly. In particular, we consider that a representation of the dangerous permission categories, placed on a 3×3 grid and marked with red and green background colours according to the corresponding accessibility requirements of an app, would probably visualise sufficiently the minimum functionality requirements of this app. Figure 10c demonstrates the proposed visual scheme for an app that will not function unless access to the Camera and Contacts groups is given. Such schemes might also visually compliment (or substitute) existing system information (Fig. 10b).

Finally, although graphs like the one presented in Fig. 4 provide insightful information about the percentage of granted permissions per category (and per device), it would be also useful to propose schemes that efficiently describe these data visually. Hence, we could create a "privacy profile" that represents each user. Figure 11 presents the profiles of 11 participants. Each profile is basically a heat map which represents the percentage of apps (per device) that were granted access to the 9 categories of dangerous permission groups. For example, participant No9 is more keen to provide access to the Calendar, Camera and Microphone, compared to other participants. Moreover, we could say that users like participant No11 or No13 seem to be more cautious when granting permissions to apps, compared to users like No3, No7 or No10.

Further work needs to be done in order to investigate if users who are more keen to grant permissions to apps are more vulnerable to malware attacks. This knowledge might assist major app distributors to fight malware expansion. In addition, further work on the usability of schemes like the one presented in Fig. 10c needs to be done, to assess their usefulness and value to the users' experience provided by online stores.

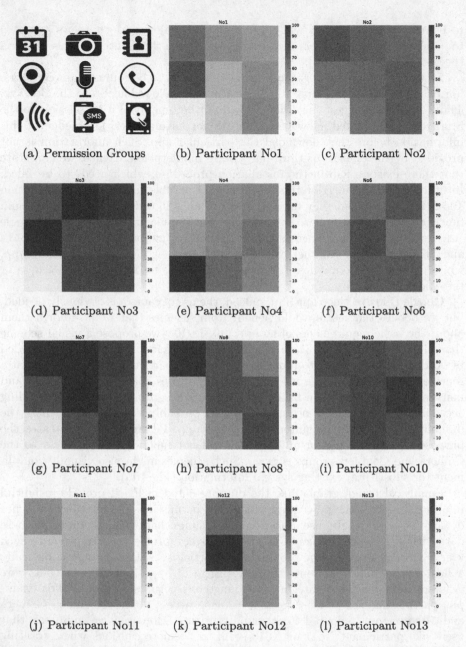

(a) Permission Groups   (b) Participant No1   (c) Participant No2

(d) Participant No3   (e) Participant No4   (f) Participant No6

(g) Participant No7   (h) Participant No8   (i) Participant No10

(j) Participant No11   (k) Participant No12   (l) Participant No13

Fig. 11. User profiles representing the accessibility of sensitive resources on their devices.

7   Conclusions

Privacy-aware users were anticipating the advent of Android's fine-grained permission model for a long time. Our previous study showed that the majority of

Android users positively adapted to this major update. This paper confirmed that most users prefer the new model. Furthermore, we confirmed that the vast majority of Android apps request access to the devices' storage and that most users are willing to permit this action. Moreover, we deduced that although people are more reluctant to allow access to resources such as their cameras or microphones, they tend to grant these permissions to specific app categories. They overcome their initial hesitation to benefit from the provided apps' functionality. We also noted that almost half of the participants in this research work did not update their apps; the other 50% of the participants seem to update their apps regularly. Furthermore, we suggested that users should be informed about the least required resources an app needs to provide its basic functionality. Hence, we proposed a visualisation scheme which could be used in online app marketplaces. Finally, this paper suggested the use of heat maps to represent users' privacy profiles. We intent to test the usability of the proposed schemes as part of future work.

Acknowledgements. This work has been supported by the EPSRC: grant number EP/N008448/1.

References

1. Global smartphone sales by operating system from 2009 to 2015 (in millions). https://www.statista.com/statistics/263445/global-smartphone-sales-by-operating-system-since-2009/. Accessed 10 Feb 2017
2. Normal and Dangerous Permissions. https://developer.android.com/guide/topics/permissions/requesting.html#normal-dangerous. Accessed 10 Feb 2017
3. Almuhimedi, H., Schaub, F., Sadeh, N., Adjerid, I., Acquisti, A., Gluck, J., Cranor, L.F., Agarwal, Y.: Your location has been shared 5,398 times!: a field study on mobile app. privacy nudging. In: Proceedings of the 33rd Annual ACM Conference on Human Factors in Computing Systems, CHI 2015, pp. 787–796. ACM, New York (2015)
4. Andriotis, P., Sasse, M., Stringhini, G.: Permissions snapshots: assessing users' adaptation to the android runtime permission model. In: 2016 IEEE International Workshop on Information Forensics and Security (WIFS), pp. 1–6, December 2016. doi:10.1109/WIFS.2016.7823922
5. Andriotis, P., Takasu, A., Tryfonas, T.: Smartphone message sentiment analysis. In: Peterson, G., Shenoi, S. (eds.) DigitalForensics 2014. IAICT, vol. 433, pp. 253–265. Springer, Heidelberg (2014). doi:10.1007/978-3-662-44952-3_17
6. Andriotis, P., Tryfonas, T.: Impact of user data privacy management controls on mobile device investigations. In: Peterson, G., Shenoi, S. (eds.) Advances in Digital Forensics XII. IFIP AICT, vol. 484, pp. 89–105. Springer, Cham (2016). doi:10.1007/978-3-319-46279-0_5
7. Beresford, A.R., Rice, A., Skehin, N., Sohan, R.: Mockdroid: trading privacy for application functionality on smartphones. In: Proceedings of the 12th Workshop on Mobile Computing Systems and Applications, HotMobile 2011, pp. 49–54. ACM, New York (2011)
8. Bettini, C., Riboni, D.: Privacy protection in pervasive systems: state of the art and technical challenges. Pervasive Mob. Comput. **17**(Part B), 159–174 (2015). 10 Years of Pervasive Computing' in Honor of Chatschik Bisdikian

9. Bugiel, S., Heuser, S., Sadeghi, A.R.: Flexible and fine-grained mandatory access control on android for diverse security and privacy policies. In: Presented as Part of the 22nd USENIX Security Symposium (USENIX Security 2013), pp. 131–146. USENIX, Washington, D.C. (2013)

10. Hornyack, P., Han, S., Jung, J., Schechter, S., Wetherall, D.: These aren't the droids you're looking for: retrofitting android to protect data from imperious applications. In: Proceedings of the 18th ACM Conference on Computer and Communications Security, CCS 2011, pp. 639–652. ACM, New York (2011)

11. Jung, J., Han, S., Wetherall, D.: Short paper: enhancing mobile application permissions with runtime feedback and constraints. In: Proceedings of the Second ACM Workshop on Security and Privacy in Smartphones and Mobile Devices, SPSM 2012, pp. 45–50. ACM, New York (2012)

12. Ongtang, M., McLaughlin, S., Enck, W., McDaniel, P.: Semantically rich application-centric security in android. Secur. Commun. Netw. 5(6), 658–673 (2012)

13. Pearce, P., Felt, A.P., Nunez, G., Wagner, D.: Addroid: privilege separation for applications and advertisers in android. In: Proceedings of the 7th ACM Symposium on Information, Computer and Communications Security, ASIACCS 2012, pp. 71–72. ACM (2012)

14. Wijesekera, P., Baokar, A., Hosseini, A., Egelman, S., Wagner, D., Beznosov, K.: Android permissions remystified: a field study on contextual integrity. In: 24th USENIX Security Symposium (USENIX Security 2015), pp. 499–514. USENIX Association, Washington, D.C., August 2015

Communicability Evaluation of Privacy Settings on Facebook for Android

Beatriz Brito do Rêgo[1]([⊠]), Ingrid Teixeira Monteiro[2],
and Andréia Libório Sampaio[2]

[1] Federal University of Bahia (UFBA), Salvador, Brazil
beatrizbr@ufba.br
[2] Federal University of Ceará (UFC), Quixadá, Brazil
ingrid@ufc.br, andreia.ufc@gmail.com

Abstract. With the widespread popularization of Facebook, which is considered the most used social network nowadays, a concern has become constant among its users: How is users' data privacy being assured, since one of the purposes of Facebook is actually the exposure of user data? Facebook provides privacy settings that help its users to preserve their information. However, users are not always able to access these settings easily. In order to analyze this question, two methods of evaluation were used: Semiotic Inspection Method (SIM) and Communicability Evaluation Method (CEM). The evaluation was carried out considering a very particular profile: users located in Quixadá, a small city of Ceará contryside, a state located in the northeast of Brazil who access Facebook exclusively by mobile phone. We concluded that Facebook has a real concern with its users' information, however, in some cases, they are not receiving this message accordingly. As result, although users understand the risks of lack of privacy, they generally did not know how to use Facebook's tools to ensure their privacy.

Keywords: Facebook · Privacy · SIM · CEM · Android

1 Introduction

The human being has a natural need to be social and has the impulse to seek what s/he lacks in other individuals. In order to support social interaction, social networks were born [1]. An example of a social network is Facebook, which, today, is the most widely used online social network [2]. In addition to the web version, Facebook provides a mobile one, which has versions for smartphones and tablets. Out of its 1.32 billion of users, 55% use smartphones as the main device to connect to the service [3]. The smartphone is a tool on the rise, as many users are adhering to it for ease of transportation and cost, advantages that a desktop environment does not have.

Due to the fast popularization of Facebook, issues related to security, integrity and protection of personal information have emerged primarily by users who do not feel comfortable about making their personal information available to other sites and take the risk of having external companies using them without permission [4]. Facebook enables this type of control to users through security and privacy settings.

From this delicate context, some questions can be made: Was there a decrease in privacy with the increase in popularization of Facebook? Do Facebook privacy settings

© Springer International Publishing AG 2017
T. Tryfonas (Ed.): HAS 2017, LNCS 10292, pp. 623–639, 2017.
DOI: 10.1007/978-3-319-58460-7_43

adequately meet the needs of its users? Do users know how to tune privacy settings to keep track of their accounts? Are users aware of the effects of the privacy settings? Specifically for this article, we are interested in evaluating privacy settings on Facebook in relation to its communicability, which is a usage quality criterion that relates to how well the interface can communicate to the user, during the interaction, the design logic, that is, communicate the designer's vision about who the user is, what their preferences and needs are, and what the system is and how the system can support them [5].

We then selected two HCI evaluation methods focused on communicability: Semiotic Inspection Method (SIM) [6], which, through interface inspection, aims to capture the message elaborated by the designer to be accessed by the user during the interaction with the system. In SIM, only the evaluator interacts with the system, playing the role of the user. The Communicability Evaluation Method (CEM) [6] attempts to identify communication breakdowns that eventually may result in inter-action problems. In addition, to apply CEM, the user him/herself must interact with the system. The evaluator only observes this interaction.

This study was carried out with people from a region in the countryside of the state of Ceará (Brazil). The selected profile was: people with low skills in using personal computers and mobile devices, regardless of their school lever, older than eighteen years old, and that access their Facebook account from a smartphone running Android operating system.

The purpose of the research presented in this article is to identify user access difficulties regarding Facebook privacy settings. As a result of the application of the two methods of evaluation, we could observe breakdowns that were identified with both methods and others that occurred in only one of them, reinforcing the importance of combining different evaluation methods to obtain more comprehensive results. In addition to that, we could point out some suggestions for improving the Facebook interface used in the study (version 28.0.0.0.15), such as: renaming the "Synchronize photos" function to a more meaningful name, changing the order of the menu options, placing "Help Center" item as the first one, among other suggestions listed below.

The remainder of the article is organized as follows: In the next section, we talk about privacy on Facebook, presenting some research work on evaluation of the Facebook privacy settings. Subsequently, there is the methodology section, where we describe the participants profile, the scenarios that were created according to the evaluated environment and the execution of the two methods chosen: SIM and CEM. After the methodology section, we present the results section, in which we describe what was found with the execution of the two methods. Subsequently there is the discussion of results, final considerations and future work.

2 Privacy on Facebook

Facebook provides several communication and socialization functions for its users. Some of them are: (i) inviting friends who are part of Facebook to ensemble their network of friends; (ii) sending messages to them through chat; (iii) sharing news, photos or videos; (iv) posting messages and (v) commenting or "liking" friends' posts.

In the mobile version of Facebook, there are two menus that refer to privacy settings. The first menu is named "*App Settings*", where you can find settings for operations that only occur in the mobile version of Facebook, such as audible warnings when one of the user's friends marks the user on a publication. The second menu is named "*Account Settings*", which holds options for actions that may occur in both mobile and desktop versions, such as the option of analyzing photo publications, useful when a friend marks some user on a photo. When this option is enabled, the photo will go to analysis, and only after the user accepts the publication, it will appear in his/her timeline.

There is a concern with issues related to privacy of Facebook users' information. This concern could be observed, for example, in an evaluation competition promoted in the XI Brazilian Symposium on Human Factors in Computational Systems (IHC)[1], held in 2012, which was themed after the evaluation of features offered by Facebook for data privacy control by its users. The competition sought a reflection on privacy on Facebook and the discussion of how HCI study field can contribute to the quality of interactions mediated by computational technologies.

Therefore, in this competition, several papers discussed about privacy on Facebook social network [4, 9–12]. The articles were split into use of inspection methods and observation methods. Two of them used Semiotic Inspection Method [9, 11], and other three papers [4, 9, 10] used observation methods, such as the CEM and Usability Test. Articles [4, 10] used the Heuristic Evaluation method to compare with the results obtained with observation methods. The paper [8] used data collection using online questionnaires and semi-structured interviews, using Content Analysis method to analyze the collected data. All researchers used methods to evaluate Facebook only for desktop environments.

In addition to the evaluation competition, other research works addressed issues with Facebook privacy, such as [13, 14]. The first one [13] was published in the IHC 2012 but not within the evaluation competition. This shows that it is a quite pertinent theme for the concern with the information that the users let available in the social networks. In this article, the researchers conducted a survey with 225 participants with questions related to people someone accept as a friend or even if users make selection of what they post. In the paper [14] presented in the IHC of 2013, the evaluation was basically composed of interviews, tasks and questions related to these.

All papers cited have important contributions to the subject. But the differential of our research is the target audience of the interior of Ceará state who are not technology experts and only access Facebook through smarthphones.

3   Methodology

In this section, the profile of the participants who were selected for the evaluation will be explained, as well as the scenarios that were created to perform the evaluation of Facebook for mobile phones. We also present in summary how the selected methods were executed, taking into account the environment and the target audience.

---

[1] http://www.ufmt.br/ihc12/#.

3.1   Participants

The participants' profile included people who have a Facebook account and who use smartphones to access their account on the Android platform. In the recruitment phase, we looked for participants older than 18 years. This age limit is due to the fact that users older than 18 years can share information to the general public, to friends, to specific people, among others options. In the account created for who is under 18 years old, the option to post messages is enabled only for friends.

It was not mandatory for the participants to have completed elementary school, but they needed to be able to read, a basic requirement to fully use any online social network. We also target people who did not have advanced computer skills. Finally, we were interested in people living in the city of Quixadá and neighboring regions, where we have this specific type of audience. Our research included people who have a Facebook account and who use smartphones to access their account on Android platform, because the public in the region most of the time owned phones with this operating system. This is shown in the research performed by Damasceno [15], which may be associated with the fact that prices of devices with Android platform are cheaper than those of iOS platform. This research was conducted in 2014, in Quixadá [15] and investigated the penetration of social networks among its users. Out of the 96 interviewees, 65% did not access any type of social network, and the rest had a Facebook account. This is an interesting fact, since Facebook was founded in 2004, and, ten years later, it was known by only 34.5% of the users considered in the research. In addition, only 8% of respondents had access to the internet for more than 5 years [15], suggesting that the public in the region is composed of users with recent experience in the use of Internet and social networks.

Then, to apply SIM, the analyzers had to put themselves in place of people who only had smartphones to access their Facebook accounts, with low technology knowledge and had little experience with social networks, and for the execution of the CEM six (06) participants with different ages, schooling and time of use of Facebook were selected, as shown in Table 1.

Table 1. Profile of participants.

Use	Age	Schooling	Facebook use
U1	34	High school	1 year
U2	55	Elementary	3 years
U3	46	High school	Less than 1 year
U4	28	University degree	5 years
U5	37	Elementary	1 year
U6	18	High school	3 years

3.2   Scenarios

For SIM and CEM, it is necessary to create scenarios to guide the activities proposed by the methods. Scenarios describe human activities or tasks in a story that allows the exploration and discussion of contexts, needs, and requirements [16]. A scenario has a plot, which includes sequences of actions and events: what users do, what happens to them and what changes occur in the environment [5]. For the realization of both methods, we adopted the same scenarios. Three scenarios were elaborated that differed only by the task proposed in each one. In the following, we describe each of these three tasks proposed to the participants:

1. <u>Enable photo sync option:</u> When enabled, each photo taken from the user's smartphone is automatically saved in a Facebook album. The photos remain private until the user chooses to publish them.
2. <u>Disable Messenger Location:</u> After disabling this option, when user is chatting, his/her location information will not be available.
3. <u>Enable reviewing photo posts:</u> When the user enables this option, s/he keeps track of his/her friends' posts on his/her timeline, so no posts will appear without his/her confirmation.

An issue to note is that the first two tasks are available only in the mobile app. The configuration of the third scenario exists in both the mobile application and the desktop environment.

3.3   Execution of Semiotic Inspection Method

The Semiotic Inspection Method (SIM) is based on Semiotic Engineering [6]. SIM is useful to evaluate the communicability through inspection, aiming to build an integrated version of the metacommunication message (the message passed by the designer about the system), identifying inconsistencies and ambiguities among the various signs chosen to represent this message. It is a non-predictive method, so the evaluator explores the artifact in order to identify problems and their causes, deepening their knowledge about the artifact [17].

The inspection occurs according to the classification of the signs that make up the interface, which are divided into metalinguistic, static and dynamic. Metalinguistic signs are those used by the designer to explicitly communicate to users the meanings s/he assigned to other signs encoded in the interface and how they should be used [5], such as error messages, descriptions of interface elements and system documentation. Static signs express the state of the system and whose meaning is interpreted independently of the causal and temporal relations of the interface [18], such as icons, menus and other interface elements. And, finally, the dynamic signs are signs that express the behavior of the system, involving temporal and causal aspects of the interface. They are linked to the interaction itself and should be interpreted by reference to it, such as animations indicating system processing.

The inspection begins with the elaboration of the metamessage corresponding to each of the three classes of signs. This metamessage can be paraphrased as described in Chart 1.

With the metamessages reconstructed, the evaluator compares the results obtained to be able to elaborate a condensed version that unifies the three versions of the metamessage. Thus, in the reporting of results, it is possible to "see" the problems encountered by judging the failures of communicability.

> *"Here is my understanding of who you are, what I've learned you want or need to do, in which preferred ways, and why. Therefore, this is the system that I have designed for you, and this is the way you can or should use it in order to fulfill a range of purposes that fall within this vision."[6].*

Chart 1. Model of the designer's metamessage

The consolidation activity begins with the synthesis of the results, divided into possible knowledge that the user needs to have to perform the task, knowledge acquired after performing the tasks and suggestions for improving the interface to the found problems [5].

3.4   Execution of Communicability Evaluation Method

The main objective of CEM is to evaluate the quality of the communication of the designer received by the user, through the interface, in interaction time. This method increases the knowledge of designers, evaluators and researchers on how users interpret the artifact. This evaluation allows the identification of communication breakdowns that may occur during the interaction of the user with the computational artifact [17].

For the execution of CEM, it is necessary to prepare the environment where the interaction will be observed. Firstly, it was necessary to use a software that made it possible to transfer the image from the mobile phone to the computer, in order to record the user interaction. So this software facilitated the whole process of capturing the images of user interaction. There was also needed a software that recorded the computer screen to later analysis by the evaluator.

Before starting the evaluation, all users were asked to sign a consent form. In addition, participants interacted on Facebook from fictitious accounts created exclusively for the tests. We realized that the use of fictitious accounts left users more relaxed on privacy concerns because, in dealing with their own accounts, users end up being afraid of what can happen to their data. Then, it was verified that the fictitious accounts helped the evaluator to discover more communicability breakdowns by the fact that the users did not inhibit when carrying out the tasks.

For a rigorous analysis of the data generated by CEM, we performed an interview before the scenarios are executed and another one after the end of the activity. Thus, the data were crossed to elaborate the semiotic profile of the system. After the preparation of the analysis, the pilot test was carried out and we consequently updated what was necessary.

With the data collected through interview and recording of the interaction, we started with the interpretation and consolidation of the results of the CEM, which is divided into three parts: tagging, interpretation of tags and elaboration of the semiotic profile.

Tagging is used to identify communicability breakdowns, that is, moments of interaction in which the user demonstrates that he or she has not understood the designer's metacommunication, or moments in which the user finds it difficult to express their intention to communicate in the interface. The CEM establishes thirteen tags [18], which relate these moments of difficulty or lack of understanding to possible user utterances, which represent the breakdowns that may occur during the interaction. The thirteen tags are: "Where is it?", "What's this?", "What now?", "Oops!", "Where am I?", "I can't do it this way", "What happened?", "Looks fine to me", "I give up", "I can to otherwise", "Thanks, but no, thanks" and "Help!". For example, the tag "Oops!" is used when the user abruptly stops an action by realizing that this is not what s/he meant. The "Looks fine to me" is characterized when the user believes he finished the desired task, even when this task did not actually finish successfully.

After tagging, the tags are interpreted, through which the evaluator becomes aware of the main interaction problems [17]. If they exist, the evaluator will be able to say not only what the problems are, but also why they occurred [5]. If there is no tag associated with the interaction it means that, within what was observed, it was not possible to identify breakdowns in the communication between designer and user.

The last step of CEM is the elaboration of the semiotic profile, which consists in achieving an in-depth characterization of the user-designer metacommunication [17]. The semiotic profile is elaborated through the reconstruction of the designer's metamessage as received by the user at the time of the interaction [5].

It is important to emphasize that SIM evaluates the emission of the metacommunication of the design, which is encoded in the interface. The MAC evaluates the quality of the reception of the metacommunication by the user [5].

4 Results

In this section, the results of the evaluation are presented. We first present whay was discovered with SIM and later the results of CEM. In SIM we can see the detailed metamessages of each task, whereas in CEM we describe the results of the three stages, tagging, interpretation and creation of the semiotic profile.

4.1 Semiotic Inspection Method

In this subsection, we describe the three metamessages generated by the evaluator, one to each class of signs (metalinguistic, static and dynamic), taking into account the scenarios that were created.

Before presenting the metamessage we will remember which are the scenarios created for the evaluation. The first was the activation of the photo synchronization option; in the second the user would have to disable the option of Messenger service locations and lastly the activation of the analysis of photo publications.

Below we reproduce the metamessage generated for the inspection of the three scenarios referring to metalinguistic signs. For better understanding, the metamessage is fragmented:

[You possible are a user who knows the term privacy, but if you do not know, you know where to look for this information on Facebook]. The application provides users with the option of *"privacy shortcuts"*, where there are several functions related to user privacy, such as *"Who can see my stuff?"*, *"Who can contact me?"* and *"Privacy Basics"*, among other options. In *"Privacy Basics"*, the designer, using metalinguistic signs, demonstrates his concern for the user, by advising him that he is in charge of his account and that will help him to have the experience that he wishes, offering to the user a small tutorial on privacy. The designer cares about the user's data and tries to inform him if he does not have the necessary knowledge about the term privacy.

[You are a person who cares about your photos available on Facebook, but does not care that your friends have access to your location]. In the first task, photo synchronization is not enabled by default, besides the designer's concern to show the user that their photos are private. When the user selects the *"Sync Photos"* option, which is on the *"App Settings"* menu, a message appears stating that the photos are private. The word "private" is bold and underlined, so that it has greater emphasis and, after synchronization is activated, the designer again informs that the photos are private. Curiously, regarding the second task, which is to disable the Messenger locale service, so that the user's location is not told to a friend by the chat, we have seen that the location information is included by default.

[Do not worry, you have full control of the situation. In addition, you access your Facebook account by both computer and mobile]. When the user performs the task of synchronizing photos, a message appears informing the user that his photos will be available when he connects to a computer. The designer assumes with this information that his users access their accounts by smartphone and also by computer. Therefore, it uses icons from a mobile phone and a computer when the user selects the option to synchronize photos, to demonstrate how the synchronization of photos works, assuming that Facebook users also own a computer.

[You are used to using aid systems when you can not understand a certain action. To help you, we've set up a help center and privacy shortcuts, which explain in detail what are the basics of privacy and our data usage policy]. Regarding the first task, the designer provides a metalinguistic sign in a question mark format, in the *"Sync Photos"* menu, in which the user, by selecting this option, will be redirected to the help center, which is a menu created for helping Facebook users when they are in doubt about a certain action. When we inspect the second task, we do not identify any information related to Messenger locale services, only a brief message that is available when the user selects the menu for the task. Already for the third task, there are two menus in the help center to assist the user, *"Publications and Markings"* and *"Privacy and timeline analysis"*, Reinforcing the designer's concern with photos of Facebook users.

Below we write the metamessage regarding the inspection of the static signs, following the same fragmented format with the evidence of the inspection:

[You are a user using knowledge gained from other interfaces. Knowing this, we use common everyday symbols to guide you]. The symbols chosen by the designer were a gear icon, which refers to *"operation"*, used to refer to settings, and a padlock icon to tell the user that his photos are private and that only he *"has the key"* and the power to decide when to open this padlock.

[You understand that the Messenger settings are not on the tab where your friends are available to chat, but in the application settings]. Because *"Messenger"* is a widely used name for chat, it is expected that this option is located in the area that shows the list of friends online in the chat. In this area, there is the same gear icon in the upper right corner. Because this static sign is also used in App settings, by association, this gear would also lead to chat settings, where the Messenger locations option would be. However, when selecting the tool, the only option that the designer made available is the possibility to activate and deactivate the chat. In this case, the designer seems not to have taken advantage of previous user experience to facilitate their interaction with the system.

And finally, below we have a reconstructed metamessage from the dynamic signs for the three tasks performed:

[You are a user who expects to sync your photos from your phone with a Facebook album, but you want your photos to be private and can only be posted when you are logged in to your desktop account]. When activating photo synchronization, the designer shows the user a message stating that the synchronized photos are private and also shows a dynamic sign in circular arrow format, which is very used to mean page update, communicating the dynamic character of this action, since when updating, if there are new photos saved in the mobile phone, they will automatically appear.

[You are accustomed to on-and-off options, so you will not have trouble making certain settings]. When you go to the *"Messenger Locations"* screen, there is the following information: *"Location is on"*. Beside it, there is a blue icon that can be turned off and on, characterizing itself as a dynamic sign, as the symbol instantly changes its color. As well as the third task, in which the user can confirm the timeline analysis, slide the ON/OFF button and the act of light (represented by the blue color) on and off, reminding to be on and off.

[You will not get immediate feedback from this setting, just when some of your friends tag you in a photo, when you can experience the effects of your actions externally]. The effects of some tasks can not be immediately perceived, because they are configurations that cause only later impacts, giving the impression of *"lack of dynamic signs"*. An example can be applied to the second task: When the user configures the Messenger locale service, he will only see the effect of this option when someone talks to him in the chat or vice versa, and he realizes that his location was not identified in the message. Although not immediate, this is still a dynamic sign, but perceived only *"outside"* the privacy setting interface.

4.2   Communicability Evaluation Method

Regarding CEM, after the evaluation with the users, the tagging stage was performed. The evaluator watched closely each video of each interaction, so that the breakdowns of communicability could be identified. Each break is associated with a tag. The graph below lists the eight tags identified in the tests, colored according to the occurrence in each task (Graph 1).

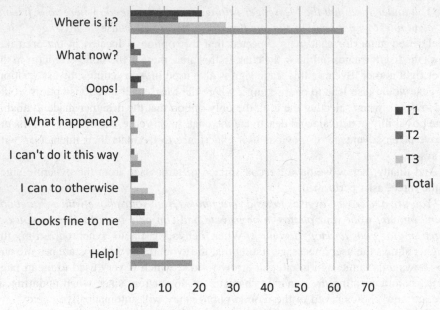

Graph 1. Tags occurrence

It is observed in the graph that of the 13 possible tags, 8 has occurred. Among the five ones that did not generate breakdowns in any of the tasks, we highlight the tag "What's this?". Its absence may be related to the fact that CEM has been executed in smartphone devices, making it difficult to identify its occurrence, since the most recurrent symptom of this tag in desktop systems is to position the mouse cursor over the waiting interface signs of a tooltip about what they mean [18]. In touchscreen interfaces, there is no mouse, nor screen tips, making it difficult to identify this tag. Next, we present the interpretation of the breakdowns in each task separately.

In the first task, all users, except U4, associated the phrase "synchronize photos" to the Facebook photo album. So everyone followed the first step of looking for where the option could be to sync photos, characterizing the "Where is it?" tag. To perform the task, the preferred interaction path would be to access the "Application Settings" menu, then select the "Synchronize Photos" option, however U2 and U6 understood that synchronizing photos would be the creation of a photo album or the viewing photos of albums. Then the two users entered the corresponding menu, where you could see the "synchronize photos" (Sincronizado) option on the right side of the "Uploads" (Carregamentos) and "Albums" (Álbuns) options (Fig. 1). In this way, the two users managed to accomplish the task, however characterizing the break "Go another way".

Users U1, U2, U5 and U6, when creating an album, thought that they had completed the task, when, in fact, they did not, characterizing the tag "Looks fine to me". For this task, U4 was the only one who did not ask the evaluator for help. All the others asked for help, characterizing the tag "Help!", because they could not understand where the function to synchronize photos would be located.

Fig. 1. Syncronize tab

In the second task, users U1, U2, U4 and U5 completed the task in a few steps. U3 and U6 users went different ways. User U3 performed a sequence of steps within menus, and in the end realized that he was not on the right path and returned to the starting point, characterizing the tag "I can't do it this way" User U6 has associated the word "Messenger" with the chat window that shows the list of friends who are online and offline, choosing the configuration gear sign. The subsequent screen, only with one option to activate and deactivate the char surprised the user, characterizing the "What happened?" tag, as shown in Fig. 2.

Fig. 2. Chat tab

In task 3, U1, U2, U3, U4 and U5 performed the same steps that characterized the same breakdowns: first the "Where is it?" tag, then the "I can to otherwise" tag. They entered the application settings menu, thinking that the solution to the task would be in this menu and then selected the *"Photo tagging (alerts enabled)"* (Marcações de foto (alerta ativado)), option, which means that when you mark a photo, the user will be warned by an audible alert, thus characterizing the break "Looks fine to me", because the users thought that they had carried out the task with success. The user U1, after this action, chose in the same menu the option *"Publications in the mural (alert activated)"* (Publicações no mural (alerta ativado)), occurring for the second time the "Looks fine to me" tag. These options can be viewed in Fig. 3. After this sequence of steps, users U2, U3, U4 and U5 have requested help, characterizing the tag "Help!".

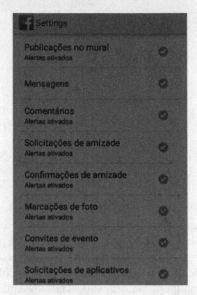

Fig. 3. Application configuration menu

Data collected from the interview

Although CEM did not establish the presentation of interview data with participants as one of its steps, we decided to present some relevant passages in this section as the interviews revealed important information about how they view the privacy issue on Facebook.

One of the interview questions was "How do you understand privacy on Facebook?". U2 said that he uses Facebook as a means of communication between him and his son who lives in another city. But when asked about what he understood about privacy on Facebook, his answer was with another question: "Like, for everything I do on Facebook, any other person who is my friend is able to see?" After an affirmative gesture from the evaluator, he went on to say that "This is not cool!", realizing the risk that he himself should be putting on his profile on the internet.

U3, when asked the same question, was much more detailed in reporting that he did not lose privacy by joining Facebook because: "I always thought that, not that it protected my privacy, but I never went any further, because I only have on Facebook [as a friend] whom I know [offline]". U3 has been unconcerned about privacy issues because it only has close people connected to it through the network. He told a case in which he even excluded some people he knew, but whom he had no close contact with and therefore did not qualify as friends.

U4, when asked if it ever used a privacy configuration tool, replied: "Actually I try to put as few things as possible, so I do not need to use any privacy tools, just put what I believe other people can see." This suggests possible users' difficulties in not knowing how to configure their Facebook, which is why they prefer to police themselves, for fear of exposing their information.

U5, when asked if she had ever been in a situation involving her privacy, answered yes: "I had to share a video of my daughter just for her boyfriend and I ended up sharing it for everybody, because I did not I knew how to put it [only] to him." This user attempted to perform an action that should be simple and, for inexperience, the opposite happened. For this reason, the concern is real whether users can configure their privacy preferences by using Facebook.

At the end of the interaction of the six users, they were asked if they had ever performed these settings, only U4 had did one of the settings, which was the one for photo analysis, but explained that it was a long time ago and that he no longer remembered how to perform the action. When asked about suggestions for improvements, two of the six users, U1 and U3, suggested changing the name "synchronize" because they did not know what it meant.

U1, when asked about what he had learned about privacy after the test, responded: "I thought everything was exposed, I did not know I had those options. [When I] have more time, I'll look to learn the other options." U6 said, "I learned that I can further secure my privacy," when asked about the same question.

U5 was very happy to learn how to set up photo analysis, whose opinion was: "I learned to analyze [the photo tags], I did not know I could, for example, if the person tagged you in a photo and you did not like the photo, so you can block your friends from seeing this picture, citing one example: "I went to the [company name] meeting once, and they took a picture, I was too fat, it was horrible, and this photo everyone saw because [I] did not know that it was not to put on my Facebook."

With all this information, we could see that users care about their privacy, as they cited cases of privacy risk, because they did not know how to configure Facebook to the best of their ability. In the next section, we present the semiotic profile, which is the last stage of CEM.

Semiotic Profile
The semiotic profile has the objective of identifying and explaining the failures in the system's communicability. As in SIM, we used as a template the message that is set out in Chart 1. Below the metamessage was reconstructed according to the evaluator's perspective from what was observed in the users' interactions with the system, always aiming to tell what the designer wanted to pass on to its users.

You are a user who cares about privacy, and we therefore make various features available that you can enjoy. We know that you use Facebook extensively, but you do not know that there are such privacy settings, and if you know they exist, you do not know where to find them. By not knowing how these settings work, you feel fear and insecurity about your data that is available in your Facebook account. By not knowing about these features, you choose not to look for the information, for fear that something bad happen with your data. The fact that Facebook handles personal information ends up leaving you distressed with every action you take, for fear that your data will be put at risk, weakening or extinguishing any desire to seek or test the functions that Facebook makes available to you.

5 Discussion of Results

With the completion of the two methods and the consolidation of the results in both, we could see that both CEM and SIM methods pointed out some breakdowns in the interface communication, both in sending and receiving the messages.

Regarding the first task, with CEM, it was seen that users did not know the function of the "synchronize photos" option, even asking the evaluator for help. But with SIM, it has been seen that there are various forms of help that support users who do not know how to perform certain actions. In a way, this help is not reaching the users to whom this research was directed. In CEM, it was realized that the users' greatest difficulty was to understand what the word "synchronize" meant, making them rely only on the word "photo" of "synchronize photos", to seek resolution of the task, and to focus on the options for photo albums. However, they ended up looking in the wrong places, difficulty that was not identified during the semiotic inspection.

For the second task, five out of the six CEM users performed the task with ease, since the path to solve this task was the same as the first task. Using this knowledge, they ran the scenario correctly, but one of the users attempted to access the chat window, which is understandable, because the evaluator, when executing the SIM in the second task, also noticed that, in this window, there is a static sign (the gear) that refers to a tool that Facebook itself uses in the settings menus.

In addition, the evaluator also noticed in SIM that the message that is displayed to the user when he selects the Messenger location service option is somewhat confusing because the designer reported that it was necessary to select a symbol before the message was sent. This message ends up confusing the user in the evaluator's view. However, CEM showed that, even with the confusing message, the user was able to perform the task without major difficulties, most likely due to previous experiences with similar on/off options.

In the third task, five out of the six users performed the same sequence of steps on CEM. As the first two tasks were performed in the application settings menu, users also sought from this menu the resolution of the third task. In this menu there is a Photo Tagging option, but this option is only to set audible alert, confusing the users.

In SIM, the evaluator discovered that the designer used the metalinguistic features to explain and guide the user so that he could protect his privacy, such as privacy shortcuts, in which there is a specific menu for notions of privacy. Facebook also has a policy that describes how it devotes itself to take care of its users' information. With SIM, Facebook's concern with user data was very evident, but with CEM it was possible to discover that this information, in a way, is not reaching the user in the way the designer intended.

5.1 Suggestions for Improvements

After discovering which breakdowns were found by the two methods, some improvements can be listed so that in the future these failures do not happen.

⑩ Change the name "synchronize" to a word that is closer to the user's vocabulary, such as sharing photos from the phone in an album, because users did not understand what the word meant. Another suggestion is to use metalinguistic signs to explain what the static sign means, a strategy that Facebook itself adopts in other actions.

⑩ Put the "*Help Center*" menu above the "*Settings*" menu, so this option would be more visible to the user. With this modification, they would possibly access this menu first, before executing the settings.

⑩ In the second task, a targeted help is required for the Messenger locale option, as it is not clear from the user message how to select this option.

⑩ Another suggestion would be to remove the blue arrow, which is located on the "*Messenger Service and Location Options*" screen, for the reason users do not understand that the blue arrow will appear when the user opens a chat window only, ultimately confusing the user. Since there are users who only use Facebook through the mobile application. This sign ends up confusing the user, since he will not deal with it in the interface he uses.

⑩ In the third task, it would be of great help not to leave the user's easy access to the option of sound notifications for markings of photos, since the user was confused with this option. If it was placed within a specific menu of sound notifications, it is possible that the user did not enter the menu, thinking that it is in the desired option.

The Facebook application for smartphones was recently upgraded to version 108.0.0.17.68 (January 2017), and even without detailed inspection, it was already possible to identify some differences, such as the "Synchronize *photos*" option, which was replaced by a standalone application, similar to Messenger, titled Moments. This first observation is evidence that some of the problems identified were revealed to be real by the Facebook team, to the point of being resolved in later versions than the one used in our evaluation.

6 Final Considerations

In this research, we performed an evaluation of the communicability on Facebook's privacy settings, using two methods of Semiotic Engineering: SIM and CEM. It is important to notice that the two methods were chosen to be applied together, in order to have a greater relevance in the results. Some ruptures found in CEM were also confirmed in SIM, but there were also a few cases in which the evaluator did not find any difficulty in performing the scenarios during the inspection, but in CEM users experienced difficulties, even asking the evaluator for help. There were also situations where the evaluator identified problems in SIM that did not materialize in CEM.

At the end of this research, it was seen with SIM that Facebook cares about users' data and that it offers a series of options that allow the user to secure their information according to their will. However, in many respects, the CEM showed just the opposite: users generally did not know that these options existed and therefore often experienced situations of lack of privacy with their information, as reported during the interview.

Therefore, it is expected that, with the results and the ruptures found, we might have contributed to future versions of Facebook interface, so that, in addition to put effort to produce a pleasing interface in aesthetic terms, they also improve the communicability concerning privacy issues, so that users can use Facebook the best and safest way.

In addition, we also see as contribution of our research, a complete example of joint application of the SIM and the CEM and also the reflection on privacy in virtual social networks.

We identify as an opportunity for future work, an analysis of the same scenarios performed in this article, as the new application update. Another option would be, after this analysis of the new version, compare the results of the two evaluations and see what has been improved. Another possible deployment, would be after discovering the ruptures of Facebook settings, use Codesign or Participatory design to analyze whether the ruptures found would be eliminated or not if the user had participated in the design. It would also be interesting to apply a similar research focused on other social networks.

References

1. de Meira, S.R.L., Costa, R.A., Jucá, P.M., da Silva, E.M.: Redes Sociais. Sistemas Colaborativos. Editora Campus (2011)
2. Oficina da Net. As 10 maiores redes sociais de 2016. https://www.oficinadanet.com.br/post/16064-quais-sao-as-dez-maiores-redes-sociais. Accessed 18 July 2016
3. Tecmundo. Facebook atinge 1,32 bilhão de usuários e 80% dos brasileiros na web. Disponível em: http://www.tecmundo.com.br/Facebook/60937-Facebook-chega-1–32-bilhao-usuarios-atinge-80-brasileiros-web.htm
4. de Souza, L.G., Sippert, T.A.S., Cardoso, A.S., Boscarioli, C.: Análise da percepção e interação de usuários sobre privacidade e segurança no Facebook. In: Companion Proceedings of the 11th Brazilian Symposium on Human Factors in Computing Systems. Brazilian Computer Society (2012)
5. Barbosa, S.D.J., da Silva, B.S.: Interação Humano-Computador. Elsevier, Rio de Janeiro (2010)
6. de Souza, C.S., Leitão, C.F.: Semiotic engineering methods for scientific research in HCI. Synth. Lect. Hum.-Cent. Inform. 2(1), 1–122 (2009)
7. Francisconi, C.F., Ggoldim, J.R.: Aspectos bioéticos da confidencialidade e privacidade, Iniciação à bioética, Conselho Federal de Medicina, Brasília, pp. 264–284 (1998)
8. Nojiri, S.: O direito à privacidade na era da informática algumas considerações
9. de Carvalho, J.V., Lammel, F., da Silva, J.D., Chipeaux, L.C., Silveira, M.: Inspeção semiótica e avaliação de comunicabilidade: identificando falhas de comunicabilidade sobre as configurações de privacidade do Facebook. In: Companion Proceedings of the 11th Brazilian Symposium on Human Factors in Computing Systems. Brazilian Computer Society (2012)
10. Oliveira, Á.S., Oliveira, A.T., Oliveira, D.S.M., Carneiro, M.P.G., Almeida, R.L.A., Darin, T.G.R.: Exposição de imagem no Facebook: um estudo sobre a privacidade na rede social. In: Companion Proceedings of the 11th Brazilian Symposium on Human Factors in Computing Systems. Brazilian Computer Society (2012)

11. da Rodrigues, K.R.H., Canal, M.C., Xavier, R.A.C., de Alencar, T.S., de Neris, V.P.A.: Avaliando aspectos de privacidade no Facebook pelas lentes de usabilidade, acessibilidade e fatores emocionais. In: Companion Proceedings of the 11th Brazilian Symposium on Human Factors in Computing Systems. Brazilian Computer Society (2012)
12. Terto, A., Alves, C., Rocha, J., Prates, R.: Imagem e privacidade: contradições no Facebook. In: Companion Proceedings of the 11th Brazilian Symposium on Human Factors in Computing Systems. Brazilian Computer Society (2012)
13. Francine Bülow, B., Selbach Silveira, M.: Eu vi o que você fez... e eu sei quem você é!: uma análise sobre privacidade no facebook do ponto de vista dos usuários. In: Proceedings of the 11th Brazilian Symposium on Human Factors in Computing Systems. Brazilian Computer Society (2012)
14. Manoel Pereira, J., Xavier, S., Oliveira Prates, R.: Antecipando possíveis implicações de privacidade na postagem de fotos no Facebook. In: Proceedings of the 12th Brazilian Symposium on Human Factors in Computing Systems. Brazilian Computer Society (2013)
15. Damasceno, F.A.P.: Avaliação do uso de celulares por pessoas residentes no Sertão Central do Estado do Ceará. 60 f. TCC (graduação em Engenharia do Software) - Universidade Federal do Ceará, Campus Quixadá, Quixadá (2014)
16. Rogers, Y., Sharp, H., Preece, J.: Design de Interação: Além da Interação Humano-Computador, 3rd edn, p. 548. Bookman, Porto Alegre (2013)
17. de Castro Salgado, L.C., de Souza, C.S.: CommEST-Uma ferramenta de apoio ao método de Avaliação de Comunicabilidade. In: III Conferência Latino-Americana de Interação Humano-Computador (2007)
18. Bim, S.A., de Souza, C.S.: Obstáculos ao ensino dos métodos de avaliação da Engenharia Semiótica. Pontífice Universidade Católica – Rio de Janeiro (PUC-Rio). Tese (2009)

Sharing the 'Real Me' – How Usage Motivation and Personality Relate to Privacy Protection Behavior on Facebook

Nina Gerber[1(✉)], Paul Gerber[1,2], and Maria Hernando[1]

[1] Faculty of Human Sciences, Technische Universität Darmstadt,
Darmstadt, Germany
{n.gerber,gerber}@psychologie.tu-darmstadt.de
[2] Faculty of Computer Sciences, Technische Universität Darmstadt,
Darmstadt, Germany

Abstract. Although social networks like Facebook have become an important part of social communication and daily life for many people, most users have concerns regarding their privacy on Facebook. In order to gain a deeper understanding of how users try to protect their private data on Facebook, we conducted an online survey with 280 German Facebook users. We used regression analyses to investigate if usage motivation and personality relate to the management of privacy settings as well as the deployment of other protection strategies in Facebook, such as blocking certain contacts or deleting a post or photo/video tag. Our results showed that Facebook users with rather lax privacy settings have a greater feeling of being meaningful and stimulated when using Facebook than users with rather strict privacy settings. Furthermore, Facebook users scoring high on extraversion and low on agreeableness tend to use more other protection strategies besides the management of privacy settings. However, no association could be found between usage motivation and the deployment of other protection strategies on the one hand, and between personality and the management of privacy settings on the other hand. The results indicate that it is important for privacy researchers as well as product and privacy intervention designers to consider the user's motivation to share personal data, because only if privacy studies and interventions account for this important factor, it is possible not only to gain a complete picture of the privacy behavior of users, but also to influence it.

Keywords: Facebook · Needs · Personality · Privacy · Privacy protection strategies · Privacy settings · Social network services · Usage motivation

1 Introduction

For many people, social networks like Facebook have become an important part of their daily life and social communication processes [42]. Despite the numerous advantages and possibilities Facebook offers to its users, many of them have mixed feelings when it comes to the disclosure of personal data on Facebook. Indeed, Acquisti and Gross [1] showed that most Facebook users had more concerns related to privacy

© Springer International Publishing AG 2017
T. Tryfonas (Ed.): HAS 2017, LNCS 10292, pp. 640–655, 2017.
DOI: 10.1007/978-3-319-58460-7_44

than to terrorism or environmental pollution. Although their privacy concerns do not seem to stop users from sharing personal information on Facebook entirely [42], numerous studies indicate that users apply different protection strategies to guard their data, such as untagging photos, deleting posts and managing their privacy settings [6, 8, 20, 41]. In order to gain a deeper understanding of the deployment of different privacy protection strategies, more research is needed regarding the influence of potentially relevant factors like personality [38] and motivation to share data [16]. To close this gap, we conducted a survey with 280 Facebook users. Using regression analysis, we took a first step in showing how personality and motivation to use Facebook (i.e. intended fulfillment of various needs through Facebook usage) can be used to predict privacy protection behavior.

Our contributions are two-fold:

- We contribute to the theoretical understanding of privacy behavior on social networks by demonstrating the importance of usage motivation.
- Our results indicate how certain personality characteristics are related to the deployment of different privacy protection strategies.

The remainder of this paper is organized as follows: The second chapter gives an overview of related work, the third chapter provides the theoretical background as well as the research questions, the fourth chapter focuses on the research methodology and the fifth chapter contains the analysis and results of our study. Finally, the research findings are discussed in chapter six.

2   Related Work

A number of studies have dealt with the deployment of different privacy protection strategies by Facebook users. For example, Debatin et al. [6] showed that Facebook users who had recently experienced a personal privacy invasion were more likely to alter their privacy settings compared to users who just heard about a privacy invasion experienced by other users. Young and Quan-Haase [41] found that university students mainly adopted privacy protection strategies that restricted access to their personal data for different members of the Facebook community, rather than strategies that would allow them to control data access for third parties. Furthermore, they showed that university students do not use fictitious information as protection strategy, since this would lead to confusion among friends and peers. Another study by Staddon, Acquisti and LeFevre [36] concerning the use of privacy protection strategies on Facebook not only showed that the controlling of post visibility is strongly correlated with the deletion of posts, but also that users who value privacy features most generally show more privacy actions.

Furthermore, the results of Peters, Winschiers-Theophilus and Mennecke [25] indicate that US users would rather remove friends from their contact list than change their privacy settings to restrict the visibility of their data, whereas Namibian users refuse from the deletion of friends due to the concern of being rude. Therefore, 50% of the participants reported that they restricted some friends from seeing all of their posts.

They further showed that US users tend to update their privacy settings usually when they are looking for or after they found a new job.

. Beyond culture, other demographic factors seem to influence privacy protection behavior as well. Female users are more likely to have a friends-only Facebook profile [37] and tend to use a more diverse set of technological privacy tools (i.e. protection tools implemented in the social network site itself) than males [7, 19], maybe because women generally have more privacy concerns related to safety (e.g., stalking) and therefore transfer their protection strategies to the online context. When it comes to teenagers, however, Feng and Xie [11] found that females are indeed more likely to set their profile to private and adopt more privacy-setting strategies, but do not express more privacy concerns. Their results further suggest that older teenagers tend to implement more privacy protection strategies (e.g., deleting someone from their friends list, deleting older posts, block people, untag photos), whereas younger adults are more likely to show a wider use of technological privacy tools than older adults [19], maybe due to greater knowledge of and skills in using these technologies.

Ross et al. [28] suggest that the motivation someone has to use Facebook (e.g., to communicate, seek social support, be entertained) might also be useful in understanding Facebook usage behavior. Using factor analysis, Sheldon [33] identified six motives for using Facebook: relationship maintenance, passing time, interacting in a virtual community, entertainment, coolness and companionship. Facebook usage for reasons of relationship maintenance was associated with a greater number of Facebook friends, whereas usage for entertainment purposes and passing time significantly predicted frequent change of one's Facebook profile. Further research on this topic [35] showed that Facebook users with high levels of self-disclosure were more satisfied with Facebook's ability to entertain and pass time. Furthermore, Hollenbaugh and Ferris [13] found that Facebook usage for exhibitionism and relationship maintenance is associated with larger amounts of disclosed personal information. They also showed that usage for relationship maintenance is associated with disclosing more breath of information in Facebook, whereas the depth of information disclosure was found to be related to the usage motivation 'interacting in a virtual community'. The results of Waters and Ackerman [40] suggest that Facebook users disclose their data to share information with others, to store information and being entertained, to keep up with trends and to show off. On the other hand, Krasnova et al. [17] found evidence for an association between self-disclosure on Facebook and relying on the convenience for maintaining relationships, building new relationships and enjoyment.

Regarding personality, Lang and Barton [18] showed that users scoring higher on agreeableness are more likely to choose direct communication with the uploader in order to remove an unwanted picture of themselves. Their results further suggest that users scoring higher on conscientiousness rather choose an indirect strategy to get rid of the unwanted picture, for example by unfriending the uploader and thereby deleting the association between the picture and their profile. Study results differ regarding the relationship of personality and general disclosure of information on Facebook: Amichai-Hamburger and Vinitzky [2] found that extraverts are less and neurotic and persons scoring high on openness to experience are more likely to disclose personal information, whereas Correa et al. [5] showed that extraverts tend to post more pictures and information about their activities. In another study [23], highly agreeable users were found to post more content about themselves, while at the same time, users scoring high on agreeableness, conscientiousness, emotional stability and introversion tend to experience more regret for posting inappropriate content in the past. Utz and Kramer [39] showed that narcissistic users (i.e. users who think they are a very special person who deserves a lot of attention) of the German social network 'StudiVZ' choose less restrictive privacy settings, but this effect did not occur for users of the Dutch social network Hyves.

3 Theoretical Background and Research Questions

3.1 Need Fulfillment

The Uses and Gratification Theory states that people decide to use a specific medium (e.g., Facebook) if it can gratify their social and psychological needs [10, 15]. Active participation in online social networks like Facebook is associated with various psychological and social needs. Three of them are innate psychological needs that, according to self-determination theory (SDT) [29], form the basis for self-motivation and personality integration: (a) autonomy, (b) competence and (c) relatedness [21, 27]. Autonomy refers to the feeling that one's activities are self-chosen and self-endorsed, competence describes the perception of being effective in one's activities and relatedness means a sense of closeness with others. Based on a set of studies that build on the most established theories concerning psychological needs, Sheldon et al. [32] identified a set of ten needs that have the potential to create a positive experience. Of these ten needs, seven have shown to be of particular importance for users dealing with interactive products [12]. In addition to the three fundamental needs postulated by SDT, these are: (d) meaningfulness, (e) pleasure-stimulation, (f) security and (g) popularity-influence. Meaningfulness refers to the feeling that one is moving toward an ideal version of oneself, whereas pleasure or stimulation addresses a hedonic desire to experience pleasure and be stimulated. Security refers to a sense of order and predictability and popularity-influence describes the ability to 'win friends and influence people' [4]; as cited in [32]. The general association between Facebook usage and need fulfillment leads us to the following research questions:

RQ1a: Do Facebook users with strict and those with lax privacy settings differ pertaining to the needs that motivate them to use Facebook (i.e. (a) autonomy, (b) competence, (c) relatedness, (d) meaningfulness, (e) pleasure-stimulation, (f) security and (g) popularity-influence)?

RQ1b: Do Facebook users who deploy certain privacy protection strategies besides the management of privacy settings and those who do not differ pertaining to the needs that motivate them to use Facebook (i.e. (a) autonomy, (b) competence, (c) relatedness, (d) meaningfulness, (e) pleasure-stimulation, (f) security and (g) popularity-influence)?

3.2   Personality Traits

Beside psychological needs, recent study results indicate that social network participation is influenced by certain personality traits [2, 3, 5, 23]. Certainly the most common model of personality is the five factor model, also called 'Big Five personality traits', which describes human personality on the basis of five dimensions: (a) openness to experience, (b) conscientiousness, (c) extraversion, (d) agreeableness and (e) neuroticism (i.e. emotional stability) [22]. Although the 'Big Fives' have been mainly used to describe frequency and intensity of Facebook usage [2, 28] or the deployment of specific Facebook functions like chats or timeline posts [30] so far, they are likely to be associated with the deployment of certain privacy protection strategies as well [18]. We therefore add the following research questions:

RQ2a: Do Facebook users with strict and those with lax privacy settings differ pertaining to their personality traits (i.e. (a) openness to experience, (b) conscientiousness, (c) extraversion, (d) agreeableness and (e) neuroticism)?

RQ2b: Do Facebook users who deploy certain privacy protection strategies besides the management of privacy settings and those who do not differ pertaining to their personality traits (i.e. (a) openness to experience, (b) conscientiousness, (c) extraversion, (d) agreeableness and (e) neuroticism)?

4   Research Methodology

We conducted an online survey with 280 German Facebook users. All questions were implemented in SoSci Survey [24] and presented in German. It took participants about 30 min to complete the whole survey. To recruit participants, the questionnaire link was sent to 270 German student mailing lists. Of the respondents, 71.8% were female and 27.1% were male (1.1% did not specify their gender), ranging in age from 18 to 45 years (M = 22.84, SD = 3.76). Five Amazon coupons á 20€ were drawn among participants. Psychology students from our own university received course credits.

4.1   Measures

Various items were used to assess need fulfillment, personality traits, privacy settings, other privacy protection strategies and demographics. To increase reliability and validity, items are based upon previously validated instruments whenever available. Item formulation prompted participants to answer as accurately as possible. To achieve this goal, formulations like 'What do you think...' or 'Could you please estimate...' were avoided, and where possible it was spoken in terms of facts ('How often do you...' or 'How many times do you...' etc.). Additionally, items that asked for content that could not be easily found by the participants included click-path indications to point to where the content of the item could be found (e.g. for item PS03 'Home → Click on the lock symbol on the top right → 'Who can see my stuff?''). Two filtering questions were

Table 1. Items used to assess privacy settings (PS) and the deployment of other privacy protection strategies (OS)

Nr.	Item
PS01	Is it possible to find your profile via Google or other search engines? Yes (6) No (0)
PS02	Have you ever changed the default privacy settings on Facebook? Yes (6) No (0) I don't know (0)
PS03	Who can see your Facebook profile and its contents? Only you (6) User-defined (selected people and groups) (3) Only your Friends on Facebook (3) Friends except Acquaintances (3) Anyone on or off Facebook (0)
PS04	Do you have to agree first if other people try to tag you in a post/photo/video? Yes (6) No (0)
PS05	Who is able to see your e-mail address? Your Friends (4) Friends of Friends (2) Everyone (0) Data not provided on Facebook (6)
PS06	Who is able to see your telephone number? *(answer options see PS05)*
PS07	Who is able to see your current location? Only you (6) User-defined (selected people and groups) (4) Your Friends on Facebook (4) Friends of Friends (2) Anyone on or off Facebook (0) Data not provided on Facebook (6)
PS08	Who is able to see your birthplace? *(answer options see PS07)*
PS09	Who is able to see your date of birth? *(answer options see PS07)*
PS10	Who is able to see your relationship status? *(answer options see PS07)*
PS11	Who is able to see your family relations? *(answer options see PS07)*
PS12	Who is able to see your employer? *(answer options see PS07)*
PS13	Who is able to see your educational institution? *(answer options see PS07)*
OS01	Do you use the blocking feature? Yes No
OS02	Have you ever deleted a post on your time wall to prevent other people from reading it? Yes No
OS03	Have you ever provided incomplete or fictitious information on Facebook on purpose to prevent other people from collection information about you? Yes No
OS04	Have you ever deleted a tag on a photo or video of you? Yes No

used to exclude participants who do not use Facebook on a regular basis and those who use it as part of their working activity and not for private purposes. Five items were used to assess the participants' gender, age, level of education, nationality and duration of Facebook usage.

To assess need fulfillment trough Facebook usage, we used the Needs Scale developed by Diefenbach, Lenz and Hassenzahl [9]. The Needs Scale evaluates the extent to which an interactive product (e.g. Facebook) fulfills the seven postulated needs that are associated with the use of interactive products (autonomy, competence, relatedness, meaningfulness, pleasure-stimulation, security and popularity-influence). Items corresponding to each need are presented as continuation of the sentence 'When using the product, I generally feel that…'. All items were measured on a 5-Point Likert scale with 1 representing 'strongly disagree' and 5 'strongly agree'.

Personality traits were assessed with the BFI-10 scale, a brief version of the Big Five Inventory developed by Rammstedt and John [26]. In this 10-item version, each Big Five personality construct is assessed with two items. All items were measured on a 5-Point Likert scale with 1 representing 'strongly disagree' and 5 'strongly agree'.

A total of thirteen items was used to measure the participants' privacy settings. Answer options matched the privacy setting options available on Facebook at the time of questionnaire development (12/20/2015). Four items corresponding to the deployment of other privacy protection strategies were developed in order to evaluate to which extent users do protect their private information from undesired (public) access. The items used to assess privacy settings (PS) as well as other privacy protection strategies (OS) can be found in Table 1.

5   Analysis and Results

5.1   Calculation of Privacy Scores

Privacy Settings. For statistical analysis, a score between zero and six points was assigned to every answer option of the privacy setting items (see Table 2). Depending on his or her answers, a privacy setting score was calculated for every participant by summing up the individual answer scores. The calculated privacy setting scores range from 15 to 78 points, with 78 being the maximum reachable. Table 2 summarizes the distribution of the scores across participants.

Other Privacy Protection Strategies. To calculate a score for the deployment of other privacy protection strategies besides the management of privacy settings, another score was calculated by summing up the positive answers for each protection strategy. The calculated protection strategy scores range from 0 to 4 points (M = 2.16, SD = 1.13), with 4 being the maximum reachable (Table 2).

Table 2. Distribution of privacy setting scores

N	280	Percentiles								
Mean	58.66	P_{10}	P_{20}	P_{30}	P_{40}	P_{50}	P_{60}	P_{70}	P_{80}	P_{90}
SD	11.39	41	51	55	57	61	63	67	68	71
Minimum	15									
Maximum	78									

5.2 Examination of the Research Questions

Need Fulfillment

RQ1a. Linear regression analysis was used to test if Facebook users with strict and those with lax privacy settings differ pertaining to the needs that motivate them to use Facebook. All seven needs were entered as predictors, whereas the privacy setting score was used as dependent variable. The resulting regression model exhibited an adjusted R^2 of .049, thereby explaining a total of 5% in the variance of privacy setting management (F = 3.039, p < .05). However, only meaningfulness was found to be of significant predictive power (β = −.274, t = −3.36, p < .001), with higher values of meaningfulness indicating the usage of lax privacy settings.

To further investigate the relationship between privacy settings and usage motivation, we compared the need values for the participants with very lax privacy settings ($\leq 10\%$, i.e. percentile 10) to the values for those with very strict privacy settings ($\geq 90\%$, i.e. percentile 90+). Therefore, a multivariate analysis of variance (MANOVA) was conducted, with the seven needs serving as dependent variables and the percentile membership as independent variable.

As can be seen in Fig. 1 the participants with very strict privacy settings showed significantly different values for meaningfulness and pleasure-stimulation compared to those with very lax privacy settings. Table 3 illustrates the need profiles of both groups.

RQ1b. Analog to research question 1a, a linear regression analysis was conducted to test if Facebook users who deploy certain privacy protection strategies besides the management of privacy settings and those who do not differ pertaining to the needs that motivate them to use Facebook. Again, all seven needs were entered as predictors, whereas the protection strategy score was used as dependent variable. The resulting regression model held no significant prediction power (F = 0.247, p = .973).

Personality Traits

RQ2a. Another regression analysis was conducted to test if Facebook users with strict and those with lax privacy settings differ pertaining to their personality. Therefore, the 'Big 5' personality traits were entered as predictors, whereas the privacy setting score was used as dependent variable. The resulting regression model held no significant prediction power (F = 1.732, p = .127).

RQ2b. Analog to research question 2a, a linear regression analysis was conducted to test if Facebook users who deploy certain privacy protection strategies besides the management of privacy settings and those who do not differ pertaining to their personality. Again, the 'Big 5' personality traits were entered as predictors, whereas the

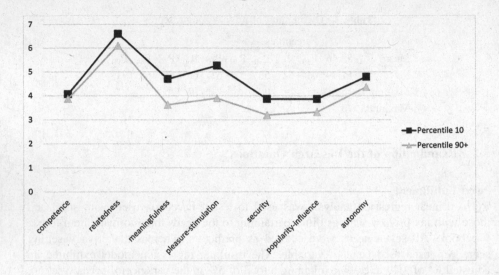

Fig. 1. Need profiles for percentile 10 and percentile 90+ of the privacy setting scores

Table 3. Results of the MANOVA testing the differences of need values for users with very strict and very lax privacy settings

Need	F-value	Sig.	Partial η^2
Autonomy	0.62	.44	.009
Competence	0.09	.77	.001
Relatedness	0.60	.44	.009
Meaningfulness	6.48	.01*	.091
Pleasure-stimulation	10.61	.002**	.140
Security	2.02	.16	.030
Popularity-influence	1.99	.16	.030

Note: $*p < .05$; $**p < .01$; $***p < .001$

protection strategy score was used as dependent variable. The resulting regression model exhibited an adjusted R^2 of .055, thereby explaining a total of 5.5% in the variance of protection strategy deployment ($F = 4.243$, $p < .001$). Two personality traits, extraversion ($\beta = .232$, $t = 3.891$, $p < .001$) and agreeableness ($\beta = -.121$, $t = -2.045$, $p < .05$) showed a significant prediction for the deployment of other protection strategies besides the management of privacy settings.

To gain a deeper understanding of the particular protection strategies deployed depending on the specific personality of the Facebook users, we conducted individual linear regression analyses for each of the four protection strategies. The regression models showed significant predictive power for the use of the blocking function with an adjusted R^2 of .022 ($F = 2.272$, $p < .05$), the deletion of a post with an adjusted R^2 of .027 ($F = 2.542$, $p < .05$) and the deletion of a photo/video tag with an adjusted R^2 of .056 ($F = 4.289$, $p < .001$). The detailed results can be found in Table 4.

Table 4. Personality traits predictor values for the deployment of other protection strategies

Protection strategy	Personality trait	β -value	t-value	Sig.
Use of the blocking feature	Extraversion	.146	2.400	.017*
	Agreeableness	−.127	−2.116	.035*
Deletion of a post	Extraversion	.173	2.856	.005**
	Conscientiousness	−.128	−2.142	.033*
Deletion of a photo/video tag	Extraversion	.253	4.238	<.001***
	Openness to experience	−.134	−2.266	.024*

Note: $*p < .05$; $**p < .01$; $***p < .001$

No significant prediction could be found for the use of incomplete or fictitious information. Figure 2 shows the personality profiles of Facebook users who deploy the
particular protection strategies compared to those who do not.

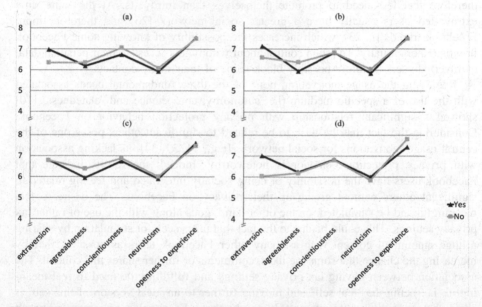

Fig. 2. Illustration of the personality traits of users who (do not) use different protection
strategies. (a) Deletion of a post; (b) use of the blocking feature; (c) incomplete or fictitious
information; (d) deletion of a photo/video tag

6   Discussion

The goal of this study was to investigate if usage motivation and personality relate to
the management of privacy settings as well as the deployment of other protection
strategies in Facebook. Our results showed that Facebook users with rather lax privacy
settings have a greater feeling of being meaningful and stimulated when using
Facebook than users with rather strict privacy settings. Furthermore, Facebook users

scoring high on extraversion and low on agreeableness tend to use more other protection strategies besides the management of privacy settings, such as blocking certain persons or deleting a post or photo/video tag. In detail, (1) higher values of extraversion and lower values of agreeableness are associated with the use of the blocking feature, (2) higher values of extraversion and lower values of conscientiousness relate to the deletion of posts and higher values of extraversion and (3) lower values of openness to experience relate to the deletion of photo/video tags. However, no association could be found between usage motivation and the deployment of other protection strategies on the one hand, and between personality and the management of privacy settings on the other hand.

Although the association between extraversion and use of privacy protection strategies might seem contra intuitive at first glance, it is in line with the results from Amichai-Hamburger and Vinitzky [2], who showed that extraverted users tend to place less information on their Facebook profiles than introverted users, which may be explained by the fact that extraverts rely to a greater extend on their social skills and therefore feel less need to promote themselves than introverts. At the same time extraverted users usually have a greater social network [26] and therefore more Facebook friends [2, 23], which increases the possibility of knowing some Facebook friends rather casually. To retain control about whom gets access to their personal data, extraverted users therefore possibly block some of their many contacts.

Regarding the usage motivation, none of the three fundamental needs associated with the use of a specific medium (i.e. autonomy, competence and relatedness) [10] showed a significant relationship with privacy protection behavior on Facebook. Considering the fact that the wish to be related to significant others poses one of the central usage motivations for social networks [e.g., 14, 31, 34], its lacking association with privacy protection behavior is noteworthy. Indeed, the results indicate that Facebook users have the possibility of being socially integrated and feeling related to significant others without giving up their privacy on Facebook. The desire to feel meaningful and be stimulated, on the other hand, goes along with the use of rather lax privacy settings. This could be due to the fact that users seek for stimulation by sharing a huge amount of content with as many other Facebook users as possible, thereby increasing the chance that someone likes, comments or further shares this content. The association between having lax privacy settings and fulfilling the need to feel meaningful, i.e. being the 'real self' and moving further to an ideal version of this self, is somewhat more difficult to interpret. It may be that a Facebook user perceives oneself as his or her 'real self' to a greater extend if this self is shared with as many other users as possible. At the same time, this form of self-disclosure prevents other people from getting a false picture of the particular user due to a lack of information. Looking at the need profiles in its entirety, another possible explanation could be that users with a more moderate need profile tend to have stricter privacy settings because as specific needs gain significant importance during the usage of Facebook, other considerations like privacy take a back seat and hence, users pay less attention to their privacy settings.

Finally, it can be said that personality is somewhat associated with the deployment of specific privacy protection strategies, whereas usage motivation (i.e. need fulfillment) is related to the management of privacy settings. Considering that most of the protection strategies investigated refer at least in the broadest sense to the interaction with other people, it sounds reasonable that personality plays a role for their deployment. Privacy settings, on the other hand, are of a more technical nature and therefore are more associated with the goals one wants to reach by using Facebook.

6.1 Implications

Our results hold several implications for privacy researchers as well as designers of privacy friendly applications. First of all, when speaking about privacy, it is important to consider the context in which personal data is provided by a user. Designers of privacy friendly applications or interventions that aim to increase a user's privacy self-protection should bear in mind that users have various motivations to share their data, for example to feel related to significant others, but also to feel meaningful or to be stimulated. If an alternative privacy-friendly application cannot provide the intended gratification, users will continue to use the established, privacy-threatening applications. Equally, privacy researchers have to consider the usage motivations and needs that the investigated user aims to fulfill, as they seem to explain some of the variance in privacy setting management. Personality, on the other hand, appears to be associated with the deployment of other, more concrete and behavior-centered protection strategies like the deletion of a post or photo/video tag or usage of the blocking feature. Hence, it is important for privacy researchers to assess a wide range of privacy protection strategies and not only focus on the management of privacy settings. Product designers should account for the fact that less extraverted users deploy fewer privacy protection strategies, maybe because they feel a stronger need to promote themselves online. Therefore, innovative technological privacy friendly solutions should enable introverted users to construct an impressive online identity without revealing too much of their private data.

6.2 Limitations

Like any survey trying to assess actual behavior, this study has various limitations that should be kept in mind when drawing conclusions based on the results. Since we did not verify the self-reported privacy behavior, it is quite possible that participants did euphemize their privacy efforts or simply did not recall their true privacy settings. However, we tried to avoid the last point by instructing the participants to check on their actual privacy settings if they were not sure about them, and added click-paths that point to where the particular content could be found. Nonetheless, we do not know how often participants use the particular protection strategies like blocking another user, and under which circumstances they do so. Further research is needed to gain a deeper understanding of the situational and motivational factors that influence the deployment of certain protection strategies. Furthermore, the BFI-10 scale, which we used to measure the big five personality traits, is known for rather low levels of reliability, compared to the long version [26]. We decided to use it nonetheless, because a methodologically satisfying measurement of personality based on a sufficient amount of items would have taken about thirty minutes, which we considered as inappropriate for the present study design. However, the low reliability of personality measurement should be kept in mind when interpreting the study results. Another limitation is the use of regression analyses based on self-reported data, which allows no interpretation of causality. Further studies are needed to provide an experimental investigation of actual privacy behavior and the causal effects of usage motivation and personality. Furthermore, we limited our research to the context of Facebook usage. Although Facebook is the most popular social network nowadays, we do not know if the results can be generalized to other privacy related contexts like the installation of smartphone apps or the encryption of e-mail communications. Since most participants stem from university populations, the sample is most likely skewed (i.e. younger, higher educated and eventually over-averagely tech-savvy), compared to the general population. Further studies should be based on more heterogeneous samples to allow for generalization.

6.3 Future Work

Our next steps will contain a more generalized approach to investigate the effects of usage motivation on privacy decisions and behavior. Since the need for meaningfulness and pleasure-stimulation seem to be associated with privacy related behavior in the social network context, it could be that other needs play a significant role in other contexts. If we are able to identify a pattern which can be used to predict whether a user pays more or less attention to non-primarily usage considerations like the own privacy, this would be very valuable for the design of privacy interventions. Equally, usage motivations/needs could be beneficial for defining the context a service or application is used in on a more general level than 'social networks' or 'e-commerce' and thus provide new insights into differences between users of the same service or application.

6.4 Conclusion

Investigating 280 German Facebook users, we found that usage motivation significantly predicts the management of privacy settings, whereas personality plays a significant role in the deployment of other privacy protection strategies such as use of the blocking feature or deletion of a photo or video tag. In detail, extraverted users tend to deploy a wider range of privacy protection strategies than rather introverted users. Regarding the management of privacy settings, the use of lax settings is associated with a greater feeling of being meaningful and stimulated when using Facebook. Product designers and privacy researchers therefore should consider the context in which users provide personal data, i.e. what motivates them to share their data in the first place. Only if privacy studies and interventions account for these important factors, it is possible to not only gain a complete picture of but also to influence the privacy behavior of users.

Acknowledgments. The research reported in this paper has been supported by the German Federal Ministry of Education and Research (BMBF) within MoPPa.

References

1. Acquisti, A., Gross, R.: Imagined communities: awareness, information sharing, and privacy on the Facebook. In: Danezis, G., Golle, P. (eds.) PET 2006. LNCS, vol. 4258, pp. 36–58. Springer, Heidelberg (2006). doi:10.1007/11957454_3
2. Amichai-Hamburger, Y., Vinitzky, G.: Social network use and personality. Comput. Hum. Behav. **26**, 1289–1295 (2010). doi:10.1016/j.chb.2010.03.018
3. Büschel, I., Mehdi, R., Cammilleri, A., Marzouki, Y., Elger, B.: Protecting human health and security in digital Europe: how to deal with the "Privacy Paradox". Sci. Eng. Ethics **20**, 639–658 (2014). doi:10.1007/s11948-013-9511-y
4. Carnegie, D.: How to Win Friends and Influence People. Simon & Schuster, New York (1936)
5. Correa, T., Hinsley, A.W., de Zúñiga, H.G.: Who interacts on the Web? The intersection of users' personality and social media use. Comput. Hum. Behav. **26**, 247–253 (2010). doi:10.1016/j.chb.2009.09.003
6. Debatin, B., Lovejoy, J.P., Horn, A.K., Hughes, B.N.: Facebook and online privacy: attitudes, behaviors, and unintended consequences. J.C.M.C. **19**, 83–108 (2009). doi:10.1111/j.1083-6101.2009.01494.x
7. De Wolf, R., Willaert, K., Pierson, J.: Managing privacy boundaries together: exploring individual and group privacy management strategies in Facebook. Comput. Hum. Behav. **35**, 444–454 (2014). doi:10.1016/j.chb.2014.03.010
8. Dey, R., Jelveh, Z., Ross, K.: Facebook users have become much more private: a large-scale study. In: PerCom Workshops, pp. 346–352. IEEE Computer Society (2012)
9. Diefenbach, S., Lenz, E., Hassenzahl, M.: Handbuch proTACT Toolbox. Tools zur User Experience Gestaltung und Evaluation. http://germanupa.de/events/mensch-und-computer-2014/tutorials/experience-design-tools.html
10. Dunne, A., Lawlor, M.A., Rowley, J.: Young people's use of online social networking sites – a uses and gratifications perspective. J. Res. Interact. Mark **4**, 46–58 (2010). doi:10.1108/17505931011033551
11. Feng, Y., Xie, W.: Teens' concern for privacy when using social networking sites: an analysis of socialization agents and relationships with privacy-protecting behaviors. Comput. Hum. Behav. **33**, 153–162 (2014). doi:10.1016/j.chb.2014.01.009
12. Hassenzahl, M., Diefenbach, S., Göritz, A.: Needs, affect, and interactive products - facets of user experience. Interact. Comput. **22**, 353–362 (2010). doi:10.1016/j.intcom.2010.04.002
13. Hollenbaugh, E.E., Ferris, A.L.: Facebook self-disclosure: examining the role of traits, social cohesion, and motives. Comput. Hum. Behav. **30**, 50–58 (2014). doi:10.1016/j.chb.2013.07.055
14. Joinson, A.N.: Looking at, looking up or keeping up with people? Motives and use of Facebook. In: SIGCHI, pp. 1027–1036. ACM Press, New York (2008). doi:10.1145/1357054.1357213
15. Katz, E., Gurevitch, M., Haas, H.: On the use of the mass media for important things. Am. Sociol. Rev. **38**, 164–181 (1973). doi:10.2307/2094393
16. Kokolakis, S.: Privacy attitudes and privacy behaviour: a review of current research on the privacy paradox phenomenon. Comput. Secur. **64**, 122–134 (2017). doi:10.1016/j.cose.2015.07.002
17. Krasnova, H., Spiekermann, S., Koroleva, K., Hildebrand, T.: Online social networks: why we disclose. J. Inform. Technol. **25**, 109–125 (2010). doi:10.1057/jit.2010.6
18. Lang, C., Barton, H.: Just untag it: exploring the management of undesirable Facebook photos. Comput. Hum. Behav. **43**, 147–155 (2015). doi:10.1016/j.chb.2014.10.051

19. Litt, E.: Understanding social network site users' privacy tool use. Comput. Hum. Behav. **29**, 1649–1656 (2013). doi:10.1016/j.chb.2013.01.049

20. Madden, M.: Privacy Management on Social Media Sites. Pew Research Center, Washington, D.C. (2012)

21. Masur, P.K., Reinecke, L., Ziegele, M., Quiring, O.: The interplay of intrinsic need satisfaction and Facebook specific motives in explaining addictive behavior on Facebook. Comput. Hum. Behav. **39**, 376–386 (2014). doi:10.1016/j.chb.2014.05.047

22. McCrae, R.R., John, O.P.: An introduction to the five-factor model and its applications. J. Pers. **60**, 175–215 (1992). doi:10.1111/j.1467-6494.1992.tb00970.x

23. Moore, K., McElroy, J.C.: The influence of personality on Facebook usage, wall postings, and regret. Comput. Hum. Behav. **28**(1), 267–274 (2012). doi:10.1016/j.chb.2011.09.009

24. oFb - der onlineFragebogen. https://www.soscisurvey.de

25. Peters, A.N., Winschiers-Theophilus, H., Mennecke, B.E.: Cultural influences on Facebook practices. Comput. Hum. Behav. **49**, 259–271 (2015). doi:10.1016/j.chb.2015.02.065

26. Rammstedt, B., John, O.P.: Measuring personality in one minute or less: a 10-item short version of the Big Five Inventory in English and German. J. Res. Pers. **41**, 203–212 (2007). doi:10.1016/j.jrp.2006.02.001

27. Reinecke1, L., Vorderer, P., Knop, K.: Entertainment 2.0? The role of intrinsic and extrinsic need satisfaction for the enjoyment of Facebook Use. J. Comm. **64**, 417–43 (2014). doi:10.1111/jcom.12099

28. Ross, C., Orr, E.S., Sisic, M., Arseneault, J.M., Simmering, M.G., Orr, R.R.: Personality and motivations associated with Facebook use. Comput. Hum. Behav. **25**, 578–586 (2009). doi:10.1016/j.chb.2008.12.024

29. Ryan, R.M., Deci, E.L.: Self-determination theory and the facilitation of intrinsic motivation, social development, and well-being. Am. Psychol. **55**, 68–78 (2000)

30. Ryan, T., Xenos, S.: Who uses Facebook? An investigation into the relationship between the Big 5, shyness, narcissism, loneliness, and Facebook usage. Comput. Hum. Behav. **27**, 1658–1664 (2011). doi:10.1037/0003-066X.55.1.68

31. Saleh, F., Jani, H., Marzouqi, M., Khajeh, N., Rajan, A.: Social networking by the youth in the UAE: a privacy paradox. In: CTIT 2011, pp. 28–31. IEEE, Dubai (2011). doi:10.1109/CTIT.2011.6107957

32. Sheldon, K.M., Elliot, A.J., Kim, Y., Kasser, T.: What is satisfying about satisfying events? Testing 10 candidate psychological needs. J. Pers. Soc. Psychol. **80**, 325–339 (2001). doi:10.1037/0022-3514.80.2.325

33. Sheldon, P.: Student favorite: Facebook and motives for its use. Southwest. Mass. Commun. J. **23**, 39–55 (2008)

34. Sheldon, P.: The relationship between unwillingness-to-communicate and students' Facebook use. J. Media Psychol. **20**, 67–75 (2008). doi:10.1027/1864-1105.20.2.67

35. Special, W., Li-Barber, K.: Self-disclosure and student satisfaction with Facebook. Comput. Hum. Behav. **28**, 624–630 (2012). doi:10.1016/j.chb.2011.11.008

36. Staddon, J., Acquisti, A., LeFevre, K.: Self-reported social network behavior: accuracy predictors and implications for the privacy paradox. In: SOCIALCOM, pp. 295–302. IEEE Press, Washington (2013). doi:10.1109/SocialCom.2013.48

37. Stutzman, F., Kramer-Duffield, J.: Friends only: examining a privacy-enhancing behavior in Facebook. In: CHI 2014, pp. 1777–1786. ACM, New York (2010). doi:10.1145/2556288.255699

38. Taddicken, M.: The 'Privacy Paradox' in the social web: the impact of privacy concerns, individual characteristics, and the perceived social relevance on different forms of self-disclosure. J.C.M.C. **19**, 248–273 (2013). doi:10.1111/jcc4.12052

39. Utz, S., Kramer, N.C.: The privacy paradox on social network sites revisited: the role of individual characteristics and group norms. Cyberpsychol.: J. Psychosoc. Res. **3**, Article no. 1 (2009)
40. Waters, S., Ackerman, J.: Exploring privacy management on Facebook: motivations and perceived consequences of voluntary disclosure. J.C.M.C. **17**, 101–115 (2011). doi:10.1111/j.1083-6101.2011.01559.x
41. Young, A.L., Quan-Haase, A.: Privacy protection strategies on Facebook. Inform. Commun. Soc. **6**, 479–500 (2013). doi:10.1080/1369118X.2013.777757
42. Zephoria Internet Marketing: The Top 20 Valuable Facebook Statistics. https://zephoria.com/top-15-valuable-facebook-statistics/

Exploring Consumers' Attitudes of Smart TV Related Privacy Risks

Marco Ghiglieri[1(✉)], Melanie Volkamer[1,2], and Karen Renaud[3,4]

[1] Technische Unviersität Darmstadt, Darmstadt, Germany
marco.ghiglieri@crisp-da.de
[2] Karlstad University, Karlstad, Sweden
[3] University of Glasgow, Glasgow, UK
[4] Mississippi State University, Starkville, MS, USA

Abstract. A number of privacy risks are inherent in the Smart TV ecosystem. It is likely that many consumers are unaware of these privacy risks. Alternatively, they might be aware but consider the privacy risks acceptable. In order to explore this, we carried out an online survey with 200 participants to determine whether consumers were aware of Smart TV related privacy risks. The responses revealed a meagre level of awareness. We also explored consumers' attitudes towards specific Smart TV related privacy risks.

We isolated a number of factors that influenced rankings and used these to develop awareness-raising messages. We tested these messages in an online survey with 155 participants. The main finding was that participants were generally unwilling to disconnect their Smart TVs from the Internet because they valued the Smart TV's Internet functionality more than their privacy. We subsequently evaluated the awareness-raising messages in a second survey with 169 participants, framing the question differently. We asked participants to choose between five different Smart TV Internet connection options, two of which retained functionality but entailed expending time and/or effort to preserve privacy.

Keywords: Smart TV · Privacy · Risks · Human factors · Consequences

1 Introduction

Smart TVs are a relatively recent innovation that, in addition to streaming traditional broadcast content, facilitate access to Internet content and services as well as video-on-demand, games and infotainment. At first glance, Smart TVs seem to deliver distinct added value, as compared to traditional televisions. A closer look reveals a number of privacy risks in the Smart TV ecosystem: (1) vendors and broadcasters routinely collect and share Smart TV usage-related data [15,18,44], (2) many vendors record and analyze speech by transmitting it to third party services to extract commands for operating the TV [25] and (3) Smart TVs are less reliably secured than desktop computers and smartphones,

© Springer International Publishing AG 2017
T. Tryfonas (Ed.): HAS 2017, LNCS 10292, pp. 656–674, 2017.
DOI: 10.1007/978-3-319-58460-7_45

[26]. In effect, consumers connecting their Smart TVs to the Internet are, perhaps unwittingly, sacrificing their privacy. There seems to be little pressure from consumers to force vendors and broadcasters to respect their privacy. Two explanations are possible: (1) consumers are unaware of the privacy risks and/or (2) consumers are aware of the risks but consider them acceptable or too unlikely to be concerned about.

The primary aim of our research was first to assess general awareness of these privacy risks. We discovered a poor level of awareness, so we proceeded to develop strategies to improve consumer awareness and also to explore the likelihood that consumers would be prepared to act to protect their privacy. Our research project's phases were as follows:

First, we explored general levels of consumer awareness of risks using an online survey. This included understanding which particular risks were considered critical, and why. This online study with 200 participants confirmed a low level of general awareness. From the participant responses we derived factors that clearly influenced participants' risk judgments. We then used these factors to craft effective awareness messages to be used in phase two.

Second, using an iterative approach, we developed two awareness messages based on the factors we isolated during the first phase, and evaluated them. One message raised awareness of usage data collection and analysis. The other did this, but also flagged the possibility of their usage data being misused. We conducted an online study with 155 participants to test the impact of these messages, as measured by their willingness to disconnect their Smart TVs from the Internet. Most participants were unwilling to do this. The most commonly-mentioned reason for this was the fact that they wanted to retain the Smart TV's Internet functionality. Even though we increased awareness of privacy risks, they valued the Internet functionality so much that the risks did not seem to concern them.

Third, we tested whether privacy-aware consumers would be willing to spend time and/or money in order to preserve their privacy, all the while retaining the TV's Internet functionality. We presented participants with a privacy-protection mechanism such as the one proposed by Ghiglieri *et al.* [18]. This mechanism installs broadcaster and vendor privacy protection before the Smart TV is connected to the Internet. Internet functionality is unhindered but the consumer's privacy risk is reduced. 169 people participated in a study to explore reactions to, and acceptability of, this mechanism. Most participants declared themselves willing to deploy this kind of privacy-protection mechanism.

Our main findings are as follows:

- We confirmed a generally low level of awareness of privacy-related risks in the Smart TV context.
- Some participants were aware that data was being gathered and analyzed, but unaware of the potential for misuse.
- Making participants aware of potential misuse is more effective than only making them aware that data is collected and analyzed by vendors (whom they may trust).

- Raising awareness, in and of itself, is insufficient. Together with awareness, people also need the means to preserve their privacy.
- Expecting people to forego all Internet functionality is unrealistic. However, they express a willingness to spend time and/or money on privacy protection as long as they can retain Internet functionality.

In conclusion, it is clear that research into the development of usable privacy enhancing technologies (PET), providing an improved level of privacy preservation while retaining functionality, is required. Awareness-raising, on its own, is insufficient.

2   Background

Publications and media have shown that Smart TV consumers are exposed to privacy risks such as the collection and analysis of usage data for various purposes. A blog [9] revealed that the privacy policy of LG contains a corresponding statement; Samsung's [33] and Sony's [36] privacy policies also contain such statements. Furthermore, published studies [14,15,17,18] showed that the Internet functionality HbbTV has been also used to profile consumers without consumer's consent. HbbTV is a standardized technique that covers video-on-demand and information services for Smart TVs provided by the broadcasters. It is supported by 97% of the current available Smart TVs [34], in Germany, the country in which this research was conducted. According to the Smart TV working group of the German TV-Platform [1] a worldwide usage of HbbTV is being contemplated. Europe has the highest coverage as of today. Other publications have shown that even the (traditional) broadcast channel of the TV signal is vulnerable and can be manipulated so that it can transport malicious data to Smart TVs in a specific regional area (e.g. manipulating HbbTV in Oren *et al.* [29]). Furthermore, Michéle *et al.* [26] showed that Smart TV media players could enable TV hacking and allow secret access to camera and microphone data streams. Indeed, in Metro [32], a news paper, it was reported that a couple was recorded in an intimate situation by hackers. The recorded video was published. More vulnerabilities have been revealed: Smart TV Apps [27], Vendor transferred voice data unencrypted [5] and incorrect implementation of HTTPS certificate validation [16].

3   Methodology — Consumer Awareness

We describe the study design, recruitment and ethics as well as the methodology for the evaluation of the free text answers for the online survey to explore levels of consumer awareness of risks.

3.1   Study Design

It comprised the following steps (see Fig. 1):

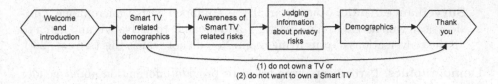

Fig. 1. Study Design.

Welcome and Introduction. First, participants were informed that the survey focused on Smart TVs. They were not briefed about the exact focus of the survey so as not to prime their responses. Information about the duration was provided, as well as the fact that there were no wrong answers.

Smart TV Related Demographics. Participants were asked whether they owned a TV. Those who did were informed what a Smart TV is and asked whether their own TV was smart. Those who did not own a Smart TV were asked whether they would like to own one. Only those who owned a Smart TV, or wanted to own one, continued. The remaining participants were forwarded to the "Thank you" page.

Awareness of Smart TV Related Risks. Participants were asked to enumerate Smart TV risks they are aware of. Afterwards, they could name measures that could be used to counteract these risks.

Judging Information About Privacy Risks. Participants were given four different risks to contemplate, one per page, in random order. For each, participants were asked to judge how critical it was. Options for the rating ranged from 1 'not very critical' to 3 'neutral' to 5 'very critical'. The option 'don't know' was also available. They were asked to justify their ratings. The request for justification appeared on the same page as the scenario description.

The displayed privacy risks were identified from the research literature and public media (see Sect. 2). The following scenarios were presented to the participants (we add one reference as an example reference for further information about the corresponding attack):

- **Broadcaster Profiling.** The TV gathers information about how long, and how often, you watch each channel. If the broadcaster offers multiple channels, it is possible that the usage information from different channels is aggregated (see e.g. [14]).
- **Vendor Profiling.** The Smart TV vendor gathers information about how you use the TV. For example, the vendor gets detailed information about which apps you use. Furthermore, it gathers information about how long, and how often, you use your TV (see e.g. [44]).
- **Voice Recognition.** If you decide to control your Smart TV with your voice, anything you say is transmitted to, and analysed, by the vendor's servers. To provide this functionality, it is necessary to transmit all utterances in the room, for processing by the vendor's servers (see e.g. [25]).

– **Surveillance Audio.** Your Smart TV is equipped with a microphone. Outsiders can gain access to the Smart TV and are able to activate it and listen to all the conversations in your living room. You do not realize this (see e.g. [26]).

Demographics. Participants were asked to provide information about gender and age.

Thank You. Finally, we thanked participants for their support and they received information on how to claim their monetary reward.

3.2   Recruitment

The study was conducted in Germany in December 2015. SoSciSurvey[1] was used as platform for the survey. The participants were recruited via clickworker[2] which is similar to Amazon Mechanical Turk but recruits in Germany instead of the USA. We paid each participant who completed the survey, and did not provide obvious nonsense answers, €2 per participant on that platform. We measured the average time with test participants. This was about twelve minutes. As Germany has a minimum wage of €8.50 per hour €2 was fair payment.

3.3   Ethics

Guidelines on ethical issues regarding research involving humans are provided by the host university. These guidelines were followed with respect to respondent consent and data privacy requirements were met. Participants first read an information page on which they were assured that their data would not be linked to their identity and that the responses would only be used for study purposes. Furthermore, using SoSciSurvey ensured that data was stored in Germany and thus subject to German data protection law. They were told that they could withdraw at any time. Moreover, they were told that all answers were valid: there was no such thing as a wrong answer. No debriefing was required.

3.4   Evaluation Methodology

We used open coding to analyze free text answers. We proceeded in the following way: First, two authors analyzed the free text answers independently and composed a list of codes. Furthermore, they clustered these codes in categories. Afterwards, the categories were discussed and the authors agreed on one list of categories as well as a mapping from code to category. These categories were afterwards applied to the free text answers by two authors. Then, the assignments were compared and discussed to agree on the categories to be assigned. It was possible to assign one answer to several categories.

   Note, all studies were conducted in Germany and questions and quotes in German were translated for inclusion in this paper.

---

[1] http://www.soscisurvey.de.

[2] http://www.clickworker.com/.

4   Results — Consumer Awareness

4.1   Sample

200 participants completed the survey. 8 were removed from the data set since they entered implausible values (e.g. data and rating did not match, empty free text fields all over the place). The survey group consisted of 104 females (54%) and 87 males (45%); 1 (1%) did not provide gender. The youngest participant was 19, the oldest 89 and the mean age was 38.9 years with a standard deviation of 12.41.

14 participants (7%) indicated that they did not own a TV. Out of the 178 remaining participants who owned a TV, 127 (71%) have a Smart TV and 51 (29%) owned a non-Smart TV. 44 (86%) of those who did not own a Smart TV would like to have one but 7 (14%) did not. 171 participants completed the survey with the questions about the scenarios.

4.2   Awareness of Risks

We assessed whether participants knew about Smart TV privacy risks. In total, 60 individual text fields for risks were cited. The average number of risks per participant was 2.14 for those who mentioned at least one risk; overall 0.16. 28 (16%) participants mentioned at least one risk; 11 (11%) of the female participants who were asked to mention risks mentioned at least one.

We analyzed the 60 free text risk-related responses in terms of two aspects: 'potential actions' or 'consequences' of a risk. The most often mentioned potential action was 'collecting data' (19 participants), 'access to camera or microphone' (17). The other categories are 'access to sensitive data' (4), 'access to network' (3), and 'TV manipulations'. These aspects were mentioned by 21 participants. The most often mentioned consequences of privacy risks are 'personalized advertising' (7) and 'being robbed' (3). The others are: 'TV getting too slow' (2), 'Child watches inappropriate content' (2), 'TV does not work' (2) and 'program could change' (1). These consequences were mentioned by 12 participants.

We confirmed a general lack of awareness of privacy risks, and concrete consequences thereof.

4.3   Risk Scenario Ratings

We analyzed how critical participants rated the displayed privacy risk scenarios. Table 1 provides, for each scenario, (1) the number of participants who answered 'I don't know', (2) the number of participants considered[3], (3) the mean value how critical the scenario is rated for all participants, all female/male participants, as well as those mentioning/not mentioning risks in the previous part of

---

[3] Note, the total numbers differ as the number of people who answered 'I don't know' may differ as well as those who were set to 'not using' differs from scenario to scenario.

the survey. The 'broadcaster profiling' scenario was considered by most of the participants as the less critical one (light gray) and the 'surveillance audio' one as the most critical one (dark gray).

Table 1. How critical a scenario is rated for different subgroups of participants and different scenarios. (available options were: from 1 'not very critical' to 3 'neutral' to 5 'very 'critical'; and the option 'don't know' was available; most critical is filled dark gray and least critical light gray.)

Scenario	I don't know	all	female	male	Risks	No Risks
Broadcaster Profiling	4	2.82 (164)	2.66 (95)	3.06 (68)	3.19 (27)	2.74 (137)
Vendor Profiling	2	3.46 (168)	3.52 (95)	3.42 (72)	3.50 (28)	3.45 (140)
Voice Recognition	10	3.97 (159)	3.99 (91)	4.00 (67)	4.07 (27)	3.95 (132)
Surveillance Audio	4	4.69 (166)	4.75 (95)	4.67 (70)	4.64 (28)	4.70 (138)
$\sum$	20	3.74 (657)	3.73 (376)	3.79 (277)	3.85 (110)	3.71 (547)

4.4 Influencing Factors

In total 684 free text answers for the justifications, with more than 7,200 words, were examined using an open coding approach. We identified the factors that potentially impact the ratings related to privacy risks. The different factors are explored in the following paragraphs:

Party Who Gathers the Data is likely to be an influential factor because many participants consider vendors and broadcasters collecting data to be acceptable: e.g. "*Vendor may take the data as long as there is no abuse*", "*I consider broadcasters to be secure*". However, criminals would use data to harm them ("*On top of that there is a danger of data being abused by criminals*").

The **type of data** is also likely to be an influential factor. Some participants were not worried about the described privacy risk as they considered the addressed usage data to be unimportant, i.e. not worth protecting as compared to other types of data: "*Don't care about usage data*", "*Inspection of usage data is relatively uncritical as long as there is no inspection of personal data such as Skype conversations*", "*Don't mind as long as they don't have access to personal data such as passwords or banking details*", "*Inspection of usage data seems uncritical*", "*I don't care about usage data*", "*The danger of abuse is minimal*", "*Information about my usage behaviour can be passed on*".

Being aware that usage data collection constitutes a privacy risk might have an influence. Some participants see no disadvantages (*"There is no disadvantage for me"*, *"I think it has no negative effects on me"*) or only consider the advantages to vendors and broadcasters of collecting and analyzing usage data:

- More reliable viewing figures: *"At least better than faked viewing figures"*, *"[..] I don't really like it, but, on the other hand, it would be a real improvement in viewing figures"*
- Better products: *"Usage data is required in order to improve products"*, *"It is important to support future development, because you can see which applications are used frequently and which not"*.

On the other hand, other participants consider any collection of (usage) data a privacy invasion (*"I totally decline any data-gathering"*, *"violates my privacy"*, *"very bad, would violate my privacy a lot. If this happened, I would not feel very comfortable"*.) as well as with terms like surveillance (*"I don't want to be kept under surveillance"*) and profiling (*"you can create a user profile"*).

Even when they are aware of a privacy risk, **being aware of possible misuses** might have an influence. Those who are aware of possible misuse mentioned different types of misuse:

- Vendors generally misuse the data: *"data can be abused"*, *"my voice could be used without my knowledge"*. Note, the last quote actually addresses an interesting aspect: *'without my knowledge'*. However, this aspect was only mentioned very rarely.
- Vendors sell data: *"It is critical; I don't want the vendor to sell my data. It is a private affair"*.
- Burglary: *"It invades definitely my privacy, no one may want that. Burglars can check if someone is at home or not. If yes, they can burglarize or check if burglary would be worth at all on the basis of information obtained. If that isn't critical enough, I don't know…"*.
- Close a Deal: *"With my voice someone could fake phone calls to confirm orders or contracts. In addition, there is a risk that not only commands to the Smart TV are recorded, but also private or business conversations are recorded"*.
- Espionage: *"I would feel spied on"*, *"It isn't ok if I, as a customer, am spied on in this way. The legislature must do something"*.

Most of these were only mentioned by one or two participants.

Considering **personalized advertising as beneficial** or **irritating** seems to be an influencing factor:

- Some like personalized advertising since it suggests items of interest: *"I'll benefit from the analysis of my usage behaviour as they provide me with tailored advertisements and special programmes for me personally"*.
- Others consider this to be a nebulous attempt to misuse their data: *"Could be evaluated for personalized advertisement and programs -> data may be sold to other companies in the media group"*.

People's **general privacy attitudes** may also have an influence. Those participants who have a negative attitude towards any type of privacy violation are, in
general, more motivated to complain. Those who are more difficult to motivate
are those that:

- use the 'nothing to hide' argument: *"I don't talk about important things I need
  to be concerned about"*, *"There is nothing I have to hide"*,
- have become accustomed to privacy risks: *"nowadays it is normal"*, *"You
  don't have to like it, but in a way it has been wildly implemented for some
  years now, hasn't it?"*, *"It's the same problem with computers. If anybody
  wants to be a criminal, there will always be a way"*, *"On the internet via
  computer or smartphone data is saved as well"*
- think it is unavoidable: *"You can't change it"*.

In summary, the following factors influence consumer ratings: the party who
gathers the data; the type of data; awareness of the fact that (usage) data is collected; being aware that collected data can be misused; personalized advertising
being considered beneficial, or not; basic attitudes.

5   Awareness-Raising Messages

In some pre-studies we tested a range of messages covering a combination of
different influential factors (see Sect. 4.4). Some included concrete consequences
other were more high level; some referred to hackers, others to vendors and broadcasters. We concluded that privacy-related awareness could best be prompted by
messages that avoid being too specific about a potential misuse as too specific
(e.g. burglary) is likely to be judged as low risk as it is considered as too unlikely
in this context. People need to be able to visualize the particular scenario and
believe that it could happen, i.e. it is realistic. Based on these pre-considerations,
we decided to evaluate the following messages:

- **Simple awareness message.** The Smart TV vendor and the broadcasters
  collect and analyze usage data (e.g., information about how, and how often,
  you use your Smart TV).
- **Advanced awareness message.** In addition to the text from the 'Simple
  awareness' Group: *It cannot be ruled out that the gathered information ends
  up in the wrong hands in order to harm you.*

Next, we wanted to evaluate how effective these messages would be and test
whether the advanced message is more effective in terms of motivating participants to protect their privacy.

6   Methodology — Raising Awareness

In this section, we explain the study's design and the recruitment process. The
ethical considerations and methodology were as described in Sects. 3.3 and 3.4.

6.1 Study Design

The study applied a between-subjects design. Participants were randomly assigned to two groups that differed with respect to delivery of the above-mentioned awareness messages. The first group saw the simple message and the second group saw the advanced message. The study was proceeded through the following steps (see Fig. 2):

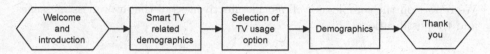

Fig. 2. Study Design.

Welcome and Introduction: Participants were informed that the study focused on Smart TVs. They were not briefed about the exact focus so as not to prime their responses. Information about duration was provided (up to 10 min) as well as the fact that there were no wrong answers. They were told that they could leave the study at any point. However, only those who completed the study earned a monetary reward.

Smart TV Related Demographics: Participants were shown information related to Smart TVs and asked whether they owned a Smart TV. Afterwards, we presented information about Internet functionality and gave them some examples to illsutrate this. We then asked them to rate whether they use or would like to use Internet-related functionality on their Smart TV on a regular basis. Options ranged from 1 'does not apply at all' to 5 'fully applies'.

Selection of TV Usage Option: Participants were shown one of the two above-mentioned awareness messages followed by an appropriate explanation of the message. Note that we did not call them simple or advanced. Participants were asked which Smart TV usage option they would prefer. Because the only truly reliable privacy protection option is not to connect the Smart TV to the Internet the following two usage options were presented[4]:

1. 'Privacy risk' option: The Smart TV will be connected to the Internet.
2. 'Privacy protecting' option: The Smart TV will not be connected to the Internet.

The **Demographics** and **Thank you** steps were as described in Sect. 3.1.

6.2 Recruitment

The studies were conducted in June/July 2016. SoSci Survey and clickworker were also used. We paid each participant who completed the studies and who

---

[4] The category names (privacy risk/protection) are only used here and were not communicated to the participants.

did not provide obvious nonsense answers according to the minimum wage of Germany a fair monetary reward (i.e. €1.40 for about 9 min). Furthermore, we made sure that each clickworker could only fill out one of our Smart TV related studies.

7   Results — Raising Awareness

We report on the sample as well as the effectiveness of the awareness messages and the justifications.

7.1   Sample

155 participants completed the study. The study group consisted of 75 females (49%) and 79 males (51%); 1 participant did not mention gender.

We only considered those participants who stated that they own a Smart TV and who rated that they use Internet functionality regularly at least with 3 (ranged from 1 'does not apply at all' to 5 'fully applies').

82 (53%) participants owned a Smart TV and used Internet functionality regularly. From these 82, 43 (52%) were made aware that usage data is collected and analyzed, i.e. were assigned to the 'simple awareness' group. The remaining 39 (48%) were assigned to the 'advanced awareness' group and were made aware that, in addition to legitimate collection and analysis, the data could also be misused to cause harm if accessed by criminals. The youngest participant in the 'simple awareness' group was 18, the oldest 65 and the mean age was 32.63 years with a standard deviation of 10.21. The corresponding numbers for the 'advanced awareness' group are: the youngest 18, the oldest 57, mean age 35.05 and standard deviation 11.20.

7.2   Effectiveness of Awareness Messages

In the 'simple awareness' group, 8 (19%) stated that they would not connect their Smart TV to the Internet anymore ('privacy protecting' option).

In the group 'advanced awareness', 15 (38%) participants selected this option. For more details see Table 2.

We did the following χ^2-tests: A significant improvement in the selection behavior could be shown between the groups 'Simple awareness' and 'Advanced awareness'; $\chi^2 = 4.00$, df = 1, p = 0.046, ϕ-coefficient = 0.221. Note, no significant difference could be found between males and females; 'Simple awareness': $\chi^2 = 4.51$, df = 1, p(exact) = 0.06 and 'Advanced awareness': $\chi^2 = 0.37$, df = 1, p(exact) = 0.74.

7.3   Justifications

The following categories of justifications for keep using the Internet were identified:

Table 2. Effectiveness of both awareness messages

Option	Simple awareness group			Advanced awareness group		
	Female	Male	$\sum$	Female	Male	$\sum$
# (%) Privacy risk option	17 (71%)	18 (95%)	35 (81%)	12 (57%)	12 (67%)	24 (62%)
# (%) Privacy protecting option	7 (29%)	1 (5%)	8 (19%)	9 (43%)	6 (33%)	15 (38%)
$\sum$	24	19	43	21	18	39

Functionality is Important: Participants valued the functionality they obtained by connecting the Smart TV to the Internet. Example quotes are:

"A Smart TV without Internet isn't useful", "I don't need a Smart TV without Internet", , "If I own a Smart TV, I want to use [the Internet] functions", "I love the Internet", "The Internet extends the functionality of Smart TVs".

Some participants balanced privacy against functionality and functionality prevailed. Example quotes are:

"I think that the advantages that I get when it's connected to the Internet outweigh the disadvantages", "It is convenient to access the Internet on my Smart TV, but there is a risk that personal data will be stored".

Don't Mind: Participants did not mind if usage data is collected and analyzed by broadcasters and vendors for various reasons. Example quotes are:

"I don't have any secrets in the selection of my programs", "I don't mind if my usage data is passed on", "[..] I don't care if someone finds out that I watch porn."

Resignation: Participants were resigned to this use of their personal data. Example quotes are:

"I think nothing is wrong", "Today, data is collected everywhere. The recording of TV usage behavior is relatively innocent.", "Since data is stored in the Internet anyway. Moreover, it's a advantage because the offers are getting more personalized.", "The risk always exists that data ends up in the wrong hand, [..]." "There isn't 100% protection", "The risk always exist that data ends up in the wrong hand, [..]."

7.4   Discussion

This study's results demonstrate that significantly more consumers would disconnect their Smart TV when they are made aware of the risks with the advanced awareness message (with harm) as compared to the simple message (without harm). Thus, for further awareness studies it is essential to communicate the potential harm and not just the fact that data is collected and analyzed.

We also gained other insights into Smart TV consumer attitudes towards privacy risks. Many would willingly sacrifice privacy in order to make use of the Internet functionality of Smart TVs either because (1) functionality is more important, (2) consumers do not mind sharing usage data or (3) consumers are resigned to privacy invasions. Note, most participants inhabited the first category.

Consequently, we were interested in whether the situation would change if privacy tools were made available. We wanted to evaluate the effectiveness of both messages in the presence of such a tool. In particular, we wanted to find out whether the advanced message was still more effective in this context.

8   Methodology and Results — Offering Functionality

The recruitment was carried out as described in Sect. 6.2. The ethical considerations and methodology were as described in Sects. 3.3 and 3.4.

8.1   Study Design

The design was similar to the first study. Participants were given options as introduced in Sect. 6.1 and also an additional three other options[5]:

3. 'Effort' option: The Smart TV will not be connected to the Internet. It will be used as an external monitor for a laptop that is connected to the Internet.
4. 'Effort+cost' option: A privacy-protection mechanism will be deployed to prevent usage data collection while retaining Internet-enabled functionality. It will cost €20 and requires about 15 min to configure.
5. 'Costs' option: A privacy-protection mechanism will be deployed to prevent the usage data collection while retaining Internet-enabled functionality. It will cost €40 and no additional configuration time is required.

The privacy protection mechanisms with costs/effort have not been marketed as yet, but a prototype mechanism can be found in [18]. The 'Effort+cost' option is supposed to be installed on an existing device (e.g., router) and the software should be purchased for €20 similar to regular protection software for PCs[6]. The 15 min configuration time is the average time a consumer may need to configure software (install it, choosing the preferences and select the right Smart TV Model). For the 'Costs' option, we considered a pre-configured bundle[7] with hard- and software which should be purchased for €40.

---

[5] We did not mention the names of the options in the study as presented here.
[6] See e.g. https://www.amazon.com/dp/B010P91LYY (accessed 11 December, 2016).
[7] See e.g. https://www.amazon.com/dp/B000BTL0OA (accessed 11 December, 2016).

8.2 Sample

169 participants completed the study. The study group consisted of 84 females (50%) and 83 males (50%); 2 did not provide gender. 97 (53%) participants owned a Smart TV and regularly used Internet-enabled functionality. From these 97, 45 (46%) were assigned to the 'simple awareness' group and the remaining 52 (54%) were assigned to the 'advanced awareness' group. The youngest participant in the 'simple awareness' group was 18, the oldest 68 and the mean age was 36.44 years with a standard deviation of 12.08. The corresponding numbers for the 'advanced awareness' group are: the youngest 18, the oldest 67, mean age 36.80 and standard deviation 12.20.

8.3 Effectiveness of Privacy Protection Availability

Table 3 reports the results for all participants. In both groups more than 67% stated that they would be willing to spend time and/or money to get both functionality and privacy. From the three available options, the effort and/or cost options were preferred, especially in the 'advanced awareness' group (75%).

Table 3. Effectiveness of both messages

Option	Simple awareness group			Advanced awareness group		
	Female	Male	Σ	Female	Male	Σ
# (%) Privacy risk option	6 (27%)	8 (35%)	14 (31%)	4 (15%)	8 (31%)	12 (23%)
# (%) # (%) Effort option	3 (14%)	3 (13%)	6 (13%)	2 (8%)	4 (15%)	6 (12%)
# (%) Effort + costs option	7 (32%)	6 (26%)	13 (29%)	13 (50%)	12 (46%)	25 (48%)
# (%) Costs option	5 (23%)	6 (26%)	11 (24%)	6 (23%)	2 (8%)	8 (15%)
# (%) Costs and effort related options Σ	15 (68%)	15 (65%)	30 (67%)	21 (81%)	18 (69%)	39 (75%)
# (%) Privacy protecting options Σ	16 (73%)	15 (65%)	31 (69%)	22 (85%)	18 (69%)	40 (77%)
Σ	22	23	45	26	26	52

We applied the same χ^2-tests as in the first study. No significant improvement could be shown between the selection behavior of the 'simple awareness' and 'advanced awareness' groups; $\chi^2 = 4.21$, df $= 4$; p(exact) $= 0.373$.

There were no significant differences between male and female selections; 'simple awareness': $\chi^2 = 1.53$, df $= 4$, p(exact) $= 0.96$ and 'advanced awareness': $\chi^2 = 4.83$, df $= 4$, p(exact) $= 0.28$.

8.4   Effectiveness of Offering Functionality

We observed a difference in the choosing behavior of Smart TV consumers comparing the first (two options) and the second study (five options). We analyzed the differences between them. We found that an increased number of consumers demonstrated a preference for a privacy-protecting connection method.

For this analysis, we combined the groups 'w/o Internet' and all effort and/or cost groups from the second study to arrive at two groups. The distribution after combining the four privacy-protecting options of the second study looks, at first glance, like a random distribution, since 26 (27%) participants selected the 'Privacy risk' option and 71 (73%) a privacy-protecting option. A 20 to 80 distribution would be expected under random choice circumstances. In the first study, 59 (72%) wanted to retain the connection to the Internet and 23 (28%) wanted to disconnect the Smart TV. Thus, the choice behavior differed significantly from a random distribution ($\chi^2 = 15.80$, df $= 1$, p ¡ 0.001) with a clear lean towards the 'Privacy risk' option.

Therefore, we interpret the choice behavior in the second study as a positive effect. Proposing alternative options that protect the consumer's privacy while retaining Internet functionality seems the most promising approach.

9   Related Work

We report on related work in the following different areas:

Mental Models of Privacy and Security. Mental models can influence people's attitude, so we list some work in this field. Mental models in the context of privacy and security have been studied from Camp [2], Dourish et al. [10] and Wash [41] as well as in different concrete areas, such as smartphones from Ophoff et al. [28], Volkamer et al. [40], Harbach et al. [21] and Elie [11], network security from Solove [35], firewalls from Raja et al. [30], secure communication from Friedman et al. [12], passwords from Weirich et al. [43], single sign on Gupta et al. [19], anonymous credentials from Wäslund et al. [42] and Harbach et al. [20], privacy settings from Debatin et al. [6], email encryption from Gaw et al. [13], Renaud et al. [31] and Clark et al. [4]. In these areas, security and privacy protection tools are increasingly available. The focus of these papers differs from this work, since mental models should help us to understand why the existing tools are not used. We explored how consumers thought about Smart TV security and privacy risks in order to establish effective and acceptable protection measures. However, there are parallels. Some reasons for not using security tools might be reasons that consumers do not complain if corresponding tools are not available or vendors and broadcasters collect usage data intentionally.

Attitudes Towards Privacy and Security. People's privacy attitudes often differ from the decisions they make. This inconsistency is called 'privacy paradox'. This issue has mostly been highlighted in the context of online privacy, e.g., from Trepte et al. and Dienlein [7,37–39]. In the context of Smart TVs, we experienced similar issues. Consumers claimed that privacy was important, but most of them also connected their Smart TVs to the Internet without any qualms.

Privacy Calculus. The privacy calculus theory is one way to explain users' privacy behaviour (referred to as privacy paradox). It states that people seek a balance between potential risks and benefits, e.g. in e-commerce from Dinev *et al.* [8], in online market places from Kim *et al.* [22] or from Lankton *et al.* in social networks [3,24]. We discovered that, in the context of Smart TVs, functionality outweighs privacy concerns.

10   Discussion and Conclusion

We reported on three studies with a total 524 participants. They evaluated Smart TV owner awareness, attitudes towards privacy risks and measures to preserve privacy.

We had anticipated general lack of awareness. Our studies confirmed this. Only 28 of the 171 (16%) participants in the first study mentioned a privacy risks in their responses and only 12 (7%) were able to name concrete consequences of privacy invasions.

We showed that Smart TV consumers were most likely to deploy a privacy protection measure on their Smart TV when the measure did not impair available functionality. They were willing to commit time and/or effort to protect their privacy under these conditions. If functionality is restricted, on the other hand, they are unlikely to deploy a privacy-protection measure. Thus, corresponding usable technologies should be offered instead of purely making people aware of the privacy implications of current technologies.

Furthermore, we find that significantly greater numbers of Smart TV owners would disconnect their Smart TV when exposed to an awareness message that mentions actual potential harm. Thus, awareness-raising endeavours should always incorporate mention potential harms of Smart TV related privacy risks. Further findings were:

- Some of our participants had become so used to being profiled and observed that they seemed to consider resistance futile.
- Others could only come up with the advantages of external agents collecting their data.
- Others demonstrated a naïve trust in vendors and broadcasters.

Limitations. All studies were conducted in Germany, where the population tends to be more attuned to privacy concerns than citizens of other countries [23]. A study with Americans, for example, might well deliver different awareness levels and responses to privacy risks. The studies relied on self-report. Participants could have given false answers but since they were anonymous it is hard to see that many would feel the need to disseminate or to fabricate responses. We tailored surveys to reflect Smart TV privacy risks. A different set of scenarios might well have revealed other factors and thus led to dissimilar messages.

Acknowledgments. This project has received funding from the European Union's Horizon 2020 research and innovation programme under grant agreement No 653454. It has also been supported by the German Federal Ministry of Education and Research (BMBF) within the project MoPPa (16KIS0343) and by the German Federal Ministry of Education and Research (BMBF) as well as by the Hessen State Ministry for Higher Education, Research and the Arts within CRISP.

References

1. Working Group Smart TV of the German TV-Platform: Marktanalyse Smart-TV - Eine Bestandsaufnahme der Deutschen TV-Plattform. http://tv-plattform.de/images/stories/pdf/marktanalyse_smart-tv_2013.pdf. Accessed 06 Nov 2016

2. Camp, L.J.: Mental models of privacy and security. Technol. Soc. Mag. IEEE **28**(3), 37–46 (2006)

3. Choi, B.C., Land, L.: The effects of general privacy concerns and transactional privacy concerns on facebook apps usage. Inf. Manage. **53**(7), 868–877 (2016). https://doi.org/10.1016/j.im.2016.02.003

4. Clark, S., Goodspeed, T., Metzger, P., Wasserman, Z., Xu, K., Blaze, M.: Why (special agent) johnny (still) can't encrypt: a security analysis of the APCO project 25 two-way radio system. In: USENIX Security Symposium (2011)

5. David Lodge: Is Your Samsung TV Listening To You? Pen Test Partners. https://www.pentestpartners.com/blog/is-your-samsung-tv-listening-to-you/. Accessed 23 Feb 2016

6. Debatin, B., Lovejoy, J.P., Horn, A.K., Hughes, B.N.: Facebook and online privacy: attitudes, behaviors, and unintended consequences. J. Comput.-Mediat. Commun. **15**(1), 83–108 (2009)

7. Dienlin, T., Trepte, S.: Is the privacy paradox a relic of the past? An in-depth analysis of privacy attitudes and privacy behaviors. Eur. J. Soc. Psychol. **45**(3), 285–297 (2015)

8. Dinev, T., Hart, P.: An extended privacy calculus model for e-commerce transactions. Info. Syst. Res. **17**(1), 61–80 (2006). http://dx.doi.org/10.1287/isre.1060.0080

9. DoctorBeet's Blog: LG Disables Smart TV features in the EU to force users to accept new oppressive Privacy policy. http://doctorbeet.blogspot.de/. Accessed 23 Feb 2016

10. Dourish, P., Delgado De La Flor, J., Joseph, M.: Security as a practical problem: some preliminary observations of everyday mental models. In: Proceedings of CHI Workshop on HCI and Security Systems. Fort Lauderdale, Florida, 5–10 Apr 2003

11. Bursztein, E.: Survey: most people don't lock their Android phones - but should (2014). https://www.elie.net/blog/survey-most-people-dont-lock-their-android-phones-but-should

12. Friedman, B., Hurley, D., Howe, D.C., Felten, E., Nissenbaum, H.: Users' conceptions of web security: a comparative study. In: CHI 2002 Extended Abstracts on Human Factors in Computing Systems, pp. 746–747. ACM (2002)

13. Gaw, S., Felten, E.W., Fernandez-Kelly, P.: Secrecy, flagging, and paranoia: adoption criteria in encrypted email. In: SIGCHI Conference on Human Factors in Computing Systems, pp. 591–600. CHI 2006 (2006)

14. Ghiglieri, M., Waidner, M.: HbbTV security and privacy: issues and challenges. IEEE Sec. Priv. **14**(3), 61–67 (2016)

15. Ghiglieri, M.: I know what you watched last sunday - a new survey of privacy in HbbTV. In: Workshop Web 2.0 Security and Privacy 2014 in Conjunction with the IEEE Symposium on Security and Privacy (2014)

16. Ghiglieri, M.: Incorrect HTTPS Certificate Validation in Samsung Smart TVs. Technical report (2014)

17. Ghiglieri, M., Oswald, F., Tews, E.: HbbTV - i know what you are watching. In: Informationssicherheit Stärken - Vertrauen in die Zukunft Schaffen, pp. 225–238. Bundesamt fr Sicherheit in der Informationstechnik, May 2013

18. Ghiglieri, M., Tews, E.: A privacy protection system for HbbTV in smart TVs. In: IEEE 11th Consumer Communications and Networking Conference (CCNC), pp. 648–653, Jan 2014

19. Gupta, S., Bostrom, R.P.: Theoretical model for investigating the impact of knowledge portals on different levels of knowledge processing. Int. J. Knowl. Learn. $1(4)$, 287–304 (2005)

20. Harbach, M., Fahl, S., Rieger, M., Smith, M.: On the acceptance of privacy-preserving authentication technology: the curious case of national identity cards. In: Cristofaro, E., Wright, M. (eds.) PETS 2013. LNCS, vol. 7981, pp. 245–264. Springer, Heidelberg (2013). doi:10.1007/978-3-642-39077-7_13

21. Harbach, M., von Zezschwitz, E., Fichtner, A., De Luca, A., Smith, M.: It's a hard lock life: a field study of smartphone (un) locking behavior and risk perception. In: Symposium on Usable Privacy and Security (SOUPS), pp. 213–230 (2014)

22. Kim, G., Koo, H.: The causal relationship between risk and trust in the online marketplace. Comput. Hum. Behav. 55, 1020–1029 (2016). doi:10.1016/j.chb.2015.11.005

23. Krasnova, H., Veltri, N.F.: Privacy calculus on social networking sites: explorative evidence from Germany and USA. In: 2010 43rd Hawaii International Conference on System Sciences (HICSS), pp. 1–10. IEEE (2010)

24. Lankton, N.K., McKnight, D.H.: What does it mean to trust facebook?: examining technology and interpersonal trust beliefs. SIGMIS Database $42(2)$, 32–54 (2011). http://doi.acm.org/10.1145/1989098.1989101

25. Matyszczyk, C.: Samsung's warning: Our Smart TVs record your living room chatter (2015). http://www.cnet.com/uk/news/samsungs-warning-our-smart-tvs-record-your-living-room-chatter/

26. Michéle, B., Karpow, A.: Watch and be watched: compromising all smart TV generations. In: IEEE 11th Consumer Communications and Networking Conference (CCNC), pp. 351–356, Jan 2014

27. Niemietz, M., Somorovsky, J., Mainka, C., Schwenk, J.: Not so Smart: On Smart TV Apps (undated). http://www.ei.ruhr-uni-bochum.de/media/nds/veroeffentlichungen/2015/08/31/SmartTvAttacks.pdf

28. Ophoff, J., Robinson, M.: Exploring end-user smartphone security awareness within a South African context. In: Information Security for South Africa (ISSA), 2014, pp. 1–7. IEEE (2014)

29. Oren, Y., Keromytis, A.D.: From the ether to the ethernet-attacking the internet using broadcast digital television. In: 23rd USENIX Security Symposium (USENIX Security 14), pp. 353–368 (2014)

30. Raja, F., Hawkey, K., Hsu, S., Wang, K.L., Beznosov, K.: Promoting a physical security mental model for personal firewall warnings. In: CHI 2011 Extended Abstracts on Human Factors in Computing Systems, CHI EA 2011, pp. 1585–1590. ACM, New York (2011)

31. Renaud, K., Volkamer, M., Renkema-Padmos, A.: Why doesn't Jane protect her privacy? In: Cristofaro, E., Murdoch, S.J. (eds.) PETS 2014. LNCS, vol. 8555, pp. 244–262. Springer, Cham (2014). doi:10.1007/978-3-319-08506-7_13
32. Rob Waugh (Metro): Smart TV hackers are filming people having sex on their sofas and putting it on porn sites. http://metro.co.uk/2016/05/23/smart-tv-hackers-are-filming-people-having-sex-on-their-sofas-and-putting-it-on-porn-sites-589924 8/. Accessed 06 Nov 2016
33. Samsung: Samsung Privacy Policy-SmartTV Supplement. http://www.samsung. com/sg/info/privacy/smarttv/. Accessed 06 Nov 2016
34. Seven One Media: Addressable TV - The Future is now. (02). Accessed 4 Feb 2016. Available from authors on request
35. Solove, D.J.: "I've got nothing to hide" and other misunderstandings of privacy. San Diego Law Rev. **44**, 745 (2007)
36. Sony: Privacy Policy for the applications and/or online services on Sony's cloud platform. http://policies.sony.net/tvsideview/pp_en.htm. Accessed 23 Feb 2016
37. Trepte, S., Dienlin, T., Reinecke, L.: Risky behaviors: how online experiences influence privacy behaviors. Von der Gutenberg-Galaxis zur Google-Galaxis (From the Gutenberg galaxy to the Google galaxy), pp. 225–244 (2014)
38. Trepte, S., Reinecke, L.: Privacy Online: Perspectives on Privacy and Self-disclosure in the Social Web (2011)
39. Trepte, S., Teutsch, D., Masur, P.K., Eicher, C., Fischer, M., Hennhöfer, A., Lind, F.: Do people know about privacy and data protection strategies? Towards the "Online Privacy Literacy Scale" (OPLIS). In: Gutwirth, S., Leenes, R., Hert, P. (eds.) Reforming European Data Protection Law. LGTS, vol. 20, pp. 333–365. Springer, Dordrecht (2015). doi:10.1007/978-94-017-9385-8_14
40. Volkamer, M., Renaud, K., Kulyk, O., Emeröz, S.: A socio-technical investigation into smartphone security. In: Foresti, S. (ed.) STM 2015. LNCS, vol. 9331, pp. 265–273. Springer, Cham (2015). doi:10.1007/978-3-319-24858-5_17
41. Wash, R.: Folk models of home computer security. In: Proceedings of the Sixth Symposium on Usable Privacy and Security, pp. 11. ACM, Redmond (2010)
42. Wästlund, E., Angulo, J., Fischer-Hübner, S.: Evoking comprehensive mental models of anonymous credentials. In: Camenisch, J., Kesdogan, D. (eds.) iNetSec 2011. LNCS, vol. 7039, pp. 1–14. Springer, Heidelberg (2012). doi:10.1007/ 978-3-642-27585-2_1
43. Weirich, D., Sasse, M.A.: Pretty good persuasion: a first step towards effective password security in the real world. In: Proceedings of 2001 Workshop on New Security Paradigms, NSPW 2001, pp. 137–143. Cloudcroft, NM (2001)
44. Zolfagharifard, E.: Is YOUR TV spying on you? Report reveals how Vizio smart televisions track your data so that it can be sold to advertisers (2015). http://www.dailymail.co.uk/sciencetech/article-3312597/Is-TV-spying-Report-re veals-Vizio-smart-televisions-track-data-sold-advertisers.html

Sharing Information with Web Services – A Mental Model Approach in the Context of Optional Information

Oksana Kulyk[2]([⊠]), Benjamin Maximilian Reinheimer[2], and Melanie Volkamer[1,2]

[1] Karlstad University, Karlstad, Sweden
[2] Technische Universität Darmstadt, Darmstadt, Germany
{oksana.kulyk,benjamin.reinheimer,melanie.volkamer}@secuso.org

Abstract. Web forms are a common way for web service providers to collect data from their users. Usually, the users are asked for a lot of information while some items are labeled as optional and others as mandatory. When filling in the web form, users have to decide, which data, often of personal and sensitive nature, they want to share. The factors that influence the decision whether or not to share some information has been studied in the literature in various contexts. However, it is unclear to which extent their results can be transferred to other contexts. In this work we conduct a qualitative user study to verify, whether the reasons for sharing optional information from previous studies [12] are relevant for the context of interacting with a commercial website. We found, that only a few of them were named by the participants of our study.

Keywords: Web forms · Optional fields · Mental models · Interviews

1 Introduction

Web forms have been a known component on websites since the 1990s. They are often used by web service providers to collect personal data of their users, which is either directly required for the functionality of the service, or serves other purposes such as enabling data analytics (e.g. for personalized advertisements or service improvements). Usually, the users are asked for a lot of information, often of personal nature, while some items are labeled as optional and others as mandatory. When filling in the web form, users have to decide, which data they want to share. The only way for the users not to share data requested in mandatory fields is either not to use the service at all, or to provide information that is fake but has a semantic that the service provider accepts (e.g. a wrong birthday but still an existing date). Users have more power in deciding whether to share information or not when the fields are optional.

A number of studies have been dedicated to the research on users' behaviour and perception regarding the web form fields. In particular, several studies focused on researching a link between the users' willingness to provide data by

© Springer International Publishing AG 2017
T. Tryfonas (Ed.): HAS 2017, LNCS 10292, pp. 675–690, 2017.
DOI: 10.1007/978-3-319-58460-7_46

filling in the web form fields that are not mandatory and the users personality traits [5,11]. The paper by Preibusch et al. [12] provides a list of reasons which might explain, why users provide data for optional fields on the website form. This list, however, is only partially supported by existing studies. Furthermore, these studies have been performed in specific contexts, such as creating an account on social lending networks. Hence it is unclear whether their results can be generalised to other types of web services.

In order to check the relevance of their list, Preibusch et al. conducted a quantitative study in [12]. One of the goals of the study has been to find out the reasons why the participants filled in the optional fields. Their results confirmed the relevance of some of the reasons from their initial list. Furthermore, the study found anecdotal evidence for additional reasons such as user extroversion or feeling compelled to complete all the fields in the form. The authors, however, did not elaborate on the additional reasons. Furthermore, being only one of several research goals of the study, the reasons of filling in the forms were the focus of only one open question, which did not allow clarifying follow-up questions. The study also focused on a specific context of the mTurk platform. As such, the participants expected that their input data will be used for statistical research (which provided additional motivation for some of them to input more), that the more data they input, the more rewards they would gain from the mTurk platform, and the authors themselves recognize that the active users of mTurk might be more inclined to fill in web forms out of interest than the general population.

In this work we conduct a user study to verify, whether the reasons for filling in the optional fields of the web forms are consistent with the initial list by Preibusch et al. in the context of interacting with a commercial website. Concretely, the scenario for our study was that the participants had to register a user account on a mock website of the Deutsche Bahn (German railways) company[1]. They were told, that the goal of the study is to evaluate the usability of the new design proposed by the company. After filling in the registration form, semi-structured interviews were conducted with the participants, where they were asked to explain why they filled or not filled in the optional form fields. The interviews were qualitatively analysed using the reasons from the initial list of Preibusch et al. as pre-existing categories. The results show which reasons have been mentioned by our participants and whether additional reasons have been mentioned that cannot be assigned to the initial list. We found correspondences for three out of ten items in the list in our interviews. We also found evidence for two additional categories of reasons that the participants gave when asked to explain why they filled in an optional field.

We furthermore looked at the reasons why the participants were reluctant to share additional data, and at the countermeasures they used, such as providing fake data, in order to avoid sharing more than they would want.

---

[1] https://www.bahn.de/p/view/index.shtml, last accessed 10.02.2017.

2 Methodology

In this section we describe the user study that we have conducted, and the methods we used to analyse the resulting interviews.

2.1 User Study

We first by describing the study design and the demographics of our participants.

Mock Registration Website. For our user study we set up a mock registration website that contained a cloned and modified registration form of the "Deutsche Bahn" company on a local virtual machine. The DNS entries in the host file on the operation system were manipulated, so that the participants were not able to tell that the website is not online. For the same purpose, the Internet connection status bar was hidden.

The form on our mock website resembled the design of the original Deutsche Bahn registration website, but contained a different set of form fields, namely, eight mandatory fields and six optional fields. The fields that were included in the form were chosen as common fields on the websites in Alexa top 50^2. Namely, we included such optional fields as title, date of birth and phone number. In additional to these fields that were commonly encountered on the websites, we also chose to include two optional fields that we rarely used in web-forms, namely, the marital status and country of origin. We further included an optional checkbox that asked whether the participants consent to using cookies.

Participants. The study consisted of 16 participants, with eight women and eight men. The youngest participant was 23 years old, and the oldest 58 years old, with 36.5 as the mean age. In order to prevent priming the participants towards thinking about their privacy, the participants of the study were told that they are going to participate in a study done in collaboration with the Deutsche Bahn, and that the goal of the study was usability evaluation of a new registration form for the Deutsche Bahn website. The participants were offered either 10 Euros or one credit point reimbursement for their participation in the study. Most of the participants rated their IT knowledge highly: When asked to agree or disagree with the statement that their IT knowledge is good, 11 participants answered that they either "strongly agree" or "agree", three neither agreed nor disagreed, and three disagreed with this statement. All but one participants answered either "strongly argee" or "agree" to the statement that their privacy is important to them (the remaining participant did not answer that question), and all but three answered "strongly agree" or "agree" to the statement that they take active measures to protect their privacy (out of the remaining participants, two neither agreed nor disagreed, and one did not answer the question).

---

[2] http://www.alexa.com/topsites, last accessed on 10.02.2017.

Study Design. After welcoming the participants, the study consisted of two parts.

Registration. In the first part, the participants were told to fill in the registration form on the mock website that we have set up. At the beginning of the study every participant had to read the same study description, describing the goal of the study, namely, usability evaluation of the registration form. The participants were then told to register themselves using the modified registration form. It was furthermore stated, that no questions during the registration process are allowed in order not to interfere the process. Still, the participants were encouraged to think out loud during the registration. The registration process was completed when the participant clicked on the send button.

Follow-up Questions. The follow-up questions were asked in form of a semi-structured interview. After the registration, the participants were told that we have an exclusive access to their registered dataset to further discuss their perceived usability of the registration form. To obfuscate the real intention of our interview and to be in compliance with our communicated research goals, the introductory questions started with usability topics. Afterwards, based on the displayed data type fields, the participants were asked a set of questions about why they have or have not filled in the optional fields.

The study concluded by debriefing and gathering the demographic data.

2.2   Analysis Methodology

Our main research goal was to find out, which reasons for filling in the optional fields from the Preibusch et al. initial list [12] were mentioned by our participants, and whether there have been any reasons not on this list. For this purpose, the interviews were transcribed and analysed using qualitative semi-open coding approach. We took the list of Preibusch et al. as the pre-defined categories and classified the participants responses in the interviews according to these categories. In case we encountered responses that could not fit into the pre-defined categories, we assigned them to new categories. Each transcript has been analysed by two independent authors, and the findings were then discussed and agreed upon among the authors. The categories were supplemented with the quotes from the interviews, translated from German to English.

As additional research goals, we decided to consider the reasons that the participants gave for not providing their personal data to websites, and the countermeasures they used when a website requested some kind of personal data they did not want to disclose. For these goals, the interviews were analysed by two authors using open-coding approach, and the resulting categories were further discussed among the authors and agreed upon. As with the main research goal, we provide a quote supporting each one of the categories, translated from German to English.

3   Results

In this section we describe the evaluation results of our study.

3.1   Reasons for Filling in Optional Data Fields

We first describe the findings relevant to our main research goal. We provide the list of the pre-existing categories and specify whether we found any correspondences to them in our dataset. We further describe the new categories that were derived from our analysis.

Pre-existing Categories. We first describe the correspondences we found in our interviews to the list of Preibush et al. in [12].

Over-disclosure by Accident. Commonly, the users do not distinguish between optional and mandatory forms, either due to the website's design or due to not paying attention to the clues that point that a field is optional. As such, a significant number of participants in our study reported not seeing the red star that appears only near to mandatory fields[3], and then mentioned that they would not have filled the data if they have seen that it is optional.

> "It was not intended, I would not have filled it in if I did not think that I had to input it."

Over-disclosure by Proxy. This item relates to the cases, where the autocomplete function of one's browser ends up filling in more data than the user intended to. As the participants in our study used a lab computer to fill in the form, over-disclosure by proxy was not relevant for them.

Limit Disclosure is Costly. It has been suggested, that some users fill in all the fields in the form, since distinguishing between optional and mandatory fields requires too much time or effort, for example, if the website requires sending the filled form first before telling whether there is data missing in some of the mandatory fields. However, none of the participants named this reason for filling in optional forms explicitly.

Building Social Capital. The studies on websites that maintain a public or semi-public (i.e. open only to friends on social networks, or to recruiters on job hunting websites) have shown [7], that some users provide more data in their accounts in order to create a better image of themselves. In our study, however, the participants did not have to create a public profile of themselves, hence, they could not build social capital based on the data they provided. Therefore, as expected, none of them has mentioned this reason.

---

[3] Note that our mock registration form used the same indicator for distinguishing between mandatory and optional fields as the real Deutsche Bahn website.

Expecting Monetary Return. The data provided by the users is often used by the companies to provide additional offers to the users such as personalised advertisements. Hence, it has been suggested that the users might input their data in order to be able potentially to benefit from such offers. A number of our participants mentioned, that they disclose such data as their date of birth, expecting special offers sent to them on their birthday, or expecting information on discounts tailored to their interests.

> "Okay, it can also present a benefit, if I, for example, register myself somewhere or fill in some form, and in this way the personalized offers can be tailored to me. This can be an advantage."

Note that although the participants interacted with the mock website, they did not attempt to surf the website in order to find the information about the exact benefits they might get from disclosing additional data. They also did not mention that they tend to research the potential benefits of data disclosure on other websites they use before they actually input their data on these websites. Hence, their expectations relied more on their reasoning and previous experience than on the information provided by the service prior to the data disclosure.

Expecting Non-monetary Return. Similar to monetary benefits, the companies might provide additional features to the user based on their input data, such as personalised recommendations of products or services or additional functionality. Some of our participants mentioned expecting such a non-monetary return in form of an additional functionality in exchange for providing additional data, such as getting phone notifications when the transport is late if the phone number is provided.

> "...while booking a bus trip in Germany on the Internet, one has to input the phone number in order to be notified about the delays. And I see a benefit in this, that I leave my phone number, although generally I am reluctant. This would be an example where I see that it makes sense for me to leave my phone number."

Similar to the expectations of monetary return, our participants neither attempted to find out whether the Deutsche Bahn provides additional functionality in exchange of disclosing optional data prior to the registration, nor did they mention researching potential benefits of data disclosure before providing their data on other websites.

Expecting Infrastructure Improvements. Preibusch et al. suggest, that the companies can use the information gathered from the users to better adjust their services to the demands of their customers. Hence, expecting such adjustments, the users might choose to provide additional data. However, none of our participants mentioned such motivation for disclosing data on web forms.

Acting Reciprocally/Altruistically. Studies have shown [11] that people who generally tend to act reciprocally also provided more data by filling in the fields in the study questionnaires. Since, however, our study focused on filling in the registration forms on commercial websites, it is not surprising that our participants did not mention the motivation to act reciprocally or altruistically as their reason for providing additional data.

Personality. Preibusch et al. suggest that for some users their personality might influence their decision to input more data, for example, if the user enjoys filling in the questionnaires. Indeed, the study in [12] included a significant number of participants who mentioned that they enjoyed participating in the surveys or find the activity of filling in the forms fun and interesting. However, none of our participants mentioned their personal preferences as a motivation for providing more data. It is worth noting, however, that a number of participants mentioned their personality traits as the reason *not* to provide their data on the websites, which we describe in Sect. 3.2.

New Findings. We further describe additional reasons mentioned by our participants but not included in the initial list in [12].

"It makes sense for them to request this information" Several users mentioned filling in the fields, that they expected to be mandatory, even though the fields were marked as optional. The expectations of the participants were either due to their previous experience with similar services, or due to their assumption that the particular data is required for the service functionality.

> "Maybe for some... maybe at the Espirit online shop, there I would think, why are they interested in my date of birth, they are only interested in what I order. [...] They do not need to know my date of birth. And here I thought, that it might be relevant for ordering the train ticket. I would relate the date of birth to the registration."

> "Country of origin... I saw that it is not mandatory... I deliberately filled it in, because I think that this is an important category for the classification. This was just my interpretation."

> "No, I think, when I fill something in, do they really need this, or not? And all that I filled in is important... so, in my opinion."

As with the case of expecting monetary or non-monetary return from providing additional data (see Sect. 3.1), the participants in this category relied on their own reasoning in deciding whether the requested data is indeed required by the service instead of attempting to get this information from the service provider itself.

"I trust that they have their reasons for requesting this information" Similar to the previous category, some participants claimed to disclose optional data if they believed that there was a good reason for the service provider to request the information. However, while the participants in the previous category based their beliefs on their own reasoning, others relied more on their trust in the service provider to use their data responsibly.

> "Now, for example, I have an airline in mind, they need some data in any case. I do not have any problems with it, since I trust that the data stays confidential with them."

Similar to the previous category, the participants neither attempted did not attempt to find out the reasons why the service collects the requested data.

Filling out Fields as Default Behaviour. Some of the participants claimed, they generally tend to fill in all the forms on the website, unless they have a particular reason not to. While these claims can be considered close to the pre-existing categories "over-disclosure by accident" and "limit disclosure is costly", we still decided to categorize them separately, since the participants neither claimed to overlook the indicator and disclose more than they intended to, neither mentioned making a conscious decision to save time or effort by filling in all available fields.

> "I just did not see any disadvantage, so I thought, I fill this in."

In particular, some stressed that they would disclose the information if the website is trusted.

> "And the fields I do not fill in, these are, for example, address stuff, but I have no concerns with the Deutsche Bahn."

3.2   Other Findings

We describe the findings for our additional research goals, namely, by providing an overview of the reasons that our participants mentioned for not disclosing their personal data, and the countermeasures they mentioned using when confronted with the request to share more data than they wanted.

Reasons for Not Filling in Optional Data Fields. The responses of the participants who were reluctant to share their data can be grouped into two categories.

Personal Feelings. A number of participants mentioned that they did not share their data due to their personality, or because they "had a bad feeling" sharing more than they considered absolutely needed. As such, this group focused on their subjective feelings and personal preferences:

> "I do not like disclosing it, but this really a very personal and subjective thing!"

Concrete Threats. Another group mentioned specific threats that they wanted to protect themselves against, such as spam mails or phone calls, or identity theft:

> "I do not like it when people just call. I have experienced this a couple of times, that someone just calls me, and I do not like it."

> "Some [companies] really try [to protect the data], but then it's like, yeah, we have been hacked, or... and this is just great. Then they have all the data, all the credit cards... this did not yet happen to me, but... this is why I do not have a lot to do with the Internet services."

Countermeasures. We asked our participants what would they do if there is a registration form on some website with mandatory fields that require data the participants do not want to disclose. The responses can be grouped into following categories:

Boycott the Website. The most obvious solution mentioned by several participants was that they would refuse to use a website, if it required data considered too private by the participants. In particular, looking for alternatives that provide a similar service but either require less data or are more trusted not to misuse the collected data has been mentioned:

> "I already had this, that I wanted to register, for example, in the online shop, and then I did not want to fill in the data. And then I did not register, and bought it at Amazon for a couple of euros more."

Input Fake Data. A solution also mentioned by our participants was to input fake data, if the real data is considered too private to disclose. The types of data that is faked, as well as the settings in which fake data is given, varies. As such, a number of participants mentioned that they input fake data often, aside from the situations when it could hinder the functionality offered by the service:

> "So I am always the one who under circumstances also inputs fake data, when it does not suit me. This is possible."

Some have mentioned that they are reluctant to input fake data into the websites owned by governmental institutions:

> "Actually, always, except for, I would say, official institutions, where it has to be correct."

Another approach that has been mentioned in the interviews was to input fake data, which, however, is not misleading. One particular example is the date of birth: as the website's intention is to find out, whether the user is older than 18, the specific age is assumed to be irrelevant, hence, fake data can be given.

"There is the Rotkäppchen sparkling wine, and when one goes to this website, then one has to input the date of birth. Maybe minors under 18 years old are not allowed to visit the website. So I could imagine. And when I look at something on the website, then I just click on some number. I mean, I am not under 18, but I just click something, since it does not matter whether I am 30, or 40, or 50 years old, for me to go there. "

It is worth noting, however, that a number of participants claimed that they never input fake data due to their personality traits.

"No, I am very honest."

Avoid Registration, but Still Use the Service. One possible solution to avoid filling in unwanted web form fields was to look for the ways to use the website functionality without registration.

"I actually never register, and continue without login. [...] They do not know who I am, what my name is, where I live and so on, and I do not have to remember any login and can always do that in another way, so to say."

Use Throw-away Contact Information. The reluctance to fill in contact information has been often mentioned by our participants, either due to privacy reasons, or in order to avoid unwanted advertisements. Hence, in order to be able to register on the websites, that demanded the user's e-mail address, some of the participants mentioned registering a separate address just for the registration purposes, that is not checked as often as their regular address.

"The e-mail address is in any case a second email address, so it is not an important one. When too many junk gets there, then it will not be read."

"Then one can have a spam e-mail. Then they can spam me as they want, that does not bother me."

While the practice of using throw-away phone numbers appears to be much less frequent than using throw-away e-mail adresses, it has been mentioned as well. In particular, one of the participants reported registering a phone number from an Internet phone company, so that the calls to this number went to the participant's email instead of going to their regular phone.

"When one has to input the phone number as a mandatory field, then I often input a Sipgate phone number, that lands in a normal mail box. [...] This is a Voice-over-IP phone number, there I get at most an e-mail, when someone calls it. But my mobile phone does not ring."

4   Related Work

For describing the related work we focus on research that studied the factors that influence the data disclosure of the users and the tools that aim to prevent the users from disclosing too much data. We furthermore describe the works in other domains that study the mental models of the users and the motive for their behaviour concerning various security mechanisms.

Reasons and Factors that Influence Data Exposure. A number of studies focused on the topic of web forms and optional fields. As such, Preibusch et al. conducted a quantitative user study in order to study the users [12] and construct our original list of reasons to expose their data. They also conducted a user study trying to gauge additional responses, but the context was also limited (the users thought that the purpose of the study was to gather and analyse their data). Their further findings include quantitative analysis whether users are likely to fill in optional fields, whether the presence of mandatory fields increases their likelihood to enter data and how long does it take to enter data.

The personality traits of the users that influence their data disclosure have been the topic of several studies. As such, Egelman [5] studied the personality traits that help predict the decision making and risk-taking attitudes of the users. The focus of other studies was more specific. As such, Adams et al. [2] studied the trade-offs that the users consider acceptable for disclosing their personal data, and Ackerman et al. studied the users attitudes towards providing data in e-commerce [1]. The study in [11] focused on the dependencies between the personality traits such as fairness or desire to act reciprocally and filling in the forms. All those studies strengthen the assumption that attitudes and personality traits should be more focused when trying to understand differences in privacy behavior.

Other researchers studied disclosure of personal data on social lending sites [4]. They argue that this exposure is related to the theory of descriptive social norms. It means that either the similarity of context, social proximity, and mimicry of success factors leads to people exposing their data because of social norms and less because of rational decisions. Kramer conducted a similar study where they look at the specific privacy in Faccbook [8]. Furthermore Korff et al. studied the effect of differences in the choice amount by changing the number of chechboxes and choice structure by varying the sensitivity of personal data items presented on privacy behavior [7]. They expect the amount and the structure to have a similiar effect on the privacy behavior compared to all day decisions like shopping. Acquisti et al. studied the extent to which the users are ready to sacrifice their privacy in exchange of a monetary return.

Tools that Prevent Data Exposure. A number of researchers focused on the development of different tools to support more privacy-aware behaviour of the users in the process of filling out web forms. Knijnenburg et al. conducted a study where they compared new and more detailed forms of auto-completion tools with a traditional one [6]. The main purpose was to revive the privacy calculus for filling out web forms. They proclaim that users may skip this privacy calculus out of convenience and therefore use the traditional auto-completion tools. Krol et al. developed a tool for alerting users when they are about to fill in an optional form [9], thus making people more aware of unnecessary data exposure.

Mental Models of Privacy-Preserving Behaviour in Other Domains. Aside from web forms, a number of papers studied the reasons why the users do not engage in privacy-preserving behaviour in various domains. As such, a qualitative study have been conducted by Renaud et al. [13] in order to derive the mental models of users regarding e-mail encryption. The study in [3] researched the reasons mentioned by the participants for not using password managers, and the study in [16] considered the reasons that prevent smartphoned users in engaging in various secure behaviour such as setting a screen lock or installing an anti-virus software. A general overview of mental models in security is provided by Volkamer et al. in [15], stressing that understanding the mental models and comprehension of security mechanisms of the users is cruical in supporting the users in their privacy-related decisions.

5   Conclusion

In this chapter we summarize our findings, as well as discuss their implications and possible directions of future work.

5.1   Summary

As the web-based services attract more users, the websites also tend to gather more personal data. The users are seldom provided an explanation on what the purpose of the data collection is, and often the website design makes it hard for the user to notice, which data is mandatory to provide for using the service. Hence, users result in filling in the optional fields on the website forms, providing more personal data than needed for their intentions.

We have conducted a study to find out the reasons, why the users fill in optional fields on the websites. We based our assumptions on what these reasons are on existing literature, namely, on the list provided in [12]. The reasons on this list, however, were either not confirmed in an empirical study at all, or the study was done in a specific context (such as the study of user's behaviour on social networks or providing data for a research survey) which is not directly transferable to other types of websites and services. Our study focused on finding out whether the aforemendtioned reasons would be relevant for the scenario where the users have to fill in the registration form on a website of a company that provides commercial services, which is one of the most common contexts encountered on the web. In our study we asked the participants to register an account on our mock registration website, which, as they were told, belonged to the Deutsche Bahn company (German Railways) that assigned our research group to conduct a usability study of their new registration form. After the participants registered an account, they were asked to explain what data they decided to share and why.

We found, that only three out of ten reasons from the initial list in [12] were mentioned by our participants when asked to explain why they filled in the optional fields in the forms. Namely, the reasons that were mentioned by our participants were *over-exposure by accident* (i.e. not being able to notice an indicator that shows whether a field is optional or mandatory), *expecting monetary return* (e.g. special birthday offers, if the date of birth is provided) and *expecting non-monetary return* (e.g. a phone notification for a delayed transport, if the phone number is provided).

We have further identified three categories that were not explicitly present in the initial list by Preibusch et al., but mentioned by our participants. In the first category, the participants decided to fill in optional fields because they believed that the service required the particular data in order to provide the necessary functionality. Despite the fields being marked as optional by the service, the participants in this category strongly relied on their own reasoning to decide, whether it makes sense for the service to request a particular piece of data, hence, whether they should provide this data. The second category, on the other hand included the statements from the participants that generally relied on trust in the service. Even if the participants noticed that some fields were optional and they could not themselves think of a good reason for the service to require some particular data, they still decided to fill in these fields since they trusted that the service would not request the data unless it had a good reason to do so. The third category consisted of the statements that concerned the default behaviour of the users. Especially if the service itself was found trustworthy, the participants decided to fill in all the fields, since they saw no disadvantage in doing otherwise.

Further findings indicate, that many of our participants were reluctant to disclose their data, due to either concrete concerns of data misuse, or a general feeling of uneasiness. Moreover, we provided a list of countermeasures that the participants would use if the website requests some data they are not comfortable sharing, such as providing fake data, registering a separate e-mail which the user rarely checks for providing it on the website or boycotting the website entirely.

5.2 Discussion and Future Work

Our findings indicate following factors that determine whether the users are likely to input their optional data. The first factor is the users' *trust* that the service would not collect data without good reason, is unlikely to misuse it and is capable of ensuring its security against external attacks. The second important factor is *transparency* meaning that it is be important for some users to understand what their data is used for before they decide to disclose it. Note, that the factor of transparency has also been found relevant in privacy-related decisions in other domains, such as in deciding to install a smartphone app if the permissions that the app requests make sense to the user [10]. The final factor is *awareness*,

688 O. Kulyk et al.

meaning that many provide more personal data then they would want to, only because they did not notice an option to do otherwise.

Note that all these factors are reflected in the EU General Data Protection Guideline [14] (GDPG). As such, Art. 5 states, that "Personal data should be [...] collected for specified, explicit and legitimate purposes and not further processed in a manner that is incompatible with those purposes; [...] adequate, relevant and limited to what is necessary in relation to the purposes for which they are processed; [...] processed in a manner that ensures appropriate security of the personal data, including protection against unauthorised or unlawful processing and against accidental loss, destruction or damage, using appropriate technical or organisational measures ('integrity and confidentiality')", which corresponds to the factor of trust as expressed by our participants. The guideline further demands that the users are provided with "the purposes of the processing for which the personal data are intended as well as the legal basis for the processing" (Art. 13), which corresponds to the factor of transparency. As our results show, our participants relied on their expectations of which benefit they would get from disclosing additional data, or what the purpose of collecting specific information was, instead of attempting to find out this information from the service itself. Still, they were more likely to disclose the data if they could think of a purpose behind its collection. The factor of awareness is addressed with the guidelines requiring the consent of the users for data processing (Art. 6). The guideline defines consent in Art. 4 as "any freely given, specific, informed and unambiguous indication of the data subject's wishes by which he or she, by a statement or by a clear affirmative action, signifies agreement to the processing of personal data relating to him or her". The participants in our study, on the other hand, overlooked the information on the website, thus providing more data than they would otherwise do.

Given our findings related to the GDPG, an important direction of future work is the improvement of communication between the service providers and the users. As such, as trust in the service provider has been shown to be an important factor for the decision making of the users, tools for trust assessment (e.g. in form of an evaluation, to which extent the service provider complies to the GDPG) and communication, possibly from independent institutions, would be helpful in supporting the users. Furthermore, our study has shown that the users rely on their considerations on what the potential benefits of their data disclosure would be, or how the service could use their data, while deciding which data to disclose. Hence, input from the service provider with this information can help the users make a more informed decision. Finally, as a number of users tend to overlook the indicators for optional fields, providing more data than they would want to, more visible indicators on the website would make sure that accidental disclosure without the users explicit consent is minimized.

Our study has further shown, that there is a discrepancy in the participants attitudes towards data disclosure. As such, while some of the participants filled in the data without having any concerns, others claimed being reluctant to disclose their data. Given that all the participants had to interact with the same website, it would be interesting to investigate the further differences between those two groups that influence their decision making and attitudes towards data disclosure. Furthermore, an interesting direction of future work would be investigating other contexts in which the users have to decide whether to disclose data. As such, it would be interesting to compare, whether the user behaviour and reasons for either disclosing or not disclosing data differ while interacting with a trustworthy website such as a well-known Deutsche Bahn company, as opposed to interacting with a small and unknown online shop or other service that might be deemed less trustworthy by the participants.

The prevalence of various countermeasures, such as using fake data, that the participants use in order to avoid filling in the mandatory fields shows that the reluctance of sharing personal data, even at the expense of the user's convenience, is a significant factor in decision making for many users. These findings suggest that collecting too much data without providing a sufficient explanation can be detrimental for the web services as well. On the other hand, since the countermeasures mentioned by our participants are not an optimal solution for every user, better tools for supporting the users who do not want to disclose their personal data are needed.

Acknowledgements. This work has been co-funded by the DFG as part of project D.1 within the RTG 2050 "Privacy and Trust for Mobile Users". This research has also received funding from the European Union's Horizon 2020 research and innovation programme under grant agreement No 653454. It has also been supported by the German Federal Ministry of Education and Research (BMBF) as well as by the Hessen State Ministry for Higher Education, Research and the Arts within CRISP.

References

1. Ackerman, M.S., Cranor, L.F., Reagle, J.: Privacy in e-commerce: examining user scenarios and privacy preferences. In: 1st ACM Conference on Electronic Commerce, pp. 1–8. ACM (1999)
2. Adams, A., Sasse, M.A.: Privacy in multimedia communications: protecting users, not just data. In: Blandford, A., Vanderdonckt, J., Gray, P. (eds.) People and Computers XV - Interaction Without Frontiers, pp. 49–64. Springer, London (2001)
3. Alkaldi, N., Renaud, K.: Why do people adopt, or reject, smartphone password managers? In: EuroUSEC 2016: European Workshop on Usable Security, vol. 18, pp. 1–14 (2016)
4. Böhme, R., Pötzsch, S.: Collective exposure: peer effects in voluntary disclosure of personal data. In: Danezis, G. (ed.) FC 2011. LNCS, vol. 7035, pp. 1–15. Springer, Heidelberg (2012). doi:10.1007/978-3-642-27576-0_1
5. Egelman, S., Peer, E.: Predicting privacy and security attitudes. ACM SIGCAS Comput. Soc. **45**(1), 22–28 (2015)
6. Knijnenburg, B.P., Kobsa, A., Jin, H.: Counteracting the negative effect of form auto-completion on the privacy calculus. In: ICIS 2013: International Conference on Information Systems. AIS eLibrary (2013)
7. Korff, S., Böhme, R.: Too much choice: end-user privacy decisions in the context of choice proliferation. In: SOUpPS 2014: Symposium on Usable Privacy and Security, pp. 69–87. USENIX (2014)

8. Krämer, N.C., Haferkamp, N.: Online self-presentation: balancing privacy concerns and impression construction on social networking sites. In: Trepte, S., Reinecke, L. (eds.) Privacy Online, pp. 127–141. Springer, Heidelberg (2011)

9. Krol, K., Preibusch, S.: Control versus effort in privacy warnings for webforms. In: WPES 2016: ACM on Workshop on Privacy in the Electronic Society, pp. 13–23. ACM (2016)

10. Kulyk, O., Gerber, P., El Hanafi, M., Reinheimer, B., Renaud, K., Volkamer, M.: Encouraging privacy-aware smartphone app. installation: what would the technically-adept do. In: USEC 2016: Usable Security Workshop. Internet Society (2016)

11. Malheiros, M., Preibusch, S., Sasse, M.A.: "Fairly truthful": the impact of perceived effort, fairness, relevance, and sensitivity on personal data disclosure. In: Huth, M., Asokan, N., Čapkun, S., Flechais, I., Coles-Kemp, L. (eds.) Trust 2013. LNCS, vol. 7904, pp. 250–266. Springer, Heidelberg (2013). doi:10.1007/978-3-642-38908-5_19

12. Preibusch, S., Krol, K., Beresford, A.R.: The privacy economics of voluntary over-disclosure in web forms. In: Böhme, R. (ed.) The Economics of Information Security and Privacy, pp. 183–209. Springer, Heidelberg (2013)

13. Renaud, K., Volkamer, M., Renkema-Padmos, A.: Why doesn't jane protect her privacy? In: Cristofaro, E., Murdoch, S.J. (eds.) PETS 2014. LNCS, vol. 8555, pp. 244–262. Springer, Cham (2014). doi:10.1007/978-3-319-08506-7_13

14. The European Parliament and of the Council of European Union: Regulation (EU) 2016/679 of the European Parliament and of the Council of 27 April 2016 on the protection of natural persons with regard to the processing of personal data and on the free movement of such data, and repealing Directive 95/46/EC (2016), http://eur-lex.europa.eu/legal-content/EN/ALL/?uri=CELEX:32016R0679, last accessed on 10.02.2017

15. Volkamer, M., Renaud, K.: Mental models – general introduction and review of their application to human-centred security. In: Fischlin, M., Katzenbeisser, S. (eds.) Number Theory and Cryptography. LNCS, vol. 8260, pp. 255–280. Springer, Heidelberg (2013). doi:10.1007/978-3-642-42001-6_18

16. Volkamer, M., Renaud, K., Kulyk, O., Emeröz, S.: A socio-technical investigation into smartphone security. In: Foresti, S. (ed.) STM 2015. LNCS, vol. 9331, pp. 265–273. Springer, Cham (2015). doi:10.1007/978-3-319-24858-5_17

Integrating a Practice Perspective to Privacy by Design

Christopher Lentzsch[1], Kai-Uwe Loser[1], Martin Degeling[2]([✉]), and Alexander Nolte[1]

[1] Institute for Applied Work Science,
Ruhr-University Bochum, Bochum, Germany
{lentzsch,loser,nolte}@iaw.rub.de
[2] Institute for Software Research, Carnegie Mellon University, Pittsburgh, USA
degeling@cs.cmu.edu

Abstract. The goal of privacy by design (PbD) is to consider privacy aspects during all steps of a software and system design process in order to foster the development of privacy friendly technology. Current PbD approaches mainly focus on technological aspects of privacy in software engineering and rarely include viable approaches that take into account the context in which software systems are built and used. The future context of use however plays a crucial role for the effectiveness of privacy and security measures. Therefore, we propose to use a socio-technical design approach based on the established method of STWT (socio-technical walkthrough). This method allows multiple stakeholders to reflect on process models they design collaboratively over multiple sessions. Based on a privacy focused analysis of models from previous workshops we adapt the STWT and corresponding modeling guidelines to incorporate aspects relevant for privacy by design.

Keywords: Privacy by design · Socio-technical systems · Participatory design

1 Introduction

Developing products and services that respect a user's privacy is a growing field of interest with advances in big data techniques, the internet of things and progress in information and communication technology in general. Cavoukian [1] is often attributed as being the first to summarize the privacy by design principles emphasizing user-centered design and pointing out the benefits of increased privacy and security awareness when systems are developed transparently and privacy is enforced proactively Privacy by design (PbD) has already been proposed as a guideline to ensure privacy friendly systems, but. the question of how these guidelines can be put into practice has become an even more pressing issue [2]. Especially, since the General Data Protection Regulation was adopted by the European Parliament [3], which makes PbD mandatory for new products. PbD emphasizes that privacy considerations have to be a part of every step of the software design process to be effective.

Despite a growing amount of work on privacy enhancing technologies, privacy strategies and privacy patterns, the adoption of PbD is still lacking adoption in practice,

© Springer International Publishing AG 2017
T. Tryfonas (Ed.): HAS 2017, LNCS 10292, pp. 691–702, 2017.
DOI: 10.1007/978-3-319-58460-7_47

especially in software development processes [4]. Gürses and Alamo [2], in line with a recent ENISA report [5], state that engineering privacy by design requires a multi-disciplinary approach in which "Data protection authorities should play an important role providing independent guidance and assessing modules and tools for privacy engineering" [2]. While there are notable advances with respect to engineering privacy requirements we see a lack of adoption of PbD ideas with respect to process-driven approaches and socio-technical design. One way to foster PbD not only on a technical but also an organizational process level is to support collaborative approaches of socio-technical systems design.

In this paper, we further elaborate on an approach that extends existing methods of socio-technical design by including privacy related aspects. We published first ideas of this approach in [6]. The approach combines collaborative process design workshops with a web-based system that fosters critical reflection and discussion on such designs.

2 Related Work

The fuzziness of the concept privacy is one of the main challenges of PbD and privacy engineering [4, 7]. There are legal, regional and cultural differences with respect to what is to be achieved by protecting privacy. And with respect to the question of how to apply PbD one can find solutions in IT Security, Software and requirements engineering, business process management and legal compliance [5]. This emphasizes the need for collaboration when systems are developed with privacy in mind to incorporate the different perspectives. Especially legal requirements for handling personally identifiable information (PII), despite the fuzziness of the concept of privacy, have led the discussions of data protection goals [8] that are meant to be workable constructs when designing process that involve PII. The data protection goals extend the widely known computer security goals (confidentiality, integrity and availability) with respect to privacy related goals such as transparency, unlinkability and the ability to intervene [8] which were recently chosen to be the standard model for data protection audits by the German conference of data protection officials. While unlinkability refers to mechanisms to enforce purpose binding, the ability to intervene requires data processors to prove that they can actually control and disrupt specific PII data flows, e.g. if required by the data subject. Unlinkability for example can be achieved by minimizing the amount of data collected. The data protection goals are in line with other, less process but more technology oriented approaches like the one proposed by Gürses et al. [9] and especially the privacy strategies and tactics developed by Hoepman et al. [10, 11]. They argue that engineering privacy by design should always be based on minimizing data since the amount and risk of PII collected within a product or process predetermines the following iterative steps of development like requirements analysis, threat modeling, security analysis and implementation. This leaves room for methods that support these iterative steps. Notario et al. [12] suggest to apply use cases as a methodology to elicit requirements. The value of use cases within that methodology is to bring together all stakeholders that have an interest in processing PII such as legal staff, business consultants, business analysts, data analysts and software architects. Vicini et al. [13] describe how methods of co-creation can be used to integrate a variety of stakeholders in a requirements engineering process, but make no use of process models which are emphasized by Notario et al. [12] as an important factor to achieve organization impact. There is thus a need for methods that bring relevant stakeholders together and make use of process models as a mutual artifact. The socio-technical design approach we propose in the following can provide a suitable solution for this gap.

Socio-technical design first became a field of interest in the early 1950s in the face of the ongoing industrialization [14]. During that time researchers realized that it is necessary to consider the social context of people in order for technology to have the desired effect. They also found that the introduction of technology inevitably has an effect on the working environment which again has an influence on how technology is used. This led to the development of a number of approaches which were subsumed under the umbrella of the term socio-technical design (STD). These approaches aim at giving "equal weight to social and technical issues when new work systems are being designed" [15]. The goal of these approaches is to bring together users and designers since thy are mutual experts or mutual lays at the same time. Practitioners are experts of the domain, while they would usually know little about privacy enhancing technologies. This is the case vice versa for the privacy experts creating a gap for both groups. In consequence discursive processes creating a discussion around a proposed design are necessary to bridge this gap.

Most STD approaches consequently focus on workshops in which current and future users of a system alongside domain experts and software developers create a conceptualization of a future system [16–18]. It is common to start conceptualization by analyzing the current state of a system or process by visualizing it in graphical models. These models are then subsequently used as a basis to identify problems and discuss future designs. Arriving at a suitable design usually requires multiple workshops as well as phases in between in which designs are reflected and tested [19]. Results from these tests then serve as an input for future workshops and future design iterations. STD can thus be perceived as a mutual adaptation process between design and its implementation in the work place.

Privacy is a multi-facetted problem that can be leveraged using organizational as well as technical means. Socio-technical design can serve as a means to consider both aspects and come up with solutions that all stakeholders agree upon when used in the context of privacy by design. Through socio-technical design it is possible to integrate multiple stakeholders into the design process and to identify problems within processes that are potentially be overlooked otherwise because they are often considered less important [20]. Therefore, legal and privacy/security experts can also help to make decisions on tradeoffs that have to be made with regard to the use of privacy enhancing technologies and usability, efficiency or implementation costs.

3   The Methodical Background: SeeMe and the Socio-Technical Walkthrough

To design socio-technical systems, modeling is at the core of our methodology. Socio-technical modeling was designed to integrate the modeling of technical and work processes and in consequence makes more topics of the envisioned practice available for design and development. It proved to be helpful to contextualize processes and situations to make topics available for discourse. Methodologies like the well-established socio-technical walkthrough (STWT) [19, 21–24] consist of the two parts: notation and method. The modeling notation we used in the project is called SeeMe. It supports the description of various socio-technical aspects such as coordination between different process participants and the behavior of human actors performing the process. SeeMe is applied during STWTs to represent and discuss the work processes. Our experience with both SeeMe and the STWT method stems from a development of about eighteen years, driven by practical application in various contexts (for a list of projects s. [16]). As the initial rationale of this still ongoing action research effort, we intended to describe the phenomena of socio-technical systems appropriately consisting of technical, organizational and personal views, as it is an important background of privacy engineering in particular. We found technical and social phenomena to be equally relevant including technically enforced behavior as well as (emergency) behavior with inevitable human decision-making and human actors creating workarounds to unpractically designed technical solutions. Therefore, our basic assumption is that it is highly relevant to describe aspects of work processes and coordination issues as part of designing socio-technical systems and making privacy by design proposals. The SeeMe notation we use is based on technically oriented modeling notations and was enriched with ways to express vagueness including incompleteness and uncertainty. The notation is designed to support:

- the visualization of complex interdependencies between the activities of users, between human work and the technical systems, and if needed it can also depict the technical components
- the creation of an integrated view on technical and social aspects
- the flexible adaptation of levels of detail in every section of processes
- the creation of a shared understanding of the socio-technical design

Using the notation SeeMe we developed methods to create models discursively. The core method is called the socio-technical walkthrough (c.f. [16] for a detailed description). The term walkthrough points to a step-by-step approach which takes place in collaborative workshops. Questions play an important role to guide the modeling and the attention of participants. Additionally, workshops are repeated to further elaborate the results. Between workshops changes to models are primarily done for aesthetic reasons in order to make models easier to perceive and understand. We will discuss this approach later as the mixed collaboration approach.

With the STWT the goal is to foster collaborative reflection and negotiation. The models are used as visible explications of knowledge, which has various facets:

Models are used as a boundary objects [21] between different perspectives. The models are a shared resource for reference. Participants can see their own perspective in the context of the environment. They can also see, understand and discuss consequences of personal behavior for others.

In previous applications the STWT has helped to foster integrated discussion of technical and organizational aspects that lead to well thought through decisions. Decisions and changes – technical as well as organizational – than lead to changes to the respective area, so that collaborative reflection on the changes improves the design.

In addition, the diversity of the participants' experience resulted in an enriched design decision. Using the STWT and extending it with Privacy by Design aspects can therefore enrich discussions about design decisions and will allow system designers to relate to the future practice that can be integrated in the design process.

The next section gives a simple modeling example to create an impression of the models used. We already proposed specific changes on the methodology [6] to adapt to the needs of privacy by design, which we will describe in the then following section.

4   Modeling an Example Process in SeeMe

We will use the design of a survey-based study by a university where participants are contacted by email and asked to use a web-based system to answer a short question-naire as a practical example for our approach. Study designs like this have to take into account local privacy regulations and – depending on local practices – have to be approved by institutional review boards or data protection officers. A process model that reflects the necessary steps is shown in Fig. 1.

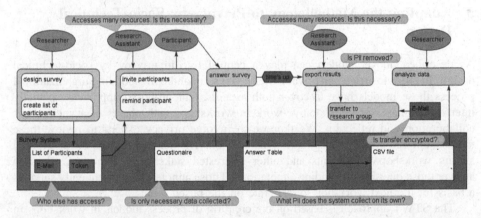

Fig. 1. SeeMe model of the survey process with added comments regarding privacy (Color figure online)

In order for a design artefact for a future system to be useful it has to cover social and technical aspects at the same time and has to be easily understood by those involved in the design. It has to be useful for those that later use it to develop software based and conduct organizational changes in order for the software to be used effectively. The SeeMe modeling notation thus can be perceived as being ideal for a task like this. It is capable of covering social and technical aspects of a process within the same visualization. SeeMe only consists of three basic elements and has been proven to be easily understandable for stakeholders. Furthermore, SeeMe also allows for explicitly displaying vagueness. As mentioned earlier this is crucial for depicting real life processes since real life phenomena sometimes cannot and should not be expressed formally. At the same time SeeMe offers all constructs necessary to depict complex decisions and can thus be used as a basis for software development.

The example process model (Fig. 1) uses SeeMe. The process involves roles (depicted as red ellipses) like participant, *researcher* and *research assistant* who execute activities such as *invite participants* and *remind participants* (depicted as yellow rectangles with round corners). The process involves *assistants* who will send out links with unique tokens, e.g. encoded within the URL to the survey to a *list of participants* (an entity depicted as blue rectangle) created by the researchers. They will also remind participants if codes were not used. When the time is up the survey is closed and the assistants export the answers from the survey systems as a CSV file and send it to the research group via email. This rather simple process of conducting a survey can pose various privacy related issues such as protecting the identity of the participants or general questions about data handling within research groups. This model in particular depicts multiple occasions in which issues with respect to privacy and secure handling of PII can arise.

Additional stakeholders that we omit in this example are third parties like the company providing the survey system or researchers from other institutions that would like to work with the raw data.

5   Adapting the Methodology to Privacy by Socio-Technical Design

As described above, models can play a central role in privacy by socio-technical design. In order to arrive at a privacy friendly system and corresponding organizational process those models have to cover both aspects. Our proposed approach especially intertwines phases of collaborative work in workshops with phases of asynchronous collaboration and reflection. We propose to involve privacy experts to review these models and add privacy related questions later on. The adapted models are distributed among workshop participants and other interested stakeholders who are asked to answer those questions by adding annotations. Those annotations subsequently serve as a basis for the next workshop to elaborate on the raised topics.

The STWT approach is based on the creation of process models in workshops in order to reflect multiple perspectives and aspects of the real work environment and the existing experience and practice. It is important to note that envisioned practice which is already documented (e.g. in Information Security Documentation) often differs from the real practice. It is crucial to understand the needs that lead to such differences. Facilitators can help to reflect the actual process in a process model. These facilitators guide workshops by asking how the participants conduct their work and what they do at a certain point in time. The contributions are integrated into the graphical process model right away. This model subsequently serves as a basis for discussion on potential improvements as well as on how the future system has to be designed to suit the work environment of current and future users. In order to arrive at a suitable design, the facilitator usually asks the users a set of predefined questions such as: "Where do you see issues with the current process?" or "What support do you need in order to fulfill your tasks?".

Altering this approach in order to fit the context of privacy by design requires some changes to the STWT. While it is considered useful for privacy experts to participate in workshop sessions, other changes should integrate a privacy perspective, too. It is necessary to focus on potentially privacy relevant aspects of work processes, to include questions regarding privacy into the design phase and to respect modeling guidelines to achieve the required level of detail. In the following section we will describe an analysis of existing models to identify requirements for guidelines towards the goals of privacy by design.

Designing a suitable socio-technical system cannot solely happen within modeling workshops. Due to the fact that social and technical aspects mutually influence each other it is not possible to analyze all potential effects of technology on a social system and vice versa. It is thus crucial to apply an evolutionary approach in which designs are created, tested and refined. Additionally, to the repeated workshops we use a web-based editor as a means to access process models that have been created during workshops and to further discuss these models using annotations. In addition, the web editor supports a question based re-evaluation of a process that can be used to ask questions related to the data protection goals or common privacy patterns [25]. This enables non-privacy experts to evaluate common privacy practices and optimize a process before details are discussed with privacy experts in a consecutive work-shop. Proposals of privacy experts might be complex so that it is necessary that the models are adapted prior to following workshops.

Such a participative process have positive effects on understanding and motivation when the process are executed [26] but especially increase the motivation for changes otherwise only perceived as obstacles [20].

6 An Analysis of Existing Models of Work Practice

To get a better understanding to what extent our process driven approach already covers privacy relevant issues and what aspects of privacy are not dealt with we analyzed the outcome of 10 previously held STWT workshop series. Over the years a changing team of process modelling experts has conducted workshops in a variety of domains ranging from logistics to insurance to health care and welfare. Each of the analyzed workshop series consists of 2 up to 11 individual workshops with a great variety of complexity of both the domains and the developed models. The analyzed workshops were conducted within one large organization. We asked two privacy experts to review the final SeeMe models and analyze them with respect to the data protection goals. The experts added comments to the process models addressing privacy problems that could emerge if the process was implemented as described. The comments the experts made mainly asked for access rights, retention and deletion of PII and missing aspects of the models to determine if an impact to privacy is present.

6.1 Results

The privacy experts added 19 annotations in total. We categorized the questions and clustered them to get an overview of common issues. The 19 questions were added to 18 distinct elements. An overview over the corresponding element types is given in

Table 1. We expected the high count of annotated entities. This relates to the SeeMe notation where entities are used to model artifacts like systems or documents that are likely to contain PII.

Table 1. Type of element

Entity	Activity	Condition	Role
10	4	3	1

The effected sub elements ranged from 0 to 12 elements while a large majority concerned elements without sub elements. The comments indicate that this is a result of a lack of detail as those elements often referred to subsystems that might handle PII but are usually omitted during the workshop phase and handled as black boxes (Table 2).

Table 2. Categorization of the added questions

Data minimization	All categories	Deletion	Access control	General question	Training	Transmission
15	2	2	2	1	1	1

The questions added most frequently referred to the minimization of data collection (e.g. "is this information really necessary?" or "are PII included?") and were connected to elements where it was unclear what types of data were actually stored or processed. A number of organizational processes required employees to make notes about what happened, for example after experts assessed safety issues of working conditions and rooms. If not regulated, more than necessary information could be stored describing potentially unsafe, personal habits of specific employees revealing them to everyone that could access the report. Thus the category data minimization is the most frequent one. An overview how often a specific category was assigned to the questions is given in Table 3.

Table 3. Meta comments assigned to the added questions

Missing detail	Access rights management	Base system	Begin of process	Collection of data	End of process	Lawfulness	External System
13	2	2	2	2	1	1	1

As already outlined above the experts did not find obvious threats to privacy but addressed potential issues that would arise if PII were involved. To determine if this is the case the experts asked for missing detail.

The privacy experts also stated apart from their annotations added that they did not find any aspects explicitly related to support the transparency with regard to the data subject or the ability to intervene e.g. if a data subject requests a copy of records or demands deletion.

7   Guiding Privacy by Design Modeling

As mentioned earlier the walkthrough to create models is guided by questions that are oriented to the work practice. From our analysis of previously created process models we know that an evaluation by privacy experts requires more detailed information as currently captured in the modeling workshops.

To provide the necessary depth of detail a two-tiered approach is necessary. On the one hand, workshop organizers have to adhere to additional modeling guidelines and questions to reduce the vagueness of the models with respect to what types of data are collected. On the other hand, the participants can add more detail to specific model parts during the reflection phase.

For example, restricting the access to a distinct group is a common measure to handle PII securely [5, 10, 27]. To enable the privacy experts to evaluate the appropriateness of such restrictions, the system access rights must be modeled with little ambiguity. To achieve this the roles with access to the system should be captured in one super role that is connected to the system itself or directly to the activity using the system and not its parent activity.

As stated above, experts were unable to assess some of the process steps and systems included in the process model because details about what type of data is actually involved was not specified. The practitioners involved in the process know best which information is handled in each step of the process and know what is actually necessary to execute it. But, a discussion on the details of each part of the process during the workshop can lead to too detailed models and extensive workshops. The more detailed a model gets the harder gets it to grasp [28]. Also, focusing in tiny details can lead to major discussion blocking the whole workshop. Therefore, participants should be asked to add additional details during the reflection phase in which they individually work on the model and annotate it. The participants need to be guided through corresponding questions while annotating the model. When using our software other stakeholders are able to view the annotation of others dissent can be expressed and resolved in the following workshop. The questions for detailing on specific parts of the model can be assigned to individual participants so all parts in question are covered.

This approach is only feasible if the participants know systems or parts in question well and can explain them easily e.g. a standard form. During the course of supporting the introduction of an information security management system (ISMS) [29] we made the experience that dedicated models for systems and their corresponding interfaces are needed to keep an overview and facilitate the creation of models including this systems. These models can easily be provided through hyperlinks in SeeMe. Providing the sub models on demand on the one hand feeds the need to know the specific details of technical systems or other artifacts to review them but on the other hand omit them if they are currently not relevant for the discussion.

To ease the aforementioned guidance needed we provide the following heuristics (Table 4):

Table 4. Overview of additional guidelines

Who	What	Goal
Facilitator	Model access to PII explicitly	Minimize data/support experts, evaluate risk level, identify the relevant legal provisions
Participants	Add details to specific model parts asynchronously	Provide necessary depth of detail to design a system respecting the needs of practitioners
Technical experts	Provide models of systems used	Provide necessary depth of detail and documenting the limiting aspects of existing systems
Privacy experts	Introduce PbD Patterns into models. One additional Focus is to provide means to enhance transparency and interventions of data subjects take perspective of the data subject	Describe/model design proposals in a way that practitioners can evaluate the effects on their practice

8   Conclusion and Future Work

In this paper we described how privacy by design can be incorporated in established, collaborative methods for designing socio-technical systems. The methods need to be adapted to the goals of privacy by design. We extended the focus of modeling to specific topics needed for privacy by design. We suggest that privacy experts should take part in workshops where processes are modelled and propose a question-based evaluation of processes to enable non-privacy experts to avoid common privacy and security issues. The methods should bridge the gap between practitioners being experts of the work practice and privacy experts which know privacy by design patterns, but have problems to evaluate (unintended) effects of these proposals to practice. Our early experience is promising with respect to this goal. The methods already prove to be useful to bridge practice-expert gaps.

In our future work of this action research project we aim to practically improve work practice to collect more experience. After including common privacy patterns into PbD plugins of the SeeMe web editor we also aim at evaluating our approach in workshops with the data protection office of a university that handles cases like those described above. We will observe the hopefully converging market of privacy patterns as to incorporate better design support with these patterns in mind.

References

1. Cavoukian, A.: Privacy by Design - The 7 Foundational Principles (2009)
2. Gürses, S., del Alamo, J.M.: Privacy engineering: shaping an emerging field of research and practice. IEEE Secur. Priv. **14**, 40–46 (2016)
3. European Parliament: General Data Protection Regulation (2016)

4. Spiekermann, S.: The challenges of privacy by design. Commun. ACM **55**, 38 (2012)
5. Domingo-Ferrer, J., Hansen, M., Hoepman, J.-H., Le Métayer, D., Tirtea, R., Schiffner, S., Danezis, G.: European Union, European Network and Information Security Agency: Privacy and Data Protection by Design - From Policy to Engineering. ENISA, Heraklion (2014)
6. Degeling, M., Lentzsch, C., Nolte, A., Herrmann, T., Loser, K.-U.: Privacy by socio-technical design - a collaborative approach for privacy friendly system design. In: Workshop on Privacy in Collaborative and Social Computing, Pittsburgh, PA, USA (2016)
7. Schwartz, P.M., Solove, D.J.: The PII problem: privacy and a new concept of personally identifiable information. N. Y. Univ. Law Rev. **86**, 1814 (2011)
8. Rost, M., Bock, K.: Privacy by design und die Neuen Schutzziele. Datenschutz Datensicherheit **35**, 30–35 (2011)
9. Gürses, F.S., Troncoso, C., Diaz, C.: Engineering privacy by design. Comput. Priv. Data Prot. (2011)
10. Colesky, M., Hoepman, J.-H., Hillen, C.: A critical analysis of privacy design strategies. In: 2016 IEEE Security and Privacy Workshops (SPW), pp. 33–40. IEEE (2016)
11. Hoepman, J.-H.: Privacy design strategies. In: Cuppens-Boulahia, N., Cuppens, F., Jajodia, S., Abou El Kalam, A., Sans, T. (eds.) SEC 2014. IAICT, vol. 428, pp. 446–459. Springer, Heidelberg (2014). doi:10.1007/978-3-642-55415-5_38
12. Notario, N., Crespo, A., Martin, Y.-S., Del Alamo, J.M., Le Metayer, D., Antignac, T., Kung, A., Kroener, I., Wright, D.: PRIPARE: integrating privacy best practices into a privacy engineering methodology. In: 2015 IEEE Security and Privacy Workshops (SPW), pp. 151–158 (2015)
13. Vicini, S., Alberti, F., Notario, N., Crespo, A., Pastoriza, J.R.T., Sanna, A.: Co-creating security-and-privacy-by-design systems, August 2016
14. Trist, E., Bamforth, K.: Some social and psychological consequences of the long wall method of coal getting. Hum. Relat. **4**, 3–38 (1951)
15. Mumford, E.: A socio-technical approach to systems design. Requir. Eng. **5**, 125–133 (2000)
16. Herrmann, T.: Systems design with the socio-technical walkthrough (2009)
17. Kensing, F., Simonsen, J., Bodker, K.: MUST: a method for participatory design. Hum.-Comput. Interact. **13**, 167–198 (1998)
18. Bødker, K., Kensing, F., Simonsen, J.: Participatory IT Design: Designing for Business and Workplace Realities (2009)
19. Nolte, A., Herrmann, T.: Facilitating participation of stakeholders during process analysis and design. In: Angeli, A., Bannon, L., Marti, P., Bordin, S. (eds.) COOP 2016: Proceedings of the 12th International Conference on the Design of Cooperative Systems, pp. 225–241. Springer, Cham (2016). doi:10.1007/978-3-319-33464-6_14
20. Loser, K.-U., Degeling, M.: Security and privacy as hygiene factors of developer behavior in small and agile teams. In: Kimppa, K., Whitehouse, D., Kuusela, T., Phahlamohlaka, J. (eds.) HCC 2014. IAICT, vol. 431, pp. 255–265. Springer, Heidelberg (2014). doi:10.1007/978-3-662-44208-1_21
21. Loser, K.-U., Nolte, A., Prilla, M., Skrotzki, R., Herrmann, T.: A drifting service development: applying sociotechnical design in an ambient assisted living project. In: Viscusi, G., Campagnolo, G.M., Curzi, Y. (eds.) Phenomenology, Organizational Politics, and IT Design: The Social Study of Information Systems, pp. 311–323. IGI Global (2012)
22. Herrmann, T., Kunau, G., Loser, K.-U., Menold, N.: Sociotechnical walkthrough: designing technology along work processes. In: Clement, A., Cindio, F., Oostveen, A.-M., Schuler, D., van den Besselaar, P. (eds.) Artful Integration: Interweaving Media, Materials and Practices, Proceedings of the Eighth Participatory Design Conference 2004, Toronto, Ontario, Canada, 27–31 July, pp. 132–141. ACM Press (2004)

23. Herrmann, T., Loser, K.-U., Moysich, K.: Intertwining training and participatory design for the development of groupware applications. In: Cherkasky, T., Greenbaum, J., Mambrey, P., Pors, J.K. (eds.) Designing Digital Environments — Bringing in More Voices, Proceedings of the Participatory Design Conference 2000, CPSR, Palo Alto, pp. 106–115. CPSR, Palo Alto (2000)

24. Herrmann, T., Prilla, M., Nolte, A.: Socio-technical process design—the case of coordinated service delivery for elderly people. In: D'Ascenzo, F., Magni, M., Lazazzara, A., Za, S. (eds.) Blurring the Boundaries Through Digital Innovation. LNISO, vol. 19, pp. 217–229. Springer, Cham (2016). doi:10.1007/978-3-319-38974-5_17

25. Kahrmann, J., Schiering, I.: Patterns in privacy - a pattern-based approach for assessments. In: Camenisch, J., Fischer-Hübner, S., Hansen, M. (eds.) Privacy and Identity 2014. IAICT, vol. 457, pp. 153–166. Springer, Cham (2015). doi:10.1007/978-3-319-18621-4_11

26. den Hengst, M., de Vreede, G.J.D.: Collaborative business engineering: a decade of lessons from the field. J. Manag. Inf. Syst. **20**, 85–114 (2004)

27. Probst, T.: Generische Schutzmaßnahmen für Datenschutz-Schutzziele. Datenschutz Datensicherheit - DuD **36**, 439–444 (2012)

28. Herrmann, T.: Kreatives Prozessdesign: Konzepte und Methoden zur Integration von Prozessorganisation Technik und Arbeitsgestaltung. Springer Gabler, Berlin (2012)

29. Loser, K.-U., Nolte, A., Herrmann, T., te Neues, H.: Information security management systems and sociotechnical walkthroughs. In: Bella, G., Coles-Kemp, L., Lenzini, G., Ryan, P.Y.A. (eds.) 2011 1st Workshop on Socio-Technical Aspects in Security and Trust (STAST), pp. 45–51. IEEE Computer Society (2011)

Detection and Auto-protection of Cache File Privacy Leakage for Mobile Social Networking Applications in Android

Hui Li[✉], Wenling Liu, Bin Wang, and Wen Zhang

Beijing University of Posts and Telecommunications, Beijing, China
lihuill@bupt.edu.cn

Abstract. A lot of privacy data are generated by using mobile social networking applications (MSNAs) and the values of user's privacy data in those applications increase with the establishment and development of big data platform, which makes MSNAs the primary target to be analyzed. Therefore, it is important to analyze privacy leakage and protect user's privacy in the MSNAs. However, the existing approaches of data leakage detection in the Android platform are not suitable for MSNAs, e.g. VetDroid are considered as an impractical means since they require users' frequent participation; TaintDroid and the detection methods based on it require the modification of Android system or the modification and re-package of the application, so the cost of the experiment will increase, and the operating efficiency of the application will decrease apparently. In this paper, we propose a privacy leakage detection tool named X-Decaf (X-Posed based Detection of Cache File) as well as an auto-protection method named ATFed (Automatic Transparent File Encryption/ Decryption) in MSNAs on the Android platform. These two methods are designed to solve the above-mentioned issues under the conditions of keeping low coupling with the Android system and posing low impacts on the original MSNA.

Keywords: Android system · Privacy leakage · Taint tracking · Cache file · X-Posed · Transparent encryption

1 Introduction

With the popularization of mobile technologies and mobile social networking, mobile social networking applications (MSNAs) have become one of the most popular activities on smartphones and tablets. In 2016, We Are Social [1] released its latest report "Global Digital Snapshot", giving its readers a glimpse at the comprehensive survey of the global Internet, social networking and mobile usage. As the report shows, the total number of mobile social media users has reached 1.97 billion with a significant growth of 17% annual increase compared with the data of 2015, accounting for 27% of the world's population. In the meantime, with the development of big data platform, when users' privacy is recognized as an asset, social networking applications have

T. Tryfonas (Ed.): HAS 2017, LNCS 10292, pp. 703–721, 2017.
DOI: 10.1007/978-3-319-58460-7_48

undoubtedly become the primary and most vulnerable targets. Tons of users' privacy data is generated in the MSNAs, however it is still uncertain whether this data has been handled carefully by the application developers. Therefore, it is necessary to have a deeper study into the privacy leakage issue and the protection mechanisms of the privacy information in the MSNAs.

The privacy leakage issue on Android platform has already drawn wide attention. Since Android is an operating system based on access control, plenty of solutions focused on the analysis and optimization of the permissions. VetDroid is a dynamic analysis platform to reconstruct a fine-grained access control mechanism and detect the sensitive behaviors of the applications on Android [2]. Shebaro et al. [3] presented a context-based access control system, through which applications can be dynamically granted or revoked certain permissions based on the specific context. Nauman et al. [4] put forward a fine-grained, user-centric privacy preserving permission framework that allows the users to selectively grant permissions to the applications installed. Wu et al. [5] proposed an effective access control scheme for preventing permission leakage in the application level and provided developers with better management of security of components. However, the user-based access control for data leakage detection approach in all these studies is considered to be an impractical means since they requires users' frequent participation.

Some other researches focus on the analysis of certain type of privacy detection and protection. CHEX is a static analysis tool which can automatically review the Android application of components hijacking vulnerabilities, thus protecting user privacy data [6]. Tan et al. [7] proposed Chips, a context-based run-time access control system to deal with the photos of applications with a fine-grained access control. Naveed et al. [8] performed a comprehensive study of privacy leakage in external devices for Android mobile phones, and proposed management approach of external equipment through a bluetooth, NFC or etc. Rahman et al. [9] and Fawaz et al. [10] studied the information leakage of geographic location and proposed corresponding protection strategies.

Besides the above-mentioned approaches, other researchers track the leakage of private data by modifying the Android framework or source code of applications. SplitDroid segregated the sensitive components of an application based on the Linux Container mechanism for isolated execution and privacy protection [11]. Tripp and Rubin [12] established a quantitative and probabilistic dual judgment model using Bayes' theorem and solved the problem of privacy judgment according to the environment of diffusion points. TaintDroid modified the Android virtual machine and the interpreter, provided a complete function of dynamic taint tracking [13]. Furthermore, researchers have also put forward more optimized schemes based on TaintDroid such as PasDroid [14] and Styx [15]. Cui et al. [16] and Zhang and Yin [17] rewrote the bytecode of Android applications to add the corresponding privacy detection strategy, realized the privacy tracking and leakage detection by means of repackaging.

Unfortunately, most of the existing schemes based on certain type of permission or privacy data are not qualified to handle the problems of privacy tracking and leakage detection as MSNAs often involve many types of sensitive system permissions and private data. Moreover, strategies based on TaintDroid need to modify the Android framework, and the approaches based on TaintDroid [14, 15] need repackage the applications, thus not only increasing the experimental cost, but also introducing a great impact on the efficiency of the applications.

To address the security problems caused by privacy leakage, we propose Xposed-based Detecting-Cache-File, namely "X-Decaf", a detection framework of MSNAs together with an auto-protection method named ATFed (Automatic Transparent File Encryption/Decryption). The detection framework first uses taint tracking and Xposed framework to innovatively monitor cache files generated during the application run-time and organize the suspected leakage path to evaluate the leakage rank of sensitive data. Then ATFed is applied to this application to offer an automatically privacy data protection under the conditions of keeping low coupling with the Android system and posing low impacts on the original MSNA. The main contributions of this paper are:

- We undertake a study of privacy data and privacy leakage. As for the MSNAs, some attack scenarios are listed and a more detailed definition of privacy leakage standard is given.
- Based on the taint tracking and Xposed framework, we propose an MSNA's privacy leakage detection framework and conduct in-depth evaluation of security and performance on popular MSNAs.
- We design an auto privacy data protection mechanism named ATFed, which automatically encrypts and decrypts the privacy cache file without the modification of Android framework and the involvement of application developers.

The rest of this paper is organized as follows. In Sect. 2, we define the privacy data and leakage standard on social applications. In Sect. 3, we present a detailed system design and implementation of X-Decaf. Section 4 presents the evaluations and discusses the experimental results. In Sect. 5, a mitigation of ATFed is proposed to solve the problem of cache file privacy and an evaluation of effectiveness and overhead is given in Sect. 6. Section 7 concludes the whole paper.

2 Privacy Data and Leakage

2.1 Definition of Privacy Data

Since MSNAs generally produce tons of data in various types during users' interaction, privacy data related to the users' private information can be involved frequently. It can be seen from the analysis result of 50 kinds of Android social networking applications in the market as shown in Fig. 1 that 6 types of data, i.e. pictures, video, voice, geographical location, contact, phone calls and SMSs are mainly involved in MSNAs and may cause potential vulnerabilities of data security. Furthermore, since media data such as images, video and voice often produce numerous unprotected cache files on storage, privacy data are defined as media privacy data in this paper, and we mainly focus on this kind of privacy data leakage.

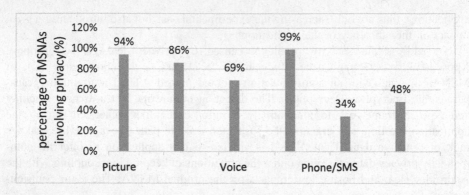

Fig. 1. Types of privacy data involved in MSNAs

2.2 Definition of Privacy Leakage

The Android system will create a separate file directory for each application in the directory of /data/data/and the data generated during applications' run-time will be kept in this default directory. Note that Android system itself provides a security mechanism to guarantee the safety of this directory. When an application accesses a file stored in the /data/data directory, it first passes the UID/GID-based DAC security checks, then the MAC check of SEAndroid. However, all these checks are not strong enough when a mobile phone is rooted and the malwares break through the Android security mechanisms to get the users' privacy data. At the same time, many other improper handlings may cause the run-time data of applications not to be stored in the corresponding / data/data directory. These operations may include: (1) The developers may arbitrarily call some system APIs (i.e. getExternalStorageDirectory(), etc.) regardless of the security mechanisms when writing an application, resulting in caching files or information documents during run-time stored in some public directory; (2) Different Android systems have different components, for example, a device with limited memory may need an SD Card memory extension, as a result, some cache files have to be stored in the public directory of SD Card. Meanwhile, the application does not use any security mechanisms, i.e. encryption or obfuscation, so any application in such devices can access the files in this directory and cause privacy leakage problems. Traditional privacy leakage behaviors refer to the application's remote collection and dissemination of user private information without explicitly notification. In this paper, we will conduct research on the privacy leakage from a new perspective and mainly discuss the applications creating cache files involved users privacy data due to its design defects and lack of proper strategies to manage these files. To have a better understanding of social software and analyze the risk of privacy leakage, the X-Decaf framework is designed for monitoring cache files of MSNAs during their run-time and future detection.

2.3 Standard of Privacy Leakage

We define the standard of privacy leakage based on the following three aspects:

Cache File Path. As mentioned in Sect. 2.2, Android system will generate cache files in corresponding paths. See in Table 1 below.

Table 1. Cache file path

Cache file path	Abbreviation
/data/data/pkg_name/	DATA_PRI
/data/data/pkg_name/(global_readable)	DATA_PUB
/storage/emulated/0/Android/data/pkg_name	SD_PRI
/storage/emulated/0/	SD_PUB

As the file storage paths can reflect the access permissions to a certain extent in Android system, we list some attack scenarios respectively.

DATA_PRI: Only the application itself can access the file path, the attackers cannot obtain the files without root permission;

DATA_PUB: Any application can access the file path and even maliciously tamper the file when it is global-readable;

SD_PUB, SD_PRI: The attackers can easily tamper a file in SD-card file directory, no matter it is private or public.

Note that the files in SD_PRI directory can be deleted with "CLEAR DATA" function under Android Settings, and unless the application manages by itself, the files in SD_PUB cannot be deleted directly. We distinguish files in SD_PRI directory from those in SD_PUB directory because it reflects the irregularities of developers.

Cache File Protection Status. According to the analysis of the above mentioned attack scenarios, it is not qualified to guarantee the security of data generated during the application run-time only relying on the file directory security mechanisms provided by the Android system itself. With such protection measures as confusion, encryption, etc., files can be better protected. Even if an attacker broke through Android system protection and make access to the files, it will still take a great cost to restore the treated files. So, the cache file protection status should be taken into consideration and thus provide important foundation for analyzing privacy leakage.

Cache File Life-Cycle. Cache file life-cycle contains the processes of cache files from generation, transfer, storage to deletion, during which they are under threat of hacker's attacks. Therefore, it is important to have a good perspective into the life-cycle of cache files. Here is a summarization of scenario simulation of cache file life-cycle:

Case 1: The cache files are generated during the application run-time, and deleted after the application exits;

Case 2: The cache files still exist after the application exits, but the application provides related functions such as "clear cache" which can be executed to delete the cache files.

Case 3: The cache files still exist and cannot be deleted even with function "clear cache" provided by the application itself.

In view of the three aspects mentioned above, we define a standard for cache file privacy leakage according to their storage path and life-cycle. The overview of privacy leakage criteria is shown in Table 2. Note that our analysis only focuses on unprotected cache files and the protected cache files are regarded as safe with the default protection applied by Android security mechanism, so there are no leakages.

Table 2. Standard of privacy leakage

	DATA_PRI	DATA_PUB	SD_PRI	SD_PUB
Case 1	MILD_LK	MEDIUM_LK	MEDIUM_LK	MEDIUM_LK
Case 2	MILD_LK	SEVERE_LK	SEVERE_LK	SEVERE_LK
Case 3	MILD_LK	SP_SEVERE_LK	SP_SEVERE_LK	SP_SEVERE_LK

According to the definition of privacy leakage standards combined with the current Android platform common attack scenario, the privacy leakage is divided into 5 levels: NO_LK, MILD_LK, MEDIUM_LK, SEVERE_LK, and SP_SEVERE_LK. More details are given as below.

NO_LK: No cache files or only protected cache files created during application run-time;

MILD_LK: An attacker can obtain privacy data only with root permission;

MEDIUM_LK: An attacker can obtain privacy data by monitoring the application run-time actions;

SEVERE_LK: An attacker can use folder tools to view files or Android File APIs directly to get privacy data;

SP_SEVERE_LK: Application cannot delete cache files even by its own "clear cache" function.

X-Decaf will study the links between private data and cache files within the application based on the above definition and privacy leakage standard, and perform analysis of privacy leakage effectively and efficiently.

3   Detection of Cache File Privacy Leakage

3.1   X-Decaf Overview

X-Decaf exploits the characteristics of the Android system, the taint tracking technology and the X-Posed framework to detect the leakage paths and the privacy data in the cache files within the MSNAs on the Android platform. It will perform a static analysis together with dynamic analysis of the application with high detection precision and only import a low impact, neither does it have a tight coupling with the Android system nor have the need to modify the application. The X-Decaf contains three components, i.e. sensitive library, taint tracking and cache file analysis, as shown in Fig. 2.

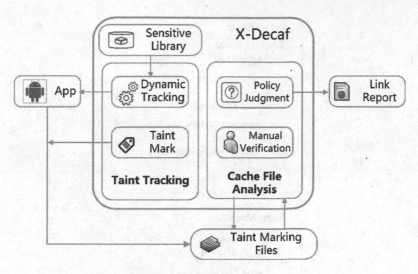

Fig. 2. Components of X-Decaf

The functions of the three components are:

Sensitive Library. After analyzing a large number of social applications on the market and obtaining the statistics of these applications' calling API, we filter and obtain those system APIs which are related to the processes for generating and spreading of sensitive data to form a sensitive function library for X-Decaf.

Taint Tracking. Taint tracking mainly consists of two parts: a dynamic tracking module first requests sensitive functions for specific privacy data from sensitive library, as a detection target, these sensitive functions are monitored by the corresponding Hook Module generated by X-Posed frames; the monitoring results are marked in the taint marking module, which achieves the file-based taint marks combing source privacy data type, source file name and appropriate strategies.

Cache File Analysis. Firstly, the manual verification performs the corresponding detection based on the definitions and standards of privacy leakage; secondly, policy judgment, i.e. an automated monitoring script, detects all taint-marked cache files generated during the taint tracking phase. The policy judgment module based on the criteria monitors taint cache file status puts out the leakage report.

3.2 X-Decaf Framework Architecture

We present the overall work-flow of X-Decaf to detect file-based privacy leakage during application run-time. It takes the following major steps as shown in Fig. 3.

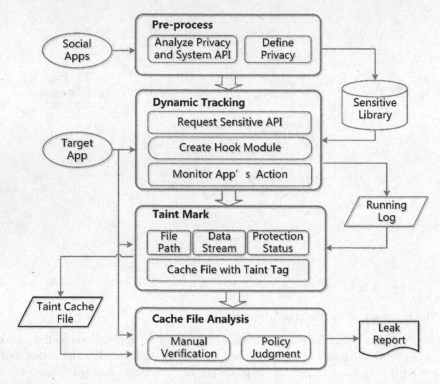

Fig. 3. X-Decaf architecture

Establishing Sensitive Library. In the early stage of X-Decaf design, we have collected and analyzed more than 100 MSNAs on the market for the relationship between privacy data and Android system API. We found that Applications usually access specific permissions and call similar system APIs in generating, obtaining and disseminating private data. For example, photo data will refer to APIs like camera service, system gallery reading, image compression, and file I/O, etc. With the help of some decompilation tools such as Apktool, IDA pro, etc., we can filter these system APIs related to the creation and propagation of sensitive data, and eventually establish a sensitive library for X-Decaf.

As we mainly analyze the cache files for the social software, the sensitive library will involve three types of system APIs including voice, pictures and video which contain large amounts of sensitive data of users' private information. Note that sensitive library will take an open sensitive API strategy of XML format for the convenience of automatic detection scripts for the sensitive functions. Figure 4 lists part of the corresponding system sensitive APIs of voice data in sensitive library.

```
<sensitive-policy privacy-type = "voice">
    <uses-permission name="android.permission.RECORD_AUDIO" />
    <uses-permission name="android.permission.WRITE_EXTERNAL_STORAGE" />
    <uses-permission name="android.permission.READ_EXTERNAL_STORAGE" />
    <class-info class-name = "android.media.AudioRecord">
        <method-info method-name = "startRecording" method-args = " "/>
        <method-info method-name = "read" method-args = "byte[],int,int"/>
        <method-info method-name = "native_read_in_byte_array" method-args = "byte[],int,int,boolean"/>
        ...
    </class-info>
    ...
</sensitive-policy>
```

Fig. 4. Sensitive API of voice (part)

Here is a more detailed description of the sensitive API strategy.

- **Sensitive-policy** tag. It is the root tag for specifying privacy policy. The attribute *privacy-type* figures out the type of privacy data.
- **Uses-permission** tag. It describes the corresponding permissions for this kind of privacy, and is similar to the declared permission in Android system.
- **Class-info** tag. It describes the name of class which contains sensitive functions, and requires a *class-name* attribute for the class name.
- **Method-info** tag. It describes the specific information for this sensitive method. Two attributes can be used for description: *method-name* and *method-args*.

Dynamic Tracking. The sensitive function contained in the sensitive library is the main detection object during the social application run-time. Dynamic Tracking module first sends a request to the sensitive functions for specific privacy data, then takes these sensitive functions as a detection target and generates the corresponding Hook Module by X-Posed framework. After the corresponding Hook Module has been loaded to the phone system, Dynamic Tracking module can monitor the application's actions during its run-time.

Taint Marking. Taint Marking module is mainly used for cache file filtering and taint marking. The major steps are presented as follows:

Cache File Filter. In the stage of dynamic tracking, X-Decaf monitors system I/O operations. Since there are tons of I/O operations during the application run-time, the taint marking module will mark too many unrelated items without the file filtering operation, and consequently affect the operational efficiency of the entire system. In order to improve accuracy of the taint marks and reduce the impact of application running, X-Decaf filters cache file with a fine-grained strategy. An example for photo data is presented. Firstly, a cache file with suffix ".jpg", ".jpeg" and ".bmp" will be classified as sensitive cache file directly. For unusual file extensions, X-Decaf will then further detect its data streams (".jpg" files' data stream begins with "JFIF"). In addition, if the application itself has already protected the cache files (using confusion, encryption, etc.), we can also mark in this case. Thus, no matter which form the cache files exist, X-Decaf can easily filter data streams, and trace all privacy leakage files.

Taint Mark. After filtering sensitive cache files, X-Decaf will mark the file with taint marking mechanism by adding TAG to these files' name. The TAG contains 3 attributes: privacy type, file hash and file protection status, in which protected file is marked with 1 and 0 means no protection. For example, an unprotected photo cache file named "cache.tmp" will become "cache_photo_hash_0.tmp" after taint marking. This handle strategy will bring the following benefits:

- Without changing target applications' data flow and control flow;
- Taint TAG can associate all the corresponding cache files with applications' data flow;
- Each same-origin cache file's protection status will be monitored.

Manual Verification. X-Decaf marks a series of cache files with taint TAG. After that, we will analyze these files manually. Firstly, we must verify if a social application has managed cache file's life-cycle by manual tests as described in Sect. 2.3. Secondly, based on the above-mentioned standards, we must monitor the cache file by its storage path and protection status to figure out whether it exists or has been removed during the test, and then perform the appropriate policy in the next stage.

Policy Judgment. Policy judgment cooperates with manual verification. Policy judgment runs as an automated monitoring script, monitoring changes of protection status, file path, life-cycle of these cache files with taint TAG, and finally outputs a leakage report according to privacy leakage criteria.

3.3   X-Decaf Analysis

Compared with the existing detection tools, X-Decaf has the following advantages:

A Lower System Coupling and No Application Modification. Most of dynamic taint tracking tools or privacy leakage detection frameworks, such as TaintDroid and its derivatives, require the modification of the Android system. The other existing tools modify application directly by bytecode rewriting and strategies insertion. However, with the development of tamper-resistant and signature mechanism, the cost of repackaging applications gradually increases. X-Decaf does not require modification of the Android platform or applications, and subtly takes advantage of system APIs as well as analyzes the correlation between privacy data and system API for data privacy leakage detection.

Multiple Types of Privacy Detection. Sensitive library provides common system API related to privacy leakage. Therefore, facing with different data privacy, X-Decaf can flexibly choose a variety of strategies to monitor simultaneously these sensitive functions.

Multi-lateral Application Test. Existing studies show that applications usually share similar API call to operate privacy data. Therefore, our X-Decaf system can easily and simultaneously monitor multiple applications on the market for certain types of sensitive privacy leak.

4 Experimental Results of Privacy Leakage Detection

In this section, we will discuss how we perform privacy leakage detection on the most popular MSNAs on the Android platform including WeChat, Mobile QQ, Weibo, Yixin, Momo and Wumi, and evaluate the effectiveness, accuracy and efficiency of X-Decaf when handling the voice, photo and video files. The evaluation is performed on Nexus5 and Nexus6 with android version 5.1.1 and the detailed analysis results are presented below.

4.1 Vertical Analysis of Privacy Leakage

We first conduct a vertical analysis of the country's most popular mobile MSNA, WeChat, by X-Decaf for privacy data leakage involving voice, images, video, etc. The analysis focuses on the data leakages of cache files and counts the number of leakage path. As shown in Table 3, X-Decaf can accurately detect a source data in the process of application run-time including generation, transfer, propagation etc. As for the corresponding cache files of image data, for example, three cache files will be generated from the same source data, *.jpg for copy of the original image, th_* for small thumbnail and th_*hd for large thumbnails. In conclusion, X-Decaf can accurately analyze the data of an application during its run-time, with no false negative and false positive of any privacy path.

Table 3. Privacy leakage of WeChat

WeChat (6.3.13)	Leakage path	Leakage path number
Voice	SD_PUB /tencent/MicroMsg//voice2/../msg_*.amr	1
Image	SD_PUB /tencent/MicroMsg/../image2/../*.jpg SD_PUB /tencent/MicroMsg/../image2/../th_* SD_PUB /tencent/MicroMsg/../image2/../th_*hd	3
Video	SD_PUB /tencent/MicroMsg/../video/*.mp4 SD_PUB /tencent/MicroMsg/../video/*.jpg SD_PUB /tencent/MicroMsg/../draft/. SD_PUB /tencent/MicroMsg/../draft/*.thumb	4

Note that ".." refers to the folder directory of application cache files due to some service logic (such as time, random number, etc.) while "*" refers to cache file name accordingly.

4.2 Horizontal Analysis of Privacy Leakage

We use X-Decaf to analyze the most popular MSNAs in the Android platform and detect whether they suffer from some kinds of leakages while handling the voice, photo and video files. The leakage reports are shown in Table 4.

Table 4. Leakage report of leakage rank and leakage path number

Name	Version	Voice		Photo		Video	
		Leakage rank	Leakage num	Leakage rank	Leakage num	Leakage rank	Leakage num
WeChat	6.3.13	SP_SEVERE_LK	1	SP_SEVERE_LK	3	SP_SEVERE_LK	4
Mobile QQ	6.2.3.2700	SP_SEVERE_LK	1	SP_SEVERE_LK	3	SP_SEVERE_LK	2
Weibo	6.3.0	NO_LK	0	SEVERE_LK	2	SEVERE_LK	2
Yixin	4.3.1	SP_SEVERE_LK	1	SP_SEVERE_LK	2	SP_SEVERE_LK	1
Momo	6.7_0413	SP_SEVERE_LK	1	SP_SEVERE_LK	2	SP_SEVERE_LK	3
Wumi	5.3.0	SEVERE_LK	1	SEVERE_LK	1	NO_LK	0

Note: NO_LK: No cache file or only protected cache file created during application run-time.
SEVERE_LK: An attacker can use file viewer tools or Android File API to get privacy data.
SP_SEVERE_LK: Application cannot delete cache files by its own 'clear cache' function.

4.3   Privacy Leakage Score

We define a grading rule for evaluating the rank as shown in Table 5 and quantity of leakage considering the types of privacy data and the number of leakage path, the score is calculated as:

$$C = \sum_{k=0}^{4} V_k \bullet n \tag{1}$$

where C refers to the score of the application of certain types of privacy data leakage, V_k is the leakage score of leakage level while n is the leakage path number of the certain type of privacy data. Based on Table 5, the privacy leakage score of mainstream social applications in voice, photos and video data can be computed, the results are shown in Fig. 5.

Table 5. Leakage score rules

Leakage level	Leakage score V
SP_SEVERE_LK	4
SEVERE_LK	3
MEDIUM_LK	2
MILD_LK	1
NO_LK	0

Leakage score is a reflection of the management of cache file including private data of an application. It is not surprising that WeChat ranks first in the leakage scoring of the three types of private data because of its abundant functions and complex business that provides related rich entertainment service.

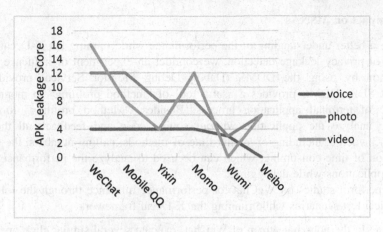

Fig. 5. Leakage score of some major MSNAs

Furthermore, we use X-Decaf to analyze the leakage about photo for the most 50 popular MSNAs. It can be found from Fig. 6 that only 4% of the MSNAs do not involve photo data, the other 96% of the MSNAs are the presence of SEVERE_LK or more, and 74% applications are SP_SEVERE_LK.

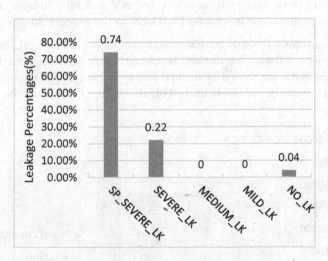

Fig. 6. Leakage statistic of photo in 50 MSNAs

The statistic fully illustrates that the current application developers often have little consideration of the user's privacy leakage and fail to comply with the specifications in the development.

4.4   Impact on MSNAs

To have a better understanding of the performance while running the X-Decaf in the process of privacy leakage detection, we conduct an experiment of influence on the application by using the DDMS (Dalvik Debug Monitor Service) provided by Android SDK. DDMS provides a useful tool of "method profiling" to monitor the run-time of terminal application process. Besides, "Method profiling" tools can dynamic analyze the application without source code and feedback all the Java methods involved, including executing time of methods, calling numbers, the overall proportion of time consuming, which can be used to analyze the performance of the social applications while debugging.

We perform studies on WeChat for performance influence through the following five typical test scenarios while running the X-Decaf framework.

Test 1: In the non-chat screen of WeChat, execute several similar click operations and analyze the overall performance of X-Decaf that influences WeChat;

Test 2: Call the camera API to take and send a picture, analyze the performance influence that X-Decaf may have in the photographing process;

Test 3: Send nine images continuously to analyze the performance impact of X-Decaf to the picture sending process;

Test 4: Send three small videos of six seconds continuously, analyze the performance impact of X-Decaf to the video sending process;

Test 5: Send three small videos of six seconds and nine images continuously, analyze the performance influence of X-Decaf to the sending process.

Each test runs for more than 20 times under the same WiFi network, moreover, the cache files generated during the test will be cleared every time when the test finish in order to prevent influence caused by manual testing, network conditions and the cache data of last test. It can be seen from the test results of Fig. 7 that under the condition of

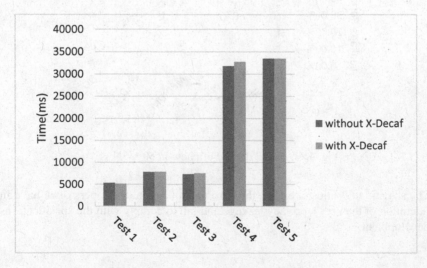

Fig. 7. Performance impact on WeChat

not modifying the application, X-Decaf only imposes very low effects on the application performance.

5 Auto-protection of Cache File

ATFed (Automatic Transparent File Encryption/Decryption) offers a general framework for protecting the cache files from leaking the user's private information by transparently encrypting and decrypting private data during the runtime without the modifications of the underlying Android framework or any involvement of the application developers. That is, ATFed will transparently encrypts the application's cache files through API hooking on the caller side. For instance, a photo taken in the MSNA will be encrypted without the application's involvement while being written into a cache file. When reading from the storage, ATFed decrypts the data accordingly.

To realize the hook process, the file IO operations both on the Java level and the native level should be considered. Specifically, most of the Java file IO related APIs eventually go through the underlying native libraries, such as libjavacore, so during the implementation of ATFed, APIs inside this native library will be detoured to our hooks and then the data will be encrypted when written to the cache files and decrypted when read. For example, the Java FileIOStream API eventually invokes the APIs inside the IOBridge class, which in turn calls the native functions inside the native library libjavacore. Then the native functions inside the libjavacore dynamically link the file IO APIs including open, read and write to libc. To make things easier, we will hook into the caller side APIs.

Figure 8 depicts the architecture of ATFed which consists of a hook module and a crypto module.

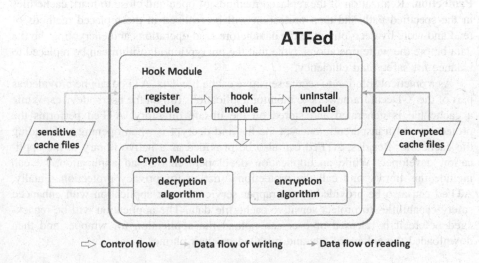

Fig. 8. Architecture of ATFed

The register module will mainly parse the ELF file and obtain the information needed to execute hook as ATFed starts works, then hook module will provide the hook functions and the backup of the original methods, finally, the uninstall module will be used to uninstall hook functions and restore the function of the original methods after the execution of the whole process. When the sensitive data of an application is being saved as a cache file, hook module in ATFed will get control of the file IO operation at first, and then the crypto module will be called for transparent encryption. Accordingly, when the encrypted cache files of an application are being read for the content of sensitive data, hook module will still preferentially get control of the file IO operation, and then the crypto module will launch the transparent decryption.

The major processes are given as follows:

Preparation. Determine the APIs (such as *read*, *write*) of the access operations in the implementation of file operations called in the system and the corresponding dynamic link library where these APIs exist. This part of work mainly relies on the analysis of Android source code including Java level and the native level, and finally we will hook into the *open*, *close*, *read* and *write* functions in the *libjavacore.so*;

Start Hook. Call the hooked function in the corresponding dynamic link library and hook module will redirect to the specified function as we have modified function addresses in the GOT (Global Offset Table) which stores the address of the global variables and functions. In this way, we replace the call of original *read* or *write* methods in the Java core codes by the call of the new implemented *read* or *write* in our program of ATFed. We realized this part in the hook module by the GOT hook technology which will analyze the dynamic link library of ELF format to get information of String Table, Symbol Table and the Relocation Table as well as figure out the address of hook functions in GOT;

Protection. Realization of the replaced methods of open and close to mark cache files in the specified path and then protection will be realized in the replaced methods of read and write by decrypting the file data before read operations and encrypting the file data before the write operations. Note that the encryption algorithm can be replaced to balance the safety and efficiency.

As a practical solution to secure sensitive cache file data, ATFed can be provided as part of the X-Decaf framework to monitor applications run on the users' devices. While a cache file is generated and stored on the unsafe directory, ATFed performs the protection and transparently encrypt the file and decrypt it when opening and reading the cache file. Besides, ATFed can also be provided as a native library to the application developer. While an application developer released an application, he can include this library and call the protection function for privacy protection. Finally, ATFed can also be provided as a wrapper service for the application with enhanced safety capabilities to protect sensitive cache file data. The application will be repackaged before it is released or user can upload the application for wrapper and then downloaded the enhanced one and installed on their phones.

6 Experimental Results of Auto-protection of Cache File

To figure out the compatibility and effectiveness of ATFed as well as the performance overhead, we conduct several simulation testing on Nexus5 with android version 4.4.4 and 5.1.1, the detailed analysis results are presented below.

As for compatibility and effectiveness, we use a test apk with file IO operation and install it on the phones. The apk is run on both the Dalvik virtual machine and the Android runtime (ART) virtual machine under protection of our system. After that, we manually interact with it and then use the "adb pull" command to pull out all the files in certain path and check whether the files were encrypted. The evaluation shows that this apk can execute normally both in Dalvik and ART, and all these files are encrypted successfully.

To evaluate the performance overhead of ATFed, we use this apk to encrypt and decrypt ten files with different sizes ranging from 1 megabytes to 500 megabytes 5 times and calculate the average time used for each operation. The algorithm we adopted is RC4. Table 6 shows the experimental results for Dalvik run-time with android version of 4.4.4 and Table 7 is for ART with android version of 5.1.1.

Table 6. Average time consumed in reading and writing operations in Dalvik

File size(M)	Without ATFed		With ATFed	
	Reading time (ms)	Writing time (ms)	Reading time (ms)	Writing time (ms)
1	4.0	4.0	26.0	26.0
2	8.0	10.0	54.0	50.0
5	6.0	24.0	122.0	120.0
10	16.0	44.0	226.0	244.0
20	34.0	84.0	436.0	480.0
50	74.0	224.0	942.0	1212.0
100	172.0	580.0	2042.0	2428.0
200	271.6	1599.8	8437.8	9190.2
350	521.2	3348.4	16153.8	17647.2
500	602.0	5573.0	21686.8	25656.6

Table 7. Average time consumed in reading and writing operations

File size(M)	Without ATFed		With ATFed	
	Reading time (ms)	Writing time (ms)	Reading time (ms)	Writing time (ms)
1	3.4	4.6	47.6	47.8
2	6.0	10.2	83.6	84.2
5	15.8	26.2	223.0	216.6
10	28.6	49.6	412.6	415.2
20	67.6	105.6	846.0	838.2
50	156.4	230.2	2111.4	2246.8
100	286.8	475.2	4176.4	4379.0
200	540.2	1592.8	8309.6	8943.2
350	932.0	3525.5	1442.6	15867.4
500	1198.8	5916.8	21565.8	23623.4

It is clear that the transparent encryption and decryption process does consume more time and have an influence on the application run-time to a certain extent, but fortunately the overhead is acceptable, as the size of a cache file in the MSNA can be much smaller than most of the test data given in our experiments. For example, the size of a general image or voice cache file in WeChat can be several hundred kilobytes or even smaller while the size of a general video file is around 2 megabytes. More specifically, a 10 s video file size in WeChat is just 1.7 M and it takes less than 0.1 s to encrypt or decrypt this cache file. What's more, the overhead can be even more positive as they are not such IO extensive in the real-world applications.

7   Conclusion

By analyzing the MSNAs from the China domestic market, we find that the developers of the current MSNAs fail to consider the protection of the user's privacy data in the development process, which is greatly different from our common sense. Typically, we believe that as the most popular mobile applications, how to protect user privacy should be considered in the MSNAs from the beginning of the development. However, experimental results show that most of the MSNAs have suffered from media privacy leakage. A solution called ATFed mechanism is proposed to protect the cache files generated by the MSNAs, so that the files can be stored in ciphertext and regarded as the protected cache files created during the run-time of the MSNA.

References

1. http://wearesocial.com/uk/special-reports/digital-in-2016
2. Zhang, Y., Yang, M., Yang, Z., et al.: Permission use analysis for vetting undesirable behaviors in android apps. IEEE Trans. Inf. Forensics Secur. 9(11), 1828–1842 (2014). doi:10.1109/TIFS.2014.2347206
3. Shebaro, B., Oluwatimi, O., Bertino, E.: Context-based access control systems for mobile devices. IEEE Trans. Dependable Secure Comput. 12(2), 150–163 (2015). doi:10.1109/TDSC.2014.2320731
4. Nauman, M., Khan, S., Othman, A.T., et al.: Realization of a user-centric, privacy preserving permission framework for Android. Secur. Commun. Netw. 8(3), 368–382 (2015). doi:10.1002/sec.986
5. Wu, L., Du, X., Zhang, H.: An effective access control scheme for preventing permission leak in Android. In: 2015 International Conference on Computing, Networking and Communications (ICNC), pp. 57–61. IEEE (2015). doi:10.1109/ICCNC.2015.7069315
6. Lu, L., Li, Z., Wu, Z., et al.: Chex: statically vetting android apps for component hijacking vulnerabilities. In: Proceedings of the 2012 ACM Conference on Computer and Communications Security, North Carolina, USA, pp. 229–240 (2012)
7. Tan, J., Drolia, U., Martins, R., et al.: Short paper: chips: content-based heuristics for improving photo privacy for smartphones. In: Proceedings of the 2014 ACM Conference on Security and Privacy in Wireless & Mobile Networks, Oxford, UK, pp. 213–218 (2014). doi:10.1145/2627393.2627394

8. Naveed, M., Zhou, X., Demetriou, S., et al.: Inside job: understanding and mitigating the threat of external device mis-binding on Android. In: Network and Distributed System Security Symposium, San Diego, California (2014)

9. Rahman, M., Ballesteros, J., Carbunar, B., et al.: Toward preserving privacy and functionality in geosocial networks. In: Proceedings of the 19th ACM Annual International Conference on Mobile Computing & Networking, Miami, Florida, USA, pp. 207–210 (2013)

10. Fawaz, K., Feng, H., Shin, K.G.: Anatomization and protection of mobile apps' location privacy threats. In: 24th USENIX Security Symposium (USENIX Security 15). Washington, D.C., USA, pp. 753–768 (2015)

11. Yan, L., Guo, Y., Chen, X.: SplitDroid: isolated execution of sensitive components for mobile applications. In: Thuraisingham, B., Wang, X., Yegneswaran, V. (eds.) SecureComm 2015. LNICST, vol. 164, pp. 78–96. Springer, Cham (2015). doi:10.1007/978-3-319-28865-9_5

12. Tripp, O., Rubin, J.: A Bayesian approach to privacy enforcement in smartphones. In: 23rd USENIX Security Symposium (USENIX Security 14). California, USA, pp. 175–190 (2014)

13. Enck, W., Gilbert, P., Han, S., et al.: TaintDroid: an information-flow tracking system for realtime privacy monitoring on smartphones. ACM Trans. Comput. Syst. (TOCS) 32(2), 5 (2014). doi:10.1145/2619091

14. Hsiao, S.W., Hung, S.H., Chien, R., et al. PasDroid: real-time security enhancement for Android. In: 2014 Eighth International Conference on Innovative Mobile and Internet Services in Ubiquitous Computing (IMIS), Birmingham, UK, pp. 229–235. IEEE (2014)

15. Bal, G., Kai, R., Hong, J.I.: Styx: privacy risk communication for the Android smartphone platform based on apps' data-access behavior patterns. Comput. Secur. 53, 187–202 (2015)

16. Cui, X., Yu, D., Chan, P., Hui, L.C.K., Yiu, S.M., Qing, S.: CoChecker: detecting capability and sensitive data leaks from component chains in Android. In: Susilo, W., Mu, Y. (eds.) ACISP 2014. LNCS, vol. 8544, pp. 446–453. Springer, Cham (2014). doi:10.1007/978-3-319-08344-5_31

17. Zhang, M., Yin, H.: Efficient, context-aware privacy leakage confinement for android applications without firmware modding. In: Proceedings of the 9th ACM Symposium on Information, Computer and Communications Security, Kyoto, Japan, pp. 259–270 (2014)

A Privacy-Driven Data Management Model for Smart Personal Assistants

Danilo M. Nogueira[1], Cristiano Maciel[1], José Viterbo[2(✉)],
and Daniel Vecchiato[1]

[1] Federal University of Mato Grosso (UFMT), Cuiabá, Mato Grosso, Brazil
cmaciel@ufmt.br
[2] Fluminense Federal University (UFF), Niterói, Rio de Janeiro, Brazil
viterbo@ic.uff.br

Abstract. Smart personal assistants are regarded as a promise to solve the problems related to the information overload faced by users in information-rich environments. Such systems make use of user data together with context information to present useful content that may help the user to perform desired actions. However, malicious use of this data could harm the privacy of the user. This work aims to propose a data management model capable of protecting the user from possible abuses in the use of collected data. Based on this idea, this work presents an analysis of the main personal assistants available for use today, and a survey on the predisposition of users to share personal information. Through this study, a privacy-driven management model was proposed and verified by a focus group composed by software engineering students.

Keywords: Smart personal assistants · Privacy · Personal context data · Ambient intelligence

1 Introduction

The popularization of smartphones has instigated the development of increasingly interactive applications. This fact is confirmed by a study published by Qualcomm [20], leading manufacturer of processors for smartphones, on the habits of mobile users in the main markets in Latin America. The study is part of an initiative to measure the degree of adoption, assimilation and use of information and communication technologies in society and showed that Brazilians have a strong acceptance of entertainment and banking services, as well as social networks. However, it makes clear that there are still large gaps to be fulfilled with the development of new applications. A niche of this market are context-aware applications, which, according to Weiser [26], can help to overcome the problem of information overload. Myers [19] argues that there has been a significant effort in both academia and industry to develop smart personal assistants (SPAs) to manage our increasingly complex, information-rich and communicative work environments. These assistants make use of software capable of analyzing information about the environment in which the user is inserted, and so can seamlessly perform the necessary actions to interact with the environment and the user [5].

T. Tryfonas (Ed.): HAS 2017, LNCS 10292, pp. 722–738, 2017.
DOI: 10.1007/978-3-319-58460-7_49

According to Carberry [8], by observing the actions of a person with the use of software agents, it is possible to deduce its plans. The recognition of such aspects can improve the effectiveness of context-aware applications and make them more inter-active. However, although the recognition of has ben a research topic extensively studied, it is not an easy task, and many open problems remain. A great difficulty for agents is to recognize the very context in which the user and his device is inserted. There is also the issue that the recognition of plans must be managed immediately to deal with possible changes of context [9].

For the recognition of the user plans, the mobile devices are omnipresent, observing the user in his private life all the time in an invasive way. In addition, user's data is collected and handled by plan recognition systems occurs in a worrying way, as there is no transparency in the management of such data by service providers, what makes the user susceptible to malicious use of such information. As Vecchiato [22] points out, there is a lack of work focusing on security issues during the extraction, manipulation and dissemination of this data. The occurrence of security breaches can further aggravate privacy issues by malicious use of the data.

Therefore, this work discusses ways to guide the development of a model for non-invasive data management, that is, to assure that the management of the user's data for the recognition of plans does not disrespect or invade his privacy, considering that he may not want that some pieces of information are accessed by personal assistants. This research was developed in the scope of the architecture proposal Devices, Environments and Social Networks Integration Architecture (DESIA). DESIA allows the manipulation of sensitive context data from sensors and mobile devices and includes emerging technologies such as social networks, cloud computing and software echosystems, emphasizing security and privacy, fundamental aspects not always covered by other architectures [17, 22].

Hence, we propose a privacy-driven data management model, i.e., a model capable of ensuring that SPAs do not commit abuses on the use of the user data collected. For the execution of this study, we conducted a survey with potential SPAs users, which made possible to propose a privacy solution for the users of these platforms. In addition, this article presents in detail the theoretical foundations that serve as the basis for this research. Moreover, we performed an analysis of the main SPAs available for use in the market. This paper brings the complete analysis of the data of the survey conducted with smartphone users, presenting the main requirements listed through the research. Finally, the model resulting from the principles raised from the research with users of a focus group is exposed.

2 Theoretical Framework

Ubiquitous or ubiquitous computing does not just mean being able to take devices anywhere, but allowing them to be present everywhere intrinsically, connected to the same network and making use of equally ubiquitous systems. Thus, for instance, with the use of ubiquitous computing, a computer that has the information about in which room it is located can adapt its behavior in a significant way [26].

To acquire information, these ubiquitous systems can make use of software agents who can sense the environment as they are deployed through sensors. Through the input of data by these sensors, the agents are also able to change the environment in which they are deployed [5]. However, despite all the agents' ability to observe the environment, they need directions to be able to make changes in the environment intelligently. These directions begin with the recognition of the actions that the user performs over time to reach a given goal [8].

The recognition of these actions, called "user plans recognition", is the main driver of any smart personal assistant, since without this ability the assistant will not be able to propose intelligent solutions to the user. As Gong reports [12], a smart personal assistant is the implementation of a computer interface with a social intelligence that would come from the agent's ability to be curious, effective, adaptive, and appropriate in interactions with the user. The implementation of a smart personal assistant involves receiving data from the user or from a software application used by the user, which allows the extraction of information and data and the processing of this information together with the profile of the user to produce an appropriate response to him.

On the other hand, due to this idea of intrinsic pervasiness to the operation of ubiquitous computing in smart personal assistants, there is a social problem embedded in this idea: the lack of privacy. Although these systems are extremely useful, your information in the wrong hands can become a problem for the user. Government officials and marketers, for instance, could make an unpleasant use of this information [26].

We can understand privacy as a condition that preserves intimate life, personal affairs and chores. In this way, the privacy of the user is a condition that aims to protect his data and personal information in scenarios related directly or not to the use of some system. Kapadia [16] states that, in order to ensure respect for his privacy, users should be in control of how their data and personal information are transferred to third parties.

In Brazil, as a guarantee for the user's privacy rights, a law commonly known as the Internet Civil Landmark was issued on April 24, 2014. This law guarantees the full exercise of the right of access to the Internet, safeguarding the right to privacy. It reinforces that the possession of personal data and the private communications by organizations providing Internet services, must respect and preserve the privacy, honor and image of the user or third parties involved in the use of such services [7].

Although ubiquitous computing may pose a risk to the user's privacy, the growing demand for systems that address the problem of information overload makes the paradigm "anywhere, anytime" the new challenge for designing and implementing the next generation of information systems. Hence, ubiquitous access to such information systems requires new concepts, models, methodologies and assistive technologies to fully exploit their potential [23].

3   Methodology

To develop this research, we conducted a literature review in the study area and conducted two qualitative studies. The first study dealt with an analysis of profiles of user personal assistants and the second one consisted in a focus group with students of Computer Science. The literature review focused on the areas of Human-Computer

Interaction and Artificial Intelligence. We reviewed articles on agents, methods of recognizing plans, privacy policies and smart personal assistants. Due to the difficulty of finding works that explored the capabilities of a Smart Personal Assistant (SPA) an analysis of the main SPAs present in the market was carried out.

The three assistants covered in this survey were selected because they are directly related to the three mobile operating systems with the biggest share on the market – Android, iOS and Windows Phone –, respectively Google Now, Siri and Cortana. To analyse the respectives SPAs, we consulted the descriptions of the functionalities and terms of use provided by each company. For a post-analysis, we elaborated a questionnaire composed of 21 questions, one discursive and the other multiple choice, which was applied to smartphone users who had smart personal assistants or not. The questionnaire was answered by 11 people invited to participate in the survey due to their differences in the use of smartphones and their social profiles. The questionnaire raised the complete profile of each participant by asking questions about the level of education, age and training area. The name of each participant was not collected to preserve their anonymity.

Based on the data collected in the survey, an analysis of privacy profiles was performed by assessing users' willingness to allow personal data sharing with smart personal assistants and their knowledge of those applications. In the next step, we elaborated a privacy-driven data management model based on the needs and fears of the surveyed users, using smart personal assistants that met the users' privacy profiles.

We validated the proposed model through a focus group study [3] with Computer Science students of the Federal University of Mato Grosso (UFMT). We divided the activities into 4 stages. In the first stage, each participant fulfilled a consent form for the participation in the focus group and a questionnaire to evaluate each profile and each subgroup. In the second step, the participants watched an explanation on smart personal assistants, the current SPA scenario and the model for data management proposed. Then the participants were divided into three subgroups for discussion, each group having a copy of the proposed model to evaluate the positive and negative aspects of its use. In the final stage, a collective discussion was opened to present their verifications of the proposed model. The result of this verification was essential for the construction of the privacy solutions that this work suggests.

4   Smart Personal Assistant Technologies

Smart personal assistants are still not very common systems and little used by lay users in technology. In today's generation of smartphones, three smart personal assistants stand out: Siri developed by Apple, Google Now developed by Google and Cortana developed by Microsoft [25]. All of them make use of ubiquitous computing and ambient intelligence concepts because they are connected to several other information services that permeate the environments that the users meet [2].

4.1   Siri

At its debut in 2010, Siri was able to connect to 42 different web services that were used to create a single response formed from the best information available from these sources. He was also able to make reservations at restaurants, buy tickets and even call a taxi, without having to open any other application [6].

The idea of its creators was that Siri was an autonomous tool that could anticipate the intentions of the user and make the information available before the user requested it. Siri could anticipate the frustration of a delayed flight by bringing in alternative flight information and other means of transportation such as train travel or car rental information. However, its creators have never been able to develop these functionalities [6].

4.2   Microsoft Cortana

Cortana had its debut in smartphones in 2014 and aimed to position itself as a personal digital assistant that could help the user to organize their daily tasks, managing meetings, reminders and other activities of the user's daily life.

To manage this information, Microsoft talked to several high-level personal assistants and found that they kept a notebook with notes on all the key information and personal interests of those they attended. The simple idea of having a notebook with personal key information has inspired Microsoft to create a virtual notebook for Cortana that stores personal information and anything that Cortana can see and use. The first time the user uses Cortana, it formulates basic questions to learn about the user's personal interests such as name, gastronomic preferences, or favorite movie types, for example. However, the user can always tell Cortana that something is not right and that it should not have access to that data.

4.3   Google Now

As part of the Android 4.1 update in 2012, Google introduced its virtual personal assistant for Android smartphones, Google Now [13]. It is a virtual personal assistant that provides information to the user via cards of the search-engine application, based on search history data, location, calendar events, and user-provided information such as favorite team, place of work, place of residence, and so on. Access to these data aims to provide more relevant information to the user [15].

At the first use of Google search-engine application, the user is asked if he wants to activate Google Now. From them on, the cards appear automatically when the wizard tries to guess what information the user will need at a given moment [5]. To provide this information, Google Now runs discreetly in the background of the Operating System, collecting and synthesizing records of searches, calendar, event locations, and travel patterns to inform and alert the user through notifications or cards in the search application [24].

Thus, Google has designed a distinctive technological line. On the one hand, there are virtual assistants who make inquiries and actions through user requests, on the other hand there is Google Now, which provides information without the need for user requests. It was rated by The Verge as the first virtual assistant that actually anticipates user needs [4].

4.4 Comparison Among SPAs

Table 1 presents a comparison among smart personal assistants. This comparison shows that Google Now is more proactive while Siri behaves in a reactive way. Like Google Now, Cortana also has a more proactive behavior.

Table 1. Comparison among SPAs

SPA	Siri	Cortana	Google Now
Platform	iOS	Windows phone	iOS, Android
Proactive	No	Yes	Yes
Parcial control of collected data	No	Yes	No
Storage	Cloud	Cloud	Cloud
Data source	Webservices	Bing	Google

One disadvantage of Siri before the others is that it only runs on one platform, while Google Now is present on both its Android and iOS, while Cortana is the only one that runs on smartphones and desktops simultaneously.

4.5 Terms of Use

Siri's terms of use [1] state that by using Siri, everything the user says will be recorded and sent to Apple so that audio information is converted into text and user requests are processed. The device may also send other information such as user name, nickname, and user contact relations, as well as song names stored on the device. At the end of the term of user, it is advised that the location of the iOS device "may also be sent to Apple" at the time the user places an order to Siri [1].

Not unlike Apple, Microsoft [18] also alerts users in their terms of use that when any voice command feature is used, he agrees that Microsoft will record and collect the voice inputs, and that the data will be used in accordance with the Windows Phone privacy policy. The Windows Phone privacy policy states that "we collect certain information to enable the features and services offered on the phone to perform the requested or authorized transactions and to display customized content and advertisements in accordance with your interests and preferences" [18]. The terms of use also state the user grants permission to Cortana to collect his current availability and share that information with others. He also grants permissions to Cortana to communicate with others on his behalf automatically.

The Google Now terms of use [13], informs the user that his Google account data and calendars are used to help him with his day-to-day activities, and that it stores information about the use of Google Search, Google Maps and other Google services, including user location and other data associated with Chrome history, websites, and applications. The terms of use also tell the user about device data that is stored by Google, such as contacts, calendars, alarms, music, movies, books, and other content. User location history is also stored, even when a product from Google is not being used. The terms make it clear that location information can also be used by any Google application and service, including ads that are displayed to the user.

4.6   Comparison Among Terms of Use

By comparing the terms of use of each smart personal assistant, it is possible to realize that Siri accesses user data only during its use, while Google Now and Cortana are always sharing information. All assistants collect personal data and store voice input data. Only Google Now accesses device data (Table 2).

Table 2. de comparação de termos de uso

SPA	Siri	Cortana	Google Now
Access to personal data	During the use	Always	Always
Collection of voice inputs	Yes	Yes	Yes
Access to device data	No	No	Yes
Communication on behalf of the user	No	Yes	No

5   User's Privacy Perception

In order to better understand the profile of the users of smart personal systems and smartphones, a qualitative survey was carried out with 11 people between August 6, 2015 and October 4, 2015. A questionnaire was answered by them to collect their views on data privacy in the smartphone as well as their intentions to use a smart personal assistant.

Google Now was presented to them as an example of a smart personal assistant. In this analysis, only smartphone users were able to contribute with their opinions, as the idea of data collection and privacy for people who do not use smartphones on a dayly basis would be too abstract.

The questionnaire had 21 questions distributed among 3 sets of questions: questions about demographic data, questions about the use of smartphones, and questions about opinions on privacy during the use of smartphones.

5.1   Demographic Data

The participants of the research have different background, 5 of them have already graduated, while 4 are undergraduate students. Among the participants with higher level, the courses of Information Systems, Pharmacy, Journalism and Administration stand out. All participants have ages varying between 20 to 35 years. Most participants are between 21 and 24 years old. Among the members of the research, 7 are men and 4 are women. All participants have smartphones and profiles on Facebook that, from 8 responses, was considered the social network where participants most provide personal information. The second most accessed social network is Instagram, which is used by 7 participants. Android operating system is the most used by participants, 6 of them. Other 5 participants use iOS. None of them, however, use the Microsoft's operating system.

5.2   Apps and Smartphone Use

On the use of mobile apps, all participants said they use Whatsapp. The second most widely used application was Waze, chosen by 5 participants. Thirdly, the Google Now and Siri applications are used by 3 participants, each. Of these, only 3 participants said they had already read some terms of use of the listed applications. In the case, only Whatsapp has had its term of use read by the users.

5.3   Data Privacy

Participants were also asked about automated reading of e-mails from Google and only 3 participants reported not knowing about this operation, 8 said they would like to turn off it. When informed that when interrupting the reading of e-mails, services like Google Now would be less accurate, only 1 participant informed that he would change his opinion and keep the reading of e-mails working.

Asked about allowing an assistant to read information on social networks, location, browsing history, e-mail content, chat content, and application usage on the smartphone, 3 participants informed that they would not allow a personal assistant to have access to any of this information.

The permission to share the location was the one that had more positive responses. As for the other information, most of the users showed resistance to share them. None of the users said that they would allow the sharing of complete informations of chat applications or e-mails content.

5.4   Smart Personal Assistants

After being exposed to a simple concept of what a smart personal assistant is and the method of operating such systems, participants were asked if they considered such methods invasive. All participants responded yes and 9 of them also agreed that the current methods would be less invasive if there were some legislation that protected the privacy of shared data. Among the participants, 9 would also consider it less invasive if it was possible to have a more accurate control of the shared information. Only one participant said that even if there was specific legislation or if it was possible to control what information to share, he would still consider the methods invasive.

At the end of the survey, participants were asked about the impact that the information in the survey brought to the intended use of applications on the mobile phone. Six of them said they would continue to use the apps the way they already used them. One participant said that he would try out some of the applications cited in the survey. One participant said that he would continue to not use these applications and 3 said that after learning about the information in the survey, they would decrease the use of those applications.

5.5   Requirements Derived from the Survey

Based on the analysis of the results, it was possible to define some requirements that a privacy-driven data management model must meet. Thus, this section presents the following requirements:

1. Work together with messaging applications, since messaging applications are very much used in smartphones;
2. Be transparent in the use of personal user data, since the vast majority of users are not aware of what happens to their data, because they do not read the terms of use;
3. Provide confidence to the user during data collection, since users are not comfortable with the operation of agents;
4. Provide transparency and control of shared data, as users are afraid to share personal data to private companies;
5. Provide information based on location data, since it is among the information that users are less afraid to share with the use of systems;
6. Give users the power to choose, since they consider invasive the methods of data acquisition;
7. Act in accordance with the laws that govern the right to privacy of the user, since the great majority of users considered that personal agents would be less invasive if there was legislation that regulated the use of the data;
8. Be considered non-invasive so that the use of personal assistants may increase.

5.6 Assumptions for the Model

Based on the requirements presented in the previous section, we define here that for the model to meet the requirements, it must:

- Allow the user to view all data collected by the system and give it the power to discard any data collected, to meet requirements 2, 3 and 7 of the previous topic;
- Provide ways to configure the presentation of collected data, to meet requirements 4 and 7;
- Indicate to the user the information that the system can infer and configure when this information will be presented, to meet requirements 5 and 6.

These assumptions were used to shape the components of the model, so that it implements a data management with privacy.

6 Privacy-Driven Data Management Model

According to [11], the goal of creating a model is to achieve simplified representation of the real world through abstraction. To do this, one must select some real-world characteristics that must be represented by the system. A good model has the same properties of the portion of reality that it attempts to represent. Since a model is a simplification, it can be studied and manipulated to find solutions to related real world problems.

For this reason and based on the concepts obtained through the literature review, the analysis of the existing applications, the survey with users, and the legislation in force, a model was elaborated to be less invasive, since it takes into account the user preferences and is protected by privacy principles.

6.1 Model Validation

For a more in-depth analysis that enabled the elaboration of a verified and less invasive model, another research was carried out, this time presenting a previously elaborated model for a focus group composed only of Computer Science students from the Federal University of Mato Grosso. The 14 people focus group was gathered to verify the model capacity, technical acceptance, and potential to support a non-invasive smart personal assistant system.

The focus group activity began with the application of a questionnaire with 8 questions to collect the profile of the participants. As for the use of social networks, the participants presented a very similar profile. The three most used social networks among the participants were Facebook with 100%, LinkedIn with 50% and Instagram with 35.7% participation.

After the application of the questionnaire, the students were presented with information about smart personal assistants in which the main assistants available on the market and some of their terms of use were mentioned. At the end of the presentation, the proposed model was presented to the students.

Then, the students were randomly divided into 3 groups composed of 4 participants each. The groups were given the task of listing positive and negative aspects of the presented model. After 45 min of discussion, positive and negative considerations were presented by all groups.

Positive Aspects
As for the positive aspects, the groups praised the model's ability to customize the data to be shared for each user profile. The ability for full control of smart assistants by the user has made the survey participants more confident and secure about the availability and use of their personal information.

Negative Aspects
Each group also presented suggestions for model improvement. The most common concern among the groups was with the amount of information indexed in the user's data repository and the impact that this would have on the consumption of the smartphone's storage capacity. To improve the understanding of the focus group participants, it was explained that the data repository only uses data present in the storage of other systems, serving only as a data library. This explanation given to the participants was used to fine-tune the definition of the data repository.

6.2 Model Description

This section presents the privacy-driven data management model for implementing smart personal assistants in ubiquitous devices (see Fig. 1), resulting from the verification by the focus group.

The model was designed to have a high level of abstraction, in order to facilitate discussions about the direct impacts to the user and not to be analyzed in the systems development and implementation contexts. However, Sect. 6.3 presents a view of the model in a layered architecture.

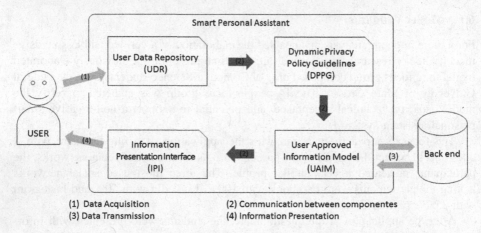

Fig. 1. Privacy-driven data management model for smart personal assistants

It is worth noting that this model idealizes a smart personal assistant with a proactive approach, in which the assistant anticipates the intentions of the user. In this way, the model can be used in smart personal assistants who already have a similar approach.

Data Acquisition

Data acquisition will be done through software agents that will apply data mining techniques to detect user information from the use of other applications. The agents will also find data through device sensors and index that information found in component called User Data Repository.

User Data Repository – UDR

The User Data Repository (UDR) can be understood as an index of all data encountered by agents during data acquisition. To allow transparency of data usage by the personal assistant, the idea of an information repository is based on the idea used in Cortana's notebook. The difference in the model proposed in this work is that, in addition to checking and managing the basic information such as user name, home and work place, the user can check and manage all the data found by agents such as: browsing history, travel data, calendar events, etc.

For instance: during data acquisition, agents can collect personal information from the user. The user, when consulting the indexed information in the UDR, decided to exclude the information from his place of work, since it is not in the interest of the plan recognition that the smart personal assistant considers such data for the inference of information. This data will then be hidden from the smart personal assistant, allowing full control of the information managed by the assistant.

Dynamic Privacy Policy Guidelines – DPPG

The Dynamic Privacy Policy Guidelines (DPPG) is a component that allows the user to manage the availability of the data to be shared with the back end for inference of information. Through the DPPG the user defines in which moments, places and situations a given data, indexed in the RDU, will be available to be sent to the back end service by the User Approved Information Model.

For instance, when the user is interested in a shorter route to go home after work, the personal assistant will be able to send the data of his location to the back end service for a period of time – for half-hour beginning 15 min before the end of the user's office hours and ending 15 min after that.

In the example, the DPPG will be configured to permit the use of location data if the user is in the workplace for a period of half an hour, beginning 15 min prior to the set time of office. This will allow the information to only leave the device if the user needs a route suggestion with less traffic to get home. If the user is in another situation, outside the workplace, at lunchtimes, etc., the information about his location will not be shared.

User Approved Information Model – UAIM

The User Approved Information Model (UAIM) is the component that sets the information patterns, to be inferred by the recognition of plans carried out by the back end service. This component allows the user to configure what information he wants to receive. It is also the component responsible for informing the user which data will be used to infer the selected information pattern. By considering that information inference is the product of the plan recognition process, UAIM is the main product directory generated by the plan recognition system.

Its communication with the back end occurs only when the information display rules are met, and the data managed by the DPPG is available for inference of information. Thus, the use of the device data network will occur only at useful times to the user, so that uninterrupted data transmission does not occur.

For instance, the user will inform UAIM that he wants to receive information about airfare values. The user will be asked if he agrees to share the search history data and the city in which he is located, so that the back end service is aware of the user's destinations and can determine the route the user will follow to make his trip in the best way possible. The user will consent to sharing browsing history only when he is at home.

Back End

The back end service is responsible for inferencing information by recognizing user plans from their personal data. It receives from UAIM the type of information that it must complete and the personal data of the user, necessary to carry out the recognition of plans. After recognizing the user's plans, it sends to UAIM the useful information understood.

For instance, the moment the user arrives at the airport during a trip, the back end service will be informed about the user's location, e-mail content and information on the best way to go to a hotel. Thus, during the recognition of plans, the back end service will recognize that the user will go to the hotel when leaving the airport. Thus, the service will consult information about the city that the user is in to decide what will be the best way to reach the hotel. After consultation, the information will be transmitted to the smart personal assistant to be displayed to the user.

Note that in the described example, UAIM is configured to inform the back end service about the user's best interest in getting to a hotel when traveling, and DPPG allows the sharing of location data and e-mails content when the user's current location is different from the city in which he resides. Thus, the service provider will have access to the user data only when the user intends to obtain a return by giving up his data.

Information Presentation Interface – IPI

The Information Presentation Interface (IPI) is the component of the system that communicates with the user to allow him to configurate the other components. The IPI presents information resulting from the plan recognition process performed by the back end service and received by UAIM.

This paper does not propose to discuss the ideal interface for communication with the user, but as an example of interaction it is suggested the presentation of the result of the plan recognition and the cards in use. The sequence of steps below demonstrates the interaction process between the user and the smart personal assistant:

1. **Demonstrate the card to the user**. During the first use of the smart personal assistant, the system must show the user the information template that will be present on the card (see Fig. 2A). The system should also inform which data types indexed in the UDR will require sharing permission to perform the plan recognition.
2. **Request the data to use the card**. If the user decides to use the card, an explicit data access request will be made for the full functioning of the smart personal assistant (see Fig. 2B). The system will obey the legal requirements regarding its responsibility in obtaining the user's data. By agreeing to the request, the user will be performing the configuration and management of the personal data in the DPPG.
3. **Send data to the back end service to perform data processing**. The system must send the data provided to the back end service that performs the recognition of the user's plans and provides the inference information.
4. **Receive the information inferred by the backend service**. In the same way that the data is sent for the back end plan recognition service, the inferred information must be sent to the SPA on the user's device.
5. **Present in card information inferred by the back-end service**. The SPA should present the card with the information to the user (see Fig. 2C). The presentation can be done in both the application and the notification system of the device.

In this example, one can note how privacy issues can be associated with the internet legal requirements, moreover, how the SPA places the user at the center of decisions by shaping their functioning according to the user's consent profile.

6.3 Layered Architecture

This section presents a view of the proposed model in a layered architecture (see Fig. 3), since this method allows to identify the main structural components of the system and the relationship between them.

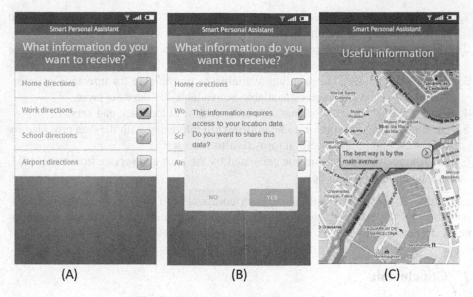

Fig. 2. Smart personal assistant interface

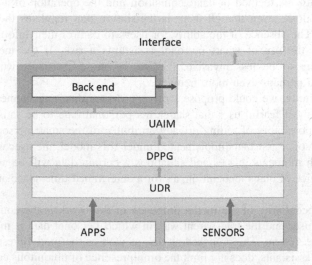

Fig. 3. Layered architecture of the proposed model

In a layered architecture "each layer only depends on the features and services offered by the layer immediately below it" [21]. Thus, it is an ideal way to present the proposal of an architecture for the model exposed in this work. We divided our proposal in 6 main layers:

1. The personal user data can be found by means of sensors present in the device and by applications that use the data;
2. Using agents, the UDR performs the process of data discovery and performs the indexation of this data, which becomes available for the above layer;
3. The DPPG classifies the data into available or unavailable for inference of information. The data classified as available is available for the next layer;
4. The UAIM selects the available data and sends it to the back end service;
5. The back end service performs the information inferecing with the data provided by the UAIM and returns useful information to the user;
6. The IPI receives the information generated by the back end service from the UAIM, thus finalizing the data flow.

In the sequence presented above, each component of the model serves the component in the layer immediately below with information and the other lower components do not have to interact with the components above.

7 Conclusion

The frequent and increasingly assiduous use of smartphones and mobile applications by people is clear. With this research, it is possible to conclude that certain users are not comfortable with the method of data acquisition and the operation of agents as invasively as it is done, even though there is legislation that regulates the use of their personal data. The absence of the ability for users to control their information before sharing makes the use of smart personal assistants a risk. If the method of data acquisition were to be less invasive, the use of these assistants would be more responsible and perhaps even more frequent.

From this study, we could propose a privacy-driven data management model that will allow the most fearful user that shares his personal data to be satisfied with the flexibility and possibility of setting privacy attributes of the smart personal assistants. With smart personal assistants implemented under this model, the user will be able to define in which moments, places and situations a certain data will be available to be sent to the service of plans recognition, all for a determined time-space and defined by the user.

The main peculiarity of the model proposed in this work is the concern with the privacy of the user and the transparent way in which personal data is maintained and analyzed by the system. The proposed model, as well as the model present in today's smart personal assistants, does not limit the omnipresence of ubiquitous computing, but in contrast, it allows the data collected by the ubiquitous devices to be controlled by the user, thus preventing the user from being vulnerable to malicious use of such data.

On the other hand, what limits the model is the lack of knowledge about the information that the user intends to receive. The model requires that, during the implementation, a library of information already exists to be displayed to this user. Another limitation of the model is the amount of information that will be sent to the plan recognition system, since the recognition of plans may be hampered by the fact that the configurations permit the sharing of few data, when in fact a larger set of data would be necessary to increase the knowledge of the system about the user with support of machine learning techniques. However, it is expected that with the application of a non-invasive model, users will adopt these assistants more frequently, increasing the amount of data collected by the system.

As a future work, a smart personal assistant implementation will be carried out following the privacy-driven management data model presented here with a more refined study of data mining techniques for acquiring user data. During implementation, the suggestions listed by the focus group will be applied such as: using a colloquial language in the description of the terms of use and making the data privacy settings grouped by categories of information available. We also identified as objects of study for future work, the analysis of communicability in the stages of configuring the system and the accomplishment of a study of the main information that a user is interested in receiving.

References

1. Apple Inc. iOS License Agreement (2012). http://www.apple.com/legal/sla/docs/ios6.pdf. Accessed 18 Apr 2016
2. Baljak, V., et al.: S-CLAIM: an agent-based programming language for AmI, a smart-room case study. Procedia Comput. Sci. **10**, 30–37 (2012). Elsevier
3. Barbour, R.: Grupos focais. Artmed, Porto Alegre (2009). (in Portuguese)
4. Bohn, D.: Google Now: behind the predictive future of search. The Verge, 29 October 2012. http://www.theverge.com/2012/10/29/3569684/googlenowandroid42know-ledgegraphneural networks. Accessed 04 Nov 2015
5. Bordini, R.H., Hübner, J.F., Wooldridge, M.: Programming Multi-agent Systems in AgentSpeak Using Jason, vol. 8. Wiley, Hoboken (2007)
6. Bosker, B.: The inside story of siri's origins and why she could overshadow the iphone. The Huffington Post, 22 January 2013. http://www.huffingtonpost.com/2013/01/22/siri-do-engine-apple-iphone_n_2499165.html. Accessed 27 Oct 2015
7. Brasil, Lei no. 12.965, 23 April 2014. Marco Civil da Internet. Brasília, DF, 24 April 2014. (in Portuguese). http://www.planalto.gov.br/ccivil_03/_ato2011-2014/2014/lei/l12965.htm. Accessed 10 Apr 2016
8. Carberry, S.: Techniques for plan recognition. User Model. User-Adap. Interact. **11**(1–2), 31–48 (2001)
9. Chaouche, A.C., El Fallah Seghrouchni, A., Ilié, J.M., Saïdouni, D.E.: Smart agent foundations: from planning to spatio-temporal guidance. Enablers Smart Cities 33–63 (2016)
10. Finger, T., Maciel, C.: A comparative study on the architecture of social networks facing users great demand. IEEE Lat. Am. Trans. **10**(1), 1208–1214 (2012). (Revista IEEE America Latina)
11. Gigch, J.P.V.: System Design Modeling and Metamodeling. Springer Science & Business Media, New York (2013)
12. Gong, L.: Intelligent personal assistants. Google Patents. US Patent App. 10/158,213 (2002)
13. Google Inc. Termos de Serviço do Google (2014). https://www.google.com/policies/terms/. Accessed 18 Apr 2016
14. Hauswald, J., et al.: Sirius: an open end-to-end voice and vision personal assistant and its implications for future warehouse scale computers. In: Proceedings of the Twentieth International Conference on Architectural Support for Programming Languages and Operating Systems, pp. 223–238. ACM (2015)

15. Ingraham, N.: Google Now: search based on time and location. The Verge, 20 June 2012. http://www.theverge.com/2012/6/27/3120727/googlenowtimelocationsearch. Accessed 04 Nov 2015

16. Kapadia, A., Henderson, T., Fielding, J.J., Kotz, D.: Virtual walls: protecting digital privacy in pervasive environments. In: LaMarca, A., Langheinrich, M., Truong, K.N. (eds.) Pervasive 2007. LNCS, vol. 4480, pp. 162–179. Springer, Heidelberg (2007). doi:10.1007/978-3-540-72037-9_10

17. Maciel, C., de Souza, P.C., Viterbo, J., Mendes, F.F., El Fallah Seghrouchni, A.: A multi-agent architecture to support ubiquitous applications in smart environments. In: Koch, F., Meneguzzi, F., Lakkaraju, K. (eds.) Agent Technology for Intelligent Mobile Services and Smart Societies. CCIS, vol. 498, pp. 106–116. Springer, Heidelberg (2015)

18. Microsoft. Política de privacidade do Windows R Phone 8.1 (2015). (in Portuguese). http://www.windowsphone.com/pt-br/legal/wp8/windows-phone-8-1-privacy-statement. Accessed 18 Apr 2016

19. Myers, K., et al.: An intelligent personal assistant for task and time management. AI Mag. **28** (2), 47 (2007)

20. Romer, R.: Qualcomm divulga dados de sua primeira pesquisa sobre conectividade no Brasil Canaltech, 18 March 2014. (in Portuguese). http://corporate.canaltech.com.br/noticia/qualcomm/Qualcomm-divulga-dados-de-sua-primeira-pesquisa-sobre-conectividade-no-Brasil/. Accessed 18 Apr 2016

21. Sommerville, I.: Software Engineering. Pearson, Upper Saddle River (2011)

22. Vecchiato, D., et al.: Using agents towards providing security on a context-aware architecture. In: Proceedings of the 1st International Workshop on Agents and CyberSecurity, p. 10. ACM (2014)

23. Viterbo, J., et al.: Ambient Intelligence: Management of Distributed and Heterogeneous Context Knowledge. CRC Studies in Informatics Series, pp. 1–44. Chapman & Hall (2008)

24. Ward, J.: Google Now. Popular Science, 15 November 2012. http://www.popsci.com/gadgets/article/201211/googlenow. Accessed 04 Nov 2015/16/17

25. Warren, T.: The story of Cortana, Microsoft's Siri killer. The Verge, 02 April 2014. http://www.theverge.com/2014/4/2/5570866/cortanawindowsphone81digitalassistant. Accessed 28 Oct 2015

26. Weiser, M.: The computer for the 21st century. Sci. Am. **265**(3), 94–104 (1991). Nature Publishing Group

Designing Privacy for You: A Practical Approach for User-Centric Privacy

Awanthika Senarath$^{(\boxtimes)}$, Nalin A.G. Arachchilage, and Jill Slay

Australian Centre for Cyber Security, University of New South Wales - Canberra,
Australian Defence Force Academy, Campbell, Australia
a.senarath@student.unsw.edu.au, {nalin.asanka,jill.slay}@adfa.edu.au

Abstract. Privacy directly concerns the user as the data owner (data-subject) and hence privacy in systems should be implemented in a manner which concerns the user (user-centered). There are many concepts and guidelines that support development of privacy and embedding privacy into systems. However, none of them approaches privacy in a user-centered manner. Through this research we propose a framework that would enable developers and designers to grasp privacy in a user-centered manner and implement it along with the software development life cycle.

1 Introduction

Donald Trump's presidential campaign was seriously damaged, when a personal conversation he had with a friend ten years ago (in 2005) was recorded and released to the public during his run in the elections in 2016 in the USA. The recording had been done without the knowledge of the two people engaged in the conversation and was released at a very critical moment in the presidential campaign [1]. This is not much different to the situation users face on a daily basis when using on-line applications to network, communicate, shopping and banking on-line, and for many other personal tasks [9]. Due to the pervasiveness of Information and Communication Technology on-line applications have become an integral part of users [7]. However, they are unaware of the plethora of sensitive information that is being collected by applications in the background, the entities that have access to those information and how securely their data is stored [40], because those systems are not designed for end user privacy. Therefore, users unknowingly become vulnerable to highly personalized scam, and identity theft [41]. For example, a cyber criminal called Peace listed 200 million of user records of Yahoo users for sale on the dark web at the beginning of August, 2016, which consisted of user names, encrypted passwords [3].

Caputo et al. [10] in their investigation on barriers to usable systems, claim that companies do attempt to adhere to theories that improve usability of systems to secure company reputation for protecting market shares. Obstructing existing user practices in systems is mentioned as one of the five pitfalls by Lederer et al. [31] that should be avoided by privacy designers to ensure usable privacy. However, other than providing lengthy, in-comprehensive data policies

© Springer International Publishing AG 2017
T. Tryfonas (Ed.): HAS 2017, LNCS 10292, pp. 739–752, 2017.
DOI: 10.1007/978-3-319-58460-7_50

and user guides [2,44], very little attention has been paid by organizations to integrate privacy as a part of user engagement with the system. A usable privacy implementation would help users better understand the system and manage their personal boundaries in interacting with systems. However, up-to-date security and privacy is a different process in an application, which the user is forced to go through [40,44].

Privacy directly concerns the user as the data owner [8]. Privacy of a system should be designed for the user (user-centered) [5] and to be *user-centric*, designers should take a step further to analyze users' expected behavioral engagement with the system, to ensure they address potential privacy risks [49]. However, current approaches for privacy design mostly concern data as an impersonalized entity [22] and ignores users perspectives and behavioral traits in embedding privacy into systems [52]. For example, Caputo et al. [10] has pointed that developers have different perceptions on what usability really means, and also thinks "developers know best", and see little or no need to engage with target users. As a solution to this problem, Rubenstien and Good [42] highlights the importance of extending the existing user experience (UX) evaluation techniques to improve usability of privacy implementations in systems. We are contributing by providing a systematic approach for software developers to design privacy as they approach the software development lifecycle with a user-centered view [17,48]. We propose a paradigm shift in developer thinking from *Implementing Privacy in a System* to *Implementing Privacy for Users of the System*, through the concept of user-centered privacy.

2   Related Work

There are many conceptual and technological guidelines introduced by researchers to support developers and designers to implement privacy in applications. Fair information practices (FIP) [47], Privacy by Design (PbD) [11], Privacy Enhancing Tools (PET) [24] and Privacy Impact Assessment (PIA) [14] are guidelines or principles that have emerged to support developers to implement privacy in systems. However, we are experiencing major privacy failures in systems and applications [29] because, these guidelines are not formed in a way that is practically applicable with the software development processes today [17]. There is a gap in privacy guidelines for developers and privacy in practice [50].

Fair Information Practices (FIP) focus on the rights of individuals, and the obligations of institutions associated with the transfer and use of personal data such as data quality, data retention and notice and consent/choice of users [47]. Here, personal data is data that are directly related to the identification of a person and their behaviors [47]. FIP is criticized to lack comprehensiveness in scope and to be unworkable and expensive [19]. This is where PbD gained its recognition. It is fair to say that PbD is an improved state of FIP [17] with focus on a wider range of requirements considering the business goals of the company [11]. PbD was introduced as a set of guidelines to embed privacy as a part of system design in the designing phase it-self [15]. It involves seven principles

[11] which focus on the developer and the company perspective of privacy rather than user perspective [11,22,52]. For an example, the last principle in PbD states that it should respect for user privacy, however it does not tell how to design privacy in a user-centric way [22,48]. Furthermore, due to the widespread of the PbD concept, it has become a fashionable idea to declare commitment to PbD, without genuine privacy interests [17]. Therefore, Davies et al. [17] highlights the importance for an integrated approach to developing PbD as a practical framework to overcome its flaws, as otherwise PbD would remain the accepted norm comprehended only by a small community of good privacy practitioners.

Privacy Impact Assessment (PIA) is a more practical approach that focus on the impact of privacy on the stakeholders of a project [14]. However, PIA is only a first step and should be followed by PbD and implementation technologies for completeness. Privacy Enhancing Technologies (PETs) are used to implement certain designs to overcome the risks identified in the PIA [24]. However, PETS can be used only after careful analysis of privacy requirements and following a systematic approach to decide how privacy should be implemented in the system. That is where the framework we propose is going to fit in. While PETs are useful in gaining insights into the technological capability in implementing privacy in systems, PbD provides the base on which privacy should be designed prior to implementation, bridging the former with latter is a timely requirement [17].

PRIPARE [30], a recent development in the field of privacy engineering, elaborates how PbD should be implemented in practice. This work address the part that was lacking in PbD in great detail. They consider a similar approach to ours defining how PbD should be applied in each step of a generic development cycle, considering environmental factors to assist development throughout. However, PRIPARE, too considers privacy only from the perspective of the application developers and organizations. Even though they encourage respect for user privacy similar to PbD, they fail to nudge developers to think in a user-centered manner, comprehend real user requirements in privacy, varying on the nature and purpose of the application, context of usage of the application, and also on the characteristics of the user group. We propose *User-Centered Privacy* with all steps in the framework proposed, centered on the user of the system.

In the framework for "Engineering privacy" [49], which proposes a solution for practical privacy implementations, the importance of understanding user behaviors in implementing privacy is heavily discussed. However, as they have proposed in their framework, it is not realistic to implement privacy-by-architecture in a system where annoymity, data-minimization and other privacy technologies are practiced to an extent where providing information, notice, and choice and access to users can be completely ignored [24]. On the other hand, Cannon [9] has provided a comprehensive guide for implementing privacy in a system addressing all parties in a company. It involves a very descriptive data analysis framework and a guide for privacy related documentation. However, this lacks a user-centric approach towards privacy and focuses solely on the development perspective. It considers data from the company perspective and ignores user's behavioral engagement with the system and their expectations and perceptions of privacy.

Furthermore, it is not defined adhering to a particular development process, or a work-flow and only contains best practices that should be followed by developers for embedding privacy into systems. Therefore it is not possible for an organization to directly apply them to the current development processes they practice. To address both these gaps we have implemented our framework on Unified Software Development Process (UP), created by Jacobson, Booch, and Rambough [18].

Iterative and Incremental software development processes [4,23,45]) are highly used today in organizations [13] due to their capability of handling varying requirements in short time periods. UP is the most descriptive form of Iterative and Incremental development processes from which the modern light scale development processes customized for has been derived from [43]. It defines steps not only for the development of a software application, but also to manage, maintain and support it throughout [43]. Therefore, we define the proposed framework (Fig. 1) on UP so that it could be easily linked to the lightweight simplified interactive and incremental software development processes that are used widely.

3 Systematic Approach for User-Centric Privacy

The proposed framework considers the phases defined in UP through which the project moves over time, with each phase containing balanced out amounts of analyzing, implementation and designing tasks involved. The four phases in the UP life cycle are inception, elaboration, construction and transition [43]. The proposed framework defines tasks to be carried out in each of these phases, so that privacy would be a part of the development process throughout.

For an example, consider developing a mobile gaming application. A privacy risk estimation for all stakeholders such as game players, developers and the company that releases the game as well as the platform that hosts the game should be done in the inception phase. Afterwards, effective data minimization in the inception phase would ensure commitment to privacy and better understanding of privacy requirements from beginning itself. This is expected in PbD, as integrating privacy at later phases would not deliver expected results in terms of privacy [11]. Analyzing of data gathering requirements and players behaviors, and the environment in which the game would be played (on phone, tablet in public places), setting privacy goals and high privacy risk mitigation designs in the elaboration phase would further strengthen the company's privacy goals and ensure usability of privacy designs [49]. Identifying any remaining privacy requirements, reviewing, user surveys and comparing players' expectations against implementation for preparing privacy policies is required in the construction phase. This would aid effective transparency in the game application being designed [25]. Testing privacy, defining privacy setting for deployment guide and accountability evaluation [12] at the transition phase would sum up the work-flow for user-centric privacy implementation in the game.

Figure 1 describes the proposed framework as a work-flow, that should be followed by the development team collectively, to achieve privacy in the system.

Each step in the work-flow is tightly bound to the next, such that the results and knowledge gained in the initial step assist the execution of the next step. Environment and change management are specifically defined in UP to support planning and management of the project [43]. This is an essential step in software development given the continuous change requirements and modification that happens in practice. We have hence included these steps in our work-flow to ensure continuous privacy commitment.

We expect to conduct a study involving application developers and end users to validate our framework, and to receive feedback to fine tune it to improve its potential for practical realization. Sections of the questionnaire that aligns with each step are embedded to show how we aim to validate the steps proposed. The full questionnaire of the study is available in the appendix.

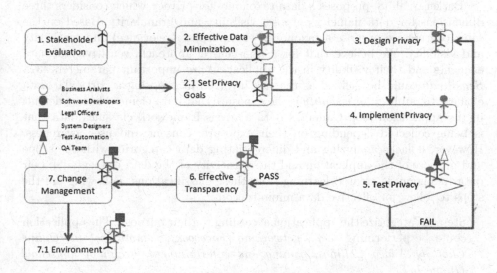

Fig. 1. User-centric privacy framework

1. Stakeholder Evaluation: PIA [24] already proposes a privacy impact analysis on the end user in designing a system. However, we propose to assess both the company and the users rather than just assessing the impact of the system to the end user. For effective privacy, all stakeholders of the system need to be analyzed in terms of their privacy expectations, responsibility and potential vulnerabilities [14], to understand their requirements, perceptions and behaviors with the system. Users and the company as an entity should be considered for their expected goals from the system being developed, their expected engagement with the system and the potential privacy impact that could arise and accountability [12]. Accountability is considered to be a strong parameter in effective privacy implementation as it ensures reliable and responsible systems [12]. A stakeholder evaluation report should be generated at the end of the evaluation and the report should be composed to be available during the latter stages. Understanding the stakeholders in terms of privacy would help designers for effective data minimization with a better view of the users expectations.

2. *User-Centric* Data Taxonomy for Privacy: *Data minimization* is a very broad statement in FIP [8]. However for effective data minimization usage of Data should be minimized in a meaningful way. Collecting a small amount of highly sensitive data that is irrelevant to the purpose of the application cannot be voted as good compared to collecting a large amount of less sensitive data related to the application. For an example users would expect a health care website to store their past health conditions, but not for a social networking site [40]. It was shown that users were comfortable with web-sites collecting their data when it directly relates to the purpose they serve [34]. To this end we are proposing the *Data Taxonomy for Privacy* for effective data minimization.

Barker et al. [8] proposes a data taxonomy for privacy which considers three dimensions for data namely, purpose, visibility and granularity. Based on the same concept we propose a taxonomy with purpose (relevance) and sensitivity and visibility. We believe that for a user-centric approach, sensitivity of data elements and their visibility in the application are important parameters [37]. *Sensitivity* could be defined as the risk involved in exposing a particular data element to public, and *visibility* is the exposure that data element has by default in the application [36]. Cannon's data analysis framework classifies data that is being collected depending on their exposure, consent and user awareness. However, it lacks analyzing and differentiating data categories with the scope and purpose of the application and the sensitivity of the data elements [9]. Our data taxonomy is created learning from these classifications. Following are the steps to follow for effective data minimization.

- Step 1: Categorize the application according to their purpose. The application could be performing *social networking (Facebook), communication (Online Chatting, Video Calling), gaming and entertainment, health or household (Home IoT)*.
- Step 2: Depending on the category of the application rank the users they expect to collect in the order of relevance to the purpose of the application [14].
- Step 3: Categorizing user-data you expect to collect from user perspective, such as *Personal Identification Data (Name, Age1), Behavioral Data collected from user (purchasing, health behavior), Financial Data, Societal Data (Occupation, Marital/Family Status) and History (Travel, Health, Occupation)*.
- Step 4: Score all data according to their sensitivity and visibility and rank: In rating privacy in Facebook, Minkus et al. [37] has shown that the privacy level of certain types of data depends on its sensitivity to the data subject and its visibility in the given application [36]. The framework already put forward by Liu and Terzi [35] to evaluate sensitivity and visibility of data elements can be applied here.
- Step 5: Looking at the rankings, if the application is collecting a data type that is less relevant to the purpose and scope of their application, which are not directly required to achieve their business goals, and have a higher sensitivity

ranking, either take measures to improve their data collection strategy or improve their application to ensure access, choice and notice for those highly sensitive data elements [9].

Through effective data minimization, analysts should aim to ensure a win-win situation in achieving both privacy and business goals as defined in PbD [14] in the designing step of the development life-cycle.

Validation Questions Proposed:

- a. What are the data elements that you collect in this application?
- b. Rank the data elements you collect in the order of relatedness, sensitivity and visibility of those data elements to the purpose the application serves
- c. For those highly sensitive data elements that are less relevant to the purpose of the application,
  - i. Is there any way that you can avoid collecting those data?
  - ii. What is the database structure they being stored? Have you evaluated the privacy risk factor in designing these databases?
  - iii. Have you considered hiding, separation, aggregation, notice and control in designing the databases?
  - iv. What are the risk mitigation strategies that you have specifically used?

Consider yourself as an end-user of the application you designed,

- a. What data do you expect this application to collect?
- b. What data are you willing to expose to the application for your benefit as a user? Create separate lists imagining you as a health-care professional registered to provide service and a user seeking medical advice.
- c. What sort of data do you think the application should specifically refrain from storing and making use of? Why?
- d. What data do you believe the application collected in the background while you were using the application?

---

3. Set Privacy Goals and Design Privacy: In designing privacy goals for their system designers should take into consideration how a user is expected to engage with the application they design. The amount of data the user is going to expose and their expected level of privacy are highly dependent on users' engagement with the application [20, 38]. Also the usability and adaptability of the privacy enhancing tools designers embed in the system largely depends on users behavioral engagement of the system. If the designers place the privacy tools in an accessible way, but not visible to the user in their natural engagement with the application it is not likely to be used. Hence we emphasize that designers and developers should focus on the behavioral engagement of users with the system, similar to how User-experience (UX) designers test and evaluate their interfaces [51]. In terms of privacy goals the designers should separately consider users' privacy goals and the company's business goals. User goals could be defined through a user-survey. As defined in PbD concepts, it is important to see privacy and business goals as common goals which should not be compromised for each other [11]. As proposed in our *effective data minimization* above and *transparency with privacy policies*, which follows the designing steps, we have shown how to achieve this win-win situation in practice.

Designing privacy is the essence of PbD concept [11]. This involves on defining the data access, retaining policies and storage of data. Through *data minimization work-flow*, designers would get an idea of the sensitivity and relativity of the data elements they access, which gives them a better position to effectively decide on the consent/choice/access options they should embed in the system. For this it is important that they understand the user behavior and user perception of privacy. Spiekermann and Cranor [49] in their framework emphasize the importance of developers understanding the *user sphere* in implementing effective privacy. User sphere means the user perception, how privacy could be breached, how users see and behave with the system. Similarly in our user-centric privacy designing approach we stress the importance of developers understanding potential vulnerabilities for the user, and the company and data breaches from user perspective and company perspective. Developers could understand these aspects through user-surveys and interviews. Defining user-centric privacy goals and designs would support developers to implement privacy into the system in a user-centric manner.

4. Implementing Privacy: Developers can incorporate existing PETs wherever applicable in achieving the privacy goals set forth by the designers. There are ample PETs that has been designed so far and technologies that are adopted to implement privacy in systems [16]. These includes mechanisms for anonymity, network invasion, identity management, censorship resistance, selective disclosure credentials and also database implementation to preserve privacy [16]. Selection of PETs are highly subjective and dependent on the privacy goals and requirements of the software being developed [24]. It is beyond the scope of this paper to explicitly discuss existing PETs. However, a fact worth noticing is that it is not possible to achieve a 100% privacy preserved system through pure architectural and technological support as suggested in the Engineering privacy framework by Spiekermann [49]. Privacy in a system should be achieved through a balanced approach with privacy architecture, policy implementation, communication and transparency as guided in our work-flow for user-centric privacy. All the implementations and designs should be tested in a process that involves real end users and other entities that are devoted for testing applications as explained in the following section.

5. Testing for Privacy: Testing is the most important section in software development. In the proposed framework we define the following guidelines to be followed in testing for privacy with a *user-centric* approach. Testing should follow the privacy implementation steps. A cycle of designing and implementation should follow in terms of failure of any of the following guidelines.

- Preserving privacy of data in applications during testing in database-centric applications (DCAs): It is argued that data anonymization algorithms as k-anonymity [32], taken to preserve database privacy seriously degrades testability of applications [21]. However, guessing-anonymity [39], a selective anonymity metric, is voted better against other forms due to the possibility of selective anonymization.
- Testing the application for potential privacy vulnerabilities: The privacy risk assessment and the information flow diagrams could be used by testers to gain an idea of potential privacy vulnerabilities. Information collections, processing, dissemination and invasion are identified by Solove as the four stages in an application where privacy could be breached [46]. QA teams and test automation teams should test the application for potential privacy vulnerabilities in these stages.
- Testing the usability of implemented privacy specific tools (privacy user-setting processes): During the initial phases of development there could be tools incorporated in the system, explicitly to reduce privacy risks. Usability of these tools should be tested against real users during the test phase to ensure their effectiveness.

6. *User-Centric* Approach for Transparency: In the current context transparency means displaying users about what data is being collected, how the data is going to be retained and used in the privacy policy [26]. However, almost none of the applications today is successful in effectively displaying these data through the privacy policy [29]. The privacy policy is incorporated by many companies as a tool to comply to legal obligations [26]. However, we believe that in transparency the true meaning is not just displaying what the application does, but also to bridge the gap between user expectation versus reality [25]. Companies can win the trust of users and users would be more open and comfortable using applications as they have knowledge on what is happening to their data in the application [33]. For this developers should perform a survey and a usability study of the developed system prior to defining their privacy policies. Rao et al. [40] in their study explains the mismatched user expectations on-line. Based on this we propose the user-centric approach for transparency through evaluation of user expectations versus real design. This way companies can get more accurate details about users, and win users trust while achieving their business goals [34], which is the one of the principles in PbD [11]. The proposed work-flow is,

- Step 1: List collection/retain and storage of data in the application.
- Step 2: Conduct a user survey with the application that covers general use-cases; information about the data the user expects the system to collect, users' understanding on how the data is stored/used by the system.

- Step 3: Identify the mismatches between user expectation versus reality; generate privacy policy with details covering discovered mismatches.
- Step 4: Conduct a readability test and evaluate the privacy policy, Flesch readability test could be used for this purpose [28] (A model that is widely used text readability).
- Step 5: Publish the privacy policy, minimize changes. In the case of unavoidable changes inform users well in advance.

Validation Questions Proposed:

- a. What information you believe the users would expect to see in the privacy policy and why?
- b. What information have you included in the privacy policy specifically to oblige for legal requirements?
- c. What information have you included in the privacy policy specifically to maintain transparency and better communication with the end user?
- d. What is the readability score of the privacy policy? (Use the Felsch Readability evaluation formula)
- e. Do you think navigation in the privacy policy an important feature?

Consider yourseld as an end user of the application you design.

- a. Do you think this application should have a privacy policy? Why?
  - i. Would you take time to go through the privacy policy of the application?
- b. Write down things you wish to see in the privacy policy of this application.
- c. Write down the most important sections you believe that should be covered in the privacy policy of this application.

---

7. Documentation: Documentation should be approached with the focus of *What information do developers need from past projects?* [53]. Cannon [9] has specified documentation requirements for privacy maintenance. However, in UP the focus is more on creating and maintaining models rather than textual documentation for quick adaptability and change management [53]. The benefit of the documents should always overweight the cost of creating it and models are encouraged as temporary documents that are discarded once their purpose is served [6]. Based on Cannon's suggestions considering the current context, we propose generating the following documents with relation to privacy design,

- Stakeholder privacy risk evaluation report: during inception
- Data flow diagram: during inception
- Privacy statement for the application end user: during transition
- Deployment guide with privacy settings: during construction
- Review document about privacy issues, risk mitigation and responsible parties in decisions made (Accountability): during transition

PbD emphasizes the importance of adopting privacy at the earliest stage in system design [11]. We highlight the importance of adopting privacy design early as well as continuing it until the very last step of the software development life-cycle. We show clearly how to achieve that in practice with a user-centered approach through a comprehensive step by step guide. Software development is rarely a single process that involves a single person [27]. Our privacy framework as shown in image 1 comprehensively captured the role of each party in terms of privacy design and implementation [27]. Most importantly the proposed framework, coins the term *User-Centered Privacy* and comprehensively emphasize how developers should adopt a user centered mentality in approaching privacy in systems.

4   Conclusion and Future Work

As on-line applications are being used to achieve simple day to day tasks, using them is not something users could refrain from due to privacy concerns. As users are getting more and more concerned about their privacy on-line, developers should focus on embedding privacy right into their applications with a user-centric approach. Through this paper, we contribute *A practical work-flow to implement user-centric privacy design*, which is a timely requirement for effective privacy designing and implementation [17]. To the best of the authors' knowledge, this is the first framework designed to specify an end-to-end work-flow to achieve privacy as a user-centric approach with current software development processes.

Interviewing software developers and designers to understand their expectations and understandings on implementing privacy is highly desirable for strengthening and fine tuning the proposed framework in a more pragmatic manner. Applying the framework to more abstract and practical development processes like agile, scrum would also help fine tuning.

References

1. Fahrenthold, D.A.: Trump recorded having extremely lewd conversation about women in 2005. https://www.washingtonpost.com/politics/trump-recorded-having-extremely-lewd-conversation-about-women-in-2005/2016/10/07/3b9ce776-8cb4-11e6-bf8a-3d26847eeed4_story.html. Accessed 14 Oct 2016
2. Facebook data policy. https://www.facebook.com/policy.php. Accessed 21 Aug 2016
3. Curran, P.: August 2016 hacks: 8 of the largest hacks, breaches and cyber incidents. https://www.checkmarx.com/2016/09/11/august-2016-hacks-8-largest-hacks-breaches-cyber-incidents. Accessed 03 Nov 2016
4. Abrahamsson, P., Salo, O., Ronkainen, J., Warsta, J., Agile software development methods: review and analysis (2002)
5. Adams, A., Sasse, M.A.: Users are not the enemy. Commun. ACM **42**(12), 40–46 (1999)

6. Anwar, A.: A review of RUP (Rational Unified Process). Int. J. Softw. Eng. (IJSE) **5**(2), 12–19 (2014)
7. Arachchilage, N.A.G., Martin, A.P.: A trust domains taxonomy for securely sharing information: a preliminary investigation. In: HAISA, pp. 53–68 (2014)
8. Barker, K., Askari, M., Banerjee, M., Ghazinour, K., Mackas, B., Majedi, M., Pun, S., Williams, A.: A data privacy taxonomy. In: Sexton, A.P. (ed.) BNCOD 2009. LNCS, vol. 5588, pp. 42–54. Springer, Heidelberg (2009). doi:10.1007/978-3-642-02843-4_7
9. Cannon, J.: Privacy: What Developers and IT Professionals Should Know. Addison-Wesley Professional, Boston (2004)
10. Caputo, D.D., Pfleeger, S.L., Sasse, M.A., Ammann, P., Offutt, J., Deng, L.: Barriers to usable security? Three organizational case studies. IEEE Secur. Priv. **14**(5), 22–32 (2016)
11. Cavoukian, A.: Privacy by design: the definitive workshop. A foreword by Ann Cavoukian, Ph.D. Identity Inf. Soc. **3**(2), 247–251 (2010)
12. Cavoukian, A., Taylor, S., Abrams, M.E.: Privacy by design: essential for organizational accountability and strong business practices. Identity Inf. Soc. **3**(2), 405–413 (2010)
13. Cho, J.: A hybrid software development method for large-scale projects: rational unified process with scrum. Issues Inf. Syst. **10**(2), 340–348 (2009)
14. Clarke, R.: Privacy impact assessment: its origins and development. Comput. Law Secur. Rev. **25**(2), 123–135 (2009)
15. Danezis, G., Domingo-Ferrer, J., Hansen, M., Hoepman, J.-H., Metayer, D.L., Tirtea, R., Schiffner, S.: Privacy data protection by design-from policy to engineering. arXiv preprint arXiv:1501.03726 (2015)
16. Danezis, G., Gürses, S.: A critical review of 10 years of privacy technology. In: Proceedings of surveillance cultures: a global surveillance society, pp. 1–16 (2010)
17. Davies, S.: Why privacy by design is the next crucial step for privacy protection (2010)
18. Fuggetta, A.: Software process: a roadmap. In: Proceedings of the Conference on the Future of Software Engineering, pp. 25–34. ACM (2000)
19. Gellman, R.: Fair information practices: a basic history. Available at SSRN 2415020 (2015)
20. Giannakos, M.N., Chorianopoulos, K., Giotopoulos, K., Vlamos, P.: Using Facebook out of habit. Behav. Inf. Technol. **32**(6), 594–602 (2013)
21. Grechanik, M., Csallner, C., Fu, C., Xie, Q.: Is data privacy always good for software testing? In: IEEE 21st International Symposium on Software Reliability Engineering, pp. 368–377. IEEE (2010)
22. Gürses, S., Troncoso, C., Diaz, C.: Engineering privacy by design. Comput. Priv. Data Prot. **14**(3) (2011)
23. Hall, J.G., Rapanotti, L.: Towards a design-theoretic characterisation of software development process models. In: Proceedings of the Fourth SEMAT Workshop on General Theory of Software Engineering, pp. 3–14. IEEE Press (2015)
24. Hoepman, J.-H.: Privacy design strategies. In: Cuppens-Boulahia, N., Cuppens, F., Jajodia, S., Abou El Kalam, A., Sans, T. (eds.) SEC 2014. IAICT, vol. 428, pp. 446–459. Springer, Heidelberg (2014). doi:10.1007/978-3-642-55415-5_38
25. Jensen, C., Potts, C.: Privacy policies as decision-making tools: an evaluation of online privacy notices. In: Proceedings of the SIGCHI Conference on Human Factors in Computing Systems, pp. 471–478. ACM (2004)

26. Kelley, P.G., Cesca, L., Bresee, J., Cranor, L.F.: Standardizing privacy notices: an online study of the nutrition label approach. In: Proceedings of the SIGCHI Conference on Human Factors in Computing Systems, pp. 1573–1582. ACM (2010)
27. Kerry Spalding, J.Y.T.: Practical strategies for integrating privacy by design throughout product development process. In: Proceedings of the CHI Conference Extended Abstracts on Human Factors in Computing Systems, pp. 3415–3422. ACM (2016)
28. Kincaid, J.P., Fishburne, R.P., Rogers, R.L., Chissom, B.S.: Derivation of new readability formulas (automated readability index, fog count and flesch reading ease formula) for navy enlisted personnel. Technical report, DTIC Document (1975)
29. Kumar, P.: Ranking digital rights: pushing ICT companies to respect users privacy. In: CHI 2016 Workshop: Bridging the Gap Between Privacy by Design and Privacy in Practice, p. 15. CHI (2016)
30. Notario, N., Crespo, A., Kung, A., Kroener, I., Métayer, D., Troncoso, C., del Álamo, J.M., Martín, Y.S.: PRIPARE: a new vision on engineering privacy and security by design. In: Cleary, F., Felici, M. (eds.) CSP 2014. CCIS, vol. 470, pp. 65–76. Springer, Cham (2014). doi:10.1007/978-3-319-12574-9_6
31. Lederer, S., Hong, J.I., Dey, A.K., Landay, J.A.: Personal privacy through understanding and action: five pitfalls for designers. Pers. Ubiquit. Comput. 8(6), 440–454 (2004)
32. LeFevre, K., DeWitt, D.J., Ramakrishnan, R.: Incognito: efficient full-domain k-anonymity. In: Proceedings of the ACM SIGMOD International Conference on Management of Data, pp. 49–60. ACM (2005)
33. Leon, P.G., Rao, A., Schaub, F., Marsh, A., Cranor, L.F., Sadeh, N.: Why people are (Un) willing to share information with online advertisers (2015)
34. Leon, P.G., Ur, B., Wang, Y., Sleeper, M., Balebako, R., Shay, R., Bauer, L., Christodorescu, M., Cranor, L.F., What matters to users?: factors that affect users' willingness to share information with online advertisers. In: Proceedings of the Ninth Symposium on Usable Privacy and Security, p. 7. ACM (2013)
35. Liu, K., Terzi, E.: A framework for computing the privacy scores of users in online social networks. ACM Trans. Knowl. Discov. Data (TKDD) 5(1), 6 (2010)
36. Maximilien, E.M., Grandison, T., Sun, T., Richardson, D., Guo, S., Liu, K.: Privacy-as-a-service: models, algorithms, and results on the Facebook platform. In: Proceedings of Web, vol. 2 (2009)
37. Minkus, T., Memon, N.: On a scale from 1 to 10, how private are you? Scoring facebook privacy settings. In: Proceedings of the Workshop on Usable Security (USEC 2014). Internet Society (2014)
38. Oulasvirta, A., Rattenbury, T., Ma, L., Raita, E.: Habits make smartphone use more pervasive. Pers. Ubiquit. Comput. 16(1), 105–114 (2012)
39. Rachlin, Y., Probst, K., Ghani, R.: Maximizing privacy under data distortion constraints in noise perturbation methods. In: Bonchi, F., Ferrari, E., Jiang, W., Malin, B. (eds.) PInKDD 2008. LNCS, vol. 5456, pp. 92–110. Springer, Heidelberg (2009). doi:10.1007/978-3-642-01718-6_7
40. Rao, A., Schaub, F., Sadeh, N., Acquisti, A., Kang, R.: Expecting the unexpected: understanding mismatched privacy expectations online. In: Federal Trade Commission PrivacyCon Conference (2016)
41. Rashtian, H., Boshmaf, Y., Jaferian, P., Beznosov, K.: To befriend or not? A model of friend request acceptance on Facebook. In: Symposium on Usable Privacy and Security (SOUPS 2014), pp. 285–300 (2014)
42. Rubinstein, I., Good, N.: Privacy by design: a counterfactual analysis of Google and Facebook privacy incidents (2012)

43. Satzinger, J.W., Jackson, R.B., Burd, S.D.: Object-Oriented Analysis Design: With the Unified Process. Thomson Course Technology, Boston (2005)
44. Schaub, F., Balebako, R., Durity, A.L., Cranor, L.F.: A design space for effective privacy notices. In: Eleventh Symposium on Usable Privacy and Security (SOUPS 2015), pp. 1–17 (2015)
45. Schwaber, K.: SCRUM development process. In: Sutherland, J., Casanave, C., Miller, J., Patel, P., Hollowell, G. (eds.) Business Object Design and Implementation, pp. 117–134. Springer, London (1997)
46. Solove, D.J.: A taxonomy of privacy. Univ. Pa. Law Rev. **154**(3), 477–564 (2006)
47. Solove, D.J., Rotenberg, M., Schwartz, P.M.: Information Privacy Law, 4th edn. Aspen Publishers, New York (2003)
48. Spiekermann, S.: The challenges of privacy by design. Commun. ACM **55**(7), 38–40 (2012)
49. Spiekermann, S., Cranor, L.F.: Engineering privacy. IEEE Trans. Softw. Eng. **35**(1), 67–82 (2009)
50. Stark, L., King, J., Page, X., Lampinen, A., Vitak, J., Wisniewski, P., Whalen, T., Good, N.: Bridging the gap between privacy by design and privacy in practice. In: Proceedings of the CHI Conference Extended Abstracts on Human Factors in Computing Systems, pp. 3415–3422. ACM (2016)
51. Unger, R., Chandler, C.: A Project Guide to UX Design: For User Experience Designers in the Field or in the Making. New Riders, Indianapolis (2012)
52. van Rest, J., Boonstra, D., Everts, M., van Rijn, M., van Paassen, R.: Designing privacy-by-design. In: Preneel, B., Ikonomou, D. (eds.) APF 2012. LNCS, vol. 8319, pp. 55–72. Springer, Heidelberg (2014). doi:10.1007/978-3-642-54069-1_4
53. Voigt, S., von Garrel, J., Müller, J., Wirth, D.: A study of documentation in agile software projects. In: Proceedings of the 10th ACM/IEEE International Symposium on Empirical Software Engineering and Measurement, p. 4. ACM (2016)

Correction to: Radicalization, the Internet and Cybersecurity: Opportunities and Challenges for HCI

Joanne Hinds and Adam Joinson

Correction to:
Chapter "Radicalization, the Internet and Cybersecurity:
Opportunities and Challenges for HCI" in: T. Tryfonas (Ed.):
Human Aspects of Information Security, Privacy and Trust,
LNCS 10292, https://doi.org/10.1007/978-3-319-58460-7_33

This chapter was originally published without the inclusion of a Funding Disclosure Statement. This has been corrected.

The updated version of this chapter can be found at
https://doi.org/10.1007/978-3-319-58460-7_33

Author Index

Printed in the United States
By Bookmasters